LEADERSHIP THE OUTWARD BOUND WAY

BECOMING A BETTER LEADER IN THE WORKPLACE, IN THE WILDERNESS, AND IN YOUR COMMUNITY

LEADERSHIP THE
OUTWARD BOUND
WAY

OUTWARD BOUND USA

FOREWORD BY JIMMY CARTER

JOHN RAYNOLDS, ASHLEY LODATO, ROBERT GORDON,
CAROLINE BLAIR-SMITH, JOAN WELSH, AND MARK GERZON
CASE STUDIES BY JIM GARRETT
EDITED BY ROB CHATFIELD, LEWIS GLENN,
CHRISTINE UMMEL HOSLER, AND KRIS FULSAAS

THE MOUNTAINEERS BOOKS

Dedicated to the three educators who brought Outward Bound to the United States:
Joshua L. Miner, Gilbert Burnett, and F. Charles Froelicher

THE MOUNTAINEERS BOOKS
is the nonprofit publishing arm of The Mountaineers Club, an
organization founded in 1906 and dedicated to the exploration,
preservation, and enjoyment of outdoor and wilderness areas.

1001 SW Klickitat Way, Suite 201, Seattle, WA 98134

"Outward Bound®" is a registered trademark of Outward Bound, Inc.

The Mission of Outward Bound
To inspire character development and self-discovery in people of all ages and walks of life through challenge and adventure, and to impel them to achieve more than they ever thought possible, to show compassion for others and to actively engage in creating a better world.

Manufactured in the United States of America

Copy Editor: Erin Moore
Design and Composition: Mayumi Thompson
Photo Credits: Frontispiece © Jon Underhill; page 18 © Kiran Nimmagadda; page 126 © Kathleen S. Lodato; page 128 © Rob Chatfield; page 222 © Robert Gordon; pages 224 and 294 © Robert Alexander.

Library of Congress Cataloging-in-Publication Data
Leadership the Outward Bound way: becoming a better leader in the workplace, in the wilderness, and in your community / Outward Bound USA ; foreword by Jimmy Carter ; John Raynolds . . . [et al.] ; case studies by Jim Garrett ; edited by Rob Chatfield, Christine Ummel Hosler, and Kris Fulsaas. — 1st ed.
    p. cm.
  Includes bibliographical references.
  ISBN 978-1-59485-033-2 (hb) — ISBN 978-1-59485-034-9 (pb)
  1. Leadership. I. Raynolds, John, 1929- II. Chatfield, Rob. III. Outward Bound, Inc.
  HM1261.L426 2007
  158'.4—dc22
                    2007027007

❂ Printed on recycled paper

CONTENTS

PART IV. TAKING LEADERSHIP INTO YOUR COMMUNITY

ACKNOWLEDGMENTS

This book was written with the assistance of many people from Outward Bound USA and The Mountaineers Books whose behind-the-scenes efforts have contributed greatly to the quality of this work. The authors would like to offer special thanks to Christine Ummel Hosler, whose patience, professionalism, and tutelage inspired excellence in all areas of the book, and Lewis Glenn and Margaret Miller for lending their vision and direction to the project from its beginning stages. Thanks also go to Rob Chatfield whose steady leadership helped translate the vision of *Leadership the Outward Bound Way* into reality.

Outward Bound USA would like to acknowledge Jimmy Carter, former President of the United States, and Mark Gerzon, author and conflict-resolution expert, for their contributions.

FOREWORD

For more than forty years, Outward Bound USA has been delivering challenging experiences to young men and women, helping them to achieve more than they ever thought possible. Filled with a powerful sense of self and the importance of service in creating a better world, Outward Bound graduates have become leaders in a wide range of organizations and endeavors of importance to our country.

The underlying principles of Outward Bound are based on the philosophy of Kurt Hahn, a German educator who escaped Nazi Germany to found schools in Scotland and Wales. Hahn believed that young people must be instructed in the "four pillars"—self-reliance, physical fitness, craftsmanship, and service and compassion—in order to reach their full potential. He believed equally that young people would respond best and assume major responsibilities when told they were needed, as opposed to required. He believed that leadership always necessitates action, whether in the form of large initiatives that can change the world or the small acts of kindness that define a Good Samaritan. The schools whose founding he inspired, including Outward Bound USA, change lives, build teams, and transform public schools based on these beliefs.

Today, Outward Bound USA is one of our nation's preeminent nonprofit experiential education organizations, providing training and personal development to more than 70,000 young people and adults each year. In the wilderness, in cities, and in schools around the country, participants learn the importance of leading from within a team and through service. They learn how to measure success in terms of the entire group completing the expedition and seeing beyond individual accomplishment. Diversity and inclusion are important elements of meeting great challenges. Differences in social or ethnic background are harnessed to overcome fear and achieve the objectives of an Outward Bound course.

This book provides a thoughtful and informative look at how the Outward Bound way has found application in a wide range of outdoor recreation, education, and business organizations. The fundamentals of Hahn's philosophy, which have helped educate millions of young men and women around the world, are brought to light in ways that can help people of all ages and walks of life take greater advantage of their own potential.

The world in which we live is in desperate need of those trained and inspired by Outward Bound . . . men and women of compassion and humility who are committed not only to efficiency and effectiveness, but to social justice and a sustainable environment. Rosalynn and I have participated in Outward Bound and support this great organization as it continues to deliver leadership skills in its unique and time-tested way.

—*Jimmy Carter*

INTRODUCTION

BY ROB CHATFIELD

A leader is a dealer in hope.
—Napoleon Bonaparte

In 1941, Lawrence Holt became the senior partner in his family's shipping company, the Blue Funnel Shipping Line. From early adulthood, Holt had been deeply concerned by the social problems of his day. In particular, he was sympathetic to the travails of seamen, whose lives were often wearisome, dangerous, and attended by meager wages. Perhaps as a result, Holt's seamen were better paid and better trained than most in the British Merchant Navy. The officers of his Blue Funnel Shipping Line, with whom he had forged a particularly strong bond of affection and trust, were among his most loyal employees. "Mr. Lawrence," as he was known, was a respected and beloved leader.

From the start of World War II, Holt's passenger steamships had been requisitioned by the British Admiralty and converted to armed merchant cruisers. The ships, crewed by officers and sailors of the Royal Navy and by seamen from the Blue Funnel Shipping Line, brought food and other critical supplies from North America across the North Atlantic. Without these supplies, Britain would have starved.

The men who sailed these steamships knew this. And so did the Germans, whose U-boats formed the "wolf packs" that hunted the slow-moving vessels. The U-boats and their torpedoes turned the North Atlantic into a killing field. They inspired such fear among the young British sailors that many refused to sleep in their assigned bunks, located below waterline deep in the belly of the ship, because that was where the torpedoes hit.

By the spring of 1941, Lawrence Holt knew he had a serious problem. The Blue Funnel Ship-ping Line had lost five of its vessels during the first three months of that year. While the great loss of life that resulted from enemy action was a lamentable consequence of wartime operations, Holt was especially troubled by the deaths of some of his younger seamen. They had survived the sinking of their ships, but when confronted with the challenge of enduring the elements in an open lifeboat, they surrendered first their hope and then their lives.

Holt was a man in search of a solution. He knew that many lives could be saved if he could give his young men the resolve, tenacity, and resourcefulness that would sustain their hope long enough for them to meet their rescuers.

Later that year, Holt was approached by an innovative educator named Kurt Hahn, a Jewish educator who had fled Nazi Germany. Hahn needed a financial backer for a nationwide program he had been developing since the mid-1930s to foster physical fitness, tenacity, enterprise, and compassion among Britain's youth—a program informed by aims of the school he had been forced, as headmaster, to leave behind in Germany. Holt quickly saw how Hahn's educational ideas could serve the interests of a nation at war while helping prepare his seamen for the rigors of the North Atlantic. Together they founded an organization that would train the young seamen and the nation's youth in the ways of self-confidence and service. Lawrence Holt would name that organization "Outward Bound," when a ship is sailing from her home port to her last and furthermost port.

By the end of World War II, fifty-two of the ships owned or managed by Holt's company had been lost at sea. Yet the training the crews of Blue Funnel Shipping Line received had made a real difference: the seamen had a high rate of survival. At a time when being sent on a wartime convoy route was practically a death sentence, Lawrence Holt succeeded in giving his men what they needed most: leadership, hope, and the skill to survive.

Leadership matters. More than sixty-five years have passed since the Battle of the Atlantic brought two determined men to a crossroads. Were it not for the war, Lawrence Holt and Kurt Hahn were unlikely to have seen their individual needs intersect to such a powerful effect. Yet these men had much in common: Holt had an abiding and genuine concern for the welfare of those he led, and Hahn was an educator of considerable resolve who understood the value of rigorous character training to the needs of youth. Both men were repeatedly able to inspire others to do what had to be done—despite hardship, danger, and uncertainty—through the compelling example of effective leadership and the notion that a positive outcome is possible even when there is overwhelming evidence to the contrary.

Outward Bound is an organization born of war that has thrived in peace. Its leadership methods strongly reflect its traditions of service, self-reliance, craftsmanship, and compassion, as well as a dedication to the proposition that in all of us exists the potential to become an effective leader. Today, more than ever, Outward Bound's inclusive, community-focused approach to leadership is needed to give hope and promise in an unpredictable world.

Importantly, this book is not just about "outdoor leadership." It is about *indispensable* leadership—the kind that you can take into your community, your school, your business, and your life. Many of its leadership lessons are informed by the work of countless educators who have immersed themselves in the great wilderness classrooms that Outward Bound pioneered in the 1940s. This book also draws heavily from the diversity of today's Outward Bound USA, which, in addition to using the wilderness as a classroom, works in cities and schools, with business leaders and educators, the academically gifted and the less so. Today, no other organization practices leadership across such a broad swath of society and in so many milieus as Outward Bound.

Whether you are a seasoned leader, aspire to become one, or are just interested in learning more about leadership, this book is for you. Every day, as we negotiate the shifting landscape of our lives, we encounter opportunities to incorporate leadership into our interactions with others. Maybe you're the mother who hopes to improve the availability of child care in her community, the teacher who wants to advance the education of his students, the college student who wishes to see positive change in a world plagued by intractable problems, or the new citizen who wants to lead her community in a fresh direction. The extent to which you are ready to take advantage of these opportunities can mean the difference between just imagining your dreams and realizing them. As Mohandas Gandhi, the great political and spiritual leader of India's independence movement, once said, "You must become the change that you want to see in the world."

Leadership the Outward Bound Way can be your guide to effecting change in your world. It offers understandable and transferable advice, anecdotes, and insight into the many challenges of effective leadership.

This book is organized to introduce you first to the fundamentals of leadership as practiced by Outward Bound. Then it explores how those principles and techniques play out in the many different contexts of your life—from the backcountry to the boardroom. This book is intended for use by the individual but also includes material, such as the thoughtful case studies, that can be used by a class or group interested in leadership.

Leadership the Outward Bound Way is divided into four main sections, each carefully crafted by an experienced leader and practitioner from within the senior ranks of Outward Bound. At the start of each section, we'll introduce you to the person who will facilitate your learning journey into a specific area of leadership.

We start first with a look at the essentials: styles of leadership, how to share authority, how to use power appropriately, and how and when to foster interdependence and promote team building. We also discuss the relationships between comfort, fear, risk taking, and decision making, as well as their impact on leadership.

Next we take leadership to the wilderness. This part of the book is a practical guide to the basics of leadership in an outdoor setting. It discusses the merits of careful planning and safety and how to be responsible for others. Mentoring, role modeling, and how to become a good follower are introduced. We also explore the importance of contemplation and self-knowledge to effective leadership.

The third part of the book examines leadership in the professional context. For years Outward Bound Professional has worked with the leaders of some of the finest and most innovative companies in America. Here we talk about the power of teams and how to build them and lead them. We learn how to create and sustain a shared culture while developing a better understanding of what motivates competitive people to see the value in working cooperatively with others. We share ideas about leading through change and how to establish direction through shared values, vision, and mission.

In the last section, we take you home: into your community. Outward Bound's relationship to community is strong and tightly integrated into much of what we teach. Here we talk about the intrinsic value of compassion and service and how to bring leadership deep into the core of your community. We discuss how to integrate

public service into the rest of your life. Ways to lead volunteers and work effectively with young people are introduced. Finally, we'll look at ways to approach political situations so that you can motivate both allies and opponents to move toward the common good.

Immediately following each section of the book is a "case study," which takes you into the thick of a specific leadership situation, challenging you to deepen your understanding of a many-sided problem. Pioneered at Harvard Business School in the 1920s, case studies have since been used at many institutions of higher learning as a method of preparing students for the management and leadership challenges of their future careers.

In *Leadership the Outward Bound Way*, we have prepared four case studies based on real-world problems. A detailed narrative quickly immerses you in the situation. A series of questions embedded in each narrative positions you as the leader of the group facing the situation: "What were the leadership decisions that contributed to the situation? What would I do now if I were the one in charge?"

Once you have carefully considered the questions posed within the narrative, you can turn to the appendix to find additional questions about the case study and more points to ponder. Through this progression, details of the case study are first fully illuminated and then carefully nuanced by guided inquiry through to a point in which you can match the vicarious experience of the case study to your own real-world situation.

We hope you find *Leadership the Outward Bound Way* a useful resource in helping to extend the possibilities of effective leadership well beyond what you know. May it challenge you to be the change that you wish to see in the world.

Hope arouses, as nothing else can arouse, a passion for the possible.
—Rev. William Sloane Coffin Jr.

PART I

LEADERSHIP FUNDAMENTALS

About the Author: John Raynolds

A graduate of Williams College who attended Stanford University Graduate School of Business Administration, John Raynolds also holds two honorary doctorate degrees in humane letters and laws. A naval officer in Korea with Underwater Demolition Team 13, he was involved in taking the team airborne—the genesis of the Navy SEALs.

Raynolds' varied career includes investment banking, West African cocoa, Volkswagen-Porsche distribution, heavy construction equipment manufacturing, venture capital, international executive searches, and not-for-profit foundations.

A trustee of Outward Bound USA from 1974 to 1990, Raynolds participated in forty-one Outward Bound expeditions and courses. When he was president and CEO of Outward Bound USA from 1981 to 1990, student enrollment increased from 7,000 a year to more than 30,000. He led Outward Bound's entry into public schools and founding of the first independent urban Outward Bound Center, in New York City. Currently 40,000 students participate in Expeditionary Learning Outward Bound in public schools, and 10,000 students take part in the New York City Outward Bound Center.

A lifelong mountaineer, Raynolds has climbed many of the world's major mountains. He is also a Golden Gloves and Amateur Athletic Union boxer, a haiku poet, and author of two books on volunteer service.

The *Wall Street Journal* featured Raynolds in

"The Stew Pot Theory of Career Building." CNN's half-hour special on Raynolds in its program "Pinnacle" aired internationally in 1988. He currently serves on four not-for-profit boards, including the Achilles Track Club, with which he has completed six New York City marathons.

Personal Introduction: John Raynolds

In 1974 I experienced my first Outward Bound trip: a weeklong course down the Colorado River to introduce corporate leaders to the basics of Outward Bound. The expedition would convince us to support Outward Bound both financially and in word-of-mouth marketing.

The trip through Cataract Canyon, Hells Half Acre, and many other rapids was fascinating, exciting, and oftentimes scary. Even though we were captains of industry, in this unfamiliar territory we all lacked confidence in being a captain on a river rapid. We were not quite sure how to do it well. Yet we persevered; though we hit rocks and screwed up in many ways, we were basically safe because the instructor was at the raft's stern to help us.

During the trip, there was a short Solo (a time for rest and reflection). We were placed separately in scenic locations overlooking the river. We could not see any of the other participants but were not far from the instructors, who could hear us if we had any trouble. We stayed out overnight with just a sleeping bag, a tarp, a water bottle, and a journal.

During that night alone, seeing the incredible stars in the blue-black sky and just the river below, I composed haiku poetry in my head; in the morning, I wrote the poems in my journal. That morning we gathered in a circle to share thoughts or experiences we had had on Solo. I offered to read my haiku poetry, but, strangely, I had stage fright—even though I was a senior executive with many life experiences, I was daunted to share something so intimate as poetry. Yet, I was encouraged by the group, and so I read my poetry.

After that first expedition, I served on the national board of Outward Bound for about ten years, and in 1981, I became the full-time CEO of Outward Bound USA. It was the most wonderful job I have ever had. I dealt with strongly motivated, outstanding people whom I admire in so many ways, plus I did something I loved. And I experienced firsthand how Outward Bound develops leaders.

Whether you are a wilderness trip leader, a corporate manager, an educator, a community leader, or simply one of those people who repeatedly seek out—or find themselves thrust into—leadership roles, you can learn from the leadership strategies Outward Bound uses in its programs. You may want to do some of the things that successful leaders have learned through their experiences in Outward Bound. You might recognize your own leadership successes and failures in some of the stories recounted in this book. You may also learn ways to organize your own life around principles contained in this section, Leadership Fundamentals.

Chapter 1, Why Learn Leadership from Outward Bound? introduces Outward Bound's origins and evolution as the world's principal leadership education organization. Chapter 2, Becoming a Leader, addresses leadership roles and styles, and Chapter 3, Communicating Effectively, deals with a leader's communication skills. Chapter 4, Building Trust, Building a Team, will help you build and nurture your teams. Chapter 5, Taking Risks and Making Decisions, will guide you in developing and exercising judgment. Chapter 6, Finding Courage, Overcoming Fear, will help you find your own leadership motivation and courage.

Outward Bound's founder, Kurt Hahn, remarked in 1965 at an address in Harrogate, England, that "Outward Bound can ignite—that is all; it is for others to keep the flame alive." I hope this book will ignite a passion in all types of leaders to keep the flame of Outward Bound's leadership lessons burning.

CHAPTER 1

WHY LEARN LEADERSHIP FROM OUTWARD BOUND?

Outward Bound has been teaching leadership around the globe for more than sixty-five years. It has done more to help young people and adults recognize the leader within themselves than any other private organization in the world. In the United States alone, some 710,000 people have learned life-changing, transferable leadership skills and strategies through Outward Bound experiences.

A few months after the terrorist attacks of September 11, 2001, Outward Bound received a remarkable letter from an alumnus.

A teacher at an elementary school about fifteen blocks from the site of the World Trade Center had recently returned from an Outward Bound boating course. The morning of September 11, in the wake of the attacks, he found himself coordinating the evacuation of students from the school.

In the frenzy of activity that warm September morning, he took off his button-down work shirt, revealing the Outward Bound tee shirt he was wearing underneath.

Suddenly a woman—someone he had never met, who was obviously very panicked—stopped him on the street outside the school. She pointed to his shirt.

"He'll know what to do," she told the man with her. "He's been to Outward Bound."

And he did know what to do. He was able to give them directions to a location nearby where volunteers were being assembled.

How did spending two weeks boating in Maine with a group of strangers prepare this man to help cope with a major urban disaster?

Simply put, through his Outward Bound experience, he learned the key task of a leader: to identify what needs doing and to organize a group of people to get it done.

Many Outward Bound trustees, alumni, and former staff are renowned national leaders in various arenas—Patricia C. "Tosh" Barron, high-level Xerox executive; Arthur Blank, co-founder of Home Depot; Candace Carpenter, founder of *iVillage.com*; former U.S. President Jimmy Carter; Marian Wright Edelman, founder and president of the Children's Defense Fund and former director of the Center for Law and Education at Harvard University; Bill Harrison, CEO of Chase Manhattan/J. P. Morgan; Antonin Scalia, U.S. Supreme Court associate justice; Lorna Wendt, founder of the Equality in Marriage Institute; and John Whitehead, former co-CEO of Goldman-Sachs and former Deputy Secretary of State of the United States—but most are regular citizens who seek out challenge and adventure. Although most Outward Bound alumni will not have the opportunity to assist in rescues as dramatic as the one described above, many of them will return home and assume leadership responsibilities that they had never considered before. And almost all will return to the leadership roles they already fulfill at home—parenting, coaching, leading teams at work and in school and government—to perform these duties even more effectively and with greater reward.

You may never attend an Outward Bound program, but through this book you can benefit from the experience of thousands of instructors and hundreds of thousands of participants who have found that they have great potential for leadership that they did not know they possessed.

OUTWARD BOUND'S ROLE IN DEVELOPING LEADERSHIP SKILLS

Why should you learn leadership from Outward Bound? There are several reasons.

Outward Bound-shaped leaders meet a real need in today's world. Compassion, self-reliance, and concern for the common good play central roles in Outward Bound's philosophy and leadership training. Leaders influenced by these values consider the needs of those who follow and who depend upon their leadership, rather than seeking only to promote personal gains, behavior we've seen recently in so many corporate and political situations. Also, in times of increased global struggle, leaders instilled with compassion for their fellow human beings and concern for the needs of others can bridge gaps in cultural misunderstandings. They can help rectify the fundamental lack of respect for others and intolerance of cultural differences that are at the root of many conflicts.

Outward Bound's leadership approach is replicable and versatile. It can be adapted to a range of leadership styles in a variety of environments and situations. There are no secrets to the Outward Bound approach. Outward Bound leaders model a transparent leadership style that allows those who follow them to absorb leadership lessons directly by watching and listening. Outward Bound's philosophy stems from the clearly articulated core values and principles of an innovative educator, founder Kurt Hahn. Outward Bound's methods are based on more than half a century of experimentation and practice in more than thirty countries. And Outward Bound's strategies are broadly applicable enough to be used in classrooms, the wilderness, boardrooms, playing fields, legislatures, and many other leadership environments.

The Outward Bound philosophy of education is also modeled on centuries of educational wisdom and experimentation, with traditions dating back to the Greeks and Romans as well as innovations taking place in classrooms every day. Kurt Hahn was a daring educator who founded several schools in Europe. When discussing educational

ideology, Hahn often told a particular story about Outward Bound's roots in traditional education. As Hahn described in a speech in London in 1960, the co-founder of one Hahn's schools, Prince Max of Baden (the last imperial chancellor of Germany), was being interviewed by a visitor to the school.

Prince Max's enthusiastic guest asked him the following question: "What are you proudest of in your beautiful schools?" He said, "I am proudest of the fact that if you go the length and breadth of the schools, you will find nothing original in them. It is stolen from everywhere, from the British public school, from the Boy Scouts, from Plato, from Goethe."

Then the enthusiastic guest turned to him and said, "But oughtn't you to aim at being original?" Prince Max rather abruptly answered, "Well, you know, it is in education like in medicine; you must harvest the wisdom of a thousand years. If you ever came across a surgeon who wants to take out your appendix in the most original manner possible, I would strongly advise you to go to another surgeon."

Outward Bound not only harvests the best traditional educational wisdom but also remains on the forefront of current educational innovation. Outward Bound developed an innovative and comprehensive proposal for school reform called Expeditionary Learning that won a series of large grants from the New American Schools Development Corporation, beginning in 1992–3 and continuing through 1996–7. The Expeditionary Learning Schools (ELS) design was eventually implemented in schools across the United States.

Outward Bound's leadership style is accessible to new leaders, as well as thought-provoking and stimulating to experienced leaders. Every year Outward Bound trains hundreds of new staff and participants in its leadership methods. Most people get the message fairly easily. The leadership skills

Outward Bound imparts are immediately relevant to situations at hand. Leadership lessons are reinforced by practice and reflection on successes and failures. For more-experienced leaders, the Outward Bound approach offers a means of refining leadership skills, as well as innovative ways of being a better leader by being a better follower.

Outward Bound uses an unfamiliar environment as the most effective classroom. In the Outward Bound Expeditionary Learning model, the expedition metaphor provides an unfamiliar, and therefore helpful, learning environment. This is one of the most successful strategies employed by Outward Bound programs of all types. In the traditional Outward Bound course, the classroom is the wilderness. But as Outward Bound programs spread to corporations and schools, different kinds of classrooms have been used with great success. Sometimes the unfamiliar environment is a social one, comprised of learners who don't yet know each other. For example, a much-publicized series of Outward Bound programs involved giving corporate executives urban experiences in large cities.

The criteria for a successful unfamiliar learning environment are simply that (1) the environment is different enough from what the learners are used to so that a certain degree of tension or anxiety is present; (2) the opportunity exists for the learners to master skills that help them meet the challenges presented by the foreign environment; and (3) success is possible only as the result of group effort.

In an address at an international Outward Bound conference in 1987, Dr. Paul Ylvisaker, former dean of the Harvard University Graduate School of Education, described how learning takes place best in environments that evoke high emotion. The wilderness environment—or the metaphorical "wilderness" environments just described—produce such emotion and are thus conducive to profound learning. Ylvisaker noted that the best learning environment is characterized by the following conditions, all of which are key components of the

Outward Bound learning environment:
- challenge and emotion
- caring and intimacy
- a high prospect of success
- an environment in which the collective and the individual come together
- an environment in which values are clear and the "value" of values is immediately demonstrable

An unfamiliar environment—whether physical, metaphorical, or social—is one that you create for your own leadership situations, and the conditions that accompany it can be used to guide your leadership approach and strategies.

Before we can discover *how* Outward Bound goes about developing leadership skills and teaching leadership, we must go back to the origins of Outward Bound to understand the unique place Outward Bound occupies in leadership training. The sections below describe its founding principles, the values that influence it today, and the ways in which those values guide Outward Bound in its leadership practices and lessons.

THE ORIGINS OF OUTWARD BOUND

"Training for all through the sea or the mountains—that is my plea."
—Kurt Hahn, in an address given to the Honourable Mariners' Company in Glasgow, Scotland, in 1947

Kurt Hahn, Outward Bound's founder, was born into a cultured Jewish family in Berlin in the late 1800s. Due to severe sunstroke he suffered in college, Hahn spent a number of lonely months in darkened rooms, during which time he experienced firsthand something that later formed his guiding educational and personal philosophy: "Your disability is your opportunity." Using this motto and some theories he drew from Plato's *Republic*, the Oxford-educated Hahn devised a plan for a new kind of school, which he later

OUTWARD BOUND'S EXPEDITIONARY LEARNING SCHOOLS

Expeditionary Learning Schools/Outward Bound create, develop, and sustain good public schools that are more active, engaging, rigorous, and humane than the norm in cities and towns where good schools are most needed. Education and leadership both have the fundamental purpose of helping people deal well with the new, with the unfamiliar, with change. At some level, education and leadership are vehicles for improving the world. That's a long-term project, and it requires constancy of behavior and values. Every teacher leads his or her class, leads his or her students. Every leader teaches his or her peers, subordinates, bosses. Whether the word we use is "teaching" or "leading," the principles and practices for doing it well are basically the same. Here are seven such principles and accompanying practices that help teachers become good teachers. They apply well to leaders who may not yet think of themselves as teachers.

Managing the self: teaching or leading by example, using examples to teach: Expeditionary Learning Schools have the principle of taking responsibility for one's own learning. The will to carry on and not give up in the face of great obstacles and difficulties is one of the fundamental behaviors taught and learned in Expeditionary Learning Schools. Good teaching requires self-disciplined teachers who, whatever else they teach, teach their students self-discipline by being self-disciplined. Good teachers also teach respect, kindness, courtesy, and strong work habits by exemplifying them. In public schools, students see their teachers every day over the course of a year or several years. If teachers are not lit up by learning, they aren't likely to light up the learning in their students. It's the teacher's job to notice and call attention to good models of all kinds. Students need models to know what quality looks like, feels like, sounds like in the work they're expected to do. Teachers can be very effective when they are transparent, think out loud, or in other ways give students a window into the teacher's thinking. The very idea that teachers are learners is important to demonstrate. A good way for a teacher to make his or her own learning process accessible to students is to work and learn alongside them, jointly researching subjects on which neither teacher nor student is expert.

Establishing a culture: Defining, exemplifying, and communicating values is one of the central requirements of leadership, and especially of educational leadership. Outward Bound's central value is profound personal development harnessed to helping others; in schools, the aim may be to develop a student culture where it's cool to work hard, do your best work, trust your teachers, and read whole books. In Expeditionary Learning Schools, tracking (the practice of placing students in different classes based on perceived differences in their abilities) is eliminated or minimized, and students collaborate with each other, critique each other, and help each other do their best work. The idea is to establish a culture (including a peer culture) of quality where nothing less than people's best work is expected.

Knowing and caring about the people: Be constantly on the lookout for ways to help students along the path to self-discovery, very often in unexpected and unorthodox ways. Expeditionary Learning Schools make use of small groups in classrooms to organize work and develop the students' abilities to collaborate and help one another. Expeditionary Learning high schools and middle schools have "crew," where small groups of students meet regularly with a faculty adviser to make sure no one is isolated or lost in the shuffle.

Knowing and caring about the content, material, and work: If you're teaching math, you should know the math you're teaching well enough to play with it. You must be curious and interested in finding out more about it, what you can do and understand with it. Expeditionary Learning Schools help teachers pick subjects that are socially charged and naturally engage students' natural connection and sense of fairness. The idea is to make assignments more compelling by finding the local connections to the overarching topics within their own communities.

Building a good team: Teachers in public schools don't generally get to choose the students who'll be in their classes. Teaching, therefore, has much to do with making the group you have into the most effective learning group possible. One important teaching skill that comes from knowing students well is knowing which students to pair or group together for what kinds of tasks. Putting the right people together for the right kinds of things is a key leadership skill in all kinds of organizations, and it comes from knowing your people well. It is high-priority, high-leverage work for a teacher in the classroom.

Committing to the mission, focusing, and persevering: Many efforts to change institutions are abandoned before they've really gotten started, thus assuring that they won't work because they are not actually *tried* long enough to work. School reform, by its very nature, requires a sustained effort. It takes more time to improve schools than is generally discussed or acknow-ledged in the press and in political debate, and it often takes longer than our political structures support. Ideas are important, but they come in a moment. Doing is what counts, and doing takes years. Outward Bound, through its Expeditionary Learning Schools program, contracts long term with schools to work closely with teachers to improve student learning, school culture, and the quality of instruction. We begin by requiring an at least 80 percent positive faculty vote from each school-partner before starting to work with them on a five-year plan, which, we have learned, is generally how long it takes to make a good school (or to make a school good) when most things are going right.

Stepping back, letting go, and bringing out the best: One reason so many children are bored in school is that teachers talk too much. In Expeditionary Learning Schools, teachers talk less and students do more. Gradually stepping back and letting the students take charge is perhaps the overarching pedagogical practice that defines the *course* of an Outward Bound course. The student moves from dependence to independence.

—*Greg Farrell, President and CEO, Expeditionary Learning Schools/Outward Bound*

co-founded with Prince Max of Baden, Germany's last imperial chancellor. Based on Plato's educational ideals, the Schule Schloss Salem, a coeducational boarding school (whose name was derived from the Hebrew word *shalom* and the Arabic word *salaam*, both meaning "peace") opened in Germany in April of 1920, with Hahn as headmaster.

Germany was in a time of despair, bordering on anarchy, with its youth particularly susceptible to opportunities that gave them feelings of power, belonging, and importance. The rise of Nazism and the German youth movement granted young people freedom and importance in society—without, as Hahn believed, their having to earn it. Hahn's intent at Salem School, as described by Josh Miner and Joe Boldt in *Outward Bound USA: Crew Not Passengers,* was to "nurture a German youth with con-

victions rooted in personal responsibility, kindness, and justice." Hahn wanted to train future citizen leaders who would stand up for what they believed to be right, "despite hardships, despite dangers, despite inner skepticism, despite boredom, despite mockery from the world, despite emotion of the moment."

Hahn's outspoken criticism of Hitler and Nazism eventually resulted in his self-exile in Scotland and England, where he battled depression over the loss of his school, his homeland, his livelihood, and his struggle for the integrity of German youth. But he summoned strength by reminding himself that his "disability" was indeed his "opportunity," and once again he founded an innovative school. This time a school just for boys (the school went coeducational in 1974), it was called Gordonstoun, and opened outside the city of

Elgin, Scotland, on the coast of the Moray Firth, in 1933. With a distinguished board of directors and some notable pupils (including Greece's Prince Phillip, who was first a student at Salem School in Germany and was later to marry the future Queen of England, Elizabeth II), Gordonstoun's enrollment grew steadily. When World War II broke out in 1939, however, the British Army commandeered Gordonstoun, and Hahn faced another setback-inspired opportunity.

At this time, British merchant ships by the dozens were being sunk by German U-boats in the frigid North Atlantic Ocean. When survivors were picked up in lifeboats, a curious thing was discovered: the older, petty officers were alive, and the younger, fitter, seventeen- to twenty-year-old seamen had died. The situation was so bad, according to Miner and Boldt, that Lawrence Holt, partner in a large merchant-shipping enterprise, the Blue Funnel Shipping Line, told Hahn that he "would rather entrust the lowering of a lifeboat in [the] mid-Atlantic to a sail-trained octogenarian than to a young sea technician who is competently trained in the modern way but has never been sprayed by salt water."

Holt, whose own children were Gordonstoun alumni, asked Hahn whether he had any idea why the younger sailors were dying and the more senior ones were surviving. Hahn replied that he believed the younger men were simply becoming overwhelmed by the frigid weather and the anxiety of an unlikely survival. When presented with challenges more extreme than any others they'd ever faced, Hahn said, the young men were giving up and succumbing, whereas the older men, who had been in touchy situations before, were not only surviving but were also able to reach out to help the younger men. By helping the others survive, they were able to access reserves of extra strength and thereby survive themselves.

Holt asked Hahn whether he could design a course combining the hardships of cold-water survival and the compassion of reaching out to help one's shipmates. Hahn said he could—and Outward Bound was born. The shipping company provided funds and maritime staff members for the founding of a new school in Aberdovey, Wales, a school designed to promote physical fitness, enterprise, tenacity, and compassion among British youth. Although the school did not exclusively train young merchant sailors to prove hardier at sea, it served a similar purpose: training generations of British youth to find within themselves the inner strength to learn to overcome emotional or psychological doubts about their abilities (or to "defeat their defeatism," in Hahn's words, according to Miner and Boldt), and to push themselves further than they thought possible.

The Aberdovey school was unique in that it provided short-term training (courses lasted only a month) that consisted of wilderness and maritime experiences, physical fitness preparation, technical skills practice, rescue training, and service to the local people. Hahn's belief was that the essence of Outward Bound was to provide "training for all *through* the sea or the mountains" rather than *for*," meaning that he was not training students to become sailors or mountaineers but, rather, by using the inherent lessons of the sea and the backcountry, the unique setting of an outdoor classroom, and the potential for increased self-awareness, he was helping students to gain life experience and develop character. This is something still emphasized in Outward Bound today: training *through* the sea, rather than *for* the sea, or training *through* the mountains, rather than *for* the mountains.

In 1962 the Outward Bound concept was introduced in the United States, when the first Outward Bound school opened in Colorado. Today, Outward Bound in the United States is comprised of five branches: Wilderness, Expeditionary Learning Schools, Professional, Urban Center, and Discovery.

Wilderness: Outward Bound's backcountry expeditions last from four to ninety days and consist of backpacking, canyoneering, canoeing, dogsledding, mountaineering, white-water rafting, rock climbing, sailing, sea kayaking, skiing, and snowboarding.

Expeditionary Learning Schools: Outward Bound's innovative school program combines rigorous academic content, learning expeditions, active teaching, and community service.

Professional: Outward Bound Professional has developed custom programs delivered in the wilderness and in boardrooms that are designed to facilitate organizational change and build professional teams in the workplace.

Urban Centers: Outward Bound's school- and community-based programs in urban centers provide students, educators, and civic leaders with cross-cultural experiences to better understand their capabilities and their value to their communities. Challenges often include visiting an unfamiliar neighborhood, working in a homeless shelter, and sleeping out in a city park, as well as wilderness components such as canoeing, rock climbing, and camping.

Discovery: Outward Bound has designed these programs to serve at-risk youth, those who have been committed by the juvenile justice system, or those who are at risk for dropping out of school, running away from home, or getting involved in criminal activity. Discovery programs involve the families of young people, as well as schools and communities that are exposed to factors, such as the street-drug culture and gangs, that stimulate delinquency.

The methods underlying the five branches of Outward Bound are guided by Outward Bound's values, educational principles, and leadership strategies.

OUTWARD BOUND'S PURPOSE

Plus Est en Vous.
(*"You have more in you than you think."*)
—*Gordonstoun school motto*

The term "outward bound" signifies the moment that a ship leaves the safety of the harbor and commits itself to the unknown challenges, hazards, and rewards of the open sea. Kurt Hahn and Lawrence Holt named their training program "Outward Bound" because they were cutting their students loose from the safety of home, family, friends, and familiar routines and thrusting them into uncomfortable, challenging, and often scary new environments. Today, Outward Bound participants leave the comfort of their familiar environments and commit themselves to the challenges and rewards of an Outward Bound program. In the process of undertaking difficult tasks in unfamiliar situations with relative strangers, Outward Bound participants learn to draw on reserves of strength that they didn't know they had, learning that *plus est en vous.*

Outward Bound aims to help people discover their strengths and act upon them, not just at Outward Bound but also when they return home to their communities, their families, their schools, or their workplaces. An Outward Bound program seeks to prepare people to better deal with the tests of strength and character that we all inevitably face in life. The Outward Bound mission has succeeded if alumni go on to become role models, leaders by example, agents of positive change, and, ultimately, more empathetic, compassionate individuals.

One of the best examples of a leader doing what he believed to be right comes from Josh Miner, Kurt Hahn's protégé who brought Outward Bound from Britain to the United States. At Gordonstoun, Miner was coaching Hahn's track team and was faced unexpectedly with a rival team showing up to compete barefoot. At first Miner was concerned, but he eventually reasoned to himself that those athletes were accustomed to practicing barefoot, and the meet was held on a grass track, so therefore the advantage didn't seem too unfair. When Hahn noticed what was happening, though, he told Miner, "Those boys can't afford track shoes. Have our lads take off theirs and start the meet over." Although Miner was initially disgruntled, he later wrote in *Outward Bound USA: Crew Not Passengers* that this was one of life's most important lessons: the example Kurt Hahn set in his "instant, uncompromising doing of what he knew to be right."

THE OUTWARD BOUND PROCESS

We are better than we know. If we can just be made to see it, perhaps for the rest of our lives, we'll be unwilling to settle for less.
—*past Outward Bound participant*

For many years, the magic that happens on Outward Bound courses seemed to most people to be a bit of a mystery. People knew that Outward Bound turned out amazing results, but nobody—even those within the organization—seemed to be able to describe how or why.

Then in 1976 two Outward Bound instructors, Victor Walsh and Gerald Golins, articulated what had previously been considered simply the inexplicable, magical success of the Outward Bound methodology. In a paper entitled "The Exploration of the Outward Bound Process," Walsh and Golins broke down the Outward Bound process into some of its key elements. The basic concept shows a willing learner facing challenges in an unfamiliar environment, solving these problems by working closely with strangers, and emerging more confident and competent as a result (Figure 1).

The presence of this structure and these conditions does not guarantee the outcome of expanded capacity (or "character development," as Outward Bound's goal is now commonly referred to), but it does provide an environment that is conducive to achieving this outcome.

Once the Outward Bound process was described in this manner, it became easier to replicate the conditions that result in character development, both within Outward Bound as well as in programs hoping to duplicate Outward Bound's success. This description also provided instructional staff—the critical link between Outward Bound intentions and actual results—with a clear framework for program structure and delivery.

The Walsh and Golins model for Outward Bound's process is straightforward: if you use your own skills to solve stressful problems with new teammates in unfamiliar surroundings, you will emerge stronger and more confident than before. Or, to paraphrase the quotation at the beginning of this section, if you are put in situations in which you realize you have more in you than you thought you did, you will forever after hold yourself to a higher standard.

Outward Bound's Guiding Principles

The Outward Bound philosophy is a unique blend of two great traditions: the Greco-Roman way of tenacity, physical challenge, courage, and perseverance, and the Judeo-Christian way of compassion, self-sacrifice, love, and tolerance. At a time when many of Kurt Hahn's contemporaries were espousing either military or pacifist values, it is no surprise that the innovative Hahn supported unconventional curricula that combined the seemingly incongruous traditions, supplemented by activities that challenged and developed the mind, the spirit, the heart, and the body. The result is that today an Outward Bound alumnus can finish an Outward Bound course saying both, "I have never felt so sorry for myself, or so frustrated, or so miserable" as well as, "I have never felt so exhilarated, so cared-for, and so concerned about others."

In the years leading up to the founding of Outward Bound, Kurt Hahn articulated several sets of values, tenets, and principles that continue to guide Outward Bound today: the four pillars of Outward Bound, the five tenets of education, and the seven guiding principles of character development.

The Four Pillars (Core Values)

In a conversation with another educator, Lester Davies, Hahn asked Davies to imagine a Roman temple whose roof served as the Outward Bound training program. Hahn described this conversation in a 1947 address to the Honorable Mariners' Company in Glasgow, Scotland: "It does not matter whether the mountains, the sea, or any other

A motivated, committed

STUDENT

is placed into a

UNIQUE PHYSICAL ENVIRONMENT

(as opposed to an accustomed environment)
and into a

UNIQUE SOCIAL ENVIRONMENT

(which allows both individuality and group consciousness; both conflict and resolution)
and is then given

PROBLEM-SOLVING TASKS AND CHALLENGES

(that are organized, concrete, incremental, and manageable, which require mastery of technical skills) and
that create

STRESS AND/OR ANXIETY

(which stimulates possibilities such as succumbing, coping, or thriving),
to which the student adapts by demonstrating

MASTERY AND/OR COMPETENCY

(because the student is motivated, is alert, has group and instructional support, and is presented with
problems that are structured to facilitate mastery),
which

EXPANDS CAPACITY AND DEVELOPS CHARACTER

(increased self-awareness, increased self-esteem, and increased acceptance of and service to others).

Figure 1. The Outward Bound Process

topographical medium is used for the activities which help to develop the boy's character," Hahn said, "[but] the roof must be held aloft by four pillars." These four pillars—rescue, physical fitness, self-reliance, and project work—formed the core values of Hahn's Aberdovey School.

Students were trained to perform rescues on sea and land as a service to their local (mostly maritime) communities. Physical-fitness training instilled confidence through improved health and vibrancy. Self-reliance was obtained by learning to "cope with the basic requirements of simple life"—meeting one's own needs, relying on one's own inner strengths and knowledge, and gaining

the confidence to look to oneself to meet challenges. Project work trained students to learn concrete skills, to develop the "sixth sense" that distinguishes "the true craftsman, the true healer, the true seaman."

As Outward Bound evolved, so did Hahn's four pillars. Today, Outward Bound's educational philosophy is held aloft by these four pillars:

1. Self-reliance
2. Physical fitness
3. Craftsmanship
4. Service and compassion

These key concepts form the historical framework of Outward Bound's core values, as well as its approach to teaching leadership. The best leaders, as Outward Bound believes, are self-reliant and physically and mentally fit. They take pride in the quality of their work, and if they choose to do something, they do it well. They willingly and enthusiastically serve others and their communities. And above all, they show compassion for their fellow human beings.

A brief look at how these values influence Outward Bound leadership situations illustrates the relationship between the four pillars and the Outward Bound leadership approach.

1. Self-reliance: As did Kurt Hahn, Outward Bound staff today model and teach reliance on one's own skills and strengths. The confidence that comes with knowing that you have the ability to solve your own problems is a critical aspect of being both a secure leader as well as a valuable member of any community. Self-reliance does not dictate isolation from or an inability to work with other people; instead, it encourages self-sufficiency, innovation, and, in Hahn's words, "sensible self-denial."

> **Leadership Situation:** *Participants are trying to decide whether they should set up tents tonight. One participant asks the leader, "Is it going to rain?" The leader has two choices of response.*
> **Response Option One:** *"I think so; you'd better put up your tents."*
> **Response Option Two:** *"This is a great opportunity to learn about cloud formations and weather patterns. Did anybody notice any cloud formations this afternoon? . . . "*

The second reply encourages self-sufficiency by giving participants the information they need to make a decision; and not just that particular night but every night.

2. Physical fitness: A leader needs to be physically and mentally fit enough to perform any leadership duties that might be required—*at the highest level possible.* Clearly, if you're a wilderness trip

leader, the level of fitness you'll need will be different from that required for the leader of an advocacy group. But Outward Bound believes that, regardless of their leadership responsibilities, the most effective leaders are those who maintain healthy bodies and clear minds, modeling a balanced life and an attitude of reasonable self-denial.

> **Leadership Situation:** *After a long day of hiking, a couple of participants approach the leader and tell her that they'd like to do a moonlight ascent of a nearby peak. The weather conditions are clear and calm, the peak is only a short distance away, and the climb is not technical. Organizational policy (as well as common sense and good judgment) dictate that nighttime activities be supervised by a leader.*
> **Response Option One:** *"That sounds like a wonderful idea, but I'm really tired after today's hike. What if we climb the peak tomorrow morning instead?"*
> **Response Option Two:** *"Wow, what a great idea. I'm tired, but I have enough energy to climb the peak with you. Let's get packed up."*

Doing the extra moonlight hike is not a requirement of the job, but it will enhance the quality of the experience for the participants, as well as encouraging future initiative on their part. The leader who is physically fit enough to lead *at the highest level possible* will still have enough energy left at the end of the day do something like this—to climb that extra peak, manage an evacuation, or do whatever else she might be called upon to accomplish.

3. Craftsmanship: Outward Bound's methods of experience-based education puts participants in situations wherein the need for specific skills is immediately apparent and wherein the application of these skills (for example, reading a map correctly, making a good decision about which route to take, treating a wound properly, interpreting weather

THE OUTWARD BOUND PROCESS 29

patterns accurately) usually results in success. Instructors promote craftsmanship by modeling high-quality work, and they encourage participants to hold themselves to high standards and to take pride in everything they do.

> **Leadership Situation:** *It's late at night, and the group has been hiking hard all day. The exhausted participants want just to flop down on the ground on their sleeping bags and pads, foregoing any camp chores until after a good night's sleep. The participants saw the cirrus clouds come in earlier that day and know that they could have rain by morning. Setting up tents would be the prudent thing to do, but they are too tired to deal with erecting tents. They ask the leader if that's OK.*
> **Response Option One:** *The leader says, "Sure, good idea; I'm tired too," and flops down beside them.*
> **Response Option Two:** *The leader says, "Sure, no problem," and then sets up the participants' tents himself.*
> **Response Option Three:** *The leader says, "That was a hard day, wasn't it? No wonder we're all so tired. But because we've seen the cloud cover develop today and could have rain by morning, we really need to set up the tents. Once I have my tent up, I'll come around and help you."*

Option Three allows the leader to show compassion for his tired group, while still modeling good camp craftsmanship and involving the participants in taking responsibility for themselves.

4. Service and compassion: Meeting the needs of another person, group, or community ignites, in Kurt Hahn's words, "the highest dynamics of the human soul." When people throw themselves into working for the common good, serving their group or community, and showing compassion for their fellow human beings, their strongest, most admirable selves come forth. Even though

their initial inclination might be just to look out for their own needs—particularly in challenging or difficult situations—people usually find that by helping others, they discover strength that they didn't know they had.

> **Leadership Situation:** *It's late in the day, and several participants are struggling to keep up with the group, although several other participants are still hiking energetically. One of those lagging behind finally suggests that they stop and make camp early. The group turns to the leader for a decision.*
> **Response Option One:** *"You're right; some people are too tired to continue. Let's camp right over there."*
> **Response Option Two:** *"It does seem as though some people are moving more slowly than others. How could we address this situation?" The leader then helps the group brainstorm possible solutions, including stopping early, taking a water and food break, or redistributing pack loads among the members of the group.*

Option Two gives half the group the opportunity to show compassion for the other half, without forcing any particular outcome. Compassion and service lose their allure when coerced.

Further examples of how these four pillars are incorporated into individual Outward Bound programs are described in the other parts of this book.

Five Tenets of Education

Kurt Hahn's progressive educational theories centered around creating well-rounded, socially responsible citizen-leaders. In pursuit of this goal, he established educational principles and practices that combine action and thought, as well as challenges that require imagination and innovation and that strengthen the body as well as the mind. He created situations that balance out students' strengths and weaknesses. Hahn articulated five educational tenets or objectives aimed at training citizen-leaders and that served as Outward Bound's mission statement for decades—"I regard it as the foremost task of education to insure the survival of these qualities."

1. an enterprising curiosity
2. an indefatigable spirit
3. tenacity in pursuit
4. readiness for sensible self-denial
5. above all, compassion

Curious leaders seek out new ideas and fresh methods, refusing to get stuck in ruts or practicing outdated techniques. Leaders with indefatigable spirits are able to maintain a positive outlook and to energize their groups when morale is low. Tenacious leaders refuse to quit when things get tough, persevering even beyond what they might think are their limits. Leaders who are willing to make reasonable personal sacrifices save energy for the common cause, rather than focusing on their own needs or aims. And, finally, the compassionate leader—one who is able to put herself in another's shoes, to demonstrate genuine empathy and caring—creates an environment of trust and mutual respect, builds a strong team, and provides opportunities for personal learning and growth.

The best way for leaders to instill these qualities in those who follow them is to model them.

Seven Principles of Character Development

At the Salem School, Hahn and Prince Max encouraged their students to develop values rooted in personal responsibility, kindness, and justice. The Seven Laws of Salem were born from this objective. The seven laws are these:

1. Give children the opportunity for self-discovery.
2. Make the children meet with triumph and defeat.
3. Give the children the opportunity for self-effacement in the common cause.
4. Provide periods of silence.
5. Train the imagination.
6. Make games (in other words, competition) important but not predominant.

7. Free the children of the wealthy and powerful from the enervating sense of privilege.

Let's look at how each of these seven laws applies to Outward Bound and can be used to improve leadership ability.

1. Give the opportunity for self-discovery. Those who know themselves, who are aware of their own values, strengths, and limitations, are most able to lead others. In order to lead effectively, you must be grounded in your own beliefs and values.

2. Make your followers meet with triumph and defeat. The best leaders build on their successes and learn from their failures. The experiences of both triumph and defeat are necessary; triumph builds confidence, and defeat fosters humility.

3. Give the opportunity for self-effacement in the common cause. Few things are more thrilling than losing oneself in a common quest, and the act of serving others is the best means of fostering compassion for one's fellow human beings. When people throw themselves wholeheartedly into a task for the good of the group—rather than for the good of the self—they bring their most powerful, admirable selves forward, which translates into a strong leadership presence.

4. Provide periods of silence. Reflection creates opportunities for self-examination and increased self-awareness. Confident leaders are self-aware and use periods of reflection to learn from past experiences and better plan for new situations.

5. Train the imagination. The most successful leaders in history have been those who were able to think on their feet, adjust quickly to change, and imagine the impossible. Leaders need to be able to inspire through innovation, adapt to accommodate new circumstances, and have the vision to nurture themselves and their groups to do things that they didn't think they could.

6. Make competition important but not predominant. Competition for the common good is usually more inspiring and rewarding than competition for individual gain. Leaders who nurture in their groups a sense of communal competition ("let's see how fast we can all make it up this mountain") create a healthier environment than do leaders who encourage individual rivalry ("let's see who makes it up to the top of the mountain first"). Leaders must be able to build a cohesive team, and encouraging competition *for* the group as a whole is more effective than promoting competition *within* the group.

7. Free the children of the wealthy and powerful from the enervating sense of privilege. The Outward Bound experience endeavors to create a level playing field on which no one is entitled to any special treatment. Participants learn that they must pull their own weight as an equal member of the group, not as a special case exempt from hard work.

These seven laws are instrumental in Outward Bound's educational-reform models today, and they also guide Outward Bound enrollment objectives and wilderness course design.

USING OUTWARD BOUND VALUES AND PRINCIPLES IN YOUR OWN LEADERSHIP PHILOSOPHY

Clearly, Outward Bound's foundations in leadership and character development are well established. But what does this mean for *your* leadership philosophy? Good news—it means that you have the opportunity to draw on these solid foundations to influence your own leadership style and strategies.

But how do you decide what to use in your own leadership situations? In order to do this, you need to be grounded in a solid understanding of your own values, convictions, strengths, and limitations. Your self-awareness will contribute to your ability to determine which leadership styles and strategies will and which won't work for you.

What Motivates You?

You might begin by asking yourself why you lead. There are no right or wrong answers to this question, but some answers will generally indicate whether you're going to enjoy leading and be good at it.

■ If you're leading because you get an ego boost from it, your participants are likely to pick up on this, triggering power struggles with your groups.

■ If you're leading because it's what you've always done and it's easier to keep doing it than to find another job, then you're likely to burn out and make a big mistake eventually.

■ If you're leading because you're used to being in charge and you aren't good at following, then you may find yourself getting frustrated when your groups begin to function independently and in situations that require the leader to take a backseat role. Or, worse, you may fail to allow your groups to develop autonomy and independence because you need to remain in charge.

■ If you're leading simply because no one else is willing to do it, you may grow resentful of your group.

Being a leader is incredibly demanding. Most leadership situations involve dealing intensely with people—not with projects, ideals, or inanimate objects—so if you're not motivated by a desire to work closely with others, you might reconsider your decision to become a leader.

But the following motivations probably indicate that you will thrive over the long term in leadership positions:

■ You want to be (or are already) a leader because you get satisfaction from seeing people experience personal growth.

■ You want to be (or are already) a leader because you love working with people, and the challenge of building teams brings you great satisfaction.

■ You want to be (or are already) a leader because you've found that accomplishing goals in groups makes you feel alive, and you hope to share this experience with others.

How Do You Apply Outward Bound's Guiding Principles?

Once you've figured out some of your leadership motivations, you can begin to identify what sort of leader you'd like to become and how you can go about reaching your goals. Now let's look at some examples of ways in which you might use Outward Bound leadership philosophy or values in your own leadership situations.

Craftsmanship

Leadership Situation: *You're the volunteer leader of a local food bank that gets lots of donations and makes up hundreds of boxes of food every day. Your group gets the job done quickly and cheerfully, but the quality of the work is inconsistent. Some boxes are missing certain items, while others contain duplicates of those same items. You want to set a better standard of craftsmanship (one of the four pillars), but there just doesn't seem to be enough time.*

Response: *You decide to ask several volunteers to join you in an extra weekly shift, which will be spent organizing the food warehouse so that boxes can be packed more efficiently and meticulously. You also institute a new inventory system, so that each box is checked before it goes out the door for delivery. You begin to emphasize the importance of accuracy over the value of speed, and your volunteers begin to slow down a bit, taking more care to make sure that boxes are packed properly rather than trying to get as many boxes out the door as possible.*

Physical Fitness

Leadership Situation: *You're the head of the local volunteer ambulance crew. Your team has some very skilled men and women, but many of them are quite out of shape. The actual work doesn't demand a high level of physical fitness (another of the four pillars), but you believe that your team could be even more valuable if your volunteers were fitter and therefore better able to reach the scene of emergencies quickly.*

Response: *You begin using part of each weekly training session for fitness training. You begin slowly, with some friendly games of basketball or soccer, but soon build up to weekly hikes and bike rides. Your crew enjoys the camaraderie of the weekly activities, and they all begin to feel better about themselves as pounds drop and muscles emerge. The ambulance work becomes easier, too, as people grow more agile, quicker on their feet, and more adept at lifting heavier things.*

Sensible Self-Denial

Leadership Situation: *You're a middle manager in a small high-tech company that is facing a rough period and has decided to layoff some of its people. You have a great team working under you, and you don't want to lose any of them, particularly because you're confident that the company will need to grow again within a few years. You investigate a bit and discover that if enough of the upper and middle management agreed to give up annual year-end bonuses, the amount saved would cover the salaries of the people who would be laid off. You wonder whether this might be a great opportunity for sensible self-denial (one of the five tenets of education).*

Response: *You don't really want to give up your bonus, but after discussing it with your spouse, you determine that though the bonus is useful, it isn't necessary for meeting your basic financial needs. You enlist the cooperation of several other managers, and you approach the board of directors with your plan. You forego your annual bonus, make more cuts in discretionary spending, and continue working with your loyal team.*

Triumph and Defeat

Leadership Situation: *You're the new coach of your son's undefeated hockey team. After a few games, you realize that your*

*team is playing way out of its league. Your
team has many more resources, more experience, and more time to practice than most of
the other teams in its league, so it is easily
beating all the teams it plays. Your players
have developed arrogant, almost condescending attitudes toward the other teams as
they easily rack up victory after victory.
You realize that your team is not learning
anything about competitiveness and, more
important, the players are not experiencing
the value of losing; you think it's important
that the kids learn about both triumph and
defeat (the second of the seven principles of
character development).*

    Response: *You switch your team to a
more competitive league. At first the kids are
devastated by their initial losses, and some of*

*the other parents are quite angry with you.
But as the pain of losing mounts, the kids
grow driven to become a stronger team. They
begin to focus on working hard at practices
in a way that they hadn't before. They lose
their cocky attitude and treat opposing teams
with respect. They feel genuinely proud of
the games they win, and they use losing
games as opportunities to critique their
techniques and strategies.*

A FINAL NOTE

Now that you've thought a bit about how Outward
Bound's leadership values and principles can influence your own leadership approach, the following
chapters can help you begin to tackle the specific
strategies and styles that make you the leader you
are, as well as the leader you want to become.

CHAPTER 2

BECOMING A LEADER

Your position never gives you the right to command. It only imposes on you the duty
of so living your life that others can receive your orders without being humiliated.
—Dag Hammarskjöld, **Markings**

Leadership can be daunting. Many people are afraid of public speaking; some lack the confidence to assert themselves; others don't value their own opinions or skills enough to think that anyone else would want to follow them. Leadership roles and responsibilities can seem vague, and the qualities that make a good leader are often elusive. Frequently, when Outward Bound instructors are addressing the concept of leadership to a group of our students, many of them express doubt about their ability to be a leader. "I'm not very charismatic," they say, or "I'm a better follower."

But when we explain leadership this way— "Leadership is seeing what needs to be done and getting a group of people to do it"—the students usually get it. Suddenly being a leader doesn't seem so intimidating or out of reach. Student leaders quickly learn to identify what needs to be done and organize their peers to do it, whether it is packing up camp, following a compass bearing, or reaching the top of a distant summit. What's more, really good leaders not only get others to do something, but they get them to *want* to do it.

In *The Leadership Challenge*, organizational leadership consultants Jim Kouzes and Barry Posner in 2002 provide a more sophisticated definition, calling leadership "the art of mobilizing others to want to struggle for shared aspirations." Once you understand the underlying goal of the best leadership—getting people to do something enthusiastically—then you can think of all leadership strategies as a means of achieving this end.

The first questions you must ask yourself are these: "Am I ready to project an image of com-petence and skill? Do I have what it takes to be a good leader?" You might begin by simply asking yourself, "Do I have the ability to mobilize people to struggle toward shared goals?"

Think back on recent leadership roles you've held. Have you motivated a group of people to do something? Led a production team at work? Started a volunteer firefighting squad in your community? Served as president of your local Parent Teacher Association? Volunteered to be your kids' scout leader? You may even have some leadership experience that you have forgotten about or that you have considered unnoteworthy. Were you the class president in high school? Or the captain of your sports team? Did you lead a church youth group? Or have you started a book club in your community? Consider any experience in which you motivated a group of people to do something.

Whatever the situation, it's possible that you already have some leadership experience or background on which you can draw. Although your "followers" and the particular situation might be different, the principles of good leadership remain the same, and the lessons you learned in your previous leadership roles can be applied to leadership positions you'll take on in the future, along with some new ideas incorporated from the Outward Bound leadership methodology.

In their book *Effective Leadership in Adventure Programming*, outdoor leadership experts Simon Priest and Michael Gass refer to leadership as "a process of influence based on power." As a leader, you hold a tremendous amount of power, which you use to influence the people in your groups.

You will adopt or embody many different leadership qualities and strategies, but ultimately all of them represent your expression of your leadership power. *How* you choose to use this power defines and characterizes your leadership style.

In 1990 the International Peace Climb, formed under U.S. leadership, was a group of climbers who worked together to summit Mount Everest and to celebrate the recent rapprochement of three of the great former national rivals: Russia, China, and the United States. It was agreed that each rope team would have a Russian, a Chinese, and an American climber and that they would all cooperate to summit together.

The group met for a practice climb on Mount Rainier. The weather turned bad, and as the group descended, the Chinese climbers got totally disoriented and were lost for some time on the mountain. The American team leader determined that these Chinese climbers did not have the expertise to climb Mount Everest and sought replacement climbers. Quickly recovering from this shock of their climbers being removed from the team, the Chinese brought in a number of talented Tibetan climbers to replace the Chinese climbers.

Once the new team began climbing Mount Everest, it quickly became apparent that the style of teamwork modeled by the Americans was something fairly foreign to the Russians, who were mostly speed-climbing champions from Europe and the Caucasus Mountains. The Russians did not have confidence that the entire group was going to summit. Their idea of a summit bid involved the strongest climbers moving quickly up the mountain while the rest of the group worked to support their efforts by moving gear and establishing high-altitude camps. The Russians attempted to climb quickly to high altitudes, but they were not interested in ferrying the loads up to establish the different high camps. Consequently, the climbing leader had to rely on the American climbers and the Tibetans to ferry loads and to keep the expedition progressing up the mountain.

With the blessing of good weather, twenty of twenty-one climbers in the International Peace Climb reached the summit of Mount Everest over a period of three days, and the Russians' theory about only the fastest climbers being able to summit was proven wrong. Although all members of the group did not demonstrate the cooperation that the campaign had been designed to promote, the expedition's summit bid was wildly successful due not only to the extra efforts of the Americans and Tibetans but, even more important, to the leader's ability to make the best of a potentially bad situation.

When faced with the diverging interests of his team members, the climbing leader of the International Peace Climb, Ian Wade—a longtime Outward Bound instructor and skilled mountaineer—had to decide how best to approach the lack of Russian cooperation in order to meet the expedition's goals. Although the expedition was designed to promote cooperation among international rivals, the leader knew that the climb would receive a lot of international attention and that attention would be more positive—and, thus, the climb would be deemed more successful—if everyone on the team reached the top. The ideal situation would have been for the leader to convince the Russians to ferry loads and for the entire team to share equally in the tasks involved in reaching the summit. The leader could also have told the Russians that they must ferry loads or risk being removed from the expedition, but this would likely have bred resentment and a dissolution of team unity, perhaps even resulting in unsupportive and dangerous climbing conditions. The leader was unsuccessful in persuading the Russians to cooperate fully, and he didn't want to use his leadership power to give the Russians an ultimatum, so he eventually compromised by using the Americans and Tibetans to pick up the slack in ferrying loads. The Russians met their personal goals of climbing quickly, the team met its goal of getting everyone up the mountain, and the expedition succeeded under the skilled management of the leader, who was faced with the potential for the expedition to dissolve when the Russians wouldn't cooperate. A difficult leadership situation was resolved successfully because of strong leadership skills and the sacrifice of others willing to follow the leader's plan.

The team leader's decision not to wield his power to coerce the Russians into something they were adamantly opposed to was deliberate. On a climbing expedition, a team leader's decisions serve as the ultimate authority, and in fact, one of the main reasons that climbing expeditions always elect a team leader is because fractious situations and disagreements occur on nearly every expedition. In this situation, the leader had to decide which decision would threaten the expedition more: coercing some semblance of cooperation or allowing the spirit of cooperation to be compromised. He decided to use his leadership power to keep the expedition moving harmoniously up the mountain, rather than insisting on cooperation and perhaps gaining it at face value but likely also breeding a slew of additional headaches that would slow progress and jeopardize the success of the expedition even further.

STEPPING UP TO FILL A LEADERSHIP VACUUM

Groups without leadership make people uncomfortable. Even in situations wherein no leadership is really needed, after a little time has passed, the subtle search for a leader will begin. When a leader does emerge, the rest of the people in the group are willing to follow, at least until circumstances dictate a change.

For example, think of the classic long line out the door of the women's restroom in any public facility. Women will stand in line for long minutes, frustrated but waiting their turn. A few longing glances might be cast at the neighboring empty men's bathroom, but no one goes beyond wishing that someone else would break the ice and use it first. So when some brave soul steps forth and actually uses the men's room, suddenly the situation improves, as half the women leave the long line and join the ad hoc leader in using the men's room.

Here's another example. If you've ever been one of the first people on the scene of a car accident, you'll know that it goes something like this: Everyone mills about nervously, wanting to help but unsure how to begin. People cluster in groups, quietly wondering among themselves what happened. Finally someone arrives and begins giving directions—"You call 9-1-1. You get everyone to move their vehicles to the shoulder. You go get the first-aid kit from the trunk of my car."—and suddenly everyone has a purpose. People are happy to help out, once someone else tells them what to do.

Because people are more comfortable in groups with leadership, if you have taken responsibility for the success of a group (whether it be friends, clients, or a group of colleagues), participants or followers will automatically look to you with some degree of confidence and respect. They believe that if you have the confidence to take on this responsibility, you probably have the skills to carry it off. Or they instinctively understand that if someone else has enough faith in your skills to put you in a leadership position, they should trust that assessment. You will retain this instinctive trust and respect until you do something to jeopardize it.

ESTABLISHING CREDIBILITY AND MAINTAINING INTEGRITY AS A LEADER

A survey by Seth Godin, described in *Wisdom, Inc.*, covered 20,000 middle and top-level managers. He asked them to rate the most important virtues of leaders. The results echo the values deeply embedded in Outward Bound. The most important value they found was ethics, and the second most important value listed by these executives was teamwork. Good leadership is inseparable from irreproachable ethics, role modeling the value of doing the right thing, and being guided by a sound moral compass.

The challenge of identifying values worth upholding and then holding yourself and your followers accountable to those values is critical to the integrity of any leader. Outdoor leader Steve Willing writes in *NOLS Leadership Education Toolbox*, "If you want to be a more effective leader, then develop your values and align your behaviors with them." Walk your talk, and your followers will feel inspired to walk it with you.

One of the best ways you can earn your followers' respect is to be a role model for the values of the organization you work or volunteer for. Successful leaders succeed in part because they demonstrate and express their commitment to values that have been deemed important by a particular group. This is as true in the outdoors as it is in the workplace, in organized religion, in the military, and in politics. People respect and willingly follow leaders who embody the chosen values of the community or group.

Whether you're an outdoor leader, a classroom teacher, a volunteer group leader, or a corporate manager, the organization you work or volunteer for will expect you to uphold certain values. As long as you demonstrate your commitment to these values, your participants will continue to trust your integrity.

AVOIDING LEADERSHIP FAILURES

Leadership breakdowns occur in all types of leadership situations, and a collapse of integrity or ethics is usually the root cause. In 1992, Wayne Calloway, the chairman and chief executive officer of PepsiCo Inc., addressed this issue in a speech he gave to a conference of the National-American Wholesale Grocers Association. He said that he had noticed a disturbing trend among the company's young recruits—they weren't getting very far as managers. When the company studied these young employees to find out why, the results were surprising:

"The biggest reasons our bright young people fail have nothing to do with intelligence, or where they went to school, or even how well they know their jobs," Calloway said. *"The biggest reasons for failure were traceable to one thing—flawed values."* He named arrogance as a major problem: people assuming they're smarter than anyone else, so they don't listen to others or their ideas. In this way, arrogance kills teamwork and learning, stopping both the individual and the organization from making progress. *"The other reasons for failure for these otherwise excellent people were along the same lines: lack of loyalty, lack of perseverance, lack of commitment."*

Note that *none* of these six reasons has anything to do with education, intelligence, or experience. They all have to do with character, integrity, and values—how you conduct your life and what's important to you.

No matter why leaders fail, their failures generally occur in one of two ways: (1) when there is inconsistency in the leader's expression of the group values (for example, when the leader doesn't model those values or is only intermittently committed to upholding them), or (2) when there is dissent among group members regarding their commitment to these values (for example, when not all participants share the group values).

When a Leader Inconsistently Expresses Group Values

To illustrate the first way in which leadership fails, let's say you preach the virtues of environmental responsibility, telling your participants that they must make as little impact on the natural world as possible. But then they see you breaking branches on a tree to make room for your tent, and they begin to lose respect for you. If you frequently fail to walk your talk, your credibility declines, you increasingly lose any influence you once had over your participants, and eventually you will no longer be able to motivate them to act.

Joe's participants loved him. He was lots of fun, full of jokes, quick to start a game. An exceptional climber and mountaineer, Joe had outstanding outdoor skills and a never-ending supply of interesting stories. He had explained all of the organization's rules to the participants, but he didn't take some of those rules seriously, and he didn't really care if the participants slipped up once in a while.

For example, participants were supposed to pack up and carry out any leftovers, but a couple of times the group threw some macaroni down the outhouse hole; Joe just pretended not to notice. Another time, a couple of kids were smoking in one of the tents, but Joe just said loudly, "Hmm, that's funny, I think I smell cigarette smoke. I must be imagining it." Joe was cool—the kids could really relate to him.

Things got a little chaotic after a while, because nobody really seemed to be in charge. The trip goal was to climb a few small peaks in preparation for a technical ascent of a dormant volcano. Joe would try to wake the participants up early, but they all just grumbled and went back to sleep. The group hiked fewer and fewer miles each day, until finally the ending destination had to be changed because there was no way they could make up all those miles. Meals were sporadic, cooked carelessly and eaten hastily, but nobody really cared. Besides, it was fun just sleeping in, swimming, playing games, and laughing at Joe's stories.

Joe's participants went home full of smiles and stories about their wacky leader. It was only in later years that any of Joe's participants wondered how such a brilliant mountaineer could have failed to lead his participants to the top of even one peak.

In Joe's situation, his participants continued to like him, but he quickly lost leadership credibility because he did not model his organization's values of challenge and environmental responsibility. Joe's group experienced a leadership breakdown because Joe failed to uphold the values that his participants and his organization expected him to model: respect for the environment and a sense of challenge and adventure.

The temptation to compromise on your (or your organization's) values is surprisingly tempting, particularly for new leaders who want to make sure that their group likes them. Turning a blind eye to a participant who is burying his leftover dinner in a hole is a lot easier than confronting him about it and holding him accountable to an environmental ethic. Laughing at a potentially offensive joke around the water cooler creates less conflict than addressing appropriate professional behavior and respect for others' feelings. But ultimately, although these failures to hold followers accountable to a set of values might result in an easier rapport with them, it does not result in leaders establishing themselves as people worth following.

When a Team Has an Inconsistent Commitment to Group Values

In the second way that leadership breaks down, dissent erupts among group members regarding their level of commitment to common values. In Outward Bound, if the students are not led to accept certain basic values, to work together to achieve a common goal, and to confront challenges to the best of their ability, there will be dissension even if the leader models these values.

For example, let's say that one of your company's requirements is that every team must complete some pro bono work each quarter. As the team manager, you organize the pro bono work and expect everyone to participate. But when the projects arrive, some of your team members balk, saying that they didn't take this job just to work for free. They refuse to help out the team with the projects.

With two groups of employees subscribing to different values regarding pro bono work, you are forced to choose between the two sets of values because you can't force people to volunteer. You have a professional responsibility to uphold your organization's pro bono work ethic, and thus you must support the employees willing to be full participants in the company goals. At the same time you must seek to hold *all* the employees accountable in some way to the value of pro bono work.

This type of leadership breakdown is what occurred on the International Peace Climb described above: some members of the team were unwilling to commit to, or had a different interpretation of, the team's value of cooperation. The team leader was faced with a leadership breakdown and had to decide between three options: whether to let the expedition dissolve, to try bringing about the unlikely result of the Russians deciding to ferry loads, or to reinterpret the definition of cooperation. He ultimately reinterpreted the definition of cooperation, by deciding that cooperation and expedition success could be achieved if the Russians climbed quickly while the rest of the team ferried loads.

USING YOUR POWER JUDICIOUSLY

In leadership situations, there are constant opportunities to either set yourself apart from your group or to join it. Let the decision about when to separate yourself from your group always be a deliberate one, one that you make in the interest of asserting your authority for a specific purpose rather than clinging to your power simply because you have it.

Joining in Your Team's Work

Remember how effective it can be to join your group when appropriate.

When I was associate director of Colorado Outward Bound and supervisor of all programs, I participated in many river-rafting trips on the Green and Colorado

rivers in Utah; these were some of my favorite adventures. The river staff was always great fun and very hard workers. Although I did not have the paddling skills to qualify as an instructor on those courses, I was still a staff person and always pitched in and helped set up camp, organized and participated in cooking crews, loaded boats, and whatever else was needed that was not technical teaching.

On rivers, there are strict protocols about taking out all garbage, including human waste. Rafters are required to bring out with them receptacles for different types of garbage, and they are required to be diligent about not contaminating the rivers and their surroundings with human excrement. Therefore, portable latrines for everyone to use are set up a little away from the campsite. These latrines are always situated out of sight of fellow campers but with a good view of the surroundings. In those days they were made up of several layers of garbage bags within a rectangular "ammo tin" (ammunition boxes scavenged from army surplus stores) with a toilet seat on top.

Every morning, these ammo-tin latrines were sealed up and placed on the supply boat, which carried all the gear but had no students on it. Washing the toilet seat and sealing up the latrine to be sure it didn't leak was something we all took turns doing, myself included.

The end of a river course, called the take-out, is a place where a road comes down to the river and there is usually a boat ramp of some type. After all the participants were met by a bus to take them back to civilization, the staff said farewell to them and was then faced with sorting and stowing the gear, dealing with all the garbage, deflating the rafts, and, oh yes, dealing with the latrine! So, being the most senior staff, I felt obliged to volunteer to carry the very full sealed plastic bags over to the designated disposal placed specifically for that purpose. It was a nasty, necessary chore, but sometimes leadership is like that! It was the best gift of thanks I could give to the hard-working instructors!

—Joan Welsh, former president of the Hurricane Island Outward Bound School

One of the most effective leadership strategies for building trust is to minimize your own use of power except when the situation calls for dynamic leadership, assertive role modeling, or executive decisions. The inclination to minimize

your position of influence is usually instinctive for compassionate leaders, but even if it's not your natural tendency, you can learn how to maintain a balance of joining your group and separating yourself from it.

One of the best examples of a leader who understood how to balance power with teamwork was the polar explorer Ernest Shackleton. At a time when the common practice on ships was for the officers and crew to eat separately (with the officers dining on gourmet meals served on fine linen while the crew ate stews and porridges), Shackleton's

SHACKLETON'S LEADERSHIP LESSONS

Due to the recent popularity of books and a movie featuring the formerly little-known twentieth-century Antarctic explorer Ernest Shackleton, the story of his amazing explorations and incredible leadership skills have entered mainstream America. Despite almost unbelievable setbacks of the proportions of a Hollywood adventure movie, on a two-year Antarctic expedition Shackleton managed to lead his crew to safety through dangerous conditions and almost overwhelming odds. All the while he maintained a sense of optimism, respect, and harmony in situations that would have driven any other leader or crew to despair, contempt, and mutiny. Powerful leadership lessons can be gleaned from Shackleton's story, as described in *Shackleton's Way* by Margot Morrell and Stephanie Capparell:

- Cultivate a sense of compassion and responsibility for others. You have a bigger impact on the lives of those who follow you than you can imagine.
- Once you make a leadership decision, commit to sticking through the tough learning period.
- Do your part to help create an upbeat environment for your team. A positive and cheerful environment is important to productivity.
- Broaden your cultural and social horizons beyond your usual experiences. Learning to see things from a different perspective will give you greater flexibility in problem solving.
- In a rapidly changing world, be willing to venture in new directions to seize new opportunities and learn new skills.
- Find a way to turn setbacks and failures to your advantage. These represent a good time to step forward on your own.
- Be bold in vision and careful in planning. Dare to try something new, but be meticulous enough in your proposal to give your ideas a good chance of succeeding.
- Learn from past mistakes—yours and those made by others. Sometimes the best teachers are the "bad bosses" and the negative experiences.
- Never insist on reaching a goal at any cost. It must be achieved at a reasonable expense, without undue hardship for your followers.
- Don't be drawn into public disputes with rivals. Rather, engage in respectful competition. You may need their cooperation someday.

*men all ate the same food together, which
fostered a sense of companionship and
group identity.*

*Similarly, Shackleton's expedition was
equipped with a limited number of toasty-
warm reindeer-hide sleeping bags and a
greater number of wool ones that quickly
grew soggy in the marine climate. When
Shackleton's ship sank off the Antarctic coast
and the men abandoned the* Endurance
*for the lifeboats, Shackleton and his officers
rotated in and out of the wool bags with the
rest of the crew, despite the fact that no one
would have much grumbled if the captain
and the officers had kept the finer reindeer
bags for their own use.*

*Shackleton had an unerring sense of
small actions that would have large effects
on team unity and trust, and he maximized
these opportunities, taking his turn chipping
ice, killing seals for food, or hauling boats
overland with the rest of his men. Yet he
still maintained his authority and ability to
command, perhaps in part because his men so
respected his work ethic and sense of fairness.*

Separating Yourself from Your Team

There is a delicate balance to achieve here. Getting into the trenches with your team will establish you as a caring, knowledgeable, and humble leader, and it will rally your team around you. But you can't join your team in every aspect of their work, or you will neglect your leadership duties. You also need to establish yourself as an authority figure so that your lead will be followed and your decisions respected. You signed on as the captain, not as the crew.

However, the way in which you separate from your team is also tricky. Isolating yourself from your team can make you seem superficial and create an "us versus them" dynamic. If you squirrel yourself away in your glass-windowed office and never set foot on the factory floor, you send the message of a great power imbalance between your team and the "big boss." If you get yourself your own hotel room while your team squeezes in four to a room, you're sending the message that your comfort is more important than theirs. If you use your participants' first names but expect them to call you "Mr." or "Ms." (unless you're working with kids in specific contexts), you're conveying the idea that you are worthy of more respect than they are.

One of the many wonderful things about the wilderness environment is that it is the great equalizer. If it's raining, the leader is getting wet, too. If the mosquitoes are biting, the leader tastes just as juicy as the participants. Participants notice this and feel more kinship with their leaders when they feel as though their leaders can understand them and empathize with them.

Coaching Rather than Commanding

If your intention, like Outward Bound's, is to teach your participants or followers the skills they need to have some degree of independence, you must move beyond having them respect you simply because you are in a position of authority. Instead, try to enable your participants to view you as a coach who helps them learn the skills they need to reach group and personal goals under their own leadership. To do this, you must use your influence as a leader to instruct and mentor rather than to direct and command.

This is a tricky balance to achieve, because you want and need your followers to respect your authority (particularly when you're working with difficult groups), but you also need them to be able to separate from your authority and begin to respect the leadership within the group. You don't want anarchy, and you don't want the type of leadership that emerges within a group because the leader is seen as ineffectual. You want to be able to step back in when necessary and have your followers listen to and respect your decisions at any time, but you also want them to learn to operate completely autonomously without your involvement.

If your followers always and only see you as

an authority figure, their success will always be connected to you. They will miss out on the unique sense of confidence that comes with succeeding on their own and discovering that *plus est en vous*—that they have more in them than they knew. Your followers' esteem for you needs to be based on something more than your position of authority.

EXPRESSING YOUR LEADERSHIP PRESENCE

Often when people imagine a leader, they envision someone other than themselves. If they are thinking about an outdoor leader, they picture a brawny, tanned, (and frequently) male, superhero. If they envision a corporate leader, they see a tall, dignified, attractive, mature man or woman in a suit.

Sometimes all it takes is a clipboard for people to identify you as a leader. When people are uncertain or lost, they look around them for leadership. If someone has a certain aura—or even something as innocuous as a clipboard—implying leadership, people gravitate toward that person for guidance.

I frequently carry a small notebook around with me to public events such as meetings or hearings, in case there is anything I want to jot down. Inevitably, someone identifies me as a leader and begins asking me questions about the process or purpose of the meeting. Even when I protest that I am among the uninitiated, just as they are, they often regard me skeptically, as if I must be trying to abdicate my leadership role. With an air of confidence and a leadership "tool" such as a notebook, a leader has no chance to just blend into the crowd.

—*Barbara, instructor for an American Management Association seminar*

But most leaders look just like you and me and everybody else. That is, leaders come in a variety of appearances: they're tall, short, young, old, beautiful, plain, strong, frail. So if most leaders look so ordinary, what identifies them as leaders? The answer is their *leadership presence*—the way leaders' mannerisms and appearances imbue them with an authority that causes them to shine, and other people to identify them as leaders.

Think about the way that actors who are satirists mimic political figures. They never mention the name of the person they're imitating and often look nothing like the politicians they're imitating, but by mimicking another person's tone of voice, speech patterns, and gestures (albeit often grossly exaggerated), satirists are able to convey to their audience who they are mimicking. They are, in a sense, replicating a politician's *leadership presence*.

Your leadership presence is a compilation of your tone of voice, your body language, your physical appearance, the way you dress, and the way you engage other people. There are hundreds of ways to effectively express your leadership presence and hundreds of ways to combine the characteristics that comprise leadership presence. That explains why some great leaders are statuesque with booming voices and some great leaders are tiny and soft-spoken. Some wear thousand-dollar shoes and others shop at thrift stores. Some gesture dramatically while others are self-restrained. Some use humor, others are somber, some are outgoing, others are reserved. Some are in wheelchairs, others are deaf or blind. The effective ones, though, have in common that they are leaders with a presence that works for their particular leadership situation.

For a long time women have struggled and today struggle still to achieve positions of leadership traditionally held by men. Initially, women thought they needed to adopt men's leadership styles and presence to be taken seriously as leaders. But as social equality between men and women has grown and women in leadership roles have become more common, many women realize that they are more effective leading with their own styles than they are leading under borrowed styles and cultivating a leadership presence not their own.

Also, for a long time the most important leadership positions—in business, education, and politics—were held by older people, who theoretically had a life perspective and wisdom not present in younger generations. But as energetic young people with innovative ideas began transforming companies, schools, and politics, the image of the elder statesman expanded to make room for the vision of the young person who has a different—but equally effective—leadership presence.

The same can be said for any minority group—whether based on gender, race, sexual preference, religion, or ethnicity. Opportunities are not yet equal and much discrimination still exists, but the leaders of tomorrow aren't necessarily going to be the people with the highest educational degrees and loudest voices. They're instead going to be people of all colors, from all backgrounds, with unique and personal leadership presences. But most important, the leaders of tomorrow will be the people who express, model, and uphold positive values and ethics common to much of society.

Enhancing Your Leadership Presence

Everything you say or do and everything about the way you look affects your leadership presence. Because we're growing accustomed to leaders coming in all sorts of outer packaging, few aspects about a person are inherently positive or negative. Still, at the same time, everything makes a statement. White hair says one thing, dyed or bleached hair says another. Tattoos speak loudly, as do unusual or multiple body piercings. Cracking your knuckles communicates a message, as does biting your fingernails. Calling people "dear" says something, as does referring to a coed group as "you guys."

You don't have control over every aspect of your appearance, so it's important to make the most of the things that you do have control over, whether they are physical attributes, tone of voice, or mannerisms. Here are some tips for enhancing your leadership presence:

Dress and groom yourself appropriately. Although we try not to be, humans are superficial characters and make judgments based on appearance. So make sure that the image you're

presenting is the one you're intending. Dress appropriately for the situation, regardless of your leadership position. For example, the CEO of Outward Bound might occasionally wear shorts around the office or in the field, but if out on a fund-raising trip, a business suit is appropriate attire. Consider the appropriateness of visible body art and jewelry, and if it seems inappropriate for a particular leadership situation, play it down.

The message here is not to hide your true self or to attempt to be somebody you aren't, but, instead, to present yourself from the start in a way that gives little reason for your followers to judge or be offended by you. Once they get to know you and you have established yourself as a credible leader, then you can relax your standards of appearance as you deem appropriate within the organizational culture.

Make eye contact. One of the quickest ways to establish your leadership presence is to make eye contact with your followers. Making eye contact takes confidence, and it says to the follower, "I see you and I want to engage with you." It makes followers feel validated and feel as though you're worthy of their respect. It also makes you seem trustworthy, open, and honest.

Maximize your best leadership attributes. Do you have an unerring sense of humor that helps groups relax and diffuses difficult situations? Are you able to foster a quick sense of intimacy and trust among participants? Do you have a particularly clear and coherent way of presenting information? Your best leadership attributes will greatly enhance your overall leadership presence, so take advantage of them. Become aware of your best leadership attributes and use them consciously until they become second nature.

Be open about your shortcomings. You don't need to introduce yourself to a new group by saying, "I'm Bob and I'm not very good at letting go of control," but neither do you need to attempt to hide your weaknesses. Once you have established yourself as a worthy leader, it can actually be very productive to share your shortcomings with participants.

Showing vulnerability makes you more real and more approachable, and the honesty and risk required to share such information shows you to be a confident leader willing to take emotional risks.

Maintain appropriate boundaries. Many people are uncomfortable when strangers touch them (a hand on the shoulder, a pat on the arm), even if the intention is not threatening. Similarly, most people are uncomfortable when others stand too close to them to speak. Step back and give people space until they invite you into it. Be sensitive to cultural differences regarding what constitutes appropriate boundaries.

Avoid nervous habits. Cracking your knuckles, wringing your hands, chewing the insides of your lips—all of these are nervous habits that will annoy your followers as well as communicate that you have a sense of anxiety or a lack of confidence. Sometimes these habits are so distracting to followers that they miss half of what you are saying because they're wondering how many more times you will toss your hair back during the course of your speech.

Watch out for potentially offensive language. You probably have a pretty good sense about blatant insults or loaded language that would offend people. But watch out for seemingly innocuous language that can alienate individuals or entire groups. For example, many women are put off by a leader's use of "you guys" to refer to a coed group as a whole.

Using Your Leadership Presence Effectively

One of the most important aspects of your leadership presence is figuring out how to use it to your best advantage. Frank Fields (not his real name), the CEO of a Fortune 100 company, got involved in Outward Bound at his wife, Elizabeth's (nor hers), urging after she'd had a very moving Outward Bound experience (recounted in Chapter 6, Finding Courage, Overcoming Fear). Here is Frank's experience using his leadership presence to effect a particular outcome.

Frank and Elizabeth adopted twenty-three teenagers under the "I Have a Dream" pro-gram in the South Bronx, agreeing that they would fund these students' college education if they could complete high school. Frank and Elizabeth also agreed to spend one day each month with the group doing various types of adventurous things together.

One Saturday morning, Frank was playing basketball outdoors in jeans and a tee shirt with a number of these students. He got a phone call from someone at the high school saying that one of the students had been arrested and was in jail and asking Frank to come down and see what he could do to help. So Frank went down to the South Bronx police station and said, "I'm Frank Fields, and I'm here to see so-and-so to see what I can do."

The desk sergeant said, "Yeah, Buster. Go ahead and have a seat over there."

Well, an hour went by, an hour and a half went by, and Frank went back to the desk sergeant and said, "Look, I came here to see so-and-so and no one has come for me."

The desk sergeant said, "Yeah, yeah. Well, have a seat. We'll get to you."

At this point, Frank went back out to his car and got his blue suit, white shirt, tie, and proper shoes and went to the men's room and changed into his business attire. He went back to the desk sergeant and said, "I am Frank Fields, CEO of such-and-such company, and I would like to see so-and-so, now!"

The desk sergeant said, "Yes, sir. Right away."

Sure enough, Frank was ushered in and allowed to have an interview with the young person, and in good time was able to get the student released on Frank's recognizance.

Unfortunately, our society oftentimes operates on values that are responsive to power rather than to what is fair. Knowing this, you can sometimes use your leadership presence to effect the influence you desire.

ADAPTING YOUR LEADERSHIP STYLE

Effective leadership takes many different forms. Napoleon Bonaparte was an effective leader, but in a much different way than was Mohandas Gandhi, Queen Elizabeth I, or Nelson Mandela. Outward Bound recognizes that different instructors lead effectively in many different ways, and these different approaches, referred to as an instructor's "leadership style," are worthy and valued.

Think about how your participants or followers would describe you as a leader. Dynamic? Quiet? Authoritarian? Laid-back? Your leadership style is simply the way in which you go about achieving your leadership objectives—or, to use the definitions of leadership described earlier, the way in which you use your power to influence your followers.

> *In one of my first courses as a very young Outward Bound instructor, I was faced with a potentially difficult group. I was about to teach a twenty-eight-day course in the all-male youth-at-risk program we used to run in Maine, and I could tell from the participants' medical files that this was going to be a group of pretty tough seventeen-year-old boys. I decided to establish an aura of authority and discipline around myself by wearing mirrored sunglasses— which I ran out and purchased two hours before the course started—for the first couple of days of the course. By hiding the occasional uncertainty that invariably showed on my face in the early part of a course, I thought, I could create an illusion of confidence.*
>
> *The whole plan backfired, of course; the students saw right through me. I was so busy trying to be someone else that I was un-able to do any of the things that had worked well for me in the past.*
>
> *—Ashley Lodato, Outward Bound staff since 1986*

Most leaders tend to have a preferred leadership style, usually the one that comes most naturally to them or the one with which they have had the most success. Your preferred leadership style can usually be identified somewhere along a continuum of leadership approaches, ranging from very directive, highly involved methods to a quite relaxed, laissez-faire manner, illustrated in Figure 2:

A directive approach marks a leader who makes most decisions alone and exerts overarching personal influence over the group.

A democratic approach is characterized by a leader who shares power with others, involving group members in decision making and problem solving. A democratic leader might consult with either the entire group or a few group members before making a decision; such a leader might also turn some decisions over to the group completely.

A consensual approach implies that the leader facilitates group decisions in which everyone voices an opinion and decisions are made through a process of consensus and compromise.

A laissez-faire approach involves the leader relinquishing leadership power to the group entirely. Good laissez-faire leadership does not promote leaderlessness or chaos but, instead, is used effectively with mature groups that possess the leadership skills necessary to govern themselves as well as the skills needed to successfully complete the task at hand.

You can probably identify your own preferred leadership style somewhere along this continuum

◄ - directive --------------- democratic --------------- consensual --------------- laissez-faire -- ►

Figure 2. The Leadership Continuum

by simply imagining your response to the following scenario:

Leadership Situation: *You're headed out to go hiking with a group of friends. No one is the official leader, but because you organized the hike and chose the route, you feel responsible for the day's success. When you get to the trailhead, you notice a "Trail Closed" sign. What is your response?*

Directive Response: *You might say something like, "Oops; sorry, gang. I guess I didn't check trail condition reports. Let's get back in the cars and drive up the road a few miles to another good trail I know."*

Democratic Response: *You might say, "Uh-oh, what are we going to do?" and ask each of your friends what they want to do. You then make a decision yourself based on the majority opinion, after everyone weighs in.*

Consensual Response: *You might say, "Well, shoot, this isn't going to work. Any other ideas?" and help your friends come up with a decision that everyone is content with.*

Laissez-faire Response: *You make the maps available to your friends, then excuse yourself to the outhouse, saying "I'll be happy going wherever you all decide to go."*

Ideally, though, you would recognize the value of being able to demonstrate *all* these different leadership styles. Good leaders are aware that although their preferred leadership style may be effective in a variety of circumstances, different situations call for different responses. And the best leaders are able to move seamlessly between leadership styles according to the needs of the situation.

Shifting between leadership styles is difficult until you become confident in your own skills and authority. If you're a new leader, you probably tend to prefer either a uniformly directive style (which showcases your skills, reinforces your authority, and generally leads to predictable outcomes) or a uniformly consensual style (which helps you feel not so alone in the leadership position because you are including everyone in the group). But as you gain more experience, you will find that you are a more effective leader if you start to adapt your leadership style to the needs of a particular situation.

OUTWARD BOUND LEADERSHIP TIPS

If you become a "friend" only—the kind of friend who understands and sympathizes with everything—you may find it difficult to say no or to direct your actions toward the objectives of the course that sometimes require actions, strategies, or interventions that your group may find unpleasant. If you become friends with some group members more than others, you will be suspected of favoritism, and many participants may be uncomfortable with your actions or directions. You are likely to lose respect and professional standing.

If you become a "boss" only—just telling the group what to do and not inviting participation in decisions—your group members may undertake the activities of the course, but they may lose the more valuable essence that stems from the building of personal relationships. They may feel invisible, unimportant, and powerless. The course is likely to lack enthusiasm and group pride.

If you become a "teacher" only—always looking for the teachable moment, directing all your comments toward course objectives, continuously impelling your students into learning opportunities—you may lose credibility as a real person with your students. They may develop immunity from the constant pressure to be intentional.

—Outward Bound Instructor Manual

Ultimately, your leadership style must be "you"—it must be authentic and reflect who you are, with all of your strengths and shortcomings. Trying to adopt someone else's leadership style wholesale is generally ill-fated: you won't "wear" the new style well, your participants or followers will see you as disingenuous, and you will have undermined your group's confidence in both your integrity and your competence. As Bill George, former CEO of Medtronics and author of *Authentic Leadership: Rediscovering the Secrets to Creating Lasting Value*, writes, "Leadership is always about character. Leadership is always about authenticity."

INFLUENCING OTHERS OUTSIDE THE LEADERSHIP ENVIRONMENT

Your actions in your particular leadership environment—whether the classroom, the boardroom, the backcountry, or a philanthropic organization—are your expression of your leadership power and influence. As a leader, you might be tempted to think that you can be "off the clock" sometimes or that you don't always need to measure up to the standards of integrity and character that others expect you to uphold. But the sometimes-tiring truth for truly great leaders is that your influence is *always* being expressed, even if you don't intend it. And your actions *outside* your leadership environment can actually say more about your leadership potential and expertise than your actions inside your leadership environment.

After retiring from Outward Bound, I was CEO of an international executive recruiting firm. It was a large and diversified company with some fifty offices around the world, and we were hired to find potential senior management personnel for a wide variety of corporations. Our job was to evaluate the true leadership potential in these candidates.

We found an interesting thing. We found that character was the most essential element for success in a corporate leadership role. Furthermore, we found that the best indicator of character was the amount of service—giving back to the community—the executive had blended into his or her career.

John Whitehead—former co-CEO of the investment banking house Goldman-Sachs, later Deputy Secretary of State, and most recently head of the project to rebuild Ground Zero underneath the former World Trade Center towers in New York—is a stunning example of a leader with both excellent corporate acumen and admirable character.

While John was co-CEO of Goldman-Sachs, certainly a fast-track and all-consuming business environment, he spent one-third of his time on not-for-profit work. His rationale was that when he served on boards of not-for-profit organizations, he got input about what was going on in the world that he could not get from his own internal executives at Goldman-Sachs. Being a part of the not-for-profit world and meeting with other board members who served on these major not-for-profit organizations broadened his outlook and made him a far more effective co-CEO of Goldman-Sachs. John used his leadership influence not just to benefit the not-for-profit boards that he served on but also to serve as a role model for others in his company who, through his work, actions, and integrity, would see the value of volunteerism or community service in their own lives.

One of the values espoused by Outward Bound's founder, Kurt Hahn, as you may remember from Chapter 1, Why Learn Leadership from Outward Bound? is the value of service. Even more important than the benefit serving others provides to the individual or community served, service releases great reserves of inner strength in the one who serves. Outward Bound has wholeheartedly embraced the value of the relationship between leadership and service and finds that its best leaders are ones who serve outside their work with Outward Bound. As a leader, you will find that such service work broadens your perspective, broadens your areas of expertise, broadens your world of contacts, and, most important, strengthens your self-image and makes you a more effective role model and leader. For more on service, see Chapter 13, Serving Others as a Community Leader in Part IV, Taking Leadership into Your Community.

LEADING OTHER LEADERS

One of the uniquely challenging situations you may encounter is the "opportunity" (remember Kurt Hahn's words from Chapter 1: "your disability is your opportunity"!) to lead other leaders. You may encounter this situation if you are charged with training peers or if you are enlisted to take a group of leaders or managers on a retreat or wilderness trip.

As you know, leaders like to . . . well . . . lead. They like being in charge, making decisions, influencing others. And frequently they have a hard time following. Typically, the more leadership power an individual holds, the more difficulty that person has in pulling *out* of a leadership role, even temporarily.

Outward Bound frequently works with groups of leaders: corporate executives, leaders in education, and civic leaders. These people have always been in charge in their daily lives, and they are accustomed to showing a decisive attitude toward decision making. When faced with the unique and challenging situations presented on Outward Bound programs, these people usually have one of two responses.

The first type of response is that they may be so disoriented by the unfamiliar environment that they become somewhat vulnerable and realize a few key things. They learn that it is OK to show fear in unfamiliar territory. They learn that it is OK not to be in charge all the time. They learn to rely on the rest of their team and on the advice of the instructor, because they do not have the knowledge to be in charge all the time. They learn that it is OK to fail and to make decisions that may be wrong. And they learn that it is OK to show ignorance and to learn and listen to the group.

The other response is that they ignore any disorientation experienced in the unfamiliar environment and attempt to continue to assert themselves as leaders, as illustrated by the story below.

Ed (not his real name) was the CEO of a large manufacturing company and a participant on an Outward Bound canoeing expedition. Ed was an experienced outdoorsman who had canoed quite a lot. He was partnered, however, with a novice canoeist. To meet his own level of skill, Ed tended to choose water routes that weren't easy for beginners, and his canoe overturned several times, resulting in great frustration and resentment on the part of both paddlers.

Eventually—thanks to some tactfully direct feedback from the instructor—Ed realized that he was giving advanced directions to someone who did not have the experience to either interpret or act upon them. Ed had initially been holding his partner at fault for all the capsizes, when in reality it was his fault for choosing routes that they as a pair were ill equipped to run successfully and for shouting directions that his partner couldn't follow.

Ed later said around the campfire that the most important thing he learned on this trip was that, whereas he was always the boss wherever he traveled in the world, on Outward Bound he was subject to compassionate and constructive criticism by staff and students alike. At Outward Bound, Ed learned to see a side of himself that he hadn't experienced in his corporate world.

Ed later became a trustee of Outward Bound USA and for years has been a staunch supporter of Outward Bound's objectives. This early experience on the canoe trip gave him some important feedback that perhaps made his leadership style more empathetic and compassionate.

What can you do when you're faced with leading other leaders, perhaps ones like Ed? There are no magic answers for dealing with other leaders, and the key is to remember that you must get a good sense of each individual's character and temperament before you do or say anything radical.

A couple of tips might help you figure out how best to approach your role as a leader of leaders. These tips are nearly as relevant for dealing with participants who have no other leadership experience, but they're especially important when leading other leaders.

Acknowledge leader-participants' leadership background and expertise. Although these participants might be entering unfamiliar territory, they are still bringing many leadership skills and attitudes with them. Acknowledge the expertise that exists in the group, and reassure participants that while they will not be expected to lead in situations that are out of their areas of proficiency, their leadership skills will be called upon and valued throughout the expedition, training, or retreat.

Clarify your role and their roles. Explain that you will be the official leader for the duration of the training or expedition and that this is a great opportunity for the participants *not* to be in charge. Don't completely remove the participants from all leadership responsibilities, however. Make them wholly responsible for some things right from the beginning, such as time management.

Provide ample information. One of the things that can make people—and leaders in particular—feel most vulnerable and most patronized is when they feel as though they do not have enough information about situations. Withholding information sets up a power dynamic in which you, the leader, hold the information and thus the power, leaving the participants in the dark and powerless. You don't need to give the participants a minute-

by-minute account of the plan for each day, but provide them with a general framework that outlines the goals of the expedition or training, an itinerary, and any other information that they might likely need or want.

Do not engage in power struggles. Cultivate a respectful and positive rapport with each individual, and avoid situations that could result in public power struggles. If you sense someone questioning your authority or attempting to seize power simply because he or she is used to being in control, approach that person directly and confront the situation in a nonthreatening manner. See Chapter 3, Communicating Effectively, for more information on power struggles.

Demonstrate a transparent leadership style. When appropriate and instructive, explain your leadership decisions to the participants. For example, you might say, "We were going to spend time this afternoon learning how to use a map and compass to triangulate, but the discussion about corporate ethics and values seemed so engaging to everyone that I decided to let it keep going. We'll do the compass work tomorrow instead."

Involve others in decision making when appropriate. Although leader-participants might not share your knowledge and skill in a particular leadership environment, they are probably quite experienced decision makers. And making decisions in a new environment with a group of other leaders can be a good learning opportunity for them. You might say, "Folks, we need to decide whether we're going to take the more direct, off-trail route to the peak we're going to climb tomorrow or whether we're going to stay on the trail, which is the longer but more straightforward route." Then give the participants the maps, make yourself available for questioning, and let the participants make the final decision.

Share your vulnerabilities, and offer opportunities for participants to do so too. Opening up about your own leadership concerns can provide a great forum for others to share similar anxieties. When leaders begin to see themselves and other leaders as ordinary, vulnerable humans, it gives them a chance to acknowledge a side of themselves that they probably usually ignore. (See Chapter 4, Building Trust, Building a Team.)

A FINAL NOTE

The saying goes that great minds think alike, but in fact, great minds *don't* think alike—that's part of what makes them great. Although many of the most commonly used effective leadership strategies and methods have resulted in history's greatest leaders, one of the key pieces to any effective leader's style and presence—the overall leadership package that he or she presents—is his or her unique approach. One of the things that will make you the strongest leader you can be is your ability to think independently and be yourself. By all means, borrow ideas, model habits, and adopt strategies from leaders you admire. But at the end of the day, the leadership package you present should be one that originates from you.

CHAPTER 3

COMMUNICATING EFFECTIVELY

One of the most important lessons Outward Bound passes on to its alumni is a visceral understanding of the inner strengths and resilience that are released as a result of reaching out to help others in need. Having seen how their strength and support helped others cope with their fears and push the limits of what they thought was mentally or physically possible, alumni return home with the confidence to face their own fears and overcome their own challenges. It is this empathetic communication style and understanding of human nature that characterizes the Outward Bound approach to leadership.

A decade after the United States pulled out of Vietnam in 1975, American war veterans started taking Outward Bound courses. The concept was the brainchild of Outward Bound instructor and former U.S. Army Colonel Bob Rheault, who commanded U.S. Special Forces in Vietnam. As a senior Vietnam War veteran, Colonel Rheault was very aware of the terrible problems that many veterans of the Vietnam War were suffering, later called Post Traumatic Stress Disorder (PTSD). Many of these veterans were confined to Veterans Administration hospitals. They had flashbacks, during which they were capable of violent acts, even to the extent of trying to kill somebody they thought was a Viet Cong soldier.

Colonel Rheault thought he knew a bit about what was going on with these soldiers and convinced a VA hospital to allow him to take a group of ten veterans out on an Outward Bound experience. He took the group out into the wilderness and conducted strenuous Outward Bound activities such as rock climbing, rappelling, long backpacking treks, and orienteering. At night around the campfire, the group talked about the experiences of the day. As the group began to meld and to work as a team, they began to share their own stories—stories of anxiety, fear, and what they had been through in combat that led them to being confined to VA hospitals.

After Colonel Rheault's first group returned to the hospital, staff psychiatrists remarked that he had been able to achieve more therapeutic recovery with these ten soldiers in a week than they had been able to achieve in group therapy in a year. Word spread through the VA system that Outward Bound was a very successful and effective way of dealing with these veterans, and Colonel Rheault eventually established Outward Bound programs in many VA hospitals throughout the country. He is currently working to reestablish the program for veterans of the wars in Afghanistan and Iraq.

Through the Outward Bound process, Colonel Rheault was able to communicate with these men—most of whom were suffering from severe mental or psychological distress—in a way that enabled them to begin dealing with the traumatic effects of the war. Outward Bound has had similar success in communicating with other groups of people who often feel alienated from mainstream America: survivors of abuse, cancer survivors, recovering drug addicts, and juvenile offenders.

A LETTER TO OUTWARD BOUND

I'm a thirty-eight-year-old male, and I was in the Marine Corps. I have shot myself in the head once and have tried several other ways to kill myself. I have used drugs since Vietnam.

I have tried to quit doing drugs and trying to kill myself for my kids, my family—it was always for someone else. Inside me I have wanted to die; I just didn't want to hurt anyone anymore, and I didn't want to hurt inside anymore.

Well, things have changed, with the help of the people from Outward Bound. They took me back to when I was young, back to the time when I was a whole person. They helped me let the good side of me come out—the bad was still there but he wasn't in control. The good was in control, and with the pride this course has given me, the trust in others and trust in myself, I didn't have to use drugs to be happy or to hide the hurt and pain inside. I learned that all the anger inside was not always anger—it was sadness and pain and many other feelings. But the biggest thing of all was, in our boat on the river, in the silence, a great joy arose. I want to live, not die.

I'm not a real smart person, so I can't use a lot of big words to tell you how much I love you all for giving me this strength to live and go on, so I hope just a real big thank-you will be enough. I wish I could say more.

—Freddie, past Outward Bound participant

Yet the Outward Bound experience is not designed to be a therapeutic one, and the instructors are not trained counselors. It is simply the strategic design of the Outward Bound process and the skill of the instructors in helping participants form meaningful, supportive relationships that enables Outward Bound to have success communicating with groups such as Vietnam veterans.

BEING A COMPASSIONATE COMMUNICATOR

Vast amounts of research have gone into leadership communication skills, much of which is incorporated into Outward Bound's curricula. But most of what Outward Bound teaches and models about good communication simply stems from the organization's belief that compassion, above all, should guide all our interactions with others.

This is what is perhaps unique about Outward Bound's approach to communication: Outward Bound's methods of expression and interacting with others are primarily influenced by a desire to communicate compassionately and to communicate with the best interests of the other person or other people paramount in our minds.

RECOGNIZING THE IMPORTANCE OF GOOD COMMUNICATION SKILLS

Have you ever been in a position where you are expected to follow someone whose directions you can't understand or someone who knows the business inside and out but can neither explain projects nor delegate authority? How many people do you know who are afraid to approach their supervisor with a problem because they think it won't do any good?

As CEO of Outward Bound USA from 1980 to 1990, I worked hard in the early years to develop a national office and staff who were competent, worked well together, and provided the necessary support to the Outward Bound schools. Outward Bound grew very rapidly during this period—we grew from 7,000 students a year to more than 30,000 students a year in a single decade—I found myself spending more and more time out in the field working with the schools, working with staff, and conducting safety reviews.

The result was that I was not in the

national office as much as I should have been, and the office was not operating as efficiently as it should have. Recognizing this and getting some help from my trustees, I brought in an outside consultant who had a look at our operating procedures to see how we could improve. The central point of what he found was that the staff really missed me because I was away from the office a lot.

However, my vice president of marketing, a wonderful man named John Greene, filled the gap in many ways. He managed people by "walking around." His method of communicating and bringing people together was to stop by their desks, pass the time of day, see how they were doing, and spend time with them. Paying attention to the office staff made them feel much more like members of the team, and morale improved.

This was a strong lesson for me: managing by walking around is a very effective way of communicating, and I had been perhaps too remote, too much in my office handling the paperwork or other things that had to be done.

In communicating with people, you have to be there for them, using personal, one-on-one contact. You cannot do it by memos and you cannot do it by telephone. You need to be face to face as a presence for them.

A vice president at a major software development firm recently complained that he was going crazy. He felt that the new boss he had ended up with after a recent reorganization was clueless. The VP told his boss's Human Resources director that he had never met a worse leader. The VP felt his new boss was a really nice guy and he understood the product, but he had no ability to simplify things and pick out three key things to focus on. And the concept of driving accountability was completely foreign to him.

Our complaints about those who lead us are frequently related to their communication skills or lack thereof. In the situation above, the supervisor had the technical knowledge required for his position and was even a nice guy, but he lacked the ability to communicate key expectations to his team.

It seems self-evident to say that to be a good leader, you must be a good communicator. But what makes communication so important to leadership? To answer that question, let's return to what we referred to earlier (Chapter 1, Why Learn Leadership from Outward Bound?) as the key task of a leader: to identify what needs doing and to organize a group of people to get it done. If the heart of leadership is the necessity of conveying information accurately to others and then persuading them to act upon it, then the ability to *communicate*—to clearly express one's thoughts and feelings in a manner that can be understood by others—lies at the core of the leader's necessary skills. Good communication skills enable a leader to do these things:

■ Convey information.
■ Develop rapport with followers.
■ Establish trust.
■ Build teams.
■ Act upon decisions.
■ Motivate and inspire.
■ Help followers find meaning in experiences.

As a leader, you use your communication skills in a variety of ways, but you use them on a daily basis in three main ways: (1) to convey information, (2) to build relationships, and (3) to make and act upon decisions. Let's look at each of these more closely.

Convey information: Leaders must be able to convey information in many situations: teaching a skill, providing information, describing a process or system, clarifying expectations, and explaining a goal.

Build relationships: Leaders need to build relationships by developing rapport and establishing trust, not just between themselves and their followers but also *among* their followers, in order to create strong teams.

Make and act upon decisions: And finally, because leadership is a constant series of decisions, leaders with good communication skills have an easier time making and acting upon decisions if they are able to effectively solicit information, communicate decisions to their group, articulate their rationale, facilitate group decision-making discussions, and assess whether team goals are being met.

A leader who is not guided by compassion can certainly perform some of these functions effectively, such as conveying information accurately and acting upon decisions. Yet the leader with a compassionate communication style will be far more successful at establishing a good rapport with followers, building teams, and helping participants make meaning out of experiences.

BEING A GOOD COMMUNICATOR

Leaders communicate in a variety of ways, but the best ones all have the following characteristics in common:
- They are good listeners.
- They are able to read and respond to individuals' and groups' energy levels and attention spans.
- They are able to appeal to learners with different learning styles.
- They understand the importance of positive feedback.

At the root of these four skills—listening, being aware of the group, appealing to different learning styles, and expressing praise or approval—is the guiding sense of compassion. Compassionate leaders respect their participants enough to really listen to them and care enough about them to be in tune with their energy levels and needs. They are invested enough in participants' personal learning and development to convey information in a way that appeals to a variety of learners. Leaders who are good communicators realize that heartfelt praise contributes to both increased self-confidence for the participant as well as a stronger rapport between themselves and their participants.

Listening

Some people are naturally good listeners, but most of us have to work at it. Think about it.

Say your colleague comes in to work on Monday and you ask him about his weekend. As he starts telling you what he did, you immediately begin mentally reminiscing about what *you* did and how you will tell him about your exciting day. Before he is barely finished, you've launched into your own story.

Or you're at a social event, meeting lots of new people. Within seconds after shaking a new acquaintance's hand, you've forgotten her name. You were concentrating on how *you* were coming across, and your attention wandered from what she was saying. Now it's a bit awkward to converse with her, and when a friend of yours approaches, you can't introduce your new acquaintance very well. It's important to look directly at the person and repeat her name at the first opportunity. People like to hear their name said.

Or you get home from work and your spouse says that he'd like to talk to you about something that's bothering him. He names a complaint about something between you and starts describing how he feels, but you've already tuned him out as you start formulating your defense.

In each of these examples, you might be *hearing* what people are telling you, but you're not really *listening*. In order to really listen, you need to clear your mind of everything except what is being said to you. In its *Outward Bound Instructor Manual*, Outward Bound offers its instructors the following suggestions for effective listening:
- Resist distractions.
- Focus on the speaker.
- Concentrate on understanding not only the speaker's words but also the feelings and attitude of the speaker.
- Suspend judgment initially (meaning is often distorted by the speaker's choice of words and by the listener's opinion of the speaker).
- Wait before responding, in order to digest the speaker's entire message.

TOOL	TECHNIQUE	EXAMPLE
Ask an open-ended question.	Probe for further information by asking a question that requires more than a quick answer.	*"What are your ideas for helping the group meet deadlines better?"*
Paraphrase.	Rephrase using your own words to confirm the speaker's meaning.	Speaker: *"I'm just going to belay—I'm afraid of heights."* Listener: *"So what you're saying is that your fear of heights is making you reluctant to rock climb."*
Check your perceptions.	Rephrase using your own words to confirm the speaker's meaning.	Speaker: *"This group is just so lazy."* Listener: *"It sounds as though you are frustrated with the slow progress of the group. Is that true?"*
Signal with your body language.	Increase the comfort level for the speaker by using your body—eyes, torso, arms—in a way that is congruent with your words.	Make eye contact. Lean forward. Relax your arms (don't cross them or put them on your hips).

Once the speaker has finished talking, you can respond in one of the following ways, paraphrased here from materials used in Interaction Associates' "Facilitative Leadership" workshop:

Being Aware of Your Group's Energy and Ability

Compassionate leaders make sure that they are aware of how their group is doing—whether they need a bite to eat, a chance to ask questions, or simply a chance to stand up and stretch in the middle of a long meeting.

It is the end of the day and everyone is tired. A couple of kids in the group haven't had any water in a few hours and are getting dehydrated. Someone has developed bad blisters but doesn't want to say anything about it for fear of slowing the group down. The group is still about a mile from camp when they run into a couple of other hikers. Starved for some adult conversation, the leader stops to chat with the other hikers, saying to his group, "I'm going to hang out here for a few minutes. You all head on down to camp and I'll meet you there later. Watch your maps carefully—it's easy to miss the side trail to the campsite." The leader strikes up a conversation with the other hikers and the group stumbles on.

When the leader reaches the intended camp an hour later, he is dismayed to find his group nowhere in sight. He finally catches up to them nearly a mile past camp, walking dejectedly. They are so tired that they have missed the campsite and simply straggled on.

The situation above had no serious consequences, but it could easily have been avoided. When the leader stopped to visit with the other hikers, leaving his group on its own, he failed to note the low energy level in his group. Had he been aware of their waning energy—which affected the participants' abilities to navigate—he would have either conveyed his instructions far more carefully, making sure that the participants could read the maps and find the campsite, or, even better, he would have continued on with them to ensure that they reached the campsite successfully. The leader's ignorance of his group's energy level led to a communication breakdown and a disheartening end to an already exhausting day.

One of the common pitfalls to which leaders frequently succumb is to place the importance of the information they need to convey over the ability of their group to absorb this information.

Think about how often you've been in a meeting or a seminar that is running late. The participants are tired, hungry, and restless, but the leader still has a lot of information left to cover so he plows ahead with his presentation.

The aware, compassionate leader would say, "It seems as though people are losing steam. Why don't we take a ten-minute break to walk around and grab a drink, then we'll meet back here for another hour. Instead of finishing the budget presentation, we'll do some small-group brainstorming about the upcoming project. Then I'll finish the lecture tomorrow."

Remember, if effective communication involves things such as *conveying information accurately, building rapport,* and being able to *motivate and inspire,* then effective communicators will realize that these things can be accomplished only with a receptive audience: participants who are alert, prepared, and physically comfortable.

You can establish a compassionate, supportive environment in which communication will be most effective by making sure that all your participants have their basic needs met. These needs, according to psychologist Abraham Maslow in *Toward a Psychology of Being,* are listed below:

1. **physiological:** hunger, thirst, shelter, etc.
2. **safety:** security, protection from physical and emotional harm, etc.
3. **social:** affection, belonging, acceptance, friendship, etc.
4. **esteem and ego:** self-respect, autonomy, achievement, status recognition, attention, etc.
5. **self-actualization:** performing, achieving, doing, etc.

Maslow's theory of human motivation claims that the lower motivations—physiological, safety, and social needs—must be met before the higher ones—esteem and self-actualization needs—can be met. So if your participants are going to learn, grow, perform, and achieve, their basic needs must also be fulfilled.

As a leader, you can communicate directly with participants—as well as observing other nonverbal signals and body language—to determine whether basic needs are being adequately met. One gauge of basic needs used by Outward Bound instructors is to assess their own condition. If the instructor is hungry, the participants are probably ravenous. If the instructor is tired, the participants are likely exhausted. If the instructor is cold, the participants might be on the verge of hypothermia.

You can employ the same system of assessment in your own leadership situations: if you're confused by the presentation, your followers are probably completely bewildered; if you're lonely, your participants are probably feeling alienated.

Appealing to Different Learning Styles

As a leader, you will develop your own strategies for getting a group's attention and presenting information. As you're developing your methods, one of the most important things to remember about communicating with groups is that people learn in different ways. As CEO of Outward Bound, I was fortunate to work with many truly outstanding instructors; one in particular remains in my memory.

Huck was a physically strong instructor in his mid-twenties who had a quiet way of presenting himself. He was not particularly vocal, but when he did speak, people listened. He was an expert at all the things the expedition was seeking to do as it went down

*the river, and he was a particularly good
rafting leader. But the thing that especially
set him apart was his ability to grab and hold
a group's attention by reciting poetry.*

*Huck had memorized the entirety of
the Alfred Lord Tennyson poem "Ulysses,"
which is more than ten pages long. It is
an especially meaningful poem for adults
because Ulysses is approaching the end of his
middle years and is feeling a diminution of
his physical abilities.*

*Huck would wait to share his poem until
we had an especially spectacular viewpoint
above the river. Everyone would climb up
onto a rock outcropping, usually to a place
where we all could sit around on top of
the cliff and watch the river rushing by.
Huck would then recite "Ulysses" (which,
coincidentally, is the source of the Outward
Bound motto—"to serve, to strive, and not
to yield").*

*It was such a powerful experience, listen-
ing under a Colorado sky to this young man
reciting a poem about an older man dealing
with his diminishing faculties. As Huck
recited the poem, some of the group would be
moved to tears.*

I learned from Huck how important it is to
have different strategies for reaching out to groups
and making points or inspiring discussions in
subtle but powerful ways.

Some Learning Styles

Most of us aren't limited to a single way of learning, but learning becomes stressful if we spend too
much time outside of our "preferred" style. Below
are some of the most common learning styles.

Visual: About 65 percent of us are visual
learners who need to *see* something in order
to learn it. If we watch someone jump-start a
battery, for example, we review this image in
our mind's eye, then attempt to repeat the skill
ourselves. We absorb information by reading
and looking at diagrams, often tuning out verbal
directions in favor of examining a visual image.
A visual learner would learn how to use a new
digital video disc (DVD) player by reading the
instruction manual.

Auditory: A third of the population is comprised of auditory learners who learn well by
hearing things and then repeating them to themselves. Auditory learners benefit from discussing
ideas. They also are easily distracted by noises,
and they frequently use white noise or other
soothing sounds to lessen auditory distractions. An
auditory learner would learn how to use a DVD
player by listening to someone give instructions.

Kinesthetic: About 5 percent of us are kinesthetic learners who gather meaning from touch
and movement. Almost everyone fits into this
category as a young child, but only a few retain
this learning style. The kinesthetic learner would
figure out how to use a DVD player by pushing
buttons and experimenting until he or she understands how it works.

Ironically, the kinesthetic, or "hands-on," approach has been touted recently as the ultimate
learning method. The assumption that hands-on
learning is most effective is currently prevalent,
and educators and leaders go to great lengths
to adopt a more hands-on style. This approach,
however, is consistently effective for only a small
percentage of the population.

Presenting Information for Different Learning Styles

The best way to present information is in a way
that is interesting, relevant, and accessible to
the learner. If you're presenting to just one person, you can tailor your approach. But if you're
presenting to large groups, you'll need to vary
your methods in hopes of appealing to a variety
of learners. As a leader, it's important that you
vary your approach in order to reach all learning
types and avoid having any one group spend too
much time outside the environment in which it
learns best.

A Chinese proverb says, "I hear and I forget; I see and I remember; I do and I understand." Outward Bound's educational process is based on the concept of learning by doing. We believe that the more actively people are involved in the learning process, the greater is their retention of the information. So you might need to initially present information in a variety of ways, but ultimately your participants are going to retain the information best if they play an active role in learning it.

For example, a visual learner might be able to tie a new knot immediately after seeing a demonstration, but if he doesn't practice that knot a few times, it's unlikely that he will be able to tie it again from memory the next day.

The *Outward Bound Instructor Manual* offers the following methods for presenting information:

Storytelling: If you've got the time and the imagination, telling stories is a great way to get your audience engaged in a topic. It can also be especially useful as an introduction to a topic or to demonstrate a point. Relaying real-life experiences can help your followers remember something.

Darryl was an Outward Bound instructor from the South Bronx who had a great sense of adventure and challenge. When Darryl—who had never been north of Maine—heard about an expedition to the North Pole led by the British explorer Robert Swan, he wanted to become a member of this international expedition. Somehow, Darryl wrangled an interview with Robert Swan and convinced him that he would be a valuable member of the team. He would be representing the United States and, as an African American, he had special reasons of his own to take on this incredibly strenuous trek.

The expedition team journeyed up into northern Canada to train for the expedition. During this training period, Darryl's feet become absolutely blistered and raw from working in his boots and pulling the heavy sleds. The doctor who was examining all

the team members before setting out on the expedition told Darryl that he was going to disqualify him from the expedition because of the terrible condition of his feet. Darryl, however, begged to be allowed to try it. There was going to be an airplane resupply along the way, and if after the first week Darryl was not making it, they could fly him out. So, with this backup plan, Darryl set off with the expedition to go to the North Pole.

Arctic travel is always difficult, and this trip was no exception. Temperatures were oftentimes -45° Fahrenheit. There were ice fields and deep crevasses to cross with the sleds. There was high wind. Everybody was stretched to their physical and emotional limits. Darryl's feet were, indeed, bloodied from the terrible blisters, and there was raw flesh on his heels. Darryl did not complain, and he did not allow himself to be evacuated out. Darryl made it to the North Pole, walking hundreds of miles in fifty-six days on bloodied feet.

After reaching the Pole and coming back to the inner city where he worked, Darryl devoted himself to telling young people and particularly young minority boys and girls to reach out for their dreams. "Look what I did! If I can do it, you can certainly do it." Darryl visited high schools in inner cities around the country, telling his story and showing slides of his epic journey to the North Pole, inspiring a generation of urban teens to believe in themselves against all odds.

Guest speakers: If you're a leader who's familiar to your followers, bring in a new voice to add to your presentation. Your followers will give a guest speaker new, refreshed energy and attention. Sometimes hearing something from a guest—particularly a distinguished guest—makes information seem more legitimate than hearing it from the same old voice.

When I was CEO of Outward Bound, the national board of Outward Bound consisted of forty trustees plus seventy members of the advisory board. This was a very large group to run an effective meeting with, so meetings had to be planned carefully and orchestrated; really, it was almost like theater. I thought long and hard about how to make one of our annual meetings special—how to give the board and the advisory board members a true flavor of what was going on at Outward Bound.

Oftentimes this was done by having Outward Bound staff or students talk about their experiences. In this meeting, Colonel Bob Rheault (remember the story earlier in this chapter about his work with Vietnam veterans suffering from PTSD?) was going to give a talk about his experience dealing with Russian soldiers who also had PTSD.

A few weeks before the board meeting, I was on an invitational river trip with a professor from a southern university who had a doctorate in French literature. He was a wonderful combination of literary man and man of action; he had been a master sergeant in Army Special Forces in Vietnam, and decorated for his service there. In talking with him on the river trip, I found that the man who had awarded him his Bronze Star for heroism was none other than Colonel Robert Rheault. I thought, "Hmm, I wonder if this professor would come up to New York and be a part of our board meeting and have a reunion with Bob Rheault?"

Well, he did come to the meeting, and when Bob Rheault was giving his speech, this professor was introduced and came up to Bob Rheault and said, "You know, Colonel Rheault, I respected you so greatly and we haven't met since you pinned a Bronze Star on my chest in 1969 in Danang Province. I am proud to be here and shake your hand." It was a wonderful

moment because Colonel Rheault had no idea that this man was going to be there, and it was an effective way of bringing something special to this presentation.

By being creative in your own way, as a leader you can come up with outside resources with a particular bearing on what you are seeking to accomplish in your leadership role with your team. So think back on your history and your acquaintances and see what might be done to create that very special moment in a meeting.

A teacher of tenth-grade English had her students read a variety of Holocaust accounts. Everyone grasped the concept intellectually that the Holocaust was unimaginably horrible, but it didn't hit home on a visceral level for most of the teens, who, after all, were born four decades after the fall of Germany.

Then the teacher arranged for a Dachau survivor to come speak to the class. In a lightly accented voice, the survivor described being separated from her parents and siblings and placed on a train. When the students left the room, most were in tears.

Discussion and debate: A well-organized discussion or debate with specific topics or questions can be a useful presentation tool. This technique works well either with ethical questions or with topics that do not have right or wrong answers.

Say you're the assistant fire chief at a rural fire department. You know that if a house catches fire, it's likely that the interior of the house will be totally destroyed unless the fire is put out right away, even if the main structure remains relatively intact. Given the response time required in rural situations, your team usually reaches a fire before the house has burned to the ground but after most of the interior has been irreparably damaged. The homeowner's insurance coverage will be best if the whole house burns down, but sometimes you are able to put out the fire before the destruction is complete.

You pose the question to your squad: "Should we put out a fire as soon as we can, or, if a house is headed toward irreversible damage, should we let it burn so that the owner will be in the best financial position to rebuild?" Your squad's discussion of this ethical dilemma is likely to be lively and passionate.

Followers' presentations: Studies have shown that when you present something, you retain 90 percent of what you presented. Provide resource information to your followers and assist them in determining what is relevant and/or essential. Followers can be creative with their presentation outlines, so allow ample time for them to prepare high-quality, engaging lessons. Provide specific guidelines, such as presentation length and objectives.

First-aid topics are great lessons to have participants present. Pair up your participants and give them access to first-aid handbooks and diagrams. Then have them each prepare a lesson on a particular first-aid topic, such as treating burns, splinting broken bones, or dealing with dehydration. Give them five minutes to present the information, followed by ten minutes of discussion, then another fifteen minutes for them to facilitate the other participants' practice of the new skill.

Skill demonstrations: This is also called whole-part-whole teaching, a presentation method for skill acquisition. After participants see the entire skill demonstrated, it is then broken down into individual parts. When all the parts are reviewed, the entire skill is demonstrated again. If a participant is having difficulty with a skill, the leader determines which parts of that skill the participant should practice. After the individual parts are mastered, then the skill is put together as a whole.

Roy has broken down the art of instructing canoeing strokes into three distinct phases:

1. *Catch—the moment that the paddle blade enters the water*
2. *Propulsion—the part of the stroke that applies force to the canoe*

3. *Recovery—repositioning for the next stroke*

Participants practice each phase of the stroke, then put the three steps together into one fluid motion. Breaking each stroke down into three parts makes it easy to identify which step is causing someone trouble, then that person can practice the troublesome step until he or she improves.

Much of this section is paraphrased from the *Outward Bound Instructor Manual*. Different learning styles have been the subject of much research, and if you're interested in reading more about this subject, consult the resources for Chapter 3 in the Bibliography at the end of this book.

Expressing Positive Feedback

The ability to express genuine approval is critical to a leader's communication skills, and Outward Bound considers praise and positive feedback to be a necessary part of the learning process. The increased self-confidence that comes from realizing success provides the inspiration and courage to reach for future successes, as well as communicating the message that the leader truly cares about the participants.

My high school marching band leader was one of the most demanding leaders I've ever worked under. A Korean war veteran, "Sarge" barked out orders to his musicians, drilled our marching routines into us with a military precision, and with a single scathing glance could quiet 200 high school students who all had an instrument in hand.

We could have hated Sarge, but instead, we stayed late after school, spent our weekends marching up and down the city streets, and gave up our vacations to attend band competitions in hopes of gaining his approval. Sure, we all liked playing our instruments, and band trips were a lot of fun, but mostly we liked how we felt about ourselves when we performed really well.

At the end of a great performance— whether a routine practice on the football field or a demonstration in front of thousands of spectators—Sarge would wave his baton with a flourish and say, "Yay, Band!" He wouldn't yell it—just say it loudly enough that the drummers in the back row could hear. But that quiet, almost emotional "Yay, Band!" made us glow. We walked around almost giddy for hours afterward, thrilled by our own abilities and reminded of them by our leader's simple declaration of approval.

—Zackary, Outward Bound instructor 1997–2000

Sometimes leaders assume that their followers or participants are aware of the leader's approval, but this is typically not the case. Anyone who has ever been a participant or a follower knows that you frequently spend time wondering whether you're doing things "right" or what the leader thinks of your performance. Similarly, if you've worked under someone who treated every action as a major accomplishment, you know that such praise can ring hollow after a while. The compassionate leader instinctively knows when approval will be interpreted as genuine and when it will seem

simply as gratuitous or insincere. A general balancing guideline is that when you, as a leader, *think* a praising thought about one of your participants, *say* it, no matter how minor it might seem to you.

For example, you're out on a wilderness trip and you're enjoying immensely the dinner that two of the participants cooked up. Tell them, "This dinner is superb—thanks for your time and creativity in making it."

Or you notice that a colleague's report is particularly thoughtful and coherent. Tell her, "I was really impressed with your report; it hit all the salient points in an interesting way."

Or after you hear an engaging presentation from another faculty member, tell him how well he kept his audience's attention.

Keep words of approval appropriate to each participant and each group. Don't concoct praise simply for the sake of praising—your listeners will see through this, and your genuine praise will be received more skeptically. And know that you may have to occasionally search for approving words for someone whose accomplishments are subtle.

Sometimes a few words of heartfelt praise can serve as emotional support. A number of years ago, I was diagnosed with a very aggressive, life-threatening form of cancer, and the Outward Bound national office put out a notice informing the Board of Trustees. I received a number of

PRESENTATION TIPS FOR NEW LEADERS

Excellent teachers develop their skills training repertoire throughout their careers. Initially, we emulate other teachers we have seen. We borrow ideas that we like. We repeat strategies that worked. We steal jokes that made the presentation more fun. Eventually, as we become more conversant with the curriculum, we can be more creative and experimental.

- Develop two or three presentations that you are very comfortable doing.
- Be yourself and try to display a relaxed and positive attitude. You will not be effective if you are using a style that is not your own.
- After a new presentation, ask a supervisor and your participants for feedback.
- Take notes right away, documenting what worked well and what you would change the next time you present the information.
- Watch and learn from others. Take pieces of others' presentations and make them your own.

—Outward Bound Instructor Manual

communications and expressions of support and compassion, but one letter in particular was especially meaningful to me. It was from a corporate CEO who was a strong national leader and had been a board chairman of Outward Bound, so he knew me well. He wrote this:

Just a brief note to say I hope you are well on the road to recovery. We all have you in our thoughts and prayers. Must be that "cowboy coffee" around the campfire on all those Outward Bound trips that put you in this fix. Well—as we all know from our experiences, we can reach way beyond our expectations, and I am sure you will!

I really have not expressed this before, but your contributions to Outward Bound have been immeasurable. You have represented to me what Outward Bound is all about: positive, uplifting, risk taking, good judgment, staying cool under pressure, strong values, integrity, adventure, and so many other things. I value your friendship, wisdom, and counsel—I always have.

You are on the track of recovery—and we are all going to do what we can to get you there.

I treasure this letter because it comes from the heart of a man I respect. It is an example of the kind of leadership that we all must be aware of as we work with people who have problems. We must try our best to say the good things that we feel about them and not wait until it is too late for our words to help such people solve their problems. It is important for you as a leader to say it *now*, to give approval, to give praise, and to extend strong feelings of friendship to somebody who needs your support.

USING NONVERBAL COMMUNICATION

Don't forget that sometimes the most powerful means of communication are nonverbal. I once witnessed effective nonverbal communication

when two groups of soldiers from different countries came together at Outward Bound.

Colonel Bob Rheault (introduced earlier in this chapter) knew that the Russians had had a disastrous experience in Afghanistan. He felt that the Russian veterans of the Afghanistan War, who are called "Afghansi," were probably suffering from the same sorts of PTSD as were U.S. veterans of the Vietnam War. He communicated with the Russian government, which gave him permission to come to the then–Soviet Union to conduct a course for Afghansi who were suffering from PTSD.

The Russian program was successful, and afterward Colonel Rheault got the idea of bringing a group of Afghansi to the United States to meet with a group of U.S. Vietnam veterans. I was invited to this historic meeting of these two groups of soldiers, neither of which could speak the other's language.

Awkward and shy smiles marked the faces of most of the men as they began to mingle without being able to understand what one another were saying. But the Vietnam veterans had brought their guitars and banjos, and the Russians had brought their balalaikas and other traditional Russian instruments. One American struck up the Vietnam-era song, "Where Have All the Flowers Gone?" The Russians then responded with a song of their own. And suddenly, back and forth, the two groups were trading songs of their combat eras in these two foreign lands.

Pretty soon, they grew closer together and then there were tears on the faces of many soldiers as they began to hug each other. Although they shared hardly a word in common, these two groups of veterans from two failed wars communicated through sharing the music of their times. The nonverbal communication among them was especially poignant. The music, the facial expressions, the tears, the hugs—all these elements broke down cultural barriers as the men began to relate to each other as one human being to another.

As a leader, remember that opportunities for nonverbal communication can be especially powerful. Colonel Rheault could have chosen to hire an interpreter and have these men come together to verbally share their memories and feelings about their combat experiences. But instead he trusted the power of their experiences to transcend language barriers and created an environment in which communication without a common language was possible and effective.

Most of us are aware that *how* we say something affects the reception of our message much more than *what* we say. This is why if you say "No!" to a child with a smile on your face, the child is likely to interpret that message as a "Yes!" Being aware of your own nonverbal messages and being able to interpret others' nonverbal signals will help you do the following:

■ Ensure that your messages are sent with the correct intent.
■ Understand others' messages more readily.
■ Build rapport and trust through your ability to communicate more effectively with others.

Your leadership presence (see Chapter 2, Becoming a Leader) is characterized by your use of nonverbal communication. There are several things to consider about nonverbal communication:

Eye contact: In American culture, making eye contact communicates a sense of confidence, warmth, trustworthiness, and interest in others. Avoiding eye contact makes you appear shifty, insecure, and insincere. However, be aware that in other cultures, eye contact can have other meanings, such as confrontation. In Japan, for instance, it is courteous to look down when meeting someone.

Facial expression: Your face is a wonderful palette for conveying messages. It can also betray how you really feel, even if your words indicate otherwise. Smiling is probably the most powerful cue, communicating warmth, happiness, reassurance, and approachability. A genuine smile is hard to mistake—it's usually a relaxed motion accompanied by a crinkling of the entire face and a warmth in the eyes. A forced smile is easily identified as masking a different emotion.

Gestures: You don't want to be perceived as a stiff, motionless robot, but neither do you want to distract or annoy your listeners by gesticulating wildly, unless the situation calls for it. Subtle gestures can communicate quite powerfully: a slight tilt of the head says "I'm listening," a sweep of the arm is welcoming, and nodding tells the listener that you sympathize.

Body position: Stand confidently but not too rigidly. Be aware that crossing your arms or putting your hands on your hips often communicates a message of impatience. Turning your back shows a lack of interest in or awareness of others. Leaning slightly forward conveys interest and warmth.

Tone of voice: Remember the Charlie Brown television cartoons, wherein when an adult speaks all the kids hear is "Wah wah wah wah wah"? This illustrates the perceived monotony of the adults' tone of voice. Your voice is an instrument that can be raised or lowered, sped up or slowed down, made shrill or low or fluid or choppy. Try varying your tone of voice according to different situations. Avoid a single tone and rhythm; it makes you seem dull or unaware of your audience.

Proximity: How close to or far from your listeners you are can affect your message. Being too close makes most people feel nervous or invaded. Look for signs that your listeners are uncomfortable with your proximity: avoiding eye contact, folding arms on their chest, slowly retreating. Too much distance creates a social barrier, eroding the rapport and trust you have built up.

Humor: Laughter releases tension and puts people at ease. The use of humor early in a leadership situation can create a comfortable atmosphere. The ability to laugh at yourself makes you seem approachable. Be aware, however, that too much humor can make you come across as insincere or untrustworthy. In leadership situations, sarcasm should be used sparingly and only when you are confident that everyone in the group will find your comment funny and no one will take personal offense. For example, make a humorous comment such as "Mmm, there's nothing I love better than finding a slug in my cereal bowl in the morning" rather than "Mmm, there's nothing I love better than burned oatmeal," which would possibly cause the expedition cooks to feel ashamed or singled out.

RESOLVING CONFLICTS

One of the nearly inevitable predictabilities of groups is that conflicts arise within them. In rare cases, groups function seamlessly as teams without a scrap of tension, but these are few and far between. And frequently it's not so much that such groups are conflict-free but rather that they are ignoring and avoiding the sources of tension that lead to conflict.

Before my husband and I were married, when we had been just dating for a year, we got the brilliant idea of taking both sets of parents—who didn't yet know each other—on a three-day canoe trip. We packed gourmet camping food, gathered all the gear, and bundled everybody in cars bound for the river.

On the first day, we had blazing sun, cloudless skies, smooth paddling, and wild blueberries for dessert. Our parents quickly became best friends, and my then-boyfriend and I congratulated ourselves on our good fortune.

The second day dawned with an ominous red sky, and by noon it was raining steadily. We sang songs as we paddled, ate cookies, and generally kept spirits high, even through a mile-long portage. But as late afternoon approached, the older generation's energy began to flag. The prospect of setting up tents and cooking dinner in the rain loomed

grimly in everyone's mind, and suddenly the trip didn't seem to be so much fun anymore.

As fate would have it, we happened upon some simple cabins along the riverbank. Stopping for a quick snack under the shelter of one of the porches, we noticed a sign informing us that these cabins were available for public use for anyone willing to simply sweep them out and restock the woodpile before leaving. When my mom read this sign, she immediately went down to her canoe and began unloading her pack. She was moving in for the night.

"Wait a minute," I protested, "I think we should discuss this as a group." We held a huddled group discussion about whether or not to stop at the cabins for the night—a discussion dominated by my mom trying to persuade the rest of us that stopping was the only sensible thing to do. She lobbied so hard that no one else could get a word in edgewise, and the friendly discussion soon dissolved into a bit of a power struggle between my mom and the rest of us. All of us wanted to stay at the cabin, but my mom's aggressive attitude about pushing her agenda made us all a bit argumentative.

We ended up staying at the cabin, and my mom spent the rest of the evening trying to placate the rest of us for having railroaded us into succumbing to her will. We were all happy to have a roof over our heads, but the tension surrounding the discussion process still lingered. I later tried to explain to my mom that it was not the night at the cabin that we resented but, instead, her domineering (all 100 pounds of her) approach to reaching the decision to stay.

—Ashley Lodato, Outward Bound staff since 1986

Conflict is not an inherently bad thing, but if it is ignored, it can escalate into situations that are unsafe or detrimental to the integrity of the group. It's important that leaders take charge of identifying the source of tension and reaching resolution.

Groups that need to work together to succeed—such as groups on wilderness trips, teams for projects at work, or firefighting squads, for example—will realize their true potential if they don't have unresolved conflicts. Individuals don't necessarily need to become best friends or take bullets for one another, but they must show mutual respect and be willing to put the good of the group above personal gain.

IDENTIFYING THE SOURCES OF CONFLICTS

So your role as a leader is to help groups resolve conflict. Where do you begin? First, you need to identify the source of the conflict.

Conflicts arise in groups for many reasons, but some of the most common are differences of opinion, differences in values, personality clashes, power issues, and hidden baggage. Most leaders aren't equipped to be psychoanalysts who can get at the root of people's issues that cause conflict—nor should they be. Yet it's important for all leaders to recognize that the conflicts they encounter in leadership situations are often, as mountaineer and author John Graham puts it in his book, *Outdoor Leadership*, "like an iceberg with seven-eighths of its mass below the water line."

Knowing that feelings, beliefs, and experiences hidden from the leader—and often hidden even from the conflicting parties—are often the root cause of a conflict may help you as leader show a little more compassion and understanding in your attempt to resolve the conflict. You don't need to identify *why* the conflict has arisen, only *what* has actually occurred and *how* to move forward toward resolution.

Encourage Responses Rather than Reactions

Fight or flee. You should also recognize that individuals typically have one of two reactions to conflict: they fight back or they flee. Fighters yell, get angry, defend themselves, and generally try to prove themselves to be in the right. Fleers acquiesce, apologize, and generally try to avoid or extricate themselves from the conflict. Neither of these reactions is particularly healthy, and certainly neither results in any sort of acceptable resolution.

Responding versus reacting. Your job as a leader is to get your participants to move beyond the "fight or flee" reactions and into an emotional environment wherein they can participate in open and honest dialog. One approach you can take when discussing conflict is to talk with participants about the difference between *reacting* and *responding*. Fighting and fleeing are both reactions: the visceral, emotional effects of an introduced stress. Discussion, clarification, and listening are all responses: ways of attempting to reach resolution.

Choosing. *It's important to recognize that individuals can choose whether to react or respond when faced with conflict.* Although the emotional reactions might be triggered by the stress, it is still the participants' choice whether to fight, flee, or respond in a manner that moves the situation toward resolution.

Prevent Conflicts

Note that *preventing* conflict is not the same thing as *avoiding* it. Prevention means creating an environment wherein conflict arises less often because the tension is dealt with in other ways. Avoidance means that conflict is ignored when it arises. The same principles that apply to establishing rapport, developing trust, and building teams (see Chapter 4) also apply to preventing interpersonal conflicts from escalating.

Model a high standard of behavior. The expectations you communicate while your group is forming set a tone for individual behavior. If people know they are expected to be mutually respectful, courteous, compassionate, flexible, tolerant, and trustworthy—and if you model these qualities—then many of the conflicts that arise as a result of people simply grating on each other's nerves in intimate working conditions will be avoided.

Encourage open communication. You can head off many conflicts simply by establishing an atmosphere of open, honest communication. If you've set a tone that encourages frank dialog and you've modeled effective use of feedback (see "Provide Feedback," below), then your participants may be equipped to deter many conflicts by addressing them before tension escalates.

For example, let's say that one member of your hiking group is always sitting down to write in her journal as soon as you reach camp, while everyone else scurries about setting up tents and preparing dinner. If your participants are comfortable giving feedback and if they enjoy a trusting rapport with each other, one participant just might be able to say to the writer, "Rachel, you're so good about keeping up with your journal; it's clear that you want to record the events of the day before you forget them. But the rest of us are trying to get camp set for the night and it's frustrating to see you relaxing. Why don't you help me get out the stoves and pick a dinner, and then you can write while we sit and wait for the water to boil?" This statement gives Rachel credit for being so diligent with her journal, gives her an opportunity to join in the camp tasks without assigning blame, and curtails the action that if left unheeded would eventually become a larger source of tension within the group.

Address power struggles. Power struggles can occur between a participant and a leader or between two (or more) participants. Power struggles in a group situation are usually the result of one of two things: (1) an individual is accustomed to being in charge and cannot relinquish control to a different leader, or (2) an individual is so disoriented by the unfamiliar situation, new people, or the stress of new skills to learn and challenges to face that he or she resorts to posturing, antagonizing, or otherwise trying to get some footing that gives him or her a sense of power and confidence.

A compassionate approach is particularly important when dealing with power struggles because many people have issues around power or the loss of it. Treat people with respect, give them choices, and give them the ability to save face. Recognize that the power struggle may simply be the individual's best attempt to meet personal needs for belonging and acceptance. If those needs are met in other ways, the power issues will likely diminish.

Avoid blame. Often we get so wrapped up in trying to figure out why something happened and whose fault it is that we are unable to move toward resolution. If an argument degenerates into a "he said, she said" dialog, it will be difficult to resolve anything. At some point, you must move beyond trying to figure out whose version of the story is true, get the conflicting parties to agree to disagree, then put your energy into conflict resolution.

Ensure that basic needs are met. This concept seems so simple, but it's easily forgotten. If individuals are tired or hungry or lonely, they frequently act in ways that causes tension or that are incompatible with harmonious interpersonal relations. Help people meet their basic needs so that they can focus on being rationale, compassionate, generous individuals. See "Being Aware of Your Group's Energy and Ability" earlier in this chapter for more details.

Provide feedback. Feedback is a method of providing individuals or groups with observations about behaviors. Constructive feedback is designed to alert an individual or group to a behavior that the feedback-giver believes could be changed with a positive effect. Bear in mind that feedback can be threatening and what is said might be easily misinterpreted. Make sure your participants know that the purpose of feedback is to improve group productivity, individual growth, and interpersonal harmony. Some suggestions for giving feedback from the *Outward Bound Instructor Manual* are these:

- **Be direct:** Talk to the receiver in the first person and be to the point. For example, "I noticed that you told Jason that you were too tired to belay him, but then you seemed to have lots of energy to run back to camp after rock climbing."
- **Be specific:** Describe behaviors that are helpful or detrimental. For example, "Just now you interrupted Bob. Why don't you let him finish, and then you can speak."

- **Own your own feelings:** Distinguish between a person's behavior and your response to that behavior. For example, "I felt frustrated when you were checking your email while we were on the phone, because I was really upset and needed someone to listen to me."
- **Be aware of your tone:** Be honest and straightforward; try not to come across as condescending. For example, "I admire your persistence, but you're still not strong enough to carry that fire hose. Let's get you on a strength training program, and in the meantime start out on another aspect of firefighting." *Not* "You're so detail-oriented that I hate to waste you on the end of a hose—let's put you in charge of equipment allocation."
- **Time your feedback:** Feedback is most useful when given as soon after an occurrence as possible, judged by the individual's readiness to listen. For example, "When you yell at me while we're in the middle of a rapid, I get even more flustered and can't follow directions. It's better for me if we talk about our plan for getting through the rapid beforehand and then critique it afterward." Forcing your feedback on someone who is not prepared to hear it is futile: "Quit screaming at me! You're always shouting directions in the middle of the rapids! We're about to hit a rock!"
- **Limit information to what a person can use and do something about:** For example, "I get annoyed when you linger in your sleeping bag in the morning, because the rest of us are always packed up to go before you are ready." *Not* "I feel frustrated when you linger in your sleeping bag in the morning, because the rest of us are always packed up to go before you are ready. And besides, you snore all night so I can't get enough sleep."
- **Balance critical feedback with supportive comments:** For example, "I admire your organizational skills—maybe I can get some tips from you sometime. I feel frustrated, though, when you go into my desk and reorganize my files because then I don't know where anything is."

Use Different Styles of Conflict Resolution

Suppose you've taken all these steps to prevent conflict and create an environment conducive to cordial group interactions, and still you find yourself with a conflict on your hands. What do you do?

First of all, as with all other leadership interventions, determine what part you will play in resolving the conflict. The leader can play several roles in conflict resolution, and these roles echo the leadership styles addressed in Chapter 2, Becoming a Leader: directive, democratic, consensual, and laissez-faire.

Arbitration (directive): The leader listens to arguments from the conflicting parties, discovers as much as possible about the situation, and then makes a decision to settle the conflict. All parties must agree to adhere to the solution the leader comes up with.

For example, say two co-leaders for a backpacking trip are engaging in power struggles. According to Leader A, Leader B has cast himself in the role of "Mr. Nice Guy" and is always having fun with the participants, joking around, and bringing out chocolate bars, while Leader A plays the role of task master and skill instructor. According to Leader B, Leader A came across as so domineering and task-oriented that he felt as though somebody had to show some compassion and lightness toward the participants.

As the overarching leader, you give both of the other leaders a chance to air their gripes and explain their perspectives, and then you eventually issue a decision: The leaders will take turns being "leader of the day." The day's leader will drive the trip agenda, organize the group into action, and intervene if needed. The other leader gets to relax somewhat that day, chat with participants, and avoid making the unpopular decisions.

At Outward Bound, arbitration like this would be a last-ditch solution if all other approaches have failed, because it essentially removes participants from the decision-making process and gives them little influence over—or investment in—the resolution.

Compromise (democratic): The leader meets with each conflicting party separately and gains concessions from each party. The leader ultimately decides how to resolve the conflict based on the best compromise that can be reached.

For example, in the parenting group you lead, a married couple are feuding about how best to deal with their "spirited" five-year-old daughter. The father thinks that the daughter is becoming a brat and that the best way to deal with her is to "give her a dose of her own medicine." So when she screams and yells, he screams and yells back. When she calls him names, he calls her a little pill. The mother is frustrated by the daughter's behavior but thinks that the parents need to model kind words and soft voices in hopes that the daughter will begin to mimic their behavior. The father thinks that his wife is too soft on the girl and that she doesn't discipline her enough.

You meet separately with first the mother and then the father, and talk to each of them about their ultimate goals for their parenting. You elicit some possible compromises from each of them separately and eventually present the parents with the resolution to their conflict. The father will stop calling the daughter names and will instead tell her about his frustration with her behaviors, and the mother will give the daughter timeouts alone in her room when she is being belligerent, instead of trying to rationalize with a five-year-old about acceptable behavior.

Mediation (consensual): The leader facilitates a discussion between the conflicting parties, all of whom share the goal of reaching an agreement. The conflicting parties, not the leader, make the ultimate decisions. The leader helps the conflicting parties go through the negotiation process by pinpointing the issue(s), clarifying the goal(s), and identifying possible solutions.

Say you're leading a canoe trip, and the participants cannot agree about the best way to portage the boats and gear from one lake into the next. Some participants think that the fairest way is for each paddling pair to carry their boat and all the gear in their boat over to the next lake. Others protest that it would be better for the stronger people to carry the canoes and for the others to haul the gear.

You facilitate a discussion that helps the participants revisit the trip goals and brainstorm all possible solutions. Ultimately, the participants decide to approach this from a group perspective, with the entire group being responsible for getting all boats and all gear over to the next lake. The group decides to let each paddling pair carry their canoe and gear. However, a volunteer offers to help one pair of smaller canoeists with carrying their canoe, replacing the smallest person, who can then help carry lighter gear.

Negotiation (laissez-faire): The leader tells the conflicting parties that they must resolve the conflict however they see fit and then removes him- or herself from the discussions. The leader agrees to accept whatever solution the conflicting parties come up with. As with other laissez-faire strategies, this method should be employed only with mature individuals who are equipped with the skills to solve the problem successfully. And the leader must be prepared to accept whatever solution they propose.

For instance, you meet with the employees of your small business to discuss the year-end holiday party. You have some money set aside for a celebration, and you want the employees to decide how to spend it. Some people want to hold a big bash at a posh local restaurant. Others want to have a potluck at someone's house and donate the money to a local charity. And a third group wants to invest the money in hopes of generating a larger fund for next year. The meeting devolves into a heated argument with your employees calling one another names and shouting at each other. These conflicts of opinion are dealt with as follows.

You get them calmed down and remind them of the constructive behaviors you expect of them. Then you remind them of the basic information regarding the party and ask them to reach a decision together by the end of the week. They come back with a decision: have the less-expensive potluck and donate the unspent funds to a local charity. As a leader in laissez-faire mode, you accept any decision your team reaches as long as it falls within the parameters you set.

Conflict resolution is an important area of expertise for a leader to master, and there are numerous resources on conflict resolution available (see Chapter 3 resources in the Bibliography at the end of this book).

COMMUNICATION PITFALLS

This chapter has at length described what effective communication entails. Frequently people confuse some of the following characteristics with good communication skills. Keep in mind that being a good communicator doesn't necessarily mean:

Talking all the time. Sometimes people mistakenly think that being a good communicator means being a "good talker." Being comfortable with talking to others is certainly a key characteristic of good communication, as is being articulate. But if you're talking incessantly, you're probably not doing that much listening. Also, if you're talking a lot, you're encroaching on your participants' potential reflection time.

Answering all questions. Outward Bound gives its students evaluation forms to fill out at the end of their wilderness courses to evaluate their instructors' performance and effectiveness. Instructors used to consistently receive low marks on "provides timely feedback." We couldn't figure it out—Outward Bound instructors give feedback constantly. Then, after talking with different students, we realized that they were interpreting "provides timely feedback" to mean "tells me the answer when I want it."

The Outward Bound philosophy is to empower learners by having them answer their own questions when the information is readily available to them. So instructors were answering questions such as, "How much farther is it to camp?" or, "How much

water do I put in the rice?" with statements such as, "Let's take a look at the map" or, "Let me help you look that up in the cookbook." In such situations, the students wanted the easy answer—"4 miles" or "two-to-one"—and thus rated their instructors low in the "provides timely feedback" area of communication skills. Being a good communicator doesn't mean providing easy answers, but it does mean spending the time it takes to help followers figure out the answers for themselves.

Avoiding difficult conversations or confrontations. Addressing interpersonal relationships is not just for therapists—it is a productive means of building stronger teams and establishing environments of open, honest communication.

A private contractor working for a university doesn't have daily or even weekly contact with her colleagues. A weeklong conference in Hawaii was the longest time she'd ever spent with this team of co-workers. During the conference, she was dismayed to discover that her colleagues spent most of their free time bad-mouthing each other behind closed doors, aligning themselves in cliques and camps, and gossiping viciously.

When the contractor expressed her concern about this negative work environment to her supervisor, suggesting that they hire a mediator to begin to sort out some of the unproductive group dynamics, he replied, "I know; it's really unpleasant, isn't it? But I can't do anything about it right now. I'm a new leader to this team, and I really need to establish myself with this group before I try to make any changes. They already think I'm a little too groovy—if I tried to get them to talk about interpersonal relationships, they would lose any respect they have for me."

Sadly, this supervisor missed the opportunity to present himself as a courageous leader (by standing up for what he believed to be right, even if it meant losing respect) and a good communicator. If he had tried to address the destructive interpersonal dynamics on his team, he might initially have lost some loyalty and possibly even some employees, but eventually the team would have emerged stronger and more able to function together productively. They might even have begun to enjoy working together.

And ironically, because the atmosphere of back-biting is so pervasive in this work environment, any loyalty the leader believes himself to have is probably a sham—his name is likely the one most frequently whispered in the backroom slander sessions. By failing to address the vitriolic atmosphere, the leader is condoning it.

Over-processing. Many people assume that good communicators are always communicating with others: asking them about their feelings, listening intently, and urging heartfelt confidences. But over-processing—digging too deep, trying too hard to elicit emotions, forcing difficult conversations—can alienate a leader from her followers. Constant overt attempts to inspire meaningful conversations or revelations can backfire, causing the followers to perceive the leader to be disin-

genuous. A good communicator will develop an ability to determine when emotional probing is appropriate and when it is overkill.

When you're thinking about how to best communicate with a group or an individual in a given situation, remember the three main tasks of good communication: 1) to convey information, 2) to build relationships, and 3) to make and act upon decisions. If you exercise your communication skills in a way that enables you to fulfill one or more of these tasks, then you are likely practicing good communication.

A FINAL NOTE

Outward Bound believes that interpersonal interactions are critical to developing increased self-awareness, and Outward Bound believes that good communication skills enable us to process and understand the meaning of our interactions with others. In the Outward Bound way of thinking, people are inherently good, want to do their best, and deserve to be treated with respect. Reaching out to help another person releases tremendous reserves of strength and courage.

■ CHAPTER 4 ■

BUILDING TRUST, BUILDING A TEAM

You are a crew, not passengers.
—*Kurt Hahn*

The 1984 U.S. Olympic Volleyball Team, according to Coach Don Beal, was made up of individual stars and prima donnas. Leading up to the games, there was no teamwork in the group. Athletes blamed each other, outside circumstances, and other people for their losses. They complained that the referees were biased, or it was a strange court, or there was jet lag, or there was funny food. The players were world-class athletes who couldn't seem to win the volleyball games they should have won. Why? Rather than playing as a team, they were out to build their own individual egos.

Coach Beal, who had heard about Outward Bound's leadership in building teams, asked Outward Bound to run a twenty-day team-building course for the U.S. volleyball team in the winter of 1983, prior to the 1984 Olympic Games. Outward Bound decided to take these San Diego beach boys on a ski mountaineering course in the Wasatch Mountains of Utah.

When the group arrived, there were twenty members, and only fifteen were actually going to be chosen for the final volleyball squad, so there was a tremendous competitive energy among the players. There were also two coaches and a sports psychologist along on the course, adding to the tension and emotions.

The athletes were novice skiers, so they quickly grew frustrated, and they transferred this frustration to their daily objectives of covering ground and getting to planned camping places, which they were unable to

meet. They were uninterested in reading the maps, and they shuffled off in different directions, frequently splitting up into small groups that did not communicate with each other. The team demonstrated the same lack of unity and cooperation in the mountains that they had on the volleyball court.

But after a few days of floundering, they began to realize that if they did not take charge of their situation, nobody else would. If they did not read the maps, they would get lost; if they did not cook the food, they would be hungry. Small signs of cooperation and cohesion began to appear. But because they had squandered so much time early in the expedition on apathy and bickering, they were woefully behind schedule. With forty-eight hours left in the program, the group still had 25 miles to travel to finish their route. Fortunately, by this time they had begun to realize they were responsible for their own actions and that they had to work together to make it back out of the mountains.

They hunkered down, set off on their 25-mile march, and made it out of the Wasatch Mountains—and when they emerged from the snowfields, they were a team. They had finally taken responsibility for their own actions. There was no one else to blame for their failures and no one else to credit for their accomplishments. When they got back on the volleyball court, they beat the Russians on their home court, and they went on to beat Brazil to win the Olympic Gold Medal in the 1984 Olympics.

What happened at Outward Bound that caused this disparate group of athletes to undergo such a stunning transformation into a high-functioning team? This was a classic example of the Outward Bound process at work (addressed in Chapter 1, Why Learn from Outward Bound?). The members of the volleyball team were challenged by the unfamiliar environment, and they learned that in order to succeed, they needed to learn specific skills and work together as a group to get themselves out of difficult situations. The experience of cooperating with each other to apply their new skills to solve real problems, as well as their eventual triumph, led to a lasting sense of team unity and increased performance.

The team-building success achieved with the Olympic volleyball team might seem a result of happy circumstance and the unique Outward Bound process, but the factors that created it can be replicated in a variety of leadership environments. This chapter will help you discover how you, too, can use Outward Bound leadership experience and strategies to build cohesive, competent teams.

UNDERSTANDING INTERPERSONAL DYNAMICS IN GROUPS

If you've had any experience as a member or a leader of a group, you probably know that there are some predictable aspects of groups. Once you understand some of these predictable characteristics, you can better prepare yourself to deal with the interpersonal communication challenges that your groups will most likely face as they evolve from a loosely organized group of relative strangers into a team.

Stages of Group Development

A lot of groups begin as a collection of strangers, but as they share experiences and struggles, they begin to knit into intimate or high-functioning teams. This happens quite predictably to groups in the outdoors because the inherent stresses and rewards—as well as the forced intimacy—of a backcountry expedition serve as catalysts for change and growth, requiring groups to transition

from one stage to the next as they successfully manage the challenges they encounter.

However, the same process happens with other groups who work closely together, especially in stressful situations, such as military platoons or relief-work teams. Corporate teams and volunteer groups frequently experience the same stages of development, but the process takes longer than in the backcountry or in the military, likely because 1) the working conditions are not as inherently stressful or 2) because the group members get a break from each other—and from the interpersonal challenges of the group—every night and on weekends. This is one reason why many corporations and volunteer groups use retreats as a team-building strategy: it brings about the intimacy that comes from being with the same people day in and day out. Consider what happened with the volleyball team.

Day One: *The athletes arrive at Outward Bound and are immediately thrust into an unfamiliar environment, in cold weather, with strange gear, and with the expectation that they will get to know a different side of their teammates. The athletes all know each other, but due to inter-team rivalry and a history of poor cooperation, few would consider any of the others friends. They are nervous about their ability to succeed: to make it through the Outward Bound course and to make it onto the final Olympic team.*

Day Five: *An argument after dinner is heated. Two of the group members have been told by the rest of the group that they are overbearing. People are tired of these two telling everyone else what to do all the time. Other group members are accused of being self-centered and lazy. The Outward Bound instructor helps the group discuss communication and leadership strategies. The two alleged tyrants agree to take on supporting roles in the group for a while: heating water, setting up tarps, etc. Although the conflict is difficult, it is productive because it results* *in increased group efficiency and more open lines of communication.*

Day Ten: *After almost a week of struggle, the athletes finally realize that no one is going to rescue them from Outward Bound—that to make it through the course means learning the skills necessary to function in the backcountry and learning to cooperate with each other. A new sense of intimacy, fostered by shared hardship, results in more harmonious relationships. Common goals and a common purpose unite and guide the group. Roles have been established, and the expedition hums along efficiently.*

Day Nineteen: *Twenty novice skiers apply their athletic prowess to completing a 25-mile journey and making it out of the mountains at the scheduled time—all without their instructors' help. All signs of earlier self-centeredness, resistance to cooperation, and bickering have evaporated. They have just accomplished something that twenty days ago they—as well as their coach—would have thought impossible.*

What accounts for a transformation like this? What process leads a group like the one described above to develop socially from being distant to having intimacy? Many researchers have identified the various stages of growth groups tend to go through that result in group competence. One of the most widely referenced findings in the leadership world is that of organizational consultants B. W. Tuckman and M. A. Jensen in their article in the journal *Group and Organization Studies*: their model is "forming, storming, norming, performing, and adjourning." In this model, as in others, members of groups start as unconnected individuals, begin to form as a group, experience conflict or instability as they sort out roles and group norms, begin to function efficiently, reach a high level of performance, and ultimately dissolve as a group.

Forming (dependency and inclusion): Individuals begin to get to know each other and

become familiar with program systems and expectations. In the backcountry, with participants learning, eating, sleeping, and working together in an environment of forced intimacy, groups grow close fairly quickly. The same thing can happen in the typical workplace as long as there are ample opportunities to work closely with others on challenging projects, but it usually takes longer.

Storming (counterdependency and fighting): As individuals grow more comfortable with each other and as the intensity of the physical and psychological challenge increases, group members begin to address conflict, sort out relationships, and question authority. After a sense of rapport and intimacy has been established, participants form opinions about the character and integrity of other group members and feel compelled to voice these opinions if they find someone shirking responsibility or attempting to dominate. Sometimes participants question the actions or decisions of the leader as the expedition or project grows harder or as they encounter challenges they think they can't tackle. In the storming phase, interpersonal conflicts frequently resemble fights between siblings, with the comfort and intimacy of the participants showing even through their dissent.

Norming (trust and structure): Resolved disagreements and personality clashes result in greater intimacy, and a spirit of cooperation emerges. A norming group works harmoniously to face daily challenges, includes all participants in group leadership in an equitable manner, and functions effectively with minimal involvement from the official leader.

Performing (working): With group norms and roles established, group members focus on achieving common goals, often reaching an unexpectedly high level of success. Late in an expedition, some natural leadership has emerged from within the group, and participants are eager to face increased challenges under this leadership. The official leader presents the group with choices and options, and frequently the group chooses to accomplish things that surpass even the leader's expectations.

Adjourning (transference): Group members

recognize that the dissolution of the group is approaching and begin to put closure on the experience, including reflecting on personal growth and transferring learnings to future situations. In the backcountry, participants frequently get a little anxious about returning to their everyday lives, having found a difficult but rewarding lifestyle in the backcountry with a new group of comrades. In comparison with the backcountry, life at home seems remarkably easy, and most participants leave their expeditions with good intentions of being more appreciative of creature comforts. Participants begin to think about dissolving relationships within the group and reestablishing connections with important people at home. With leader encouragement, participants reflect on strengths they found inside themselves and potential ways to act upon these strengths at home.

Adjourning happens a little less formally in the typical workplace, where the group isn't actually dissolving. Yet frequently a group that has just completed a long or challenging project (for example, the end of a trial or election, or the completion of a big marketing campaign) needs to bring some closure to the experience and, in a sense, adjourn that phase of the team's working relationship.

Applying These Concepts

Why does any of this matter? Shouldn't you just turn each group loose to do its own thing?

That's certainly one option. But the most successful, high-performing groups are frequently the ones that have been allowed to experience all these stages of group development. The groups that struggle in pursuit of goals often emerge as the strongest.

Don't take shelter from the storming phase. The storming phase can involve participants questioning the leader's authority or the value of the expedition or the project. Participants might also begin to form cliques, aligning themselves with others who share their habits or values and thus aligning themselves *against* others in the group. Although the storming phase can often be frustrating or frightening for the leader, it's a crucial part of the group development process. And although the temptation is to gloss over conflicts, restore group harmony, and make everyone happy, it's best to let the storming phase run its course. The leader who realizes this will spend the storming phase teaching the group how to communicate effectively, resolve conflicts, and make cooperative decisions.

Don't get stalled in the norming phase. Another reason to understand the phases of group development is so that you can nudge your group from the norming phase into the performing stage. A common breakdown occurs when groups get so comfortable in the norming phase that they fail to reach the performing stage.

For example, your hiking group that has been successfully knocking off 10-mile days might continue to do so, with plenty of time at camp for swimming, fishing, or just hanging out. They enjoy the expedition immensely, but they never know the exhausted elation of a 20-mile day, the thrill of a sunrise at the top of a glacier, or the simple joy of figuring out exactly where on the maps they are after they've spent the entire day "lost" in dense underbrush.

Similarly, you might be the president of the volunteer board of an independent school. Your board members are successfully raising funds and promoting the school, so they're doing their job adequately. But you think that the board experience would be enhanced for them—as well as providing an additional service to the school—if board members were to organize and facilitate an annual education summit for the teachers, even though it will mean a lot of extra time and work.

There is nothing really wrong with what either group is doing. Participants who complete outdoor programs that end with a friendly group of people doing fun things together usually go home contented with the experience; board members who successfully support a school through financial means usually feel that their time has been justified. But if the leader's goal is, like Outward Bound's, to instill participants with a greater sense of confidence, having done things that they didn't know they could do, then the group that fails to really perform is being shortchanged.

The way to facilitate the transition from norming to performing is to give the group greater challenges and responsibilities. For example, you might increase the mileage or the difficulty of the terrain. Or you could present the idea of the education summit and enlist volunteers to serve on the planning committee. In order to meet these challenges, the group must move into a higher level of functioning.

See the larger picture. Armed with this basic knowledge about groups, you can begin to understand your group's development, predict future needs, and monitor your group's progress. Not every successful group passes through each of the five phases of development, and some do so but not sequentially. But this model illustrates what is a remarkably predictable evolution experienced by most thriving groups. There isn't room enough in this section to provide more than this snapshot of the stages of group development; but if you're interested in learning more about Tuckman and Jensen's five-phase model, consult Simon Priest and Michael Gass's *Effective Leadership in Adventure Programming* (see the references for this chapter in the Bibliography at the end of the book).

BUILDING YOUR TEAM

Remember the old system of choosing teams that you experienced during elementary-school ballgames, wherein the two team captains would take turns choosing players for their teams? Well, in most circumstances, you're probably not going to have this opportunity to select your team from a lineup of available players. Sometimes leaders do find themselves in this situation—such as when they start a new business—but most likely you will be either inheriting a preexisting team (for example, you get promoted to a management position) or creating a team from a group of strangers brought together by circumstance. Regardless, your task is to take this group of people and nurture it into a high-performing team. If you do get the opportunity to hand pick your team, you can learn more

about its development in Part III: Taking Leadership into Your Professional Life.

Set the Tone

The first day of an initial encounter with a new group—the first few hours in particular—are a study in nerves, social awkwardness, and second thoughts. You can almost hear the thoughts of the participants as they go through the process of meeting the other participants and sizing up the leader(s): "What have I gotten myself into? Are any of these other people like me? How am I going to be able to do the things the leader talks about doing?"

CREATE AN ENVIRONMENT CONDUCIVE TO CHALLENGE AND LEARNING

The first job of leaders is to create a friendly, welcoming environment; to put participants at ease; and to inspire the confidence of participants for the leaders. Setting the tone for a successful experience begins with the first moment that the participants encounter their leader, so the leader's communication skills must be used to full advantage from the moment the leadership situation begins.

Break the Ice

As a leader dealing with new groups of people and new situations in your business life, your home life, or your social life, you need to establish a comfortable rapport with and among people in groups. This is commonly referred to as breaking the ice, but what it's really about is breaking down barriers that prevent meaningful connections with others—the kinds of connections that come from sharing vulnerabilities, hopes, and fears. As the leader, you need to begin to establish an environment of openness and trust among participants, setting the stage for future intimacy and the strong bond that comes from such close relationships.

However, you can't just sit a group of strangers in a circle and ask them to share vulnerabilities or other private details of their lives—well, you can, but you might not get very many responses. You

> ### ICEBREAKER: A COMPASS CHALLENGE
> Try a challenge activity such as this: The participants arrive and discover an envelope with a compass and a note telling them to go east to find their leader. The group must figure out how to use the compass and then walk in the right direction until the leader is located. Make sure the challenge is designed for success, even if it also results in a little frustration. In this example, if the leader thinks that the group may not know how to figure out where east is, there should be some directions in how to use the compass included in the envelope.

> ### ICEBREAKER: SHARING A MUTUAL INTERVIEW
> An effective sharing activity involves splitting group members up into pairs and then giving each half of the pair three minutes to "interview" the other half. Then have each pair reverse roles for another three minutes. When everyone reconvenes, each person introduces the person they interviewed.

need to begin the process of building a team by offering a brief, light-hearted opportunity for people to start to get to know each other in an informal setting. Close teams are formed by people who know, respect, and trust one another. Once group members learn each others' names and a few details about one another, they will feel more comfortable initiating one-on-one conversations, which will take them one step closer to true group cohesion.

It's useful to start with an initial welcome, followed by some sort of introductory name game—an icebreaker with the goal of everyone learning the names of other people in the group and getting past the initial awkwardness of unfamiliarity. Typical icebreakers include activities such as those below and in this section's sidebars. You can find additional icebreaking activities and discussions in the resources section for Chapter 4 in the Bibliography at the end of the book.

Fun activity: This is any activity designed to simply share names, ease the tension, and be a little silly. Examples include group members introducing themselves and then shouting out each others' names as they throw a ball around the circle of people, or simply saying your name and an adjective that describes you: "Hi, I'm popular Pedro." "Nice to meet you, popular Pedro; I'm joyful Jasmine."

Challenge activity: This is an activity designed to get the group members working together immediately. Such an activity offers the added benefit of giving the leader, as well as the group members, a sense of the leadership strengths within the group. Challenge icebreakers should be designed to demonstrate what the group can accomplish when people work together. This is a metaphor for meeting a shared goal, but most important, it allows the participants to interact with one another and break down barriers of shyness.

Sharing activity: This is an activity designed to help participants learn a little about one another. The level of sharing required should be determined and modeled by the leader and should be appropriate to the situation.

For example, the leader might say, "Hi, I'm Rachel, and the worst job I ever had was scooping poop up from behind the elephants in a parade." Such sharing encourages one level of intimacy, whereas something such as "Hi, I'm Greg, and I struggled with stuttering when I was a kid" encourages a deeper level. Only skilled facilitators working in very specific settings—and *not* in introductory team-building situations—should model initial sharing of things such as "Hi, I'm Lisa, and I'm a victim of abuse."

Once the ice—the barrier to social connections—is broken and the group suddenly no longer consists of complete strangers, you can begin to orient the participants to the schedule, logistics, and program goals that will drive their group situation, whether it is a wilderness expedition, a class project, or some other challenge or goal.

Establish a Supportive Environment

A "why are you here?" discussion in the first few hours can be instrumental in setting a positive tone. Not only is this a time when participants can talk about their motives for being involved with this group (as well as hearing others' motives), it's also a forum for sharing fears or concerns about the upcoming experience. The leader's role in these initial discussions is to ask appropriate questions, facilitate the conversation, and model the values of empathy, respect, and sensitivity to others' needs. You might ask a couple of questions such as the ones below and invite group members to share their thoughts.

- What (if any) reservations or concerns do you have about this project (wilderness expedition, or whatever)?
- How do you usually react or respond in situations in which you feel nervous?
- How can I or the other participants help you address these concerns?

The reasons for sharing concerns are these: (1) to help participants gain better personal insight into their own feelings; (2) to establish the group as a sympathetic and supportive entity; and (3) to create an environment of open communication, trust, and compassion within the group. If taking risks and expanding comfort zones are critical elements of your goals for your group, these things are best undertaken in a supportive environment. If nervous participants realize that they are surrounded by a supportive network, consisting of the other participants and the leader, they are more likely to be able to accept challenges, to learn, and to grow.

Finally, remember that there are many different ways to begin the process of forming groups and building teams. Sometimes all it takes to set the right tone is providing an environment that allows participants to communicate freely.

Create an Environment of Trust

As a leader, you must find ways in which those you are seeking to lead gain trust in you as well as gaining trust in the rest of their team members. People often refer to the sense of trust created among platoon mates in the military—a trust so iron-clad that each soldier knows that another is guarding his or her back, and each would probably risk taking a bullet to save another's life. In fact, many who study the psychology of war remark that an interesting transformation occurs in platoons. At some point, the soldiers in a platoon say that they are fighting for the life and safety of the soldiers around them, not for the cause that the war revolves around.

Fortunately for you, you're probably not going to have to create such a climate of trust that your followers would take bullets for one another. But you do want to inspire in them a sense of selflessness and concern for their teammates that is strong enough that they will willingly sublimate their own desires for the common good.

Demonstrate competence. First, you must demonstrate your own competence, not just in helping the group achieve its goals but also in your ability to maintain a safe emotional environment. If people are going to trust you—to put them on a cliff on the end of a rope, to sail in high seas, to tackle a controversial new project at work—they need to feel sure that your skills are adequate and that you have a strong sense of responsibility and personal accountability. They need to make sure that you are going to watch out for their best interests and, further, that you are going to put their well-being above your own. This concept is addressed in "Establishing Credibility and Maintaining Integrity as a Leader," in Chapter 2, Becoming a Leader.

Share a personal vulnerability. Next, one of the best things a leader can do to initiate a sense of intimacy among participants is to share a personal vulnerability. Sharing appropriate personal information creates an atmosphere of warm, genuine human connections. Let your participants see you as a person with opinions, emotions, and vulnerabilities. You must maintain your professionalism, but this does not mean being socially aloof and impersonal.

For example, a particular situation might lead you to share that you have a strained relationship with your parents; however, it would generally be inappropriate for you to share that you and your spouse are having marital troubles. Another great example of this comes from a new chairman of the board of directors for one of the Outward Bound schools.

At the first board meeting, this new chairman, who was the managing partner at a major law firm in southern California, led the board members through the business discussions of the day and the different tasks that had to be accomplished. Then he did a most unusual thing. He shared with the group that he had always suffered from "imposter syndrome," a term used by psychologists to indicate a person's feeling that he is an outsider, that he is not one of the inner circle but is instead outside it looking in, and that if people really got to know him, they would reject him.

Here was a remarkably successful attorney sharing with this group that he had always suffered from this feeling and that even though he was the leader of a major law firm, he felt inadequate in many ways. The rest of the board members were so overwhelmed by this new chairman's honesty that they would have walked through fire for him after he shared his vulnerability and sense of inadequacy.

This sense of not being in the "in" group is something that many people relate to, even if they have held many leadership positions or even if they

would be deemed highly successful by others' standards. As one Outward Bound alumnus writes:

> *My ability to interact with others has also changed significantly. Before Outward Bound, I did not know myself. I masked my feelings of inadequacy by telling people things that were not true but made me seem like everyone else. I now feel confident in sharing with others what is different about me and what makes me unique. As a result, I have been privileged to see both the quality and quantity of my personal relationships increase significantly.*
> —Sam, past Outward Bound participant

Hearing the leader express a vulnerability says to the group, "I am going to take a personal risk here and share one of my insecurities. I am trusting you to be respectful of my feelings. You can expect the same from me." It also models a culture of sharing and emotional risk taking.

State expectations. Much can be communicated through the leader modeling trust and respect, as well as sharing personal vulnerabilities. But it's also a good idea to state this information right up front—to tell participants what you expect of them in terms of their courtesy and respect toward others and in terms of their sensitivity and confidentiality.

In the group's first meeting, the leader can communicate or revisit the project or expedition's objectives. Many participants may be unaware of what is expected of them in order for them to have a successful experience, either individually or as a group. Group norms as well as personal rights and responsibilities should all be discussed in this initial meeting.

For example, you might discuss your organization's harassment policy and your own expectation of mutual respect. Or you could address a code of conduct and expected work ethics. The expectations you communicate to your participants will depend upon your particular leadership situation.

While it may seem to you that some of these

social norms and rules are obvious, to others they may not be. Clearly communicating expectations and rules right off the bat prevents potential future misunderstandings. Most important, it establishes the concept of the group—the independent, democratic learning community composed of the individual participants—and lays the groundwork for participants feeling obligated to and responsible for this group.

Foster one-on-one connections. The leader can also create opportunities for one-on-one connections within the group. As people learn about each others' backgrounds and personalities, and witness each others' strengths and shortcomings, they begin to trust one another more. They begin to see the rest of the members of their group as ordinary, fallible human beings just like themselves. And they begin to feel a sense of warmth and caring from and for each other. Ample opportunities for people to work in pairs or trios or simply spend time getting to know each other, fosters strong one-on-one links that ultimately lead to strong group ties. One Outward Bound participant describes the intimacy she developed with her peers on her Outward Bound course:

> *I found myself interacting easily with other people my age. I had never before communicated so freely with other teenagers. We learned how to give constructive feedback to each other. For example, if there was something someone did not like about me, that person told me. If someone felt I was conducting myself improperly, I heard about it. My positive contributions to the group were also noticed and affirmed. Other people in the group depended on me, and I depended on them. I learned in real time how everyone must work together to make the team function at its best.*
> —*Sophia, past Outward Bound participant*

The reality is that teams with strong interpersonal connections function far more effectively than those with superficial relationships, even if the project or goal doesn't seem to demand a high level of intimacy. So any time and energy spent on creating a climate of trust and intimacy will pay off in the eventual accomplishments of the team.

Prevent conflicts. Finally, it's important to recognize that within any group, particularly larger groups, it's likely that not everyone will form a bond with everyone else. Furthermore, everybody might not like everybody else. Although one of your roles as a leader is to encourage interpersonal connections that will unite your group, you are also responsible for being in tune enough with your group to recognize when interpersonal friction exists and to take steps to ameliorate potential conflicts.

Storming as a phase of group development differs from actual conflict in that it allows sharing of differences, as in a family, with an outcome of greater understanding. The leader must differentiate between this growth element and real conflicts that could harm the group's performance.

You might head conflicts off before they start by strategically pairing people to work on individual tasks together. Or you might need to address interpersonal tension directly among the affected parties. Regardless, you should not attempt to force bonds that do not seem to be forming naturally. For more on this topic, see "Resolving Conflicts" in Chapter 3, Communicating Effectively.

TIPS FOR PUTTING PARTICIPANTS AT EASE

Learn and use names: Memorize your participants' names *before* they arrive, and put names with faces as you meet people. Begin to use participants' names freely as soon as you've met, even if you occasionally use the wrong name. It will help cement their names in your memory, and it will encourage participants to learn their teammates' names more quickly.

Memorize trivia: Memorize one nonconfidential thing about each participant *before* they arrive (for example, Joe lives in Manhattan, Jim worked in the Philippines, Maria speaks Spanish). This kind of information is usually available through enrollment or application information. Knowing one thing about each person gives you a conversation starter should you need one ("So, Joe, what's it like living in a big city?") as well as a link for establishing connections and conversations within the group ("Jim, you and Willy both spent time in the Peace Corps, didn't you?")

Treat people as individuals: Despite the necessity of group identity and unity, people like to be seen and treated as individuals. This means holding individuals, not the group, accountable for unacceptable practices as well as singling out individuals for praise above and beyond group accomplishments. If people start to think that individual behavior doesn't matter and that the leader notices only group actions, people begin to care less about their own conduct, and group performance suffers.

Check-in regularly: Taking moments at regular intervals to check-in briefly with each participant communicates to them that you notice and care about their well-being. This doesn't have to be overly time-consuming. If you're on a wilderness trip, simply walk along the trail next to each person for a few minutes each day, or stroll around the campsite while dinner is being cooked and ask "How are you doing?" or "How are things going for you?" If you're leading a team at work, use breaks in between meetings to check-in with team members to find out what they think of the group's progress or how they view their own role in the group. If you have a co-leader, you can divide up the group and have each leader check-in with half the participants.

Address the Concept of Teamwork

There are many different definitions of teamwork. To some, like the Russian climbers described in Chapter 2, Becoming a Leader, teamwork means everyone doing what he or she excels at in the interest of success. For others, teamwork means that everyone shares equally in the work and responsibility. To some it means that everyone pulls his or her own weight. So when you tell your participants that you expect them to work as a team, you need to clarify what you mean by that.

You might start by asking your participants what the term *teamwork* means to them, then use their responses to launch a discussion about the kind of teamwork that you will be trying to cultivate during this expedition or project. If the participants' definitions of teamwork are radically different from the climate you are trying to create, you may need to provide a rationale for your particular agenda.

The nineteenth-century philosopher William James coined an interesting phrase to describe the teamwork atmosphere that we try to create at Outward Bound: "the moral equivalent of war." According to an essay of the same title by James, war "satisfied a primitive longing which will never be extinguished—the longing to lose yourself in a common cause which claimed the whole man." James hated war, but he believed that combat brought about "strenuous honor" and developed the individual's ultimate mental, psychological, and physical talents. Furthermore, because there was no personal gain to be had from combat, individuals threw themselves wholeheartedly into the common struggle, stifling their own desires to serve their teammates and the common good. William James challenged educators to find a "moral equivalent to war"—similar opportunities that would bring out the best in people: their full energy and attention, their best efforts, and their compassion for their fellow human beings.

Outward Bound expeditions try to create similar opportunities to bring out the best in our students. Challenging tasks that require the participation of every member of the group—such as reaching the top of a distant summit or negotiating the way through a froth of white water—inspire a similar sense of team unity and loss of oneself in the common cause. If this resembles your definition of teamwork, you'll need to clarify this to your participants, reminding them that it's not the attainment of the peak or the completion of the project that is the eventual goal but, instead, the experience of camaraderie, cooperation, and selflessness that are required in order to reach the objective.

Unite Your Team with a Shared Vision

The common cause referred to by William James is a powerful glue in bonding your team together. Although it's possible to create a strong team focused on achieving a goal that doesn't hold any particular meaning for team members, the best way to unite a team is through common struggle for a shared vision. This is how grassroots organizations working for political, environmental, or social change are formed: people with similar values and visions begin to work together to achieve common goals.

Possibly the most famous shared vision of the twentieth century was Dr. Martin Luther King Junior's view of a world of racial equality, which he proposed in his "I have a dream" speech, and it united entire generations of teams of civil rights workers. Similarly, John F. Kennedy's brief presidency inspired the idealism of the 1960s, with young Americans asking what they could do for their country and joining philanthropic enterprises such as the nascent Peace Corps (which, incidentally, used Outward Bound staff, methods, and ideology in its early training programs).

We'd all love to conceive a shared vision as lofty and a means of expressing it as articulate as those of Dr. King's or President Kennedy's, but most of us will have to settle for slightly more everyday, although no less heartfelt, dreams of team goals. This vision of great things to come—an image of success—should be vivid enough to inspire your team to struggle to achieve it. If individuals and teams are going to push themselves to work hard, perhaps sacrificing some of their own desires in order to achieve team goals, then the eventual goal needs to be worth their struggle. Share your vision with your team, then create opportunities for them to adapt it to fit their own ideas of success.

In college, I rowed on what proved to be an undefeated crew team. Our coach, whom we adored, didn't fill our heads with visions of national championships or gleaming trophies. Instead, she simply asked us to "make the boat go fast."

At first, many of us didn't really understand what she meant by this. Of course we were going to make the boat go fast—that was the whole purpose of racing. But as she coached us to better technique and, more important in sweep rowing, synchronized movements, we suddenly began to feel what our coach meant. The boat started going really fast. At times we seemed to skim over the water as the eight rowers moved in perfect harmony, each oar blade dipping into and out of the water at the same moment.

Once we felt what it meant to "make the boat go fast," we held this vision in our heads and used it to guide us to victory after victory. Our success went to our heads a bit, and we got a little cocky, but mostly we enjoyed the feeling of moving in precise synchronicity with seven other rowers and sharing the thrill of victory with teammates who felt like extensions of ourselves.

—Ashley Lodato, Outward Bound staff since 1986

In creating your shared vision, don't forget to address the role of failure as well as success. Images of success naturally inspire and guide, but failure can be a strong motivator, too. Although failure can be disheartening for a group, it can also increase motivation to succeed in future ventures. This is how the underdog sports team can make a strong comeback, winning the entire tournament.

Failure also serves an important purpose in team building: it causes participants to lean on each other for emotional support, which makes them grow closer and stronger as a team. You don't want your team to be driven to succeed only because the image of failure is so terrifying or inconceivable, but neither do you want your participants to believe that the complete measure of success is whether or not they reach the intended goal.

Use Internal Competition

As we saw with the U.S. volleyball squad at the beginning of this chapter, internal competition can have a divisive effect on groups. But internal competition can also be used quite successfully to unite and motivate groups, as long as the team is competing to improve and strengthen itself, to better its best performance. As Josh Miner and Joe Boldt note in *Outward Bound USA*, Kurt Hahn claimed that competition was good as long as it "taught a lesson of 'the good ally' and teamwork, modesty in winning, and resolution in defeat." One Outward Bound instructor describes an impromptu challenge encountered on a wilderness canoeing course that inspired a sense of internal competition:

We were paddling down the Rio Grande with a semester course, when we came around a bend and saw an unusual sight on the Mexican side of the river. A cow was stuck in the mud—almost to the tops of her legs—and two Mexican ranchers were trying to pull her out, with little success. The twelve of us—two strong Outward Bound instructors and ten robust college students—pulled over to see if we could help. None of us spoke very good Spanish and the ranchers didn't speak any English, but we communicated through a few words and gestures that we would try to help.

Well, we dug and pushed and pulled for what seemed like hours, but that cow was good and stuck. The language barrier seemed to melt away and we were chatting and laughing with the Mexican ranchers. We still had many miles left to paddle that day, but there was no way that our students were going to leave that cow stuck in the mud. They had been presented with an unexpected challenge and they were going to face it, darn it!

While the students had many ideas for freeing that cow, none worked until someone finally got the idea of using the rope from one of our throw bags [used for canoe rescue], and we eventually pulled that cow out of the mud with a great suction sound. Cheers all around! Our students were filthy, covered with mud and cow muck, but they were as jubilant as if they had just won a gold medal. The competition to find a solution that worked was successful. The energy, innovation, and teamwork present while we worked to free that cow were mind-boggling.

—Jon, Outward Bound instructor since 1990

Many of the activities on an Outward Bound wilderness expedition require teamwork mixed with internal competition for success: getting the whole group to the top of a technical peak, for example, or moving six canoes and a mountain of gear from one lake to the next. Students vie with one another to show the best aspects of the skills they've learned and to achieve their task in the timeliest manner. Undertakings such as these involve every participant, and a sense of completion is experienced only when the whole group has reached the top of the mountain or the other side of the portage. The internal competition is inspired by time goals, the uncertainty of success, and the desire to triumph against the odds.

Other unexpected situations often arise that inspire this sense of teamwork and internal competition, such as arriving at a river crossing and finding the water too deep or swift to cross. The group might send scouting parties up and down the river to find alternate crossings, which prompts the separate parties to try to be the first to find a solution. Or the group might attempt to construct a raft out of wood and scavenged materials. Or you might have two or more groups competing to build a raft and then use it to complete a race around a short water course. Again, internal competition is inspired by a sense of urgency and uncertain success.

ESTABLISHING A LEADERSHIP TEAM

As if leading isn't challenging enough, frequently you're put in a situation wherein you are co-leading with someone else. Although a co-leader gives you a sounding board, a source of moral support, and another set of hands and pair of eyes to share the leadership burden, a co-leader also gives you yet another relationship that must be forged and another team that must be built. But establishing an open and productive leadership team is just one more aspect of your professional development as a leader, and it will serve only to better your general team-building skills.

If you have a co-leader, building a strong relationship with your co-leader is one of the most important tasks you'll face. A strong leadership pair can inspire its team to great accomplishments, whereas a leadership team characterized by disagreements, power struggles, or other interpersonal tension threatens the integrity of the entire team. Many Outward Bound instructors headed out on three- or four-week courses often say, "As long as my co-instructor and I get along, everything else will be OK." The flip side of this situation is that if you and your co-leader don't get along, three weeks can seem like an eternity.

Develop Open Lines of Communication

To establish and maintain a unified leadership team, the most important aspect is open lines of communication. If you and your co-leader feel comfortable addressing disagreements, giving and soliciting critical feedback from each other, and confronting tensions as soon as they arise, you will establish a strong foundation from which you will be able to solve all your interpersonal issues. Sometimes it's tempting to ignore challenges to the working relationship, particularly if the leadership situation is a temporary one (for example, co-leading a two-week expedition). But if significant issues are swept under the carpet, the effect destabilizes the group and threatens the success of the expedition or project.

Establishing these open lines of communication involves beginning conversations prior to the arrival of your participants. Before going out in the field on courses, Outward Bound co-instructors address topics such as the following (from the *Outward Bound Instructor Manual*):

Personal strengths and weaknesses: Co-leaders can help nurture each other's strengths and ease the stress of their weaknesses. For example, one leader might share that he is incredibly organized and manages time well but gets very frustrated with participants when they seem to be floundering. His own organizational and time-management skills cause him to have a very low tolerance for others' bumbling. He knows that experimentation and some amount of hesitation is necessary for the group's development, but he needs his co-leader's help in nipping his frustration in the bud before he expresses it to the group. The co-leader might say to him, "You seem to be getting angry. Why don't you go take down our tent while I try to get the group organized?" Or "I think that the discussion the group is having right now is more important than meeting our next time goal. Let's delay for a while and let them keep talking."

Personal values and goals: Co-leaders can support each other in meeting personal goals that affect the course. For example, one leader might have a goal of spending more one-on-one time with participants and getting to know each of them on a deeper level than she typically does on a course. The co-leader can support the other leader in taking time to do this by supervising group activities that allow the other leader to pull participants aside one by one. The co-leader can also revisit the goal with the other leader regularly, checking to see what progress has been made.

Leadership styles: It is exceptionally important that co-leaders know what each other's preferred leadership style is (see Chapter 2, Becoming a Leader). If one leader prefers a directive style and the other is more laissez-faire, an interesting but not always compatible dynamic is created. Leaders with similar leadership styles need to encourage each other to experiment with different styles according to different situations. Leaders with vastly different styles need to discuss how they will avoid sending mixed messages to the group.

Expectations and potential hesitations about working together: Frequently, when you meet a new co-leader, you have initial hesitations about working closely with that person. Perhaps he seems to make a joke out of everything, or maybe she seems to need to be in control all the time. Addressing these issues before they crop up in the actual leadership situation will make it easier to discuss them when they do arise. For example, "Remember when I said that I was worried that you trivialized things by joking about them? Well, today I had that concern again when you . . . "

Communication between co-instructors: It's important that co-leaders determine beforehand how they are going to make decisions, resolve conflicts, and intervene in group actions or discussions. Otherwise, for example, frequently one leader will jump in at the first sign of dissent, while the other leader would prefer to let the group make an attempt at resolution. Some leadership teams agree that unless there is an imminent threat to life or limb, the leaders will consult with each other before either intervenes. Others take turns being the official leader each day, and that leader makes all decisions about interventions for the day. Others decide that the most conservative opinion will always prevail. Note that this final system sounds good at face value, but in reality what often results is groups not being pushed to achieve their full potential, because the conservative instructor prevails and opportunities to push the group beyond what they thought was possible are consequently limited.

Ultimate authority: At Outward Bound, if one instructor is not clearly the senior leader, one of the co-instructors must be designated as the ultimate authority, responsible for overall quality and safety of the course. In the unlikely case of an unresolved decision, the designated leading instructor would make—and be accountable for—the final decision.

Maintain Harmony in the Leadership Team

When building a leadership team with another leader, don't forget that you are establishing a *working* relationship and that it is probably going to be a lot of *work*. Sometimes you fall into perfect synchronicity with a co-leader, but most often you have to work through a lot of differences. Some tips for maintaining a harmonious co-leading relationship are these:

Present a unified front. Address disagreements privately. Deliver criticism outside of participants' presence. A unified leadership front inspires trust and confidence from participants; an unstable leadership team jeopardizes this trust.

Give each other space to lead. Determine who is going to teach what and who is going to lead what, then step back and let each other teach and lead. It's tempting to add your own two cents' worth on a topic that your co-leader has just covered, but resist the temptation unless what you are adding is *critical* to the participants' understanding of the topic. Most often, it isn't.

Create regular opportunities to review the working relationship. Commit to regular check-ins with each other to see how things are going. Provide each other with regular, timely feedback.

A FINAL NOTE

Now that you've learned various ways to build trust and establish teamwork—such an important part of your leadership success—you and your team are ready to face risks together and hone decision-making skills.

CHAPTER 5

TAKING RISKS AND MAKING DECISIONS

A ship in harbor is safe—but that is not what ships are built for.
—John A. Shedd, Salt from My Attic, *1928*

Sometimes being a good leader means taking risks. In fact, some of the most successful leaders say that leadership is a dance—a delicate balancing act involving the potential hazards and rewards of risk taking and the apparent safety and security of the status quo. Stephen Anton (not his real name), the executive director of a small, nascent Central American microcredit organization describes his struggles with needing to expand the company but lacking the financial resources to do so at strategic times.

I started a microcredit organization in Honduras in the aftermath of 1998's Hurricane Mitch, which had nearly devastated an already impoverished rural population. We gave small loans to rural women to start up businesses in their villages. The organization was initially funded through private donations and grants acquired in the United States, but our eventual goal was to reach sustainability (with the women's interest on loan repayments eventually covering operating costs) within a number of years.

In microcredit, you have to continue to grow and expand the program, particularly in the early stages, because if you don't, you will never reach sustainability. Also, our loan system involved a borrower getting three loans of progressively increasing amounts, and the women's business plans depended upon receiving the second and third loans. But growth involves money, and we frequently experienced tight cash flow, due to a decline in donations or a delay in receiving grant funds.

On one occasion, we were expecting a $100,000 donation to arrive in January, and we were counting on that money to carry us through several months of staff salaries and loan expansion. But January arrived and the money didn't. When February came and there was no sign of the money, we wanted to be prudent and spend less in case the donation didn't come through. But we knew that in microcredit, arresting growth before you reach sustainability is usually a death knell for the organization because donors don't want to perpetually fund an organization that isn't progressing toward financial independence. So we had to decide whether to stop growing and wait for the check to arrive or to keep spending money and expanding loan opportunities for our clients, hoping that the promised funds would arrive.

We decided to risk it, and we kept growing. We raised smaller donations more aggressively to cover some of our operating costs in the meantime, and we stopped paying my salary, as well as that of the development director. It was tough. We put off paying many of the organization's bills, and the development director and I both delayed payment on many of our own personal bills. We felt that we were doing the right thing because we were able to generate enough money to keep giving the women their loans and paying the salaries of our native staff, but we were haunted by the thought of running out of money and ruining the organization, which would have meant ruining the hopes of the hundreds of rural women who were improving their own and their families' lives with these small loans.

Fortunately, the promised donation finally came through, but not until May, after we'd wondered for five months whether the risk we'd taken had been too great. We faced many similar situations over the years, and we always decided to prioritize the continuation of loans over immediate financial solvency. And the organization thrived as a result.

The way you approach risk is an important characteristic of your leadership style. This chapter provides information that may help you evaluate your own relationship with risk, assess the potential risks of particular actions, assess your judgment, and make effective decisions.

TAKING LEADERSHIP RISKS

One reason why people either shy away from or gravitate toward leadership positions is that leadership involves risk. Leaders risk disapproval from their followers if they make unpopular decisions. They risk alienation from their followers if they aren't able to establish a rapport of respect and trust. They risk harming their own and their organization's credibility if they spearhead failed projects. And they risk being held liable if one of their participants gets seriously injured.

But with uncertain risks also come the potential for certain rewards—and this is what draws those who can cope with risk into leadership situations. The triumph, honor, and satisfaction that come with successful leadership experiences are intoxicating. Being a respected leader who effects positive change in people's lives or communities is a thrilling and gratifying experience.

Risk to Participants

Leaders' primary responsibility is the well-being of their followers, so as a leader you should always consider the risks that any particular action or activity will pose to your participants. The wilderness context presents many obvious physical risks to participants as a result of inherent dangers, bad luck, and poor leadership decisions; when you're thinking about risk management, it's usually these types of risks that come to mind.

As the CEO of Outward Bound, I once joined a group of fourteen- to fifteen-year-old students who were preparing for the final challenge of their Outward Bound course: an ascent of the South Sister, a 10,000-foot nontechnical but vigorous climb in the Oregon Cascades. The students were going to spend the night on top of the South Sister, and they were discussing what they thought they should bring. The discussion was very much dominated by the fact that the students did not want to carry much weight up the mountain. If left to their own devices, it's possible that they would have headed off with a windbreaker and a few granola bars each. But the staff had to consider the risks of the climb and of spending the night at high altitude and then weigh those with the participants' desire to travel fast and light.

They finally reached a compromise, getting the students to take sleeping bags, ice axes, helmets, and a rope in addition to a little food. The climb was successful, and the students had the minimum equipment necessary to keep themselves safe. They finished the climb tired, hungry, and a little chilly but completely healthy and elated and proud of themselves that they had completed a strenuous climb and spent the night out on top of a mountain with a minimalist strategy.

There are also risks to participants in all types of leadership situations, regardless of whether or not there is any real likelihood of sustaining a physical injury. An entrepreneur with a great idea and a little capital might start up a small company and lure several acquaintances away from their stable jobs. If the company flops, those friends are suddenly unemployed. Or the chairman of the board of a nonprofit organization might persuade the rest of the board to host an unusual type of fund-raiser. If the fund-raiser is not successful, the board members are disheartened. And sometimes the risks to the participants include bodily harm, as in the case below, with the employees of the Central American microcredit organization described earlier in this chapter:

> One day the credit officers were held up at gunpoint just after making their weekly loan repayment collections. The thieves obviously knew exactly where the credit officers would be and when they would be transporting large amounts of cash; they also knew that there was very little likelihood that they would be pursued and held account-able for the crime. The credit officers were unharmed but very shaken up and reluctant to return to the area where they had been robbed, aware that the thieves were probably emboldened by the previous day's success.
>
> But the executive director felt that it was very important that the organization show its commitment and loyalty to the borrowers (poor rural women), so the next day he made the credit officers go back to the same place. This time, though, the executive director accompanied the credit officers on their collection rounds. The director didn't have any special ability to prevent another robbery, nor was he likely to thwart an ambush, but his presence reassured the credit officers, showed them that he took their personal safety seriously, and gave them the courage they needed to continue. Most important, it reinforced the director's commitment to the organization's mission—to help rural women achieve financial independence through entrepreneurship—to both the borrowers and the employees.

With these risks to participants, though, also comes the possibility of rewards for them. A small-town civic leader who fights against corporate development pressures—despite the citizens' interest in bringing better job opportunities to the region—may see the residents experience a renewed commitment to the small-town values that make the community a desirable place to live. The manager of a team at a large company who initiates change in the corporate culture might hear the staff discussing how much more pleasant the work environment is. A student pushed to excel by an inspirational teacher may go on to make more of herself than she ever would have dreamed. A promising athlete may find the support she needs from a coach to try to make it in the professional leagues, as is illustrated by the story of a young dancer.

> A high schooler named Patricia (not her real name) was a dedicated ballet dancer. Starting at about age ten, she was the best dancer in town and in fact became the best dancer the town had ever seen. Her dance teacher was committed to Patricia's development and urged her to seek a position in a professional dance company after graduating from high school. Patricia had dreams of dancing professionally, but other than her teacher, everyone else tried to convince her to go to college. "Dancers have short professional careers," her friends told her. "When you can no longer dance, what will you fall back on? What if you get injured? A college education will serve you better than chasing a position with a dance troupe."
>
> Fortunately for Patricia, her dance teacher persevered and eventually provided the support Patricia needed to get a position with a professional company right out of high school. Suddenly Patricia was living her dream, dancing professionally. Had it not been for her inspirational teacher who convinced her to follow her dreams rather than succumbing to the pragmatic advice of

her friends and family, Patricia would have probably gone on to college and spent the rest of her life wondering "what if . . . ?"

This young dancer's teacher took a risk in encouraging Patricia to follow her dreams. The teacher risked the disapproval of the dancer's parents as well as the potential anger of Patricia had she not succeeded with a professional company. But the teacher saw that these risks paled in comparison to the potential feelings of satisfaction and pride—both for her and for Patricia—if the dancer were to make it, and the teacher decided to use her leadership influence to support Patricia in becoming more than she thought possible.

As you're considering what risks a particular activity or course of action poses for your followers, remember that your followers are going to be more willing to take these risks because they trust you: they trust your judgment, your skills, and your concern for their well-being. It's up to you to make the final decisions about what risks you are going to subject your participants to, because your sphere of influence as a leader is so great.

Risk to Leader

Some leadership decisions put participants' physical and emotional well-being at risk, and some leadership decisions put a leader's integrity or reputation at risk. In many situations, it is this latter category of risk that is harder for leaders to commit to because of the personal nature of the possible consequences. But it is precisely these types of situations—opportunities for leaders to stand up for what they believe to be right even in the face of opposition—that Outward Bound founder Kurt Hahn strived to inspire leaders to seize: "Effect what they have recognized to be right, despite hardships, despite dangers, despite inner skepticism, despite boredom, and despite mockery from the world."

In the winter of 1988, I pondered a watershed decision for Outward Bound's future. The wilderness programs had grown by leaps and bounds in the 1980s, and I felt it was time for Outward Bound to again reach out and take two major steps: (1) to enter the public school system with programs embodying our unique pedagogy and curricula to develop self-esteem and leadership in young people; and (2) to found Outward Bound centers in urban areas, where the need for such an opportunity was so great among young people.

This was risky business—I didn't know whether the Board of Trustees would support me or not. I was pretty sure that introducing this subject would put my job on the line, and I started thinking about polishing up my resume. Many of Outward Bound's staunchest proponents were adamant that the Outward Bound experience could occur only in a wilderness setting. To introduce Outward Bound into mainstream education and into the inner city, they argued, would simply not work; you needed the inherent unfamiliarity and tension of the wilderness environment to bring about the personal growth and self-confidence Outward Bound was known for. If I didn't understand this, they might say, I wasn't an appropriate leader for the organization.

But I was convinced that Outward Bound could have a positive influence in both these nonwilderness settings, and I decided to take the risk and promote the initiatives. At our spring board meeting, I took a deep breath and made a speech urging the board to adopt these two new missions. To my great relief, an influential board member said, "I'll work twenty-four hours a day for this mission!"

The resulting initiatives—Expeditionary Learning Schools and Urban Centers (both of which are discussed in Chapter 1, Why Learn Leadership from Outward Bound?)—grew into some of Outward Bound's most successful and effective programs.

In your leadership career, you will face—or

you may currently be facing—opportunities to take risks that, if successful, would result in improved conditions for your company or your team. You might be thinking of starting up a new program to benefit an underserved segment of the population. You might be rallying for curriculum reform within your school or academic department. Or you might be trying to introduce an emotionally healthier environment for your colleagues. Any of these types of ventures requires courage, initiative, and a willingness to risk your position.

Risk to Company or Organization

Leaders are in a position to make decisions and take risks that can bring a company or organization great success or jeopardize its very existence.

Outward Bound had originally been a program for only male participants. When it decided to run a pilot program for women and girls in 1965 in the United States, there was a general outcry. The public at large, as well as many of the Outward Bound staff, just didn't believe that women could handle the rigors of an Outward Bound expedition. Many tried to dissuade Outward Bound from pursuing the path of coeducation because it would, they said, dilute Outward Bound's reputation as the premier school for wilderness challenge.

Of course, the young women ended up excelling at expedition challenges and generally proved themselves to be as hardy as the men, and the threat to Outward Bound's reputation was successfully avoided. But it took a visionary leader and a supportive board, willing to risk the organization's image for something it strongly believed would work, to institute such a dramatic change.

Interestingly enough, Outward Bound experienced similar opposition when only three years later it launched a program for adjudicated youth (youths convicted of a crime in juvenile court and sentenced to probation, community service, or a term in a juvenile detention facility). Again, the pilot program met with success, and again, the leaders of the school proved to have taken a reasonable risk.

With the rash of corporate accounting scandals of the early twenty-first century, it has become obvious that, in the United States at least, many leaders are willing to risk company reputation and solvency for personal financial gain. Most companies don't have the ability to ride out poor-risk situations as easily as the ones that have been featured in recent accounting-scandal news. Most companies must rely on their leaders to take calculated risks based on an interest in serving the company and ensuring its continued existence rather than on an interest in personal gain.

But company leaders also have a responsibility for serving the organization's mission, and sometimes doing so entails taking risks. For example, say you are the editor of the only local newspaper in a small town. The majority of your readers might be fairly socially conservative, but there is probably a strong liberal element in the town, too. You feel an obligation to serve both audiences, even if sometimes appealing to one means alienating the other. You therefore risk printing occasional controversial editorials in the hopes of promoting greater tolerance and understanding, even if you lose a few readers in the process.

Sometimes the risks to a company are quite difficult to weigh. For example, take the recent situation of some university law schools that refused administrative support to military recruiters on campus due to the military's "don't ask, don't tell" policy regarding sexual orientation. Law school officials claimed that hosting military recruiters condones this discriminatory policy, which contradicts the universities' policies against discrimination. The military argued—successfully—that schools that accept federal funds should also provide support for military recruiting activities on campus. One defensible thing for these universities to do would be to reject federal funds because the strings that come attached to them are incompatible with their own antidiscrimination policies. But doing so would mean that none of the students could receive federal loans and grants, which would not only jeopardize the universities' enrollment but would also put them at risk of being able to serve only the wealthy, which would be incompatible with their missions of diversity. Either option ends up alienating a segment of the population, thereby making the decision a complicated one.

The Role of Risk in Outward Bound Programs

When I was asked to serve as CEO of Outward Bound in 1980, the organization was struggling to define the role of risk in its programs. Outward Bound had developed its uniquely successful reputation by putting people in extremely challenging situations, so the general public was aware of the risks associated with Outward Bound. Some of these risks were very real, such as climbing technically difficult peaks and tackling ambitious winter routes.

As discussed in Chapter 1, Why Learn Leadership from Outward Bound?, a challenging learning environment is critical to achieving Outward Bound's outcomes. In *Ascent: The Spiritual and Physical Quest of Legendary Mountaineer Willi Unsoeld*, by Laurence Leamer, Unsoeld, a mountaineer, Outward Bound instructor, Peace Corps director, and educator, says, "Risk is at the heart of all education." But as the country's largest and most respected outdoor education organization, Outward Bound also had a moral and legal obligation to examine its risk management strategies very closely. Those of us who worked at Outward Bound didn't want the courses to avoid risks; we wanted them to undertake calculated risks in a manner that would be appropriate for an organization leading the field of outdoor education.

Over the years, we realized that the challenging learning environment we sought could be achieved without the extreme degree of risk that was then present in Outward Bound programs. The tension that leads to personal growth and character development is also accessible in less inherently dangerous situations. And because wilderness travel is already fraught with unavoidable hazards, choosing the most difficult expeditions possible was simply complicating the risk factor in a manner that might have become unacceptable

for the flagship organization, had we not chosen to reassess its relationship with risk.

So we began to focus more on the importance of preparing Outward Bound participants to deal with hazards by training them rigorously. Activities that had been considered fairly risky for a group of novices following two experienced leaders were perceived in the realm of acceptable risk when undertaken by a group of participants who had learned the skills necessary to complete the activity safely. Tom Price, an educator who worked with Outward Bound founder Kurt Hahn in the 1960s, put it this way (from the Outward Bound Instructor Manual):

> One must distinguish between adventurousness and recklessness. The principle here should be not to restrict activities within safe limits. Anyone can make adventure training safe by taking all the adventure out of it. [The principle] should be to prepare [participants] by technical training and physical fitness to deal with the danger competently.

So Outward Bound evolved from emphasizing activities that had a high element of objective risk into focusing on elements that have a strong degree of *"perceived risk"*—activities that can be managed with an acceptable amount of risk but that put participants out of their comfort zones and make them feel on the edge, such as rock climbing and rappelling.

Outward Bound's activities didn't create extraneous adrenaline rushes, such as you would expect from bungee jumping or skydiving; all Outward Bound activities remained closely linked to the skills required for the wilderness expedition. Neither did we dumb down our programs to a level where we could guarantee absolute safety. We examined our program goals and figured out how to balance program safety with program quality. If the balance began tipping in either direction, either safety or quality was compromised. Either the program was extremely safe but not very successful in delivering intended outcomes, or the quest to achieve these outcomes became so rigorous that the program grew unsafe.

The balance between pushing the limits of exposure to risk and ensuring a vibrant learning environment is best illustrated by a story in *Ascent*, by Laurence Leamer, about Willi Unsoeld, who promoted the early Outward Bound programs to potential students and their parents. "I can't guarantee you your son won't die," he was notorious for telling parents bluntly, "but I can guarantee you if you continue to stifle him, his soul will surely die." His message was clear: profound personal and spiritual growth depends upon an element of risk.

Other profound changes involved instituting a more rigorous training program for staff; collecting and evaluating statistics on lost student days due to injury, illness, and dropping out; and informing participants in great detail about the inherent risks present in the programs they enroll in. So risk remains a very real and necessary aspect of the Outward Bound curriculum, but it consists of calculated risks undertaken in the interest of meeting program goals.

Weighing Risks

The bravest man is the one who weighs all the risks and, when they become greater than the object is worth, has the courage to turn back and face that other risk of being called a coward.
—father of a Gordonstoun schoolboy, as told by Kurt Hahn at the annual meeting of the Outward Bound Trust, London, July 1960

As a leader making decisions, you'll constantly need to weigh the risks associated with any particular course of action.

I participated in an expedition to Denali— Mount McKinley, in Alaska—a number of years ago. Rising 17,000 feet above the Alaskan plain, Denali is a very challenging mountain to climb. Its severe storms and Arctic cold are similar to conditions encountered in the Himalya. We had been on the mountain about ten days and were within a day's climb of the summit, eager to reach the top and celebrate the attainment of our goal. At this point, however, the weather turned ugly, and a massive front moved in with heavy snowfall. The snow fell heavily for two days as we sat trapped in our tents, and by the time the storm had passed, we had about 4 feet of new snow on the ground. The last section of the climb was a rather steep headwall up to the summit ridge, and the loose new snow created a high risk of avalanche. Our climbing leaders tested the snow and said that it was too unstable and that we should turn around.

We were devastated. Many of us had made great personal sacrifices of time, energy, and financial resources to climb this mountain, and we were determined to reach the top. But the climbing leaders looked at the snow conditions, evaluated the risks of proceeding, and decided that we should turn back. Crestfallen, we acquiesced to the leaders' decision.

In retrospect, this was clearly the right decision. Avalanches were prevalent on that section of the climb, and the consequence of continuing could easily have been a loss of life to our party.

So how do you go about weighing risks? If you're a linear thinker and a visual learner, you might consider making a simple list of pros and cons, with the potential positive outcomes of a particular decision listed on one side of the page and the potential negative results on the other. Then think through each outcome and determine whether that outcome is likely, possible, or highly unlikely. If you end up with a lot of likely outcomes in one column and a lot of highly unlikely outcomes in the other, then you can probably take a chance on that particular course of action.

Another method is to reconsider similar situations from past experience. It's possible that you've

TAKING RISKS: AN ANALYSIS SYSTEM

The system that Outward Bound has developed for assessing whether or not to paddle particular white-water rapids can be used as a model for assessing your own potential risks. In the Outward Bound model, you approach a rapid and scout it (look at the rapid from shore), breaking it down into the following steps:

1. **The Entrance:** Where is the best place to start? How easy will it be to get your boat there?
2. **The Rapid:** What moves are necessary? How much will you need to maneuver your boat? How precise will you need to be? Do you and your participants have the skills to execute these maneuvers? How many standing waves are there? How big are they? Is there any danger of swamping your boat or knocking it over? How many holes are there? (Holes are hydraulics formed by current and obstacles, such as rocks, that can be large enough to pose a hazard.) How easy are they to avoid? If you can't avoid them, are you equipped to tackle them safely and competently?
3. **The Runout:** What does the bottom of the rapid look like? If a boat were to be upside down at the bottom of a rapid, are there any dangers to the swimmers?
4. **The Dangers:** What are the hazards that will jeopardize the safety of a run: rocks, swift current, cold temperature, other dangers?
5. **Protection Plan:** What will you do to provide a safety net for paddlers who capsize or run into other difficulties (such as getting stuck in a hole, getting broached on a rock, etc.)?
6. **Plan:** Are you going to run the rapid? How? If you don't make your intended line, what is your backup plan?

A risk analysis system can be applied to many other situations, such as a corporation changing a product name or introducing a new product line or pricing strategy, or a not-for-profit organization undertaking a capital campaign or a new program element. As you get ready to "scout" the potential course of action you're contemplating, consider the following factors:

1. **The Entrance:** Where is the best place to start? How easy will it be for you to get there? Does starting there set you up for success in the best manner possible?
2. **The Action:** What particular action steps are required to execute your plan? Do you and your participants have the skills and experience to complete these tasks? What are the obstacles facing you? How easy are they to avoid? If you can't avoid them, are you equipped to overcome them?
3. **The Aftermath:** What are the potential repercussions of this course of action? Are there likely to be any unexpected consequences?
4. **The Dangers:** What hazards might you, your followers, and your company or organization face en route to completing this action? How serious are these hazards?
5. **Protection Plan:** How are you going to protect your followers, yourself, and your organization if everything doesn't go according to your plan?
6. **Plan:** Are you going to move ahead? How? What is your backup plan?

—Outward Bound Instructor Manual

done something like this before, and you can draw on your experience and wisdom. We like to think that we avoid making the same mistakes twice, but oddly enough it's often just as we make the same mistake a second time that we realize, "Hey, wait a minute, I've done this exact same thing before."

You might also just make an intuitive decision about whether the potential rewards are worth the potential risks to your participants, yourself, and your organization. Ask yourself whether the course of action you're considering seems to you to be the right thing to do. If part of being a leader means standing up for what you believe to be right, then you need to examine all your actions through this filter. Standing up for what you believe is right is frequently the harder course of action, and it may be easier to allow yourself to be deterred from this path simply because it is daunting. But if you are compelled to choose what seems like the honorable path, then you must have courage and take a chance.

After you've made the decision, listen to your instincts. If you're feeling good and solid, move forward. If you have a small flutter of misgiving, you might want to reevaluate. You might not end up changing your mind, but at least you will have given your intuition a chance to weigh in.

Finally, once you've chosen a path and started down it, don't spend a lot of time looking back over your shoulder wondering "what if?" But *do* spend time looking in front of you and from side to side to be aware of new information that might affect your course of action. Just because you've chosen to move in a particular direction does not mean that you should continue blindly toward your original destination. Frequently, new information emerges that makes it more prudent to change your course of action than to continue on.

Situations such as this are quite common in the wilderness: you start up the peak on a cloudless day, but storm clouds begin to brew and you head back down early; or you reach the section of white water you're scheduled to paddle, and recent runoff has changed the river from Class II to Class IV, so you decide to portage around the rapids. If you run into similar situations, evaluate the new information and decide whether it affects your risk-versus-reward equation enough to alter your plans.

Those interested in more complex risk analysis models can consult John Graham's *Outdoor Leadership* and Simon Priest and Michael Gass's *Effective Leadership in Adventure Programming*, both listed in the references for Chapter 5 in the Bibliography at the end of this book.

DEVELOPING JUDGMENT

At the core of maintaining a healthy balance between calculated risks and an ethical obligation to safety lies *judgment*. Judgment is the ability to apply knowledge, past experience, and logical reasoning to make a decision when there is missing information. Everything you do as a leader—from communicating to intervening to establishing rapport to facilitating activities—rests on your ability to consistently demonstrate good judgment.

However, good judgment is an elusive quality to develop, and it's frequently hard to define or identify, although lapses in judgment usually become painfully obvious. The effects of good judgment are similar in all types of leadership situations: appropriate challenge, healthy interpersonal relationships, achievement of goals, personal growth, reward. But the consequences of poor judgment can vary widely, depending upon the leadership context. In the wilderness, poor judgment can result in devastating or fatal accidents. In the classroom, poor judgment can cause disillusionment or despair. In the workplace, poor judgment can create unstable or dangerous working environments or severe financial strains.

Can good judgment be taught? Experts disagree. Some people believe that only years of experience in your particular leadership field and solid reflection on successes and failures can result in solid judgment. Others argue that you can learn good judgment if you have common sense, if you're trained well, and if you are able to learn from others' mistakes. A more accurate way to put it is to say that good judgment can be *developed* rather than taught; this allows for both past experience and training to cultivate and influence your judgment. In other words, you can develop good judgment in the same way you might develop good social skills: you learn from experience, from watching others, and from having someone instruct you in accepted behavior.

Judgment in Leadership Situations

Without sound judgment, even leaders with superior technical skills and keen interpersonal skills can put themselves, their participants, and their organization at risk in some situations—for instance, when embarking on a backcountry trip. Outdoor leaders' judgment is called upon countless times each day as they make decisions about routes, weather, and participants' physical and psychological safety. Some of these decisions can be made by following the policies laid out by the organization the leaders are working for (if that's the case), but even so, most organizations require their leaders to draw upon inner resources of experience and common sense in order to make a sound ruling. And sometimes even the presence of an institutional policy cannot replace good judgment.

> *While packing up the first-aid kit on Day Eight of a sea-kayaking course, Gary realized that the epinephrine (a prescription injection critical to the treatment of anaphylactic shock, which is an often severe and a sometimes fatal systemic reaction in a susceptible person to a specific antigen) had been inadvertently left behind in the van at the resupply the day before. Organizational policy dictated that "student travel shall not take place without the presence of two doses of epinephrine in the first-aid kit," but acquiring another supply of epinephrine would require that one of the instructors complete a 25-mile solo paddle, much of it across open water. None of the participants had a known anaphylaxis-inducing allergy, and bees were not common in the area in June. Gary needed to decide whether to adhere to company policy or whether the risks of compliance were greater than the risks of proceeding without the required epinephrine.*
>
> *Gary consulted with his co-instructor and discussed the two options: proceed without the epinephrine, or send one instructor out for the epinephrine. They considered both options' impact on the safety of the participants, the safety of the staff, and the*

quality of the course. Based on their experience and the information they knew about the open-water crossings and the students' medical backgrounds, they determined that the chance of something happening to the solo paddler was greater than the chance of a participant having an anaphylactic reaction to an allergen. They decided to proceed without the epinephrine and acquire some at the next convenient opportunity.

Although this decision resulted in Gary breaking a policy, it was upheld by the program director upon debriefing afterward. Gary's rationale was sound; he showed good judgment.

But aren't we just talking about common sense here? Can't leaders with a good head on their shoulders keep themselves and others safe? Not necessarily. In *Teaching Leadership and Decision Making*, senior Outward Bound instructor Caroline Blair-Smith describes the relationship between common sense and judgment:

> *When you use common sense, you base decisions on the results of past experience. When you exercise judgment, you base decisions on the results of past experience, other experts' past experience . . . and extended reflection on the implications of that experience, including a close examination of the relationship between probable causes and effects.*
>
> *The difference between judgment and common sense is the difference between problem solving primarily with foresight or hindsight. Judgment develops through practice, reflection, and the connection to a wider base of knowledge: other instructors', case studies and accident reports, and personal development plans.*

In the sea-kayaking situation described above, common sense alone would have not enabled Gary to make the best decision. Without the experience to weigh the two different risks, his knowledge of the likelihood of an anaphylactic reaction, and his prediction that the organization's administration would uphold his decision, Gary might have made a different decision.

Like the wilderness, some leadership environments have objective hazards that can cause injury or death if leaders exercise poor judgment. A fire chief must assess the likelihood of a burning building collapsing before he sends his crews of firefighters in. Military leaders determine whether the capabilities of their platoons are enough to defend themselves when fighting behind enemy lines. Industry foremen evaluate the attentiveness of employees using potentially dangerous machinery. But even in a physically safe work environment, the consequences of poor judgment can still be serious and have lasting, damaging effects.

Classroom teachers, for example, are in a position every day to influence the decisions that young people make for themselves. A teacher who exerts a negative influence over a student could be eroding the student's sense of self-awareness or confidence. Similarly, a corporate manager who uses poor judgment in a big business decision could be sending the company on a course of bankruptcy, which ultimately would lead to job losses and devastating effects for employees. Perhaps the stakes aren't as high in some leadership contexts as they are in others, but they still can be pretty pricey.

Assessing Your Judgment

So how can you tell whether you have good judgment? And if you don't have it, how can you get it? Determining whether or not you have good judgment is a rather vague process. Some people might even say, "If you have to ask, you don't have it." Yet, there's more to it than that.

A general guideline might be to simply consider the experiences you've had and the decisions you've made in your leadership field and to assess their processes and outcomes. If you've made the same big mistakes more than once or if you frequently end up wishing you'd done things

differently, your judgment might be lacking. If, on the other hand, you've been pleased with the way things have worked out for you based on the choices you've made, you probably have good judgment.

Another way of assessing your judgment is to ask your co-leaders and your employer whether they think you've got good judgment. If they say no, ask for examples of specific instances when you might have exercised poor judgment.

Even leaders with a history of excellent outcomes and sound decisions agree that good judgment is something that needs ongoing development. So whether you determine that your sense of judgment could use a little refinement or you're just looking to continue your good track record, the following suggestions can help:

Get experience. Experience is the best teacher. Get into the classroom, dig your hands in as a new manager, jump right into civic leadership responsibilities. If you're an outdoor leader, go on as many expeditions as you can. No amount of training or study can substitute for firsthand experience.

Reflect on your mistakes. Although it might be painful or embarrassing, reflecting on your mistakes and trying to determine where you went wrong will help you avoid making the same mistake again.

Learn from others' mistakes. Talk to others in your field—other teachers, civic leaders, outdoor leaders, business leaders. Ask them about poor decisions they've made and whether they know what they could have done differently. Examine case studies and read annual accident reports in your field; for instance, outdoor leaders can turn to *Accidents in North American Mountaineering* and the *American Canoeing Association River Safety Report* (see Chapter 5 resources in the Bibliography at the end of this book).

Work with mentors. If you're a teacher, you can ask other faculty members to observe you in your classroom and provide critical feedback. Ask your mentors how they make their decisions. Outdoor leaders can co-lead trips with more-experienced leaders in order to learn by watching them use good judgment. Ask them about their rationale for making certain decisions. Ask them to critique your decisions.

Trust your instincts. This is a tricky bit of advice, because sometimes our instincts lead us astray—and if you find yourself involved in one epic experience after another, perhaps your instincts are betraying you. But many good leaders say that when they are about to make a particular decision, a tiny flutter of dread or a nagging feeling is just enough to indicate to them that they are about to make a bad judgment call. Pay attention to these warning flags, and if things just don't feel right, change your plan. At the very least, pause long enough to reexamine your decision or plan. It's possible that you have forgotten a critical aspect or have neglected to think through the outcome.

Relying on Policies Versus Judgment

One of the most important decisions you—or the organization you work for—will need to make regarding your approach to managing risk is whether that approach is going to be primarily policy-driven or judgment-driven. Being policy-driven means that you rely on precise instructions in order to guide your actions and decisions. Being judgment-driven means that you rely on your ability to apply knowledge, past experience, and logical reasoning to select a course of action. Both approaches have benefits and drawbacks. Relying on judgment gives you more freedom, but it also gives you more responsibility and accountability. Relying on policies gives you more organizational support, and the benefit of combined institutional wisdom, but it also limits your creativity and choices.

Here's an example: Outward Bound has debated for years about what to do to prevent foot injuries in the field. Because foot injuries—often even minor cuts and blisters—usually result in participants departing the program early (because being able to walk and stand is critical to participation), Outward Bound has prioritized keeping foot injuries to a minimum.

Outward Bound used to have a policy dictating that "shoes will be worn at all times except when in tents." When strictly adhered to, this policy prevented virtually all foot injuries. But it quickly became exceptionally difficult to enforce because it seemed so rigidly ridiculous. For example, it's wonderful to remove your feet from your boots and stick them out in front of the fire on a cold winter night. Sitting in a canoe in the middle of a calm lake never seemed like a situation in which shoes were necessary. And participants who wanted to jump out of their canoes and into the lake for a dip—where their feet were never making contact with solid ground—had to put on their shoes first.

Eventually we changed the shoe policy to "footwear will be worn when the potential for foot injury exists." This gave Outward Bound instructors the freedom and responsibility to make judgments about when participants should wear shoes, rather than having to either break policy or require that the participants wear shoes in unnecessary situations.

Any legitimate organization needs to have some policies, of course. Policies give the staff some guidelines for consistency, and policies set standards for operations. And it's important that staff follow policies if there are any. An organization with policies that are not consistently practiced loses credibility, as well as placing itself in a position of liability.

For example, if Outward Bound staff consistently failed to enforce the original shoe policy described above, it would become easier for them to fail to enforce other policies, perhaps more important ones. Once a climate of ignoring policies is established, it becomes pervasive and arbitrary. Or if an instructor failed to enforce the original shoe policy and a participant cut himself severely while wandering around barefoot, the participant as well as Outward Bound could be held liable for the injury.

MAKING DECISIONS

Leadership is a constant process of making decisions. You can spend all the time in the world preparing for things in advance, but when the unexpected knocks on your door, you will spend still more time making decisions. You get good at making snap decisions, and you get better at mulling things over for a while. You learn when it's important to act quickly and when you should sleep on something. Most of all, you grow confident with your own ability to come up with solutions and put them into action, even when faced with situations you had never dreamed of.

> *When I was directing a program for Outward Bound, an unexpected situation arose at an inopportune time. Forty kids from a school district about twelve hours away had just finished a three-week canoeing course, and they were eager to go home. The bus that was supposed to retrieve them never showed up. A series of phone calls revealed that the bus company had confused the departure date and was planning to pick up the students the following day. Suddenly we had on our hands forty kids who were tired of camping and ready for TV and junk food, as well as eight instructors who were looking forward to a break from the kids.*
>
> *After spending a few moments in denial, certain that something would happen to salvage the situation, I gathered together my course directors, as well as some of the instructors, and we brainstormed possible solutions. We investigated several options—including putting the students in hotels for the night—but finally we determined that the only reasonable solution was to keep the students at the basecamp for another night and persuade a few of the instructors to keep working for another day. It all worked out fine, due to the valiant efforts of the staff and the amazing resilience of the students, but it was an experience that I would not want to repeat.*
>
> —*Ashley Lodato, Outward Bound staff since 1986*

Preliminary Factors to Consider in Decision Making

Make easy decisions quickly and save your decision-making energy for those times when a situation is so complex that it warrants careful consideration. When you are faced with a complicated scenario, consider the following factors before you begin brainstorming possible solutions; this assessment will help you get a clearer picture and a more objective grasp of the situation.

Reality of the situation: You will make the best decision in any given situation if you have a strong grasp of what's really going on. It takes extra time to come up with the most accurate assessment possible, but the time spent figuring things out will pay off when you come up with the best solution for the particular situation.

In the early days of wilderness instruction at Outward Bound, trip leaders used to say that if something unexpected came up and nobody was on the verge of losing life or limb, then it was time to sit down and smoke a cigarette. Nowadays we just advise leaders to remove themselves from the group and the situation for a moment, which has the same effect as the cigarette (without any of the health risks): it pushes the leader to take the time to think rationally instead of reacting.

Step back and assess the situation. Is the canoe really lost forever, or is it simply broached on a rock around the bend? Is everyone on your production team jumping ship, or have a few key resignations just made it seem that way? Try to gather as much information as you can that will help you get the clearest picture possible of the situation.

Participants' limits: As participant skills and abilities improve, the risk-to-reward ratio becomes more balanced. This is why a rock climb that might be considered inappropriate for participants on the first day of a climbing trip might be perfect for the fifth day. The rock itself doesn't change, but your participants' ability to climb it successfully does, not only because their physical climbing skills improve but also because their ability to push the limits of what is psychologically comfortable for them increases. So the decision to tackle the rock climb on the first day would be considered too risky because the participants might get so scared and so disheartened by their inability to make much upward progress that they are unwilling to rock climb for the rest of the trip. The decision to climb the rock on the fifth day would be considered a reasonable risk.

Leader's limits: Similarly, your skills and experience as a leader affect the risk-to-reward ratio. Let's say you're a new manager who wants to implement some radical change around the office. Instead of having people specialize and work independently on most projects, you'd like more endeavors to be undertaken by small teams. You have the sense that this would result in increased productivity as well as the staff's increased satisfaction in their working environment. But you think that the change would initially be received with skepticism or hostility and you're not quite sure how to go about initiating it. You don't yet have the skills or experience to guide the transition smoothly, so you decide that the risks of moving ahead (alienating your staff, losing the chance to establish credibility, possibly failing at the entire transition because you don't really know how to implement it) are greater than the reward of increased productivity and satisfaction. You decide to wait a year to try out your great idea.

Leader's emotional investment: Sometimes leaders get so caught up in their own emotions or personal desires surrounding a particular situation that it impedes their ability to make the best decision. Emotions not only cloud the reality of the situation but also provide an almost irresistible lure to choose a particular course of action. In order to be a caring, compassionate leader, you need to be vulnerable to emotion, but you also need to be able to control your emotions and personal desires when the situation demands it, such as when making decisions.

For example, let's say a particular participant on a trip you are leading is essentially ruining the trip for everyone else. You've worked hard with this participant over the past week and you've developed a rapport with him, but his behavior remains inappropriate for the expedition. You

believe that if he could just pull his act together, he could complete the expedition and really benefit from the experience. This participant probably needs to be removed from the expedition, but you've invested so much time in him that you don't want to think about that possibility. The reality is, however, you need to control your emotions about this participant and rationally evaluate how his behavior is affecting the overall quality of the expedition, then make a decision.

Involving Participants in the Decision-Making Process

Unless you plan to be a completely autocratic leader, making all decisions by yourself, you will need to employ all your communication skills when it comes to making decisions.

Even if you plan on making all decisions independently, you still will need the ability to communicate these decisions in an articulate way to your group. It's likely that there will be times when you will need to make many decisions spontaneously and/or independently—for example, when a lightning storm is approaching quickly, when two employees are about to come to blows, or when a major logistical complication threatens to ruin an entire conference.

But more frequently you will have enough time and the educational justification to involve the group to some degree in the problem-solving and decision-making process. You need to be able not only to make good decisions and act upon them quickly, if necessary, but also to guide your group through its own process of making decisions.

Choosing a Decision-Making Style

How exactly do you go about deciding what to do? Sometimes the best decision will simply come to you through instinct and experience. But often you will have the time and opportunity to deliberately think through which response, intervention, or course of action will most effectively address the particular situation. In such times, you can use one of the four methods used to establish a leadership style (see "Adapting Your Leadership Style" in Chapter 2, Becoming a Leader). Like leadership styles, decision-making styles can be directive, democratic, consensual, or laissez-faire. Consider the following scenario:

I once worked as an outdoor professional on a three-week canoeing trip for a midwestern college's outdoor recreation semester class. There were twelve students, two professors, and two outdoor leaders. The concept of consensus was very important to this college's philosophy, and almost all decisions on the expedition were made by consensus.

One decision in particular sticks in my memory. Late one afternoon we stopped at the top of a rapid; there was a campsite above the rapid as well as a campsite below. We gathered in a circle to decide whether or not to run the rapid before stopping for the night. The group quickly split into three factions: (1) those who wanted to run the rapid and camp at the bottom; (2) those who wanted to stop immediately, make camp, and run the rapid the next morning; and (3) those who wanted to leave the boats at the top of the rapid and carry our things down to the lower, better campsite, then return to the empty boats first thing in the morning to run through the rapid.

The two groups that did not want to run the rapid that afternoon did not think that we had enough time to scout and run eight boats through safely. We stood in a circle for more than two hours as the students and faculty worked through their consensus process, finally deciding to run the rapid and camp at the bottom. It took precisely twenty minutes to run the rapid successfully with loaded boats—approximately one-sixth the time it took us to make the decision.

—Larry, Outward Bound instructor since 1985

Factors to Consider in Choosing a Decision-Making Style

One strategy when deciding how much participant involvement to elicit in a particular decision is to consider three factors: timing, importance of the process, and importance of the outcome.

Timing refers to how quickly a decision must be made. Situations that require an immediate decision by a leader and might not allow time for participant involvement usually involve safety or company integrity: a canoe is about to plunge over a waterfall; participants are about to light a stove with a noticeable gas leak; the company president has just been arrested; the building has just received a bomb threat.

Importance of the process refers to the level of benefit to be gained by gathering participant input and by the decision-making practice itself. For example, a manager dissatisfied with the current grant-writing process might ask employees to brainstorm a new system. Eliciting group input in making these types of decisions is shrewd because it gives employees ownership over what can be otherwise seen as drudgery, and it also gives them valuable group decision-making practice.

Importance of the outcome refers to whether all end results are equally acceptable or whether some are intolerable. For example, the members of a customer service team might have a democratic 9-to-1 vote that results in one poor soul having to consistently deal with the most unpleasant customers; this outcome would be unacceptable and thus should not be put to a vote.

A Four-Tier Model

A host of decision-making models exist, and many of them are addressed in Priest and Gass's *Effective Leadership in Adventure Programming*. Outward Bound frequently refers to a four-tier strategy, ranging from complete decision-making autonomy resting with the leader, to the leader abdicating complete decision-making power to the group. Below are these four decision-making methods, paraphrased from the *Outward Bound Instructor Manual*.

THE DECIDE METHOD

One of the simplest methods used by Outward Bound instructors to coach their students through the problem-solving and decision-making process is the DECIDE method:

D: Define the problem.
- Is there a mutually agreed-upon problem?
- What is the desired outcome after solving the problem?
- How long do you have to come up with a solution?
- What is going to be the hardest obstacle to surmount—the "crux" of the problem?

E: Educate yourself.
- Gather facts.
- Identify alternatives through brainstorming (list all possible solutions without judgment).

C: Consider your options.
- List the advantages, disadvantages, and consequences of each option.
- What is the worst thing that could happen with each option? If that worst thing happens, could you live with it?
- Consider each option within the context of your own values, goals, abilities, and needs.

I: Identify your choice.

D: Design a plan to carry out the decision.
- List steps that need to be taken.
- Identify ways of handling obstacles.
- Determine which people are going to take responsibility for which tasks.

E: Evaluate the decision.
- What happened?
- Are you satisfied with the outcome? Was it what you expected?
- What would you change if you were to make that decision again?

—adapted from Outward Bound Instructor Manual

These methods can also be used within the group by a participant leader. In these situations, the official leader hands off specific leadership functions to a participant leader or a series of participant leaders. All of these decisions, then, need to be ones that have a range of acceptable outcomes and no immediate urgency for completion.

Directive: The leader decides alone. The leader weighs the information available, the potential outcomes, and the situation, then makes a decision and announces it to the group. This approach is wise when the decision must be made quickly and when the outcome is critical.

Democratic: The leader consults with select others (generally the designated participant leaders of the day) and together they decide. The leader empowers these others, and they all decide together and announce their decision to the rest of the group. This approach works well when the process and the outcome of the decision are of equal importance.

Consensual: The leader involves the whole group in the decision. The leader provides information regarding the decision to the whole group and helps the group reach a compromise. With this approach, the leader must be willing to live with whatever decision the group makes. This approach is very time-consuming, and it works best when the process of making the decision is more important than the outcome.

Laissez-faire: The leader turns over decision making to the group. The leader provides all relevant information to the group and tells them to make a decision. The leader then removes him- or herself from the decision-making process. With this method, the leader must be comfortable with not only whatever decision the group makes but also whatever process the participants use to reach the decision. This approach is used most effectively when the group has the maturity and skill to reach reasonable and mutually agreeable decisions.

Avoiding Decision-Making Pitfalls

A common mistake in any sort of group is to employ a democratic or consensual style as the preferred decision-making strategy. "We value the group process," the thinking goes, "and we want participants or followers to be involved and invested, so we should all play a part in almost all decisions." Such thinking results in lengthy group discussions about what color the cover of the annual report should be, whether to eat spaghetti or rice and beans tonight on the expedition, and whether to allow employees to bring their dogs to the company picnic. Democracy (the majority rules) and consensus (everyone compromises) are useful methods in many situations, but most decisions are more efficient if made in a more autocratic manner; the value of having such decisions made effectively usually outweighs any benefit gained by soliciting everyone's input on every decision.

A FINAL NOTE

The Canadian hockey great Wayne Gretsky famously commented that "you miss 100 percent of the shots you don't take." Sometimes taking a risk is less about assessing the objective hazards of the risk and more about simply being willing to fail. You might convince yourself that a particular course of action is fraught with dangers when in fact you're simply afraid that your action is going to lead to your failure.

If you find that you're rationalizing a lot with yourself and coming up with many, many reasons why you shouldn't take a particular risk, ask yourself whether you're simply trying to avoid missing a shot. And if this is the only real risk, you might instead put your energy into gathering up your courage to take the shot. You might miss the shot, true, but you also might make it. And the more shots you take, the more you're going to make.

CHAPTER 6

FINDING COURAGE, OVERCOMING FEAR

Leaders are ordinary people, and they fear the same things that ordinary people fear: public speaking, appearing foolish, loss of control of a situation, not being liked, exceedingly bad luck, standing up for what they believe is right even when it is the minority opinion, and heights, to name just a few. But because leadership demands frequent exposure to some of the very things that many people fear most, leaders are constantly confronted with daunting situations.

> *When I taught my first Outward Bound course, I was so nervous that when I met my students for the first time, I introduced myself by the wrong name. My co-leader gave me a funny look but didn't say anything. I had to decide whether to admit my mistake immediately, thereby making my anxiety even more apparent, or just continue on, hoping that no one would remember and that I could slip my real name in at some point.*
> —Renee, former Outward Bound instructor

To be an effective leader, you must find courage and overcome your fears. This is not to suggest that you will be able to eliminate your fears or that you will discover a whole new courageous persona inside you. Rather, you must learn to recognize the acts or situations that cause you the most anxiety, then choose to face—rather than avoid—your fears and identify ways of coping effectively with them; *this* is finding courage. In Leonard Zunin's words in *Tempered Radicals,* "Courage is all too often mistakenly seen as the absence of fear. Courage is seeing your fear in a realistic perspective, defining it, considering alternatives, and choosing to function in spite of risks."

After finding your leadership courage and facing your fears, you may still be afraid of the same things, but you will have learned to cope with those fears and move beyond them into action, rather than letting them limit you.

IDENTIFYING YOUR FEARS

In order to start learning to deal with your leadership fears, you must have a clear idea of what it is that you're afraid of. You can't solve a problem if you don't know what it is, right?

When you think about leading, what do you worry about? What makes you anxious about taking responsibility for a group of participants or followers? Although there are many reasons why leaders get nervous, most of us can identify our leadership fears among the following list:

- having some major disaster occur under our leadership
- not being liked or not being respected
- losing control
- being seen as incompetent
- failing

Sometimes we identify a particular fear, but upon deeper examination we discover that the real fear is actually something else, something more profound. For example, many people are indeed afraid of heights, which makes rock climbing a terrifying experience for them. But often enough, it's not the fear of heights that prevents people from rock climbing; it's the fear of not being able to reach the top and thus not succeeding. Similarly, in leadership situations, many leaders say that they are afraid of asking for help, when what they really fear is appearing weak as a *consequence* of asking for help. Others might say that they are afraid to stand up for an unpopular idea that they believe is right, when what they really fear is being ostracized as a result of expressing an unpopular view.

This is not to suggest that you must go through psychoanalysis to identify the root cause of your fears. But the better understanding you have of *what* frightens you, the better prepared you will be to begin to overcome those fears and function in the face of them.

FACING YOUR FEARS

Facing your fears means making a commitment to learning to work with them rather than avoiding them. It's actually a very simple concept, but it's incredibly difficult to implement.

> *Ask yourself for one moment what your feelings have been on the eve of some act involving courage, whether it has been physical courage, as it is commonly called, or moral or intellectual . . . What has happened to you? If [this act] has really called forth courage, has it not felt something like this? "I cannot do this. This is too much for me. I shall ruin myself if I take this risk. I cannot take the leap, it's impossible. All of me will be gone if I do this, and I cling to myself."*
>
> *And then supposing the Spirit has conquered and you have done this impossible thing; do you find afterward that you possess yourself in a sense that you never had before? That there is more of you?*
>
> *So it is throughout life . . . you know "nothing ventured nothing won" is true in every hour; it is the fibre of every experience that signs itself into the memory.*
> —*J. N. Figgis*, Outward Bound
>   Readings Book

When we're afraid of something, we turn into expert procrastinators, avoiders, and excuse-makers. Yet we all know how wonderful we feel when we tackle an obstacle rather than steering clear of it. Usually the sense of relief is so overwhelming that we wonder why we delayed so long in dealing with it.

After I had served as a deck officer during the Korean War in the Navy's Amphibious Forces, which conducts sea-to-land invasions, I was twenty-two and seeking a challenge. So I volunteered for the Navy Underwater Demolition Team (UDT)— now known as SEALs (sea, air, land)—and awaited assignment to the sixteen-week training course.

The UDT training program, whose West Coast base is in Coronado, California, had added parachute-jump training, becoming the most rigorous training regimen in the world. More than a third of the course's participants wash out. I was deeply afraid that I wouldn't measure up to complete the course.

I asked a senior UDT officer what caused most trainees to fail. He told me that they couldn't tolerate the cold water off the California coastline when called upon for long ocean swims or night operations in the surf.

The fear of washing out and failing was far more terrifying to me than cold water, so I began to take steps to get more comfortable in cold water. I started swimming daily in the ocean, and several times a week I filled my bathtub with ice cubes and ice water. I soaked and shivered.

Soon I began to develop tolerance for cold and to feel confident that I could handle the ocean water; and sixteen weeks after I began the training program, I graduated.

Facing your fears requires summoning up courage and taking a leap—a leap of faith believing that you possess the inner strength and the skill to endure the experience. But it doesn't need to be a blind leap, because you can use some of the following strategies to help you.

COPING WITH YOUR FEARS

If you've identified your fears and you've chosen to face them, it's time to learn some strategies for overcoming them. Remember, we probably are not going to *eliminate* most of our fears. But we can learn how to make them manageable, how to function in their presence, and how to prevent them from limiting us. We do this by considering the following five strategies used by Outward Bound for coping with fears:

1. Expand your comfort zone.
2. Isolate the source of the fear into manageable steps.
3. Reframe the experience.
4. Visualize success.
5. Get support.

Let's take a detailed look at each of these strategies.

Expand Your Comfort Zone

Probably the most effective way you can begin to deal with your fears is to increase the number of things that you're *not* afraid of. This doesn't mean taking up a lot of nonthreatening hobbies but, rather, expanding the boundaries of that "safe harbor" that was mentioned in Chapter 1, Why Learn Leadership from Outward Bound?

Outward Bound refers to people's "circles of comfort," shown in Figure 3. In this three-ring bull's-eye, the inner ring represents the "*comfort*

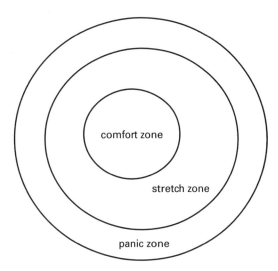

Figure 3. The Circles of Comfort

zone"—the space where people face few fears, where acquaintances and routines are familiar, and where challenges encountered are known and easily met. For most of us, the comfort zone is our everyday lives: our homes, our friends and families, our jobs, our social networks, and our hobbies: our daily routines. We might occasionally do things that make us a little nervous ("today I'm going to run 6 miles rather than 4" or "tonight I'm going to leave my daughter with a new babysitter"), but still, we're pretty sure that we're going to be able to succeed in these undertakings without too much extra effort.

The middle ring of the bull's-eye represents the "*stretch zone*"—the space where people step (or are pushed) out of their comfort zone and into situations that make them anxious. The stretch zone is a place that many people visit occasionally and a few people enter frequently. The stretch zone includes any activities or situations that call forth the classic signs of anxiety: elevated blood pressure and pulse, nervous sweat, trembling hands, thoughts tumbling in the brain. Stretch-zone situations vary from person to person, because people have different levels of comfort with different things. But often stretch-zone activities include things such as delivering a big presentation at work, seeking out new friends, asking for a raise, confronting a difficult relationship, admitting an addiction—anything that requires people to reach inside themselves and muster up courage in order to cope.

The outer ring of the bull's-eye is the "*panic zone*"—where the fears called forth by activities or situations cause people to fall apart or shut down completely. Most people are simply unable to function in the panic zone; they're no longer looking inside themselves for hidden strength because they've jumped straight into survival mode. The panic zone is vastly different for different people. For some, being stuck in an elevator would constitute a panic-zone situation, whereas others are able to parachute off the tops of skyscrapers without too much anxiety. Some people can comfortably lead troops into battle, whereas others panic at the thought of testifying in court. Not much learning or growth occurs in the panic zone because people in it are simply fighting for control.

> *There is no stress in the world.*
> *Repeat: There is no stress in the world.*
> *Surprised? Think about it. Where would*
> *you go looking if you wanted to find some*
> *stress? The Gobi Desert? South Wales?*
> *Chengtu, China? Stress is something that*
> *happens inside you. It's a product of how*
> *you perceive, define, and react to the world.*
> —*Earl Hipp,* Fighting Invisible Tigers

People learn and grow the most when they spend time in the stretch zone, with frequent retreats back to the comfort zone to refortify themselves with calm nerves and doses of courage. When people edge into their stretch zone frequently enough, they will soon discover that the boundaries of their comfort zone shift and expand, often to include activities that they previously found to be in their stretch zone. Suddenly things that used to be challenging or anxiety-producing become part of the everyday routine, and the comfort zone is larger, more encompassing, more spacious.

Similarly, at times when people drop out of the stretch zone and into the panic zone, they gain experience with getting control of the emotions and physiological changes that occur in the panic zone. As people learn to better cope with extreme anxiety, they panic less, the fear subsides, and the boundaries of the stretch zone expand to include some formerly panic-inducing situations or activities.

> *As president of Outward Bound, I traveled a great deal in the field to our different schools and led what we call Invitational Expeditions for national leaders. These were both men and women whom we wanted to enlist as supporters of Outward Bound, so we took them on these mini Outward Bound courses.*

> *Usually, when these expeditions were held at a school base camp, there was a ropes course as part of the experience for our invitees. The ropes course is essentially an adult-size jungle gym high in the air, where participants are protected with climbing gear as they swing on ropes, balance on cables, etc. Now I have always had trouble with a particular aspect of our ropes courses around the country: the balance beam. A balance beam is a log about 50 feet long suspended perhaps 30 or 40 feet in the air on wires that allow it to swing, so it is not stable. Of course, you wear a harness that you clip into a safety wire above you, so if you lose your footing you are not going to fall all the way off and be injured. But this activity always scared me to death. As I led a group of invitees through a ropes course, I thought it was proper for an employee of Outward Bound to wait until they all had had their chance, so I was the last one to go through the course. So by the time it was my turn to go on the balance beam, my anxiety level was extremely high. I just knew that I had to set as good an example as I could, but by the time I got onto the balance beam after waiting for everyone else to do it, I had what we called "sewing machine legs." My legs were shaking—and, of course, that is the worst thing to experience on the balance beam because then the log begins to shake too. So my anxiety was a very real factor, but I had to push through it.*

> *I knew I was not going to get hurt. Though some Outward Bound activities appear life-threatening, safety systems are in place to address objective hazards and prevent injury, even though you think you may fall off the cliff or fall off the balance beam or whatever. So I learned that I could take a deep breath and just go forward and not think about falling off, and I never actually did fall off the balance beam.*

This was a case in which my anxiety was ill founded but still very real. In your leadership role, you may feel anxious about making a public speech to a group of people or carrying out some activity that you are not entirely confident that you can do well. But still, you need to just take a deep breath and press on and do the best you can. Your group is going to be supportive of you because they may sense your anxiety and will respect you for the fact that you are just like them—anxious about something and yet pushing through it. So just pull up your socks and go for it.

It's important to know that simply moving in and out of the stretch and panic zones is not enough to overcome the fears that lie within you. Otherwise, people with severe agoraphobia (fear of crowds) would simply have to go out in crowded places time after time and their fear would evaporate. Certainly, frequent exposure helps, but it doesn't usually solve the problem. The time spent in the stretch and panic zones must be deliberate and focused for it to be productive, with attention paid to the source of the fear, the response it induces, and potential strategies for coping with the fear.

We all have different comfort, stretch, and panic zones. These are the principal differences that account for the different boundaries of our comfort zones:

1. **Perception of difficulty:** how manageable we perceive particular situations or activities to be
2. **Skill or knowledge base:** how equipped we are with the knowledge and/or skill to deal with these situations
3. **Self-confidence:** how confident we are in our own abilities to cope
4. **Familiarity:** how familiar we are with the situations or activities

Let's look a little more closely at each of these.

1. Perception of difficulty: Some people assess situations and see possibilities and opportunities for success, whereas others see the pitfalls and chances of failure. It's similar to the "glass half full, glass half empty" outlook on life, wherein two people can consider the same situation and come up with radically different assessments of its difficulty and likely outcome. Some reasons for this include how skilled they are, how self-confident they are, and how familiar they are with the situation, of course, but much of it is simply due to

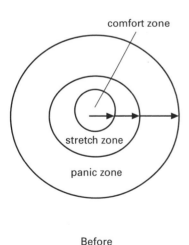

Before

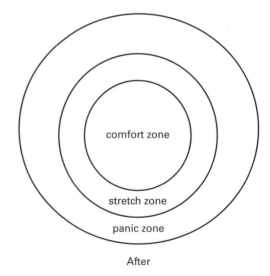

After

Figure 4. Expanding the Circles of Comfort

the way in which people tend to view challenges. Leaders who learn to view challenging situations as opportunities for success rather than occasions for possible failure are taking the first step toward widening their circles of comfort and diminishing their fears.

> *In some areas where Outward Bound runs canoeing courses, there's a lot of wind. Sometimes the wind blows so hard that it's impossible to paddle, so expeditions get wind-bound and have to stay at a campsite for a day or even two. As a new instructor, I was really nervous about getting wind-bound because I envisioned all the hassles it would cause us: we'd get behind schedule, the students would go stir-crazy, and we wouldn't have enough to do to fill up all the down time in camp.*
>
> *But then another instructor helped me take a different perspective. Being wind-bound is an opportunity to refine skills. Students get quality time learning to bake dinner in a Dutch oven over coals and to set up tents so that they withstand the wind.*
>
> *Wind-bound days also make it necessary to paddle at night, when conditions calm down, in order to stay on schedule. Night paddles can be unique and beautiful experiences, and they require the students to pay close attention to navigation.*
>
> *So my fears about being wind-bound diminished as I began to view these situations as an opportunity for skill development rather than an inevitable loss of mileage and increase in restlessness.*
> — *Dave, Outward Bound instructor*
>   *since 1993*

Kurt Hahn's leitmotif "your disability is your opportunity" serves Outward Bound students and staff well. In situations that might cause many people to give up before even starting, people who choose to view changing conditions as opportunities for learning and growth are overcoming mental barriers and setting themselves up to succeed.

2. Skill or knowledge base: If you do not have the knowledge or specific skill to deal effectively with a particular challenge, that challenge is going to seem far more daunting than if you have the skills to cope with it. Many new teachers are afraid of their classes getting unruly and out of control because they haven't yet developed the disciplinary skills to manage a large group. Many new outdoor leaders are nervous about taking their groups on cross-country travel (away from established trails) because they do not have the refined map and compass skills that they need to manage such difficult navigation. Once leaders have the skills needed to deal effectively with specific problems or challenges, some of their fear of these problems evaporates.

> *When I first started teaching white-water canoeing courses for Outward Bound, I was terrified that some of my students would capsize and wrap their boat around a rock (a not uncommon situation in which a submerged plastic canoe bends around a rock midstream due to the force of the current). I hadn't yet mastered the skills needed to deal with wrapped canoes.*
>
> *But after a few more staff trainings, I learned to unwrap boats skillfully and quickly.*
> — *Rebecca, former Outward Bound*
>   *instructor*

Outward Bound puts a lot of emphasis on skill mastery, for both its instructors and its students, because mastering skills is a critical element to developing the leadership confidence necessary to combat fears.

3. Self-confidence: Self-confident people are the best equipped to find courage and overcome fears. They don't necessarily have any fewer fears, but they are imbued with the assurance and certainty that they will be successful at quelling those fears. It's a chicken-or-egg dilemma, however: is confidence a result of overcoming fears, or are fears overcome by confident people? Regardless, the two are inextricably linked. Self-confident leaders have probably overcome many fears in their life and will continue to do so successfully because their self-assurance about their own abilities and strength of character will enable them to do so.

> *In 1941, World War II raged in Europe and the clouds of war gathered over the United States. My father was the founder and CEO of Unipress, a small manufacturing company that made steam-generated pressing machines for commercial laundries and dry cleaners. Steel to make the machines was in short supply, so a major contract with the U.S. Navy was critical to Unipress's survival.*
>
> *My father traveled to Washington, D.C., to meet the Navy procurement officer, who said, "Your equipment is very good, but we need pedal-operated presses for our ships, not steam-activated ones." This request could have potentially killed any hope of a contract, but my father was confident that he could make design changes and build the presses the Navy wanted. He said, "Well, you must want our model PA180, which is pedal operated. I'll bring the drawings and specs by for you tomorrow morning."*
>
> *So he stayed up all night erasing steam lines and drawing in pedal mechanisms. He redrew the specifications, and the next day he got the contract that carried Unipress all through the war. His quick thinking and confidence in his ability to adjust fast carried the day.*

Confidence is one of the most important leadership characteristics, no matter what the leadership situation. One reason that Outward Bound is so successful at training leaders and at teaching leadership skills is that its programs are designed to help people discover their strengths and act on them, to develop character, and, ultimately, to build confidence.

4. Familiarity: A lot of fear is simply fear of the unknown. Once situations or challenges become more familiar to us, they lose some of their mystique and frightening characteristics. Think about learning to drive. Now, driving is an activity that is actually fraught with danger, and when you're a new driver, you're aware of these hazards. You white-knuckle it on the steering wheel, creep cautiously into traffic, meticulously look both ways several times before pulling out, and allow other drivers the right-of-way at every opportunity because it gives you a chance to breathe. But after you've been driving for a while, you grow comfortable—albeit sometimes too comfortable—with the inherent risks. Because you're so familiar with it, you lose your fear of driving even though the dangers persist. The same is true for many of the fears you face as a leader: as you grow accustomed to them, you become immune to what you perceive to be their more frightening characteristics.

> *As a program director for Outward Bound, I spent a little time doing environmental advocacy at our state Legislature. The first few times I testified in front of committees, I was a shaking bundle of nerves. Even just reading a written statement, I was stricken with anxiety. The formality of the hearing process, the grandeur of the legislative halls, the row of suits in front of me, my voice booming through the microphone—the whole situation was incredibly daunting.*
>
> *But after I did it a few times, the scene became familiar and more comfortable to me. I learned the routine, I found my place in it, and I ceased to be so anxious. I never relaxed completely, but I grew comfortable enough that I didn't dread testifying for days beforehand, as I initially did.*
>
> *—Ashley Lodato, Outward Bound staff since 1986*

Familiarity *does* help diminish fears. But you want to be careful that you don't let familiarity overshadow any real dangers that might be an inherent part of a particular situation, especially when you're in a leadership position. Familiarity should help you deal with challenges that you *perceive* to be difficult; it shouldn't make you grow complacent about situations that pose inherent dangers. The previous example of driving is a good example of this: overconfident drivers can become inattentive to the road and traffic conditions, causing accidents. Here's a wilderness example: lightning storms in the wilderness are inherently dangerous. You may be exposed to lightning enough that you grow comfortable about your ability to avoid it and keep your group safe from it, but your familiarity should not allow you to believe that you are immune to its dangers or that it is simply no longer a threat.

Isolate the Source of Your Fear into Manageable Steps

Often, viewing a challenge in its entirety is intimidating, whereas viewing it as a series of tangible, manageable steps makes it less daunting. An Outward Bound instructor describes how she took a perpetually daunting experience and separated it into increments:

When I first started teaching Outward Bound courses, I got worried sick about the first two days. The first forty-eight hours is the time when the tone for the entire course is set—when you have to prove yourself as a confident and competent instructor or risk losing the trust and respect of your group. It's also the time when you establish group norms and standards for behavior. So you have to be friendly and approachable but also firm and in control; you have to indicate that the trip ahead is going to be exciting and fun but that it is also going to require a lot of hard work and first-rate expedition behavior. I used to get really stressed out about how I could ever

manage to establish such an atmosphere.

Fortunately, Outward Bound's standard practice is for instructors to design a forty-eight- or seventy-two-hour plan before each expedition begins. The plan details which skills will be taught, which discussions led, and which activities facilitated—by which instructor and when. You make the plan before the students arrive, so you can think deliberately about teaching progressions and how to hold discussions and model behavior that will set the right tone.

So during those first few days, you have that forty-eight-hour plan right in your pocket for easy reference. It doesn't eliminate the stress, because you're still thinking, "Are they going to like me? Am I teaching this effectively?" But since you always have to focus your attention on what you're teaching or saying next, you have less time for self-doubt.

—Terri, Outward Bound instructor since 1987

Or think about giving some sort of public speech. Maybe it is your bid for an elected office. Maybe you have to deliver an inspirational talk to your new employees at work. Many of us get a bit overwhelmed when we even think about approaching a podium and launching into a speech in front of a crowd; we might even feel sick.

As CEO of Outward Bound, I was often called upon to deliver speeches. These included college commencement addresses and talks to business schools and various conventions. I found it invaluable to write out my speech, then deliver it out loud in private places. I'd time the speech to fill in my allotted time slot. I'd deliver it out loud three times, until I knew each segment almost by heart and I wasn't tied to the written page.

When speech time came, I felt comfortable with what I wanted to say. The audience

*would feel my comfort level and relax, too,
which helped make the speech more effective.*

By sitting down and brainstorming the topic of your speech, spending a few days writing your speech, and practicing its delivery, you break the daunting task down into manageable steps. You might even envision yourself walking down the aisle and up to the podium. By the time your speech rolls around, you might still be nervous about so many people listening to you, but you will be confident about your speech and your ability to deliver it well.

Reframe the Experience

One of the strategies that Outward Bound frequently uses to help participants gain control over their fears is reframing experiences—casting experiences in a different light—which gives participants the opportunity to focus on a new set of challenges rather than dwelling on the ones that are causing them so much anxiety.

Because sometimes, despite one's best efforts, a goal is not reached.

I spent three years as president of the National Peace Garden Foundation doing my utmost to raise the funds necessary to build this inspirational and educational addition to the national mall area in Washington, D.C. Two former presidents, Jimmy Carter and George Bush senior, joined our board of directors. Former Secretary of State Colin Powell and author and Nazi concentration camp survivor Elie Wiesel were advisors. There was every reason that this project should be a success. But try as we might, we couldn't attract the major gifts necessary to build the Peace Garden. I felt dismayed and discouraged when we had to give the ten-acre proposed site back to the National Park Service.

But the founder of the project, a wonderful woman, Elizabeth Ratcliff, who had dedicated thirteen years of her life to the goal, reframed

the experience for me. She said, "You did everything you possibly could. You couldn't have done more. The timing was against us, with the World War II memorial raising more than $100 million. While wars have constituencies, as we saw with the memorials for Vietnam and Korea, peace is everybody's business, and hence no specific group's responsibility. So don't feel bad. We are all grateful for what you did. It was a shining cause, and you carried the torch. Thank you."

Hearing these words said in a compassionate way reframed my sense of failure to a sense of service to a nobler cause. It made all the difference.

You may find it hard to reframe an experience when failure is involved, because you are too close to the experience. Seek the counsel of a respected outsider to help you reframe what you've been through. It's OK to seek help. It does make a difference.

Visualize Success

Despite the simplicity of this idea, visualizing yourself succeeding—as opposed to dwelling on fears of failing—is a remarkably effective way to convert the negative energy of a fear into positive energy. Here's long-time Outward Bound educator Ashley Lodato remembering her first attempt at rock climbing.

When I rock climbed for the first time, at age fifteen on an Outward Bound course, I was terrified—terrified that the rope would break, terrified of the height and exposure, and probably mostly terrified (although I never would have admitted it at the time) that I wouldn't make it to the top, that I would fail, that I would look foolish in front of my peers.

On my ascent up the rock face, I slipped a couple of times, became frustrated, and eventually began to cry. As I grew more tired and discouraged, I let my fear of the activity overwhelm me. I eventually lowered off the climb, convinced that I would never rock climb again.

But I did. A new boyfriend who was passionate about climbing entered my life, and I found myself climbing more and more often. Fortunately, my boyfriend was not only a good climber but also a patient instructor and coach who encouraged me to work through my fears.

But when I got into difficult climbing situations, I still experienced moments of panic and I occasionally shut down. I knew that if I was going to keep climbing, I needed to get a grip on my fear. So how did I do this?

The solution came to me in a kind of haphazard way. I attended a lecture given by Royal Robbins, one of the pioneer Yosemite rock climbers and mountaineers. During the lecture, Robbins described how he and his climbing peers wanted to push climbing to a new level, but due to the poor quality of the ropes available at the time, they couldn't risk taking big falls or the ropes might break. Robbins described how he came up with a system of visualization for himself: he looked at a problem, pictured it in his head, and visualized himself succeeding. He would literally look at a climb or a series of moves and picture himself moving upward, step by step, until he was past the difficult part.

The next time I went climbing, I tried this. I reached a hard move, then visualized a mental movie of myself pulling and stepping myself through the move. It worked! And I realized that before this, I had always reached hard moves and pictured myself falling off them. Once I began to visualize myself succeeding, I began to climb with more confidence, more grace, and much less fear. Now, more than two decades later, I climb for fun. I still experience moments of intense fear, but I don't panic and I don't let my fear overwhelm me.

— Ashley Lodato, Outward Bound staff since 1986

Visualizing success on a regular basis also translates into increased self-confidence. Once you begin to regularly view and think of yourself as successful, you meet with more triumphs, and you begin to feel more self-assured.

Get Support

Although you may feel alone in the face of your fears, you're probably not the first person to have felt this way, and you certainly won't be the last. Talk to others about your fears, ask for advice, get some help. If your biggest fear is asking for help (thereby risking rejection), it may not be a reasonable step for you yet, but for everyone else, getting some support can be critical in learning to cope in the face of fear.

When I was directing a small environmental education program, a friend of mine approached me for some advice. She was the faculty outdoor program advisor at a local private college, and she wanted to start an accredited outdoor education degree program at the college. But her initial proposal to the faculty board had not been met with resounding success, and she was feeling a bit disheartened and nervous about trying again to promote the program. We talked on and off for weeks about educational outcomes and justifications for the program.

By the time my friend had to face the faculty board again, she had in front of her a proposal for an academically demanding, expedition-based semester course. Infused with renewed energy from our brainstorms and with confidence in the strength of her proposal, my friend convinced the faculty board to support the program, which eventually became a respected and coveted part of the college's academic offerings.

— Sara, Outward Bound instructor since 1996

Sometimes all we need is the proverbial "a little help from our friends"—a reminder that our ideas are good or that we are capable of doing the things we have set out to do. Knowing that someone else supports your ideas or believes that you can succeed can make the difference between triumph and failure.

HELPING YOUR FOLLOWERS FIND THEIR COURAGE AND FACE THEIR FEARS

> *Come to the edge.*
> *We might fall.*
> *Come to the edge.*
> *It's too high!*
> *COME TO THE EDGE!*
> *And they came,*
> *and he pushed,*
> *and they flew.*
> —Christopher Logue

Your role as a leader is to push your followers or participants and help them fly, even if they are afraid. The same strategies that you use to overcome your own fears can be employed to help your participants or followers find their courage and deal with their own fears.

Expand Their Comfort Zone

Nearly everything that is done on an Outward Bound program expands people's comfort zone. For some people, simply sleeping out in the woods in a tent or working intimately with a group of people they don't know is enough to launch them into their stretch zone. But after a few days, the sleeping bag is a familiar and welcome place and the strangers have become friends. For most people, activities such as rock climbing and off-trail navigation make them a bit anxious, and it is only after they have learned the skills applicable to these chal-

lenges and faced them a few times that the activities become more comfortable.

Let's say that you're a volunteer leader of your local Parent Teacher Association (PTA) and you want to cultivate more intimacy within your group of volunteers. Your idea is that if parents shared with one another the struggles they face with their children, it might help identify some key areas for collaboration between the PTA and the school. Yet sharing this information makes the other parents nervous; they haven't done it before, they're uncomfortable sharing private matters, and they signed up for the PTA, not group therapy.

But you forge on, sharing some of your own experiences with your kids and with the school. The other parents are awkward at first, but once they get used to the routine and once they are reassured that other parents are not judging them, they relax a little. Eventually, most parents are comfortable talking openly about challenges they've experienced with their kids. You have just helped to widen their comfort zone.

Isolate Their Fears into Manageable Steps

Your participants or followers usually have less knowledge than you do about a particular activity or challenge they're afraid of, so they may need to have the activity broken down in great detail in order to work through their fear of it. Here's another story from Outward Bound leader Ashley Lodato.

> *My husband and I took my sixty-year-old parents on a canyoneering trip (rappelling down through slot canyons) a few years ago. My mom is afraid of many height- and rope-related activities, and canyoneering*

COPING WITH YOUR FEARS

- Expand your comfort zone.
- Isolate the source of your fear into manageable steps.
- Reframe the experience.
- Visualize success.
- Get support.

probably represented the culmination of her fears. Before she backed over any edge, we had to point out every aspect of the anchor and safety systems, demonstrating the strength of the ropes, describing the redundancy of the anchors, and explaining how the entire system was ludicrously well equipped to handle her featherweight self. When she was finally reassured, she would start out.

Rappel rope clenched in both hands, she inched slowly backward, talking to herself every step of the way. "Rope can hold 2,000 pounds, rappel backed up by belay, slowly feed rope through this hand, brake hand if I need it, feet up, flat on the rock. . . . " As we peered over the edge, we could watch her glacial progress as she inched down the cliff. At the bottom, as soon as she was confident that she was back on flat ground, she would burst into a wide grin and say, "Ha! Cheated death one more time!" She had a brief respite while the rest of us dropped over, and then it was time to start getting scared about the next rappel.

From my mom's perspective, she faced imminent death every time she rappelled over an edge, and nothing we said could really convince her that it was the safety of the ropes and anchor system, not sheer luck, that had prevented her untimely death. But she rappelled dozens of times on that trip, facing over and over the thing that scared her most. She needed a lot of coaching, and she needed to talk herself through each step of the process, but she did it, and with great pride and triumph.

—Ashley Lodato, Outward Bound staff since 1986

Without this painstaking reiteration of the process, this rappeller would have been paralyzed by fear. But the separate, distinct steps of the process gave her something to focus on, and she

completed numerous rappels, albeit one minuscule step at a time.

Reframe the Experience for Them

Remember, the key is to help your participants or followers view the situation they're afraid of in a way that gives them something new to think about, so they don't focus on their fears instead.

I was once, as a staff participant, on an Outward Bound course that stopped one afternoon along a shore so that we could climb around behind a 100-foot cliff and prepare to rappel down it, lowering ourselves down the steep rock face while attached to a rope. Several of the students had already descended the cliff and were gathered below when I noticed that Elizabeth, a fifty-three-year-old participant, was sitting alone near the start of the rappel with an unhappy look on her face. I said to her, "Elizabeth, you have an odd look on your face. Can you tell me what's bothering you?"

She said, "Yes. I have a Ph.D. in youth education. I teach troubled youth in the Westchester School System. My husband, who is CEO of a Fortune 100 company, is a successful man. I think I know who I am. But I have acrophobia [a severe fear of heights] and I don't know why I have to back off this cliff."

I replied, "First of all, Elizabeth, you don't have to do this if you don't want to. I'm not going to force you to back off this cliff because I can see how frightened you must be. Lowering off this cliff is not going to tell you who you are. But," I continued, "if you do decide to break through this very real fear of yours, and you do rappel down the cliff, you will forever have that knowledge in your hip pocket—that you rappelled the cliff even when you were terrified. Maybe you'll never use that knowledge, but maybe someday you'll be in a situation where knowing you did this will give you the courage to deal with an even more dire situation."

Elizabeth thought about this for a little while and said, "You know, I think you're right. I'm going to try." She got her climbing harness on and was given some extra instruction, and then she started to back off the cliff. She fell and banged her knee, and she was in tears, but she went on down the cliff. When she got to the bottom, all her fellow students were in a circle to receive her, and most of them were in tears as well because they realized that this was a true breakthrough for her. She had overcome a very real and terrifying phobia to take this 100-foot rappel, and they were in effect validating this powerful experience for her.

Elizabeth was a pretty savvy student, and she probably realized the implications of my message pretty readily. If she chose to rappel off the cliff, she would be banking away an experience of having overcome a fear—the confidence that she could muster up the courage to do something that terrified her. And taking this a step further, if she chose *not* to back off the cliff, she was allowing her fear to limit her, and this would be a lesson she would carry with her as well.

For a more advanced understanding of reframing experiences and using metaphors, consult Stephen Bacon's book *The Conscious Use of Metaphor in Outward Bound*, listed in the references for Chapter 6 in the Bibliography at the end of this book.

Help Them Visualize Success

Your followers might not have any experience with visualization, so it will probably seem a little corny to them at first. But if they agree to trust you and then make an attempt at visualizing their success at a particular challenge, they will probably be pleasantly surprised at the results.

On Outward Bound sea kayaking courses, students are required to practice a "wet

exit" (tipping upside down in the water and releasing themselves from the kayak) before undertaking any expedition travel. Because they are wearing spray skirts that seal onto the cockpit opening, many students feel trapped and are anxious about feeling stuck in the kayak with their head underwater.

So after I demonstrate a wet exit for my students, I ask them to sit in their boats on dry land, wearing their spray skirts. I tell them to close their eyes, and then I guide them through a visualization of the entire wet exit process, from paddling the kayak out into the water through holding their breath, tipping over, releasing the spray skirt, pushing out of the boat, and bobbing up to the surface. I tell the students to actually pop their spray skirts, and when I get to the part where they are resurfacing above the water, some of them even wipe the "water" from their eyes. After that, we get out into the water and complete the wet exits.

—Josh, Outward Bound instructor since 2000

Visualizing this process gave the kayakers a dry run of an activity that caused some of them anxiety. Once they got the feel for the pressure it takes to release the spray skirt and got a clear picture of themselves swimming free of the boat and reaching the surface of the water, they felt as though they had actually practiced the wet exit. This made doing the real thing seem a lot more accessible.

When you first start talking people through visualizing a successful experience, you will probably be pretty self-conscious and your delivery may be rough. But close your eyes, too, and relax into your descriptions. Try to visualize the situation yourself, and details will come more easily to you. Speak in a low, soothing voice at a moderate pace. Keep practicing at visualizing aloud; you'll get better.

Offer Them Support

Your participants or followers should feel comfortable going to you for support when they are feeling anxious, but you should also be aware enough of their emotional states to approach them if you think they're struggling. Remember, though, that you are not their only source of support. If you've developed a strong sense of group identity, participants should be able to turn to each other for encouragement as well. And frequently, another participant can provide peer support that is more effective than the leader's support.

A few years ago, Outward Bound convinced Life *magazine to send a senior managing editor on a short Outward Bound expedition that involved canoeing down the Rio Grande on the Texas-Mexico border. This was a white-water trip, and soon canoes began to capsize. The editor came to me on Day Two of the trip and said he was too frightened to go on. This was bad news for the publicity we had counted on.*

A staff leader and I spent several hours talking with the editor and finally came up with the following solution. He would ride in the middle of the canoe with the two best canoeists. We would all stay as close as safely possible. We would carry the canoes

around rapids he felt totally uncomfortable about.

Well, he stayed on the course, and there were no more capsizes. He wrote a feature article for Life, *which was wonderfully favorable for Outward Bound. It was a success for everyone.*

The act of eliciting support from the staff and other students in the group and knowing that there were other options enabled this editor to face his fears and get back in the canoe.

A FINAL NOTE

Remember, courage is not something you're going to simply find, no matter how hard you look. And your fears are not simply going to go away, no matter how long you ignore them. Courage is something you summon, calling it up within yourself, when you decide to take a potentially overwhelming situation and tackle it straight on. And though your fears will likely remain with you, they will diminish in importance as you learn to turn them into something that fuels you rather than something that holds you back.

Trust your instincts and capabilities. Something called you to become a leader; you have to believe that you have it within you to be a good one.

CASE STUDY 1
THE PALESTINIAN-ISRAELI UNITY PROJECT

by Jim Garrett

Sometimes in an actual leadership situation, we experience a difficulty that motivates us to change leadership strategies. Consider, for example, the following description of an actual Outward Bound course that occurred a few years ago. When one instructor, Dave Genova, was frustrated with the way Outward Bound courses were delivered, he was motivated to make a change, and the result was a new project that he led with Naomi Ederr, a Jewish Israeli, and Rima Sharebi, a Palestinian Israeli, under the leadership of course director Billy Roberts.

As you read the narrative below, try to put yourself in the shoes of these leaders. Pay particular attention to the decisions made, to the interaction between the participants and their leaders, and to the communication among the leaders. Also think about the discussion questions interspersed throughout the narrative and how you might have responded to these incidents if you had been there yourself. In the appendix at the back of this book, you'll find follow-up questions that revisit these discussion questions, providing more food for thought and encouraging you to think more deeply about this scenario.

An Outward Bound instructor, Dave Genova, felt frustrated by what happened when two Outward Bound crews passed each other on a forest road. The participants of one crew, which was on a school contract course, were all black. The participants of the other crew, a public enrollment group, were all white. After the crews had passed each other, a girl in the white crew said casually, "I'm glad there aren't any n——s in our group." Many other students nodded in agreement.

When he heard this comment, Dave asked himself how that could have happened on an Outward Bound course, when Outward Bound's fourth pillar is service and compassion.

QUESTIONS

1. How ready are you to deal with conflict? Have you had the experience of being a leader of individuals or groups who just could not get along with each other?
2. What experience have you had with discrimination? Have you been a victim of another's biases? Have you been a perpetrator of discrimination yourself?
3. How would you react to the task of spending several weeks in charge of leading an expedition with a mixed group of teenagers, half boys and half girls? What sort of support would you want? What if half the participants were white and half were black, or the group were a mixture of people from traditionally opposed groups?

This incident, and Dave's reaction to it, precipitated a whole new project. Dave resolved to address a leadership vacuum by establishing a more considered approach to diversity and social issues at Outward Bound. He realized that Outward Bound's courses present the opportunity to address diversity issues. The relationships built on Outward Bound's courses can transcend social boundaries and offer a new perspective on what society might be like.

With support from North Carolina Outward Bound School board members, who agreed that that the school could do a better job of walking its talk, the first Unity Project course was designed by Dave Genova and Ian Randall in the 1990s for high school students in the southeastern United States. The Unity Project would attempt to reconcile Outward Bound's power to increase self-concept (self-confidence and self-reliance), with the Outward Bound core value of compassion for others. The course element that would be introduced to achieve this reconciliation was serious discussion about issues such as race, gender, and sexuality, within a group that had been deliberately formed for its social diversity.

Students and instructors would work to build a learning culture in which they engage in meaningful dialog and a culture that represents an ideal community that participants want to take home with them. The interdependence and human relationships that students would experience on such a course would offer the foundation for a more pervasive emotional and spiritual connection to the welfare of others. Social awareness would allow the students to perceive the need for action. Confidence, tenacity, and leadership skills would allow the students to take the action needed. The Unity Project's vision, expressed in *The Unity Project—Community Project Workbook* by Jesse Pitt (see the references for Chapter 6 in the Bibliography at the end of this book), was that its participants would return to their home communities empowered and equipped to initiate compassionate social change.

QUESTIONS

4. What are the values and ethical principles that your organization espouses? Does your organization walk the talk? Or have there been times when you felt that a better job of living up to those standards could be done?

5. What does the word *compassion* signify to you? Are effective leadership and compassion compatible? How can compassion be beneficial, not only when working with youth, but when working with adults, especially in a business context? Might a compassionate leader be a real danger to the bottom line?

Based on the success of eight years of Unity Project courses for American high schoolers, the North Carolina Outward Bound School partnered with Breaking the Ice, an international nonprofit foundation that brings people together from different cultures, viewpoints, or sides of a conflict in the hope of overcoming the barriers of mistrust, misunderstanding, and fear that are the root causes of conflict and violence in our world. Together, they developed the Palestinian-Israeli Unity Project.

The first PIUP course was conducted in 2005 for students from high schools in Haifa, Israel. Ten students, half of them Jewish Israelis and half Palestinian Israelis, were selected by Breaking the Ice after careful screening to ensure both their own full commitment and their parents' endorsement of their participation in the program. The course would include a two-week-long wilderness expedition in the Appalachian Mountains of western North Carolina.

The participants' families were fully informed that the course would be very challenging—physically, mentally, and emotionally—and that the participants would be expected to wrestle with difficult and divisive social issues, discussing them openly and honestly. Upon their return to Haifa after the course, the students would be expected to continue meeting with their crewmates and to participate with them in organizing and completing at least two community service projects in the following year.

The students from Haifa were thoroughly briefed about what their Unity Project course would involve. They were told that their course would start at the Outward Bound base at Table Rock north of the city of Asheville. They would carry all their gear and supplies in backpacks, sleep under the stars or under tarps, and learn to navigate through the backcountry with map and compass. They would work together as a group on a service project, and spend much of their time hiking, rock climbing, summiting, and rappelling.

QUESTIONS

6. Can you imagine any ways in which so small an initiative as the Palestinian-Israeli Unity Project could make a difference against so seemingly intractable a problem as the Arab-Israeli conflict? Why even bother?

7. How much information do you want to know—*need* to know—about the backgrounds of members of any group you lead? Would it be helpful to know, for example, that there are Christian as well as Muslim Palestinians? How much do you know about Israel and its population? Would an awareness of information like this make your job as leader easier? More effective?

8. What are some of the thoughts you would expect the students from Haifa to have as they head west to the United States? What sorts of "culture shock" might they experience upon arrival in Atlanta, or at Table Rock, deep in the North Carolina mountains?

The Unity Project course was designed to build a safe, inclusive community that everybody would love being a part of, and prepare students for meaningful independence later in the course. The instructors sought to impel the participants to experience their decisions, one another, and this adventure to America as adults completely responsible for their own actions, decisions, and emotions. They tried to set the crew up with a high level of honest communication and a crew culture in which they felt comfortable talking with each other about some serious and deeply emotional topics.

To a large extent, the instructors' personalities and demeanors helped form crew culture along that trajectory. The Unity Project's organizers encouraged the instructors to challenge themselves and to think critically and creatively about how they could facilitate emotional safety and not further alienate historically oppressed people. The course instructors were given the task of moving a group of diverse students to the point where they could engage together in productive dialog about their different perspectives. This was a challenging team-building and trust-building assignment.

Some specific exercises were included in the curriculum, according to the project's 2006 report. Throughout the course, Jewish students were paired with Arabic students to belay or to do partner interviews or complete camp jobs together. Mixing the group intentionally along these lines was intended to create "authentic" opportunities for each of them to experience the other.

The messages that the kids from Haifa had been told their whole lives, according to Unity Project course director Billy Roberts, were ones of division and separation. So the Unity Project course wanted to draw their attention to what they had always been told was real and what they had therefore come to believe. The course was intended to help students come to grips with the conflict between the societal values and prejudices they had grown up with and what they were now experiencing through contact with "the other" on the course. The course hoped to show them that they could trust each other and, through human-to-human connection, through shared tasks, and through open dialog, that the societal values that had been drilled into their heads back home could be overcome.

QUESTIONS

9. Unity Project course director Billy Roberts is convinced of the importance of instructors' personalities and demeanors to shaping team culture. Which of your own personality characteristics have you found to be most conducive to facilitating emotional safety in the group you are leading?

Early in the 2006 Palestinian-Israeli Unity Project course, the trip's leaders tried to create an atmosphere in which the students would be willing to take the risk of being open and honest. One of the course instructors, Dave, believed that to truly lead people from one mindset to another takes personal contact and direct individual experience, so that night he modeled the desired behavior by telling his own life story.

He told students that he had been raised in a family with strong prejudices, so he knows that moving beyond ignorance is a lifetime journey. He described what it was like as a white adult to adopt and raise an African-American child, and he added that he is just a human being on a journey, like anyone else, like them. Then the other two instructors talked about their personal experiences as well. They hoped that these personal recollections by the leaders would stimulate the students to tell their own stories.

Real progress toward mutual understanding and acceptance came through several students' experiences during the first day of rock climbing at Table Rock. Sana, a Palestinian girl who was being belayed on a climb by Miriam, a Jewish girl, was petrified by the climb, and she was nearly freaking out. At the debrief after the climb, Sana pointed out that her life had been in the hands of a Jew.

Later, Levi, a Jewish boy, was in the middle of a multipitch ascent when he was stung in the hand by hornets from a nest he encountered halfway up the pitch. Startled and in pain, he let go of his holds and fell. His belayer, Shafik, successfully stopped his fall, and Levi was able to get back on the climb. During the debriefing, Levi said his friends back home would say he was crazy to put his life in an Arab's hands.

Because these students had always been told, "Don't trust the Arab; don't trust the Jew," these were true "ah-hah!" moments for Sana and Levi.

But course participants experienced the true breakthrough on Day Ten.

On Day Nine, the students had finished their "final expedition," which they had largely planned and conducted under their own leadership, and that night they gathered at a high camp deep in the mountains of the Pisgah National Forest. Their instructors asked the students to join in a role-playing activity called "Walk in My Shoes." After explaining the ground rules for a productive group dialog, the instructors asked the students to consider, "What would your life be like as that person? What would it really be like to be Jewish? To be Palestinian?" The idea was to invite students to role-play the perspective of the other and try to tell the group their new understanding of the dynamics between Jews and Arabs—sort of a basic debate exercise.

But that night, the students really resisted telling their own stories. Instead, they presented extremist points of view and superficial stereotypes.

QUESTIONS

10. In your own leadership roles, how easy is it for you to share life experiences with your co-workers, your employees, or your students? What are the potential risks of sharing? What are the potential benefits?

11. What are the signals that you look for to assess the energy and engagement levels of your participants? Do you consider such elemental factors as mild dehydration or hunger or the natural tendency for the mind to lose focus when the body is digesting a meal?

The next morning, one of the instructors, Dave, checked in with his supervisor, Billy, by cell phone to tell him how things were going. Billy agreed to come out to the group's location to discuss the situation with the instructors. They realized that the approach to the previous night's discussion had been oversimplified. Certainly, the challenges to the conversation were compounded by a strenuous day and the late hour, but the real impediment was too much instructor input and opinion.

In the face of such emotionally charged issues, it bears repeating: make sure the students are doing almost all the talking. One of the first principles of effective communication is being a good listener. Put another way: the instructor's opinion regarding the content of whatever is being discussed is of disproportionately little importance. Leaders need to always be mindful of creating an open space in which their students feel validated and comfortable in vetting and refining their ideas.

Together the instructors reached the decision to alter the plan for the day—which had been to go right back to the cliffs for more rock climbing—and instead really focus on the "nut," the core purpose of the project. They set up a framework for continuing the discussion, telling the students that the night before, people had been picking obvious, simplified presentations.

Through many years of working with Outward Bound students, Dave had learned that real change in students' attitudes, outlooks, and behavior can be fostered by the course leaders. So the instructors urged the students to take responsibility for the discussion and to share, in deeper ways, their own personal thoughts, feelings, and life experiences, just as the instructors had done when they told their own stories the night before.

QUESTIONS

12. What did Billy's leadership bring to his instructors in the field? As a leader, how much authority for the actual running of the group do you feel comfortable turning over to those who report to you?

13. By changing the agenda from the planned activity on the morning of Day Ten—more rock climbing—the instructors short-changed the students out of a longer high-impact climbing experience. Would you have decided to make that trade-off?

What do you guess the students' reactions were when the change was announced to them?

At last, the students were willing to tap into some deep places and bring out some honestly difficult truths to share with each other. Among the poignant stories shared by the students were these:

Jacob, who is Jewish, broke the ice; he talked about what he experiences when he takes the bus in Haifa: he always feels as though he's going to die from a suicide bomber. So he gets on the bus, pays his fare, looks among the passengers to see who looks suspicious—sort of a "functional paranoia"—and then goes for a seat near the back or the front of the bus, where there's a better chance of surviving a suitcase bombing. Mona, a Palestinian, and Jon, who is Jewish, each talked of best friends and older brothers who had been killed. Another Palestinian student, Raef, talked about Palestinian schools, which have no money for supplies and repairs.

It was during this dialog that Marwan, a Palestinian, was able, through tears, to share with everyone his vivid memory of a devastating experience he had had on the group's international flight from Haifa to the United States. His seat assignment placed him in a row next to a family with two young children, and Marwan enjoyed talking with and entertaining the two little kids. But at one point during the long flight, another student from the Unity Project group walked past Marwan's row and spoke to him in Arabic. The children's mother quickly rushed her children away to other seats, where they would not be in contact with "the enemy."

When students reached this deeper level of inquiry, Dave observed that real change in perspectives and attitudes had occurred. Many

of students from both groups tended to use the phrase "That's politics!" Yet saying those words permits avoidance of the harder job of compassion and walking in the other's shoes. Or, as *The Unity Project—Community Instructor Manual* puts it, "People often express a stifling resignation to injustice by saying, 'That's just the way things are.' " Dave pushed back, reminding students that this is *not* politics; it's about real life-and-death matters.

The conversation that morning lasted for more than three hours. The students really heard one another's stories, commenting, "That's real!" The in-depth dialog had finally gotten going. The students and their instructors went deeply into what their society was telling them in the form of segregationist messages. To paraphrase Kurt Hahn, the previous days' activities, followed by these discussions, had impelled them into value-forming experiences.

As the students experienced the highs and lows, the plusses and minuses, of the course, they began to realize that "the others" are real people and that they don't just have to hate the other side because their friends and relatives hate them. So, at this point more than half-way through the course, a true breakthrough in the students' thinking about one another occurred, accompanied by expressions of deeply felt emotions and a desire to contrast knowing in the head with knowing in the heart.

By the conclusion of that morning's lengthy dialog, Billy could see that the students had begun to recognize that they can change the future, but that they must first understand why the old biases exist. Then they can move toward the future; they can develop leadership of their own.

QUESTIONS

14. How hard is it for you to let your students or clients do most of the talking? Why?

15. Was the mother of the two children who were seated next to Marwan on the airplane right to do what she did and in the way she did it? Was she wise? What kind of world is she creating for her children?

16. Of the various personal experiences recounted here, both by adults and by students, which do you think had the greatest effect on the students, freeing them to engage in authentic dialog across the ethnic divide?

17. As my twelfth-grade religion teacher, Dr. Firor, used to say: "Nothing's *real* till it's *local*." What do you make of these ideas? How do these sayings help to explain the breakthrough on Day Ten?

When a Unity Project course's objectives have been accomplished, the students are then living their perfect community and looking ahead to transferring this back home. They have embraced compassion and a commitment to serve. They have a realization that bringing about change in their lives back home will be hard and require moral courage. They have the deep sense of self, collective solidarity, and belief in human potential that will be needed to carry this off. Each person is actively engaged in the process of recognizing injustice and working against it.

The Unity Project students do not head directly home at the end of the wilderness phase of their trip; instead, they travel to cities in the southeastern United States to meet with groups at schools, colleges, and civic organizations to share their Unity Project stories and their plans to make a difference when they get back home. During the final day at Table Rock, the students planned how they would present their course experience in Atlanta and Charlotte, and they also thought ahead to ways they could work together back in Haifa to carry the Outward Bound values and ideals to their families, their schools, and their city.

QUESTIONS

18. What kind of support will the Unity Project students need back home to help them achieve their vision of initiating compassionate social change in their home communities? What does your answer to this question suggest about ways you can support the people you lead?

The two groups of students continued their contact back home. They put on presentations in all the schools in Haifa—most of which are segregated—where they told their peers, teachers, and communities what the Unity Project course had been like and what they had learned from it.

Hani Nahhas, a student from the 2005 Unity Project, described what he had gained from the experience: "The Outward Bound course made me feel about things in a way I never thought I would feel. I felt how it is to be alone in the wilderness with 'your enemy' and to see that this 'enemy' is like you. It made me think that we should tell everyone in Israel that our enemy is like us, but only with different political thoughts."

Another 2005 participant, Yael Federman, said, "I think that I can truly say now that I'm looking at people as people, although it's hard sometimes, and the easiest way is to put them in categories. This is the start of our change, and more people should have the possibility to have this hard adventure. It wasn't perfect, not even close, and we have a lot of work to do—but it is the best start that we could have ever asked for."

In 2006 the Unity Project participants also committed to work together on community service projects. Every year in mid-December, for example, Haifa has a big street festival, an all-holiday celebration. The Unity Project alumni made plans to help prepare the area and to get peers to attend the celebration with them. So on a person-to-person basis, the positive effect of the Unity Project has already grown and spread.

Most of these students were sixteen years old when they took the course, which means that within two years of returning home the Jewish kids will go into the Israel Defense Force. No doubt their military experience will be informed by what they learned in the mountains of North Carolina.

All the students, whether Jewish or Palestin-ian, returned home to a very complex social context, one that presents them every day with huge political, religious, ethnic, and economic challenges, none of which can be successfully addressed without a commitment to understanding and cooperation—and a spirit of unity. The Unity Project's course report states that the students developed a greater understanding of how complex the racial dynamics are between Arabs and Jews, a greater willingness to resolve the conflict, and a greater commitment to confront racial and identity group stereotypes. They understood that a fundamental step of progress toward resolving conflict comes from changing their own attitudes toward the other as much as it does from changing the overall cultural attitude toward tolerance of diversity in Israel. Students became more aware of their potential to be leaders and agents of positive social change. They left the course feeling empowered to go home and make a difference in their communities.

QUESTIONS

19. Reflecting on the entirety of the Unity Project and the particulars of the work with the students from Haifa, what changes in your own outlook on leadership are you prompted to make? Which parts of your leadership style or your approaches to working with diverse groups are affirmed by this case study? What would you consider changing or modifying? What are the take-away lessons for you?

PART II
TAKING LEADERSHIP INTO THE OUTDOORS

About the Author: Ashley Lodato

Ashley Lodato, who grew up in the eastern Cascade Range of Washington State, went on numerous camping and hiking trips with her parents from a very young age. After completing a twenty-eight-day Outward Bound course when she was fifteen, Ashley developed her own passion for the backcountry and began taking her friends out into the woods with her on weekends. She now spends as much free time as possible hiking, climbing, skiing, and white-water kayaking.

After earning a bachelor's degree in English and Italian literature from Stanford University and a master of arts in English from Western Washington University, Ashley taught high-school and college-level English in California and Washington.

Since 1986, Ashley has worked for Outward Bound schools in Maine, Montana, Texas, and Washington, instructing courses in backpacking, white-water and flat-water canoeing, canyoneering, and rock climbing, as well as directing programs, writing curricula, and coordinating special projects. She has spent more than a thousand days in the field with students and just about as many out in the woods on personal trips. She has also been a spokesperson and freelance writer for numerous land conservation and stewardship projects in New England.

Ashley lives in Washington's North Cascades with her husband and two children.

Personal Introduction: Ashley Lodato

The first time I took real responsibility for others in the outdoors was at age fifteen, on my first Outward Bound course. While we were on a sailing expedition, woefully calm conditions quickly put us behind schedule. Toward the end of the expedition, we realized that if we were to get back on schedule, we must row through the night with the favorable tide, taking a shortcut through a maze of islands and shallow reefs—and I was the student leader that day.

The navigation was tricky, but even more difficult was keeping group spirits up as we grew increasingly tired of rowing in shifts through the foggy night. I threw all my energy into motivating my fellow students and getting the stronger ones to help those who were really exhausted. At one point, everyone wanted to quit and drop anchor, but somehow I convinced them to continue. I felt sure that we would all be happier in the morning if we pushed on toward our goal rather than quitting because we were tired. People took turns taking short naps while others rowed, but I didn't sleep a wink the whole night—I was too keyed up with the challenge and the responsibility.

We reached our destination just before dawn, and although we celebrated our triumph as a group, I felt a special sense of accomplishment and an almost giddy pride in my fellow sailors. That experience helped me realize how rewarding leadership can be, and it was then that I decided I wanted to become an Outward Bound instructor.

I have since instructed hundreds of Outward Bound students on dozens of courses, and although each group has its own unique character, most of them share similar experiences. Each time I watch a group of erstwhile strangers work together to solve some expedition-related problem or push themselves further than they thought they could in order to achieve a particular goal, it reinforces my confidence in Outward Bound's leadership methods. Although these methods have been developed within the framework of long wilderness-based expeditions, they are flexible enough to be applied to a wide variety of outdoor leadership situations.

So whether you're leading day trips, taking your family camping, or teaching extended wilderness expeditions, this section of the book will help you incorporate Outward Bound's effective leadership strategies into your own outdoor leadership style. Chapter 7, Preparing to Lead an Expedition, looks at the logistical side of a leader's expedition planning. Chapter 8, Taking Responsibility for Yourself and Others Outdoors, focuses on the interactive skills you need while leading others out in the woods. Chapter 9, Going Solo, gives suggestions for incorporating solitude and reflective time into your leadership training and expeditions. These three chapters provide strategies gleaned from Outward Bound that you can use in your own leadership, as well as ways that you can employ the Outward Bound method of student leadership to further your participants' leadership experience.

CHAPTER 7

PREPARING TO LEAD AN EXPEDITION

Remember the first time you organized your own camping trip? It probably went something like this: You and the other neighborhood nine-year-olds gathered up sleeping bags, tents, flashlights, and cookies and retired to the backyard. You pitched the tents and settled in for a long night of telling ghost stories. After eating the cookies, though, you realized that you were thirsty, so one of you made a trip back to the kitchen for juice and water. Someone who was too cold in a flimsy sleeping bag went back inside to collect some extra blankets. A little while later, you all made a trip to the house to use the bathroom, lingering long enough to wolf down some hamburgers that your mother just happened to have ready. Finally, around 2:00 AM, rain started pouring, and your saggy tents began to leak. You all threw on your shoes and evacuated to the house, where you spent the rest of your "camping trip" on the basement floor.

Despite its lack of logistical precision and your final retreat to civilization, however, that trip was remembered as a great success, and you found yourself bitten by the camping bug. Since then, you have started to organize camping trips for groups of friends, or perhaps you're even working as an outdoor professional. Suddenly you've become an ad hoc or official outdoor leader. However, you don't necessarily think of your expedition planning as exercising your leadership skills. Isn't leadership what you do out in the backcountry, rather than what happens beforehand in the grocery store or gear rental shop?

Although it might seem as though some of the behind-the-scenes preparation for outdoor trips does not require leadership skills, in fact it is one of the first opportunities to demonstrate your competence as a leader. Why? Key elements to being a good outdoor leader are appearing organized, confident, and capable so that your participants look at you and think, "That gal really has her stuff together. It's obvious that she knows what she's doing. I feel very safe going out in the woods with her."

This is important because when you take people out in the woods, it's likely that you're going to ask them to do things that might be scary or uncomfortable for them, whether it's sleeping outside, rock climbing, or hiking off-trail. You will be most successful in leading people through these experiences if they trust you and believe that you are competent.

The first impression your participants have of you is *not* the shining image of you fearlessly guiding them to the top of a peak or showing them how to light a fire with wet wood. It is at the pre-trip meeting when you are discussing the logistics of the upcoming trip. If you come across as scattered and unprepared, it will take a lot of fearless guiding and wet-wood fires later on to earn their trust and respect. Above all, you need to inspire confidence in your participants, and the key to establishing this trust is projecting a competent, skilled image from the first contact your participants have with you or your organization. You can use some techniques from Outward Bound leadership methodology to help you project this image.

The Outward Bound approach to leadership is two-part. First, we want our instructors (because Outward Bound is a school, we call our group leaders "instructors" and our participants "students") to model organized, compassionate, and professional leadership. We want our instructors to excel at mobilizing students to work together to achieve shared goals.

The second part of this two-tier leadership strategy is what makes Outward Bound different from many other outdoor programs. Outward

Bound wants our students to graduate from their Outward Bound courses as better leaders than they were before. In fact, we want our students to finish their wilderness courses having spent the last few days of their expedition under their own leadership, with the instructor offering merely background support.

Of course, the end goal of most of Outward Bound's wilderness programming is character development—increased competence and confidence—not leadership. But we believe that by facing real problems, solving them with newly learned skills, and making decisions that matter, our students emerge more aware of their strengths and more able to use them in a variety of situations. They learn, as Outward Bound founder Kurt Hahn was fond of saying, that *plus est en vous*—that they have more in them than they know. This translates into better leadership skills, too, as students grow better able to make sound decisions, better able to communicate effectively, and better able to motivate their peers to get things done. In learning to be better leaders, Outward Bound students are also developing character. So not only must Outward Bound instructors be superb outdoor leaders, but they must train their students to be effective leaders too.

At Outward Bound, we feel that two factors are key to our unique success: (1) our focus on inspiring students to *want* to work hard to achieve personal and group goals; and (2) our use of student leadership and real student responsibility to cultivate increased competence and confidence. Simply completing a wilderness expedition, learning some new skills, and having fun are not enough. Our students must emerge from their courses having willingly struggled to accomplish things they might not have deemed important before and having become caught up in the exhilaration of doing so under their own leadership.

This chapter addresses that goal as well as the basic skills you need for outdoor leadership, from first-aid certifications to decision-making methods. In addition to these technical and interpersonal skills, you also need proven, sound judgment and an environmental ethic. Let's begin by looking at what skills you need to have before you go out in the woods and how you can integrate Outward Bound's leadership strategies into your expedition planning.

ASSESSING YOUR LEADERSHIP SKILLS

Plenty of outdoor enthusiasts head out on nontechnical backcountry day trips with little more than a love of the outdoors, a lunch, and a bit of equipment. But if you have agreed to take responsibility for others' well-being in the backcountry—particularly on extended trips—you need something more than that. Your participants will arrive at the start of your trip with a variety of outdoor skills and backgrounds; some will have been backpacking for decades, but others will have never camped outdoors. Some will have never slept in a sleeping bag before. But most will adapt remarkably quickly to the unfamiliar environment of the backcountry, as long as you are able to help them make the transition.

So what skills does an outdoor leader need to have in order to take others out on trips? It's a good question, with a complex answer. There are currently no national criteria in the United States for wilderness leadership certifications. Although there are some nationally recognized industry standards (for example, cardiopulmonary resuscitation—CPR—and Wilderness First Responder certifications), each outdoor leadership organization defines its own criteria for its outdoor educators. For instance, although required competencies vary for different activities and environments within Outward Bound, minimum requirements for all field instructors include CPR and Wilderness First Responder certification, technical competencies for specific activities, and some experience in teaching and/or leadership.

If you are employed by an organization, you must meet that particular organization's minimum standards. If you are volunteering for an organization or simply leading a group of acquaintances into the backcountry, you should weigh your skills and experience against the type of trip you plan to take.

BASIC BACKCOUNTRY SKILLS

Technical Skills

- first aid: basic wilderness first aid and CPR
- navigation: ability to read a topographic map and use a compass
- backcountry travel campcraft and skills
- relevant technical competencies for particular activity

Interpersonal Skills
Some background in:

- communication
- problem solving
- decision making
- facilitation

MINIMUM TECHNICAL SKILLS

Trip Length	Short (1–3 days)	Medium (4–10 days and/or very remote)	Long (2 weeks or more)
First-Aid Skills	CPR plus Basic Wilderness First Aid	CPR plus Wilderness Advanced First Aid	CPR plus Wilderness First Responder or Wilderness Emergency Medical Technician
Navigation Skills	<ul><li>Identify basic features on topographic map</li><li>Follow trails</li><li>Measure distances and estimate travel times</li><li>Calculate elevation loss and gain</li></ul>	<ul><li>Previous skills, plus</li><li>Orient map, using compass or points on land</li><li>Perform basic route planning</li></ul>**Off-Trail Travel**<ul><li>Take and follow a bearing</li></ul>	<ul><li>Previous skills, plus ability to:</li><li>Select off-trail route</li><li>Account for declination</li><li>Triangulate</li><li>Use GPS (although it is no substitute for an ability to read a map and use a compass, an understanding of how to use GPS is handy)</li></ul>
Backcountry Travel Skills	<ul><li>Deal with weather challenges (lightning, wind, rain, heat, snow, etc.)</li><li>Know search and rescue basics</li><li>Manage major stream and river crossings</li><li>Manage evacuation</li></ul>		
Backcountry Campcraft Skills	Minimum-impact practices, including:<ul><li>Travel techniques</li><li>Campsite selection</li><li>Campsite setup</li><li>Cooking</li><li>Waste disposal</li><li>Animal-proofing camp</li></ul>	Or: Leave No Trace training (see "Modeling an Environmental Ethic," below)	
Technical Competencies	Relevant technical competencies for:<ul><li>Water-based travel (canoeing, sea kayaking, etc.)</li><li>Snow- and ice-based travel (skiing, snowshoeing, glacier travel, etc.)</li><li>Winter travel (snow- and ice-based travel, plus cold-weather challenges, etc.)</li><li>Rock climbing (traditional methods, not just gym-based)</li><li>Mountaineering (glacier travel, rock climbing skills, etc.)</li><li>Canyoneering (rappeling, anchor construction, rock climbing, etc.)</li><li>Backpacking</li></ul>		

MINIMUM INTERPERSONAL SKILLS

	Outdoor Trips of Any Length
Communication Abilities:	■ Establish rapport
	■ Create environment conducive to learning and cooperation
	■ Convey information through verbal expression
	■ Listen effectively to others
	■ Persuade
	■ Resolve conflict
Problem-Solving Abilities:	■ Identify a problem
	■ Specify a desired outcome
	■ Brainstorm solutions
	■ Select and effect the best solution
Decision-Making Abilities:	■ Employ different decision-making methods
	■ Match appropriate decision-making methods to specific situations
Facilitation Abilities:	■ Help participants reflect on experiences
	■ Transfer lessons from experience to participants' "real" lives

The longer, more technical, and more remote the trip, the more developed your outdoor skills need to be.

Outdoor professionals often refer to two different types of skill sets required for outdoor leaders: technical skills and interpersonal skills. Technical skills are those that relate directly to doing any outdoor activity, such as setting up anchors for a rock climb, paddling a kayak, or taking a compass bearing. Safety-related skills such as first aid, search and rescue, nutrition, and evacuation management generally fit into this category of technical skills, too.

Interpersonal skills, on the other hand, are those that address the social and psychological well-being of participants; these skills might include facilitating a group discussion, resolving a conflict, or making a decision. Paul Petzoldt, a former Outward Bound instructor and founder of the National Outdoor Leadership School (NOLS), coined the term "expedition behavior" in his book *The New Wilderness Handbook* to refer to those sets of skills that relate to interpersonal relationships and other facilitative or "people"

skills. Outward Bound instructors tend to use the two terms—"interpersonal skills" and "expedition behavior"—interchangeably.

At a minimum, before embarking on any backcountry travel, a leader should have the technical and interpersonal skills outlined in the accompanying chart. These two skill sets are further detailed in a separate chart for each type of skill, technical and interpersonal. In addition, interpersonal skills are addressed in more detail in Chapter 8, Taking Responsibility for Yourself and Others Outdoors.

Finally, but most importantly, you must consistently demonstrate good judgment if you take responsibility for others in the wilderness. To determine whether you have good judgment, consider the experiences you've had and the decisions you've made in the backcountry. If you've had lots of epic experiences and many near-miss accidents, your judgment might be lacking. For more on judgment, see "Developing Judgment" in Chapter 5, Taking Risks and Making Decisions, in Part I, Leadership Fundamentals.

MODELING AN ENVIRONMENTAL ETHIC

As an outdoor leader, you are obligated to demonstrate a fundamental respect for the natural environment, a willingness to travel and camp in a way that minimizes human impacts, and a commitment to holding your participants to this same standard. New outdoor leaders may be surprised to learn how many people harbor misconceptions about backcountry practices and what conscientious efforts are required to minimize the human impact. "Can't I just bury my leftover food?" a student asks. "Won't an animal come and eat it?" Or, "My dad taught me to dig trenches around my tent in case it rains; why can't we do that here?" There are a lot of unacceptable and antiquated backcountry behaviors being used, and you need to find a way to modify them into low-impact practices.

On the first day of an Outward Bound course, my group was being dropped off at a trailhead. We had quickly sorted through clothes and equipment, stuffed gear into backpacks, and jumped into the van with a minimum of teaching so we could reach our campsite near the trailhead as quickly as possible. There were outhouses at the base camp where we had packed up, so I hadn't yet delivered my standard "How to Poop in the Woods" talk.

At the trailhead, after we unloaded the van I stood for a moment talking with the van driver, confirming our pickup time and place two weeks hence. When I finished, I gathered the students together to talk about campsite selection, water purification, and pooping in the woods. It soon became apparent that two students were missing.

I could hear their voices coming from a nearby stand of trees, so I walked over to call them back. As I did, I realized that they were answering nature's call behind a couple of large pines. I overheard one girl ask the other, "What are we supposed to do with our toilet paper?" The other

girl answered, "Oh, just fling it out in the woods; that's what I did."

Ignorance, lack of proper equipment, and indifference are the three main causes of improper techniques for backcountry camping and traveling. The first two causes are fairly easy to deal with: Participants who want to bury their leftover food are simply unaware that this is no longer an accepted practice; once coached in currently accepted methods, they will likely change their behavior. Participants who think they need to trench their tent have probably never slept in a tent with an adequate rain fly pitched expertly in a dry location; once properly equipped, they will realize that trenches are unnecessary.

However, the third cause—indifference—is the root cause of the most objectionable of high-impact violations. Consider the omnipresent beer cans along any major roadside. Do people who throw their aluminum cans out of car windows think that this is an acceptable waste-disposal method? Probably not. It's likely that if there were a police car behind them, they wouldn't do it. Are they lacking a proper place to dispose of the cans? Again, probably not; they can always throw away trash at convenience stores or gas stations. Most likely they are throwing their cans out of the car window because they just don't care about litter or littering; they are simply indifferent to the impact.

The trick is not just to get people to follow impact techniques and etiquette, but to get them to *care* about doing so. Outdoor leaders can dictate rules and model an impeccable backcountry ethic, but if participants are not intrinsically motivated to practice appropriate backcountry conduct, they will likely follow the leader's example only when the leader is monitoring them.

One of the quickest ways to turn participants off from the idea of minimum-impact techniques is to preach to them about such practices being necessary for the continued existence of natural resources. If participants were coming in with logging trucks or backhoes, there might be cause to fear for the survival of the forest. But a mound of unburied toilet paper, a blackened fire ring, or a moat trenched around a tent have very little short-term impact on the natural resource itself or even on the animals whose habitat is affected.

So who are we protecting when we pack out our trash, bury our waste, and sweep a campsite for bits of microtrash and food scraps? The answer is this: other wilderness travelers—those who are using the backcountry concurrently with us and those who will come in the future. Indeed, most minimum-impact camping practices are directed at protecting natural resources not for the sake of the resource itself, but for the sake of others who enjoy the resource. As environmental author Stephen Simpson writes in an article in the *Journal of Experiential Education*, "The practice of minimum impact often is no more than extending the social responsibility expected of people in the city to the new setting of the backcountry."

Trip participants are justifiably suspicious of a code of conduct that requires them to pick up spilled sunflower seeds in order to avoid altering the natural diet of the red squirrel. Furthermore, they are unlikely to hold themselves to this code when they are not being observed. But an explanation that leftover food scraps mar the aesthetic, pristine nature of the wilderness for the next user—ideally, such an explanation is coupled with actual evidence of someone else's leftover trash—can serve to inspire a personal ethic and commitment to thoughtful backcountry habits. If participants care what a campsite or trail looks like when *they* reach it, they are likely to care enough to leave it as tidy as possible for the next visitor.

Professional outdoor leaders must hold themselves and their participants to a high standard of minimum-impact practices for several reasons.

■ **We travel in large groups.** Large groups make it difficult for every individual behavior to be noticed. While the leader is busy demonstrating how to wash a pot without discarding any food particles onto the ground, a participant some distance away could be tossing leftover pasta into a stream. If a long line forms at the outhouse, a participant could decide to forego the facilities and instead leave unburied waste on the ground behind a tree.

■ **We travel with novices.** Many people who participate in organized outdoor programs don't have the knowledge, experience, or equipment to travel in the backcountry alone. This means that they are generally unfamiliar with standard minimum-impact practices and must be instructed in what might seem to be very basic methods to most experienced wilderness travelers. But there are so many things to be taught that we often miss a few or do not teach them quickly enough, and the resulting ignorance often results in poor minimum-impact practices, as in the earlier example of the girls flinging toilet paper into the woods.

■ **We are role models and trendsetters.** As soon as a handful of respected institutional groups start following a particular practice, it gains momentum and other followers; soon it becomes considered an industry standard—a widely accepted method. Changing an industry standard to a less harmful practice requires deliberate discussion, decision making, and public education, as well as a significant transition period.

One of the most successful campaigns to get outdoorspeople thinking about their impact in the backcountry and promoting minimum-impact practices is the Leave No Trace movement. Leave No Trace was started by the U.S. Forest Service in the 1970s, but it gained momentum in the 1990s when an appealing public education curriculum was adopted. Today, four federal agencies—the Bureau of Land Management, the U.S. Forest Service, the U.S. Fish and Wildlife Service, and the National Park Service—and several private organizations fund and administer the Leave No Trace program, which supports organizations and individuals in adopting and adhering to practices that minimize human impact in the backcountry.

LEAVE NO TRACE PRINCIPLES

- Plan ahead and prepare.
- Travel and camp on durable surfaces.
- Dispose of waste properly.
- Leave what you find.
- Minimize campfire impacts.
- Respect wildlife.
- Be considerate of other visitors.

PARTICIPANT LEADERSHIP OPPORTUNITIES

- Give each participant some background information about one of the Leave No Trace principles. Ask them to design mini-lessons to teach the principle to the rest of the group.
- Involve participants in making decisions that involve human impact. For example, if your campsite choices include a heavily impacted area of fragile plants or a pristine site with hearty grasses, you could facilitate a discussion about which site would endure your group's impact better and ask participants to make the decision.

Leave No Trace promotes seven basic principles that can be applied to nearly any backcountry environment and situation, as shown in the sidebar. More information about Leave No Trace ethics can be found by consulting the environmental ethics resources for Chapter 7 in the Bibliography at the end of this book.

It's important to recognize that no matter how pure our intentions are, simply by traveling in wilderness areas, we make a deliberate decision to have an impact on pristine places. And once that decision has been made, the burden of minimizing the impact as much as possible becomes the responsibility of the leader.

ORGANIZING A TRIP

Ernest Shackleton spent several years amassing men, supplies, and funding for his now-famous journey to Antarctica on the *Endurance*. Most big Himalayan expeditions take six months to a year just planning the logistics of their trips. But in all likelihood, organizers of most backcountry trips don't have that much time. Departure on a backcountry expedition may be imminent, and planning needs to start right away. Although the price of mistakes in most expedition planning is likely

not as high as what Shackleton had to contend with, there is probably a lot less room for error than you might think. Consider this outing:

My friend Saranne and I recently headed out on a day hike. Saranne and I had been on dozens of day hikes together in the past eight years, including numerous winter ascents in New Hampshire's Presidential Range and ambitious 20-mile loops in the Sierra that our friends deem "death marches." We didn't have a map for this particular hike—just a description in a guidebook. But we're experienced hikers and the trails are generally well marked, so we didn't worry too much.

On the way to the trailhead, we ran out of gas. Fortunately, we had a spare gallon in the back of the truck, so we arrived at the trailhead without further incident, pausing along the way at the end of the U-shaped route to drop off a bike to run the shuttle after the hike.

Once we were on the trail, we realized that the route description was inadequate for the variation of the hike we had chosen. After hiking for more than an hour downhill when we were pretty sure we were supposed to be ascending, we admitted to ourselves that we had gone off track. Retracing our steps, we eventually found the overgrown trail that we would have noticed had we paused to scout more thoroughly.

Eventually, at the end of the hike, Saranne jumped on the bike to ride back to the truck at the other trailhead. She was gone a long time—longer than it should have taken to ride 4 miles. Eventually I realized that I had failed to give her the key to the canopy of our truck, so she was unable to stow the bike in the back. When Saranne finally made it back to me, I saw that she had had to completely dismantle the bike in order to fit it in the passenger seat of the truck beside her. (She couldn't just ditch the bike and return for it after picking me up, because we barely had enough gas to make it back to town to a gas station, let alone to drive back and forth on a dirt road to retrieve a bicycle.)

After coasting the truck downhill for 18 miles in order to conserve gas, we asked ourselves, "What else could go wrong today?!" We had our answer soon enough: the nearest gas station had burned to the ground while we were out hiking.

Being the organizer of a trip requires experience, forethought, and—well—organizational skills.

As the leader of an expedition, you are responsible for the safety and quality of the experience, and a fair amount of that burden rests on your organizational ability. An ill-prepared or improperly equipped expedition is almost always doomed to failure. The good news is that, with a reasonable amount of backcountry experience, a modicum of common sense, and a few great checklists, even someone prone to organizational mishaps can put together a well-organized trip.

If you're working for an outfit, it probably has time-tested institutional organizational systems you can rely on to help you prepare for and execute its expeditions smoothly. If not, you need to create and refine your own systems and checklists that will help you hone your organizational skills.

The following sections, while not comprehensive, will at least get you thinking about what needs to be done to prepare for a backcountry expedition.

Researching What Needs to Be Done

First of all, it's essential to start planning early. Trip planning always takes longer than you think it will, so it doesn't hurt to get a lot of the legwork out of the way early. That way, as the trip departure date approaches, you will not have to run around trying to decide where to go or to find maps but, rather, will be able to help your participants prepare for the trip.

TRIP PREPARATION "TO DO" CHECKLIST

- **Trip expectations**—participant goals, leader expectations, standards for expedition behavior, safety and risk management information
- **Participants**—who, how many, how old, medical conditions, other concerns
- **Trip logistics**—how long, where, when
- **Safety**—route, weather, environmental concerns; evacuation routes; backup plan; emergency communication; outside assistance
- **Paperwork**—land-use permits, maps, participant permission and medical release forms (if leading minors), leader permit or license (if required)
- **Food**—how much, what, preparation methods
- **Equipment**—individual gear, shared gear, first-aid kit, technical equipment
- **Transportation**—getting to and from trip location

Even if you are quite familiar with the area you plan to visit, you will probably need to begin your expedition planning weeks—or even months—before your trip. Two or three days prior to any Outward Bound course start, the instructors arrive at the base camp to prepare for the course. They get familiar with their students' profiles, plan the expedition route, look at evacuation options, pack food, organize gear, gather maps, attend safety briefings, and discuss their own leadership partnership. This "course prep" time is busy, and the to-do list is long.

But the two- or three-day prep time required for an Outward Bound course is deceptively short because of the amount of information amassed over the more than sixty-five years that Outward Bound has been in business. Existing institutional knowledge about course areas, required permits, and evacuation routes expedites the planning process. Food packing and equipment systems are standardized, with rations stocked and gear ready to be pulled. Staff trainings and years of personal experience prepare instructors to plan for expeditions quickly and efficiently. And many other expedition planning tasks—such as making camping reservations and obtaining permits—are accomplished by Outward Bound administrators months prior to courses. Although much of your expedition planning can be accomplished a couple of days prior to your departure, too, everything will go more smoothly—and you will establish yourself as a more competent leader—if you devote some time to trip organization long before the departure date.

A critical decision you must make first is figuring out which is more important to you: a particular set of goals for the trip, or the makeup of the group members. If you decide to focus on specific objectives, then you must choose participants who are committed to these same goals. If it's more important to you to enjoy the backcountry with a particular group of people, then you will need to involve these people in identifying the expedition's goals or, at the very least, get them to accept the goals you've established.

If you are leading an institutional trip—for example, for your college outdoor program or for a local outing club—it's possible that you will not have any input into either the trip makeup or the expedition goals. Some suggestions for handling this situation are provided in "Leading a Trip for an Institution," later in this section.

Selecting Your Companions and Group Size

Most backcountry adventurers agree that *who* you travel with is as at least as important as *where* you travel on a wilderness expedition—if not more so. In the happiest of circumstances, your best friends share your attraction to the wilderness.

I once had a college boyfriend who hated any type of backcountry recreation. He didn't mind driving three hours to a trailhead, but once we were out of sight of the car, he grew impatient and gloomy. I was determined to change him, so that we could both enjoy the wilderness areas that I loved. After many aborted day-hiking trips (somehow on the drive to the trailhead, we always got sidetracked and ended up at Disneyland or Fisherman's Wharf), I finally decided that a romantic camping trip to the beach would be the best way to unleash what I was sure was simply his untapped passion for the wilderness.

Our beach camping trip was splendidly planned, sumptuously provisioned, and flawlessly executed. On the way home from what I thought had been a wildly successful experience, my boyfriend turned to me and said, "You owe me big time for this." It was our last venture into the out-of-doors together.

However, if your friends don't share your love of the outdoors (or until you make new friends who *do* share your interests), your trips will probably be most successful—and enjoyable—if you undertake them with people who at least have an interest in, if not a passion for, the backcountry. If you know a lot of people like this, you're in luck: grab a few folks who have the same days off and start planning your expedition. What if you don't know any such people? Check out a local outing club or post a note at a nearby outdoor retailer or your neighborhood food co-op.

Consider limiting your group size to four to six people until you are comfortable leading larger groups. Fewer than four people won't give you enough leadership opportunities to challenge you and help you develop leadership skills, whereas seven or eight others may initially stretch your leadership abilities to an uncomfortable degree. Although leadership strategies can certainly be employed in tiny groups, most leadership experts agree that some sense of a group or team is necessary in order for true leadership skills to be utilized. Without at least four core participants, the diversity of ideas and opinions is limited and the sense of "group" is diminished; with more than twelve people, consensus is impractical and group management and individual skills instruction are extremely difficult.

Your group size will sometimes affect your route options. Many backcountry areas have established group size regulations in order to minimize environmental impacts and social impacts to other travelers. When you're researching route options for your trip, be sure to inquire about group size limits (see "Obtaining Reservations and Permits" later in this section).

Another group size consideration is the optimal ratio of leaders to participants. Many states have laws governing leader-to-participant ratios; be sure to research your state's regulations. The industry standard with many outdoor leadership organizations is one leader for every five or six participants. When young participants (thirteen years or younger) are involved, a more comfortable ratio is one leader for every three or four participants.

Identifying the Goals of the Trip

Even when you're just going out with a group of friends, it's a good idea to clarify the goals of the trip. When you're officially leading a trip for an organization, it's imperative. What outcomes do you hope to achieve from this expedition? A rigorous hike covering many miles? An ascent of a scenic summit? A bonding experience with fellow hikers? A traverse of a dramatic ridge? An opportunity to refine outdoor skills in a realistic setting? A relaxing weekend in a beautiful backcountry location? Clarifying the goal(s) of the outing will allow everyone on the trip to be a fully informed (and, you hope, a fully invested) participant. It will also enable you, as the leader, to be candid about focusing your energy on achieving these goals.

You're so excited about an upcoming trip to the desert. You plan to use the cool early mornings to hike to various rock cliffs, then spend the afternoons climbing in the shade. Once out on the trip, however, you realize that your friends have different expectations. They're on vacation, and they want to sleep in. Before you know it, the routine is established: sleep late, make a gourmet breakfast, finally hit the trail at about 11 o'clock, and hike through the blistering heat all day. You cover a reasonable daily mileage, but you rock climb only once during the whole week. You didn't realize that you and your friends would have such different ideas about what a trip should be like.

At Outward Bound, we usually hold a meeting on the first night of the expedition to address personal and institutional goals. "Why are you here?" we ask our students. "What do you hope to achieve?" Answers vary from the general ("I want to meet some new people and have fun outdoors") to the concrete ("I hope to learn enough skills to take my family on a 20-mile backpacking trip") to the intangible ("I hope to clear my head and sort out some of my priorities"), but as long as the students' goals are compatible with the institutional objective of character development and can be accomplished

PARTICIPANT LEADERSHIP OPPORTUNITIES

■ Give participants the responsibility of ensuring that specific daily goals are met. For example, if a particular day's goals include having some reflection time in a scenic place, ask one or two of the participants to select the location.

■ Pair up participants and have them ask each other about their progress on personal goals. Questions that they might ask each other include these: Which goals have you met? Which ones haven't you met? What is preventing you from achieving these goals? How can I or the group help you achieve these goals?

within the confines of a backcountry expedition, we find that their aims can be accommodated.

An introductory meeting well in advance of your trip will enable you to address goals and objectives of the expedition. If you, or the institution you're working for, have determined the goals of the trip, this is the time to announce these goals to the other participants and either elicit their concurrence or allow them to withdraw from the trip. If you are determining expedition goals based on participants' interests and opinion, you can use the pretrip meeting to share ideas and collectively determine some objectives. Some questions you might ask include these:

■ Why do you want to go on this trip?

■ What (if any) are your goals for this trip?

■ How do you usually go about achieving your goals?

If you are working for an organization, expedition goal-setting is not an entirely democratic process. As a representative of that organization, you must adhere to some institutional expectations regarding expedition outcomes. For example, Outward Bound instructors operate under the expectation that they will facilitate a "value-forming experience" that leads to character development. All of their leadership strategies, then, are directed toward this educational objective. Other goals can be accommodated (for example, "I want to reach the top of a rock climb," "I'd like to make some new friends," or "I hope to keep a detailed journal"), and in fact many of them actually result in increased self-confidence or self-awareness. But the primary leadership focus is on achieving character development, not on rock climbing or building friendships or self-examination.

Depending upon the type of trip you're leading, it may be appropriate for the trip to focus on some of your own goals. Ultimately, your objective as an outdoor trip leader should be to conduct a safe and rewarding trip for everyone involved. But if your own particular goals for the trip can be accomplished in the process—and if your ambitions don't conflict with organizational or other participants' goals—then the enthusiasm you direct toward achieving these aims can often serve as inspiration for others. For example, you might have your eye on a particular peak in the Rocky Mountains, and you have the good fortune to be leading a trip in that area next week. In this case, incorporating a personal goal into a trip agenda might be appropriate.

Often, however, such focus on personal goals detracts from a leader's ability to be in tune with the trip's participants and to act in their best interests. Continuing the preceding example, you might get so focused on reaching Longs Peak that you make decisions that compromise the safety or quality of the trip, or you might push your participants harder than they should be pushed. It is probably most effective if you share your own goals as a possible framework for designing the trip but let participant and trip goals drive your decisions, letting go of specific personal outcomes and putting your leadership energy into your participants.

Communicating Risk-Management Expectations

As important as communicating the goals of the trip is conveying expectations for risk management and safety. You should explain the inherent risks present in the backcountry, as well as describe your qualifications and training that will help you either avoid or cope with hazards. Participants should be joining the trip from a position of "informed consent": they acknowledge the risks and decide to participate in the trip nonetheless.

Communicating such information prior to a trip serves a couple of purposes. Most importantly, it brings to the forefront the issues that are frequently great causes of concern among backcountry travelers, particularly novices. It establishes safety and risk management as a legitimate topic of discussion and instruction, making it acceptable for the trip leader to offer safety advice and direction and for the participants to ask questions and express concern without appearing overly anxious. It also brings participants into the risk-management equation. The trip leader is still ultimately responsible for safety, of course, but informed participants can take greater responsibility for their own and others' safety than those who are ignorant. And finally, organizations that inform their participants about risk potential stand on more solid legal liability ground than those who fail to acknowledge risks.

An unanticipated benefit of revealing information about safety and risk management is that informed participants are generally more prepared to maximize their experiences. At Outward Bound, we discovered that when we clearly spelled out the risks and challenges our students would be facing on their backcountry trips, students arrived better prepared physically and emotionally for their courses than they had when we had disclosed little about what they should expect. Now, the Outward Bound students who review the information we send them tend to be able to derive more from their experiences than those who arrive uninformed. They are prepared for and excited about pushing themselves, and they view the challenges they face at Outward Bound as opportunities for learning and growth as opposed to hardships to be endured.

Selecting an Expedition Route

Once you have decided on your group and your goals, you can begin the process of figuring out where you want your expedition to go. Although the expedition planning process can be interesting and even enjoyable, it is often overwhelming or even frustrating, particularly when more than two people are involved. One way to streamline the expedition planning process is to have the leader devise a couple of different expedition plans and present these ideas to the group for a decision, rather than involving the entire group in the brainstorming phase. Look in guidebooks, talk to other outdoor leaders, and find out what the great trips are in your area. Write down two or three expedition plans that all provide opportunities for the various goals of the trip to be met, then facilitate a discussion that will result in a decision about the expedition plan.

Roy is notorious for his unique expedition plans, for both his groups and his personal trips. He can look at a map covering an area that has been traveled by multitudes of other people and devise a completely new, original expedition. Some of his expedition plans are so wacky that it is only his enthusiasm for them that gets his co-leaders and participants excited about the trips. But this method does not work for everyone, and in fact it doesn't work for most people.

Once a couple of other leaders decided to follow Roy's example and devise a unique expedition. They were getting tired of traveling the same old routes, and they relished the opportunity to take their next group on a route that no other group had ever done before. They came up with a plan that involved canoeing on a familiar river for a few days, then spending the better part of two weeks traveling up a small, remote stream that no one had ever explored.

This stream turned out not to have enough water in it to float a canoe. After six hours traveling upstream, pulling the boats over numerous beaver dams, and thrashing through thick alders on the banks, they called it quits. The reason that no one else had ever traveled there finally became painfully apparent.

So much for the unique expedition. Not only was it disheartening for everyone to abandon the expedition plan so early in the trip, but it also reflected poorly on the leaders. To the participants, the leaders appeared ill prepared and incompetent. Unless you are like Roy and you possess a particular talent for designing and facilitating unusual expeditions, you should probably stick to routes that have been done successfully by other people, if not by you.

Most importantly, choose your expedition route(s) to accommodate the goals and abilities of the trip participants. Find out as much as you can about your participants' interests, goals, and medical history before you design the expedition routes. If a group is made up of participants who all want to climb a lot of peaks, take them into a mountain range with several attainable summits. A group with a history of knee injuries might spend more time in valleys or on higher traverses, avoiding lots of strenuous downhill. Miles of

cross-country travel will appeal to participants who want to refine their map-and-compass navigation skills. Glacier travel will interest those who want to learn mountaineering.

It's also possible to design an expedition that can accommodate a range of goals. For example, you might hike a few miles into a campsite that has several day-hiking options in the vicinity. Set up a base camp, then those who seek reflection time can relax near camp while others might ascend a nearby peak, hike over to a lake for a swim, or explore an adjacent drainage. The diversity of options will appeal to various interests, and you all will still be able to enjoy the group camaraderie in the evenings.

Below are some tips for expedition planning.

Balance challenge with comfort, a technique we call "dunking and drying." When planning a rigorous expedition route and/or a challenging trip itinerary, one of the things you should consider is how to balance challenge with comfort. At Outward Bound we subscribe to what we call the "dunk 'em and dry 'em" philosophy, which means that when designing our expeditions, we think about balancing physical or psychological rigor ("dunking") with some ease and comfort ("drying"). "Dunking" activities and processes require people to experience anxiety and stretch a little; "drying" allows people to move back into comfort zones to let the new experiences settle a little.

This scenario might take the form of hiking two or three days for long mileages, then having a rest or layover day; another example would be

PARTICIPANT LEADERSHIP OPPORTUNITIES
- Present several expedition options at the pretrip meeting, and place the decision entirely in the participants' hands. (For this to work, you must select expedition plans you will be happy with no matter what is decided.) Facilitate a discussion that will help them reach a decision, but don't let your own preferences influence the outcome.
- Teach participants some basic map interpretation skills and involve them in determining daily mileage goals, travel routes, etc.
- Allow opportunities for participants to suggest itinerary changes or ways to use layover days.

following an anxiety-producing activity (such as rock climbing) with some reflection time. This method is similar to what physical trainers recommend for developing muscle: alternating vigorous, muscle-stretching workouts with rest days or low-impact days.

Whether you deliberately adopt a "dunking and drying" philosophy or simply make a conscious effort to design a balanced expedition plan, your best strategy for a powerful experience is to plan both challenging and relaxing experiences into your expedition. The tough day taxes the mind or the muscles (or both); the moderate day allows the mind or body to recover and grow stronger.

Establish bailout points. Of course, you plan to execute your expedition exactly as you have designed it, but it's always a good idea to have a backup plan in case things don't go as you expect. When you're going over the maps of your expedition route, carefully consider any side trails, drainages, or shortcuts that could be used as bailout options if weather, injury, or general slowness warrant an early departure from the backcountry. Familiarize yourself with the landscape surrounding your expedition route, and mark potential bailout routes on your map.

If you're carrying only the maps that cover the area you plan to travel in, get at least a general idea of what is covered on the adjoining maps. Consider carrying one set of large-scale maps (1:100,000 or 1:250,000) of the area and don't use these for daily navigation, but pull them out if finding a shorter route to a road or trailhead becomes necessary.

If you're planning a one-way expedition that has no feasible options for adjusted mileage or early departures, you might reconsider your route choice. Being locked into a daily mileage requirement or being committed to making it across a particular terrain is often a recipe for disaster. Rather than being able to demonstrate compassionate leadership and adapt your itinerary to accommodate participant abilities, inclement weather, or other unexpected circumstances, you are forced to march onward, often putting your group at risk for the sake of making it out to your destination trailhead. Your participants could finish the trip exhausted and disgruntled; you can come across as heartless and unrealistic.

Flexible route options also allow you to add mileage if the group is particularly fit and ambitious. Flexible routes also give you the option of climbing extra peaks or exploring new terrain if you have the time and energy.

Timing the Expedition

Timing your expedition can be as simple as planning a trip around a particular set of dates that all participants have free. Or it can be as complicated as selecting specific dates based on the likelihood of favorable weather and relative solitude and maximizing the aesthetic value of the area (for instance, visiting an alpine environment in July when the wildflowers bloom). If you're headed out on an extremely popular route, you may need to time your trip according to the reservations you are able to obtain. If you and your participants have the luxury of a completely flexible schedule, consider the following factors when planning the dates of your expedition:

■ What season is considered prime for your particular expedition? If July and August are the best visiting months, consider going in June or September to minimize exposure to crowds. Find out if there are any limiting factors to the "shoulder" seasons (such as snowpack, mosquito hatches, etc.).

■ When are there likely to be fewer people visiting the area?

■ Plan your trip for weekdays, if possible. Depart Monday and return Friday, before the weekend crowds arrive.

Obtaining Reservations and Permits

Before visiting any backcountry area, you'll need to find out who owns the land and what, if any, regulations apply to its recreational use. Backcountry permits, fire permits, and parking permits may all be necessary for day or overnight use. A local guidebook will often provide regulations and permit information, but such policies can change frequently, and your book may be outdated. Check online or contact the land agency for accurate information. See Chapter 7 resources in the Bibliography at the end of this book for map sources and contact numbers.

Consider asking yourself the following questions:

- Who owns and/or manages recreational use on the land that I plan to visit?
- What permits do I need to visit this area—backcountry permit, fire permit, parking permit, etc.?
- Where can I obtain these permits? How much do they cost?
- Is the permitting process different for commercial and noncommercial groups? If so, which group type is mine?
- What regulations apply—group size limits, off-trail travel policies, fire regulations, camping restrictions, etc.?
- Do I, as a trip leader, need any special qualifications in order to lead a trip here? (The answer may be different depending upon whether you are leading a group of friends or working as a paid leader.)
- Are reservations necessary? If so, how far in advance do I need to reserve?

You may find that many of the most popular backcountry areas require reservations that must be made months in advance, particularly for summer trips. If you are unable to plan that far ahead, consider visiting less popular areas.

Ignorance is no excuse for violating land-use guidelines. Although it may be tempting to try to "poach" campsites or sneak into backcountry areas without a permit and avoid rangers, it is not an admirable leadership practice, aside from being illegal, and does not inspire respect from your participants. And it not only reflects poorly on your leadership integrity but also jeopardizes the use of the area for everyone. Some of those poached sites, you were counting on, also might not be available!

Planning for Communication and Evacuation Options

No one heads out into the woods with the intention of needing a rescue or some other form of outside assistance. But many novice backcountry adventurers don't think about acquiring the knowledge and/or resources they need to be self-reliant in an emergency *before* they embark upon their journey. You, on the other hand, need to have a clear plan for coping if something goes seriously awry. This includes knowing what communication options you have for seeking outside assistance as well as what evacuation routes and methods are available to you in your expedition area.

The advent of cell phones has had monumental effects on backcountry recreation. It is all too common these days to see hikers on top of remote peaks calling in to their office to gloat about the view—or, sadly enough, to see people standing at trail junctions, cell phone in hand, seeking directions for which path to follow. Indeed, many of today's travelers consider a cell phone to be the only item they need in their survival kit.

If your buddy gets injured outside the mall, no problem: you whip out your phone, call 9-1-1, and sit back and wait a few minutes until the ambulance arrives. But because modern technology is still far from foolproof, in an emergency in the wilderness, even if you're lucky enough to get cell phone, radio, or satellite phone coverage, you still probably have to deal with stabilizing an injury, preparing the injured person for transport, evacuating the patient to definitive care, or all three of the above. Any phone contact you might be able to make with emergency services will expedite only the management of the emergency once the outside assistance meets up with your group—which may not be until your group has returned to the trailhead.

As a responsible leader, you need to know the communication points and evacuation options for your expedition route. It's a good idea

DAY	DAILY PLAN	MILEAGE	CAMPSITE	COMMUNICATION	EVACUATION ROUTE
1	hike from Rte 16 over Carter Dome to Perkins Notch	6 mi	Perkins Notch	cell phone from top of Carter Dome or seek assistance of caretaker at Carter Notch Hut	down Highwater Trail to Wild River Campground
2	hike Wild River Trail to Blue Brook	8 mi	Blue Brook	no cell coverage; seek assistance from campground host at Wild River Campground	down Highwater Trail to Wild River Campground
3	hike Basin Rim Trail to Baldface Circle Trail	9 mi	Baldface Shelter	cell phone from N. or S. Baldface Mtn., or hike out to Rte 113 and use private phone	continue down Baldface Circle Trail to Rte 113
4	hike out to Rte 113	1.9 mi	home	no cell coverage from shelter; hike out to Rte 113 and use private phone	continue down Baldface Circle Trail to Rte 113

to write them down, too, so that the information is located somewhere other than in the back of your brain. Your evacuation plan doesn't need to be a complicated format, as long as it contains the necessary information. See the accompanying chart for what a typical Outward Bound expedition plan with communication and evacuation options looks like.

Share the communication and evacuation information with your participants. It won't cause them to worry about the possibility of an injury or evacuation; rather, it will make them feel secure that there *is* a plan in case something goes wrong. Also, in the off-chance that *you* are the injured party, at least the participants will know the evacuation plan.

Finally, don't forget that even with reliable cell phone coverage and easy evacuation routes, it's still best to avoid emergencies. See "Keeping Your Group Safe" in Chapter 8, Taking Responsibility for Yourself and Others Outdoors, for strategies for managing risk in the backcountry. Here are some additional tips for being prepared in case of an emergency:

Gather local knowledge. Find out as much as you can about the area you plan to visit. Find out where a seasonal ranger is stationed, which peaks have semireliable cell phone coverage, and where there is a shortcut down to a trailhead.

Leave an itinerary. Everyone knows that when they go out into the backcountry, they should tell someone else where they're going and when to expect them back. But a surprising number of people—most, in fact—either fail to do this or else change their plans without telling the backup person of the change. For an individual adventurer, failing to leave an itinerary with someone else is careless; for an expedition leader, it's negligent. Leave an accurate itinerary with a friend or your employer and inform that party of any changes to the itinerary as soon as you are able. If your expedition ends up needing to be located, at least someone will know where to start looking.

Remember, you're not alone. Although you need to have the knowledge and presence of mind to organize and direct an evacuation if one is necessary, you don't need to carry it out single-handedly. Your participants can help you manage an emergency situation if you give them clear instructions.

Familiarizing Yourself with Your Participants' Profiles

If you have access to participants' medical profiles or trip applications, it's important to familiarize yourself with this information before heading out into the woods. Such information, in addition to helping you plan an appropriate expedition (see "Identifying the Goals of the Trip," above), can help you attend to your participants' well-being in the backcountry, diagnose conditions when illness or injury occur, and even save lives.

If you're leading a loosely organized group, or you're working for an organization that doesn't collect participants' detailed medical information, you should create your own tools for gathering pertinent health-related information from participants. You can have the participants provide this information at the pretrip meeting. Obtain the following information:

- health insurance information
- normal pulse
- normal blood pressure
- known allergies and severity of reaction: environmental (plants, pollens, insects?), food (nuts, wheat, shellfish?), drug (iodine, sulfa drugs?), etc.
- medications currently being taken (dosage and frequency); what happens if medication is not taken due to lost or forgotten dosage?
- diseases or conditions currently being treated
- medical history: broken bones, surgeries, hospitalizations, heart condition, gastrointestinal illnesses, migraines, etc.
- typical level of physical activity

Designing a Teaching Progression

As the leader of an expedition, particularly one composed of novices, you'll need to teach a lot of skills in the first couple days of a trip. Although most of these teaching topics will present themselves as participants begin asking you questions the minute you get to the trailhead ("Which trail? How many miles? How steep?") or into camp ("How does this stove work? Will you help me set up this tent? Where should I go to the bathroom?"), you'll find that things work better and the pace of

---

PARTICIPANT LEADERSHIP OPPORTUNITIES

- Assign one or two participants each day to become familiar with the communication points and evacuation options for that day's expedition route. If something should happen, these participants should be able to tell you where the nearest help can be located.
- Simulate an emergency situation and have participants identify possible ways to manage the evacuation.
- Ask your participants to teach something to the rest of the group. Find out what expertise there is within the group. Someone will know how to sew on a button, someone else will be able to identify the Little Dipper, and another will know how to treat burns. Provide time (and materials, if necessary) for preparation, and then have participants learn from each other. Note: if a participant is teaching something that you would usually teach (such as using a compass or lighting a stove), make sure beforehand that the participant is providing accurate information.

DAY ONE	DAY TWO	DAY THREE
Start: welcome and introductions, name-recall activity, overview of the plan for the day, questions	Wake up, cook and eat breakfast, Break camp, pack up, sweep camp	Wake up before dawn for a peak ascent, eat a cold breakfast, load day packs
"Duffel shuffle": ■ make sure that participants have appropriate and adequate personal clothing, footwear, and gear ■ look at group gear ■ look at food if prepacked, or pack food if not	Review plan for the day: ■ navigation lesson: route, mileage, elevation loss/gain, water sources, rate of travel ■ identify lunch site goal or time, ■ identify campsite goal ■ identify other goals for the day ■ determine roles (participant leadership, navigators, etc.)	Technical peak ascent: ■ safety considerations ■ navigation ■ technical information ■ pace, timing, turnaround time
Pack backpacks		
Overview of expedition route for whole trip		
Travel to trailhead	Hit the trail: navigation work en route, rest breaks, snack breaks, lunch, pack adjustments	
Adjust backpacks		
Tips for group travel: trail etiquette, pace, rest breaks, etc.		
Other possible teaching topics along the trail: ■ lost and alone procedures ■ water purification, hydration ■ first-aid lessons (hot spots, blisters)	Other possible teaching topics along the trail: ■ first aid: rescue breathing, sprains/strains ■ lightning procedures ■ weather patterns ■ thermal regulation	Other possible teaching topics if time: ■ navigation (compass, taking and following a bearing, triangulation) ■ natural history (local ecosystems, flora/fauna) ■ environmental ethics

Hike to camp	Navigation lesson: look at route, mileage, and elevation gain/loss	Debrief peak ascent (optional): see Chapter 8
Campsite lessons: ■ campsite selection ■ division of labor: set up camp, cook dinner, clean up, hang food, etc. ■ site setup: tents, kitchen area, food hanging line, fire (if necessary) ■ human waste disposal: outhouse, catholes, or other hygiene ■ stove use and safety ■ cooking dinner	Hike to camp Reflection time in camp	Hike back to camp
Eat dinner, clean up	Campsite lessons: ■ campsite selection (if different from first night) ■ different people cook and set up camp ■ first aid: burns	Campsite lessons: ■ campsite selection (if different from other nights) ■ different people cook and set up camp
Evening discussion (optional): See "Identifying the Goals of the Trip" ■ clarify expectations for conduct (ideally following up on pretrip meeting or pretrip information disseminated) ■ discuss plan for tomorrow	Eat dinner, clean up	Eat dinner, clean up
	Evening discussion (optional): ■ check in about the day—what went well, what needs to change? ■ plan for tomorrow (early start for peak ascent, get out of camp quickly, what to bring) ■ Go to bed early for predawn start	Evening discussion (optional): ■ check in about the day—what went well, what needs to change? ■ check in about trip so far—meeting expectations? ■ plan for tomorrow Evening lesson (optional): ■ astronomy ■ night hike

PREPARING FOR TRIPS WITH MINORS

If you're working as an outdoor professional, your employer will have obtained enrollment and medical forms from your participants. If your participants are minors, additional paperwork will be required. Such paperwork may include the following:

- "informed consent" form acknowledging the inherent risks present in wilderness travel, to be signed by a parent or guardian
- medical release form with health insurance policy information, to be signed by a parent or guardian
- travel information, if participants will be traveling to the program start independently
- information about typical concerns for parents, such as sleeping arrangements, dispensing prescription medications, going on a Solo expedition (see Chapter 9, Going Solo), etc.
- information about communication options for parents explaining whether or not, when, and how they will be able to communicate with their children during the trip (for example, mail, phone, messages left with program staff, etc.)

PARTICIPANT LEADERSHIP OPPORTUNITIES

If the structure of your trip and your institutional resources allow it, consider involving participants in the preliminary logistics. Break into four teams: food, group equipment, permits, and maps.

- The food team gathers input regarding people's preferences, allergies, and so on; they then design a menu, purchase the food, and package it appropriately for stuffing in backpacks.
- The group equipment team calculates how many tents are needed, how much fuel, etc. . . . and so on.
- The permits team figures out what permits are needed from which agencies, obtains the permits, and spreads any costs among the group.
- The maps team decides what maps are needed and obtains them.

Each team needs your guidance, but many hands make light work of the sometimes mundane chores of packing food and gathering equipment. And being involved in expedition planning is one of the best ways for your participants to learn some of the skills they'll need in order to lead their own expeditions.

instruction is not as frenetic if you plan out your teaching progression ahead of time.

One of the ways that Outward Bound instructors demonstrate competent leadership and begin to impart leadership skills to their students is by modeling a clear, logical teaching progression with expedition skills. Outward Bound instructors call these initial teaching progressions their "Three-Day Plan" or "Seventy-Two-Hour Plan," and they list in detail what subjects will be taught, by which instructor, and when. That way, the instructional relationship runs smoothly because all instructors know what they are responsible for teaching, and topics are presented in a logical and timely manner. During these first three days, nearly all of the basic concepts of backcountry travel are covered, from stove lighting to water purification to toothbrushing to wildlife encounters to what to do if a participant gets separated from the group.

The sequence of the topics of each three-day plan is designed to match the itinerary of each expedition. For example, if your group is camping near a potable water source your first night, you don't need to teach water purification until the need arises. But there are themes common to all expeditions. You can adapt the three-day plan shown in the accompanying chart to meet the needs of your expedition and to match your participants' knowledge and abilities.

Leading a Trip for an Institution

If you are leading a trip for an institution, such as a university outdoor program or a local outing club, it's likely that you will not be able to choose either your trip participants or your expedition goals. In such situations, you must clarify several questions:

- Is there any sort of participant screening done prior to trips? If so, what guidelines are used?
- What educational or other types of goals will you be expected to address?
- What is the anticipated leader-to-participant ratio? Is this ratio appropriate for the activity, location, and maturity of the participants?
- What policies and protocols will you be expected to adhere to?

You may find that you disagree with some of the goals, policies, or protocols dictated by the organization you're working for; however, you have a responsibility to adhere to them. You may find that some of the participants are not necessarily people with whom you would choose to spend time; however, you have a responsibility to be courteous and welcoming to them and to give them all equal amounts of your leadership energy.

The process of planning a trip for an institution is almost identical to the process of planning a trip for a group of friends. The only real difference is that you will likely have the benefit of the institution's organizational systems, such as expedition area information, food planning resources, and equipment stocks. The pretrip meeting becomes even more important, because it is an opportunity for participants to meet each other, learn more about the trip, and establish confidence in you, the professional outdoor trip leader.

If you find that the burden of working as a professional outdoor educator—usually leading someone else's trips with a random group of participants—is

too great, you may decide to stick to leading trips for friends, coworkers, or family members.

If your organization does not use such information, or if you are a self-employed outdoor professional, you should consult with an attorney for advice about your legal and ethical professional responsibility and liability. The only circumstance in which no paperwork would be required is an informal trip, such as taking your children's friends on an overnight camping trip—but even in that situation, it is advisable to have a signed note from the parents granting you permission to supervise and seek emergency medical attention for their children.

Packing for the Trip

Once you've done all the route and evacuation planning for your trip, packing your packs should be the easy part, right? Right, as long as everyone has adequate clothing and gear and you don't forget the food and stoves.

Providing Equipment Lists

One of the best ways to demonstrate your compassion as a leader is to provide your participants with information about and access to the clothing and equipment that will keep them comfortable out on a trip. You may have your own systems all worked out perfectly, from your down jacket to your fleece socks, but you must also pass this information on to your participants and help them pull together their own equally comfortable gear. Being out in the wilderness can cause enough anxiety in itself, but inadequate clothing creates even more discomfort. In order to benefit from the experience, your participants need to have their basic needs met, and one of these is ample clothing and equipment to keep them comfortable and dry.

I was once enlisted to lead a trip in the Sierra for a private high school whose leader had gotten sick at the last minute. All the preparations, from route planning to packing the backpacks, had already been done. I met the group at the trailhead literally four hours after I received the plea for help. We introduced ourselves, I asked which of the teacher chaperones was carrying the first-aid kit, and we threw our packs on and set off down the trail. As we walked, I marveled at my luck in avoiding the most unpleasant part of any expedition: planning and packing.

When we reached camp, however, my self-congratulation turned into dismay. The participants began pulling their clothing and equipment out of their backpacks and I saw thick cotton sweatshirts, blue jeans, and gigantic D-battery flashlights. At this point, I knew what the sleeping bags were going to look like before I even saw one get rolled out: flannel-lined rectangular cotton bags more suited for a backyard sleepover than a fall trip at 8000 feet. And when the first snack was pulled out (sweetened papaya spears, ten pounds of which served as our only snack for the entire four-day trip), I knew that I should have somehow involved myself in packing for the trip despite my late conscription.

To their credit, the participants were largely uncomplaining, and we had a perfectly decent hike. But the participants were pretty chilly a lot of the time, and much of my energy went into keeping them active and figuring out ways to insulate them from the cold ground at night. And a lot of the time, I was wrestling with inner debates about whether I should keep my warm fleece jacket on or lend it to a participant and spend the evening shivering myself.

Numerous resources address the topic of what to put in your pack when you've finally decided to head outdoors. The secret to good packing is to identify the things you really need and to pack only those items. That way, you'll be prepared but you won't be hauling an unnecessarily large pack around. But learning to identify what you really need comes only with experience, and the more experienced you are in the backcountry, the more comfortable you will be in taking fewer items. Chapter 7 resources in the Bibliography at the end of this book provide several versions of packing lists, as well as philosophies about gear weight, fabric selection, and function.

Once you've determined what gear you and your participants will need to take on your trip, disseminate this information to participants as soon as possible, so that they have ample time to collect the necessary gear. If you're working with novices, provide specific details about each item of gear; for example, don't just list "three pairs of socks," but list "three pairs of midweight wool or polypropylene or other synthetic socks—no cotton." Encourage participants to borrow, rent, or shop at thrift stores so that equipping themselves for the trip remains affordable. If you have access to clothing and equipment that can be loaned, such as from a university outdoor program, let participants know what gear is available for loan.

Inspecting Gear: The "Duffel Shuffle"

The next step is to ensure that your participants have the right *amount* of the right gear, and there is really no way to make certain of this without physically inspecting each person's equipment. Otherwise, the item that you listed as "synthetic long underwear" could end up being cotton waffle-weave long johns that will be absolutely useless once they're wet.

There are a couple of ways that you can tackle the equipment inspection, but whatever system you use, it's critical to make sure that when the group heads out on your expedition, all participants are carrying appropriate amounts of suitable equipment. Your responsibility for your participants' well-being begins with ensuring that they're adequately equipped, and your job of taking care of them in the wilderness will be a lot easier if you take time before the trip to deal with gear.

One method of gear inspection is the way Outward Bound instructors begin their courses: with a "duffel shuffle," a process in which the leaders help participants sort through their personal clothing and equipment to determine whether the participants have the appropriate clothes and gear for the expedition. This is also a chance for leaders to help participants pare down the heaps of clothes they hope to bring into a manageable stuff sack that will be conducive to backpacking. A good, thorough duffel shuffle with novice backpackers can take up to two hours, so allow for this extra time.

Here's the way a duffel shuffle works. The participants move into a wide circle or some other arrangement where everyone can hear and see the leader. If you're outside, you can spread out some small ground cloths or sleeping pads on the ground—something on which your participants can pile clean clothes (no sense getting clothes dirty any sooner than necessary). If you're inside, you can use a clean floor for this purpose. You read items off the equipment list—the exact same list that you sent the participants before the trip—and participants remove each item from their suitcase and place it on the floor or mat. You walk around the group and look at the items, making sure that they are appropriate for the conditions or terrain. Sometimes actually feeling the item may be necessary; for example, make sure that rain jackets feel as though they can shed rain and that sleeping bags have enough loft for the expected nighttime temperatures. Take care not to make participants feel uncomfortable about your handling their personal equipment, but get a good look at things to make sure that they have the right stuff; it will be important out in the woods.

What if a participant doesn't have the proper item? Tactfully explain why a particular item is inadequate. For instance, you could say, "This breathable rain jacket is perfect for most alpine environments, but because our trip is happening in the rain forest, let's find you something that is really waterproof."

Ideally, you'll be working for an organization that will have equipment available for loan. If so, you simply lend a suitable replacement item. If not, you might find out whether anyone else in the group has extra equipment that could be lent. Or you might have things you're willing to loan. If you're regularly leading trips on your own, it wouldn't hurt to start a small lending wardrobe. You can find a lot of excellent outdoor wear at thrift stores, for instance. If none of these options works and there is still time before the start of the trip, you might need to ask the participant to purchase or rent suitable gear elsewhere.

What if a participant doesn't have enough equipment? Again, tactfully explain why the

---

EQUIPMENT PACKING TIPS

■ **Use a checklist.** My friend Landon keeps his personal and group equipment lists on his personal digital assistant (PDA). Geeky, yes, but it's effective, particularly for someone who doesn't keep his pack ready at all times anymore. The checklists ensure that he doesn't forget those easy-to-overlook-but-essential items such as a sleeping bag or a spoon, and having the lists on his PDA ensures that they are easily edited or printed for others' use.

■ **Encourage sharing.** Every participant doesn't need a large tube of toothpaste, a bottle of sunscreen, or a can of insect repellent. Participants can team up in pairs or trios to share such items.

■ **Encourage loaning.** Many people come overequipped for trips. It takes a bit of shrewdness, but you can frequently assess whether people would be willing to loan extra items of clothing to someone who doesn't have adequate gear. Approach potential lenders quietly and ask how they'd feel about loaning a particular item to so-and-so for the duration of the trip. Read their body language and if it seems uncomfortable, quickly drop the subject and find another source.

participant might want more equipment. For example, you could say, "Hmm, temperatures have been pretty chilly up in the mountains lately, and it's been raining. I think you're going to be happiest if you bring four pairs of socks rather than just two. Let's see if we can find you a couple more pairs." Then repeat the process described above to help the participant obtain necessary gear.

What if a participant has too much equipment? The thought of leaving behind things such as a clean tee shirt for each day of the trip, deodorant, and D-battery flashlights is often inconceivable to participants. Explain that you think they are bringing too much gear. For instance, you might say, "Wow, you have a lot of really nice equipment. But it's looking like your pack is going to weigh more than 60 pounds by the time we add food and camping equipment, and I don't think you'll be happy carrying that much weight. Let's see what we can pare down." Help these participants weed out the extra items, put them in a bag, and have them feel how much extra weight you helped them eliminate; out on the trail, these participants will quickly realize how extraneous these items are. It's possible that these participants will be willing to lend some of this extra equipment to someone else, if needed.

Doing a Quicker Gear Inspection

Another, quicker option for equipment inspection is to simply ask participants to spread out the things they've brought on a mat. Walk around and quickly sort through their equipment, suggesting that participants leave behind particular things and helping them supplement their supply if necessary. There is less participant involvement with this method, but if time is tight, it's an effective system.

You must make absolutely sure, however, that you don't fail to notice if a participant is missing a critical item. For example, if a participant doesn't pile a headlamp on the mat and you don't notice it's missing, you'll have an uncomfortable situation once you get out in the woods and realize the mistake.

Planning Food and Cooking

One of the greatest pleasures of a backcountry trip is sitting down to a well-cooked, well-earned meal. Whether you've packed simple whole foods or gourmet, freeze-dried extravaganzas, it all tastes good in the wilderness—provided you prepare it properly.

Backcountry food and nutrition is a huge topic that cannot be adequately addressed here, but, fortunately, there are numerous excellent resources on this subject. The Chapter 7 food and cooking resources listed in the Bibliography at the end of this book can help you familiarize yourself with various food-planning systems. As you experiment with different systems, you will likely find the one that works best for you.

As a leader, you need to decide how to cook the food you're bringing: in small groups, or in one large pot? This decision may seem insignificant, but your food-preparation system will actually have a great impact on your trip. Neither system is superior, but each has its own benefits and drawbacks.

One large cooking group: Cooking as a single large group takes a long time, but it fosters a sense of community and ultimately saves weight (because you minimize the total number of stoves and pots the group must carry). Cooking in groups larger than ten or twelve people, however, is extremely difficult to do well on typical backcountry expeditions; the exception to this are trips with extensive logistical support systems, such as rafting trips or large mountaineering expeditions.

Several small cooking groups: Cooking in small groups of three or four is more efficient and enables more people to become proficient cooks, but it can create a sense of segregation unless cooking groups are rotated frequently.

If your cooking equipment allows for either option, you could present both systems to your participants, explaining the pros and cons of each system. After a discussion about what outcomes your participants might hope to achieve from their food system, decide which method is more suitable.

OUTWARD BOUND INSTRUCTORS' FAVORITE FOOD TIPS

- **Plan ahead:** While dinner is cooking, plan your food for the next day. If you're planning a long day with an early start, select a no-cook breakfast and put it aside. Sort the food you'll need for tomorrow on the trail into one or two other stuff sacks. Plan simple meals for long days, and use easy days to prepare the more time-consuming meals.

- **Eat often:** At home we think about eating three square meals per day, but in the backcountry you will use your calories more efficiently if you eat five times per day: breakfast, morning snack, lunch, afternoon snack, and dinner. If you are exercising vigorously, you will also find yourself less ravenous and cranky if you eat more frequently throughout the day. Eat before you get ravenous.

- **Pack individual snack bags:** Rather than having one large bag of trail mix to be pulled out for a midmorning snack to be shared among the group, divide the large bag into individual snack bags for each participant the night before. That way everyone can snack throughout the day according to individual needs, rather than waiting for a group-determined snack break. This approach also minimizes germ-sharing.

- **Keep snacks accessible:** Pack lunch and snacks in the top or side pockets of your packs for easy access.

- **Start slow-cooking food early:** Presoak foods that take a long time to cook, such as dried beans. As soon as you get to camp, put the beans in a pot of cold water. Then when you're ready to cook them, they will have absorbed some of the water, thus reducing the cooking time. If you are camping at the same place for multiple nights, put the beans to soak in the morning.

- **Oil the pot:** Prior to cooking starches or grains, rub the inside of your cooking pot with margarine or oil. This makes cleanup easier and prevents boiling over.

- **Be creative with leftovers:** Think of ways to use leftovers creatively and appetizingly. Leftover split pea soup can be thickened with a few potato flakes and spread on crackers for lunch. Leftover rice can be kneaded into bread dough, fried up with spices, or made into rice pudding by adding milk, sugar, raisins, and nutmeg or cinnamon. Have everyone bring a screw-top hard-plastic (Nalgene-type) container instead of a bowl. Then if there are leftovers, you can store them in people's containers for later consumption.

- **Make hot drinks for more than one person:** When making tea or cocoa, make a full pot for several people. Use two or three tea bags, or mix several large spoonfuls of instant cocoa into the pot. This uses fewer tea bags or cocoa than if all the participants mix their own drink in their own mug.

- **Drink, drink, drink:** You need water to digest your food, particularly with a diet that doesn't include a lot of juicy, fresh fruits and vegetables.

- **Use dried fruits and vegetables:** Rehydrated dried fruits and veggies can make a potentially bland meal seem almost gourmet. Even if you don't have access to a food dehydrator, you can make your own dried fruits and vegetables in the oven. Place thin slices of raw produce on parchment-lined cookie sheets and bake on low heat (200°F) until they are crisp. In camp, throw handfuls into soup, pasta, or grains while cooking to add color and flavor. Our favorites include carrots, beets, onions, olives, mushrooms, zucchini, apples, cherries, apricots, and bananas.

A separate cooking group for leaders: From a leadership perspective, another food decision is whether or not you, the leader, will cook and eat with your participants. On a short trip or with very young participants, it makes sense for the leader to share food with the rest of the group. But on a longer trip, particularly with a group of mature adults, it can be very productive for the group if the leaders separate themselves from the group food scene. It gives participants complete ownership of the quality and timing of their own meals and an increased sense of independence.

The leaders can't withdraw themselves from the group food system until the participants have the skills to prepare their own meals, of course, but if you have quick learners and if your meals aren't exceptionally complicated, you could cook with your participants for the first three or four days of the trip and then start cooking your own food separately. If you use this system, make sure that the food you bring for yourself is identical to the participants' food. It can breed resentment if you're eating freeze-dried sirloin tips while the participants are cooking up beans and rice.

A FINAL NOTE

Before you go through the process of planning an expedition for a group, give yourself a few practice runs by planning some personal expeditions or trips with a friend or two. Work through the kinks of route planning and permitting, get comfortable with your gear, develop some simple but tasty meals, and perfect your own campcraft skills. Without the pressure of being in an official leadership role, you will gain the experience you need to operate as a competent and confident leader when you finally do take a group out into the woods.

PARTICIPANT LEADERSHIP OPPORTUNITIES

In the backcountry, food becomes a favorite topic of conversation, and having it prepared well, in appropriate quantities, at suitable times brings everyone on the trip great joy. Thus, food and cooking provide one of the greatest participant leadership opportunities around. Yet leaders who are overly involved in food preparation tend to assert their presence in subtle but powerful ways. One of the best ways to empower participants is to hand responsibility for the food over to them as much as possible.

- **Involve participants from the beginning:** Have them help with food preparation right away, even with menu planning and shopping, if possible. Help them create a system for food storage and organization.
- **Provide suggestions:** For instance, you could say, "We might want to choose a quick dinner because we're doing a night hike tonight." But always let participants decide what to eat for particular meals.
- **Encourage and support creativity:** If participants want to cook quesadillas at lunch rather than eating cold tortillas and cheese, why not? (Make sure your fuel supply is sufficient.) If participants want to make pancakes for dinner and macaroni for breakfast, let them.
- **Step out of the way:** If you're the kind of leader who always hovers over the stove because you're perpetually hungry, pack yourself a few extra energy bars and eat one as soon as you get into camp. That way you will be able to step back and let the participants have control over the preparation and timing of the evening meal.

CHAPTER 8

TAKING RESPONSIBILITY FOR YOURSELF AND OTHERS OUTDOORS

OK, you've done most of the work of expedition planning; the food is packed, the maps are folded, and your participants are standing at the trailhead with their packs on, ready to hike. Half a dozen or so pairs of eyes now look to you for leadership. Suddenly you realize, "Wow, these people expect me to do something. What am I supposed to do?!"

First of all, remind yourself what the function of a leader is. Chapter 2, Becoming a Leader, refers to leadership as "the art of mobilizing others to want to work together to achieve shared goals." Author and mountaineer John Graham provides a similar perspective in *Outdoor Leadership,* calling leadership "the capacity to move others toward goals shared with you, with a focus and competency they would not achieve on their own."

So your responsibility out in the wilderness is to organize others to get things done—better yet, to get them to do things with enthusiasm. You've already had some experience doing this by planning for your trip—expedition planning can be a daunting logistical feat, and you've gotten that done. But expedition planning deals mostly with gear (which is static and generally predictable), and now that you're out in the woods, you're dealing mostly with people, who (unlike gear) are dynamic and often unpredictable.

Whereas Chapter 7 focuses largely on the logistics of expedition planning, this chapter presents the "human" side of outdoor leadership, beginning with some leadership basics for the outdoors. Other sections of this chapter discuss the group dynamics of and leadership strategies for outdoor expeditions including interpersonal communication, leadership styles, and facilitation skills. Last, this chapter examines some specifics for leading an expedition.

So whether you're an aspiring outdoor leader, a committed volunteer leader, or a seasoned outdoor instructor looking for new techniques, this chapter helps you take a look at the interpersonal side of outdoor leadership.

LEADERSHIP BASICS FOR THE OUTDOORS

No matter what type of outdoor trip you want to lead—as a professional leader for an outdoor organization, as a volunteer leader for a community group, or as an informal leader of outings with your friends—you must consider some fundamental principles of human interaction, many of which are addressed in Part I, Leadership Fundamentals. Examining your leadership motivations, establishing and maintaining credibility, communicating effectively, and understanding different leadership styles are among these. In an outdoor leadership context, it's also important to be able to fill a variety of roles and understand how to employ a flexible leadership approach to best meet the needs of a particular situation.

Examining Your Motives for Being an Outdoor Leader

Maybe you're the kind of person whose favorite place to be is out in the woods, in the desert, or on the rock. Perhaps you realized that you can earn a living doing your favorite activities, so you immediately set out to get a job as an outdoor leader. Your technical-skills resume is impressive, and you are articulate and charismatic, so you were hired by an organization right away. You're about to spend the summer doing what you love and getting paid for it.

Or say you work long hours in the office but spend every weekend in the mountains. Your boss recently asked you to lead a company team-building camping trip. You'll get to use work time to plan and lead the trip for a dozen of the company managers. If it goes well, it will be an annual event.

In either of these scenarios, you've got it made, right?

Perhaps. But as the start date of your first trip approaches, you begin to wonder what you've gotten yourself into. Sometimes moving from being a competent outdoor adventurer to a competent outdoor leader requires a bit of a mental shift.

Try asking yourself why you want to be an outdoor leader or, if you already are one, why you do it. There are no right or wrong answers, but some answers might indicate whether you will enjoy and be good at leading in the outdoors. For instance, if you're leading because it's a way to get paid to be in the mountains, you'll quickly realize that being responsible for a group of people in the mountains is vastly different from—and harder than—being in the mountains on personal trips. For other motivational indicators, see "What Motivates You?" in Chapter 1, Why Learn Leadership from Outward Bound?, in Part I, Leadership Fundamentals.

Any sort of leadership role is demanding, and outdoor leadership is particularly draining, both emotionally and physically, because you can't escape from it at night or on weekends as you might do with another type of leadership job. Most of outdoor leadership is dealing with people—not summiting peaks or exploring uncharted terrain—so if you're not interested in working closely with others, you might want to reconsider your decision to become an outdoor leader. But the motivations listed below probably indicate that you will enjoy a satisfying experience of outdoor leadership:

You want to be (or are already) an outdoor leader because you get satisfaction from seeing people do things in the wilderness that they didn't know they could do.

Or maybe you love working with people, and the wilderness brings out people's true nature in a way that can't be accomplished back in civilization.

Or perhaps you've found that being in the wilderness makes you feel more alive and at peace with yourself, and you want to share this experience with others.

Establishing Credibility and Maintaining Integrity as an Outdoor Leader

As discussed in Chapter 2, Becoming a Leader, in Part I, Leadership Fundamentals, people tend to trust those in leadership positions until the leaders do something to jeopardize this trust and respect. As an outdoor leader, you have a responsibility to maintain your participants' trust by modeling and upholding the values of your group or the organization you're working for. The values your participants and/or your organization expect you to model as an outdoor leader are probably things such as the following: respect for others, an environmental ethic, and a sense of challenge and adventure. By demonstrating your commitment to these values, you establish your integrity.

As mentioned "Avoiding Leadership Failures" in Chapter 2, Becoming a Leader, leadership failures generally occur when either (1) the leader does not consistently uphold group values or (2) the group members do not uniformly subscribe to these values. In either situation, both the integrity of the leader and the success of the trip are jeopardized.

To illustrate the first way that leadership breaks down in an outdoor context, imagine that while you're getting packed up, you ask participants to leave behind all electronic ties to the outside world—cell phones, pagers, PDAs (personal digital assistants)—because you want everyone to live in the present and put their emotional energy into the trip. But then your participants notice that you're using the trip's "emergency" cell phone to call your mother to wish her a happy birthday. Your participants are resentful that you have set a double standard and that you expect *them* to put *their* emotional energy into the trip while you continue to maintain your personal outside life. There will be some double standards that your participants will understand and accept as part of your job, but others will seem simply unfair. When you promote double standards that participants consider unjust, your credibility as a leader suffers.

The second type of leadership breakdown might look something like this in the wilderness. Let's say that one of the objectives of your trip is to complete some trail work as a service project. But what happens if some of the participants decide that they aren't interested in participating in any trail restoration projects—they just want to eat, sleep, and knock off each day's mileage? You are suddenly faced with two "camps" of participants subscribing to different values regarding service, and you are forced to choose between them. You have a professional responsibility to uphold your organization's service ethic and thus must "choose" to align yourself with the camp of members who are still willing to perform trail work. Your integrity forces you to side with these participants, yet you have a similar moral responsibility to maintain a good relationship with those participants who simply want to hike. Your challenge now is to hold all the participants accountable to the value of service without alienating the participants who are rejecting it.

Maintaining your integrity can be a tricky business if you allow yourself to succumb to many blatant double standards or if your desire to be liked by all your participants clouds your ability to uphold particular values. But your trips will ultimately be more successful—and you will develop into a more confident and effective leader—if you model a high and consistent standard for personal behavior.

Learning Your Many Roles as an Outdoor Leader

In the same way that a brilliant classroom teacher can make a subject fascinating or dull regardless of its nature and content, an outdoor leader has the ability to determine the success or failure of a backcountry expedition regardless of weather and other circumstances. It's both a tremendous power and a tremendous responsibility. But what exactly does an outdoor leader *do* out there in the backcountry? The answer is more complex than most people might guess.

Whenever I'm on a plane and the stranger next to me engages me in conversation, he or she inevitably asks me what I "do." When I respond that I'm an Outward Bound instructor, people unfailingly have one of two reactions. They either look puzzled and wonder what Outward Bound is—in which case I give a brief description of Outward Bound and the instructor's role and return to reading my book—or else they sigh wistfully, "Oh, that must be so much fun."

I think that when people picture Outward Bound instructors on the job, they envision us paddling happily down a placid river, joking with our students on top of mountain peaks under cloudless skies, or sitting around a campfire passing out marshmallows. No one sees us scanning the horizon as we debate whether an approaching storm is going to hinder our summit attempt, or mediating a conflict between two quarrelling adults, or figuring out how to coax some student leadership out of a group of introverts.

It's true that some of the time on the job—such as when the sun is shining, the students are happy, and I'm looking forward to a good dinner in camp—I think, "They pay me to do this?" But most of the time, the work is very demanding. I have to be in tune with the weather, with a co-instructor, and with the emotional and physical energies of a group of students. I have to create an expedition that is challenging but realistic. I have to build rapport with individuals and help them reach their goals while concurrently creating a sense of group identity and shared goals. It's rewarding, far more than any other job I've had, but it's incredibly challenging, too.

*And I get only one chance to do it right for
each group of students. If I mess up, two or
three weeks later those students are gone and
they haven't had the best Outward Bound
experience that they could have had.*

*So when a stranger on the airplane tells
me how much fun my job must be, I just
smile and nod. I guess it all depends upon
your definition of "fun."*
— *Sarah, Outward Bound instructor
since 1995*

An outdoor leader wears many hats, as illustrated in former Outward Bound instructor Ken Kalisch's book *The Role of the Instructor in the Outward Bound Educational Process*. A snapshot of Kalisch's book shows us a multifaceted outdoor leader who is a "skill trainer, program designer, translator, group facilitator, and one-on-one counselor." In this chapter, we use "interpreter" for translator, and "coach" for one-on-one-counselor, and we've added the concept of follower, a key role at times for any good leader. The roles are sometimes hard to separate from each other, but at any given moment an outdoor leader may be performing one or more of these particular functions.

Although not every outdoor organization requires its leaders to wear so many different hats, many outdoor leadership job qualifications have been modeled on the Outward Bound instructor profile. According to Kalisch's model, the instructor's role includes the functions described below, which can be applied to any outdoor leadership position. As you think about your own role as an outdoor leader, consider your ability to perform these functions.

Skill Trainer

A critical distinction that you as an outdoor leader—or your employing organization—must make is whether your role is that of a skill trainer or a guide. A *skill trainer*'s goal is to teach participants how to take care of themselves, camp, and travel safely in the backcountry. A *guide*'s goal is to take care of participants and lead them safely through the backcountry. A guide might do a bit of skill training, and vice versa, but the two roles have markedly different goals with respect to participant independence and responsibility. Outward Bound, of course, calls its leaders "instructors" for the express reason that they are skill trainers, teachers, and educators, not simply guides. There are a couple of reasons why you might make this same decision to instruct and train participants, rather than simply guiding them.

First, the primary role of an outdoor leader is to lead a group safely through a backcountry trip, and the best tool for ensuring participant safety is to teach the participants how to do things well in the woods. Think about it: if you are the only person out there who really knows how to light a stove, read a map, or interpret weather patterns, then the burden of participant safety falls entirely on your shoulders. If, on the other hand, participants all know how to set up a dry tent in the rain, identify the early signs of hypothermia, and set up a fixed line, then you have a whole lot of eager assistants in safety management.

Second, and more importantly for Outward Bound's purposes, learning skills and using them to solve real problems gives participants a sense of confidence, which supports Outward Bound's ultimate goal of character development. Consider the following scenario:

*It's raining, and your group has just
straggled into camp after a long day. As
participants scurry about putting on warm
clothes and setting up tarps, Sarah notices
that Joey is just standing there, staring dejectedly at the ground. After a quick conversation with Joey, Sarah organizes the other
participants to get some hot water going. She
helps Joey change into dry clothes, feeds him
some trail mix, and sits him under a tarp with
a mug of hot tea. Later that evening, Joey
thanks the group for helping him come back
from the brink of hypothermia.*

> ## TIP: THE TEACHABLE MOMENT
> Seasoned outdoor leaders frequently refer to the "teachable moment"—when the conditions, the conversation, or the social environment in a group presents an opportunity to teach something relevant. The classic teachable moment might be something like this:
>
> The group is sitting down for lunch on the second day of an outing. One participant glances overhead and wonders, "Why are there all those thin, wispy clouds in the sky?" The leader seizes this opportunity to deliver an impromptu lesson in interpreting cirrus clouds and planning ahead for impending rainy weather.
>
> Take advantage of these teachable moments whenever they arise, even if they present a divergence from the planned teaching progression—and they usually do.

The participants are empowered by having helped Joey through a tough time and by realizing that they are strong enough to cope when conditions are challenging. If you had helped Joey, the end result for Joey would have been the same: he would have become warm again. But the opportunity to empower the other participants, particularly Sarah, would have been missed. It is this sense of confidence—derived from realizing that they possess the skills to deal effectively with a particular problem—that Outward Bound seeks to promote in its students and that you can instill in your participants if you choose to train them rather than take care of them.

The balance you strike between being a skill trainer and being a guide will depend upon you or your organization's mission and the type of participants you are dealing with. But most participants will appreciate learning, at the least, the outdoor skills that apply to meeting their basic needs in the wilderness. So even if you're in a guide role, you should offer participants opportunities to learn at least the basic personal-care skills related to dressing appropriately for the conditions, getting enough calories, and staying hydrated.

Program Designer

In designing your outdoor program, you are responsible for considering participant needs, abilities, and goals as well as institutional curricula and goals. You also have to create an experience that is effective, meaningful, and replicable. Outward Bound instructors have a lot of support in program design, and, depending on how well established the organization you're working for is, you may have similar support.

However, no matter how much guidance you have in designing your program, once you're out in the field, you will need to adapt and modify your carefully constructed curriculum according to participant needs or changes in the physical or social environment. The successful program designer will be able to assess when the planned itinerary or program will meet participant and trip goals and when the itinerary should be changed.

I once had a group of fifteen-year-olds who were the fastest hikers and most proficient campers an instructor could ever dream of. At first, the other instructor and I would take a break to give the group some space, but once it took us more than an hour to regain a ten-minute lead we had given the group, so we quickly discontinued that practice. Tents would be set up and water boiling within twenty minutes of reaching camp, and packing up the next morning was almost as quick.

The only problem with this group was that as soon as there was any genuine leisure time, the students would start squabbling. The girls bickered among themselves, the boys picked on the girls, friendships blossomed and flared, and general negativity was the prevalent social norm. As long as there was a task to keep them occupied, the students functioned together harmoniously, but as soon as they were left to their own devices, they quickly dissolved into nitpickers and bad-mouthers.

After trying every method we knew to address this lack of group unity, the other instructor and I realized that the best option was simply to keep them busy. That two-week course became an exercise in program design for us, as we constantly adapted the itinerary and activities to accommodate the students' needs. They were such fast hikers that we ended up adding almost 60 miles to the original itinerary. And because we needed to keep them gainfully occupied virtually all of the time, we taught advanced technical skills that we wouldn't normally teach on a fourteen-day course, such as constructing a Tyrolean traverse over a stream crossing and making a raft out of scavenged materials to cross a pond.

—Gretchen, Outward Bound instructor, 1999–2002

An awareness of your participants' abilities, as well as your ability to accommodate unexpected situations, will make it possible for you to make effective changes in your program design. For example, you might be planning an ambitious peak ascent on Day Four of an outing, but when dawn breaks that day, you notice big thunderheads in the sky. Here, the motive for changing the itinerary is obvious and irrefutable, and the experienced leader will have a backup plan for the day. But what if the day breaks gloriously clear, yet you are aware of friction within the group that you sense might limit the participants' ability to work as a team to reach the summit? The need to

change the itinerary in this situation is more subtle but just as compelling, and again the experienced leader will choose to address the friction instead of bagging the peak.

Interpreter

For an Outward Bound experience to be successful, it must be value-forming, which means that it must inspire the students to use what they have learned about their own strengths and abilities and influence their decisions and performance in other situations. Occasionally your participants will grasp this intuitively on their own, but more frequently they will need you to help them link the relationship between themselves and the experience. As a leader, you will need to, in Kalisch's words, "play an instrumental role in helping each learner translate his raw experience into organized words and concepts which in turn will embellish the experience with meaning and significance." In other words, your participants will often need you to help them find meaning in an experience.

I remember hiking for 5 miles behind a participant who was really struggling with her pack, with the steepness of the trail, and with the rapid pace of the rest of the group. The participant never complained, but I could tell that she was really working hard to maintain her calm. When we reached the top of the peak—bare and windswept, with views stretching all around us for miles—this participant burst into tears. "I've never done anything like this before," she sobbed. "I've never seen anything so beautiful. I didn't know that such a thing was possible."

As we hiked down from the summit, I asked the participant what she meant when she said that she didn't know that such a thing was possible. She told me that as a rather sedentary smoker, she had expected to struggle with the physical aspects of the course, but she hadn't really understood that reaching the top of the mountain would produce such a flood of emotion. The heart-pounding struggle to the top, the beauty of the view, the near-disbelief that she had reached the top under her own steam—all had released in her feelings that she had never had before.

I then asked her what she thought that this might mean for her life. She was silent for a long time and then responded that at home, she frequently didn't begin projects or didn't try things, because she thought that the effort wouldn't be worth the end result. "This morning," she said, "was no different. You told us that we would have a hard, steep hike up to the top of the mountain. I thought to myself, 'Is it worth the struggle just to sit on top of a mountain?' To me, the answer at the time was clearly 'No!' And if I had had a choice, I wouldn't have chosen to climb that mountain. But having been on top, I know how wonderful it felt, and I would do it again in a second. The reward was well worth the struggle. I hope that I can take this memory home with me—the desire to undertake something difficult even if I don't initially think that the reward will be worth the effort."

This participant might have reached this realization on her own, without my further questioning. But she also might have just gone home with the memory of the beauty of a windswept summit, a bit sad that she might never feel such joy again but unaware of what effect this experience could have on the rest of her life.

"Fun," "eye-opening," or "entertaining" experiences might suffice for noneducational outdoor programs, but if the experience you're structuring is to be educational, most likely you need to be involved in helping participants figure out what, if any, meaning the experience holds for them. See

"Interpreting the Meaning of Experiences" later in this chapter for more on this subject.

Group Facilitator
As noted in Chapter 4, Building Trust, Building a Team, in Part I, Leadership Fundamentals, groups move through fairly predictable stages of development, some of which require leader intervention. Although some groups just "click," functioning almost effortlessly as an effective unit, most realize their potential more fully under the nurturing guidance of the leader, who, as Kalisch notes, makes "interventions as needed to stimulate and encourage the development of positive relationships among group members." The proverbial "well-oiled machine" usually needs someone—the leader—to oil it in order for it to run smoothly.

Once I was trailing a group of seventeen-year-old boys on the final expedition of their course. It was Day Twenty-four of a twenty-eight-day course, and this was a fairly strong group; they were generally respectful of each other, and some good friendships seemed to have formed without the debilitating presence of cliques. Arguments were rare and were usually resolved quickly in a surprisingly mature way.

I came around the corner on a trail and noticed the group standing in a circle, packs off, postures aggressive and defiant. There was some sort of heated discussion underway, and as I walked closer I realized that they were arguing about the compost bag, which lay at the boys' feet in the center of the circle. The compost bag was a plastic bag, weighing about five or six pounds, full of the leftover food from the past week. It wasn't the most desirable object to have in one's pack, but it wasn't leaking or smelly or anything like that.

The boys were shouting at each other and swearing a lot; the argument didn't seem *to be nearing resolution. I had to decide if I should intervene or not, and after some deliberation, I decided to remain partially hidden behind a tree. It was late in the course, the group had been functioning effectively, and the boys had the skills and maturity to resolve the issue effectively on their own, which they ultimately did. Had it been earlier in the course, I would have stepped in to facilitate a more rational, respectful discussion.*

Out in the woods, you will spend a lot of time debating—with yourself or with a co-leader—whether or not to intervene in a particular situation, how to intervene, and when to intervene. Intervening is a skill that requires some finesse as well as an understanding of the likely results of a particular intervention. Before intervening, you must consider both the importance of the outcome of the situation and the value of the process.

Coach

Most of us have had an influential "coach" in our lives—someone who encouraged us to push ourselves, to set ambitious goals, and to do things that we didn't think we could do. The outdoor leader's role as a coach is no different. Because backcountry expeditions can be intense experiences, they cause stress and anxiety for some participants. It is your responsibility to help participants cope with this anxiety in a way that produces meaningful, lasting growth. This coaching takes the form of helping the participants explore emotions, set and achieve goals, solve problems, develop confidence, and become more self-aware.

For example, one participant might be reluctant to serve as the group's navigator. You ask the participant a few questions and learn that he's nervous because interpreting the maps is such a large responsibility and he's not sure that he can do it accurately. He has a history of messing up important projects at home and at school, and

he's pretty sure that he would mess up navigating too. You ask him what's the worst thing that can happen if he messes up the navigation, and he responds that the group might get lost. When you reassure him that it is early in the expedition and that you won't let things go that far, he relaxes.

You pair him with another participant who has good map interpretation skills but a quiet, humble leadership presence. Together the two participants complete the day's navigation successfully. You set the participant up for success by pairing him with someone supportive, and the successful experience will bolster his confidence the next time he's in a similar situation.

You don't need to be a cheerleader, providing constant and unconditional encouragement. Instead, you can first encourage participants to become self-reliant and able to meet their own basic needs. Once participants are more physically comfortable in the backcountry, they can begin to deal with the emotions that are creating their stress or anxiety. Your role is to provide authentic praise and timely critical feedback and to encourage self-reflection and self-awareness. Such coaching works only if there is a trusting rapport and a climate of intimacy between you and the participants. The participants need to trust you and to know that when you ask probing questions, deliver critical feedback, or encourage potentially upsetting self-examination, it is because you care about each participant's experience.

Follower

The leader plays an incredibly important role in the backcountry. Sometimes, however, the best leader is a humble follower. A backcountry experience led by a leader with a huge ego can be fun, adventure-filled, challenging, and engaging. But if you're trying to encourage participant competence and group independence, your participants must learn to rely on themselves and on each other, not on you. If you want to transfer leadership responsibility from yourself to your participants, you must frequently take a backseat role. In short, you must be willing to follow.

Still, even the humblest leaders need to be aware of the effect their words and actions have on others. Despite all efforts to maintain a backseat role, the leader still has a lot of influence. If you're not careful to maintain a low profile (once the participants are competent enough to provide their own leadership), your power and influence can prevent your group from becoming independent.

Some ways to diminish your influence are (1) connect with participants on a personal level, (2) show some vulnerability, and (3) consistently encourage participant leadership responsibility by stepping back and being willing to follow.

If you become *too* intimate, *too* vulnerable, and *too* much of a follower, however, you run the risk of becoming an ad hoc group member. You must walk the fine line between being too aloof and separate from participant interactions and being too close. Leading backcountry trips is an emotionally demanding experience, and there aren't a lot of social outlets for the leader. The result is occasionally that the leader is tempted to become another group member to satisfy a need for companionship. This is a particular danger when leading peers or when working without a co-leader (who can satisfy the personal and professional need for camaraderie). It's fine to be friendly with participants, but you must always maintain a professional distance. Strategies for demonstrating good "followership" without compromising professional distance include these points:

Empower participants early in the trip to assume simple leadership functions such as waking the group up, keeping track of time, carrying the maps and first-aid kit, etc.

Support participant leaders by setting them up for success. Encourage and coach them, and if you have to give critical feedback or second-guess their decisions, do it privately.

Pitch in on all camp chores, such as cooking, dishwashing, hanging food bags, etc. You can help without dominating or appropriating someone else's responsibility.

Allow participants to challenge you without interpreting it as a threat to your authority. Consider participants' opinions thoughtfully and be prepared to change your mind or your plan if necessary.

Admit your mistakes openly and without excuses. If you made a navigation error, tell the group what happened and apologize for the delay or detour. You might be able to turn the situation into a navigation lesson by analyzing the source of your error.

———————

You will find that you can cultivate positive relationships with the greatest number of participants and lead most effectively if you consider your role to include all of the functions described above. Leaders who see themselves as only a skill trainer or as only a coach compromise their ability to help their group and their participants achieve their goals most effectively.

So, going back to the question we asked in this chapter's introduction ("What am I supposed to be doing out here?"), you might find it helpful to remind yourself of these six main functions an outdoor leader performs: skill trainer, program designer, interpreter, group facilitator, coach, and follower. When you find yourself in a situation in which you're not sure what you should be doing, ask yourself which function would best help achieve participant, group, and expedition goals.

For example, if you're standing at the trailhead and everyone is looking at you expectantly, it's time to pull out the maps, become a skill trainer, and give a navigation lesson. If a participant is struggling with the emotional and physical demands of the expedition, it's time to act like a coach. And if the participants are reading the maps, getting themselves to camp, and starting to cook dinner, you should just fade into the background as a follower.

Adapting Your Leadership Style in the Outdoors

As discussed in Chapter 2, Becoming a Leader, in Part I, Leadership Fundamentals, your leadership style is simply the way in which you go about motivating others to get things done. Remember the leadership approaches described in "Adapting Your Leadership Style" in Chapter 2? Your preferred leadership style can usually be identified somewhere along that continuum ranging from very directive, highly involved methods to a quite laissez-faire manner.

A **directive approach** in an outdoor context might take the form of the leader waking the group up in the morning, directing two participants to cook breakfast, organizing the rest of the group to get packed up, walking at the front of the group to set the pace, making navigation decisions, deciding when to stop for lunch, etc.

A **democratic approach** on an expedition might involve the leader enlisting some participant leadership and including the participant leaders in decisions about how far to hike each day, where to stop for breaks, and which route to take.

A **consensual approach** in the backcountry involves the leader briefing the group about a decision that needs to be made—for example, whether to hike on trail or cross-country the next day—and then helping the participants reach a compromise that everyone can live with.

A **laissez-faire approach** in the outdoors might involve the leader giving participants the maps, showing them the campsite for that night, and then following them.

You can probably identify your own preferred leadership style somewhere along this continuum, but you need to be able to shift smoothly among the different approaches to best respond to the needs of a particular situation.

GROUP DYNAMICS ON EXPEDITIONS

Once you understand some of the predictable characteristics of groups (see Chapter 4, Building Trust, Building a Team, in Part I, Leadership Fundamentals), you can prepare yourself to deal with the challenges that you will most likely face out on an expedition.

As discussed in "Understanding Interpersonal Dynamics in Groups" in Chapter 4, the reason that groups begin to knit into intimate or high-functioning teams so predictably in the outdoors is because of the inherent stresses and rewards—as well as the forced intimacy—of a backcountry expedition.

The transformation from polite distance to social intimacy is described in Chapter 4 as a process of forming, storming, norming, performing, and adjourning. After a group of strangers spend a few days forming—getting to know each other, getting used to the routine of the backcountry, and learning how to cope with the challenges of an expedition—the storming phase begins: participants form opinions about the character and integrity of other group members and feel compelled to voice these opinions if they find someone shirking responsibility or attempting to dominate. Sometimes participants question the actions or decisions of the leader as the expedition grows harder (longer mileage, more difficult terrain, etc.) or as they encounter challenges they don't think they can tackle (rock climbing, technical peak ascent, river crossing, etc.). In the storming phase, interpersonal conflicts often resemble fights between siblings, with the comfort and intimacy of the participants showing even through their dissent.

A group in the backcountry that is norming works harmoniously to face daily challenges, includes all participants in group leadership in an equitable manner, and functions effectively with minimal involvement from the official leader. A group that has had a productive storming phase, with interpersonal issues resolved, will generally sail smoothly through the norming period and into a highly rewarding performing phase, when they cooperate and push themselves to achieve more than they might earlier have thought possible. For example, they might hike two days' worth of mileage in a single day, or they might choose to climb a peak that wasn't on the expedition plan.

The storming phase can frustrate or overwhelm an outdoor leader because it can involve participants questioning the leader's authority or the value of the expedition: "I came to have fun!" they complain, "so why do I have to hike 10 miles every day?" Participants might also begin to form cliques, with those who are looking for a relaxing expedition aligning themselves against those who want to rise early, hike hard, and cover a lot of ground. Although newer leaders in particular might feel ill equipped to resolve the issues that arise during the storming phase, it is a crucial part of the group development process. A leader who recognizes this stage and allows the group to experience it—as long as it does not evolve into a chaotic situation entirely beyond the leader's control—will enable that group to become stronger and achieve more of its goals.

Similarly, the performing phase can feel threatening to leaders, especially if the participants have really developed the skills necessary to operate fairly autonomously. The participants' growing independence destabilizes the leaders' sense of authority on the trip and often causes them to question their role on the expedition. But if the leaders remind themselves that the participants have achieved this highly desirable state of performance due (at least in part) to the leaders' skill, then this phase will give leaders an opportunity to reflect on their success.

The most successful, high-performing groups have usually experienced all these stages of group development. Even the phases that seem most intimidating to the leaders—and possibly most frustrating to the participants—should be allowed to occur naturally if a group is to realize its true potential.

These stages of group development are generally common to groups whose participants possess a certain level of emotional maturity and the ability to see the relationship between actions, consequences, and personal responsibility, although the time required for each group to move through the various phases tends to be proportional to participant age. That is, the older and more mature the participants, the longer it will take them to move into—and out of—each stage of development, particularly the storming phase. If you're working with middle-school students or young teens (who do not possess the emotional maturity of older teens and adults), you may find it useful to review the sections "Moral Development," "Behavioral Characteristics," and "Recognizing Gender Differences" in Chapter 15, Leading Youth in Your Community, in Part IV, Taking Leadership into Your Community. Young adolescents present unique characteristics that affect both individual behaviors and group dynamics in the backcountry, and their movement through these phases of group development is not entirely predictable.

Responding to the Stages of an Expedition

One reason that the Outward Bound philosophy can be applied so successfully to so many different groups in different circumstances is that it responds to and takes advantage of the predictable pattern of group development described above. Each phase of a group's development calls for a different leadership strategy, which forms the basis of the Outward Bound expedition framework. Outward Bound expeditions are structured around a central progression: from that of participants as student-learners to that of participants as ad hoc expedition leaders. This transition occurs as instructors train students in all the technical and interpersonal skills they need in order to effectively manage their own expedition as a group. As the students grow more competent, the instructors more frequently take a backseat role.

If your goal is to train your participants to assume leadership for your expedition, think about the expedition in three phases: early in the expedition, or the Training Expedition; the middle of the expedition, or the Main Expedition; and late in the expedition, or the Final Expedition. Each of these phases calls for a different level of leader involvement, progressing from a directive style to a more laissez-faire approach, as described above.

EXPEDITION PHASE	STAGE OF GROUP DEVELOPMENT	LEADER ROLES AND STYLES	EXAMPLES OF LEADER INVOLVEMENT IN INSTRUCTION AND GROUP DYNAMICS
Early Expedition (Training Expedition)	Forming	Skill trainer, guide; directive approach	▪ Teaching skills ▪ Making decisions about the route ▪ Modeling superb campcraft and Leave No Trace practices ▪ Clarifying goals and expectations ▪ Intervening before natural consequences occur ▪ Answering questions directly
Middle Expedition (Main Expedition)	Storming	Active coach; democratic approach	▪ Coaching in skill development ▪ Providing feedback and making observations ▪ Allowing nonserious natural consequences to happen
	Norming	Consultative coach; consensual approach	▪ Answering questions with statements such as "someone in the group knows how to do that" ▪ Providing opportunities for authentic participant leadership ▪ Supporting the group in accomplishing goals
Late Expedition (Final Expedition)	Performing	Backup coach, safety net; laissez-faire approach	▪ Designing an expedition that will allow participants to use technical and interpersonal skills they've been practicing ▪ Increasing responsibility and challenge ▪ Allowing participant leadership, giving real responsibility ▪ Intervening only when participants are on the brink of unsafe or unethical practices

You should make your eventual goal clear to your participants, so they're not bewildered when you begin to give them more responsibility and so they can begin the process of learning to depend on themselves and on the group, rather than on you. The chart at left provides suggestions for leader involvement on an expedition modeled after the Outward Bound progression.

Early: The Training Expedition

Early in your expedition, you will be very busy disseminating information, creating a positive learning environment, teaching basic expedition skills, modeling impeccable expedition practices, and making navigation and safety decisions. Your participants will be getting to know each other and learning to live and travel in the backcountry, absorbing information, practicing expedition skills, and developing a sense of judgment (the forming phase). Natural consequences—such as students getting wet due to a poorly set-up tent—are not allowed to happen. You are a teacher and guide during the Training Expedition.

Middle: The Main Expedition

The middle of the expedition is a good time to ramp up the intensity of the experience with more physically demanding challenges. As the expedition intensifies and as participants grow more comfortable with each other, conflicts arise (the storming phase) and participants can begin to practice effective communication, problem-solving, and conflict-resolution skills. As group behaviors and the daily routine become familiar, participants can be involved in more decision making and goal setting (the norming phase).

During the middle of the expedition, you should allow natural consequences to occur if the following conditions are present: (1) there are no significant safety implications; (2) natural consequences are a result of failing to use skills that have been previously taught—for example, neglecting a pot boiling on the stove and having dinner get burned; and (3) the value of experienc-

ing the natural consequence outweighs the value of any inconvenience endured as a result—for instance, allowing a group to hike a couple miles in the wrong direction and then having to backtrack. You can then discuss the consequence and coach the participants about how to avoid having it happen repeatedly. During this phase, encourage participants to rely on each other more for information and support—for example, "You have a question about today's route? Why don't you ask Bob? He's carrying the maps today, and he's very familiar with the route." Your role is that of a consultant and coach during Main Expedition.

Late: The Final Expedition

The last couple days of an expedition—or the last day, for shorter expeditions—is a chance for the participants to draw upon all that they have learned throughout the outing and to assume responsibility for virtually all aspects of the expedition—they are in the performing phase. As a leader, your involvement is limited; participants make all major decisions and act upon them, with you intervening only when a compromise of safety or trip quality threatens. Limit your involvement to coaching participant leaders, so that the group relies on members rather than on you. It's important that you allow natural consequences to happen during this phase, providing that the participants have the information and experience to prevent the mishap and that the consequence is not severe. During this phase, you are a coach of participant leaders and you are a safety net.

Another way of understanding the leader's role during this progression of an expedition is to look at the leader's response to the same situation if it were to occur during each of the three different expedition phases.

Situation: The participants are laughing and chatting as they approach a trail junction. Without stopping to consult a map, the participant in front takes the southern fork, heading downhill, and the rest of the group follows. The leader knows that they should have taken the northern fork.

Leader response early in the expedition: As soon as the participants pass the junction, the leader calls out to them, "Hey, you all, why don't we take our packs off here and look at the maps?" Using the opportunity as a lesson in both navigation and decision making ("Why didn't anyone think to look at maps when you passed the junction?"), the leader guides the participants through understanding that the northern fork is the one they want.

Leader response in the middle of the expedition: For fifteen or twenty minutes, the leader lets the participant walk in the wrong direction before saying casually to the participants with the maps, "I've noticed that we haven't had a map check in a while. Maybe we should take a map break pretty soon." When the maps are produced, the leader asks questions that help the participants figure out where they are and where they went wrong. If the participants don't think of it on their own, the leader suggests that they routinely stop to check maps at all trail junctions.

Leader response late in the expedition: The leader follows the participants down the southern fork until they realize on their own that they have taken a wrong turn or until he or she determines that there is no further learning or benefit to be gained by proceeding in the wrong direction.

Transference: Adjourning the Expedition

A fourth phase, transference, is brief but critical. It corresponds to the adjourning phase of group development discussed in "Stages of Group Development" in Chapter 4, Building Trust, Building a Team, in Part I Leadership Fundamentals. As the end of an expedition draws near, Outward Bound instructors guide students gently through thinking about incorporating into their home lives what they have learned—and often who they have become—on their Outward Bound course. If the students can assimilate the fundamental principle of Outward Bound philosophy—"you can do

more than you think you can"—into their lives at home, then their Outward Bound course has truly been successful, and lasting character development has been achieved. Otherwise, the whole experience exists in students' minds as an isolated incident in which a remarkable, but nontransferable, level of performance was reached.

In the trail-junction situation described above, the leader's response during the transference phase might be to ask the participants to look back on it (if it was a moving incident at the time): "Remember when you walked 6 miles in the wrong direction? What was your response to that incident? How can use you use what you learned then in future situations?" The important thing is that incidents used as examples, or metaphors, for transference must be situations that resulted in some collective or personal lessons at the time; otherwise, the participants have no meaningful frame of reference for transferring what they've learned on the expedition.

The Stages of Shorter Trips

What if you're thinking, "Wait a minute; I have only five days, not three weeks. How can I possibly model my expedition on the same progression that Outward Bound uses?" Although the Outward Bound model works best with expeditions of at least ten days, a progression of skill development and leader intervention can be applied to shorter trips as well, provided the participants are either mature, quick learners, or semicompetent outdoorspeople. You might not get a multiday period at the end of the expedition in which to test your group's skills, but even a participant-directed final hike out to the trailhead will build on navigation, time management, and group travel skills learned earlier in the trip, which will in turn lead to feelings of independent accomplishment.

The following suggestions, taken from the *Outward Bound Instructor Manual*, can contribute to a group's feeling of autonomy, even in situations in which the leader is physically present:

■ Participants decide when to get up in the morning and when to leave camp.

- Participants make all decisions involving food: when and where to eat, what to cook, etc.
- Participants interact with outside agencies encountered: rangers, etc.
- Participants treat all minor injuries, provided they have the appropriate knowledge.
- Participants make all navigational decisions, including daily route, where to stop for lunch, campsite selection, etc.
- The leader allows the group to go off-route or "get lost" for a while before intervening, if such a mishap is a result of carelessness, not because participants don't have adequate map interpretation skills.
- The leader allows all nonhazardous natural consequences to happen—again, provided that the consequence is a result of carelessness, not lack of knowledge.

So even if you have only a few days, you can use your role as a skill trainer to prepare your participants to assume responsibility for some of the leadership functions of the expedition. Even simple things—such as setting an alarm clock and waking up the rest of the group in the morning—can contribute to participants' feeling of leadership power and a group's perception of its own autonomy.

LEADERSHIP STRATEGIES ON EXPEDITIONS

This section gives you some tips for providing the most successful expeditions for your participants. Begin on the right footing, keep everyone motivated in positive ways, and help your participants realize that mistakes are just learning tools on the road to success.

Setting the Tone

The beginning of a wilderness trip can be a scene of joyful anticipation, with friends giddy with excitement about the upcoming expedition. Or it can be a tense logistical time, with the leader scurrying about in attending to last-minute details while the participants stand around awkwardly, unsure about what they should be doing. Or it can be a time of wide eyes, dread, uncertainty, and nervous anticipation. As a leader, you should be prepared to deal with any of these scenarios.

While a group of experienced comrades setting off on an adventure together creates the most relaxing atmosphere, most official trip leaders will find themselves at some time dealing with a group of nervous novices who need to be transformed into motivated, informed, and prepared participants. The tone-setting strategies addressed in Chapter 4, Building Trust, Building a Team, in Part I, Leadership Fundamentals, can help you design initial interactions that will create the emotional and social environment you're seeking for your trip, but the following additional considerations are important when preparing a group for a wilderness expedition:

- **Acknowledge the unfamiliar physical and social environment:** Not knowing who you're with or where you're going is a disorienting experience. Also, even though the woods might seem like home to you, they are a scary place for many people. Acknowledge this apprehension. Try saying something as simple as, "Right now it's hard to believe that you all will know each other better than you know most people, but in two weeks you'll be surprised when you remember that you haven't known each other all your lives. Pretty soon these other people will seem like family and the wilderness will seem like home." This will help people relax a bit as they realize they're not alone in their uneasiness—and it's perfectly normal.
- **Acknowledge concerns and fears:** During your introductory talks and preparations, off-handedly name the things that people might be concerned about—not being physically strong enough, seeing a bear, not fitting in, jumping in cold water, using an outhouse. Later, when you have time for a longer discussion and when participants have a bit more information about the trip and a bit more comfort with the environment, discuss fears and concerns in more detail. See "Create an

Environment Conducive to Challenge and Learning" in Chapter 4.

■ **Provide information:** People without information lack power and choices. Give your participants information about the trip. Tell them about the plan for the day. Show them the entire expedition on a map. Explain what a piece of equipment is as you pack it into their bags. Show them the food, tell them about outhouses and catholes, display the first-aid kit. You don't need to provide excruciating details, but giving people basic information about where they're going, who they're going with, and what they'll be doing communicates to them that they will be in a position of informed power on this trip.

■ **Use humor:** Laughter puts people at ease. An appropriate use of humor can diffuse some of the nervous energy that surrounds groups of strangers preparing for a trip together. Joke about how thick the mosquitoes are, kid about the food as you're packing it (for example, tell the story about putting dried mashed potatoes on your granola instead of powdered milk), laugh about the day you woke up with a slug stuck to the inside of your sleeping bag.

■ **Present yourself as vulnerable:** An outdoor leader can come across as an entirely different breed—an intimidating superhuman who is completely at ease slogging through swamps or walking all day carrying a sixty-pound backpack. By presenting yourself as someone who used to struggle with wilderness challenges or who can't sleep through a thunderstorm or who wanted to bring a curling iron on her first wilderness expedition, you show yourself to be approachable and accessible to your participants.

■ **Meet basic needs:** This can't be emphasized enough. People whose basic needs are not met cannot focus on assimilating new information. Introduce yourself and participants to each other as quickly as possible (meet the social need for belonging). If your participants arrive at the start of your trip hungry, give them a snack and some water before jumping into equipment lessons. If it's raining, set up a tarp and give participants rain jackets. If the bugs are biting, let participants get their insect repellent out of their suitcases.

The environment you create at the beginning of the trip sets a tone for the entire expedition. Take special care to make sure you are beginning to build a community of openness and trust, communicating clear expectations, and demonstrating a caring and compassionate attitude toward your participants.

Motivating Your Participants

Although many outdoor programs achieve their missions through either coercion ("You are *going* to climb this mountain") or "challenge by choice" ("You can choose whether or not to hike up this mountain—either way is fine"), Outward Bound believes that the most profound learning takes place when students are motivated to achieve great things because they believe that to do anything less is morally indefensible. Former military colonel and Outward Bound instructor Bob Rheault (remember him from Chapter 3?) refers to this as giving students no honorable way out of anything less than full participation in all course activities.

Impelling Students as a Leadership Strategy

Central to Outward Bound's leadership philosophy is the idea of *impelling* students to face challenges, accept responsibility, and take risks.

It's Day Eighteen of a twenty-two-day Outward Bound course, and the group has been briefed on the route for the final expedition. As is typical with a high-functioning group, the instructors have given the students a "Point A to Point B" route briefing; that is, the instructors have identified the starting and ending points for the final expedition on a map and have told the group that they have four days to make it to a checkpoint about 35 trail miles away. As the instructors fade into the background, the students cluster around the maps and begin to examine routes and measure mileage.

Group A decides to follow the Appalachian Trail, which goes directly from Point A to Point B, hitting five big peaks along the way. The route is strenuous, with several thousand feet of elevation loss and gain and a significant chunk of exposed ridge walking. Group A plans to cut about 5 miles off the distance by traveling off-trail for part of one day, linking together two parts of the trail by a bushwhack through an old clear-cut.

Group B chooses to walk from Point A down a logging road 10 miles to connect with a paved state route that will take them 50 miles to Point B. The route will involve 60 miles of road walking but almost no elevation gain or loss.

Group A makes some navigation errors on their bushwhack and ends up not saving any mileage, but they make up the distance lost with a night hike, which turns out to be pretty challenging. Their steep climbs are rewarded with spectacular views, and they end the expedition feeling tired but proud.

Group B spends four days trudging single-file down the shoulder of a paved road, ducking into fields and gravel pits for camping. For them, the final expedition ends as a mileage countdown, with students finishing the route with blistered feet, no big high points, and no improvement in expedition skills.

The two groups described above have the same starting point but markedly different outcomes. What can account for the difference? In Group A's situation, the students were motivated to tackle big challenges in order to achieve unprec-

edented success. In Group B's situation, the students were content to find a loophole that would allow them to take the easy way out (although the jury is still out on which is harder—30 miles of mountainous terrain or 60 miles of road walking) while technically still accomplishing the task set before them. It seems that Group A had some inner drive to perform, whereas Group B did not feel *impelled*—driven—to accept a challenge that might have given them the chance to learn and grow.

The Outward Bound instructor's job, then, is to present students with challenges that require them to stretch their emotional and physical limits in order to succeed. *Impelling* requires that the instructor expects every student to be fully committed to giving his or her full effort to the challenges of the course, relative to each student's own physical and emotional abilities. So the instructor's role is not to get every student to the top of a rock climb, for example, but instead to make each student feel driven to give a 100 percent effort to a rock climb, regardless of whether he or she reaches the top.

Impelling your participants means that you cannot give them an easy way to avoid a challenge, because this deprives them of a chance to grow. It's a fine line between impelling and coercion, though, and ultimately the decision whether or not to participate needs to be each participant's. Do not humiliate, coerce, or threaten participants who choose not to participate in a particular activity.

You can still respect individual choice, but doing so does not mean that you should make it easy for participants to refuse to try. This requires that you make a value judgment. You are stating very clearly that you expect participants to give their best because you believe that there is more to be gained from full engagement than there is from a random sampling of activities.

Using Intrinsic Motivation as a Leadership Strategy

One Outward Bound instructor tells a story of being impelled by the senior instructor he was working with and how that influenced his ability to motivate his students similarly:

> *I was a pretty new instructor—I think it was my second or third course. On the first night of this course, the wind was really blowing, a light mist was starting to fall, and students were kind of scattered around the campsite, trying to get warm clothes on and find the food bags. My co-instructor, Gary, and I agreed that I would set up our tarp while he helped the students get out of their wet hiking clothes, then we would all meet to light the stoves and start dinner.*
>
> *I hastily set up our tarp with a few loose tautline hitches and a couple of tarp strings just wound around tree trunks. The tarp was flapping around a bit, but it was functional and would keep our stuff dry until after dinner when I could fix it. In the midst of helping students find their raincoats, Gary came over and glanced pointedly at the tarp I had just set up. He then looked at me and asked simply, "Is this your best?" Then he walked away.*
>
> *It wasn't my best—I knew it and Gary knew it—and I was sort of embarrassed to have been noticed doing work I wasn't proud of. I think of Gary all the time now, whenever I am tempted to cut corners or take the easy way out of something. "Is this my best?" I will ask myself, and if the answer is no, then I start over. The Earl of Chesterfield said that if something is worth doing at all, then it's worth doing well. I try to live by this and inspire my students to live by this, too.*
>
> —*James, Outward Bound instructor since 1999*

This feeling of wanting to do one's personal best simply for the sake of it lies at the heart of Outward Bound's motivational philosophy. We want students to strive to do their best—to hold themselves to high standards—because they are *intrinsically* motivated to do so.

So many of our students operate in environments that rely on *extrinsic* motivation—striving for an external reward: getting good grades to please parents or get into college, being popular with friends, working hard to earn more money. At Outward Bound, we want students to throw themselves wholeheartedly into their expeditions, tackle challenges head on, keep pushing when the going gets tough, and find it in themselves to do more than they thought they could simply because *they feel driven to do so.*

Ultimately, we hope that students will transfer this internal motivation to the rest of their lives. Once bitten by this bug, Outward Bound alumni, we believe, will continue to seek out opportunities that allow them to demonstrate their strengths, proving to themselves that *plus est en vous*—there is more in them than they know.

Understanding the Roles of Success and Failure

As noted in Chapter 1, Why Learn Leadership from Outward Bound?, one of Kurt Hahn's seven principles of character development is to see to it that young people experience both success and defeat: Make participants meet with triumph and defeat. If participants are really to absorb the idea that *plus est en vous*, a balance of success and failure is necessary. An endless string of successes means that challenges are not sufficient to require the participants' deepest reserves of strength or courage. Nor does a host of failures provide participants with the confidence they need to continue to tackle challenges.

Outward Bound's methodology hinges upon something we call "the success experience." Formal education, according to Outward Bound thinking as stated in the *Outward Bound Instructor Manual*, "perpetuates in some students a constant chain of failures," whereas Outward Bound's expeditions and series of graduated challenges are designed to set students up for success: to provide them with the skills and opportunities to solve genuine problems successfully. You can create "success orientation" in the following ways:

Provide Authentic Challenge Appropriate to Participant Ability

People feel good when they accomplish something difficult, and they feel great when they accomplish something that they previously thought impossible. You should present challenges that require participants to stretch their limits of physical and mental strength in order to accomplish them. These challenges are different for every group and are often different within a group. If the challenge is too great for a particular group, or a particular participant, at a particular time, then failure is likely (see "Interpret Failure in a Positive Light," below). But if the challenge is too inconsequential, too easy, then the sense of accomplishment is diminished. The leader's responsibility is to gauge participant and group abilities and design challenges that test these abilities. For example, hiking 2 miles might be a major accomplishment for a group of twelve-year-olds, but you'd need to increase this mileage to 12 or 15 miles for a group of healthy college students.

Use Autonomy to Achieve Success Independently

Participants must earn their own success; success that is "delivered" (in other words, the participant who is hauled up a rock climb on a tight belay) is hollow and condescending. This does not mean that the leader cannot assist groups or participants; indeed, one of the roles of the leader is coaching. But the successful outcome must ultimately rest with the participant. The leader must walk a fine line between supporting and rescuing.

Reflect on Mistakes

Mistakes play a critical role in experiential learning; they provide the learner with a frame of reference for future experiences. Mistakes are *not* failures—they are setbacks en route to the accomplishment of a challenge, not the failure of the entire undertaking. A participant who takes a careless bearing that results in the group hiking 4 extra miles will likely remember to be more meticulous next time (as long as this person is aware of the relationship between that bearing and the extra hiking). One pot of burned oatmeal is usually enough to inspire a group to watch the stoves more carefully. The leader's role is to help participants reflect on mistakes and figure out how to file these experiences away for future reference.

Interpret Failure in a Positive Light

Similarly to learning from mistakes, interpreting failures in a positive light gives participants learning experiences to draw on in the future. "At least you tried" is the common form of interpreting failure in a positive light, but it will carry more weight if you take a more sophisticated angle on reframing an experience. Failures should not be diminished ("it's not a big deal") or excused ("it wasn't your fault"), but, instead, they should be interpreted in a way that salvages the successful aspects of the experience. The leader's responsibility is to provide this perspective to the participant(s) after a failure.

For example, if one of your participants struggles on a rock climb and fails to reach the top, you can help the participant to view the climb as a series of challenges, with the participant having successfully surmounted many of those obstacles before finally succumbing to the challenges near the top. You could also note that you observed the participant working hard to maneuver past some of the most difficult moves on the climb and that it's possible that the participant got so tired working on these crux moves that he or she didn't have the stamina to complete the climb. And if the participant was giving the climb every ounce of personal physical and mental strength, then the participant was pushing him- or herself to the absolute limit, which is a success in itself. Learning to cope with failure (real or perceived) is just as important as experiencing success.

LEADING YOUTH OUTDOORS

Although most of the leadership strategies and concerns outlined above (as well as in Chapter 4, Building Trust, Building a Team, in Part I, Leadership Fundamentals) apply to participants and groups of all ages, some additional tips for working with youth, particularly those in the eleven- to fourteen-year-old age bracket, are detailed in "Leadership Strategies for Working with Young People" in Chapter 15, Leading Youth in Your Community, in Part IV, Taking Leadership into Your Community. Some of those leadership strategies are outlined here:

- **Build trust:** As a leader, tell the truth. Be honest. Listen.
- **Develop credibility by maintaining an appropriate role:** You can be friendly, but you can't be a peer.
- **Set the tone for a positive group culture:** Model the behaviors and actions you are trying to instill.
- **Work to provide a culture of inclusion:** Create situations that require all group members to be involved in order for the group to succeed.
- **Develop youths' independence:** The key to building successful citizens is to nurture responsible adolescents as they try out their autonomy and to give them opportunities to practice this independence.
- **Turn over control:** Be supportive as you gradually relinquish control. Allow for both success and failure.
- **Let go:** Avoid power struggles.

Use Consequences, Not Punishment

You can employ consequences as an educational tool to help participants become aware of the effects of their actions on themselves and their group. The beauty of natural consequences in the backcountry is that they demonstrate the relationship between actions and results, as well as teaching participants what to do the next time they are in a similar situation. For example, if participants set a tent up poorly and it rains, they get wet; next time they will pay more attention to their tent setup. Or if participants choose to sleep late in the morning, they often end up hiking into the dark to reach camp; tomorrow they will decide to wake up earlier.

Consequences can also be used when a natural wilderness event does *not* emerge as a result of an action. For example, if a participant buries leftover food, the most harmful consequence would be a bear visiting camp in the night, digging up the food, tearing down the food bags, and ripping into all the supplies. But fortunately (or unfortunately in terms of participants learning a lesson), this does not often happen. Instead, you could impose a consequence that is connected both to the participant's violation of minimum-impact practices and to the rationale behind these practices: for instance, asking the participant to dig up the food and pack it out to the next resupply point.

Consequences work well in a context that focuses on success because they put the participants entirely in control of what happens to them. Whereas a punishment is usually arbitrary, meted out by an authority figure, and often humiliating, a consequence is logically connected to participant behavior and allows participants to maintain their dignity—the self-esteem that is critical to a successful experience.

LEADING AN EXPEDITION

Whenever I lead a backcountry expedition I find my thoughts subtly but automatically ordering themselves into two streams of consciousness. There are my surface thoughts, which bounce back and forth from the relevant to the frivolous: "Will we be able to ford the next river? Should I put on more sunscreen? Are the participants looking at their maps? I wonder what we'll have for dinner?" And then there are my subconscious thoughts, which stem from the realization that I am responsible for the safety and quality of the backcountry expedition. My subconscious thoughts address the big-picture issues that follow here, such as keeping my participants safe, helping my group reach its goals, interpreting meaning from experiences, holding participants to high standards of conduct, solving problems and making decisions. Whether such thoughts come automatically to you or have to be deliberately placed on your mental agenda, it's important to remember the many responsibilities of the outdoor leader.

Keeping Your Group Safe

While you are instructing, coaching, and empowering participants, you must also have a commitment to keeping your group safe. The sections "Risk to Participants" and "Weighing Risks" in Chapter 5, Taking Risks and Making Decisions, and "Dealing with Safety Concerns" in Chapter 15, Leading Youth in Your Community, all address safety issues. This section provides additional points to consider when you are responsible for others' well-being in the backcountry.

The first time I taught a New Staff Training (introductory training that new Outward Bound instructors go through), I wanted everything to happen perfectly. I wanted to model my excellent leadership skills, I wanted the route to be challenging but realistic, and I wanted the new staff to see how flawlessly an Outward Bound expedition could be executed.

The first two days of hiking lived up to my expectations; the participants were avid learners, they began to knit into a strong

social group, and we covered dramatic terrain seemingly effortlessly. But lightning storms on the third and fourth days put us woefully behind schedule. Finally, we reached a point where, if we were going to make it to our destination to begin canoeing on time, we would have to hike 21 miles one day with a substantial amount of elevation gain and loss.

We rose at 3:00 AM and began hiking. Everything went well until about noon, when the lightning storms started again. We spent most of the afternoon and evening alternately hiking and sitting in a lightning-safety position, waiting out the passing storms and covering very little ground.

At 8:00 PM, we still had 9 miles to go and people were pretty tired; we had been on the move for seventeen hours. The best thing to do would have been to make camp, get a decent night's sleep, and arrive late at our canoeing meeting. The new staff needed a physical and mental break from the rigors of the day, and it would have modeled good leadership that they could later emulate when they were in similar situations with their own groups. But I had the idea fixed in my head that we needed to stay on schedule, so I didn't suggest that we stop. And the participants, of course, would never have suggested stopping—after all, they were new staff looking to impress their director.

We hiked through the rain with our headlamps on until midnight, a dreary trudge punctuated by frequent lightning storms that seemed to be right on top of us. At one point, the trail turned into a stream, and we were walking in knee-deep water for almost a mile.

Fortunately, no one got injured (or worse) that night. Despite their exhaustion, none of the participants stumbled in the dark or slipped on wet ground. Almost miraculously, it seems, no one got struck by lightning or ground current. Everyone made it safely to the canoeing rendezvous, but this can be attributed only to sheer luck and participant stamina, not my leadership skills. I let my commitment to the original plan cloud my judgment about what was safest and most prudent for my group. I not only failed to be a good role model, but I also put my group in danger.

The information available on managing risk and safety in the backcountry is extensive (see Chapter 7 resources in the Bibliography at the end of this book), and the topic is far too broad to be covered effectively here in a few paragraphs. But you can apply the following general concepts that Outward Bound instructors use to keep groups safe in the wilderness.

Be Prepared

Obtain appropriate training. Bring adequate supplies and equipment, and know how to use them.

I once taught a three-week trip on the Rio Grande for a midwestern college. When I met the participants and the canoes at the river, I immediately noticed that some of the boats had no flotation devices in them. We were miles from anyplace to buy flotation devices, and it would have been a major logistical hassle to get some, so we convinced ourselves that it would probably be OK to go without.

And it was, for twenty days. But on the twenty-first day, at the rapid just above the takeout, one of the nonflotation boats capsized and was washed under an undercut ledge, along with the two participants who were paddling it. Time slowed down and stretched out as neither the boat nor the participants reappeared downstream as we expected them to. Finally the gasping participants popped up and, much later, the canoe did as well.

Devoid of flotation, the heavy boat had pressed down on the participants, trapping them momentarily under the boat, which was wedged under the ledge. Those long seconds we spent waiting for the participants to emerge were the longest seconds of my instructional life. Even though everything turned out OK, I wished we had spent the time and effort before the expedition to get flotation for all the boats.

Anticipate Problems

As you move through the day, be aware of problems that could arise and think through possible solutions: Could this talus slope slide? Is that river crossing too deep in the middle? Are any of these old burned trees likely to blow down on the tents tonight?

An old friend who was a pilot used to make me sit in the copilot seat with the charts. At any given moment, I needed to be able to point to a place where we could safely make an emergency landing if necessary. He didn't expect to need the emergency landing, but he wanted to know exactly where it was if he did need it.

Stay Focused

As the leader, you can't let down your guard. When others are joking as they make a descending traverse across a glacier or are goofing around as they exit a rapid, you must be alert to potential hazards. Keep yourself hydrated, well fed, and dressed appropriately for weather conditions. Although you don't need to be paranoid, you must view almost every activity or undertaking as a potential accident.

I remember once standing around with my co-instructor, chatting while our students loaded up their canoes in the small eddy near our campsite. The eddy had a moderate upstream current in it, but we didn't pay any special attention to that; after all, it was an eddy. Suddenly we heard shouts,

*and we saw in disbelief that one of the full
boats had capsized and wrapped around a
partially submerged rock. No one ever would
have guessed that an accident could occur
here, but all of a sudden we had a minor
emergency on our hands.*

Be Aware of Your Own and Your Participants' Energy

Most of the accidents that occur in the backcountry are the result not of major environmental disasters but, instead, of individual conditions such as fatigue, dehydration, or simple carelessness. You cannot single-handedly keep your group safe—each person needs to be functioning at a high physical and mental state. People who are exhausted, dehydrated, too cold, too hot, or hungry make poor decisions. Stay on top of your own mental and physical energy, and help your participants meet their basic needs so that they can stay sharp. A friend and Outward Bound instructor tells of a time when this lesson was reinforced for her:

*Sometimes when conditions are calm and
my groups are behind schedule, I push
them to paddle late into the night to reach
our intended campsites. One time I pulled
into camp with my participants at 2:30 AM,
jumped out of the canoe, and went up to
make sure that the campsite was unoccupied,
leaving the participants to unload the boats.
When I returned, I learned that somehow one
pair had let a boat loose by mistake, and we
lost the canoe. We found the canoe the next
day, but we lost a day in searching all over
the lake for it and ended up even more behind
schedule than we had been in the first place.*

*I learned from that, indeed. I learned
that while it's good to push my participants,
it's more important that the leader is "on"
and has the big-picture vision to see what's
happening. I think I was too tired and was
more focused on quickly unloading the boats
so that we could set up camp and get to bed,*

*and I forgot that my participants needed to
be watched more carefully. I suppose it's a
good lesson, because the alternative might
have been that I was up at the tent site and
one of the participants slipped into the water.*
　　　—Leila, Outward Bound instructor
　　　　since 1999

Stick to the Plan Unless You Have a Rational Reason to Change It

Problems frequently arise as a result of spontaneous changes to a plan. Many a mountain disaster has resulted from failure to adhere to the turn-back hour. Countless broken ankles have been the result of groups deciding to hike out to the trailhead in the dark to make it into town for a burger and a shower instead of staying in the woods for another night as planned. Stick to the plan unless there is a compelling reason to do otherwise.

*I once encouraged a group to push a little
in order to get ahead of schedule and reach
our destination earlier, without thinking
through the possible complications. Instead
of stopping at the planned campsite, we
headed to a river crossing that would have
been straightforward the next morning, but
by early evening it was verging on impassable due to the volume of snowmelt that had
occurred during the warm day. We had an
epic crossing, and when we finally made it to
the other side, everyone was exhausted and
some were in tears.*

*We promptly stopped to camp in a
horrible little mosquito-infested hollow, and
everyone slept poorly. Confronting us first
thing was an icy pass, which turned out to
be too treacherous to ascend until the snow
softened around midday. Had we stuck to
the original plan, we would have crossed the
river at its lowest—early morning—and
hit the pass in prime conditions at noon.
Instead, we reached our destination at the
same time we would have had we followed*

the original plan, but with most of the participants terrified, frustrated, or spent.

Change the Plan When Necessary

Conversely, stay alert for those compelling reasons that would make it prudent to change plans: deteriorating weather conditions, flagging participant energy, insufficient leader skill and experience. Don't let your ego force you to persevere with the original plan if your instincts tell you that you're making a poor decision. In the New Staff Training situation described above, when I pushed my group to complete the day's mileage despite participant exhaustion and repeated lightning storms, my desire to have everything progress precisely as I had planned it overruled my common sense. The result was that I compromised both the safety and the quality of the expedition, not to mention failing to instill in the new instructors the message that sometimes it's better to change the plan.

Don't Exceed Your Limits

You should never take leadership responsibility for others in terrain, activities, or situations in which you yourself are not personally comfortable; this includes leading groups or individuals who might have special needs that you are unprepared to meet. Leading others is *not* the time when you should push your own limits, stretch your comfort zone, or attempt to accomplish some outdoor feat at which you have previously failed. Your big challenge on any trip is to make sure that you and the people you are traveling with have a safe, fun, and rewarding experience in the backcountry.

The perfect scenario for your first stint as an outdoor leader is to take a small group of motivated people to a backcountry area with which you are quite familiar. With a route you know, you can focus most of your energy on being an effective leader and cultivating your leadership style, rather than having to agonize about navigation decisions.

The first time I took on an independent outdoor leadership role in the backcountry, I was fifteen and I had just returned from my first Outward Bound course as a student. After backpacking, canoeing, and sailing in Maine for twenty-eight days, I considered myself to be somewhat of an outdoor expert, particularly compared to the rest of my high-school friends.

My best friend, Shannon, agreed to accompany me on an overnight backpacking trip to Stuart Lake, near Leavenworth, Washington. We didn't have drivers' licenses yet, so my mom dropped us off at the trailhead, after we promised to do nothing more than hike into Stuart Lake, spend two nights, and hike out.

Within an hour on the trail, Shannon and I ran into some much older male hikers who convinced us that Colchuck Lake was much more scenic than Stuart Lake and that we should instead make Colchuck our final destination. Colchuck was indeed beautiful, and we had a wonderful camping trip, in spite of losing much of our food to a chipmunk and failing to light a fire successfully.

But we didn't even have maps that covered the Colchuck Lake area. Furthermore, we spent our second day hiking up a steep pass that was essentially a loose talus slope, partially covered with snow. I had no experience traveling on loose rock and was in no position to take someone else up that pass. Fortunately, no harm was done as a result of changing our camping plans, although the outcome could have been entirely different had we had any trouble or had our parents needed to find us for some reason.

Use Common Sense and Good Judgment

This sounds obvious, but a surprising number of backcountry accidents occur to sharp, savvy wilderness adventurers who simply decide to do something as a group that they wouldn't do as individuals. The reasons vary: giving into peer pressure, presuming there's safety in numbers, wanting not to appear cowardly, or assuming incorrectly that someone else in the group has the skill to lead the group safely through the particular obstacle. But the outcome is usually that the entire group gets in over its head and no one knows how to get out.

Some experienced mountaineers cited by Simon Priest and Michael Gass in *Effective Leadership in Adventure Programming* refer to this as the "risky shift phenomenon": the idea that when people are in groups, they tend to make riskier decisions than they would alone. As the leader, your responsibility is to stop the group before it undertakes something that you can't manage safely. If someone needs to swallow his or her pride and say, "I don't think that we can do this safely," that person needs to be you.

> *I was teaching a white-water canoeing course in the Rio Grande once with a group of adults. The river was characteristically low, and we spent most of our time dodging exposed rocks. On the last night, however, it rained and the river swelled and filled its banks. All of a sudden we were confronted with some real white water—white water that would have been fun and perfectly safe to run with a group of experienced paddlers but that I thought would be immensely risky for novice paddlers who had trained in much lower-water conditions.*
>
> *When I explained to the participants that we were going to have to portage the final stretch of river, many were incredibly angry. They viewed the newly flooded river as a fun-filled opportunity and resented me telling them that they couldn't run it. It wasn't comfortable being the bad guy, but it was the sensible decision to make.*

Avoid Disasters

Your most valuable safety-management tool is to avoid emergencies. The time you spend teaching participants how to live comfortably and safely in the woods will be more than compensated by the fact that you'll save time in not having to deal with injuries or emergencies. Certainly, teach first aid and search and rescue techniques, but these should serve only as complements to the lessons on how to use gas stoves properly, how to move through talus slopes safely, how to scout rapids, how to interpret weather patterns, how to cross deep streams, and many other backcountry safety techniques.

The deeper you are into the backcountry, the more conservative your decisions and practices regarding risk management should be. Train your participants in what to do in case of emergencies, but act in ways that prevent this training from being put to the test. One Outward Bound instructor describes a classic disaster-avoidance decision:

> *I was teaching a dog-sledding course in Maine and, as frequently happens in January, we had a winter thaw. Our plan had been to travel on frozen lakes and rivers, but with the thaw, we knew that there would be open patches of water all over the place. With good scouting, smart dogs, and quick reflexes, we knew that we could avoid the open patches, but every minute of travel would have required constant attention. We decided instead to avoid the lakes altogether and shift our expedition plan to using trails in the forest.*
>
> *—Jon, Outward Bound instructor since 1990*

Adhere to Policies and Standard Procedures

If you're working or volunteering for an organization, stick to the policies and procedures prescribed by the organization unless there is a compelling reason to do otherwise. Usually these policies are not arbitrary; they're based on institutional experience and industry-standard practices. Only rarely is it safer to stray from policies than to follow them. If you find that your organization has a policy that is consistently hard to follow or is one that you disagree with, address this with your managers when you are not in the woods. A seasoned outdoor leader has this to say about his realization that policies often exist for a good reason:

I was working for a program that had a policy requiring leaders to assess the stability of glaciers prior to teaching students self-arrest skills on them. This is good common sense, and normally I would have done exactly this, but I knew that another group had been practicing self-arrest on the glacier the day before. So rather than hiking from camp all the way up to the glacier to check things out myself, I simply asked the leader of the other group what the conditions were like. The other leader told me that conditions were good, so the next afternoon I took my group up to the glacier.

Late in the afternoon, a significant amount of snow and rock released above the group, and one participant was struck lightly with falling debris. No injuries resulted, fortunately, but I was chastened. I had incorrectly assumed that because conditions were stable one day, they would remain stable. Because snow stability can change on a daily basis due to temperature differences, the policy requiring independent assessment of conditions was warranted. Had I made my own independent assessment of the glacier, I might not have chosen to take my group up there.

—Jeff, Outward Bound instructor since 2002

Before embarking on any unusual activity, think about how you would explain your decision to your supervisor. Although this practice is a bit vague to be a guiding safety modus operandi, it might serve new outdoor leaders well as a system of checks and balances.

When I was the director of an Outward Bound program in Maine, one of the senior instructors once told me that whenever

she was considering leading her group in an unusual activity—paddling at night, bivouacking on a summit, swimming with packs across a river—she always asked herself, "How would I explain this decision to Ashley?" If her rationale was sound, the conditions favorable, and the backup plan reasonable, then she would proceed with the activity. If, upon examination, any of her motivations or methods seemed sketchy, she would alter her plans.

Consider Safety in Relation to Trip Quality

The flip side of keeping your group safe is that you don't want safety to become such an overriding concern that you spend the whole expedition huddled in camp or confined to the trail, playing it safe. The *safety* of the wilderness expedition shouldn't compromise the *quality* of the expedition.

For example, let's say you are hiking along a trail when you come to a stream crossing with a bridge that has been washed out. You assess the stream crossing by looking at it and then crossing it yourself; having determined that the water is only shin-deep and moving slowly, you think your group can safely cross without the bridge. It's true, someone might slip and fall or twist an ankle, but you are predicting that you can manage the crossing in a safe way, and even a bruise or a twisted ankle wouldn't be disastrous. You are weighing the safety of the situation against the benefit of being able to continue along your way, as well as the benefit of teaching your group about stream crossings.

But let's say you get to the washed-out bridge and discover that the stream is almost waist-deep, moving quickly, and extremely cold. You assess the safety of the situation and realize that there is too much potential for a serious accident. Even though turning around will be disheartening for the participants, you decide that in this situation, the benefit of being able to stay on track does not outweigh the safety considerations, so you turn around.

KEEPING YOUR GROUP SAFE

- **Be prepared.** Obtain appropriate training. Bring adequate supplies and equipment, and know how to use them.
- **Anticipate problems.** Think through possible solutions.
- **Stay focused.** Be alert to potential hazards. Keep yourself hydrated, well fed, and dressed appropriately for weather conditions.
- **Be aware of your own and others' energy.** People who are exhausted, dehydrated, too cold, too hot, or hungry make poor decisions. Stay on top of your own mental and physical energy, and help your participants meet their basic needs so that they can stay sharp too.
- **Stick to the plan.** Unless you have a compelling reason to do otherwise, stick to your original plan. Problems frequently arise as a result of spontaneous changes to a plan.
- **Change the plan when necessary.** Be alert for those compelling reasons that would make it prudent to change plans: deteriorating weather conditions, flagging participant energy, inadequate leader skill and experience. Don't let your ego overrule your common sense.
- **Don't exceed your limits.** Never take leadership responsibility for others in terrain, activities, or situations in which you yourself are not personally comfortable.
- **Use common sense and good judgment.** Do not do anything as a group that you wouldn't do as individuals. Stop the group before it undertakes something that you can't manage safely.
- **Avoid disasters.** Train your participants in what to do in case of emergencies, but act in ways that prevent this training from being put to the test.
- **Adhere to policies and standard procedures.** Your organization's policies are based on institutional experience and industry-standard practices. It is almost always safer to follow these policies than to stray from them.
- **Consider safety in relation to trip quality.** The *safety* of the wilderness expedition shouldn't compromise the *quality* of the expedition.

The wilderness has many inherent risks, but you—with proper training, solid experience, and good judgment—are in a position to balance risk with reward. Some outdoor leaders get so focused on safety that they fail to do any of the things that can be most rewarding in the wilderness, even if they are qualified to lead such activities: off-trail travel, peak ascents, night hikes, stream crossings, days with long mileage. Always consider safety in relation to the quality of the trip.

Helping the Group Reach Its Goals

The best—and most meaningful—kind of success is one that is achieved fairly by employing your own wit, skill, or strength. If you emphasize participant-driven accomplishments, such experiences transfer most readily to your participants'

lives at home. In order to facilitate this, you must think of yourself primarily as a coach when helping a group achieve its goals. If you play too prominent a role in the attainment of the goal, then the success is undermined. Worse, the success becomes *your* success, with the participants playing only supporting roles—rather than the other way around. But if you are too laissez-faire, then frequently the goals are not achieved and the participants do not get the thrill that comes from accomplishment.

On a recent backpacking course, we had reached our intended campsite early and the participants were excited about some free time to swim, write in journals, and generally get to know each other. Just 1 mile (but almost 1,000 feet of elevation gain) from our campsite were some spectacular ledges where the other leader and I thought it would be great to bivouac. Because we were already at the campsite that had been our goal for the day, we didn't feel as though we could push the participants hard to move on. Instead, we proposed it as an option to the participants, but after a brief discussion they decided that they would rather stay put. The other leader and I were really excited about the idea of a bivy on the ledges, but we resisted imposing our agenda on the participants. We were disappointed in the group's decision, but we thought that it was more important to honor the group decision-making process than to coerce the participants into pushing on when they had already made their campsite goal.

As it turned out, it rained just before dawn the next morning and the ledges were engulfed in clouds. Had we compelled the participants to push on to the ledges the night before, the participants not only would have been disgruntled at having been persuaded to relocate camp, but they would have had to scramble to pack up their sleeping bags when the predawn drops started hitting. We already felt confident about the choice we had made to prioritize the group's goals over our own agenda, but the rain and obscured view reinforced our decision!

What follows are several principles that can guide a leader who is trying to coach groups through successful experiences.

Clarify Goals and Elicit Commitment

First of all, your expedition goals must be clearly defined, and your participants must be committed to working to achieve these goals, as addressed in Chapter 7, Preparing to Lead an Expedition. As the expedition progresses, you should constantly revisit these goals, clarifying them within the context of the expedition and making sure that the participants are still dedicated to them.

For example, let's say your participants all agreed at the pretrip meeting that learning to navigate off-trail is an important goal for them. As you prepare your daily map briefings and navigation lessons, you can remind the students of the off-trail navigation goal, using that as a rationale for bushwhacking through dense undergrowth or spending a lot of time making sure that each participant can triangulate competently. Ask participants if the expedition plan and the lessons are meeting their needs and helping them achieve their goals. If you sense—or hear outright—that commitment to a particular goal is flagging, then you should revisit the goal.

Revise Goals if Necessary

Although you shouldn't compromise on the wider goals determined by your employing organization, often it is necessary to revamp specific group goals. Sometimes participants get enthusiastic about a particular goal without really knowing what it entails. Sometimes participants commit to a goal because they see everyone else doing it. Sometimes priorities simply change. Whatever the cause for revamping, it is your responsibility as a leader to help participants stay committed to meaningful and attainable goals.

For instance, the group in the preceding example that was so enthusiastic about learning to navigate off-trail may realize after a couple of days that they are surrounded by stunning peaks that they won't be able to climb if they continue their quest for bushwhacking and complex compass work. You can help them either revise their goal—"maintain a balance of bagging peaks and bushwhacking"—or shift gears completely—"climb every spectacular peak in this valley."

You should be careful not to support a group in revising its goals every time the going gets difficult. After all, much of the process of achieving any goal is difficult and not immediately rewarding. You need to have the vision and foresight to determine whether the achievement of the goal will compensate for the hardships endured en route or whether the process of attaining the goal is no longer productive.

Intervene When Appropriate

Intervening when a group wants to revamp its goals is a delicate task, and the longer you lead wilderness trips, the better you will become at it. Sometimes a situation begs for an intervention, even when the group is perfectly content with the way things are going.

Late in the afternoon of Day Five, our participants were getting tired. The group had already hiked 8 or 10 miles, much of it steeply downhill, and several participants had sore knees. One participant had slipped during a stream crossing and much of his gear was wet, so he was anxious to make camp and dry things out. Another participant was looking forward to some free time in camp so that she could write in her journal, catching up on the events of the course so far.

The plan the participants had come up with that morning was to hike to an alpine meadow where my co-instructor and I knew that there would be a spectacular view of the full moon rising that night. The participants, however, were beginning to talk about stopping to camp early. Although they were initially excited about the prospect of reaching the meadow and had shaped most of the day around attaining that goal, they were starting to convince themselves that camping early would be more prudent.

My co-instructor and I had to make a choice: support the group in camping early or encourage them to stick with the original plan. We took a gamble and persuaded the group to stick to the original goal and push on to the meadow. There was a bit of grumbling, but people shouldered their packs and moved on purposefully. It was a good decision; when we reached the meadow, everyone was elated

and people who had been complaining of aches and fatigue suddenly got a second wind. When the moon rose that night, casting the mountains around us in a purple glow, the participants were high on the view and proud of themselves for pushing on to reach their goal despite their weariness.

In the situation above, my co-instructor and I had to gauge whether the value of reaching the meadow and camping in an extraordinary place was greater than the value of letting the group make the decision to revamp the plan for a newly proposed goal of time to write in journals, rest sore knees, and dry things out. Based on past experience with other groups and what they knew of the aesthetics of the meadow, we predicted that the participants would ultimately be more satisfied with having pushed on to achieve the original goal—as turned out to be the case. In this situation, my co-instructor and I deemed that achieving the original goal—as well as camping in a splendid location—was more important than the group decision-making process.

Evaluate Success

So your group reached the top of a mountain: they cheered, hugged, passed around chocolate, and sat around enjoying the view. Later that day, when you are safely down or in camp that evening, take some time to debrief the experience. Identifying key decisions and factors that contributed to the successful experience will make it more likely to be replicated in future experiences. Also, evaluating the success will assign ownership of that success to the participants, rather than having it seem like a random fluke of nature. In your evaluative discussion, consider including the following questions:

- What did you do?
- How did you do it?
- Consider your original goal—did you do what you set out to do? If not, why not?
- What were the key factors that contributed to your success?

■ If you were to do it again, what, if anything, might you do differently?

Learn from Failure

In the process of striving to meet goals, you and your group will undoubtedly have both successes and failures. The same principles that are used to help individuals cope with failure also apply in helping groups deal with letdowns and fiascos. See "Understanding the Roles of Success and Failure," above, for more details.

Interpreting the Meaning of Experiences

One of the ways that a backcountry expedition can be most powerful is by participants *learning* something about themselves during their experience and then *transferring* this learning to their everyday lives back home. In order for this learning and transference to occur, participants must reflect upon experiences. Put simply, it looks like this:

LEARNING = EXPERIENCE + REFLECTION

One of the facilitative options available to you as a leader is to help participants figure out what—if any—meaning a particular experience holds for them. Although there are hundreds of ways to reflect upon experiences, the three methods most commonly used at Outward Bound are also the most easily adapted for your own use.

A Directive Approach: Learning by Telling

The directive approach involves the leader speaking for the experience. This method assumes that the leader has made some observations about individual participants or about the group, and this perspective gives the leader a way to interpret the experience for the participants. Interpreting the experience includes sharing observations about participant behaviors, making connections between these behaviors and general group dynamics, and advising participants how they can apply this knowledge to other parts of their course or their everyday lives. For example,

at the end of a day of rock climbing, you might circle up the participants and say something such as this:

> *"I noticed that a few of you did not belay anyone else, yet you climbed several climbs and required that others belay you. I also saw several of you napping in the shade all afternoon, rather than being active participants in the rock climbing. How do you think these behaviors affect your performance as a group?"*
> —Outward Bound Instructor Manual

You must exercise caution and not attempt to tell participants what they got out of an experience (for example, "You learned trust while being belayed by Joe")—that technique is usually perceived as presumptuous, condescending, and formulaic. After all, experiences themselves do not hold consistent, explicit meaning—they don't mean the same thing every time for each participant.

Instead, making simple observations and asking a few pointed questions will usually result in the participants reaching the same conclusion that you have, at the same time validating the participants' opinion and securing their investment in the learning. For example, saying, "Joe, I noticed that you were reluctant to climb at first, but as the day progressed you were willing to go up on the rock. Why do you think that is?" will usually be a lot more productive than saying, "Joe, I see that you learned to trust your teammates today."

There are two main reasons for using the directive approach: (1) when there are group dynamics issues that need to be addressed, or (2) when you think that telling the group or individuals about what you've observed will result in personal growth or increased performance as a team.

A Democratic Approach: Learning by Guided Reflection

The democratic approach involves participants reflecting on the experience together. In this method, the leader guides a discussion after an activity, asking the participants to reflect upon what they've learned as individuals and a group. This is a traditional approach toward learning through reflection: frame an activity, complete the activity, discuss the activity. Some sample debriefing questions include the following:

■ What was done? Why? Was it worth it?
■ How did the experience relate to your expectation of it?
■ What were your fears? Were they overcome? Were they justified?
■ What were the highlights? What were the hard times? Why?
■ Would you do it again?
■ How did the group work together? Who were the leaders? Were some people hard or easy to work with? Why?
■ What did *you* contribute?
  —*Outward Bound Instructor Manual*

A debrief would never include all of these questions. You would pick one or two of the questions that you think have the greatest likelihood of helping individuals or the group make use of what they learned during the activity.

A word of caution about debriefing. As Outward Bound-like experiences grow more popular in schools, communities, and workplaces, participants are learning what responses are typically expected of them. These days, if you gather a group after a rock-climbing day and simply ask, "What did you learn today?" you are going to hear "trust," "confidence," "reaching my limits," and other such programmed responses tumble out of participants' mouths before you have even finished asking the question. It's possible that the participants *did* learn trust, confidence, etc., but in order to ensure that they are *really* making these connections—and not just spewing out what they think you want to hear—you will need to ask probing questions that require more sincere reflection: "So you learned trust. What happened today that made you learn trust?"

A Laissez-Faire Approach: Learning by Doing

The laissez-faire approach involves letting the experience speak for itself. Using this approach also requires that you not have any particular goals regarding the outcome of the experience. However, using this approach does not mean just jumping from activity to activity without structuring any reflective time. The experience can speak for itself only if there is an appropriate time for it to make itself heard.

For example, at the end of a day of rock climbing, you might urge the participants to push themselves on one last climb before taking down the ropes. Then you would turn the participants loose to walk back to camp. If the experience was important enough, the participants might discuss it on their walk.

Or you might give the participants some journal writing time at the base of the cliffs before sending them back to camp. Again, though the journal writing would not be guided, if the experience was impactful enough, presumably the participants would reflect on it in their writing.

Former Outward Bound instructor Rusty Baillie famously advised, "Let the mountains speak for themselves." He, as well as many other Outward Bound instructors, believe that the inherent grandeur of the mountains (or rivers, canyons, seas, etc.) provides its own message that might result in personal growth on the part of those who experienced it.

But the mountains don't necessarily speak to everyone, and often participants on intense and challenging outdoor programs are so focused on the activities and intensity of the experience that they are simply unable to reflect on the experience without some guidance. Although studies show that many Outward Bound alumni, years down the road, derive meaning from their experiences on Outward Bound or other programs, sometimes a simple, timely nudge in the direction of reflection is all it takes to get people to make immediate, life-changing realizations about themselves.

In general, "letting the mountains speak for themselves" is an approach that is best used deliberately but intermittently throughout an expedition, interspersed with methods that require more active reflection. This laissez-faire approach is most appropriate when you sense—through observing participant behaviors and hearing participant comments—that a particular experience has been impactful but doesn't seem to require any further exploration by the group.

The classic example of this is a group sitting on top of a summit, awestruck by a breathtaking view, saying things to each other such as, "I can't believe we just climbed all the way up here" and "I've never done anything so hard or so magnificent." Despite the clichéd descriptions, moments such as these are surprisingly common in the backcountry. In such situations, it's likely that participants are going to continue to reflect on the experience long after it's over, even without your prompting.

———

As with leadership styles discussed in Chapter 2, Becoming a Leader, in Part I, Leadership Fundamentals, methods of framing and debriefing are most effective when used deliberately in specific situations. Try to determine which debriefing approach will give your participants the best chance to learn and grow from each experience.

Priest and Gass's *Effective Leadership in Adventure Programming* provides a thoughtful and thorough account of the evolution of facilitation in outdoor programming; this book can be useful to the new facilitator, particularly for those working in recreational, developmental, or therapeutic programs, which have objectives that differ from those of educational programs like Outward Bound.

Solving Problems and Making Decisions

Although they are frequently described as two separate processes, problem solving and decision making generally go hand in hand, particularly in the wilderness. Solving a problem usually involves identifying the problem, brainstorming so-lutions, and then making a decision about which course of action to take. In the backcountry, with the dynamic forces of individual personalities and a constantly changing environment, numerous problems are solved and many decisions are made every day. In fact, outdoor leadership is to some extent a long process of solving problems and making decisions: "What's the problem? How shall we fix it? Where should we go? What should we do? How shall we do it?"

Once I led an expedition on which we had to portage our canoes around a long stretch of class V white water. We arrived at the portage midmorning; the plan was to walk our backpacks down to the end of the white-water stretch, about 2 miles away, leaving the canoes and food packs at the beginning of the portage. We would then return to the beginning, eat lunch, and spend the afternoon carrying the canoes and the food packs down to the end of the portage.

We made our 2-mile backpack and left the packs before returning to the canoes and food packs. When we got back to the beginning of the portage, though, we realized with dismay that our food packs were missing. Some local construction workers told us that they had recently seen a truck with two teens in it speeding away from the beginning of the portage, so we figured that they had nabbed our food packs thinking they would be full of sleeping bags, tents, and other valuable camping equipment.

We had a problem: three days of expedition were left, and we now had no food. What should we do?

Because the problem presented an excellent opportunity for participant problem solving and decision making (and indeed, some of the participants accused the other leader and me of arranging for the food to be stolen to increase the challenge of the course!), we coached the group through the process of figuring out what to do.

It was easy to identify the problem and name the desired outcome: problem—no food; desired outcome—get food. There were other complicating factors, such as no cell phone service and no road access to the end of the portage. The participants brainstormed possible solutions, ranging from fasting to foraging and fishing to hitchhiking 70 miles to the nearest convenience store and buying food for twelve people for three days.

Finally, after considering the merits of all options, we decided to send one leader to hitchhike to a phone to call back to base camp and request a resupply while the rest of the group portaged the canoes. We would then paddle down the river to a road-accessible resupply spot. We knew that it would take most of the day for the phone call to be made, food to be packed, and the resupply to be driven out to us, so we were facing at least eight hours without food, but none of the other options offered any more comforting prospects.

Portaging is hard work; when we finally met up with our resupply, we were ravenous but happy to have solved our problem successfully. At the end of the course, a few of the participants reported that dealing with getting our food stolen was one of the highlights of the course for them!

Mountaineer John Graham, in his book *Outdoor Leadership,* says that "systematic thinking, common sense, and intuition are the keys to making good decisions." Add reflection on successes and failures (also known as learning through experience) to these three traits, and the result is a recipe for consistently good decision making.

Most capable outdoor leaders become good decision makers and problem solvers because the job entails leadership autonomy. Without a supervisor, mentor, or peer group readily accessible, outdoor leaders need to make hundreds of independent decisions, the ramifications and outcomes of which usually become immediately apparent. In order to make your own decisions, you need to be able to identify the situation or problem, consider the available options, and select a course of action that best addresses the situation.

When you are trying to pinpoint the situation or problem, remember the four factors addressed in "Preliminary Factors to Consider in Decision Making" in Chapter 5, Taking Risks and Making Decisions. Identifying the (1) reality of the situation, (2) participants' limits, (3) leader's limits, and (4) leader's emotional investment in the situation will help you get a more objective grasp of a complex problem. Once you have a clearer picture of the situation, you can begin to brainstorm possible solutions.

You can also use the decision-making strategies outlined in "A Four-Tier Model" in Chapter 5, Taking Risks and Making Decisions, in Part I, Leadership Fundamentals, to help you determine an appropriate course of action for any given situation: a directive approach, a democratic style, a consensual method, or a laissez-faire attitude. Let's review each of the four decision-making methods, with examples of how you might make decisions in a wilderness context using each method.

Directive: leader decides alone. This approach is useful when a decision must be made quickly or when participants do not have the knowledge, experience, or skill to be involved in the decision.

Wind is picking up on the lake, and the participants are rafted up in a flotilla, consulting the maps. They are still a half mile from shore, and they are novice canoeists, not ready for big swells or whitecaps. You point them in the right direction and tell them to paddle hard toward shore because the importance of reaching shore quickly outweighs the benefit of the navigation practice.

Democratic: leader consults with select others and together they decide. This approach is useful when participants have information or opinions that could affect the decision and when empowering participant leaders is important.

You show the participant leaders tomorrow's campsite on a map and then turn responsibility over to them for making a travel plan that will enable them to reach that campsite by the next evening. The participant leaders must determine what time to wake up, which route to take, and when to stop for breaks, etc. and then inform the rest of the group about the plan.

Consensual: leader involves the whole group in the decision. This approach is useful when you have plenty of time, when there is a range of acceptable outcomes, and when the decision-making process is as important—or more so—than the actual decision.

The group is camped in a saddle between two accessible peaks, and the weather is good. The plan is to climb one peak the next day and one peak the day after. You give the participants the route descriptions and tell them that they must decide which peak to climb first. You help facilitate a discussion that leads to a decision everyone is content with.

Laissez-faire: leader turns over decision making to the group. This approach is useful when participant ownership in the decision is the most important factor. It should be used only with participants who have the knowledge, experience, and maturity to make an acceptable decision.

The leader gets word that a bridge along the planned route has been washed out, about 4 miles down the trail. The leader knows that it might be possible to cross the river on foot near the bridge, but upon arrival the foot crossing also might be determined

to be unsafe. The leader gives the group this information, as well as the information that a safe crossing exists 8 miles upstream, which would involve backtracking. The leader tells the group that they must decide whether to backtrack immediately or to stay on course and hope that the river crossing can be safely completed near the bridge. After asking if there are any further questions, the leader then retires to his tent, telling the group that he'll hear the decision from them in the morning.

A final factor to consider when solving problems and making decisions in the backcountry is the dynamic wilderness environment. A decision that served you well on your last trip may prove disastrous on your next one—even if the situations seem identical—if you do not carefully reconsider all the circumstances.

For example, you might be accustomed to pulling your canoes completely up on shore when you reach camp for the evening. But at one site, thick brush and boulders prevent you from doing this easily, so you decide to leave the boats tied to a tree, floating in the water. The next morning, no problem: The boats are still there.

So the next time you camp at this site, you just leave your boats in the water. It's windier than it was last time, though, and the boats spend all night rubbing against the boulders on the shoreline. The next morning, many of your boats have holes in them.

One canoeing trip leader describes a decision he and his supervisor made, based on past decisions, that had very different results:

My program has been launching canoe trips at the same put-in for twenty years with no incidents. One day, however, we arrived at the put-in and found that the river seemed to be running higher than normal. But my supervisor pointed out to me that we always used that boat launch, so we loaded up our canoes on the shore and shoved off.

Within minutes, I knew that we had made a bad decision. The water was up in the trees along the shore, there were no eddies, and the current was faster than I'd ever seen. Our novice canoeists were no match for this river, and sure enough, one boat capsized. The boat and paddlers were quickly swept downstream, and as the other leader and I raced to catch up with them, another boat tipped.

Everything ended up working out, with no serious injuries and just some lost gear and frightened paddlers. But had we simply thought through our decision to launch in light of the new information—the high water level—we certainly never would have been in that situation in the first place.

    —Joseph, Outward Bound instructor,
    1989-1991

Weather, environmental conditions, impassable trails or routes, wild animals—all are dynamic aspects of the wilderness environment that make it necessary to not base your decisions solely on past experience in a given situation.

Modeling Decision-Making Styles

Your participants can learn to be good leaders by watching and listening to you, particularly if you're working with another leader. If you and your co-leader have a transparent decision-making process, your participants can absorb a lot of information about how leaders make decisions.

Leader A: *"What do you think about this wind—can we safely cross the lake?"*
Leader B: *"Hmm, it's not too bad yet, but it looks like it's picking up a little. I'm a bit nervous about that open stretch through the narrows."*
Leader A: *"Yeah, me too. We'd probably make it—I think the group's paddling skills are pretty strong right now. But if someone capsized, they would get washed down the*

lake pretty quickly, and we might all get separated."*
Leader B: *"What if we crossed from here to that island, and then from that island to the far point? That way we wouldn't have any really long stretches, and we could get behind the lee shore of the peninsula."*
Leader A: *"Well, it's a lot longer that way, but I think you're right."*
Leader B: *"OK, gang, let's get the boats loaded up. Here's what we're going to do. . . . "*

The rationale behind the decision is not a mystery or a closely guarded secret held by the leaders. The leaders are comfortable with batting ideas back and forth with each other without worrying about appearing indecisive in front of the participants. When confronted with a similar situation, the participants will have the background to walk themselves through the decision-making process and make a sound decision. This sort of interaction also combats the idea that leaders simply always know exactly what to do. It shows participants that leadership—can be a process based on reason, logic, and judgment.

Having High Standards for Personal Conduct

Many outdoor organizations ask participants to sign some sort of code of conduct, committing to a particular standard of behavior during their course: showing respect for others and for the environment; refraining from the use of tobacco, alcohol, or drugs; following safety guidelines; etc. Prior to your trip, you or your organization should establish behavior and conduct guidelines to which all participants will commit. You, and possibly a core group of key participants, can decide what behavior would be detrimental to the success of your trip based on the physical and emotional atmosphere you would like your trip to have. Then communicate these guidelines to all participants and elicit their compliance, either formally (by having them sign a document establishing their commitment) or informally. Along with guidelines for conduct, you should also address the consequences of failing to honor the agreed-upon standards for behavior. Some things to consider include the following points.

Discourage Alcohol, Tobacco, and Drug Use

A clear head and fast reaction time are critical to the safety of participants on outdoor programs; thus, most organizations allow no alcohol or drug use on their expeditions. Many also have no tolerance for tobacco use because of the fire danger posed by cigarettes as well as the environmental impact of cigarette butts being strewn about. Second-hand smoke is another growing concern, as well as the behavior modeled for younger participants.

Your organization, if you are affiliated with one, may have its own policies regarding drug, alcohol, and tobacco use on trips. If so, as the trip leader you are responsible for enforcing these policies.

If the institution doesn't have such policies, or if you are leading a trip for an informal group of friends or acquaintances, the issue of such policies is probably something that you should address at the pretrip meeting. Introduce the subject and then determine whether the presence of or absence of alcohol, tobacco, or drugs will be an issue for anyone on the trip. Try to reach a compromise that everyone can live with. At the very least, educate participants about the risks associated with alcohol, drug, and tobacco use. For example, in addition to impairing judgment, alcohol is a vasodilator and can lead to hypothermia by giving you the illusion of warmth in your extremities while diverting heat away from your core.

Discourage Intimate Relationships

The grandeur of the wilderness and the quick camaraderie formed among people spending every waking and sleeping hour together can often be a recipe for blossoming romance. Leaders might fall in love with other leaders, participants might find a kindred soul within their group, or a leader and a participant might sense a spark of attraction. But new romances on most outdoor trips are

inconvenient at best and painful or unprofessional at worst.

With the exception of groups of friends taking a trip together, an intimate relationship between a leader and a participant is unacceptable, even if both are above the age of consent; obviously, an intimate relationship between a leader and an underage participant is both illegal and unprofessional. The inherent power of the leader, the vulnerable position of the participant, and the precarious nature of any new relationship combine to create a situation that is unfair to all participants and that puts the quality of the entire expedition at risk. If a leader and a participant become aware of a mutual attraction, they should explore this after the expedition is over. Many organizations have policies defining the length of time (frequently, six months to a year) that must elapse between the end of a trip and the initiation of any personal communication between a leader and a participant.

Romances between co-leaders on trips are a stickier issue, because in many organizations, the most experienced leaders are often married to or romantically connected with the other most experienced leaders. People who spend 200 days each year in the field leading trips frequently become involved with someone else who does the same work. And although many organizations make an effort to keep personal and professional relationships separate, sometimes the best leadership pair for a particular expedition is composed of an existing couple. In such situations, it's imperative that both the organization and the leaders address the issue of their working relationship prior to going out in the field.

With the exception of courses designed specifically for couples or families, intimate relationships among trip participants are discouraged on Outward Bound courses because of the inherently exclusive nature of such relationships. There are two reasons for this.

First, we have found that one of the most powerful catalysts for self-discovery—and, thus, character development—is for participants to be able to operate without the burden of preconceptions. If no one knows you or your background, there are no expectations that you will behave in a particular way, and you are free to behave as you really desire. Generally, this results in people being greater and doing more than they thought they could; their strongest self emerges.

Second, group process plays an important role at Outward Bound, and a clique or romantic couple undermines this process in much the same way that a voting bloc can undermine the political process. Asking Outward Bound participants to refrain from intimate relationships is a reasonable request because in most circumstances they begin as total strangers, with no preestablished intimacy or personal connection.

Most likely, however, you will be leading a trip with participants who know each other or who are already intimately involved. In this case, try to encourage as much mingling as possible during the planning process and during the actual expedition. For example, ask one half of a couple to help with the food planning and the other half to help collect gear. Or split up a pair of best friends by assigning one to cook dinner while the other sets up tents.

Encourage Mutual Respect

Harassment, intimidation, or offensiveness of any sort are, of course, completely unacceptable in any environment and particularly on a backcountry expedition, wherein many participants already feel a bit apprehensive or out of their comfort zones. Early in the trip, address the topics of tolerance and respect for others, and then model behavior that sets the right tone. Be aware of language and actions that innocently exclude or stereotype, such as addressing your whole group, which is likely co-ed, as "you guys" or asking a few strong males to help you move a log blocking the trail.

Encourage Acceptable Social Norms

One of the curious things that often happens on backcountry expeditions is that some people relax their standards for social norms. Apparently,

as their hands and faces get a bit dirty and the memory of "civilization" fades, their standards of civility also diminish with each step away from the trailhead. This often manifests in the form of vulgar language, racy jokes, a propensity to discuss bodily functions with great gusto, or all of the above. Perhaps this is one reason that British safari travelers always dine with tablecloths, pause for a proper tea, and dress for dinner even in the bush: the trappings of civilization create a refined atmosphere and encourage travelers to remain courteous even in the wilds.

You should consider addressing this subject, though it might seem trivial, at your pretrip meeting. A collectively agreed-upon set of social norms for your trip will set the tone for a polite, civilized, and emotionally safe environment for everyone.

But even the best-laid plans can go awry, and at some point in your leadership career you will be faced with an uncomfortable situation: handling unacceptable behavior in the backcountry. How you address unacceptable behavior will both challenge you and define you as a leader.

Discourage Unacceptable Behavior

One of the least enjoyable but most important aspects of outdoor leadership is dealing with behavior that is in some way detrimental to the success of your trip. There are many ways for participant behavior to negatively affect a trip, and if you spend long enough in the outdoor leadership field, you will likely encounter them all.

If you have set up some guidelines and expectations for behavior prior to the trip, you will have a head start in identifying offensive behavior and helping the culprit to recognize this behavior as objectionable. Chances are, pulling the perpetrator aside, identifying the behavior, and describing the effect that this behavior is having on the rest of the group will induce an apology and quickly rectify the behavior, particularly when the perpetrator is a mature adult. For example, you might say, "Hey, Roy, have you noticed that Jennette is pretty uncomfortable with the jokes you've been telling this morning?" Or this: "Jennette, you might not realize this, but when you complain about how many miles we have scheduled for today, it puts a damper on other people's enthusiasm for the hike."

If discreet, polite, and well-timed observations don't result in improved behavior, it's time to employ some of the tools in your interventions toolbag. First of all, you should probably ponder *why* a participant is behaving in a way that undermines the quality of the expedition. What *motivates* people to behave in a particular way? In *Control Theory in the Classroom*, William Glasser writes that "all of our behavior is our constant attempt to satisfy one or more of five basic needs that are written into our genetic structure." He then identifies these basic needs as the following: to survive, to belong and love, to gain power, to be free, and to have fun.

If a participant is acting out on a trip—exhibiting inappropriate or unacceptable behavior—it is often because some basic need isn't being met. If you are able to determine what that person needs and how you can help meet that need, the troubling behavior often resolves itself. As an outdoor leader, you're certainly not expected to be a psychoanalyst, but frequently in the backcountry you can discern some pretty basic things about human needs.

In the example above, Roy might be making off-color jokes because he thinks it is the only way he can get attention from other group members. Roy might be lacking a sense of social acceptance or self-esteem. As the leader, you might be able to draw Roy into helping with navigation or leadership, thus assigning him some power and, with it, a sense of belonging and respect. Similarly, Jennette might be complaining about the daily mileage because she is suffering from terrible blisters. Help her clean and dress her blisters and take some of the weight out of her pack, and perhaps her griping will diminish as she realizes that someone is watching out for her well-being.

Although it's an unpleasant prospect, you should be prepared for the possibility that one day you will lead a trip with a participant whose behavior is so intolerable that there is no other solution than for you to ask that person to leave—or to expel the person from—the trip. This is never pleasant, and it almost always results in complicated logistical maneuvering; this is where the bailout plan you designed (see "Organizing a Trip" in Chapter 7, Preparing to Lead an Expedition) comes in handy. But the effect of tolerating a person whose behavior is seriously diminishing the quality of the experience for everyone else is usually much worse than any hardship suffered as a result of the expulsion. Don't make the mistake of keeping an inappropriate participant on the expedition simply because it's uncomfortable or inconvenient to expel that person—or because you believe that person will benefit from the experience despite the behavior. If a participant's behavior genuinely warrants expulsion and you keep that person on the trip, the continued presence is likely to negatively impact or even ruin the experience for other participants. Before you go out into the field, clarify your organization's policies and procedures regarding removing someone from a trip.

For additional information about handling unacceptable behavior when working with youth, see "Dealing with Inappropriate Behavior" in Chapter 15, Leading Youth in Your Community, in Part IV, Taking Leadership into Your Community.

Leading Groups with No Official Leader

Unless you're a professional outdoor educator, most of the time that most of us spend outside is likely to be in the company of people we know well in places we're familiar with. We take our kids canoeing; we get out on an annual backpack trip with our spouse; we climb or ski on weekends with our friends. Many of our trips are likely to be repeat performances of trips we've taken in the past. We have favorite places that we know well and return to often, and we have our traditions and habits that we repeat faithfully. We probably even pack the same favorite meals year after year. Indeed, many of our favorite outings are simply attempts to replicate prior great trips.

With such trips to familiar places with people we know well, why then is leadership necessary beyond simply organizing the food and equipment and making sure that the stoves work? Don't things just go smoothly if you know where you're going and you know that the other participants are going to work well together? Most of the time, things do go smoothly. With a collegial group and a familiar itinerary, the trip is likely just to "run" itself. Most of us simply head out with a group of friends for a day or a week without designating a leader, partly because we don't immediately see the need for one and partly because no one wants to assume that responsibility.

It was Day Eleven of a twenty-day sailing trip up the inlets off the coast of British Columbia (not an Outward Bound expedition). We were bound for Bute Inlet, a remote fjord that serves as a drain for wet glaciers and wild, untouched mountains. Although all four of us were experienced sailors, there were certain inevitable hazards on our trip that we had accepted.

First, the Danielle *was a pretty dinky boat, one better suited to a lake in upstate New York than to the wild seas off British Columbia. Second, there were major logging operations in the areas where we were traveling. Very frequently, we would see logs that had escaped their shipping barges and were floating aimlessly with the tides. These logs, especially the upright ones (known as "deadheads"), could easily do some damage to our paper-thin hull. Because of this, we didn't sail at night.*

But our momentum was halted when Gretchen caught her thumb between the lowering engine and the hull. We all came to the conclusion that her thumb was broken and that we needed to get her to a hospital. Assuming that the engine worked, we figured we could probably motor to inhabited Quadra Island, some 30 miles away. That

would get us there by 10:00 PM, ready for an early visit to the emergency room the following morning. It was 5:00 PM, and we didn't want to pull into the port at dark. We struck the sails and motored, praying for favorable weather.

At about 8:00 PM I took the tiller, while the others munched in the cabin. When I took over, the seas were calm and the outboard engine was running smoothly. As we motored across a major channel, the northern terminus of the Strait of Georgia, the winds shifted to the south and for the first time that day, we experienced some swells. A quick glimpse at the chart led me to realize that we were situated above some hundred miles of open sea, enough fetch to give Danielle *quite a ride. As we motored on the swells, winds and precipitation all were on the rise.* Danielle *was feeling a bit overwhelmed.*

Although I was alone on the deck, the rest of the crew knew the situation as they (and their dinner) were getting tossed around the cabin. Had there been a designated leader on the boat, he or she probably would have said something such as, "Hmmm. The winds are pretty fierce in this channel. Perhaps it would be safest if we did an about-face and headed to the hospital amid the calm seas of the morning." But no such words were mentioned. As individuals, we wanted to be in civilization that night; this desire outweighed any notion of group safety. Deep down, we all knew what we should have done, but everyone's silence reinforced our onward progression.

It was getting dark. . . . We were at the mercy of the deadheads now. Clive was strapping down the deck gear, and we were all wearing our personal flotation devices. Gretchen, with one hand useless, stayed below and navigated by chart and GPS. Dave was holding down the engine in the water, to prevent it from stalling when we went airborne between swells. We were still 5 miles from port, a solid hour of terrifying gales. My glasses were now stained by the spraying salt water. I prayed that the engine didn't die. We didn't even have our main sail up for stabilization, and at this point it would have been too dangerous to set it.

Why didn't I say anything? This was absolutely stupid. A 22-foot sloop in swells like this? If I had been by myself, I surely would have turned around. Why didn't I mention anything? Perhaps because I wasn't the designated leader. But then again, nobody was.

That hour took forever. Trying to keep Danielle *in line against the force of the swells, I swore I was about to fracture the wooden tiller. In between waves, I imagined capsizing and brainstormed how we could ferry ourselves to shore. Chances of survival in that situation would have been bleak. Every once in a while the engine began to sputter, and everyone's face went blank.* Danielle *would then resubmerge and instill momentary confidence. Why didn't I say anything???*

With the port within a half mile, the swells began to ease. What a relief . . . and inside a few minutes, we were tied up to the dock, hugging each other, swearing that we'd never do that again. We walked onshore to the bar of an inn, and within minutes we were listening to the Stones over cold drinks. We didn't deserve this pleasure. We had just played Russian roulette with a garage-sale outboard engine.

—Jeff, Outward Bound instructor since 1999

The Leadership Vacuum

A major concern for many outdoor leaders recreating in their free time is the leadership vacuum that seems to arise when several outdoor pro-

fessionals are freed from the responsibility of caring for others. Most experienced outdoor leaders, when in the field with students, are efficient and decisive, able to make quick and sound decisions, galvanize a group into action, deliver critical feedback, or speak up when something seems amiss.

But put them in a group in which no one is the official leader, and suddenly those same people are responding to questions with "I don't care—either way is fine with me" or "Whatever everybody else wants to do," standing around with coffee cups for hours in the morning instead of getting camp packed up, or waiting for someone else to point out that the crevasses seem unusually large and open for that time of year.

Designated or Ad Hoc Leader?

Many organizations combat this leadership vacuum by designating leaders for all official staff trainings and staff trips. But still, most of us have been on numerous unofficial trips with other outdoor leaders when the absence of a designated or even ad hoc leader cost us time, efficiency, or even safety.

The fact is, groups function better with leadership. So even though designating a leader can undermine the relaxed, off-the-clock environment that people desire, having a designated leader usually pays off in terms of facilitating a more efficient and harmonious expedition. If an emergency arises or a difficult situation presents itself, a group with someone ready to step into a leadership role is likely to handle the situation or emergency better than a group that flounders in the leadership vacuum until an ad hoc leader—often the person you would *least* want as a leader—steps in to fill the vacuum.

I was on a personal trip, and we became wind-bound on a huge lake, up in the eastern Arctic. We were OK with lying low for the first day or so, but after that we became pretty antsy, and some folks were concerned about timing to get to the end of the river to meet our flight out, return for jobs back home, etc. We spent a lot of time hemming and hawing about what to do, and eventually two folks came up with a plan to hike overland (with our boats and gear, etc.), which would hopefully get us to a place where we could put back on the lake in a more sheltered space.

A couple of people were really excited about the challenge. Although most of us didn't relish the thought of a long portage, we recognized that it was the only reasonable option if we were to stay on schedule. But one person really didn't like the idea, and he was very vocal about it. What ultimately was decided was that we wouldn't go. We decided not to go because one person really didn't want to go, but this somehow ignored the fact that half the group was really keen to go and all of the rest except for one were willing to go.

This situation made me realize that the previous six or seven weeks of that trip had involved this type of decision making all along. I called it making a decision to meet the lowest common denominator. In fact, all through the trip we had made decisions that reflected the least amount that any one person was willing to do but rarely honored the few folks who wanted to do more than that.

Another example of this was when we were hungry. If one person was hungry, then everyone had to stop and eat. That one person wasn't encouraged to grab a snack and hold on but, rather, the entire group would stop, despite others wanting to push on a bit farther. People were not so comfortable being the one to push the group, or in particular an individual within the group, in the absence of a leader, and so we often resorted to meeting the needs of the lowest common denominator in our decision making.

—Leila, Outward Bound instructor since 1999

No Leader?

If you really can't bear the idea of naming an official trip leader for your trips with friends, at the very least consider the following questions before you all go out in the woods together:

- Who will serve as the chief first-aid person if there is a major medical situation?
- Who will be in charge if there is an emergency?
- Who will manage an evacuation if one is needed?
- How will our group make decisions?
- Who will provide direction if our group gets stuck with a particular decision?

Leader of the Day?

If you're with a group of competent outdoor leaders, another option is to take turns being the "leader of the day," and if any difficult situations arise or if any emergencies present themselves, whoever is the leader that day will take charge of the situation.

THE EXPEDITION "GODDESS"

One group of friends on a staff trip decided to designate one woman as the "goddess." Most major safety decisions were made by the official staff trainer, and many other important decisions were made by democracy or consensus, but the group decided that if at any point they became bogged down in the decision-making process, then Kristen—the goddess—would make a decision and they would all abide by it in the interest of efficiency. Kristen wasn't the "leader," but in certain situations, she played a critical leadership role.

A FINAL NOTE

Most Outward Bound instructors breathe a sigh of relief when the trip planning, introductory activities, and gear packing have been accomplished and the group is finally standing at the trailhead or river launching area. The backcountry, after all, is where the magic—the challenges, triumphs, teamwork, camaraderie, and physical beauty—of an expedition unfolds. As a leader, you are responsible for putting your participants in situations that allow this magic to happen effectively. It can be a daunting responsibility. But the research, training, and planning you've accomplished have prepared you to do your job well. You see a half dozen or so pairs of eyes looking to you expectantly and you realize that you know what to do to make this backcountry expedition a success.

CHAPTER 9

GOING SOLO

During my fifteenth summer, I decided to go on an Outward Bound course. I didn't really care where I would go or what I would do, so my parents helped me pick out a course. My only requirement was that I didn't want to do a course that had a Solo. I had heard of Outward Bound's signature Solo activity—a period of hours or days spent alone in the wilderness with minimal provisions—and I wanted no part of it. Two days alone in the woods? Who would I talk to? Being away from a phone for a month was going to be bad enough without spending forty-eight hours of it totally incommunicado. For a fifteen-year-old who passed notes to her friends in the school hallway on an hourly basis (in the days before text messaging) and spent several hours on the phone each evening discussing the events of the day, the idea of a Solo was completely unimaginable. I simply could not wrap my mind around the concept of two entire days without significant human interactions.

Somehow my parents either failed to fully investigate all the details of the course they eventually picked or they neglected to mention to me that it did indeed include a Solo. In any case, about fifteen days into my twenty-eight-day Outward Bound course in Maine, I found myself sitting alone beside a stream, a clear plastic tarp strung up in the woods behind me. My only consolation was that although I was unaccompanied, I wasn't alone. Like thousands of Outward Bound students before me and thousands to follow, I was going Solo.

UNDERSTANDING THE SOLO EXPERIENCE

Solo generated a reputation for Outward Bound as a survival school, probably because the primary thing that mainstream Americans knew about Outward Bound was that one of Outward Bound's unique activities was a period in which participants camped alone, equipped with adequate but limited food, shelter, and equipment. So how did Solo get started at Outward Bound, and what's its purpose in Outward Bound courses?

The Origins of Solo at Outward Bound

Outward Bound founder and educator Kurt Hahn introduced the idea of solitary reflection as part of the academic schedule at the Salem School in Germany in 1920. Hahn believed that regular periods of silence and solitude were necessary for true learning. So each Sunday, students and faculty took a quiet two-hour walk alone to commune with nature and reflect on their lives.

The period of solitude was later adopted by Outward Bound in the United States, but it became a "night alone," in which each student camped alone overnight, isolated from the other students. But on the second U.S. Outward Bound course's scheduled "night alone," the patrol director received word the night before from the camp chef that food deliveries up the mountain had been delayed and that the base camp was running out of food: there would be no resupplies for at least three days. However, no one was worried. "Oh well," replied the patrol director, "that will give me a chance to do something I've been wanting to try anyway."

The patrol director gathered the students together, taught them a few things about edible plants and berries, and placed them at half-mile intervals along a stream. Three days later, the students returned to the group camp jubilant, having had profoundly successful experiences. Subsequently, the original "night alone" became a standard forty-eight- or seventy-two-hour Solo on Outward Bound courses in the United States, and Solo has remained an integral course activity ever since.

Solo at Outward Bound Today

Although Solo has a reputation of being a "survival" experience, the purpose of Solo is not—and never has been—survival. Instead, Solo on Outward Bound courses provides an opportunity for rejuvenation, reflection, and the experience of solitude in the wilderness.

It Allows for Reflection

Although the Solo is integral to the overall Outward Bound experience, its more important legacy is emphasizing the significance of the relationship between experience and reflection. As addressed in Chapter 8, Taking Responsibility for Yourself and Others Outdoors, the Outward Bound philosophy maintains that profound and lasting learning takes place when personal experiences are reflected upon. In this light, Solo—in addition to providing a generally welcome and well-deserved break from the physical and interpersonal rigors of the Outward Bound course—offers an opportunity for participants to reflect on their Outward Bound course and their life, in an environment with few distractions. It's a chance to digest what they have learned about themselves on their Outward Bound course so far.

It Isn't a Survival Ordeal

Reflection is a high-level cognitive function that cannot take place if basic human needs have not been met. Or, as the *Outward Bound Instructor Manual* puts it, "Cold, wet, hungry, or uncomfortable souls do not contemplate their role in the universe. They are more likely to be thinking about McDonalds." Thus, students on Outward Bound Solos have access to rationed but sufficient food, plenty of water, and clothing and shelter for staying warm and dry. Fasting is always an option—never a requirement—for those who seek an extra challenge for the Solo experience.

Typically, Outward Bound students complete about twenty-four hours of Solo for each week of course length, up to a maximum of seventy hours. Instructors check on students periodically, but interactions are generally brief and limited to a quick assurance that the student is OK and doesn't need anything.

Solo and Leadership

But wait a minute. If Solo is all about being alone and dealing with yourself, and leadership is all about dealing with groups of people, what's the connection between Solo and leadership? Can having a Solo experience make you a better leader? The answer is yes, for several reasons.

It Develops a Unique Awareness of and Comfort in the Wilderness

Being truly alone outside for a period of time gives you a unique appreciation for the wilderness (more on this topic is in "Seeing Solitude as a Window to Your World," below). Also, doing a Solo cultivates a fundamental comfort in the backcountry that comes from really knowing that you are relying completely on your own skills and inner strength (for more about this, see "Learning to Depend on Your Own Inner Resources," below).

It Forms Values

One of Outward Bound's basic assumptions about leadership is that you lead most effectively when your leadership style is based on values rather than on power, fear, or coercion. Values are formed by understanding yourself and by having experiences that allow you to see the connections between yourself, other people, and the natural world. Solo, as well as ongoing personal reflection, is one of these experiences. It gives you an opportunity to know yourself better, which leads to value formation. Once you are grounded in your own values, you can lead by example and by modeling these values.

It Develops Compassion

A Solo also gives you a chance to be a bit vulnerable or scared. The leader who is occasionally nervous or vulnerable is more likely to be able to demonstrate compassion and empathy for participants than the leader who never feels anxious. Although a Solo shouldn't put your life in jeopardy, somehow the simple act of being truly alone outdoors, with the darkness and sounds and elements, serves to remind you of your humanity. Having felt insignificant or scared can help you to become a more empathetic and compassionate leader.

It Builds Self-Awareness

As shown in Chapter 7, Preparing to Lead an Expedition, understanding *why* you like to lead is an important aspect of outdoor leadership. Your motivation for leading greatly influences your leadership style, as well as the effect that style has on your participants. If the reflection time on Solo is used deliberately, it can help you get a clear view of what motivates you to lead. Ultimately, you need to understand why you lead so that you can determine whether the reasons are personally meaningful for you. If your motivations for leading correspond with your priorities, values, and goals for yourself, then a leadership role is likely to be a comfortable one for you, one in which you will find personal satisfaction and professional success.

It Builds Self-Confidence

Finally, Solo builds self-confidence, which translates into a stronger leadership presence. Many people discover that what they fear most about Solo is being alone with only themselves for company. They're afraid that they will become bored with or depressed by their own thoughts. Doing a Solo can give you the happy realization that you are actually pretty pleasant company. You may be more interesting or funny than you thought. You might find that you enjoy thinking your own thoughts, carrying on mental conversations with yourself, or letting your creative mind wander. One Outward Bound alumna describes how she discovered an artistic side to herself on her Solo:

On Solo, I learned to minimize external stimulation and be more attuned to myself.

Had I had a book with me, I probably would have read it. Instead, as I sat by myself facing a spectacular vista of the Snow River Glacier and the surrounding mountains, I felt inspired to sketch the scene before me. In spite of a lifelong conviction that I cannot draw, I succumbed to the temptation and was delighted with the result.
—Monika, past Outward Bound
    participant

Such discoveries build the self-confidence that comes with believing that you are a stimulating, intelligent person. This, coupled with an increased comfort in the wilderness, can give leaders the self-assurance and self-reliance they need for success in being responsible for others' backcountry experiences.

Learning to Depend on Your Own Inner Resources

The difference between loneliness and solitude is your perception of who you are alone with and who made the choice.
—Anonymous

In addition to providing a chance to rest and reflect upon the Outward Bound experience, Solo also gives Outward Bound students the opportunity to see that they have the strength of character to mentally and physically thrive alone in the wilderness. Students who had never camped outdoors before their Outward Bound course, students who are afraid of the dark, students who don't like to get out of the tent at night for fear of encountering a bear—all complete a Solo, and many find it to be one of the most rewarding aspects of their Outward Bound experience.

One of Outward Bound's founding principles is the concept of self-reliance. At no time on an Outward Bound course is this principle more significant than during the Solo. Solo is not a survival experience, but it does require that students draw on inner strengths in order to benefit from the experience. Students often don't fully understand what a huge challenge Solo is until they are out in their individual site, very alone, with darkness approaching. Being alone outdoors can be at once frightening and exhilarating, boring and stimulating, trying and rewarding. The chief challenge of Solo is dealing with these conflicting emotions without being able to process them with anyone else. A student on an Outward Bound course in Utah shares a journal entry from her Solo:

> The journey eventually led us all into the depths of a canyon where we each spent twenty-four hours alone. We were allowed to bring only a sleeping bag, a gallon of water, some food, and a notebook for writing. Sitting alone on the canyon ledge did not frighten me, and I thought more in that one day than I have in two weeks during my life at home. The journey through my soul was hard; I faced things about myself that I wasn't able to confront before.
>
> Looking at the depths of Labyrinth Canyon, I stared into the heart of my fears. Fear stared back through red eyes, which, like the colors of the canyon, slowly changed through the day to a glowing yellow. As the moon began to rise over the steep canyon walls, so did my feelings. The flaws I saw within myself shamed me, but the virtues I began to see built me up. I felt so strong and beautiful and amazing—but with a sense of humility that was also overwhelming. I realized that by accepting myself, others would accept me, and by loving myself, I am invincible.
>
> The next morning as the sun rose, I sat in my sleeping bag watching the sunrise; my heart was calm and filled with such strength, clarity, and freedom—total utopia. I reentered camp that same morning a different person, with a deep sense of humility, strength, and, most important, love.
>
> —Annemarie, past Outward Bound participant

The Inner Challenge: Dealing with Yourself Alone

What is necessary, after all, is only this: solitude, vast inner solitude. To walk inside yourself and meet no one for hours—that is what you must be able to attain.
—*Rainer Maria Rilke,* Letters to a Young Poet

Solo is demanding in many ways. Participants must construct their own shelters with minimal materials; they have to ration their meager food supplies carefully; and they have to hear the sometimes frightening sounds of the wilderness. But the most difficult part for most people is dealing with their essential aloneness—the loneliness, fear, and boredom that accompany almost every type of solo venture of any great length. After a surprisingly small amount of time has been used up in shelter construction, campsite exploration, and a hearty nap, participants need to figure out what to do with the rest of their time alone.

When Solo rolls around on Outward Bound adult courses, for people twenty-one years old and up, we commonly hear our students argue for an abbreviated Solo period, saying things such as, "I live alone; I spend plenty of time by myself" or "I already spend a lot of introspective time; I came to Outward Bound to get *out* of my own head."

But few of us spend the kind of alone time that a backcountry overnight Solo allows: truly alone, with few outside distractions. Back home, we find many amusements to occupy unscheduled alone time: we flip through magazines while waiting in the doctor's office, read the covers of tabloids while we wait in line in the grocery store, and listen to music while sitting in traffic. Even those who live alone are surrounded by sounds—the refrigerator humming, the radio playing in the background—or distracting reminders of connections to other people: the telephone, the computer with email, the mailbox. It's almost as though our fear of being alone with our thoughts drives us to create diversions that will keep our minds occupied elsewhere. Or, in Anne Morrow Lindbergh's words in *Gift from the*

Sea, "Instead of planting our solitude within our own dream blossoms, we choke the space with continuous music, chatter, and companionship to which we do not even listen. It is simply there to fill the vacuum. When the noise stops there is no inner music to take its place."

However, on a backcountry overnight Solo, most participants are surprised to discover that they are better company for themselves than they anticipated. Without a magazine to divert their thoughts, they find meaningful ways to occupy their time. They remember things they hadn't thought of in years. They make life lists for themselves: things they want to accomplish before they die. They make plans to repair troubled relationships, sometimes even writing letters to family or friends with whom they have had a falling-out. And they think about who they are and who they want to become. They discover that *plus est en vous*—that they have more in themselves than they ever expected.

The Outer Challenge: Dealing with the Wilderness Alone

The other great challenge of any solo expedition is mustering up your courage to listen to the sounds of the wilderness, which become amplified in the face of solitude. A squirrel running past your tarp in the dark can sound surprisingly like a moose. The distant barking of coyotes becomes, in your imagination, a howling wolf pack. And many Solo participants have awakened in the night certain that a bear is devouring their food, so loud are the sounds, only to discover that a family of mice is busy gnawing its way into the gorp.

Weather imposes another daunting physical and emotional challenge. Rain threatens to soak those who set up a shoddy shelter; lightning storms remind students of their own mortality. The inner fortitude required to remain calm when you are frightened and alone is considerable. Participants who "survive" such scary encounters do so by relying on the reserves of strength that they have discovered and exercised during their wilderness expedition.

Before embarking on Solo, participants should be well equipped with the campcraft skills they need to set up a snug campsite for themselves and keep themselves comfortable and dry. But they must also draw on the other skills they have learned on expeditions: inventiveness, self-reliance, and tenacity.

Reaping Rewards in Retrospect

The difficulty and unique challenges of Solo are what make it rewarding, but sometimes that realization comes only with hindsight. After they have caught up on sleep, rinsed out their socks, and written a few letters in their journals, most participants do not sit relishing the solitary reflective time of Solo. But afterward, particularly at home, they begin to digest the relative enormity of what they accomplished, and they feel a sense of pride. Kurt Hahn, in a journal article from the late fifties, tells a story that sums up this sense of deferred gratification:

> *I know few boys who do not draw strength, and retrospectively also joy, from an arduous expedition carried out to a definite goal. I remember once asking a boy, who had sailed in our schooner around the Shetlands and Orkneys and encountered three gales, "How did you enjoy it?" He said, "Magnificently, except at the time."*

This, for many participants, is how they enjoy Solo: in retrospect.

Finding Unexpected Outcomes

Of course, some people simply hate Solo, both at the time and in retrospect. They're too bored, scared, or lonely to focus on anything other than the minutes ticking by until they can be reunited with the rest of their group. These are the people who usually return from Solo with nothing written in their journal except for lists of what they plan to eat when they get back to civilization.

Similarly, it is possible to enjoy Solo without

deriving any real lasting benefit from it. Although completing a Solo is a noteworthy feat, it is no guarantee of profound reflection. It is possible to spend forty-eight or seventy-two hours writing letters to friends in your journal, recalling the all words to "American Pie," and building stone walls around your campsite. In other words, it is possible to keep yourself occupied for an extended period of time with anything other than deliberate contemplation.

Although Outward Bound likes to believe that everyone benefits from Solo, even if they don't realize it at the time, it is the participants' prerogative to enjoy or detest, take advantage of or squander the Solo experience.

Seeing Solitude as a Window to Your World

For many Solo participants, the time alone in the woods (or desert or canyons or . . .) brings sharper focus to the natural world. With no one else to talk to and none of the distractions of civilization, people begin to notice things such as bark beetles gnawing on pine trees or fish skimming under the surface of the water. The woods become alive in a way that they are not when we are in the presence of other people. Participants become fascinated by things that would usually slip by unnoticed if other people are around: a bird song, ripe berries, an ant carrying a crumb.

Perched on rust-colored slickrock, I watched the sun slip steadily behind the huge canyon walls that rose before me. The orange glow of the sunset brought out the red-gold hues of the giant sandstone cliffs that seemed to be reaching for the turquoise sky . . . I was camping solo for three days in one site. It was on this Solo that I learned the value of solitude. Solitary time in nature can guide one to realize the splendor and significance of the natural world.

My campsite was in the corner of a small side canyon, where two walls that didn't quite meet in a corner formed a chimney.

On the second evening of my trip, I climbed up the chimney and onto a broad shelf in the canyon wall. It was when I was sitting there, on that shelf, contemplating the scene before me, that I realized and acknowledged the beauty of solitude and the power of nature. Sitting under the moon's glow, I felt pleasure after relaxing during the day in the warm glow of the sun. It was slightly chilly. The moonlight illuminated the cliffs against the dusky blue sky. A gentle breeze brought the scent of sage and juniper to my nose. I wished I could stay forever . . . but I also missed hearing the sounds of human voices. How could three days of solitude feel so fleeting, yet so long, all at once?

But I didn't regret that I was alone. It seemed to highlight the natural cycles of the earth. It was incredible to me. I remember thinking, "The Earth lives! It breathes!"

I'd read a quote by naturalist Jeff Anderson earlier that day that referred to the natural processes taking place on the canyon floor. . . . I could sense those cycles too. I experienced them too, by noting what types of rock were in which stage of the rock cycle, knowing they would break down and become one with the Earth's core before rising and cooling once more. Or by feeling the sand that blew into my eyes, knowing that once it had been solid rock and would be again. Or simply by seeing the sun rise and set each day.

When I described nightfall on that second evening in my journal, I wrote of the way external life cycles seemed to influence my own natural rhythm. "Now it is dusk," I wrote. "The sun is sunken behind the canyon wall and as the temperature drops, my energy goes too. As the moon slowly rises above the opposite wall of the canyon, stars begin to peep out one by one as the light changes and fades. Soon I'll crawl into my sleeping bag, cozy until dawn, when the

changing light stirs my spirit once more,
awakening my senses to the circle of life."
    —*Tessa, past Outward Bound participant*

Ironically, however, even surrounded by the natural world at its most dynamic, much of Solo participants' time is occupied with thoughts of the civilized world. Solo gives many people a surprisingly vivid, unfiltered look at their world at home. Life on the trail, when compared with decisions about careers or relationships, financial struggles, and unstable world politics, suddenly seems appealingly simple. You walk, eat, sleep, and then rise to repeat it all again. Consequences of actions are usually logical and immediately apparent; there is very little angst or unfairness associated with decisions. Although you might occasionally crave a soft bed or a hot shower, the challenges of life in the wilds are much less complicated than those at home, and the rewards are so much richer: a breathtaking view, the thrill of exploring the unknown, the exhausted satisfaction of a 20-mile day.

So why come home at all? Why not stay out in the wilderness, where a dry pair of socks or a hot cup of tea can bring immeasurable joy? Because, as the late legendary mountaineer Willi Unsoeld said in an address to an education conference in 1978, "That isn't where it's at."

For the vast majority of us, "life" is back at home, out of the wilderness, with our friends, families, jobs, struggles, and pursuits. We go out into the wilderness for fun and to experience its infinite beauty and simplicity, but we also go, perhaps subconsciously, because what we learn out there helps us deal better with our lives back in civilization. "The final test," continued Unsoeld, "is whether your experience of the sacred in nature enables you to cope more efficiently with the problems of man. If it does not enable you to cope more effectively with the problems—and sometimes it doesn't; sometimes it just sucks you right out into the wilderness and you stay there the rest of your life—then when that happens, by my scale of value, it's failed."

Being alone in the wilderness enables us to see our world and our place in it with more clarity than we can achieve at home. Once we begin to understand ourselves, we have more to offer others and more ability to help participants translate their experiences in the wilderness into lessons they can apply at home.

PLANNING YOUR OWN SOLO

It is a difficult lesson to learn today—to leave
one's friends and family and deliberately
practice the art of solitude for an hour or a
day or a week . . . and yet, once it is done, I
find there is a quality to being alone that is
incredibly precious. Life rushes into the void,
richer, more vivid, fuller than before.
—*Anne Morrow Lindbergh,* Gift from the Sea

Okay, so you're convinced: you want to do a Solo. You've had it with the rat race, with deadlines, with other people: you're ready to strike out on your own for a little peace and quiet in the backcountry. Or maybe you've been wishing for years that you could take to the woods because you want to live deliberately, to paraphrase Henry David Thoreau. In any case, you've decided that you are ready to spend some time alone outdoors, but you're not sure how to go about it.

Decide on Solo Traveling or a Stationary Outward Bound-Type Solo

The first thing you need to figure out is whether you are looking to complete a solo trip or you are seeking a more stationary solo experience. If you're not sure, probably the most straightforward way to make this decision is to ask yourself what outcomes you're seeking from the experience. If self-reflection, contemplation, and self-awareness are your goals, then you are probably seeking an Outward Bound-type Solo experience. If you're interested in covering some ground and facing the challenges of traveling alone in the backcountry, then you probably want to take a solo trip.

The difference between solo traveling and an Outward Bound-type Solo might seem subtle. After all, you'll be alone either way, relying completely on yourself. But the logistics of camp-craft, travel, and navigation consume a surprisingly significant amount of time and mental energy when you are traveling alone, particularly if you don't do it very often. You can easily devour a couple of days being thoroughly engaged with routefinding, campsite setup and takedown, and simply gawking at the scenery. The next thing you know, your trip is over and you haven't accomplished the reflection you were hoping for.

On long solo expeditions, though, travelers may find that they spend so much time alone in camp or on the trail that they are able to complete some profound reflective time. At some point, the expedition logistics become so routine that they can accomplish them almost without thinking, thus allowing ample time for contemplation.

The Logistics of an Outward Bound-Type Solo

Most people simply do not have time for lengthy solo trips. If you're seeking a truly deliberate experience in reflection and self-awareness and you have only a couple of days (or less), you're probably looking for a stationary Outward Bound-type Solo.

Where to Go for an Outward Bound-Type Solo?

One of the beauties of an Outward Bound-type Solo is that because you won't be on the move, you don't have to go far from home to do it. In fact, if you have a large and secluded backyard and you have the willpower to totally cut yourself off from your home, family, and other distractions, you could even do your first Solo without leaving your own property. After all, as we all know now, Thoreau went only a mile out from his mother's house to complete what is now regarded as one of the most influential solo experiences of recent history!

But if you can manage it, it is preferable to remove yourself from familiar surroundings and get yourself into the wilderness, if for no other reason than to cut yourself off from an easy escape route. The desired setting for an Outward Bound-type Solo is an aesthetic backcountry area, isolated from other people, the more scenic the better—a vast, unspoiled view tends to promote lofty thinking. But plenty of profound self-reflection has taken place under tarps on the edge of clear-cuts or in dense underbrush, too. The important thing is to be outside, alone, with a feeling of isolation or seclusion. Find a place where you can legally camp and where you expect to see no one else.

What to Bring on an Outward Bound-Type Solo?

The lists of what to bring and what to leave behind vary according to how willing you are to strip down to the bare essentials. On a Solo, many people discover that the things they would consider to be absolutely essential are surprisingly simple to do without—or they're difficult to do without, but the value of going without them outweighs the convenience of having them. For example, cries of dismay usually answer the Outward Bound instructor's suggestion that students leave their flashlights behind on Solo. But most people discover that they can do everything for which they need light during the day and that they experience night more fully without a light source.

What to bring: as little as necessary!

- plenty of water—at least two quarts per day, more if you plan to fast, or a water bottle and purification system if you'll be camping near water
- sleeping bag and simple tarp or tent
- adequate clothing for the season and environment
- journal and pen
- whistle
- optional: minimal food (about 500 calories per day)
- optional: headlamp, candle, or flashlight
- optional: sleeping pad

What to leave behind: as much as possible!

- books
- watches
- crafts and hobbies—knitting, paints, cameras, etc.

A NOTE ABOUT FOOD ON AN OUTWARD BOUND-TYPE SOLO

The trick with your food supplies is to bring enough that you are not consumed by their absence, but not so much that you are distracted by their presence. You don't want to spend your whole Solo drawing hamburgers in your journal and planning out what you'll eat when you return, but you also don't want to waste valuable reflection time cooking elaborate meals for yourself. You'd be amazed by how much time you can spend fiddling with a stove, getting water boiling, preparing, eating, and cleaning up from a meal.

- **Go raw:** Except on winter Solos, Solo food should not require cooking. Bring a small bag containing food such as bagels, cheese, nuts, trail mix, powdered drink mix, and fresh fruit.
- **Go without:** If you are able to fast without becoming consumed by thoughts of food, then fasting is a superb challenge that can enhance the Solo experience. Drink at least two quarts of water per day, and move carefully to avoid becoming light-headed. If you have any health issues, consult your doctor before fasting.

- iPods, MP3 players, PDAs, handheld electronic games, etc.
- cell phones, pagers, etc.
- excess food
- alcohol, tobacco, other stimulants
- anything else you would consider a distraction or impediment to the Solo experience

How to Begin?

Once you've packed your tiny little bag, go to your designated campsite and set yourself some arbitrary boundaries. About 200 square yards is usually sufficient—enough space to feel as though you have an adequate campsite but not so much area that exploring it will take you any significant time. Set up your tarp, drink some water, and start being alone.

And then what? Just sit around and contemplate your navel? Probably the first few hours of your Solo will pass blissfully. You'll set up a tidy campsite, organize your belongings, clean your fingernails, and protect your meager food supply from rodents. Then you'll take a nap, wake up, and start getting bored.

This boredom is a key component of Solo because it leads to the kind of self-reflection and contemplation not easily accessed in the presence of the distractions of our lives at home. Take advantage of your boredom and use the time to think deliberately about things that you don't often consider: your values, your goals, your fears, etc. If you find writing to be a productive method of reflection, use your journal. The following questions can get you started on your reflecting:

- What do I appreciate about my life?
- What do I want to change?
- What holds me back from making these changes?
- What am I afraid of?
- What is my vision for my biggest, wisest, most admirable self?

    —*Outward Bound Instructor Manual*

You could also think about the relationship between Solo and leadership and reflect on questions that pertain to your own leadership background and skills:

- What are the most important values in my life? Am I living according to those values? How? If not, what is holding me back?
- Who do I admire most as a leader? What could I do to emulate that person in my life?
- How have I served as a leader of others in the past year? Are there ways I have disappointed myself in my role as a leader? What do I want to improve on?
- Are there new leadership roles that I've been avoiding that I'm ready to take on now?

The Logistics of Solo Backcountry Travel

Although the outcomes of a solo expedition are generally pretty different from the outcomes of an Outward Bound-type Solo, a leader can derive tremendous benefits from traveling in the wilderness alone. The primary benefit to the leader is that solo travel tests and sharpens your backcountry campcraft and navigation skills, thereby increasing your confidence and comfort in being in the backcountry.

The more time you've spent outside doing the things that are an inherent part of wilderness travel—setting up a tent in the rain; getting into warm, dry clothes within three minutes of reaching camp; protecting your food from animals in a site with no trees—the more effortlessly you'll be able to complete these tasks when you have a group of participants with you. This means that you will be able to direct your energy into helping participants get their needs met, rather than having to focus on your own needs and routine camp chores.

Planning a solo trip is in most ways much easier than planning a trip with others because you don't have to consider others' opinions or preferences when making decisions. You travel to an area that *you* want to visit, pack foods *you* like to eat, take the equipment that *you* think works best, and design an expedition route that accommodates *your* goals. Although some of the work that is usually distributed among three or four group members becomes your sole responsibility—for example, food planning and packing, equipment procurement, route planning, etc.—the amount of time you save by eliminating the group decision-making process more than compensates for the extra logistical planning you end up doing for your solo trip.

Once you're out in the woods, executing the solo trip is similarly easy: you stop to rest when *you're* tired, camp where it suits *you*, wake up when *you're* ready, etc.

How to Carry It All Yourself?

There are some logistical aspects of solo travel, though, that are more difficult or complicated than group travel. The most obvious of these is that you alone must carry everything you need. All of the "group gear" weight that is usually distributed among several people suddenly falls on your shoulders—literally. Stove, fuel, first-aid supplies, tent . . . all of it goes into *your* pack.

This weighty reality causes most solo travelers to either acquire exceptionally lightweight gear or go without. Consult the resources for Chapter 7 in the Bibliography at the end of this book for ideas about lightweight gear and food.

What If Self-Rescue Is Necessary?

There are, however, potentially graver risks for the solo backcountry traveler than carrying a heavy pack. Traveling alone in the wilderness leaves less room for error than accompanied travel does, and the more difficult and remote the terrain, the more the risk increases. What you do alone in the backcountry depends upon your skill level, your confidence in your own abilities, and your willingness to accept the consequences of error or bad luck. Consider the story of Aron Ralston, eventual self-amputee, who tells his story in *Between a Rock and a Hard Place*.

When Aron sat in a Utah canyon with his right arm pinned between a boulder and the canyon wall, he spent hours agonizing about how soon he could expect outside help to arrive, given that no one knew where he was. "Usually," he writes, "I would leave a detailed schedule of my plans with my roommates, but since I left my home in Aspen without knowing what I was going to do, the only word of my destination I gave was 'Utah.' After becoming trapped in a remote, little-traveled canyon, one of Aron's first thoughts was that he had made a big mistake. "No one who will suspect I am missing knows where I am. I violated the prime directive of wilderness travel in failing to leave a detailed trip plan with a responsible person. . . . I am alone in an infrequently visited place with no means to contact anyone."

Aron's self-rescue was remarkable, requiring inventiveness, courage, and perseverance: after being stuck for six days, he amputated his forearm with a pocket knife to free himself, rappelled out of a canyon, and hiked 7 miles across the desert floor until he encountered help. But had he left an expedition plan with a friend or relative, he would likely have been found and rescued much sooner, possibly with his arm still intact.

Solo travelers usually get into trouble not by tackling challenges that are so difficult they should not be risked alone, but instead by running into unexpected complications or, like Aron, encountering a case of extreme bad luck. If you're going to travel alone in the wilderness, you can make more conservative decisions, but the most important thing you can do as a solo traveler is to leave detailed information regarding your trip with someone you trust. That way, if something does happen to you out in the backcountry, your chances of receiving outside assistance are greatly increased. Although it may seem excessive, leaving the following information will expedite an evacuation and help any potential rescue parties come properly equipped to assist you, should you need it:

Detailed route plan:
- trailhead where you plan to park
- trailhead where you will exit, if different from above
- estimated daily plan, including side trips and campsites

Equipment list:
- what kind of gear you're carrying
- how much food and fuel you have
- how warm your sleeping bag is, etc.

Vehicle:
- make or model
- license plate number and state

Departure and return details:
- departure date and time
- planned return date and time

Emergency information:
- when to worry if you're not back; allow some time after your estimated return time, just in case you're fine but slow or to give you the flexibility to extend your trip a bit. For example, you might plan to return on Day Three, but you would tell your friend not to worry until Day Four.
- who to contact—local sheriff, local rescue squad, 9-1-1, etc.
- any relevant medical conditions—diabetes, anaphylactic allergies, etc.
- any emergency contact equipment you're carrying—cell phone, signal mirror, etc.

How to End?

Remember to contact your trusted friend as soon as you return from your trip. Many chagrined solo travelers have discovered that the cavalry is out combing the woods for them while they kick back in the hot tub of a local hotel.

Once you're back home, you might spend some time reflecting on your solo trip. Think about what you did and how successful (or not) the trip might have been if you had been leading others; ask yourself questions such as these:

- Was the route an appropriate one for a group? Are my technical skills adequate for leading a group on this expedition?
- Did I make any decisions that I would not have made if I were leading others? Which ones?
- What would I do differently if I were to lead a group on this trip?

PLANNING A SOLO FOR OTHERS

For many decades, an overnight or multiday Solo was an activity unique to Outward Bound courses, but now many organizations are incorporating the experience into their trips. You may decide to do the same thing, but you should first consider whether it is an appropriate activity for your particular trip and participants. Some questions you should ask yourself when deciding are these:

Will an overnight Solo help further the

goals of the trip? If the lessons learned and the experience gained on a Solo will help participants achieve personal and group goals, the Solo is appropriate.

Is the trip long enough to justify an overnight Solo? If your trip is shorter than five days, you should probably stick to other forms of solitary reflective time; see "The Mini Solo" sidebar and "Shorter Solo Options" later in this section.

Is a night alone in the woods appropriate for these particular participants? Participants younger than fourteen are generally not ready for an overnight Solo. Participants with special circumstances—for example, survivors of abuse, etc.—or emotional instability may not be suitable for a Solo.

Can I set up a safe situation for an overnight Solo? The answer to this will depend on the area you're traveling in and any inherent risks of the season, terrain, and other factors. For example, grizzly bear territory is frequently considered to be unsuitable for Solos.

If you've decided to include a Solo as a part of a trip you're leading, you'll need to articulate *why* you want to include a Solo. This may be hard to do if you haven't completed a Solo yourself. Doing your own Solo might help you understand how a Solo can be used as a valuable expedition activity. If you use your own Solo to reflect on your life, beliefs, and values, you may become a more grounded and self-aware leader. And equally important, having done your own Solo gives you some credibility with your participants when you explain to them why they're about to go spend the night alone in the woods with limited supplies. Doing your own Solo is another way of walking your talk. See "Planning Your Own Solo," above, for suggestions for setting up your personal Solo.

Researching What Needs to Be Done

Once you've decided that a Solo will be part of the trip you're leading, you'll need to do some planning beforehand.

Select a Location

This is sometimes harder than you might think, particularly if you have a large group. You need to find a place that won't see a lot of traffic from other hikers and that has a private spot for each group member. You want to give your participants a sense of isolation as they move about their sites, but you also want them close enough together that if something happens to one participant, the others will hear that person's signals for help. Wooded areas and those with varied topography work best for Solo locations.

Get Permission

First of all, make sure that your employer or trip sponsor knows about and approves of your plans for including a Solo. Second, get permission from the land manager of the area where you plan to do the Solo. Some backcountry areas have restrictions on camping outside of designated sites; these are generally inappropriate for a Solo.

Spread the Word

Don't spring a Solo on your participants as a surprise, or you may have a mutiny on your hands. Solo is something that can be very scary for people, so you should make participants aware of your plans at the pretrip meeting at the very latest. Also, if you are leading minors, some parents have concerns about Solos, and you need to give them time to ask questions and become reassured about your intentions. See "Preparing for Trips with Minors" in Chapter 7 for additional considerations for supervising minors in the backcountry.

Gather Gear

You don't need much extra gear for the Solo aside from what you'll already have with you, but each participant will need some way to make a shelter. Tent flies or 10-foot-by-10-foot tarps with cord work well. You'll also need no-cook food rations and empty plastic bags for distributing that food, as well as individual water purification systems

THE MINI SOLO

Outward Bound instructors frequently use a "Mini Solo" early in the course in order to begin to prepare students for their overnight Solo. We plan a short travel day for the fifth or sixth day of the course, which gives us several extra hours that we can use in the middle of the day for the Mini Solo.

After locating a scenic spot where students can be somewhat isolated from each other, we tell them to collect their journals, water bottles, and a sleeping pad to sit on, and we spread them out in the woods for a few hours. We might assign them a couple of journaling questions—"How is the course going for you so far?" "Are you achieving your goals?" "If not, why not?"—or we might not. Some students write in their journals, some sit quietly thinking, and others sleep. But most return to the group refreshed by spending this time alone and less nervous about the overnight Solo to come than they were before.

The Mini Solo can also be used on short trips in place of an overnight Solo or with participants who are not ready for an overnight Solo.

(iodine drops or tablets are more convenient than filters). If individual whistles are not part of your standard equipment, it's useful to have one whistle per participant during Solo. Finally, it's nice to welcome participants back from their Solo with some sort of tasty treat, so plan ahead to pack a special food item.

Incorporate Reflection into Your Expedition Plan

Solo works best when it is the culminating experience in a series of reflective opportunities. Set your participants up for successful Solos by planning to give them tastes of deliberate reflection throughout the expedition. Provide journal time in the evenings, take moments of solitude on top of peaks or in other scenic areas, or allow occasional solo hikes (on which participants hike alone, about fifteen minutes apart from each other). The more familiar your participants are with solitary reflection, the more they will enjoy and benefit from their Solos.

Calculate Trip Timing and Length

Solo is most effective when it occurs about two-thirds of the way through a trip. If Solo is done too early, participants are not ready for the emotional and physical break from the group and the expedition. A good ratio for a Solo is about eighteen to twenty-four hours of Solo for each week of a trip. For

instance, a two-week trip would have a thirty-six- to forty-eight-hour Solo. Solos longer than forty-eight hours are generally unproductive for anyone under eighteen years old, and most people have extreme difficulty with Solos longer than seventy-two hours.

Plan So Participants Won't Go into Solo Exhausted

Sending exhausted participants off to Solo is somewhat pointless, because they will likely just sleep the whole time, unless you have a two- or three-day Solo, which allows them to catch up on their rest and still have time for reflection. The most valuable things that can come out of Solo are increased self-awareness and self-confidence, and these will not result from sixteen hours of shut-eye. Plan for Solo to occur after a reasonable travel day. Participants are likely to sleep more than usual on Solo anyway, but you want them to be awake enough to have plenty of time for reflection.

Setting Up a Solo

Getting participants out on Solo is a lengthy process, and it's important that you allow ample time for it; otherwise, participants feel rushed, which often leads to feeling anxious about the experience. Numerous Outward Bound Solos have begun in the dark due to instructors underestimating the time required to set it up, and though this is a dramatic start, it's not an ideal way for participants to begin the experience. If you have specific individual sites already picked out, you should allow at least two hours to brief participants and escort them to their sites. If not, you may need to allow up to half a day to properly set up the experience.

Scout Individual Sites

If you have picked out a general area but you need to scout for individual sites, you should allow at least one hour, plus ten minutes for each site you need to scout. So if you have six participants, you should allow two hours to scout sites. Your participants can occupy themselves with cooking a meal and sorting through their gear while you scout sites.

You'll need about 200 square yards of territory for each participant, preferably separated from the next nearest neighbor by at least 1,000 square yards. You don't want to have participants hearing each other cough, but you want them to be able to hear a yell for help. Mark each site with a piece of flagging tape so that you can locate it when you return with a participant.

Brief the Participants

The Solo briefing should consist of two parts: the "hows" of Solo and the "whys" of Solo. Even though you've made your participants aware that you're planning to do a Solo during the expedition, it's important to spend time right before the Solo discussing your reasons for including this activity. It seems more logical to start your briefing by talking about the rationale for Solo, but unfortunately most participants cannot think about the "whys" of Solo until they have the full logistical picture. Their minds are too full of "What do I do if I see a bear?" and "How much food do I get to take?" to think about "What do I hope to reflect on?" So it makes sense to address logistics first and rationale second. The following list of topics for a Solo briefing can be adapted to fit your participants and Solo area.

Logistics: Begin by describing the process—"I'm going to take you out to a specific site, show you the boundaries, see if you need any help setting up your shelter, and then leave. I'll check on you every twelve hours, then come to collect you when Solo is over. Here's what I want you to remember while you're on Solo:

"Safety: Drink lots of water, avoid sudden movements if you're fasting or feel faint, and set up a shelter to protect you from the elements.

"Rules: No swimming, no climbing trees, no traveling outside the boundaries of your site. Follow minimum-impact practices, particularly regarding campsite setup and waste disposal.

"Emergency response: Wear your whistle around your neck at all times. If you have a life- or limb-threatening injury or a situation that cannot wait until the next check-in, blow your whistle loudly in three short blasts, wait, then blow three short blasts again. Repeat until help arrives. If you hear a whistle being blown, blow your whistle too. The whistle chain will make its way to me, so I can respond.

"Packing list: (See "What to Bring on an Outward Bound-Type Solo?" above, for packing suggestions to give your participants.)

"'What if . . . ?': Now it's time to answer your questions. . . . "

Rationale: Address why *you* chose to incorporate a Solo on this trip. Acknowledge your participants' feelings of anxiety and fear. Ask participants what they are looking forward to and what they might be dreading about Solo.

Some leaders like to offer optional assignments for Solo. Examples of such assignments include "Write a letter to yourself, which will be mailed to you in six months" or "Reflect on the course so far. What have you learned that you can use at home?"

Ritual: This isn't a necessary part of the briefing, but including some sort of ceremony or ritual prior to sending participants off to be alone gives Solo a special significance and often helps participants transition more smoothly from the anxious, busy logistics of packing to the quiet solitude of the Solo. You could read a quotation or escort participants to their sites in silence.

During Solo

The time when participants are on Solo is undeniably fun for the leader. You get a bit of a break from the rigors of the expedition, you get to sleep in, and you get a chance to be with your own thoughts for a while, even if you are co-leading. All you really need to do during Solo is check on your participants every twelve hours or so. With young participants or for those with physical or emotional health issues, you should check more frequently: at least twice per day. Here are some other things you might do during Solo if you have time and energy:

Evaluate the plan for the rest of the trip. Will the original plan meet the goals of the trip, or does the expedition need revamping?

Clean house. Repair any damaged gear, give the pots a good scrubbing, clean the bandage wrappers out of the first-aid kit.

Spend a little time with each participant. Visit everyone on their Solos, staying long enough (about a half hour) to have a short interview with them about the trip and the Solo, but not so long that you detract from the experience of solitude.

Check in with your co-leader. How is the working relationship going? Are there any issues to resolve? Provide feedback on each other's leadership.

Cook up some treats for the participants' post-Solo meal.

After Solo

Welcome your participants back from Solo with a special meal. Allow conversation to flow freely around the meal; you'll find that participants informally debrief their experiences quite effectively this way. If you choose to have a formal debriefing of the experience, consider asking participants to share answers to one or two of the following questions:

■ What was your Solo like?

■ Did anything surprise you about Solo? What?
■ Did you learn anything? What?
■ Was Solo a valuable experience for you? Why or why not?

You might also simply read another quotation about solitude.

Shorter Solo Options

If you can budget only eight to twelve hours for a Solo, you have a reasonable alternative during daylight, waking hours.

The Twelve-Hour Daylight Solo

If you want to include a substantial Solo for your participants but an overnight one is not appropriate or not logistically feasible, consider an all-day Solo. Camp in a location that has some privacy. In the morning, wake participants up very early and send them out for the day with their sleeping pads, water bottles, journals, and a little bit of food. Return to collect them around dinner time.

You wouldn't want to do this on an expedition that already includes a Mini Solo, but the benefit of the Twelve-Hour Daylight Solo over the Mini Solo is that the extra six to nine hours of time alone usually guarantees that some reflection will take place, whereas a Mini Solo could turn into just a three-hour nap. A Mini Solo is most effective when it is used as a precursor to a longer overnight Solo; a Twelve-Hour Daylight Solo can be used when you don't have the time, resources, or appropriate participants for a longer Solo. Although the experience of a Twelve-Hour Daylight Solo doesn't include the challenge of a night alone, it will still provide a significant opportunity for solitary reflection without all the logistical hassle of an overnight.

The Twelve-Hour Nighttime Solo

Many an Outward Bound instructor has determined that the only way to work Solo into a busy expedition schedule is to send participants out after dinner to spend the night alone and then collect them early the next morning. Although this practice provides participants with the challenge of a night alone, there is very little, if any, time for reflection incorporated into this plan. Participants set up their shelters, sleep for eight or ten hours, pack up, and reunite with their groups. If you have only eight to twelve hours for a Solo, the benefit of having these be daylight, waking hours far outweighs any expedition time lost. The Twelve-Hour Nighttime Solo rarely produces much impact or lasting benefit for participants.

A FINAL NOTE

I have few clear memories of my first Solo, but I do remember feeling exceptionally proud of myself once it was over. I also know that it gave me the confidence and incentive to pursue outdoor recreational activities on my own. I have spent a lot of time alone in the woods since then, and although my solitary time in the backcountry has evolved into hikes with a baby or a toddler in a backpack, I still crave time alone outside, proving that sometimes the things I dread the most are the things that I end up valuing above all else.

The wilderness is, of course, filled with challenges to be undertaken and hazards to be reckoned with. But the confidence that I can face these challenges has made me a competent leader and given me a contented spirit. And ultimately, the knowledge that the wilderness exists as a sanctuary provides me with a sense of fulfillment. Whether I'm introducing a group of teenagers to a backcountry expedition, taking my kids on a canoe trip, or simply hiking around an alpine lake alone, I know that wilderness travel has influenced more than just my leadership skills—it has shaped my character.

CASE STUDY 2
SEA KAYAKERS STRANDED IN DARKNESS AND FOG

by Jim Garrett

Often we don't realize what an impact minor leadership decisions can have in the wilderness until we experience their consequences in an actual outdoors situation. Consider, for example, the following report based on a real incident that occurred in August a few years ago. It is presented as if it had been written by the assistant instructor of an eight-day sea kayaking trip along an inhabited coastline off southern Ireland for adults who are an average of thirty-six years old. To disguise the actual incident for the protection of its participants, the names of all persons and locations have been significantly changed.

As you read through the report, try to put yourself in the shoes of twenty-nine-year-old assistant instructor "Shannon Robinson," and envision your reactions as if you were actually experiencing what she describes. Pay particular attention to the decisions made by the trip's leaders, to the interaction between the participants and their leaders, and to the nature of the communication between lead instructor "Zachary Tyler" and his assistant, Shannon, who only a year before had been a course participant herself. Also think about the discussion questions and about how you might have avoided the incident if you had been there yourself. In the Appendix, you'll also find follow-up questions that revisit these discussion questions, providing more food for thought and encouraging you to think more deeply about the situation.

Yesterday morning, Tuesday, at the start of Day Six of our Boundless Experiences Inc. eight-day kayaking course in the waters of southern Ireland's Baltimore Bay, we finally pushed off from Ringarogy Island three and a half hours after we had rousted everyone from their tents. I was really looking forward to our last long day of paddling and our return to our base on Cleare Island, which lies between Baltimore Bay and Long Island Bay. Although the distance from Ringarogy Island to Cleare Island is only about a dozen miles (20 kilometers or so) as the crow flies, we faced a route of 20-plus miles (35-plus kilometers) among the islands of the bay, with several crossings of open water, particularly on the final leg of the trip, the 0.6-mile (1-kilometer) passage from the Calf Islands group to Cleare Island.

This "final expedition" day would definitely be a demanding one, not just because of our late start, but mainly because small-craft warnings for southwest winds of 15–20 knots were posted for Ireland's entire southern coastline. What's more, the waves were already choppy and up to 3 feet (1 meter) high, and rain was forecast; air and water temperatures meant that we would need to guard against hypothermia. In addition, our group had once again had a short night of sleep: We had arrived late at Ringarogy Island on Monday, Day Five, finally turning in at 11:00 PM, then rising at 5:30 AM yesterday morning. So I had reason to share some of the students' apprehensions about the day ahead of us.

As assistant trip leader, I thought back to how important the close, supportive, compassionate communications from my own instructors had been when, as a student, I had taken my first Boundless Experiences course last year. So I checked in with the six women and six men of our crew, who ranged in age from nineteen to fifty-eight, while they were preparing their breakfast, so I could give them a pep talk while assessing their physical condition and their spirits.

Then I reported to Zachary, our very experienced forty-year-old leader. Zach and I discussed the plans for the day, and he made the judgment call that, even though the weather conditions, travel distance, and group fatigue levels were not ideal, we should still go ahead with our course's scheduled plan to have this "final expedition day" be led by the students. That way, the participants would have opportunities to stretch themselves and to make good use of the expedition skills they had been taught.

In the first few days of the trip, we had given the group thorough instruction in paddling skills, navigation (with lots of map-and-compass practice), capsizing and recovery, lightning drill, and the use of ropes, knots, life vests, etc. Still, we knew that, given the weather conditions, we would want to stick pretty close behind the students as we paddled, just in case we might need to lend a hand or resume leadership at some point. Forty-three-year-old Roddy, the elected captain for Wednesday, Day Seven, eventually got the crew and gear organized, and we departed from Ringarogy Island just after 9:00 AM.

A couple of hours after launching, when our fleet of four single and five two-person ("tandem") kayaks was heading west across open water toward Hare Island at the entrance to Goose Island Channel, thirty-five-year-old Nash, in one of the single kayaks, capsized. Instead of staying in close convoy with the rest of the group, in spite of our repeated instructions to do so, he had once again split off from the group. But he successfully performed a wet exit, and the crew rallied quickly to help him get back into his kayak. His boat was pumped dry, and the crew continued on toward Hare Island, arriving there at 1:30 PM in time for a late lunch.

At lunch we wanted to update the base on our progress, but we also wanted to save our two-way radio's aging batteries for emergency use, because the very-high-frequency radio's rechargeable batteries had not been swapped at the start of our expedition for ones that would maintain their charge longer. (Our course had begun the same day that another course had ended, so our boats and equipment had been immediately redeployed without adequate time to ensure that all equipment was accounted for and in good running order.) So Zach used his cell phone during lunch to call the base and change our estimated time of arrival from 3:00 PM to 5:00 PM. No one answered the phone at the base, so he left a message and planned to call again later in the afternoon.

QUESTIONS

1. Knowing the distances to be covered and the challenges that the group was likely to encounter, do you think Zach's decision to stick with the objective of providing the students with the chance to run a student-directed final expedition was a sound one? Why or why not?

2. What strategies could Zach and Shannon have used to keep students such as Nash from repeatedly splitting off from the rest of the group? What might Nash's objectives have been? Why *did* he disregard instructions so annoyingly? Was it just an ego trip for him? Could there have been other reasons or needs that he was attempting to satisfy by repeatedly splitting off from the group?

3. When Zach and Shannon were unable to communicate with their base because the rechargeable batteries for the VHF radio had not been replaced with newer ones that would maintain their charge longer, what possible alternatives could Zach and Shannon have tried besides resorting to Zach using his cell phone? What could they have done when they were unable to contact

their base as the afternoon wore on and their crew fell further and further behind

schedule? (Note that the course area for this trip was along an inhabited coastline.)

At 2:30 PM, I again tried to contact base, this time with the radio, but again, no luck. I decided to put on my paddle jacket over my wet suit and noted that most of the students had also opted to wear wet suits for the rest of the day. Once the crew had scouted the site to make sure they had left no trace of their visit, we finally set off, leaving Hare Island at about 3:00 PM, with some 8 miles (13 kilometers) farther to go to reach base.

By late afternoon, we had reached the mouth of Goose Island Channel where it opens into Roaringwater Bay, and it was raining hard. The students rafted up in the middle of the channel, bringing all their kayaks together and holding on to one another's boats so that they could check their maps and compasses, since, as had often been the case, they were having trouble agreeing on exactly where they were and what course to follow.

I paddled up to them to remind them about the requirement that they had to be out of channels whenever they rafted up to stop and plan their next moves. Zachary came over to tell me in front of the students that, since this was not a heavily traveled channel, it would be OK to ignore the standard practice. I felt frustrated to be corrected so publicly, since I believe that students learn best when their leaders consistently apply safety-related rules and procedures. But, as the assistant leader, I knew that it was my job to follow Zach's lead and, for the most part, to keep my concerns to myself.

The group made pretty good time heading southwest past the string of small islands in outer Roaringwater Bay, and then they headed out into Long Island Bay. Even so, we were now way behind schedule—it was 5:30 PM—so Zach moved up ahead of the students, taking the lead and urging everyone to keep up the pace behind him as we continued southwest into the wind toward the Calf Islands.

By about 7:30 PM, when we could not see the sun setting because of the clouds and the beginnings of fog out on the bay, we were just off Calf Island East, and Cleare Island was only about 3 miles (5 kilometers) farther on. Twenty minutes later, we were moving down the east shore of Calf Island West, in fog and dwindling daylight, so we tightened the convoy, leaving only about 100 feet (30 meters) between the front and back of our line. Now we were faced with wind and waves both coming in from the south, our direction of travel to reach Cleare Island, which was about 0.5 mile (1 kilometer) away across this final stretch of open water.

Zach called us together and checked with everyone to see how we were all doing and whether everyone was prepared to make the final push to reach Cleare. Because he was very familiar with the area from his many trips there, Zach estimated that the crossing would take only about ten minutes. While some of the students had earlier complained of being very tired and sore, none of us spoke up with the feeling that we should consider a bailout plan.

Zach gave the group the heading of 180 degrees magnetic and firmly stressed the need to maintain a close convoy formation. Kelly, who was both tired and concerned about the coming darkness, asked that another, stronger tandem kayak be appointed to stick close beside her and her partner, but Zach assured her that we would all stick together closely, so such a buddy system would not be needed.

A few minutes before 8:00 PM, as we moved south beyond the end of Calf Island West for the crossing to Cleare Island, we were enveloped in fog and buffeted by choppier waves, although the wind had dropped somewhat. Zach, guided by the compass mounted on his kayak's deck, headed the convoy, and I took a position in the middle of the back half of our now 40-foot-long (12-meter-long), nine-boat line.

QUESTIONS

4. What might have led to Zach correcting Shannon in front of their students? Should he have avoided undermining her role as assistant leader? How? Could Shannon have responded responsibly in any other way?

5. Why do you think Zach changed his leadership style at 5:30 PM for the crossing of Long Island Bay? Was this an appropriate time for this change? An appropriate leadership style for the conditions?

6. What might have motivated Zach to want to press on to make the final short crossing from Calf Island West to Cleare Island, even though conditions were worsening as darkness came on? Could he have been fueled by a desire to keep to the original course plan, which had the crew overnighting at Cleare on the night of Day Seven? Might Zach have been motivated by a "horse-headed-back-to-the-barn" syndrome? To what extent could his self-assurance that he knew these waters from his many trips in the area have given him a (subconscious) conviction that he could find Cleare Island even if blindfolded? Could anticipated peer approval for successfully meeting the challenge have played a role in his decision?

7. Might Kelly's gender have contributed to her not insisting on having a buddy? Did Zach's refusal of Kelly's request for a stronger tandem-team buddy exhibit compassionate leadership? What might have motivated Zach's response to Kelly? How could Zach have handled the situation differently? Should Shannon have tried to influence Zach's decision?

Shortly after we started the crossing to Cleare, we saw a green navigation buoy off to our left, but in the gloom, we couldn't make out its number. Zach believed it was buoy Number 13, which would confirm his sense that we were right on course.

By this time, however, darkness and fog had made it impossible for Zach to read his deck-mounted compass, so he tried using the direction of the parallel rows of incoming waves as a navigation aid. He was unaware that we were experiencing refracting waves: a condition in which the lines of waves make an arc as they swing past a point of land. The result was that, once we had moved out into open water, the waves were actually coming in more from the west, rather than due south as they had been when we were back along the Calf Islands' shorelines.

The waves were now 3 feet (1 meter) or more high, and we were having some difficulty maintaining close convoy without being bumped into each other by the waves. We were also having real trouble seeing each other because of the fog and the darkness, so we started shouting back and forth along the length of our convoy line to maintain contact.

Zach called me up to his boat to confer and to ask me to read his deck-mounted compass, which he could no longer see clearly in the waning light. The compass indicated that we were now headed west, rather than south. But to make sure, Zach borrowed a handheld compass from Roddy, who was in the closest boat; the handheld confirmed that we were 90 degrees off course. By this time Zach, like the rest of us, was stretched pretty thin from fatigue and, possibly, dehydration, so it was understandable when he turned his kayak around and headed north for a few minutes. Then, realizing his mistake, he did a 180-degree turn, and we followed him south, continuing to use voice contact to keep together.

QUESTIONS

8. Should Zach have known about the phenomenon of refracting waves? Would Boundless Experiences have been wise to include such knowledge in its requirements for its trip leaders? If Shannon knew about refracting waves, should she have spoken up and told Zach about them?

9. Once it became apparent that the group would be traveling in fog and near-darkness, what might Zach and Shannon have done to ensure they could still navigate and communicate with their crew? Did the crew's lateness contribute to a lack of on-the-spot preparations for changing conditions?

10. At what point(s) during the afternoon could Zach have checked in with his assistant leader and crew to ensure adequate hydration and energy? Should Shannon have urged Zach to also remain hydrated and have a snack?

Now, though, a new concern arose: We could clearly hear the sound close by on our right of waves crashing onto rocks. When he actually saw the rocks, Zach guessed that we might be next to the northern end of Cleare Island, and he shouted for all of us to gather next to his kayak. But two tandem kayaks didn't show up, and the rest of us, already very apprehensive, were screaming back and forth as we tried to bunch our boats together while they bounced and dipped in the waves. The students were becoming increasingly panicky about the chaotic conditions.

A minute or two later, at about 8:30 PM, a flare illuminated the gloom. Zach told me to remain with the pod of boats, and, shouting and blowing his whistle, he rapidly set off toward the rocks in search of the missing students, soon finding one of the kayaks right next to a rocky ledge. Students Martin and Margaret told him that the two women from the other kayak, Kelly and Ruth, were standing on the ledge, with their kayak pulled up beside them, and that they had set off the flare. Zach told Margaret and Martin to paddle back to the pod, using whistles and shouts to guide them. Since we were close by, Margaret and Martin quickly joined the pod.

Zach could now see Kelly and Ruth's silhou-ettes on the ledge, so he yelled to them above the din of the waves to ask whether they were OK. They replied that they were and that they would be able to stay where they were, in spite of the rising tide and the breaking waves. Zach assured them that they would be helped off the ledge as soon as possible.

He then returned to the pod, again locating us by using whistle and voice signals, where he briefed us on the situation. He directed me to get his jacket out of the rear hatch of his boat (doing so himself would have been an unstable maneuver), so that he could get his flashlight. I got the jacket, but because of the turbulent water, I could not reattach the hatch cover, and it was lost overboard. Zach got his headlamp out of his jacket pocket. The pod had now floated dangerously close to the ledge, where we could see Ruth and Kelly shining a flashlight in our direction; Zach told us to paddle off and raft up again farther from the ledge.

Once we were rafted up again, Zach removed his cockpit's spray skirt, in spite of the waves splashing over the boats, to reach under his rear deck to retrieve the two-way radio, which he then used to call the Cleare Island base. In an even voice, he informed the volunteer on duty of our situation and requested that a motor vessel be quickly sent out to assist. Because our rafted-up kayaks continued to drift toward the ledge, student Charley grabbed on to a fisherman's buoy to "anchor" us in position within sight and sound of the women stranded on the ledge.

It was now approximately 9:00 PM. Fifteen minutes later, when Zach radioed the base again to check on the rescue effort's progress, he was informed that the motor vessel *Endurance II* was about to leave the dock. By 9:45 PM, however, there were still no signs that help was on the way.

QUESTIONS

11. If Kelly and Ruth hadn't fired a flare, how might Zach have located the two missing kayaks? What were his options under these conditions? What about Charley grabbing onto a buoy? Was that a good idea?

12. What could Zach and Shannon have done to calm their panicky crew? How might the crew have reacted if Zach and Shannon couldn't locate the two missing kayaks?

13. Was it a good decision for Zach to leave Kelly and Ruth on the ledge and rejoin the pod? Should he have gotten onto the ledge himself to check out their situation and their condition?

14. Besides not being able to read his deck-mounted compass, what other vital equipment did Zach not have readily accessible? Could he have done something differently to avoid losing a hatch cover and risking capsizing to obtain his gear?

Twenty minutes after that, I set off one of my emergency flares, and soon we could make out a large motor vessel coming toward us out of the darkness. I set off a second flare, and shortly thereafter we could hear a megaphone from the big boat identifying it as the *Endurance II*.

Because of the dangers posed by the ledge and the surf, the crew of *Endurance II* kept the big boat several hundred yards (several hundred meters) away, launching an outboard-powered inflatable boat with three staff members aboard. The inflatable quickly came over to the pod and towed all the kayaks over to the big boat, where we tied up our kayaks. Then the twelve of us—ten students and two instructors—climbed aboard; we were wet, cold, and exhausted but, at last, secure.

Meanwhile, Ruth and Kelly, who had now been on the ledge for more than two hours, continued to whistle and flash their light toward the big boat. Our course director, who was piloting *Endurance II*, shouted over to them to assure them that they were about to be rescued. Just before 11:00 PM,

the inflatable with the three staff members nosed in as close as possible to the ledge. Carrying a life ring attached by a long line to the inflatable, staff member Patrick, wearing a wet suit, swam and waded about 30 feet (9 meters) across the ledge, much of which was now awash, to reach the two students.

Patrick swam Kelly and Ruth, one at a time, over to the inflatable, where they were pulled aboard. They were quickly driven to *Endurance II*, where they were found to have no physical injuries, although they were obviously very scared. Further, though they had been immersed in waist-deep water for much of their ordeal, they were experiencing only mild hypothermia, since they had been wearing full wet suits and booties.

So our crew finally arrived at the Cleare Island base, at approximately 11:40 PM, more than fourteen hours after our morning launch from Ringarogy Island. We were quickly and efficiently met by the base's staff and treated to warm drinks, sugary snacks, dry clothing, and sleeping bags.

Careful assessment by senior staff members determined that none of us would need professional medical attention. By midnight, all the students were bedded down; thoroughly worn out but hugely relieved that this traumatic near-miss had ended safely, they looked forward to a long and uneventful sleep.

And now it's the next morning, Thursday, Day Eight, and I'm really trying to figure out what I could have, should have, done differently, right from the start of this course. What could I have done or said to Zach and our crew that might have kept those two women off that ledge and might have meant that none of us now would be gathered for a critical-incident debriefing? We didn't need to be here; things needn't have gotten to this point. Where should I have intervened? Where could I have changed things so that this trip might have ended up with only smiles and a complete sense of accomplishment, instead of being so traumatic an experience for Ruth and Kelly—and, in fact, for all of us?

QUESTIONS

15. What should Shannon have done differently? Where could she have effectively intervened?
16. What learnings can you derive from this case that you might use to inform your thoughts and actions in future outdoor leadership situations?

PART III

TAKING LEADERSHIP INTO YOUR PROFESSIONAL LIFE

About the Author: Robert Gordon

Bob Gordon is president of Outward Bound Professional and on the senior management team for Outward Bound USA. Under Bob's expertise in leadership and team development, with a focus on action learning, Outward Bound Professional has been an industry leader, providing powerful insights into the behavior of leaders and teams in challenging situations. Bob has designed and delivered programs for chief executive officers and senior managers at Xerox, Motorola Cellular, and the Institute for Civic Leadership, to name a few. He teaches seminars for the University of Maine's Conference and Institutes Division and is a keynote speaker on Leadership at the Edge.

A leader with Outward Bound since 1981, Bob has instructed hundreds of programs in the United States and internationally, including Scotland, Italy, and Costa Rica. He was director of marketing at Hurricane Island Outward Bound and has served in Outward Bound's Discovery and Wilderness programs.

Bob attended Oregon State University, where he was first introduced to climbing and Outward Bound, and earned a bachelor's degree in business administration from the University of Southern Maine.

An avid sailor and climber, Bob was a member of the 1991 American Karakoram Expedition to Gasherbrum II. Bob currently lives in Camden, Maine, with his wife, Maureen, and their two children.

Personal Introduction: Robert Gordon

In 1981, as a student at Oregon State University, I was bitten by the climbing bug, and I spent every opportunity at Smith Rock or in the Cascade Mountains. At Smith Rock, I met a leader from OSU's Outing Program whose nickname was 5.11 Evelyn (5.11 is a climb rating, and at that time, anyone climbing 5.11 was extremely good), and her boyfriend, Bill. Evelyn was an amazing climber and a real character, and I discovered she was also an instructor with the Northwest Outward Bound School.

After hearing about Outward Bound, I was fascinated by the thought of testing yourself in the wilderness with a group of strangers and gaining new technical skills. With Evelyn and Bill's encouragement, I signed up for a sailing program with the Hurricane Island Outward Bound School in Rockland, Maine. I met my twenty crewmates: a diverse band, from the United States and Europe, ages eighteen to twenty-five, who were all coming together for the first time. Some had been sent; others had signed on willingly; one was a Morehead Scholar; another was a tough kid from inner-city Boston.

Our instructors quickly split us into two groups in two pulling boats: 30-foot-long, ketch-rigged, double-ended center-board sailboats. The plan was to sail in convoy to Canada and back over twenty-six days. During that time, we were supposed to learn how to sail, navigate, and become a team. Over the next three weeks, we experienced mutinies against the staff, hardship beyond belief as we rowed through the night in the pouring rain, and moments of sheer exultation as we accomplished seemingly impossible tasks.

On the trip I experienced firsthand what it means to get others to willingly do what you want them to do—what it takes to lead. I learned about my own strengths and weaknesses as a leader and a team member, with forthright feedback from peers. It was also not what I had expected. I had thought I would learn new technical skills such as sailing and navigating—which I did; the team and leadership skills were an unexpected gift.

The power of that experience motivated me to pursue my passion for working with individuals and organizations in situations that require leadership and teamwork and to look closely at what practices and factors increase success and performance.

This section of the book delivers valuable lessons for new managers, experienced leaders, or small-business owners. It is based on my experiences and those of my incredible colleagues at Outward Bound, especially Caroline Blair-Smith, who worked with me on this section of the book. It captures real stories and best practices we've gathered over twenty-five years' working with some of the world's top companies. Chapter 10, Team Building in the Workplace, provides skills and insights into how to build a team on the job. Chapter 11, Workplace Communication Skills, tells you how to share information effectively at work. Chapter 12, Managing Change in the Workplace, describes how to lead and manage change in your company. We hope you will incorporate these lessons as you lead others at your workplace for a greater good.

CHAPTER 10

TEAM BUILDING IN THE WORKPLACE

As a natural outcome of the success of Outward Bound's wilderness programs, many organizations—corporate, governmental, and nonprofit—over the past thirty years have asked Outward Bound to help them develop high-performing teams. Gordon French, director of organizational development at Cox Communications, stated on the North Carolina Outward Bound School website in 2005 that if workplace leaders want great financial skills, they should go to Wharton Business School at the University of Pennsylvania; if they want to learn about business theory, they should go to Harvard Business School; but if they want to develop great leadership and team skills, "nothing has the impact of an Outward Bound expedition, where in three or four days they begin the transformation from being managers to becoming leaders."

This chapter discusses team building in the workplace. Though it touches on many topics covered in other parts of this book, its focus is on workplace leaders—including leaders of newly assembled teams, existing teams they have newly joined, or former teams—and the skills they need to enhance their team's productivity by working together better.

WHY USE OUTWARD BOUND PROFESSIONAL'S ACTION-BASED TRAINING AND DEVELOPMENT?

Effective workplace team-building and leadership development programs focus on creating lasting changes in behavior, improved results, and a good return on investment. So why should you use Outward Bound's experiential learning for workplace team building, training, and leadership development? Most people know about Outward Bound's experiential learning activities, which range from team initiatives to high-impact activities such as rock climbing or search and rescue, to multiple-day sailing or mountain expeditions. Many people think of these activities in the context of youth opportunities or alternative vacations—but they also apply to workplace training.

Outward Bound has found that using a proven methodology of experiential and theory-based learning, combined with the conscious use of metaphor, can build high-performing teams and leaders faster and more effectively than any other approach. Outward Bound's team-building programs strengthen organizational culture, accelerate organizational performance, and improve results—results that may include profitability, market share, and increased efficiency . . . or simply a more cheerful mood around the water cooler.

Think about some of your best learning moments or lessons—in the classroom, on the job, with a sports team, or in any other situation. Most likely, your learning emerged from a situation that required you to solve a problem, not merely think and talk about it. Similarly, in Outward Bound programs, teams work together to solve problems under adverse conditions or in simulated challenges requiring creativity, problem solving, excellent communication, and action. Combine that methodology with some of the best thinking and practices used by teams and organizations today—teams of corporate executives and organizations such as manufacturing companies (General Electric and Avery Dennison, to name a couple)—and add to that the artful use of metaphor and storytelling, and sit back and watch the learning environment come alive.

When Angus S. King Jr. was sworn in as governor of the state of Maine in 1995, he had a lot on his plate. Getting elected as an Independent against an incumbent Democrat and a Republican candidate who went on later to the U.S. Senate was no small task for a businessman and public-television host.

King, a lifelong student of leadership, was also an alumnus of Outward Bound Professional. He had attended the Leadership Maine Program, which is dedicated to building leaders to address the state's economic challenges. After his election, King brought his newly assembled team together for a three-day team-building retreat with Outward Bound Professional in Maine. The team members came from as far away as Oregon. Most did not know each other; most didn't even know King personally. King wanted to pull his team together as quickly and cohesively as possible. To work and communicate well together, everyone had to know one another's individual and collective strengths and liabilities.

Imagine being told that your first job assignment was to meet your new boss, team, and colleagues in the White Mountains of Maine in the middle of February, when temperatures of -20°F are unremarkable. The team was excited . . . and a bit apprehensive, whether they admitted it or not. They must have been asking themselves, "What does any of this have to do with my job?"

If practice really does make perfect, as the saying suggests, we should be able to get continually better at our jobs just by doing them day after day. Since we learn best from experience, then managing teams well ought to be a simple matter of practicing management. Why, then, did the governor of Maine choose the winter woods as his team-building classroom? Why are more and more organizations finding tremendous professional and personal rewards in time that's invested in leaving the workplace to study teamwork and leadership ultimately intended for the workplace?

As the preceding chapters of this book indicate, we don't really learn through experience alone: we learn through reflecting on our experience, and the lessons take shape as changes in how we think and, consequently, how we behave. Good experiences are, at best, inconclusive, and we are all capable of doing the same dumb thing over and over again. The only experiences we learn anything from are the ones that challenge our assumptions and persuade us to look at the familiar in a new light. Outward Bound programs take people out of their familiar environments and communities and bombard them with enough truly important choices that it soon becomes inevitable that assumptions get challenged.

Angus King's newly formed group assembled on a cold, dark evening with a foot of fresh snow on the ground at Outward Bound's Mountain Center. The Outward Bound staff welcomed them briefly and asked participants to assign themselves to three different cabins hidden in the woods, to find them using a map of the property, and then to meet back at the center. This first simple initiative was a way for the participants to meet their cabin mates, release some anxiety (through action) about the next couple of days, and start the team-building process.

Back at the center, the team helped prepare, serve, and clean up after dinner, with Angus happily running the Hobart dishwasher. The informal time doing dishes together is often when conversations about family and other experiences flow naturally—the team development process had begun, though not one formal activity had yet taken place.

Later that evening, the group gathered in the barn for a kickoff, starting with introductions that asked them to share who they are—not their resume, but who they really are: the people and events that shaped them as leaders and what values guide them on a daily basis. The evening also included a talk led by Angus about expectations, which began to establish how this administration would conduct itself. The group was clearly excited about the challenges ahead. King's rhetoric painted a picture in their minds about what this team could be and do. The activities of the next two days would begin the process of turning rhetoric into reality, but we'll leave this team for now and come back to them later.

WHAT TYPE OF TEAM-BUILDING PROGRAM DO YOU NEED?

If you've decided to devote time and resources to improving teamwork around the workplace, the next step is to define what that looks like in your organization. Curiously, many managers are at a loss to describe what type of workplace team they would like to build or what behaviors a high-performing team in their organization would exhibit; they struggle to articulate what exactly they are looking for. Begin with an assessment (or *scoping*) process to determine the goals and objectives of a training program for your team. If you don't know where you want to end up, it's hard to know where to start on the road to getting there.

Assess Your Team

In the early stages of team building, it is critical to hold off on choosing a training-program design or team-building solution until you have done a relatively thorough assessment of the team and your organization's development. Good assessment in team and organizational development is similar to a good medical diagnosis: both allow you to treat the real problems, not just the symptoms.

Sometimes Outward Bound has been called in by a manager to fix a team that has conflicts between team members. For example, "Joe and Dan aren't getting along, and it is affecting the performance of the team." Often, our assessment process reveals that the underlying issue is actually a lack of clarity around roles and boundaries that the manager needs to address. The manager was looking for a workshop on conflict resolution, but what was needed was a training program focused on team leadership. In "Choosing a Team-building Program," later in this chapter, we provide a team leadership model that can be used to develop high-performing teams—but first you need to assess your team. The program will be as effective as your assessment is accurate.

Define "Team"

Workplace teams are groups of people who share a common set of goals and *metrics*—the way they measure success. They may or may not work in the same building or even on the same continent. Yet the success or failure of their efforts depends on their ability to work well together.

Not all workplace groups are teams, however. Many people use these terms interchangeably, but the differences between these concepts are both substantial and subtle. Groups don't have a common set of measures and a common purpose. Many workplace committees, for example, are groups, not teams. The individuals' participation within that group is not central to their jobs.

The classic scenario is when a training-program facilitator welcomes a group and presents the goals and objectives for the day, which might include, say, improving team performance, building a high-performing team, or improving team communication. The facilitator instantly knows he or she is in trouble when eyes roll, arms cross, and participants give each other that knowing look that says, "But we're not a 'team'."

Regardless, such a group can benefit from improved teamwork, communication, sharing of best practices, and collaboration. The opportunity for groups to improve their performance is every bit as real and large as it is for teams. But acknowledging the difference between a group and a team is important to enrolling the training-program participants in the process from the beginning and getting them to buy into the program. In this chapter, we focus on teams and use that word exclusively, though many of the principles we discuss can be used to bring groups together as well.

Get to Know Your Team

If you are new to the team you are leading, have an initial conversation with the individual members (or, if the team is large, the key stakeholders) to learn more about their goals, concerns, and objectives. During these conversations, you will get a sense of the culture and organizational values that hold the team together—or that need to be changed in order to support a new direction or vision. You can also learn some of the internal and external forces affecting the team, whether those forces can be controlled by the team, or whether those forces need to be addressed in any way.

If you already know your team well, you may have a clear picture. All the same, asking questions might deliver some surprising revelations. Besides, people like to be asked what they think. Effective strategies range from formal or informal interviews to more elaborate tools.

Interviews

Confidential interviews allow team members to talk in a safe environment about their goals and objectives for themselves and the team, to describe what works well and what needs to change, and to indicate what they perceive to be the obstacles that face the organization. Interviews give team members a sense of the importance of their perspective and allow you to identify and prioritize the opportunities and challenges facing the team as seen by the team members themselves.

These interviews needn't be formal. You can casually check in with the members of the team when you happen to meet at the coffee machine. However, the content of interviews must be confidential, and any reporting, whether verbal or written, should focus on themes; no response should

be connected directly to any specific interviewee.

The sample interview in the sidebar was used by a group that needed to develop alignment (see "Check on Team Alignment" later in this chapter) on their strategic initiatives and direction. This sample interview, which takes about thirty to forty-five minutes, combines an analysis of strengths, weaknesses, opportunities, and threats (known as SWOT) with some open-ended questions designed to provide insight into and knowledge of the business and the team.

Surveys

Less time-consuming than interviews because you can collect information from many people at once, surveys are another great way to get a snapshot of your team's current reality. A well-done survey allows perceptions among team members to be compiled and studied anonymously and collectively. Surveys also provide a benchmark from which you can measure gains and losses over time.

Surveys, these days, are often done online, so they may feel more confidential. But online or not, written surveys are less personal—filling out a form doesn't encourage as much individual investment as being interviewed one-on-one by someone interested your ideas and asking intelligent follow-up questions.

A multitude of excellent surveys are available that can help you assess your team from a variety of angles such as employee satisfaction, team performance, skills inventory, and learning needs (see Chapter 10 Resources in the Bibliography for two recommended surveys). You can also develop a customized survey. The sidebar presents a sample survey, the Team Alignment Profile (TAP), we use at Outward Bound Professional. In the survey, employees are asked to circle the number that best reflects their opinion. For simplification, in the chart below only two or three statements have been included in each category.

After the surveys are collected, the information is tallied anonymously. Responses are averaged and the standard deviation taken. The use of average and

SAMPLE INTERVIEW

Begin by creating the context for the conversation. Make sure each interviewee knows everyone else and what they do. Then discuss how long the interview will last, the kinds of questions you'll be asking and opinions you'll be seeking, and how the information will be used to move the team and/or organization forward. Assure confidentiality as far as possible, acknowledging that in a team that's been together a while, some opinions will be easily ascribed to their holders whether their name is assigned to that opinion or not. Then ask each interviewee the following questions, adding other questions as appropriate:

1. What is your sense of the organization and the level of alignment (support) on each of these issues?
   - the company's mission—what you do
   - the company's vision—where you want to be
   - the company's values—its guiding principles
   - the company's strategic plan—a three-year plan for achieving its vision
2. Do you feel engaged in the larger organizational objectives?
3. As you look at the business, what are each of its following characteristics?
   - strengths
   - weaknesses
   - opportunities
   - threats
4. How effectively do different areas of the business work together? How can this be improved to take the business to a higher level of performance?
5. What do you see as the top two priorities for the business over these next intervals?
   - six months
   - twelve months
   - twenty-four months
6. What can the leadership team do more of, do less of, or stop doing? Any other coaching or thoughts?
7. For this training session to be an overwhelming success for you, what needs to happen?
8. What does "what needs to happen" look like?

standard deviation together tells a leader not only how much his or her employees (as a body) agree with the statements, but how much alike, or *aligned*, their experiences are. Results from the Team Alignment Profile help indicate the areas in which a leader might want to work most with his or her team.

360-Degree Feedback Instruments

The term *360-degree feedback instrument* describes where the feedback and insights come from: all around you. In most cases feedback is solicited and received from your boss, your peers, and your subordinates, and even from some of your company's customers. At Outward Bound we have developed the Leadership Development Profile with Psymax and we also use PDI's Profiler and Management Research Groups' Leadership Effectiveness Analysis. These 360-degree instruments are powerful and effective tools for identifying individual and team strengths and developmental needs.

Outward Bound Professional has found it essential that this type of tool is presented as a developmental opportunity for the individual: the information is confidential, and each recipient decides whether he or she wants to share the

TEAM ALIGNMENT PROFILE (TAP)

Simplified TAP questions	Disagree			Neutral			Agree
Clarity of Organizational Purpose							
1. I have a clear understanding of my organization's purpose and goals.	1	2	3	4	5	6	7
2. My performance objectives are linked to larger organizational objectives.	1	2	3	4	5	6	7
Unifying Commitment							
3. Those with whom I work are unified in a sense of common purpose.	1	2	3	4	5	6	7
4. Those with whom I work believe that achieving team goals will contribute significantly to their personal success.	1	2	3	4	5	6	7
Collaborative Climate							
5. We understand and appreciate each other's skills and expertise.	1	2	3	4	5	6	7
6. We support one another in compensating for our individual weaknesses.	1	2	3	4	5	6	7
Turning Information into Action							
7. We have access to the information we need.	1	2	3	4	5	6	7
8. We consider alternative perspectives that challenge our assumptions.	1	2	3	4	5	6	7
9. We effectively execute our action plans.	1	2	3	4	5	6	7
Effective Decision Making							
10. Decisions are made in a timely manner.	1	2	3	4	5	6	7
11. Decisions are made with appropriate levels of input from others.	1	2	3	4	5	6	7
Communication Skills							
12. I communicate openly and honestly with my colleagues.	1	2	3	4	5	6	7
Individual Perceptions							
13. I am open to receiving feedback from others.	1	2	3	4	5	6	7
14. I am confident taking considered risks at work.	1	2	3	4	5	6	7

data, and if so, with whom. If a 360-degree feedback instrument is not presented properly, the results—which can be seen as an assessment, perhaps tied to compensation—causes people to be generous or cautious in their responses. When the tool is presented as something for the benefit of the recipient and honored as such, we see a high degree of acceptance of and personal investment in the process. As with most things, the integrity of the process is everything.

The most beneficial feedback sessions using the gathered data occur when participants are willing to share their strengths and developmental opportunities with other members of the team, with the entire team, or with a coach. This can be done openly or privately; it depends to a large degree on the team and their established level of trust. Whoever administers the instrument needs to maintain an environment that is safe physically, emotionally, intellectually, and vocationally.

Unless individuals can translate the learnings from their 360-degree feedback instrument into im-provements in the workplace, the whole exercise is academic. To apply this tool to the workplace, the information needs to focus on leadership skills as observable behaviors. The Outward Bound Leadership Development Profile shown in Figure 5 is a 360-degree feedback tool which identifies twenty-one leadership skill sets from seven key leadership development areas.

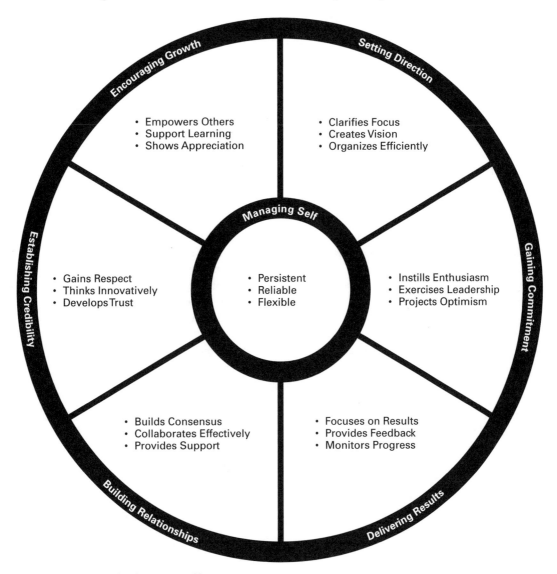

Figure 5. Leadership development profile

Outward Bound Leadership Development Profile. The Leadership Development Profile is an effective way to assess individual leadership skills as well as to develop a composite of the team's skills through a 360-degree feedback process that gathers information from all the major players in your working environment: your boss, your peers, your subordinates, and even your company's customers. The next several paragraphs describe each section of Figure 5, beginning with "setting direction" and working clockwise around to the center.

Setting direction. Every organization needs to have its mission, vision, and values established, and everyone looks to the company leaders to either deliver that vision or facilitate the process of generating it collectively. As a leader you need to know where you want to go, and your followers also need to know where you want to go—and therefore where they are heading. Oftentimes Outward Bound's assessment tools reveal misunderstandings here. A leader cries, "But I've *told* them so many times!" Somehow, they weren't hearing it. Clarify the organization's focus, create a vision, and organize efficiently.

Gaining commitment. Get people committed to the team by sharing your passion and building their trust in you. Reach out to let people know that they're important and really make a difference. Leaders don't *make* people do what the leader wants; they make people *want* to do what the leader wants, and feel valued for doing it. When people talk about what energizes them about a good company, they generally rave about the company's people and, more specifically, about the values of the people. There has to be a fit between the values of the organization and the individual. That fit is easier to accomplish if the values are clear and the company's actions match the company's words. Instill enthusiasm, exercise leadership, and project optimism.

Delivering results. Set incremental goals and meet them. Deliver measurable results. What you measure is what people will put the most effort into, so make sure you're measuring the right things. Vision is necessary, but it's also important to set a plan and manage it. Make sure there's follow-through on commitments, and check in on results. Focus on results, provide feedback, and monitor progress.

Building relationships. Investing your time and developing an awareness of yourself and others builds relationships and can have tremendous payoff in the form of committed employees, suppliers, and customers. People like to do business with people they trust and will even pay more for a service or product knowing that you are there to take care of them when needed. Build consensus, collaborate effectively, and provide support.

Cindy Makin-Brown is one of Outward Bound's senior program managers; she has mastered the skill of building great relationships. Returning clients consistently request to have Cindy work with them on their team-building program. So what is it about Cindy that makes for these great relationships time and again?

First, Cindy shows that she genuinely cares about the clients as people. For instance, in quiet moments between activities, she asks repeat clients about a spouse's career change or a child's success in athletics, calling on her memory of details from a discussion months earlier.

In her role as program facilitator, she is there to support and coach them as well as to provide honest feedback in a constructive manner. Her many years of consulting experience in team and leadership development are evident in the way she consistently picks out underlying problems and brings them to people's attention as opportunities instead of faults. By focusing on and defining the real issues as opposed to the symptoms, Cindy brings people to a place where they can hear each other, look honestly at themselves, and work through tough issues.

Last, she helps them find creative ways to work together and gives them the skills to keep doing it long after the program ends.

Establishing credibility. Having a strong moral compass, following through, and being good at what you do—not just being the expert—are all part of establishing credibility. Knowing your business and bringing the right people together to achieve consistent results creates a track record that others trust. Don't forget that you can also establish credibility if you are quick to acknowledge when you don't have the answer. Bringing in other expertise to assist you isn't an admission of incompetence, and bluffing will lower your credibility faster than just about anything. Everyone casts a leadership shadow: how people see you, trust you, think about you—all the unspoken things. Observable behaviors—such as cutting corners instead of going the extra mile to solve problems, cast noticeable shadows, and your credibility depends on what these shadows look like. Gain respect, think innovatively, and develop trust.

Encouraging growth. Are you really taking an interest in developing your people? Some leaders get a sense of security out of not helping their subordinates to grow. Having stagnant followers may seem to make a leader indispensable. Actually, helping your followers expand their skills ensures that you have good people around you and makes it possible for you too to move up. If you're indispensable in your current role, you may be overlooked for promotion! In the long term, company stability relies on plans of succession. Who would fault anyone for wanting to move up? Empower others, support learning, and demonstrate appreciation.

Martin Guitar is a six-generation maker of some of the finest production guitars in the world. Talk to almost any musician, and he or she will give you the rundown on the long lineage of Martin guitars, including the renowned D-12 guitar model. Based in the foothills in Pennsylvania, Martin Guitar

has been turning out beautiful instruments for the past 174 years. However, when the current chairman and chief executive officer, Chris Martin IV, great-great-great-grandson of the founder, took over the business in 1986, the company was struggling. Production methods were outdated and the selection of models was limited.

Chris quickly put his business administration degree to work by assessing the company and marketplace. He believed that having signature models by famous musicians would be a strong selling point to aspiring musicians whose heroes played a Martin, but first he needed to get those musicians to agree to the use of their names. For most of them, supplementing their own income was not a compelling enough factor, so he donated a percentage of the proceeds to their favorite charities. Chris also realized that a lot of people who dreamed of having a Martin couldn't afford one, so he added less-expensive models, including the Martin Backpacker, to the company's offerings.

Chris recognized that he needed a workforce dedicated to and passionate about making the best guitars in the world, so he invested substantial money and time in their professional development. Outward Bound Professional has run multiple team development programs for Martin Guitar for nearly twenty years. Chris personally embarks on two or three five-day team development expeditions with twenty colleagues every year. There, he spends time getting to know them and listening to their ideas on how to improve the company. Employees are blown away by the CEO spending five days with them, asking them how to improve the company. Chris trusts his people so much that he recently handed over the day-to-day management to a new president, Keith Lombardi. Chris remains the CEO, and his efforts have reenergized and grown the company that bears his name into a thriving business today. A more in-depth look at Martin Guitar is featured in the case study at the end of Part III.

Managing self. Knowing and sharing your own strengths and weaknesses is a precept to leading others. A leader can create a supportive environment by modeling the need for support as well as a self-reliant approach to getting support in a timely and appropriate manner. However, the energy needed to put in long, challenging days that require all your attention can come from only one source: you. Take care of yourself—it's a phrase we use all the time, even as a casual farewell, but how many of us are actually good at it? With all the commitments of running a business or a team, there just aren't many hours left in the day, especially if you have a family, are working on your education at night, or are volunteering on boards and committees. So we are always impressed when we see someone who does it well.

Before Chuck Hewitt took the post of chief operating officer for Jackson Laboratories, a leading biomedical research firm in Bar Harbor, Maine, he was the head of strategy for Cianbro, a large East Coast–based construction firm, and then chief operating officer for the state of Maine under Governor King. Prior to these posts, Chuck was president of Maine Audubon and headed a pharmaceutical firm in Ireland. His resume is a litany of very demanding positions that have required him to put in long hours in a sustained manner, and he's, well, somewhat beyond middle age.

Yet Chuck is active and fit, loves the outdoors, and is one of the most grounded, compassionate, and energized leaders we have worked with, one who really goes out of his way to take care of the people around him. Despite all his professional demands, Chuck makes the time to exercise regularly,

eat right, and pursue his passions, which include being an avid and excellent skier. Staff members have spotted Chuck barrelling down a double-black diamond run at Maine's Sugarloaf Mountain in the harshest conditions, with a huge smile on his face.

So how does he do it? He makes the time to take care of himself and makes it a priority in his life, just as he does his most important business tasks. Chuck's dedication to his health makes him a profoundly caring, compassionate leader.

When you make taking care of yourself a priority, it is not a selfish act, and you should not feel guilty about it. It's a matter of time management and prioritization. Others are counting on you. So take out your calendar and start scheduling time to take care of yourself. Be persistent and reliable.

SET THE STAGE FOR TEAM BUILDING

Successful team building depends on the relationships between workers and their leaders. Developing relationships is challenging, but with an understanding of the common patterns of the process and the tools to enhance trust and flexibility, you can create an environment wherein everyone brings out the best in one another.

Understand the Stages of Team Development

The stages of team development are discussed in Chapter 4, Building Trust, Building a Team, in Part I, Leadership Fundamentals: forming, storming, norming, and performing. While those stages of team development are as true in the workplace as anywhere else, it is helpful to understand how things may play out differently at work and what you, as a leader, can do to reduce the amount of storming and move your team into the performing phase more quickly. The sections below give workplace focus to the stages of team development.

Keep in mind that team development is not a

simple one-way progression. Change tends to toss teams back a stage or two. For example, budgetary constraints might cause frictions that had lain dormant to erupt, requiring the team to storm again; personnel changes might cause a team to re-form itself all over from the beginning. Also, different parts of a team can be in different stages. Leaders need to be aware of these different stages and the transitions between them and be aware when they themselves may be initiating a transition from one stage to another.

Crossbeam Systems, a technology-sector provider of Internet security, was in the start-up phase in 2002. Their newly formed senior management team was a group of hand-picked individuals brought together to grow the company quickly in a very competitive but growing market. The team was working through a leadership transition: their corporate executive office and founder was stepping aside as a new CEO stepped in to guide the company through the growth phase. The new CEO approached Outward Bound Professional to run a team-building retreat focusing on relationship building and team development.

The senior management team's retreat was a series of team initiatives and a ropes course experience in the middle of winter in New Hampshire. Conditions were definitely challenging, and the team encouraged, coached, and supported each other as they worked their way through the course 30 feet off the ground in the middle of a blinding snow storm. The new CEO encouraged the senior management team to take the lessons of the Outward Bound program back to the workplace: to embrace the challenges and issues they face, to acknowledge conflict and engage differences from a positive perspective, and to talk to each other as a way to work through misunderstandings and to reach consensus. The team developed

operating principles and revisited them as needed.

Over the past four years, players have come and gone. The team has had to form and re-form itself to deal with the different challenges that each stage of growth has presented. Through it all, their foundation work as a team gave them confidence in the process and the tools to make it go as smoothly as possible.

Forming

Team operating principles are often created during the forming phase. You can facilitate the forming stage by holding events that encourage people to get to know each other: Barbecues, bowling, or other sorts of outings are all great, but you don't have to leave the office to make progress. Meetings that include time for introductions and sharing stories, job shadowing, and cross training are all ways to promote mutual understanding in the context of an ordinary work day.

An electrical manufacturing company was looking to streamline production. This company's project teams were not intact work units but were cross-organizational teams assigned to work together on joint projects as part of their personal development. Their managers applied very little structure to bring these teams together during the forming stage, and so the teams jumped straight into projects without developing any operating principles. Conflicts quickly emerged over leadership, decision making, and inequities in team contribution. The project teams would have worked together much more smoothly if they had spent some time early on doing some team development work.

Instead, that is what Outward Bound did with them—somewhat after the fact. The results were immediate, due to a solid process that focused on forming, accepting, and minimizing the negative effects of storming, achieving norming, and then developing effective operating procedures and principles that allowed performing.

Storming

When the storming phase rolls around, don't over-react; instead, seek to discover the root causes. This conflict is not only normal, it's necessary if the team is to move beyond a superficial level of interaction. The conflicts are often really confusion about the division of people's responsibilities. (Incidentally, a surprising majority of conflicts in the storming phase are around role distinction, overlap, and interaction, as described in the GRPI (goals, roles, procedures, interactions) model in "Create and Ensure Organizational Alignment" later in this chapter.)

For instance, one team working with Outward Bound Professional was deep into the storming phase over the roles of account executives and client service representatives. The conflict centered around who could talk to the customers and when, and it was not as simple as it may sound; the very sophisticated product required the team to step back from their predefined "roles" and really think about what was best for the customers. The team had to patiently work through a number of different scenarios and variations before they could develop an acceptable set of guiding principles.

You as a leader and other individuals in your team will probably receive feedback during the storming phase that will require changes in behavior, communication, or organizational structure. You will need to step back (especially if your leadership is being challenged!) and be a careful listener. You may want to bring in an outside perspective to help you have the "ah-ha!" moment and come out the other side. As you address these issues, you begin the team's norming phase.

Norming

You can help your team during the norming phase by being open to making changes. The norming phase is usually when teams revisit their operat-ing principles, which are often created during the forming phase. These principles will change and adapt with the team as needs, priorities, and play-ers change.

One team we worked with was slow in re-sponding to internal staff and external customers, which created a great deal of dissatisfaction and loss of sales opportunities—and this got back to the head of the company. The issue was brought to everyone's attention, and eventually a same-day-response operating principle was agreed to and put in place, with the appropriate support system to make it happen.

Performing

The team that achieves the performing stage may require a change in the way the leader interacts with the team. More mature teams often need less direct leadership and more encouragement as they work to meet the needs of the clients.

For example, your high-performing sales team at this stage knows what to do and needs to stay focused on cultivating and closing sales. Hav-ing done the hard work of getting your team to this level, you can then step back and let them do what they're good at. Too much involvement from you at the performing stage is guaranteed to be counterproductive.

Create an Environment for Teamwork

Few things are more important to a successful business than good leadership. The ability to pull people together around a common goal and to execute tasks flawlessly is something that all organizations strive for. Outward Bound believes that leadership is a skill that can be taught and learned. Anyone can learn to lead in a way that fosters excellent teamwork; it is not an innate talent or something that certain personalities are better suited to than others. More than anything, leading a team successfully involves awareness of others' needs and strengths, a willingness to show appreciation, and a commitment to taking the time to listen and provide direction when needed.

Lead with Flexibility

Whether you become the leader of a newly assembled team, join an already existing team as its leader, or become the leader of your current team, you will need to approach your role with your eyes and ears wide open. You must repeatedly step back from your business tasks to take as objective a look as possible at your team, your goals, and your business environment and decide what type of leader or leadership style is needed at any given point. The questions to ask yourself are these:

- What type of leader is needed to take my company to the next level, whether that means growing to a larger business, increasing profits, or taking the company public?
- Do I need to be a visionary leader or a tactical leader?
- Do I need to have a solid grasp on my industry?
- Is it more important to be a team leader or a facilitative leader? (See more on facilitative leadership in the Interaction Associates model below.)

Over the years, Outward Bound has consistently observed that great leaders, irrespective of personal leadership style, ask insightful questions that help teams get to core problems and think about solutions. The best leaders are flexible in their approach. If leaders are too inclined to play only to their own strengths, they may find themselves anachronistic as their organization evolves.

Remember Crossbeam Systems, the technology-sector provider of Internet security described earlier? The founder and CEO was a brilliant engineer—he developed the original technology and products that brought the company into the marketplace. However, for the business to become a worldwide provider of Internet security solutions, another type of leader was needed. Crossbeam needed a team builder, a facilitative leader who had experience growing a business rapidly. The company made a deliberate transition in leadership styles as the needs of the organization changed.

Develop Followership and Trust

Leadership and *"followership"* go hand in hand. Developing followership, which can also be called *managing up*, is an important skill for getting your job done. By actively following, all workers apply their skills and energy to their team's goals rather than merely taking instruction and doing tasks by rote. Active followers are as busy providing their managers and teammates with information and their unique perspectives as they are with fulfilling their literal job descriptions. Great teams understand that not everyone wants to (or can) be a leader, so the team needs members to be excellent followers: people who take initiative and are constantly looking for ways to move the team forward. Followers should ask themselves and each other, "Are we looking out for the rest of the team?" It's not OK just to do your job. It's really about looking out for one another: "Why would I let someone walk into a big hole?" You aren't moving forward as a team if you're pulling people out of holes.

Does your organization have a culture in which followership is strong? Do you let others know you're available to help? Do you ask, "What can we do to support one another?" As a leader, you have a big hand in creating the workplace culture. Model the way; and when it's happening, talk about it and recognize it. "I thought that was great when you . . ." When it's not happening, discourage it. "This isn't a place where you can just say, 'It's not in my job description.' Here, we expect people to pitch in."

Teams that struggle with followership often struggle with trust. One of the best models we have found for starting some dialog about trust in teams is Stephen R. Covey's Emotional Bank Account model from *The Seven Habits of Highly Effective People*. This model, while simple in concept, is powerful in action and readily understandable by just about everyone.

The premise of the Emotional Bank Account model is that every interaction you have with someone is either a deposit or a withdrawal into your bank account of trust for one another. You make deposits through making and keeping promises and following through on commitments (such as delivering the new engineering drawings on time), through acts of compassion, through respectful feedback, or through lending a hand. Withdrawals from the trust bank may be a result of forgotten commitments (such as not following up with a client's new price quote on a project) or a comment that inadvertently hurts feelings. Every behavior you exhibit, whether big or small, either increases or decreases the trust that those around you have in you—either by a lot or a little. If you build up a large balance of deposits, you can make the occasional withdrawal by showing up late or missing a deadline, but it is important to remember that you can "go bankrupt"—others' trust in you can be completely withdrawn. Your trust "credit rating" is your most valuable asset.

Another way we see the issue of trust played out directly and metaphorically is when teams are climbing a rock face on their Outward Bound program. On the cliff, each climber has a belayer who has them on belay. Belaying (from the French, meaning "to hold fast") is the act of protecting your climbing partner with a rope and anchors to prevent a dangerous fall. Back at the workplace, each person wants to know who is "on belay" for them in the same way as when they were on the cliff. No one can take risks if they don't know there's someone there to protect them from a serious fall.

Understand Strengths and Appreciate Differences

Teams that are diverse in race, age, and gender have tremendous strength in today's business climate. Markets and customers are more diverse than ever, and diverse teams are inherently better able to address and adapt to the needs of these audiences. Your major job as a leader is recognizing what you've got when you look at your team and the individuals in it. You must view people as individuals—you have to get to know them. Spending time with your team is an important start, but the tools and instruments described in "Get to Know Your Team" earlier in this chapter can help provide you with a quick and objective snapshot of individual skills, personalities, and styles.

With regard to diversity, we at Outward Bound Professional cannot stress enough the importance of having it be part of the fabric of your organizational makeup. As the climate we work in becomes more and more global, the demand for organizations that are diverse and truly global is critical. I recently returned from Greece, where Outward Bound Professional was working with an international insurance company, one of whose criteria was that we deliver the program with a global team. As a global organization with operations in thirty-two countries, we were able to fly in a team that was diverse in age, gender, nationality, and race from Europe, Asia, and North America to deliver an outstanding program with a team that mirrored our client's diversity.

Create and Ensure Organizational Alignment

Whether you run a project team, own a small retail business in Montana, or are a senior executive at a large multinational accounting firm in New York City, you need to get everyone moving in the same direction. This is called organizational or team alignment. It is a powerful force that reduces conflict and builds a sense of common purpose and focus.

Alignment is different from agreement: when individuals agree to *support* something—even if they don't necessarily agree with it—they are in alignment on that issue. For example, if employees are aligned on their company's goals, they have a clear understanding of what those goals are, how the goals will be measured, and how the goals will be achieved.

What you are aligning toward really depends on what type of organization or team you are leading. The core elements of Noel Tichy's Team

Leadership model, also called the GRPI model, are described in *A Model for Improving Team Effectiveness* by Michael Brimm et al.:

Team charter: What are our purpose, mission, vision, and values?

Goals: What are our individual and team goals? Are they clearly understood? Are they specific, measurable, attainable, realistic, and timely (summed up as SMART)?

Roles: What are our roles? Are they clear and appropriate?

Procedures: Do we have the right processes, systems, and procedures in place? Do they address how we will do our work? Do they address how we will resolve conflicts, meet, and make decisions? Do we have good team operating principles in place?

Interactions: Do we trust each other? Do we trust the organization? Do we like our work? Do we embrace and resolve conflict? Do we frequently check for team and organizational alignment?

Check for team alignment: Check each of the above areas for team alignment. Rate each area for quantifiable comparisons. A simple survey using the GRPI model above and a scale of 1 through 5 can be done confidentially if needed.

By checking for alignment on a regular basis, you can quickly address lack of alignment, and the conditions driving it, before it creates performance and morale issues. Checking for alignment also will help you figure out where you need to spend your limited leadership time.

Run Great Meetings

During the dot-com heyday, Outward Bound had the chance to work with some very exciting new organizations that were full of young, bright, very technically competent people but whose strengths generally didn't include a lot of leadership experience. These companies were clearly a new generation. Even their names—Razor Fish, *Upstream .com*, and others—seemed designed to obscure or intrigue rather than enlighten. Meetings within these companies were often about who had the best or most creative idea, and meetings were dominated by who could talk the loudest. In that go-fast environment, it was infuriating to those workers to have to spend so much of their time in ineffective meetings.

If you want to get a reaction out of a team, just ask them whether they have ever been to a lousy business meeting. Hands fly upward, and everyone in the room can tell you what not to do. Many even confess to having run a lousy meeting or two themselves. The rest, if they're honest, will nod knowingly. It's kind of like the sailor who swears

EXERCISE: FINGER-SHOOT CHECK-IN

For an instant check-in (especially with smaller project teams), try the old schoolyard finger-shoot: On the count of "one, two, three, shoot," everyone holds out the number of fingers on one hand that indicates their answer to the question.

For instance, the leader might say, "Let's do a finger-shoot on whether you understand the role of everyone on this project. Five means 'Got it; let's go do it'" and one means 'Hold everything; I really need to review the roles to work effectively." Now the leader can get clarification on people's thoughts, especially those whose response was a one or a two. Anything below a three probably needs attention.

Admittedly simple, the finger-shoot has a number of benefits. Because everyone delivers their answer simultaneously, there isn't the temptation to just go along with the majority if you see a problem or are just feeling a little clueless. In the finger-shoot, louder voices don't prevail over quieter ones; everyone's input is equally forceful and articulate.

TIPS FOR WORKPLACE MEETINGS

- **Determine and communicate the purpose of the meeting.** Is the meeting needed to share information, to brainstorm, or to make a decision? Is a meeting needed, or could the goal be accomplished in another way?
- **Make sure the right people are invited to the meeting.** Whose job is directly related to the purpose of the meeting? Who has the critical, relevant information? Who will be needed to implement decisions that the meeting generates? What is at stake: budget, product, territory, client interests? Who owns a piece of what's at stake?
- **Send out the agenda in advance, with topics and time allocations.** Invite the group to comment on or add to the agenda.
- **Determine who will facilitate the meeting and who's responsible for the outcome, decisions made, and timekeeping.** Do you rotate the position of facilitator, or does the most senior person always facilitate? When might you need to bring in an outside facilitator?
- **Be clear on the decision-making process.** Are you looking for consensus? Are you looking for input about a decision that you will ultimately make, or are you looking for feedback on a decision that you have already mostly made?
- **Establish meeting ground rules and create a safe environment.** Have a plan in place for curtailing side conversations, irrelevant tangents, and people who take more than their fair share of speaking time. If people are not observing the team operating principles, call them on it gently but firmly. Make it OK to challenge and disagree.
- **Record action items, who is responsible for them, and what their time lines are.** Make a list of items that need to be addressed later.
- **Check in regularly.** Ask something such as, "Are we addressing the right issues?"
- **Use questions effectively.** Model inquiry, advocacy, and reflection.
- **Manage the group.** Acknowledge the contributions of know-it-alls, politely cut them off, and invite someone else to speak: "Great idea, Fred, but I'd really like to get Susan's perspective." Redirect the devil's advocate, thank her for her contribution, and challenge her to adopt or try on the opposite perspective. Test her opinion with the rest of the group: "How many people see this similarly to how Beth does?" Devil's advocates are great at testing assumptions, but someone who does it consistently may not be representing a real concern. Draw out the quiet introverts—they're assuming that if you don't ask, you're not interested. Make space in the conversation and allow for silence—some people can't think and listen at the same time.

he's never run aground: don't believe him.

Meetings necessarily consume a lot of people's time, and in business, the difference between good and bad meetings can be measured in results. With some forethought, planning, and practice, however, almost anyone can run a great business meeting. Once you have experienced great meetings, your tolerance for poor ones goes down precipitously. The sidebar gives you some tips to get you started on the road to running a good business meeting—or (better yet!) maybe even deciding that a meeting isn't needed at all.

Be Deliberate in Your Decision-making Process

Like many leaders, you may feel as if you do only two things: solve problems and make decisions. That is probably your reality about 90 percent or more of the time. Leaders spend time every day considering decisions on a new product offering, a hiring opportunity, where and how to spend advertising dollars, business strategies, and what to do for lunch. Making all these decisions would be easy if you could use the same process for every type of decision—but you can't. There are five distinct ways to make decisions (also see Figure 6,

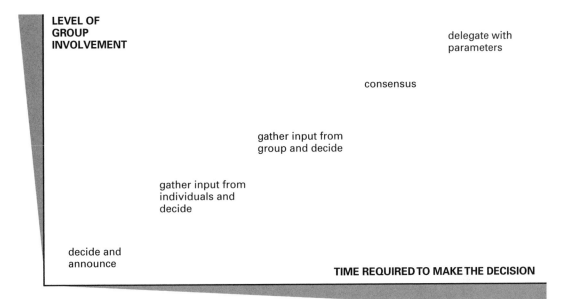

Figure 6. Interaction Associates model

Interaction Associates model, from the *Facilitative Leadership®️ Workshop Manual*):

- ■ You can make the decision and let others know what you decide (decide and announce).
- ■ You can check in with individuals and then make your decision.
- ■ You can check in with the team and then make your decision.
- ■ You can use consensus to reach a decision with your team.
- ■ You can delegate decision making, with parameters.

You may begin to make a decision one way and need to fall back on another method. But before we go further, it's important to clarify what consensus decision making means. People often confuse it with majority voting, which it is not.

What Is Consensus?

Remember the discussion on leadership styles in Chapter 2, Becoming a Leader, in Part I, Leadership Fundamentals? The definition of a consensus decision is that everyone—every single person on the team—agrees with *or agrees to support* the decision being made. As you might imagine, reaching consensus takes some time and opens serious dialog and debate. The payoff, though, especially on important decisions, is the total support of the team.

If you cannot in the first round reach consensus as a team, you can open the discussion back up and wrestle with it until everyone can agree on or at least support the decision; if you just cannot reach consensus, you can hold a vote or simply make the decision as the leader. (This, by the way, is a great forcing technique: "If you can't reach a decision today as a team, then I will.")

What's an Appropriate Level of Involvement?

Leaders should seek the maximum appropriate level of involvement from team members, recognizing that the more people who are involved in a decision, the more time and effort will be required to make the decision, with the payoff being a greater degree of support for the decision. *Appropriate* is the key word here. Appropriate involvement makes people feel valued and engaged instead of left out and nonessential. Inappropriate involvement leaves them feeling put upon or expected to waste time on a decision you or someone else should have made already. And, of course, deciding who should be involved in any decision is part of the equation.

Whose Decision Is It Really?

It is essential that you are clear when a decision is yours to make and when it is the team's decision. At Outward Bound Professional we have observed numerous occasions when a team was solicited for their thoughts, and they contributed enthusiastically, thinking they were making a team decision. In fact, the leader was just looking for input and ended up making a different decision than the one the team had put forth. The outcome of this could have been avoided if only the leader had told the team up front that their input would be helpful but that the final decision rested not with the team, but with the leader.

Which Method Should You Use?

Be clear about which decision-making method you are using, but also make sure that you are comfortable with all of them. That way you're not as likely to get stuck in single decision-making mode.

Jim was a thoughtful and passionate team leader who ran a thriving nonprofit. Jim prided himself on having a strong, inclusive team culture, which led him to use a consensus decision-making approach for nearly all team decisions. During Outward Bound Professional's interviews with individual members of the team, they described meetings as painful—not because they couldn't reach agreement, but because they just wanted Jim (whom they respected and trusted) to take a position and make some of the difficult decisions. They were under a lot of pressure as a team to turn the organization around financially, yet they felt no sense of urgency from their leader.

Moreover, the consensus process sometimes went on forever.

To be efficient and keep your team engaged, be clear about expectations and decision-making ownership and be versatile in your decision-making style and mode. As much as we all like to be involved in the decision-making process, we also like to be quick and efficient.

Measure the Right Things

People will focus on what is being measured, so make sure you have the right measures and incentives in place.

During a recent marketing and sales campaign, Outward Bound had recruiters going out to large events to promote our programs and collect leads: prospective Outward Bound course participants. The goals of the recruiters were based on the number of leads they captured. So our clever and responsive recruiters developed all kinds of innovative ways to get people at these events to fill out inquiry cards indicating interest in the program. People were filling in cards to win a jacket or piece of equipment, with no intention of ever taking one of our wilderness courses. The number of leads was huge; the only problem was that the quality of the leads was low. The concept was fine, but the measures and incentives did not match the desired result. We needed to get good-quality leads.

After reviewing the campaign, we made some adjustments. We realized that if an incentive for filling out the inquiry cards was a raffle ticket to win a wilderness program, people would have already prequalified themselves as someone who would like to do an Outward Bound course versus, say, win a prize. Another step was to visit venues such as sporting events, ski areas, and trade shows with a high proportion of serious outdoor enthusiasts. Not surprisingly, this resulted in a higher number of qualified leads that translated into participant sign-ups.

It is critical to make sure that in addition to measuring sales, profits, and overhead, you are measuring the nonfinancial aspects of your business that add value in other ways. The Balanced Scorecard introduced by Robert Kaplan and David Norton in the *Harvard Business Review* in 1996 is a way to measure not only the financial results of your organization but also the intrinsic and some-times value-driven aspects of your business that are imbedded in processes, customer perspectives, learning, and growth.

Many organizations—for example, Patago-nia, an international outdoor clothing retailer—measure their environmental contribution by the quantity of recycled materials used in their products. They also give their environmental contribution the same level of importance as their return on capital—if not more. Some companies focus on their investment in people and their corporate goal to be a learning organization by measuring the number of hours their employees spend on professional development in a class-room or other training environment. And then there's those many organizations that talk about their dedication to the environment and their people, but without metrics such as those just described, in the end it's just talk.

Do you have the right measures in place? An organization and its leaders may be frustrated with their teams' performance and consider ineffective teamwork to be the root cause. On close inspec-tion, however, you might find that the measures and rewards of the organization do not focus on teamwork as much as on individual performance.

For example, a sales organization was trying to shift its culture from one of individual contributors and competitors to a team-oriented environment that would serve its national clients better. The reasons for making the change were clear and

well articulated—including streamlined processes, reduced points of contact, and reduced paperwork and documentation—but the change wasn't happening.

When Outward Bound Professional asked about incentives and measures, it became clear that the company was still using the old incentive system, which rewarded individuals instead of the team, out of reluctance to change too much too quickly. The result was that the behaviors of the staff were stuck in the old culture of competition instead of the desired collaborative environ-ment because the measures did not support the changes.

Our recommendation was to address the root cause of the problem, which was a mismatch between the incentive plan and the desired behaviors. We delayed the program until the new incentive plan was introduced which rewarded team contribution and then conducted the team development program, which was a huge success.

Outward Bound has found that people will focus their efforts on the aspects of their job that correspond to the measures by which they are evaluated. Even when management has expressed a desire for team collaboration, employees will not act on that stated preference unless it is specifi-cally included among their performance criteria or review measures. Well-known management authority Peter Drucker said, "You can't manage what you can't measure."

Use Adversity and Challenge

Putting teams or individuals into challenging situ-ations—whether running a challenging river or sailing up the coast of Maine to Canada in an open boat—that require them to dig deep has been at the heart of the Outward Bound learning experience since the organization's beginning. People's desire to learn is heightened by challenges that are real and relevant. That same premise can be applied in the workplace through *stretch projects*, special assignments that are above and beyond the workers' skills or usual scope of responsibilities. Stretch projects take participants outside their comfort zone and into the learning zone, as described in Chapter 6, Finding Courage, Overcoming Fear, in Part I, Leadership Fundamentals.

Is there someone on your team who has potential that you would like to see grow and expand? Send that person into the field on special assignment with one of your top salespeople to do some customer research. Or assign that person to a committee responsible for the coordination of a special event. These kinds of special projects accelerate development because they require people to use skills in new ways or to acquire new ones.

Creating action learning teams to tackle business challenges is a great way to help your team develop analytical and problem-solving skills while addressing real workplace dilemmas that can benefit from a fresh set of eyes. Researching new markets, troubleshooting production issues, or addressing other persistent problems requires team members to gain a deeper understanding of the business, and it forces them to look closely at leading organizations and what makes them successful.

CHOOSING A TEAM-BUILDING PROGRAM

Once you have completed a thorough assessment of your team and identified the type of program your team needs, you can make a good decision about the best program design for your team. The team may need a program that focuses on teamwork, leadership, change, and communication, for example. All the stakeholders, including the participants, must agree on the purpose, goals, and objectives of the program. This is achieved upfront during team assessment and program design, which is done immediately with the participants in any leadership development process.

You may decide to design your own team-building program or work with a provider who will create a customized program for your team.

The length of the program and the activities you choose depend largely on the program's purpose; the need of the group, team, or organization; and the participants' skill levels. If the program's purpose is to build relationships among new team members, the design will be very different from a program focused on creating strategic alignment around a major change initiative. A program designed to recognize and reinforce the positive behaviors of a high-performing team requires a lot less time than a program for a low-performing team looking to improve its performance and skills. A team that is essentially working well together will get a lot out of a one-day team-building program, but a group that is in need of some serious team development will be better served by an ongoing multiphase engagement that enables skills acquisition, practice, coaching, and additional development over twelve to twenty-four months, which allows for the learning and practice of new skills, with ongoing reinforcement.

Effective team-building and leadership development programs for the workplace must provide opportunities for team members to work together in a different context. The different context may be an unfamiliar environment, a foreign task, or a reshuffled hierarchy. Business-oriented programs may not venture into the wilderness or even leave the building, but they must provide a different context, which creates the metaphors from which the lessons are drawn.

Programs can include a mix of experiential learning activities—from team initiatives to high-impact activities such as rock climbing or search and rescue to multiday sailing or mountain expeditions—combined with sessions and models that focus on your team's needs. Models provide a common language and structure that allow large teams to work from the same basis, with systems that can be used and maintained with consistency within a large organization. These models have the added benefit of being proven to provide an underpinning based on best practices, which can be adapted for individual organizations.

One of the major requirements of working with adult learners (which most workplace participants are) is the need to share the big picture with them and to answer any questions straight up. Obviously, if something specific about an activity requires that you not disclose it for fear of giving away the solution to an exercise, just say so. We have found time and again that adult learners need to know the big picture. We often try to keep children in the moment so they can focus on the task at hand, whereas adults are very good at focusing on the task at hand once they know the big picture.

Types of Programs

Center-based programs offer many advantages, but you must determine what type of engagement will best serve your learning objectives. Other options include insight seminars, wilderness expeditions (see Part II, Taking Leadership into the Outdoors), and multiphase engagements.

Center-based: Getting off-site to a retreat setting often sets the stage for inspired thinking and new energy and shouldn't be discounted when looking at the cost/benefit analysis of taking your team away from the office for two to three days. For example, Outward Bound Professional offers programs at our Leon L. Bean Mountain Center in Newry, Maine, in the White Mountains. Our 400-acre base has a post-and-beam lodge, cabins, a dining hall, classrooms, a course for ropes exercises (essentially an adult-size jungle gym high in the air, where participants are protected with climbing gear as they swing on ropes, balance on cables, etc.), climbing walls, and numerous peaks, rivers, and streams.

Insight seminars: These short, one-day sessions typically focus on one or two well-defined learning objectives that can be targeted through a well-designed session. Insight seminars have the advantage of location flexibility because they can be done almost anyplace that has adequate indoor or outdoor meeting space. They tend to use portable team initiatives or problem-solving

exercises that are extremely adaptable, depending on the group's needs. These exercises can range from those with no physical challenge at all (such as "Color Blind," a communications exercise developed initially for traffic control operators; see the sidebar in Chapter 11, Workplace Communication Skills) to others that are mentally, socially, and physically challenging (including the "Spider's Web," a strategy planning and team-building exercise that requires the team to get everyone through a woven web or over a rope).

Multiphase engagements: These programs are delivered in segments over a long time frame. They can combine experiential and content-based modules with retreats and center-based activities. Often, the modules are woven into an experiential leadership curriculum using a series of team problem-solving exercises that grow in complexity over a three-day retreat. The exercises begin with a focus on team formation and move on to leadership, communication, problem-solving, collaboration, and teamwork skills. The three-day retreat lays a solid foundation for the remainder of the program and accelerates by months the participants' relationship-building process through the twenty-four-hour-a-day immersion in the experiential learning process.

Recruiting and Retention Programs

Getting and keeping the right people on your team is one of your most important jobs as a leader in your organization. The right people will determine the success of your business, and these decisions are important at every level in the organization. Reducing turnover can save you in financial terms and in time spent on recruiting, hiring, and training. These costs are significant for large organizations and equally important for small organizations that cannot afford to make a bad hire.

Although one of Outward Bound Professional's clients recruited from excellent universities, its success rate in finding and keeping the best employees was not acceptable. The business wanted to improve its process of hiring recent graduates educated in logistics and materials management. Outward Bound's solution was to develop an experiential assessment program as part of a one-and-a-half-day interview process that also included a plant tour, interviews, and a review of individual assessments.

During the program, candidates performed under pressure as members of small teams completing a series of team problem-solving exercises that required leadership and communication. Leadership was sometimes allowed to emerge naturally; for other activities, leadership was assigned. Observers from the organization, as well as Outward Bound facilitators, recorded interactions and performance on a predetermined set of criteria that included teamwork, leadership, initiative, and communication skills. Participants were aware of the process up front, and they quickly got comfortable with the staff and observers. For the most part, their behaviors soon became natural.

After the session, our facilitators convened with the company's managers and reviewed the candidates' performance in the session as well as how they interviewed, how they scored on standard evaluations, and how they managed themselves with others during the interview and assessment sessions. Through a rigorous process, the group was narrowed, and some received offers.

The results have been outstanding, not only providing better candidates but also improving company and program retention dramatically. We are now in our eighth year with the program, consistently delivering great candidates. Participants express appreciation for the investment of time and resources in the process by their organization and credit it with building their interest in working for the company.

Alignment Programs

Sometimes leaders think they have done an excellent job of laying out their company's new organizational vision and strategy to their senior team and the rest of the organization. During our interviews with members of the senior team, though, it can become very evident that the vision and strategy are not shared and that the team clearly has not fully bought into the vision and strategy. We find that a multiphase engagement can be effective in these cases.

One CEO in the service industry had used taglines, talking points, and the whole nine yards to align his company, so initially he felt disbelief, anger, and frustration when his efforts failed. As soon as the dust settled, however, he quickly asked what he should do to get the team enlisted and provide them with a feeling of ownership of the plan. Based on Outward Bound Professional's assessment, we recommended a multiphased approach.

To start off, at their annual two-day all-staff retreat, we focused on the cross-organizational teamwork and communication that would be needed to implement the strategy. The program included a series of initiatives designed to build collaborative team skill and a search and rescue exercise that required cross-team communication.

The second phase was a two-day off-site session for the senior leaders, wherein we focused on clarifying the strategic direction and vision. In this working session, the senior team developed the strategic plan and action steps, assigning various pieces to members of the team. Through this process, which included a series of team initiatives that highlighted the need for agreement on the mission, vision, and values, team members gained ownership. In addition, members of the senior team received feedback via a 360-degree-feedback assessment of their own leadership capabilities and skills.

This phase was followed by a series of

working sessions and coaching sessions to get the plan to a finished state that could be rolled out to the entire organization at the next all-staff retreat. The senior team had, in turn, included many of their staff in their development of the plan, and the upper management group was enrolled and on board.

The response was phenomenal, with strong ownership by and leadership from the senior team. Surveys and employee satisfaction scores showed dramatic improvement, as well as business results based on sales and profitability.

Team-Building and Individual Leadership Skills Programs

The challenges of your business require the skills and conviction to constantly look for ways to do things better. As an individual and as a leader in your business, focusing on and investing in the development of these skills will pay off by keeping you competitive in an environment that is constantly changing and becoming more global every day.

Leadership Maine is a program for leaders from around the state conducted by the Maine Development Foundation. The goal of the multiphase, fifteen-day program spread over nine months is to educate leaders from different sectors around the state on the issues facing the Maine economy and to build the skills and relationships to address them. The session focuses on a combination of education about the challenges (identifying the need), development of leadership skills, and creation of a network of statewide leaders who can reach out to one another to work collaboratively on the these challenges.

The goals of the Maine Development Foundation are commendable. The same concept of identifying needs and building relationships to address them also applies to your organization, no matter what size it is.

Develop a Vision for Yourself, Your Team, and Your Organization

Before you can identify people, skills, and behaviors to meet challenges, you must have a vision

---

EXERCISE: ACHIEVING TEAM ALIGNMENT

A seemingly simple exercise at first glimpse, the "Helium Stick" requires a team to work together on a set of common goals and measures.

The goal of the exercise is to lower a horizontally oriented lightweight aluminum pole (a pole from a mountaineering tent works well) to the ground as quickly as possible—a time measurement—and with the highest level of quality, as measured by "customer" contact, represented in this case by each member of the team maintaining constant contact with the pole "customer" by supporting it on their outstretched forefingers.

Teams struggle to accomplish this seemingly straightforward task. The pole rockets to the ceiling instead of going to the floor, people start blaming each other, and everyone talks over one another. Slowly, after refocusing and starting over a few times, leadership emerges, communication improves, and the team comes together to execute the task successfully.

During the post-action review, we ask the group why they think we use this particular exercise. The response generally includes the need for teamwork, good communication, and perhaps recognition of either organically emergent leadership or assigned leadership. We then explore what was needed to create team or organizational alignment with a group of ten to twenty and the difficulties of doing so, and from this very real experience we springboard into the challenges of getting and maintaining team alignment in an organization of seventy or 7,000 people.

in place of where you are going. The Leadership Maine program described above combines experiential and content-based modules aimed at building leadership skills and strategic relationships among Maine's leaders. They also practice developing and expressing a vision.

A key module during the Leadership Maine program's kick-off session is a personal visioning exercise that includes a "stand and deliver" component wherein participants develop a vision, which can be work- or nonwork-related, that they express ("deliver") to their small triad team or, if they are willing, to the whole group. The exercise is usually introduced using a video of Dr. Martin Luther King Jr.'s "I have a dream" speech, a powerful example of a compelling vision that inspires everyone to think big. Participants practice and deliver their speech, taking turns as presenter, coach, and coachee. The coach offers feedback to the presenter, and then the coachee provides feedback to the coach on his or her coaching skills, which completes the learning cycle.

Many participants find this exercise to be one of the more challenging activities, pushing them outside their comfort zone. Having a vision and inspiring others to develop their own should be priority for leaders or members of a team.

FOLLOW-UP: BUILDING TEAM MOMENTUM

Few experiences are more satisfying than working with a team and seeing them gather and embrace new skills. Let's say you have invested time, energy, and money in getting your team built and working effectively. You've done off-site retreats and workshops and had some great people in to work with your team. You've gone out to observe other companies. Still, you are worried about slipping back into your old ways and not moving forward, certainly not at the pace you had hoped for. Fortunately, not reverting to old habits as day-to-day demands threaten to sweep you backward is a matter of practice and determination.

While team-building and leadership-development workshops are important catalysts for igniting change, it is back at the workplace where your real efforts begin. As a leader, a big part of your job is reinforcing the learning, revisiting the action plans, and rewarding change. You need to be disciplined about setting up ways to check and measure progress.

Tina was the head of Human Resources at a small start-up company. On her return from a team-building program, she created a sheet with the key elements for running an effective meeting and taped it to all the conference tables. She encouraged those who had also participated in the program to step up as meeting facilitators to develop their skills and to model good meeting practices. The quality of their meetings improved dramatically, and with it, their sense of professionalism. Tina did a great job of supporting and modeling the team's newly developed skills and not letting them go back to their old ways.

Significant change is challenging, requiring continual reinforcement and reassessment. It's one thing to go through a workshop; it's quite another to actually teach the material. As a leader, look for opportunities to teach and develop your team.

Below are some ways to reinforce what your team has learned in its program.

Use Facilitated Meetings

Following a program that is designed to initiate change, it's often helpful to have an outside professional help facilitate the next steps and monitor the action plans. Often our clients bring us back into their office right after the off-site program to create a conducive environment, like the one established during the off-site, where team members can be honest and open and engage in productive dialog. The other big benefit of using an outside facilitator for team sessions is that it frees up leaders and other team members to be fully engaged in the process and not distracted by the task of facilitating.

Develop and Implement Action Plans

The action plan captures what you will do to move your organization forward. It not only reinforces the key actions that need to take place but also serves as a list against which you can measure progress as you tick off the items completed. The action plan must clearly identify what needs to take place, who is accountable for it, and the time line in which it will be accomplished. Don't include anything that is not realistic and achievable.

Revisit the action plan on a regular basis. Many managers find it useful to delegate the action plan to someone who will be disciplined and persistent in keeping it in front of the whole team, including the manager.

Use Coaching

Imagine having someone on your team who cares about your development, someone with no other purpose than to help you to grow and understand your strengths and opportunities, to help you develop new skills and help you improve your performance, to help you thrive. Basically, this is a coach. Of all the areas in which you can invest time and money, coaching generates some of the best returns.

Years ago, when Outward Bound first started offering executive development programs, coaching had a certain stigma around it—coaching was a remedial topic reserved for those managers who needed "fixing." Today, life coaches and career coaches help keep us focused on areas we are striving to develop. Having your own coach no longer suggests that you're not making the grade—it is now a status symbol that says you have arrived.

However, you needn't run out and hire a coach. There are lots of ways to participate in a coaching process, from engaging peer coaches to enlisting a mentor or coach from your personal and professional network. Look for someone you respect and who will be honest and open with you—not only regarding your strengths but also your developmental needs and blind spots. Focus

your coach by asking him or her specifically to observe an area or skill you are trying to develop.

For instance, if you know you need to communicate more effectively with your team on strategic direction, have your coach observe you the next time you speak to the team about the big picture and where you see the business heading. Similarly, if you are struggling with an individual, role-play with your coach a difficult conversation that you need to have and ask for feedback. Good coaches help you pinpoint specific behaviors that need to be reinforced or changed and get you to think about different behaviors and approaches.

A senior manufacturing team had some overlapping roles on a large design project that would provide years of future business. At the same time, the team had to do business as usual. After a spirited senior management meeting, one of the functional heads, Joe, was second-guessing his relationship with Dave, the project lead. Having been at the meeting, our staff observed that any tension Joe was feeling about lack of support was misplaced, and during our coaching session we encouraged him to check in with Dave one-on-one.

Later that afternoon, we received a call from Joe saying that he and Dave had had an excellent discussion, clarifying some significant concerns, and were in total alignment on resource allocation. Had we, in our coaching role, not encouraged Joe to engage in a simple yet effective inquiry process, he could have let his relationship with Dave disintegrate on the basis of a simple misunderstanding.

LEADERS ARE LIFELONG LEARNERS

This chapter focuses on workplace leaders, including leaders of newly assembled teams or teams they have newly joined, and the skills they need to build high-performing teams and enhance their team's productivity by working together more effectively. Whether you're a new or experienced leader, the keys to success are having a clear vision; creating team alignment and commitment around the mission, vision, and values; and establishing clear goals, roles, procedures, and trusting interactions. As a team leader, do everything possible to get the right people on your team and keep them there.

The best leaders and their organizations are hungry for knowledge and looking for ways to improve, whether that means acquiring new computer skills, quality training, or a fundamental change in strategy. Always ask, "What can we be doing to get better at what we do?"

One could spend a lifetime studying leadership and team development. The most impressive individuals and companies we encounter are those who are truly lifelong learners. Angus King, the governor of Maine who after his election brought his cabinet and staff to our mountain base in the dead of winter, is an excellent example of a lifelong student of leadership.

The Outward Bound program with Angus King's group was about establishing a team profile and putting the learnings to use. It was hard to tell what was scarier for them: having to share feedback with peers, or hanging from the ropes course belayed—and literally protected by a rope—later in the day by a brand-new teammate. The days were long and hard—mentally, physically, and emotionally.

The program culminated with a final challenge that was pertinent to their new roles. The participants had to organize as several media teams with an administration team to create, produce, and direct a five-

minute media session that would take place on their return to Augusta, Maine. The sessions, which were taped by a professional film crew, were as close to the real thing as we could get. The sessions needed to capture and communicate the outcome of the three-day retreat and its value to the people of Maine. Teams produced them in an intense and time-pressured environment, working with people they may have known less than seventy-two hours.

At the end, the team was "challenge ready." They had established roles and expectations, team-operating principles, and a culture of cross-department interface. They had practiced and tested these agreements through some initial storming during the team initiatives and ropes course and had met challenges in adverse conditions. All this time, they lived close together in cabins heated with a small woodstove that needed stoking throughout the night.

When the real story hit the media, Angus was quoted as saying that the three days spent together in the Maine woods was the equivalent of "working six months together behind desks in Augusta. We went from being a dozen individuals to a close, high performing team almost overnight. We are ready to tackle the challenges facing the state of Maine."

The King administration went on to be one of the most popular and innovative administrations in the history of the state of Maine, which, for example, was the first in the nation to put a laptop computer into the hand of every seventh and eighth grader. Angus King won a second term as governor easily.

CHAPTER 11

WORKPLACE COMMUNICATION SKILLS

Quality communication and effective information sharing empowers, enlists, and motivates your team members and company. This chapter explores skills and best practices for communicating and sharing information with employees. In this chapter, communication involves not only the act of sharing information inside and outside your organization but also the use of more subtle clues, feelings, and emotions that we all continuously use to interpret others' meaning.

Information is power. Therefore, it is easy for people to associate their value to an organization with the level of information they are privy to. For this reason, and because it is very easy to undercommunicate and very difficult to overcommunicate with your team, when in doubt, communicate.

ELEMENTS OF COMMUNICATION

People interpret your meaning through your words, tone, and body language. This is often referred to as the *communication mix*. Many studies have been done on the relative importance of these three variables, and they all agree that a large majority—more than half—of understanding comes through body language. The speaker's tone is the second most important, and only a very small percentage of the message delivered is understood through the meaning of the words themselves. In other words, the aspect of communication that we tend to focus on most when speaking—our words—is the one with the least impact on how it's received.

Words

Thinking about the words we use is fairly simple, which may be why this element of the communication mix gets the most attention. We have a choice of vocabulary, sentence structure, and grammar, and we naturally modify these in response to what we believe about our audience. When addressing line workers on the assembly floor, you might choose a slightly different vocabulary and, perhaps, grammar from what you would choose for addressing a corporate board member, even if the content you are communicating is identical. In the literal, professional world of business interaction, you might think that choosing words that say what you mean is enough to ensure good communication, but that's far from the case.

Tone

By changing the tone in which you deliver your message, you can drastically change your message. In the context of the communication mix, tone includes the volume and inflection of your voice and the pace of your speech—and it is integral to understanding. We focus on tone automatically when we know words aren't important, such as when addressing small children or animals.

Think about scolding a puppy that has just produced a puddle on your grandmother's oriental rug. The puppy doesn't understand your words, but if you use a low-pitched, slow, sharp, stern voice, you let the puppy know you aren't pleased. Compare this to the voice that you use with the puppy after it successfully does its business outside. The puppy still doesn't understand your words but will strive to repeat the behavior that produced your high-pitched, cheerful, quick, welcoming tone.

It's important to remember that tone's effect on your message isn't limited to kids and puppies—we all have a visceral, positive reaction to a cheerful tone and a guarded, hesitant reaction to a gruff one.

Body Language

Body language is perhaps the most complex aspect of the communication mix. It includes elements such as eye contact, gestures, posture, dress, facial expression, tension, and energy. For example, the son of one of Outward Bound's instructors recently took his road exam for his driver's license. When the boy walked out of the examiners' room, his mother could tell—before her son said any words in any tone whatsoever—that he had not passed the exam; his shoulders were slumped, his eyes were focused toward the floor, and he shuffled his steps. On his second attempt, however, he walked out of the exam room with a bounce in his step, grinning from ear to ear, looking his mother right in the eye—obviously he had passed!

IMPLICATIONS OF TECHNOLOGY IN THE COMMUNICATION MIX

Today's technology has a large impact on how we communicate in the business world, because it limits our scope of communication from its natural spectrum of words, tone, and body language. Many corporate teams exist in a virtual setting. Opportunities for face-to-face interaction are expensive and time consuming; hence, they're a rare occasion. Regularly scheduled meetings are conducted via conference calls, while daily interactions happen in the form of emails.

These realities have significant ramifications on the productivity of our efforts to communicate. Even a well-managed conference call relies solely on words and tone; even a video call does a poor job of capturing body language. Email has the greatest potential to be misunderstood, because it relies solely on the written word.

In today's evolving business world, it becomes ever more important to invest in building the relationships of team members so that there is a foundation of trust and understanding to help compensate for the limitations of high-tech communication. See "Forums for Communication" at the end of this chapter for some tips on making high-tech communication media more effective for your company.

CONSIDER YOUR AUDIENCE

Who is your audience? How you best communicate a message often has less to do with the content of the message than with the targeted audience. Audiences may be individual people or collections of lesser or greater diversity. Your audience might be members of your team, your boss, your shareholders, your board, or the general public. Your message will be perceived best by people who feel you are addressing their concerns, and to do this well, you have to know something about them—or infer it from what you know about people in general. This section explores the challenges of communicating with your audience in mind.

When your leadership role requires you to communicate a message to your organization, you need to decide who should hear that message. Whom you choose to communicate with largely depends on whose skills and perspectives you need to bring to the table and who will be affected by the subject at hand.

Audience Size

Sometimes the size of your audience is beyond your control—for example, when you wish to address the general public or you're trying to land a particular client. But when your audience consists of people within your organization, you have some choice in how you select the group to whom you'll present your message.

There's a tendency to want to keep the group you need to communicate with small, because that would seem to make it easier to manage the sharing of information and simplify its delivery—but err on the side of inclusiveness. By including more people or more types of audiences, you actually maintain *more* control over the information because more people hear it directly from you at the same time and in the same context. Leaving people out of the communication loop may do far more damage than taking the time to include them. When you spread the word wider, people feel informed, and this enhances transparency and commitment and just avoids hurt feelings.

> *A financial services firm was recently going through a significant restructuring process as a result of being acquired by a larger, more powerful company. It wasn't a very friendly process, and the top managers were thoroughly distracted from their usual responsibilities as they wrestled with a lack of control over their own destinies.*
>
> *There's a legal nondisclosure period in such cases, and the chief executive officer didn't share much information with his management team. By not talking about it, the CEO left them to focus on their own worst-case scenarios: the management team was naturally filling in the communication vacuum with all kinds of possibilities, some real and some pretty far-fetched. They worried about the new corporate culture they were entering, about losing their independence and the trust of their own clients, and even about losing their jobs.*
>
> *Outward Bound Professional worked with the CEO to facilitate dialog at a series of offsite team-building and planning sessions, with the goal of sharing as much information as possible without compromising the need for confidentiality on certain strategic issues. The CEO had to learn to slow down and connect with his people. Once they were communicating well, the team could stay focused on the one thing that they had the most control over and that would affect the future of the organization the most: delivering great financial results.*

Keep the circle small *only* when the outcomes are momentarily uncertain, information is not complete, things are changing fast, or there's a lot of anxiety attached to an issue. Large-scale personnel decisions might fall into this category,

as would anything with significant confidentiality consequences.

However, be careful not to create sweeping justifications to excuse not communicating well when the message is awkward or to put off announcing bad news. If the situation is going to be uncertain for a significant length of time, it's best to communicate that things are uncertain, the reasons for the uncertainty, and when you expect to have an update. Weigh the costs and benefits before you decide to withhold information. When in doubt, communicate.

Social Styles of Audiences

Your audience, no matter what type or size it is, consists of a range of personalities, or *social styles*. The Wilson Learning Library's *The Social Styles Handbook* categorizes people into four quadrants: Analyticals, Drivers, Expressives, and Amiables. By nature, people of each social style respond best to different types of communication. The Wilson Learning Library model usually focuses on one-on-one interactions, but we find it also provides an excellent checklist when you have a diverse audience so that you are sure to connect with everyone at some level (see the chart on pages 258 and 259). Let's look at what defines each style.

Analyticals need data. They want the facts. They are focused on tasks and are logical thinkers who often prefer to work alone.

Drivers, on the other hand, work at a fast pace, see the big picture, are not as interested in the details, and can be very competitive.

Expressives focus on relationships and people. They are optimistic and want to be inspired by you. These folks tend to be fast paced and spontaneous, and they love being in the spotlight. Expressives can generally be counted on to be the life of any interaction or gathering, be it in a social or business setting.

Amiables move methodically. They have a tendency to want to be inclusive with a strong emphasis on relationships. Amiables want to avoid conflict and may delay making decisions, but they won't let anyone be left out.

Each of these styles has positive attributes and opportunities for improvement. These are marked on the chart with the two symbols derived from the plus-delta model explained in Chapter 12, Managing Change in the Workplace.

COMMUNICATE WITH YOUR AUDIENCE

Now that you know who your audience is, you must consider whether one message will work for everyone or you'll need to target each audience separately or in appropriate groups. Each audience may require separate communication to address the same issue from a different perspective.

Tailoring Your Message to Your Audience

What will concern, interest, or motivate each audience most: knowing the *who*, the *what*, the *why*, the *when*, or the *how*? Is your audience interested in details, or do they need a high-level overview? How will they use the information? Will your message require an immediate action or behavior change on their part, or is it just for background?

For instance, if Outward Bound institutes a change in medical screening policy that affects the way we work with participants who have heart disease, we need to focus the information differently for different people.

The technical specialists—climbing instructors, for example—need to know that when working with clients with heart disease, they must adhere to the policies that restrict the activity level of such people during our programs.

The Outward Bound risk management committee needs to know the change in policy and the reasons—best available data, medical expertise, etc.—behind the change and to be assured that the change will both support safe participation and result in less risk to the organization while providing a quality program experience to the participant and the other team members.

The clients themselves need to under-stand the reason for the restrictions and be reassured that they will still learn useful skills and be valuable participants.

Each client's physician needs to be educated on the nature of our programs and the modifications that can be made to reduce the risk to the patient, so he or she can make informed judgments.

The board of directors needs to be assured that the screening process and strategies for delivering programs are serving the mission.

Clearly, all these audiences have both needs in common as well as distinct needs that have to be addressed separately. The same memo can't go to everyone—the person distributing the information has to step into another's shoes and consider what they need to know to work effectively with the issue.

Focusing Content for Your Audience

Making sure you have the right content for your audience will go a long way toward ensuring their receptivity to your message and building your credibility. Include the right level of detail for each audience, and have additional details for those who need or want it. Be prepared.

For instance, when Outward Bound provides certified First Aid or First Responder (more advanced medical emergency) training for our staff, we need to be sure that the content is focused on procedures and equipment that are relevant to the program environments—desert, sea, center-based, backcountry—and are hands-on. The training needs to focus on injuries and illnesses that staff might see in those environments, with an appropriate amount of time spent on highly unlikely but really serious issues. The training needs to be practical, with a lot of scenarios and practice activities, or these experiential educators might wonder why they couldn't just read the book.

Also, we need to train our staff to use

equipment that they can actually carry in the field. We don't need to train people to use equipment found only in ambulances—in the unlikely event that we need one, we'd call one. The training maintains people's focus because they can see how the skills we're presenting are relevant to their work, and the skills are presented in the most accessible and memorable way.

Speaking Your Audience's Language

When Outward Bound presents a team or leadership development program for a client, we take the time to understand their language and culture and adjust our communication content appropriately.

One of Outward Bound Professional's longterm clients is deeply involved with Six Sigma, an improvement methodology originally created by Motorola. Six Sigma has a language, metrics (measuring) system, and approach that are all highly defined. When we deliver programs to this client, we weave the content, concepts, and language of Six Sigma throughout the program to reinforce their learning objectives. The communication and words that we use become very powerful in the client's application and acceptance of the programming. This ensures that the learning leaves the program site and is taken back to the workplace.

Using jargon may show that you understand your audience—if you use it right. Misuse jargon, and you can lose credibility or alienate everyone in the room who can't understand what you are trying to say.

Addressing Your Audience's Social Styles

Considering what content your audience needs is only part of being a purposeful communicator. You also need to consider the form of that content, and one way to approach this is to appeal to the different social styles within your audience. Let's look at how to address an audience from the perspective of Wilson Learning's four social styles (described earlier in this chapter).

Analyticals prefer a written form of communication to which they can respond. They want to know *what* you will do to get things accomplished and details about your plan. When addressing an Analytical, explain your logic and ask questions that reveal a clear direction. Be sure to provide solid, tangible, factual evidence and give Analyticals time to think before they must respond. When working with Analyticals, be thorough and well prepared.

Drivers want to hear about the big picture and *when* things will happen. They want to know how you are going to move the organization or project forward. It is important to address Drivers in a professional, businesslike manner. Be direct in your speech; stick to the facts, not personal feelings. Provide options, and when possible, let Drivers make the decision. Above all else, be efficient and competent.

Expressives are big picture–oriented as well, but they want to hear *how* things will impact employees, customers, and relationships. Show Expressives that you are interested in them as people by supporting their ideas and opinions. Let them talk—and try not to argue with them, as you will seldom win.

Amiables are interested in the details and *who* will be impacted—not only them but the organization too. Like Analyticals, they need time to digest your communication. On change issues, they want to be reassured that support systems are in place. To develop trust and credibility with Amiables, show them that you are actively listening and focusing on the human element of any project.

An Audience of One

Even very good, very smart people sometimes don't take the time to think about who their audience is and how to send their message, yet they'd be so much more effective if they did.

For example, if you are an Expressive who has just won a new account with a high-profile client and are meeting with your corporate financial officer, who happens to be an Analytical, how might you want to share this exciting news, and what might you want to emphasize? In this instance, the

Expressive would by nature be inclined to focus on the great excitement of having such a client and the wide array of opportunities opening because of it. Given the audience, though, the Expressive would do far better to emphasize the numbers, details, margins, and benefits of the relationship, all backed with data based on sound analysis.

Here's another example:

The plant manager of a manufacturing business was an elderly ex-football coach who was very much a Driver. He got where he was by insisting on respect and absolute loyalty to his way of doing things.

A new member of the team had some ideas for improvements around the factory and was eager to share them with the plant manager. When the new team member walked into his boss's office and asked him if he had a few minutes, the manager responded, "Yes," without looking up from his computer screen. As the new senior team member began to explain his ideas, the manager could have listened actively—made eye contact, nodded his head, and repeated phases back—asked a few questions to indicate that he understood the new ideas, and thanked the new team member for his interest in making process improvements around the plant.

Instead, when the manager finally did look up from his computer screen, he responded with a raised, aggressive voice and demanded to know why the new team member felt that these changes would be positive. Without waiting for the startled man to answer, he proceeded to tell his new team member that "challenging the system" was not an attribute of a team player.

The new team member had entered the plant manager's office with the purpose of offering creative suggestions for improving the process, not challenging it. When he left the office, he vowed never to take the initiative to share his creative ideas with the

plant manager again. He would do what was asked of him and leave it at that.

The plant manager, by responding as he preferred to be addressed—in the direct, confrontative style of a Driver—had shut down potential future contributions from his employee. Had he taken the time to find out more about his new team member and gained a sense that his style was more of an Amiable type, the plant manager may have been able to adjust his response. And while he might not have liked the ideas that were presented, at that meeting he would not have cut off his employee's drive to take initiative in the future.

When you are working with a single person whom you don't know well (a new client, for instance), be resourceful about getting some useful information about how to present your information. Call the person's assistant and ask, for instance, "Is he a big-picture guy, or does he focus on numbers and details?" The assistant definitely knows the answer and will think more of you for not wanting to waste his or her boss's time. If you are visiting the prospective client's office, look for clues: Are the walls filled with pictures of teams (Amiable) or diplomas (Expressive)? Are the furnishings simple and the walls blank (Driver), or do you see the latest in every technical device imaginable (Analytical)?

A Larger Audience

Communicating with a group is similar, except that it is likely that you will be dealing with all four of the social styles. In an effort to reach out to each style, think about keeping a fast pace (Driver), being nonthreatening (Amiable), taking a fun approach (Expressive), and being sure that your material is well researched (Analytical).

There's an added, somewhat hidden benefit in preparing a presentation with all four social styles in mind: it shows you whether you really know your material well enough to make an effective presentation. Do you know where the data come from and how the information will affect people?

Are you comfortable enough with the subject to have fun with it and also keep the presentation moving from salient point to salient point? If you can present an issue only in your own preferred style, it may be because you have looked at it from only one perspective, and you will lose three-fourths of your audience.

Your goal as a leader should be to make others feel safe and comfortable so that they can be their best. Think about how you can adjust your own style to be more in line with the styles of those around you. Rather than appearing rigid and inflexible, work to appear open-minded and flexible. You don't need to change the content of your message. Simply strive to speak in a "language" that others will understand and want to listen to. Being versatile with social styles ensures that your voice is heard, reduces relationship tensions, and helps to build more productive and trusting working relationships. In fact, as others recognize your concern and efforts to respond to what it is they value, many will reciprocate your effort to adapt.

High-performing teams are made up of a full range of social styles wherein individuals value and depend on the strengths of other team members. Throughout the duration of any project, financial quarter, election, etc., changing situations draw on the strengths of the various social styles. Initially, it will be important for the team to establish a vision and a long-range outlook—a strength of the Drivers and the Expressives. The Amiables will want to work to build relationships among the newly formed team, while the Analyticals will strive to establish processes. Over time, the need for the various particular social talents of the team will ebb and flow. By the project's conclusion, the Drivers will have pushed for the final results, the Amiables will have provided the support for the final push, the Analyticals will have documented every step of the way so that it can be easily repeated, and the Expressives will have ensured that the well-deserved celebration and recognition of effort rewards everyone. A strong leader recognizes and values each of these con-tributions, inspiring each individual to continue to contribute their unique set of strengths to the good of the team.

CONSIDER YOUR MESSAGE

All our lives, we've been learning to communicate to be understood and get what we need. You might think that by the time we enter the business world, we would be great at communicating without much conscious effort. Ironically, it is this tendency to just communicate without proper consideration of the content of your communication that is the source of much workplace miscommunication. Let's begin by considering the desired outcome of your communication.

Being Clear on the Purpose of Your Message

To be effective, communication needs to be deliberate. Being purposeful will go a long way toward ensuring that your message hits the mark. Being deliberate ensures that you don't inadvertently send a message you didn't mean.

A group of highly charged and motivated energy traders had made the long trek from Texas to Maine to develop team skills and to build stronger relationships between junior and senior executives. The turbulent waters of West Branch of the Penobscot River, which offers some of the best and most challenging stretches of white water in North America, has rapids aptly named the Exterminator, the Crib Works, and Big Heater Rapid. The difficult rapids tested even the fittest of our group of hard-charging, go-getter traders. They were challenged to avoid flipping the raft or dumping themselves into the river, as well as to work together to surf a raft on smaller rapids.

Surfing a raft is a fun technical maneu-ver that requires a team to paddle their boat upstream onto the back side of a wave that forms downstream of a rock where the current reverses and flows upstream. Surfing

ANALYTICALS
Emphasize meaning and concepts
+ Seek information and opinions
+ Observe process
+ Make decisions based on facts
+ Prefer to gather information before deciding
+ Can be creative and innovative
△ Can be slow to decide or paralyzed by insufficient information
△ Can delegate many tasks in order to focus on one
△ Have to guard against noninvolvement or unrealistic ideas

If your leader or supervisor is an Analytical, honor the leader's need for information but also request that your leader tell you how and when he or she will decide.

If a group doesn't have an Analytical, it will miss significant learnings that come from observation, or it will miss alternative perspectives. Analyticals develop processes for the group and ensure that the group adheres to policies. Too many Analyticals in a group may allow opportunities to pass.

DRIVERS
Emphasize action and direction
+ Give information and opinions
+ Easily make decisions
+ Often "keep the vision"
+ Take a stand and make things happen
+ Usually speak directly and appreciate direct feedback
△ Can be impatient with a decision-making process
△ Will sometimes decide without input
△ Might make mistakes by moving without adequate information
△ Can appear too impersonal

If your leader is a Driver, be as direct as possible with that person. Bring problems and opinions to your leader and allow him or her to make the decisions.

Mature Drivers are nonreactionary individuals with much ability in the other quadrants, but without maturity, Drivers may provide too much structure and direction for the group. If a group does not have Drivers, it must pick up Driver functions or the group will fail to meet far-reaching goals.

AMIABLES

Emphasize caring

+ Build and sustain community and teamwork
+ Build rapport and commitment
+ Seek consensus and feedback
+ Praise and show concern for others
+ Show respect for others' opinions, needs, and actions
Δ May not take a stance that puts relationships at risk
Δ May focus on relationships to the detriment of decision making
Δ Can put insufficient emphasis on their own needs

If your leader is an Amiable, ask him or her to be specific in outlining expectations. Encourage critical feedback and let your leader know that you want to hear his or her viewpoint. In a leader, Amiable preferences are powerful when combined with other quadrant functions.

Caring—the focus of Amiables—is essential to group functioning. If the group has many Amiables, however, it may not take enough risks to move forward significantly. The group may avoid conflict to the point that there is a lack of genuine connection.

EXPRESSIVES

Emphasize emotional connection

+ Voice ideas passionately and energize others to follow
+ Motivate people with a sense of mission
+ Often are good at solving interpersonal problems
+ Hold energetic dialogs and enjoy expressing their points of view
Δ Can be emotionally bound to their own ideas, losing objectivity
Δ Can create a highly emotionally charged environment by challenging and confronting others' assumptions

If your leader is an Expressive, know your own stance and opinion and voice it. Ask your leader for concrete examples to back up his or her ideas. Mature Expressives can be charismatic leaders.

Groups need Expressives in order to really be creative, innovative, and keep "the pot stirred." Mature Expressives can detach or attach themselves as needed. If immature or too strong within a group, they can be overly reactive or so impassioned with their ideas that they lose touch with reality. A group with a surfeit of Expressives may be functional but somewhat lackluster.

a raft with six people takes a great degree of skill, teamwork, and determination to hold the boat at the right angle, and by the end of the day our group was pumped by their success in executing the maneuver on their own. That day together on the West Branch had provided a great opportunity for senior and junior executives to work side by side.

As we gathered around on the riverbank at the end of a beautiful day, it was the perfect moment for the leader of the group to recognize the efforts of the team members, many of whom had clearly been well outside their comfort zones on the river and were extremely pleased with their accomplishments. It was an opportunity to recognize individuals for pushing themselves and to celebrate how well everyone had worked together.

The stage was perfectly set. Yet the leader immediately blew it by making a flippant, offhand comment about the day and then proceeding to let everyone know how great he and his particular raft group were. Then instead of enjoying a cookout on the beach with his team, he left the program early with his top four managers to go into town to party.

Saying with sincerity something as simple as "I'm really proud of you guys" after such an exciting day would have been a grand-slam home run. In the blink of an eye, he lost the opportunity to display the leadership that would have brought the group together. Instead, he let the group down and left the air filled with a palpable downer.

Is the purpose of your communication to inform and share information, gather input, set and clarify expectations, announce a decision, inspire and motivate the troops, or respond to someone else's communication? What do you want people to know after you've finished your speech, memo, or email? How should they behave differently? What should they keep doing that's working so well?

Timing Your Message

Release information as early as possible to avoid information coming out through less-reliable channels and to maintain greater control over the message. Even in the days before the Internet and cell phones, rumors traveled fast. We at Outward Bound, a field-based organization with staff and bases in remote regions of the United States and throughout the world, have felt the speed of what we affectionately call the "Coconut Wireless." Informal information travels fast and assumes all sorts of forms along the way. The only way to communicate solid information is to get the official word out faster.

Repeating Your Message

It can't be said enough: communicate, communicate, communicate. In his book *Leading Change*, John Kotter states that you need to communicate your message at least *ten* times in order for the message to be heard and retained. Most of us don't get it the first time, and we certainly don't remember it in a way that we can repeat it with accuracy. This is the reason we often see politicians or advertisers saying the same thing over and over again. When you adopt this tactic, you may feel like a broken record at times, but your message just won't sink in any other way.

For instance, one of Outward Bound's clients, a highly successful credit card company, had a message that they repeated constantly and in many different ways in meetings, trainings, materials, and screen savers: "Think of Yourself as the Customer." They even painted it over doorways throughout the organization. This tactic made it clear to us, as outsiders, that everyone in the organization understood the importance of customer service and the customer.

Here's another example:

Jim Quesnel is a senior manager with Avery Dennison's global operations division who uses two phrases over and over: "raise the bar" and "no risk, no reward." As a former site manager, Jim knows what it takes to run a successful manufacturing operation, and he engages Outward Bound Professional for help with recruiting and developing leadership talent.

During these programs, which begin with simple problem-solving exercises and culminate in rock climbing, the participants set and then execute a variety of goals. After each exercise, the group huddles to share what they have learned during the process so that they will be even better on the next task. Jim presides over these debriefs, constantly repeating the phase "raise the bar." His message to the firm's future leaders is that in order to achieve great success, they must continually set a high standard.

Jim also tells them, "No risk, no reward," believing that the feeling of accomplishment is greater when they just miss the "raised bar" than when they achieve a goal that was set to a lower standard. He sends this clear message to the participants throughout their trainings, both in his verbal communication and by his own participation during the programs.

In a similar vein, on a rock climb establishing a goal that is beyond a point that an employee thinks he or she can reach requires, in Jim's mind, the same motivation and drive as an employee setting a production quota that is deemed to be a stretch.

Delivering Your Message

Above all, when communicating in the workplace, be yourself. Striking an artificial or overly positive tone will obscure your content by reducing your credibility. People can't listen to what you say if they're wondering what you're *not* saying. When you thoughtfully present information with which you're comfortable and target it with your audience in mind, you can't help but be engaging.

Outward Bound facilitated an off-site strategic planning and team-building session with the senior management team of a top research laboratory. As we observed the group, we sensed that the head of the physical plant wasn't as comfortable with speaking in front of the group as the other team members were. In the team activities, he was shy and reserved, rarely offering his perspective unprompted. Later in the session, all the team members were supposed to present their business plans and strategies for supporting the growth of the organization, and we anticipated that his presentation would be poor, if not painful, to watch.

When his turn came around, though, we were all in for a surprise. He had the group riveted with his plain-spoken, common-sense approach to some very complicated plant needs driven by growth and demands of the laboratory environment. It was immediately obvious that he knew his stuff and, more importantly, knew how to connect with the people who were responsible for keeping the lab clean, which in their business is absolutely necessary. He walked the rest of the management team through the steps needed to complete a series of projects, and his comfort, confidence, and dry, self-deprecating style of humor was effective and engaging. The best part was that he was just being himself.

Some people can just stand up and deliver information, and they seem simply to get it right every time. Most of us need to work at it—and be ready to change delivery styles if our efforts don't go well initially.

Reading Your Audience's Reaction

You need to be ready to take action on spontaneous feedback. Some is explicit, such as questions that beg for more information and detail. You can read some feedback through your audience's

EXERCISE: TUNING UP YOUR FEEDBACK RESPONSE

This exercise, called "Clear and Grounded," gets people in your organization tuned up and focused on making spoken presentations. Here's how it works:

Divide into small groups of five or six people, and ask everyone to think of a topic they would like to share with their small group. It could be something related to your company's business, such as the rationale to buy a new piece of equipment, or it could be a personal topic, such as how to prune an apple tree properly.

Once everyone has determined their topic, they take turns presenting it to their group; the group's task is for each person to raise his or her hand to signal when they feel the presentation is clear and grounded. When everyone has raised their hand, the presenter is finished. In other words, when the presentation makes sense to the audience, the presenter is clear. When the presenter is comfortably solid with the information and getting to the root of the subject, he or she is grounded.

Once all the group's hands are up, the audience coaches the presenter on behaviors that made them feel the presenter was clear and grounded. They'll describe elements of body language, facial expression, word choice, speaking cadence, and a whole host of other things you couldn't possibly cover in a lecture on public speaking. After the presenter gets coaching, it's the next person's turn.

This exercise is subjective and just a little stressful—fun but edgy. It forces a speaker to focus on the audience, which gives immediate and relevant feedback, while striving to connect with the audience. Presenters look for cues ranging from body language and facial expressions, such as an understanding nod or the "open-mouthed trout," to signal their connection or lack of it. If this exercise is framed as a coaching and feedback exercise, the tone will be playful and positive. Try it out and have fun with it.

body language: glassy eyes or subtly exposed wristwatches that suggest you'd better get to the point and move on. See the sidebar for a coaching exercise on audience reaction.

Simplifying Your Message

The feedback-response exercise in the sidebar also helps you avoid the pitfall of going on about a subject longer than you need to. Strive to be memorable instead of comprehensive. Don't be tempted to tell all you know about a subject. Instead, engage the audience with an arresting presentation of the three or four things that you most want your audience to know when they walk away. The best communicators take complex concepts and make them simple and comprehensible. Boil it down to essentials; put the broad principles in common sense, accessible examples.

Sound bites are an extreme example of an idea boiled down to its essence. Sound bites provide themes and direction that guide an organization's and individuals' behavior. Make sure that people know what the sound bites mean in real, actionable terms.

Jack Welch at General Electric would say, "We're going to be boundary-less," meaning that the different departments would understand and be involved in each others' processes. He would also say, "We're going to be Number One or Number Two or we're not going to be in it," meaning that, of their fourteen business units, if one wasn't first or second in their sector, GE would get out of that business.

Using Executive Dialog

The word *dialog* usually means a conversation between two people, wherein each person spends some time talking and some time listening. Dialog between any two people has a feedback process built into it, if you are tuned to it. The back and forth of a normal conversation allows you to hear and explore the other viewpoints being shared.

But sometimes dialog is unsuccessful. Have you ever had a frustrating workplace conversation in which you couldn't understand the other person's viewpoint at all? Have you felt as though you were metaphorically beating your head against a wall and still couldn't seem to make a connection with someone?

Some of these metaphorical walls are the result of the realities of today's business world: Global corporations span multiple world cultures. Small, local companies hire from a cross section of the socioeconomic spectrum. In both of these situations, understanding among people within the organization is hampered by significant differences in perspective. Barriers to good communication can be overcome only with a lot of deliberate effort and a strong will to understand.

In the lingo of organizational development and performance, *dialog* means a conversation that is done well—in other words, one that provides all parties with insight into one another's perspectives. This type of dialog—sometimes also called *executive dialog*—can help you break down those metaphorical walls in the workplace to communicate and reach agreements more easily. Chris Argyris, who has done some of the best work around dialog with the Ladder of Inference model, as described in *Overcoming Organizational Defenses,* presents three dialog tools that are easy to master and understand with some practice (the key being practice): inquiry, advocacy, and reflection. Pete Senge, in *The Fifth Discipline*, also covers this well.

Inquiry is the use of active questioning to gain understanding of the other person's viewpoint; it requires a sincere desire for understanding. If, through body language, tone, or choice of words, someone shows enthusiasm, hesitancy, or trepidation about a proposed action, turn your observation into a question. You might ask, "What is it you like about this proposal?" or "What concerns you about the proposal?" or "You seem to have a strong reaction to the proposal; why is that?" By asking deeper questions, you learn more about how the other person sees or hears the proposal. You will likely learn more about the other person, the proposal itself, and how it resonates in your organization. This avoids the situation wherein you disagree with someone only to discover that you were each judging the issue on differently defined terms or that one of you had an important piece of context that was unknown to the other.

Advocacy is the act of taking a stand and putting your point out there. For example, you might say, "I think we need to do a better job serving our clients, and I recommend we conduct a survey to see where they think we need to improve." By advocating for your ideas, rather than never mentioning them at all, you make sure that they are heard in a forum where they might get realized. Your opinion about an issue may be painfully obvious to you because it is part of the reality of your everyday job, but you can't assume that everyone has the same view you have. You are in the best position to argue your position, and it's part of your job to give your team the benefit of your perspective.

Reflection is the act of asking yourself, "Why am I responding this way? What is it about this person or idea that I connect with or that bothers me?" If your feeling is negative, you might ask yourself, "Is the idea or recommendation the problem, or am I just turned off by the presenter because he or she reminds me of someone I once had a difficult time with?" By shelving your thoughts on the issue itself and just reflecting on your own reaction, you may find that you can move beyond a sticking point, because the source of the problem isn't relevant—it's just a connection that's in your head. For example, you might be reacting negatively to a proposal because it was tried once before and didn't work; on reflection, you might realize that it was good idea that was just executed poorly. The team, which has much better experience now, might pull it off flawlessly this time. To use reflection well requires noticing your inner dialog (see below).

By highlighting the tools of executive dialog, members of a team focus on communicating more effectively, with the goal of improving their team performance and problem-solving capability, becoming—in other words—a high-performing team.

Using Inner Dialog

Inner dialog is the voice in your head that narrates your reaction to what's going on around you. Right now as you read this, you may be asking yourself, "What are they talking about?—I don't talk to my-self" or "Yeah, I do that all the time . . . so what can I do with that information?" This type of thought helps you relate information to your own reality and may encourage you to read or listen further. However, some inner dialog is less productive un-less you hear it and decide to act on it.

Have you ever been in a meeting, sitting there thinking what a waste of time it is? Then during a break, perhaps you have shared your assessment of the meeting with some of your colleagues and how you would improve it. Of course, when you return to the meeting, it won't have improved, and you'll be having the same thoughts once again. All that thinking never translates to improvement because the thought never leaves your head in a productive form. For the meeting to improve, you have to speak your thoughts *during* the meeting. Explain why it's wasting your time. Discuss what would make the meeting more productive.

When people share their inner dialog, they find that inquiry and advocacy become easier, too. By voicing their inner thoughts, people don't have that valuable information swirling around in their heads—they get it out onto the table. High-performing teams share their inner dialogs to increase the quality of their communication and team effectiveness.

The first step to sharing inner dialog is to acknowledge it and get people aware of and com-fortable with the concept, much as we did with the

example above. Talk about the hypothetical bad meeting—you'll find everyone's been there. A lot of time gets wasted in the conference room if the most productive part of the meeting happens by the coffee machine during a break.

A group that learns to share inner dialog effectively can make the most of each other's strengths. They get the benefit of everyone's heart-felt thoughts, expressed in such a way as to help the process at hand.

FORUMS FOR COMMUNICATION

Forums for business communication span a spec-trum of communications technology, from actu-ally walking around your workplace and talking to people to teleconferencing. Used correctly, all these methods are effective. Although we don't touch here on every one of these methods, we highlight a few tips that can help you make a real difference in the effectiveness, morale, and culture of your team or business.

The Personal Touch: Informal Conversations

Some of the best forums for communication are the informal ones that we often take for granted, such as "just walking around" the workplace. By getting out of your office, you become more con-nected to what is going on in your business and can see firsthand what some of the challenges are. When you take the time to reach out and connect with your staff informally, you learn a lot from people by sharing their concerns and their excel-lent ideas for ways to improve the business. Many times, stumbling blocks can be addressed right then and there, and this sends a strong signal to those working with and for you.

On one occasion, as I was walking around the office I came across some of our program staff who were pulling their hair out trying to figure out how to move some sea kayaks and other equipment around on very short notice. They were trying to accommodate a client during one of our busiest time periods when all of our equipment was tied up. As we discussed the situation, I asked if anyone had called the client to see if they had any flexibility in their schedule or if anyone had called a local outfitter to see if we could rent some kayaks. No one had, as they assumed the client had no flexibility, after a couple of quick calls, we were able to accommodate the client, who did have some flexibility, without the additional cost of renting gear.

The quick fix that is often a result of walking around serves as a teachable moment as well as an opportunity to demonstrate and enhance your connection with your team.

The head of a large New Jersey financial firm made a point of regularly having lunch with small groups consisting of a cross section of employees—or with selected individuals—as a way to connect with people and to keep his

---

EXERCISE: HOW DIALOG AFFECTS COMMUNICATION

To explore and highlight the usefulness of dialog, Outward Bound uses an experiential exercise called "Color Blind." The group sits at a table or in a circle, blindfolded. The facilitator randomly passes out all but two of a set of shapes, so that each person has two or three shapes. Each person can trace the shapes with his or her hands but can't see the shapes. The facilitator then asks the team to identify which two pieces from the set are missing. The rules are these: The group must keep their blindfolds on; they may touch only their own pieces; if they ask what color any piece is, the facilitator will tell them; they have thirty minutes to solve the problem.

Because the task is left somewhat vague (for instance, what does a "set" consist of?), the team must define both the problem and the solution process. Immediately, inquiry, advocacy, and reflection are brought into play: People query one another to help establish what the solution steps are. People with ideas about how to proceed must actively advocate for their recommendations as team members interrupt each other and launch off in different directions of thinking and reflection.

For example, should they describe the shapes first or determine how many pieces there are all together? When should they ascertain the colors? Is a shape that one person describes as a "funny, lopsided barn" the same as what another person calls an "arrow," or are they completely different shapes?

Discussion about how to proceed flies around the group. Whenever someone asks a teammate to explain his or her thought process, the group understands that person's idea better. Good inquiry might reveal an aspect of the problem that no one else noticed, or it could illuminate the flaws in someone's thinking.

While all this is going on, each person has an inner dialog about what is most important and how that might be conveyed to the group, along with a bit of inner dialog about personal frustration with the problem, the process, and the communication taking place. How inner dialog gets communicated—if at all—is telling, and it contributes either positively or negatively to progress toward the solution.

For instance, if someone is developing a suspicion that the "set" consists of five shapes each in three different colors, then voicing it will allow others to consider the idea and whether it accords with what they've been thinking. Someone else may request that everyone be more careful to let each speaker finish before responding. On the other hand, if someone voices only frustration with the challenge or another person, nothing is learned and a lot of negativity gets broadcast.

During the exercise, the facilitator often coaches the group on the use of dialog so that they are able to experience the benefits in a learning scenario.

finger on the pulse of the organization. When the CEO with a Lear jet shows up in the company cafeteria and eats with the people who answer the call-center phones, he creates an atmosphere of approachability that sends a strong signal throughout the organization that everyone is valued and important.

Another benefit of this practice is that the CEO can get the unvarnished perspective of those on the front lines of various parts of his company without the information filters inherent in the corporate hierarchy.

Such front-line people are closest to the organization's problems and customers, and more often than not, they have the best insight into what solutions are most feasible and will keep the clients happy. Satisfied clients and workers who feel valued and connected keep the company healthy, and its leaders greatly benefit from the perspective of their unfiltered, unvarnished opinions. This kind of display of approachability opens up avenues of communication that would otherwise be blocked.

Speeches

Giving speeches is essential to a leadership role because it allows you to get a message out to a large crowd, whether in the workplace or for a public occasion. Speeches afford you control of the information about serious issues because people hear it directly from you. Speeches can even be taped and broadcast elsewhere or later.

Speeches can build you up as an expert in your field. If you are already a well-known expert, you can imbue your subject with credibility by speaking about it passionately.

With a great speech, your leadership can inspire, focus, and motivate the people who work for or with you to do things they didn't think possible. Speeches can develop trust and rapport on a large scale. By creating a vision of the possibilities, you can inspire people to do amazing things.

Planning a Speech

To get the best effect from your speech, it's important to have a plan. Some people can produce a great impromptu speech, but most of us need to do our homework before we can stand up and deliver our message. As outlined earlier in this chapter, you need to tailor your information and presentation according to your intent and your audience. Be yourself: Use words you ordinarily use. Use humor that is accessible and genuine. Translate other people's ideas into your language in a way that doesn't disparage the source or the audience.

Practicing Giving Speeches

The many training opportunities for speech giving are invaluable because the only way to get really good at making speeches is to do it. Trainings provide an environment in which the feedback is ready and the mistakes don't matter. Become comfortable with giving speeches, because they are an important part of leadership, and if you avoid giving them, you'll lose opportunities to communicate your vision and inspire your team.

Delivering a Speech

When you give a speech, you're in the spotlight, so it's important that the speech be from your heart, because your body language and tone will be there for everyone to see and hear. Avoid the major pitfalls of making speeches by being professional, using appropriate language and humor, and making sure your messages are positive or constructive.

Speeches are not a forgiving forum: professionally, you are very exposed, and you can't take back your words. However, this should inspire you to work on your speaking skills rather than scare you away from making speeches. It is the speaker's vulnerability that makes good speeches so powerful, because it's impossible not to equate the quality of the speech with the quality of the speaker. Leaders are most inspiring when they are being themselves and when they are deliberate.

Seizing the Moment with the Right Speech

Outward Bound staff have wonderful opportunities to speak to groups of people. Participants are curious—if not anxious—to hear what we have to say, and the wild settings in which Outward Bound courses are offered are inspiring. Because our programs take place outside of most people's usual environment, we can often choose moments for speeches that allow us to fulfill participants' immediate needs: we provide information when people really want and need it—for example, rope-handling instruction at the beginning of a climbing session, or tips on how to relieve yourself in the woods at the beginning of a wilderness expedition. To take advantage of the perfect place and moment requires some ability to deliver a speech on short notice, but more important is the ability to be in touch with people's needs, whether they've voiced them or not.

Having a sense of what your people need does more than allow you to make them more comfortable: it allows you to encourage and motivate them, because people are most likely to take risks that fulfill a perceived need. The right speech at the right time makes all sorts of challenging things possible.

A team of L. L. Bean's senior managers gathered on the coast of Maine for a three-day executive development program. The primary focus of this sailing and rock-climbing program was to integrate some new people into the organization as quickly as possible. The team included a number of veterans who had worked at L. L. Bean for many years, many of whom were very accomplished outdoorspeople.

Our plan was to sail from Outward Bound's base in Rockland to Hurricane Island, our base in the Fox Islands—a distance of about 12 miles. When our two-boat convoy headed out into West Penobscot Bay, the wind had increased to a gusty 25 to 30 knots out of the southwest, making for a fast, wet, and bouncy crossing of the bay.

After two hours, we pulled into the lee of the White Islands, a small group of spruce-clad granite domes that provide the first shelter after crossing the bay, and dropped anchor. We rafted the boats together, and the Outward Bound staff quickly discussed their assessment of the L. L. Bean team's skills and needs. The staff agreed that the crossing had fully engaged the lifelong and first-time sailors alike and that both boats' crews were working well together. The individuals in the group had shown their potential, and what they needed most was an opportunity to prove themselves.

The setting was perfect for a motivating "challenge speech," a speech about the value of rising to confront the challenges we face during our lives. As the boats swung at anchor in the lee of the White Islands, from which we could see the rolling whitecaps and breaking waves exploding on the exposed rocks, kicked up by wind now gusting to 30 knots. The team assembled in an oval by sitting on the gunwales of one of the rafted boats, and the Outward Bound staff presented in the challenge speech that followed two options for the team to consider.

The staff opened the speech by praising the team's performance on the crossing, noting how much technical skill the team collectively possessed and how well they had worked together to use it. Then the staff laid out the original plan (more or less) as well as an option made possible by the team's performance and a happy coincidence of high tide at midnight. Sitting hip to hip on a small boat that they had just sailed through rough weather, the team listened attentively.

The original plan was to sail the last mile to Hurricane Island, honing their teamwork and seamanship skills along the way. Then they would rock climb on the dramatic Hurricane Island quarry cliffs.

SPEECHES: THINGS TO REMEMBER

1. **Consider your intent:** What do you want people to remember?
2. **Consider your audience:** Choose a large group when you want to spread a general message far and wide; choose a small group to tailor your message to a very specific audience.
3. **Select a tone that fits:** Do you need to be serious, humorous, urgent? Should you be formal or informal?
4. **Use consistent body language:** Dress, stand, speak, and gesticulate in a way that matches your tone.
5. **Pick the setting:** Use an auditorium for acoustic reasons. Choose other settings for their symbolic value: under the company sign, around a flagpole, on the shop floor, at the launch site, etc.
6. **Use visual aids:** Choose visuals to illustrate your point, not to make your point.

The option was to sail to the other side of Vinalhaven, the southern of the two main islands in the middle of the Fox Island archipelago. The team would position themselves to navigate in the dark through a tiny tidal passage called the Mill River and then sail back to Hurricane Island. The Mill River is navigable only when the tide is highest (on this night, that would be midnight) and requires taking the boats' masts down to pass under a bridge at the narrowest point. Because the bridge is only a couple of feet wider than the boats, the crew needs to have the boat perfectly lined up as they row toward the bridge and then bring in their oars at the last moment and glide through. This route requires impeccable communication and boat handling—the approach to the bridge is peppered with unmarked rocks and mudflats—and they would be there in complete darkness except for the spot lights on the boats. Last, taking this option would require the boats to sail around the clock to arrive at Hurricane Island in time to climb the next morning.

The end of the challenge speech delivered the framework for how the team should make the choice, with a bit of a caveat. Outward Bound staff told the team that they must

arrive at their decision by consensus, then pointed out that there were some really strong sailors and outdoorspeople in the team who could—by force of confidence and enthusiasm—easily get other team members in over their heads. "The choice is yours, because you've earned it," the Outward Bound staff said, "but you have to make sure that everyone's up for it, and you must take care of each other."

This challenge had the desired effect of slowing the process down and getting the team engaged in a great discussion. Though the need to navigate the Mill River at high tide meant they couldn't discuss their decision at great length, they shared their personal approaches to challenge and risk and used executive dialog to engage in a very healthy debate that included everyone. Listening to them, the Outward Bound staff reflected that the topic could just as easily have been on retail strategy, and this particular discussion would serve as a great model for future team dialogs in the workplace.

The team chose the Mill River option, which turned out to be a great adventure that pushed the team hard. They were underway for forty-two hours, with only a couple of catnaps. They continuously checked in with each other and took care of one another's needs. When they arrived at Hurricane Island, they enjoyed telling the island climbing staff where they'd been in so short a time and seeing the climbing staff's jaws drop. A compelling challenge presented flawlessly in an effective speech had inspired the team to embark on a route that was improbably difficult—and to do it well.

Emails and Memos

All workplaces, even Outward Bound's, are inundated with these convenient—but sometimes insidiously troublesome—forms of communication. Emails and memos are quick and easy to produce and can send a message far and wide in your organization with very little effort. But because they are so easy to send, emails and memos invite trouble when people don't put enough thought or time into writing a professional memo before hitting the "send" button.

When sending business communications, always be professional and businesslike. The casualness that many people use when writing emails can give the wrong impression. Casual messages may leave the receivers wondering whether you are taking them seriously enough, or the receivers may consider you presumptuous in your relationship with them.

Granted, for some close business associates and long-term relationships, a more casual approach is appropriate, but err on the side of professionalism, especially in new client relationships. Being so formal may seem rigid, but it builds trust and credibility. You can deepen the relationship over the phone or in person.

Remember that emails are one dimensional. Your body language and the tone of your voice aren't available to help the receivers interpret your intent. You can use *emoticons*, the informal system of using punctuation marks and diacritical marks in particular patterns to express the writer's feelings. For instance, a colon and a close parenthesis can denote a smile in this way—:)—but emoticons

are undeniably informal (cute, even) and a poor substitute for tone and body language.

Another pitfall with email especially is that it can be forwarded or sent to the wrong person or address with the push of a button, and once an email is sent, it is difficult—if not impossible—to recall it. As with speeches, once your idea is out there via email, you can't take it back. Many business relationships have been damaged and confidential information mistakenly shared by sending email to the wrong person or organization. Many email messages are better delivered in person or by phone, especially on sensitive or difficult topics that can be upsetting or misconstrued by those receiving the message. If you have a sensitive or hot topic to discuss, make a phone call or, better yet, do it in person.

Town Meetings

The town meeting is a mass public assembly that serves as a great way to get all hands on deck and engaged in a large group dialog. The benefit of the town meeting is that everyone hears the same message, without the normal loss of intent as information gets passed down through the business hierarchy.

Holding a town meeting allows a leader to clear up misperceptions, lay out a course of action, get the pulse of the group quickly, and engage people's hearts and minds. You may call a town meeting to share important breaking news, to celebrate a recent success, to create a sense of urgency around organizational performance, or to look at process improvements. Specialists or guest speakers can be called upon to answer questions in their area of expertise.

The best town meetings are a combination of information sharing and engagement with response. You can jump-start the engagement process by getting the agenda out prior to the meeting. You can also seed possible questions or topics of discussion ahead of time to help those who may need time to think and formulate their questions, concerns, and suggestions for improvement. Part of a town meeting can include a small-group brainstorm on specific topics, the notes from which may be shared in the meeting or distributed afterward. A prudent leader will conclude the meeting with an explanation of his or her plan for addressing the inevitably long list of important topics and questions that did not get addressed!

Video Conferencing

While video conferencing has not been widely used in most small businesses, the technology is quickly changing and is readily and inexpensively available. Video conferencing can be a very effective cost-saving tool, especially by eliminating the cost of travel required to bring people to one site. Video conferencing can never replace the power of bringing people together on a regular basis to build working relationships in person, but replacing your current telephone conference calls with video conferencing allows body language and visual cues that are such an important part of the communication mix.

Video Recording

Video messages serve a similar purpose as video conferencing, but video recordings lack the dynamic interaction possible via video conferencing. It is easy to create a simple video message for those times when you can't be there yourself due to other commitments, when you have multiple sites scattered around a large geographic area, or when you need to send the same message repeatedly—for example, in training videos for new hires. Even though you can't be there in person, a video message from you is more powerful and personal than your memos, emails, written announcements, or manuals. Video messages allow you to be more personal and to connect emotionally. They also leave a permanent record that can be revisited.

Symbolic Acts

Symbolic acts are a very powerful means of communication. Symbolic acts are those in which someone does something unexpected or above and beyond the call of duty, and the effect of a symbolic act is greater than the effect that anything that's written or said could begin to have.

Symbolic acts can be small or large: a small symbolic act might be coming out of the corner office to help unload a critical shipment; a large symbolic act could be jumping on a plane to go meet with a distressed client. These acts send a loud message: the first, that we all pitch in; the second, that going the extra mile makes the difference between a merely satisfied client and one who is a raving fan.

During tough times and budget cutbacks, the CEO of a fairly large manufacturing company asked his team to consolidate support staff in their departments in a focused effort to save costs. He led the way by moving his assistant into a shared pool that served the entire senior team. Although he could have easily justified his need for a personal assistant, he made the first move and set a personal example of what he wanted to see in his organization.

Walking the talk is demonstrated through symbolic acts. When his ship was crushed in the Antarctic ice, and before his team began the impossibly long and arduous march to safety, Sir Ernest Shackleton modeled the extreme need to take only necessities by giving up his most personal and valued possessions. The international outdoor clothing retailer, Patagonia, models a company value of being gentle on the environment by embracing recycling and supporting a myriad of environmental organizations and causes. Ask yourself, "What have *I* done lately to walk the talk?"

Storytelling

Storytelling also is a very powerful means of communication. In a way similar to symbolic acts, storytelling inspires us to do more than what seems possible. Many companies are full of lore that impels us to take initiative to get things done or to dream big. Storytelling in a similar way inspires us to do more than we may have thought possible. Many organizations are full of lore that impels us to take initiative to get things done or to dream big.

One story I had heard and have now told many times over the years to aspiring entrepreneurs is the story of the founder of a local Maine furniture company with a national reputation. The founder was still in college when he had a vision of using modern boat-building techniques for outdoor garden furniture based on the design of some pieces that were on his family's coastal estate. The techniques included a finish called Awl-grip that had never been used for garden furniture due to its cost and the skill required to apply it. The young founder knew that Maine had an abundance of skilled boat builders and craftsmen and that these skills should, in theory, be easily transferable. So he decided to place a $10,000 advertisement in The New Yorker *to promote the product. He was overrun with orders before the company was even up and running and had to quickly scramble to meet demand. Weatherend Estate Furniture is still going strong today after close to twenty-five years. The current CEO is an alumnus of an Outward Bound Professional open enrollment program who uses this inspiring story to encourage his staff to continue to take risks.*

LISTEN AND ASK QUESTIONS

For all the power of a great vision and effective communication such as speeches and symbolic acts, the most important skills of a truly effective leader and communicator are listening and asking great questions. Both require the discipline to stay focused on the speaker and to withhold judgment and the formulation of a perfect response until you have heard the message and digested it completely. Your best leadership doesn't consist of offering solutions or instructing people in solving problems but, rather, asking people how they would solve the problem and then asking follow-up questions to explore their thinking. Great workplace leaders excel in the arts of listening and asking insightful questions.

EIGHT KEYS TO SUCCESSFUL COMMUNICATION

These eight key practices are in use by businesses and leaders who do an excellent job of communicating.

1. Speak to and connect with your audience.
2. Communicate your message with intent and purpose.
3. Say it again: communicate, communicate, communicate.
4. Be authentic and be yourself.
5. Be clear and grounded.
6. Engage in dialog; ask questions.
7. Have small and large communications; have formal and informal communications.
8. Use multiple media to get your message across.

CHAPTER 12

MANAGING CHANGE IN THE WORKPLACE

The first law of organizations is that every system is perfectly designed to produce the results that it produces. If we wish to achieve a different result, we have to change something. Such changes in the workplace are proactive: leaders want a different result, so they plan for a change to achieve this.

All too often, however, organizational changes come about as a consequence of a crisis: the market or technology of your field changes; impending bankruptcy forces you to make difficult cost-reducing changes you wanted to avoid; or some other external change necessitates making a change within your company.

Whether an organizational change is proactive or reactive depends on the ability of the business's leaders to anticipate that change. If you are driving the change or were otherwise able to see it coming, you have more choices in how to help your organization—and, more importantly, its individuals—through the resultant transition. Undeniably, we would all choose to have more options rather than fewer, but even in the face of the totally unpredictable, if you see transition as a complex process, it will help you understand how much difference your good leadership can make.

UNDERSTANDING ORGANIZATIONAL CHANGE

Much of the work that Outward Bound Professional does with its corporate clients, whether the goal is team building or leadership development, focuses on the individual rather than the organization as a collective. This is because, though change in the workplace encompasses an organization's systems and its teams, in order for real change to take place, it is the organization's individuals who must be willing and able to change.

We often use William Bridges's model from *Managing Transitions* as a framework for explaining how change in organizations works. This model helps leaders understand the processes that they and their subordinates go through, so they can manage expectations accordingly. Bridges describes change as situational, and transitions are the human response to change. The table below illustrates the difference:

In other words, organizational change can happen only if people move successfully through transition. Therefore, managing the human aspects of the process is an essential aspect of leadership: unmanaged transition makes change unmanageable.

These interpersonal aspects of leadership are often called *soft skills*, but they're not "soft" in the sense of "easy." The soft skills are actually the hard part of organizational change.

Manage Transitions

During transitions, people go through three phases: letting go of the old ways, moving through a neutral zone, and embarking on the new ways.

Letting go: Your team members have to be convinced to let go of the old ways. That's the first phase of managing their transition and making it possible to implement an organizational change. They may be letting go of old routines, methods, names, emblems, or locations. If the change is more than superficial, they will also be letting go of traditions, workplace communities, and even assumptions—aspects of work to which people develop significant emotional attachment.

One of our long-term clients was undergoing a fairly significant restructuring and asked us to come in to help facilitate the process during a staff retreat. Jim and Jeff

CHANGE	TRANSITION
Situational	Psychological and emotional
Happens out in the world	Happens inside human beings
Starts with beginning; finishes with ending	Starts with ending; finishes with beginning
Focuses on embarking on new things	Focuses on letting go of old things

were two of the regional managers with the company. The proposed restructuring had them changing from an organization structured around geography to one organized around business services divisions. The timeline for the restructure was very quick and we coached the general manager, Steve, to meet with Jim and Jeff prior to the retreat to give them some time to work through the proposed changes. We also assigned pre-readings to the whole group to help people think about how they react to change, including Spencer Johnson's "Who Moved My Cheese," an excellent book exploring the reaction to change as seen through the experiences of three very different mice.

Interestingly, Jim when hearing about the proposed changes was in a bit of disbelief and clearly needed time to process what the changes meant. He had been running a successful region and the change was going to require him to travel more and to focus on a different set of skills.

Moving through the neutral zone: After people have let go of the old ways and before they embark on the new beginning, there is a neutral zone, a time when team members have let go of the old but haven't yet fully adopted the new—and moving through the neutral zone takes time. The letting-go phase and the neutral zone are easy for leaders to overlook, because leaders have had far more time to think about the change and so their transitions happen much earlier. Leaders are often a phase or two ahead of their teams.

While Jim was being forced to move quickly on the proposed change, he used his time in the neutral zone to gather information. He met at length with Steve to get a deeper understanding of the reasons and strategy behind the change. He also met with his inner circle of advisors, colleagues, and family to get their perspective and spent some quality time with Jeff as they would be working much more closely in the future if he agreed to move ahead. Jim had been with the company a long time and was a very valued employee, so much so that he would have other options if he decided not to move forward in the new role.

Embarking on new beginnings: Much of this chapter discusses the strategies for making this phase of transition, when team members begin to adopt the new behavior the workplace change requires, go smoothly. Your employees will react to the very idea of change in varying ways, and you will need to recognize and manage these differences to move the organization through the neutral zone and into the new beginning as quickly as possible so that the business continues to perform during this period.

After a process of wrestling through all of the realities of how the new role would change his current situation, Jim decided that he would move forward in the new position. At the time he made the decision it was clear that Jim was just emerging from the neutral zone and still had some lingering questions; however, what he projected to the group

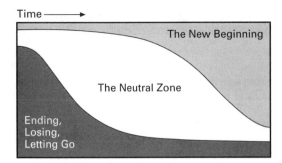

Figure 7. Phases of organizational change

during the retreat was an excitement and
enthusiasm for the new challenges ahead. As
the two-day retreat unfolded through a series
of discussions and experiential activities
focused on the change, Jim shared, "I must
admit that at first it kind of took me by
surprise. It was really important for me to
understand the rationale and strategy behind
the change and to know that I could support
it with everything I can muster. Once I
worked my way through that I started to get
energized by the new challenges ahead."

Too often, leaders expect followers to forego
transitions and to leap headlong into change. Instead, leaders should be ready for the range and
progression of emotions that come with transition.

Manage Fear

Organizational change is intimidating. The people
you are leading are often scared *by* the prospect of
change as well as being afraid *during* the change
process. But they don't fear change itself; they fear
how the change will affect them.

One of the things that fuels fears is people's
tendency to fill in voids of communication with
assumptions that are often based on faulty information. The way to manage these fears is to communicate early and often, using many (if not all)
the methods outlined in Chapter 11, Workplace
Communication Skills. By communicating early,
you give your people time to process the change

and to work through the transition phases.

Share the facts, including what you know as
well as what you don't know. In times of change,
your people deserve and appreciate honesty, even
if it means finding out that their position is going
to be eliminated. Communication can eliminate
some of the uncertainties of change—and when
it can't eliminate them, you can at least name the
uncertainties and reassure workers that their leaders are working to find answers. Your reassurance
around the points of concern is crucial to a successful transition period.

*A major health-care firm enlisted Outward
Bound Professional to help them through a
tough period after they had lost a contract
that was 8 percent of their total revenue.
They gathered their top 140 leaders from
around the country for an Outward Bound
Professional off-site program that was
designed for team behaviors. The company
knew that to get its people to rally around
a change, the people first needed to rally
around one another. People were anxious
about the changes, even to the point of being
concerned about keeping their jobs.*

*The senior leadership spoke up at the
beginning of the program and admitted that
they didn't know what the changes would
be, but that something had to change. They
asked their people to get on board and be part
of the process of determining how to solve the
problem. They acknowledged the uncertainties
and enlisted people in resolving them.*

A structure of two-way communications is
a must during the change process so that people
going through the change have a forum in which
to communicate their hopes and concerns and feel
heard. By acknowledging their fear, you create a
safe place to discuss the things causing the fear.
Even if these things can't all be addressed, they
can at least be shared, which in itself is helpful.
By sharing information, addressing concerns, and

listening to recommendations, you build trust in your leadership and in the process.

Good communication from the top of the company down through middle-level managers and onward is essential. Better still, your quality communication of the challenges your organization faces can enlist your workers as resources to help develop solutions.

Manage Reactions

Your employees will react to the very idea of change in varying ways, and you will need to recognize and make use of these differences.

Early adopters of change: There will be some employees who perhaps have been clamoring for change for months. You will want to enlist these people.

A client Outward Bound Professional works with recently shifted their email system from one software provider to another to take advantage of the added features which included a shared calendar and scheduling feature. While not a major change in the overall scope of things it was interesting to observe how different people embraced the new technology. Tony was a classic techno adept and was already using the system on his own. He had his calendar up and shared with his team before most members got home the first day the system was up and running. He was always willing to share tricks and user tips with anyone who was interested.

Late adopters of change: There will be employees whom you will need to actively enroll in the new change; and most likely, this will require you to convince them of the need for change and of the merits and sound strategy of your plan.

Mary, on the other hand, had just gotten used to the current system and was quite happy with all of the features it offered. She couldn't imagine what advantages the new

system could offer but was open to learning more if she had to. She embraced early on the new email function, but the thought of scheduling meetings online when she could call or walk down the hall didn't make sense at first. That was until she started to see how easy and convenient it was. It took a couple of months to get Mary on board, but once she saw the benefit to her work flow she became a believer.

Resisters to change: You may also have employees who will need to be brought along through emotional and intellectual appeals outlining the benefits and viability of the change.

John was another story altogether. He had been using a paper planner and calendaring system that had worked for him for years. The possibility that his calendar could be erased or altered with the push of a button worried him deeply and raised his resistance to the new online system. The idea that others could view his work calendar or possibly schedule his time was just over the top and he said so. Needless to say, John was a challenge. The last time we saw John he was still running both systems, the old and the new. Perhaps, over time and with experience with a system that proves to be reliable he will convert fully. In the meantime, everyone else at the company is now trying to pull John along.

SEEING AND COMMUNICATING THE NEED FOR ORGANIZATIONAL CHANGE

Leaders are well placed to recognize and even anticipate the internal and external drivers of change. Here's an example of anticipating versus simply reacting to change:

On the rugged coast of Maine, a small boat sails a direct course for its destination. The sails are precisely set for the angle of the boat's course relative to the direction from which the wind is blowing, and with the favorable tide now flowing, the boat will be snug in harbor before sunset. The crew has adjusted everything on the little boat according to the environment so that their goal will be met on time.

This state of perfection lasts only as long as the environment doesn't change—and in business as well as the weather on the Maine coast, change is inevitable. The wind will change direction, pick up speed, or drop entirely; the favorable tide (predictably) will slow, cease, and then reverse itself.

A novice crew may fail to notice these changes. If the wind changes to a less favorable direction, they will notice a decrease in the efficiency of the sails or realize that they are going to be late.

A more seasoned crew will anticipate some changes (tide) and respond immediately to others (wind), adjusting sails and course to maximize the boat's performance in the new conditions.

A master mariner will anticipate the changes based on close observation as well as long experience, setting the boat's sails according to the present environment and the boat's course according to the likely future one. This sailor may sail a longer distance as drawn on the nautical chart, yet arrive in harbor sooner.

Anticipate Change

As a leader of your organization or team, your job is to scan the horizon so that you may prepare for and lead the change process in a proactive, not reactive, way.

Crossbeam Systems, a leader in Internet security protection, asked Outward Bound Professional to work with their senior leadership team to build alignment around their growth strategy as they went through a transition period. At this point, they were going from their start-up phase, in which they were still led by the founder, who had a strong technical and engineering background, to a growth phase. The founder and his team had developed the technology and products in their introductory line and were very good at getting the first generation of their product to market. The founder (and chief executive officer) and his board realized that he probably was not the best person to take the company to the next stage of growth.

It was exceptional that so successful an individual recognized the need to step aside for the good of the organization and for his own best interests as well. A number of factors allowed the founding CEO to recognize the need for change. One was an understanding that the skill set that had made him so adept at starting the company was not ideal for growing the business. In this case, the entrepreneurial and engineering skills needed to develop the product were different from the skills needed to build a business that could compete and grow in a global market. Marketing, sales, manufacturing, and distribution systems were needed to "go to scale"—to expand the company exponentially—in the fiercely competitive field of Internet security. With the company's projected growth, its need for a leader who had experience leading and managing a much larger organization (and the people within it) was critical.

The founder recognized these needs and knew that, as a principal shareholder, he had much to gain in stepping aside so that the business could grow rapidly. With this insight and the encouragement of his board, he brought in a new CEO, who had experience running start-ups and larger organizations. The new CEO did an excellent job of working with the founder to communicate the changes to the employees, and laying out the vision and strategy needed to grow the business to the next level.

Communicate the Reasons for Change

A leader's first task is to explain not the organizational change itself, but what's driving it. It's essential that everyone affected by the change understand the reason for it—but it's not enough to just explain it.

Because change inherently leads to disruption of familiar structures and routines, a change itself can be seen as the cause of the "problem." The change must be presented as the solution, not the problem. It is all too tempting to try to save time by skipping the explanations of the need for the change and planning for it, diving straight instead into the actions of change. The result will be confused, unhappy people who see the change as the problem.

Explain the "Return on Change"

The benefits and viability of any given change are sometimes called the *return on change*. Only with a thorough understanding of the need for change, the subsequent plan, the strategy for change, and the return on change can your people make an informed choice on whether to stay and work through the change or to move on.

Outward Bound USA recently changed its structure from a collection of independent schools to a consolidated organization, no longer structured geographically, but around the five distinct programs we offer. The change was driven by a long list of desired benefits, including streamlined decision making, improved marketing, single points of contact for fund-raising with large national donors, strategic focus by program, and reduced overhead and costs. There was also a list of concerns regarding this proposed change, including the disintegration of regional school affinity and loyalty, loss of local program focus, and loss of a regional marketing focus.

EXERCISE: CHANGING THE GOAL

In an Outward Bound team-building exercise called "Find a Tree," participants are divided into teams of eight to ten people, and each team is shown a different tree: their goal. They are told that they will be led to a starting line approximately 20 yards away from their tree, and they need to get their entire team to that tree with everyone blindfolded and within an allotted time frame. The team has a five-minute planning session in which they may strategize and practice moving together blindfolded.

When a team is about halfway to its tree, Outward Bound facilitators call a timeout, pull two people from the team and remove their blindfolds, and show them a new tree that is now the goal, also giving their team an additional ten minutes to reach the goal. Then the two are reblindfolded and returned to their team.

At this point, the performance of the different teams varies widely. In some teams, the two who reentered immediately assume the leadership role and try to drive their team to the new goal. In other teams, the two people who know where the new tree is call a halt and explain the situation to the whole team. They fill the team in on what has changed and why, then ask for a few minutes to measure steps or get their bearings (or whatever the team's first strategy was originally). Some pairs even solicit input from their blindfolded teammates.

The teams who exhibit the first behavior keep moving, but it takes them a long time to reach their goal, and if arguments don't actually break out, some members of the team give up contributing their ideas. The teams who use the second strategy have to stop action for a while, but when they get going again, they reach their goal efficiently and with happy, engaged people.

On very close examination and after a long process, it was determined that the return on change warranted making the conversion and that many of the concerns associated with the change, having been identified through the study, could be addressed in the new structure. Through extensive study, involvement of the staff throughout the organization, and an aggressive communication effort—including town meetings, memos, Intranet sites, small-group meetings, email updates, concept or white papers, business plans, and speeches—staff members were able to make informed decisions about the change, to add valuable input, and to voice concerns—and, in the end, to make an informed choice whether to stay and work through the change effort or to move on to new opportunities outside of Outward Bound. The understanding of the changes was important: it allowed people to work through the changes in an informed and less stressful way.

CREATING READINESS FOR ORGANIZATIONAL CHANGE

Most of us are creatures of habit. People have an innate tendency to want to keep doing things as they've always done them, even if the world around them has changed and the old way doesn't work nearly as well anymore. The philosophy of staying the course is reassuring—but also very limiting.

As a leader, you create readiness for change by creating a sense of need and urgency, building confidence, and fostering a culture that seeks continuous improvement. Begin by gauging your team's readiness for change so that you know how much effort to put into building readiness.

Instill a Sense of Urgency

Sometimes you need to do little if your organization is already crying out for change. Your employees may be looking at the competition and asking for changes in products and approach. If the sense of urgency already exists, you can move ahead with building confidence.

On the other hand, you may have your work cut out for you as you create readiness for change. In his book *Leading Change*, John P. Kotter says, "Conducting business as usual is very difficult if the building seems to be on fire. But in an increasingly fast-paced world, waiting for a fire to break out is a dubious strategy." As you communicate the need for change and paint a picture of the new vision you have for your organization, sometimes you need to raise the urgency level of your team's desire for change.

Require your people to talk to unhappy customers, suppliers, or shareholders, so they hear the ugly details for themselves. Hold people accountable to a broader measure of performance. Publish in newsletters and declare in speeches a more honest discussion of the company's challenges. Set goals so high that they cannot be achieved by the current mode of operation. Once you have created a sense of urgency, you then can take the next step.

Build Confidence

You need to build confidence among your people that the changes you are proposing are practicable and will lead to a better way of doing business. Share stories of other organizations' successes with change. Paint a picture that is positive and realistic, and provide the information that people need to understand not only the reasons for and the process of the change, but their role in it as well.

At Crossbeam Systems, the Internet security provider, the simple act of discussing the stages of organizational development and the types of skills, people, and structure needed during each phase of change helped people to remain objective and to decide if they wanted a place at the table. Some people love start-ups, while others love mature organizations with all of their systems and controls in place. In providing lots of information, you empower people to make informed choices and feel some degree of control over their destiny.

Foster a Culture of Continuous Improvement

Last—though perhaps most important—as a leader, you should work to create a culture of change and continuous improvement. An organization that truly always seeks to be better is, by definition, accepting of and eager for change.

During Outward Bound Professional's team-building program with the Crossbeam Systems team, our first focus was on the principles laid out in Chapter 10, Team Building in the Workplace. The next module focused on giving on-the-spot, timely feedback. The group spent part of the day on a ropes course (an adult-size jungle gym high in the air, where participants are protected with climbing gear as they swing on ropes, balance on cables, etc.) coaching each other through the obstacles and the other part on team initiatives that provided everyone with a chance to observe and coach each other in problem-solving action, while building relationships and a foundation of trust.

At the close of the day, we had the group engage in a feedback process in which each person partnered up with every other person on the team and gave each of them coaching on what that person might do more of, do less of, or stop doing altogether to improve their contribution to the team and the organization. The exchanges were purposely kept short, and rotations were managed by a facilitator with a timer, with the understanding that if people needed more time, they would circle back later on their own.

The feedback was feared at first, but it was done with the explicit objective of helping each person to improve, and many people found it far more helpful than the standard annual review. The feedback module was received so positively that it has become part of every program this organization does, and the continual communication practice has helped them manage themselves

through change. They have created a culture of continuous improvement, making them flexible in the face of change.

Another technique for creating a culture of continuous improvement is the plus-delta model, explained by Interaction Associates in its *Facilitative Leadership Workshop Manual*; this model is a tool that Outward Bound Professional usually introduces early in our programs. Here's how it works: after an exercise, the participants gather around a big notepad with a two-column page, as shown in Figure 8.

On the left-hand side, the participants list the pluses: all the things that went well. These may include best practices that they want to see continue (such as a leader soliciting input before proposing a strategy) or innovations that they want to incorporate into their mode of operation in the workplace (such as a leader calling a halt during an activity to see if anyone has ideas about how to improve the process).

In the right-hand column, the group lists areas for improvement. It is important to note the power of language here. The right-hand side is not for things that went badly or things that don't work. Delta is the scientific symbol for change, and the delta column includes those opportunities. Thus, an entry might read "Take the time to listen thoughtfully to all team members' ideas during the planning phase to avoid having to start

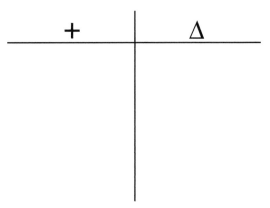

Figure 8. The plus-delta model

again" rather than "Jumping right into the task wastes time and makes people feel left out." The content of these two types of observations might sound the same, but the first example is something people can act on, and action produces change.

The plus-delta model has become part of the fabric of many of the organizations that Outward Bound Professional works with. By constantly looking at what works well and what could be changed or done differently next time, whether on a small or large scale, you create mental mindsets that are more open to initiating and engaging in change.

SUPPORTING ORGANIZATIONAL CHANGE

Organizations whose systems don't support change can only react to external changes. Building an organization that supports change means the organization can be more creative and enable your people to make proactive changes rather than just reacting to external forces.

Make Room for Creativity

In order for a system to support more proactive change, there has to be room for creativity. With change comes a huge opportunity for engaging everyone creatively in designing the new process, system, or organization.

A great exercise you can do is to ask people to use a clean sheet of paper and to envision the change from scratch, as if you were starting all over. Even if such a clean, dramatic approach is not going to be the reality, this exercise often identifies significant, creative improvements that can actually be made without having to totally start over.

Another technique is *breaking the frame*, an expression that means being open to doing something not only creatively but profoundly differently. In other words, if you don't like the answer you're getting, ask a different question. This involves a certain amount of risk, but when companies are unwilling to take risks, they find themselves unable to innovate.

A small, regional accounting firm wanted to effect a change in its corporate culture so

that people would want to work hard simply because it's the right thing to do for the clients. This attempt at change failed because the senior managers didn't put any incentives in place for working hard.

The middle managers heard what the senior managers said, but they also noticed that those words weren't backed up with corresponding actions. Middle managers asked themselves, "Why should I spend the extra time [working hard] unless I get paid for it?"

Meanwhile, the senior managers were saying to themselves, "Until we see that a manager is willing to go the extra mile, we're not going to put him or her in the bonus structure." Of course, there were some middle managers who were willing to work hard for the clients; those people left the company for one that rewarded such efforts.

The accounting industry is highly regulated, and there isn't a lot of room for creativity. In this field, a system that rewards creativity and moves away from the paradigm of paying employees according to billable hours is really breaking the frame. Not all firms are brave enough to take the risks to overcome such obstacles, but finding a way to encourage creativity supports proactive change.

Remove Roadblocks to Change

If you find roadblocks in your path, you will have to remove them. Roadblocks come in many shapes and forms; your first job is to figure out which ones are real and which ones are perceived.

Real roadblocks: Is the hurdle money? Is it that you don't have the right people at the table? Maybe it is a matter of training and education. Or are there regulatory issues that need to be addressed or changed?

You will need to probe some of these questions deeply. If your organization has been around for awhile, there may be "obvious" answers to these questions that just aren't true anymore. Your ability to correctly identify and remove these real roadblocks to change will have a tremendous impact on your effort.

Perceived roadblocks: Very often the most difficult roadblocks for an organization to overcome are not specific issues so much as sets of assumptions that drive actions. Once they're around for a while, assumptions often take the form of perceived sacred cows that are seen as untouchable. Because your job as a leader is to set the boundaries or parameters for change, don't be afraid to put "non-negotiable" issues on the table. Then you must be willing to engage in the highly charged debate that is sure to follow.

> When Outward Bound decided to consolidate nationally, the emotional debates about what was and was not on the table were numerous and wide-ranging. Everything from seemingly small items to major infrastructure decisions needed to be handled with great care and sensitivity (and commitment of time), due to their highly historical and symbolic impact.

Considerable leadership is needed to manage these tumultuous conversations. You will need to take on the tough decisions and discussions—some of which may have been sidestepped for years, even decades—to challenge sacred cows and put to rest those that obstruct your organization's path into the future.

Lead Proactively

Whatever the roadblock is, your proactive leadership can make the difference between long delays, frustrations, and failures versus obstacles overcome, a building of momentum, and a series of success stories that can be celebrated and shared. Being proactive in the face of significant change is especially challenging, because it so often requires change at the leadership level—and these are difficult decisions for leaders to make!

> Moss, a manufacturer of tents and awnings, had been a small, privately held company

> from its inception. In 2003 its founder and owner sold the company to a venture capital firm specializing in revamping static companies and selling them at a profit after only a few years. Moss suddenly went from a culture of family spirit to one of corporate expectations focusing on profit margins. A visionary leader was brought in to build on the family feeling of valuing each employee, while at the same time demanding exceptional performance.
>
> Working with Outward Bound Professional, the senior management team created a twelve-month leadership development program for twelve folks from all levels of the company, from stitchers to vice presidents. The results of this program were that a foundation of employees felt valued by their company and at the same time gained the skills necessary to help drive Moss to be able to reach the lofty annual goals that had been set for them.

The people you're leading need to be supported through the organizational change. Encouraging creativity, removing roadblocks, and fostering leadership skills throughout the organization will provide that support.

IMPLEMENTING ORGANIZATIONAL CHANGE

While making a particular organizational change, you emphasize a lot of research, perhaps purchase some software, and prepare everyone. You must choose an approach for implementing change, then establish waypoints against which to measure progress, and finally communicate how the change will happen.

Choose a Strategy

There are a number of ways to implement change, and which approach you choose depends on the size and scope of the change. For instance, putting in a new management information system is an example of a fairly large project. Scope could entail making a change in one state versus around the country, as for a nationwide insurance company, for example.

Small incremental changes: These are made over time and are often a matter of fine tuning something, such as your website. There is certainly a place for incremental change. However be sure that these incremental changes are not just a way to avoid the tough decision of starting over on something in which you have invested time, energy, and money but which may need to be abandoned in order to start afresh.

Phased or step changes: These require getting distinct pieces in place and then proceeding with the next steps as time and money allow. An example would be a medium sized retailer who has decided to renovate its storefronts in order to remain competitive and appeal to changing tastes in the marketplace. Their plan is to renovate all thirty of their stores over a three year period, and for financial and strategic reasons they decide to start with their showcase stores in their top ten markets.

Rapid changes: These are strategies in which you move as quickly as possible, knowing full well that the change is going to be disruptive at best and that by moving quickly, you hope to get it behind you as soon as possible. This last option sounds risky, and it is—budgets will be stretched to the breaking point and problems will emerge from nowhere. However, there are times when the merits of moving quickly far outweigh the costs of dropped balls or the stress that can come with rapid change. We often see this with clients that have recently gone through a merger and are still living with many unknowns and with two sets of systems. Even deciding which benefit plan will be in place going forward can create angst amongst your staff. Sometimes you just need to make a decision and then move quickly to communicate and complete the changes allowing everyone to move forward confidently.

Establish Waypoints

Once you have decided on an approach, map out the steps that will be involved. No matter which approach you choose, establish waypoints in order to break the journey into manageable pieces. It is critical to establish waypoints and measures to gauge progress, in much the same way that a sailor breaks a voyage down into sections that can be measured and reached in a comprehensible time period. Establishing waypoints provides two important aids to change.

First, the waypoints provide realistic steps that are easier to get people's heads and hands around. Your employees will need something to hang onto during the disruption that is part of the change process, and having these pieces in place gives everyone a guide and handhold to grasp. By creating waypoints, we are able to make the change process less daunting. Second, waypoints provide goals that can be acknowledged and celebrated when they are met.

LEADING RATHER THAN MANAGING ORGANIZATIONAL CHANGE

In *Leading Change*, John P. Kotter says, "Producing change is about 80 percent leadership—establishing direction and aligning, motivating, and inspiring people—and about 20 percent management—planning, budgeting, organizing, and solving problems." It is easy to be beguiled by the promise of the substantial benefits that will be realized by a change in structure, technology, or new systems. Based on that promise, some leaders jump in head first (or, more accurately, pocketbook first) to implement the change, only to realize that the process of purchasing new structures, technology, or systems—as difficult as those choices might have seemed at the time—were not even half the battle. The real challenge is getting the users of this new structure, technology, or system to swear off their old ways and embark on new behaviors.

> *For example, Outward Bound's sales team made the conversion to an electronic sales tracking, or customer relationship management, system from a manual system—or several manual systems, actually, each*

somewhat particular to each sales represen-
tative. Naturally, there were substantial
benefits to being able to see current and
future sales levels as well as being able to
look across accounts to see instantly who
else is working with the same or similar
organizations nationally.

Getting everyone to embrace and use
the system was the challenge, though.
People develop favorite ways of doing
things; their methods work for them, and
it is hard for them to let go of these. The
new system takes time and energy to
enter data, and at first, it feels as though
it couldn't possibly be worth the trouble.
A change of this type requires continued
emphasis on the benefits of the change,
training for the new system, and support
for the change process.

Support New Behaviors

In estimating the cost of new changes, leaders often leave out the cost of training, education, and the associated ramp-up time needed to fully realize the potential of the change. Instead, they stumble through the implementation period, frustrated by their staff's resistance to embracing the new system—but leaders must own the problem. They would be far better served to invest in the time, energy, and training to get people comfortable with the new system.

Use Forcing Agents

When adopting new procedures, a leader can use incentives or consequences—called *forcing agents*—designed to reward the desired behavior or to eliminate undesired behaviors. Imposed deadlines can be a huge incentive to get people to move forward with a change. For instance, knowing that the current software system will be phased out and converted by a specific deadline is a serious forcing agent when we believe that the deadline is real.

In the case of Outward Bound's customer
relationship management system, the only
way to access new leads generated by our
website and toll-free numbers is by log-
ging in to the system and pulling them up
electronically. This represents an insuperable
incentive for active use of the system.

SUSTAINING AN ORGANIZATIONAL CHANGE

Sustaining change requires active management. In the John P. Kotter quotation given above, he puts a leader's emphasis during change implementation primarily on leadership: creating change is 80 percent leadership and 20 percent management. The sustaining phase, Outward Bound argues, requires a shift in emphasis more toward management in order to ensure that forward momentum is maintained. To sustain the change, you emphasize the management of the systems, ensuring that they work and that everyone is using them.

Celebrate Successes

Take the time to celebrate small and large successes. We can get so focused on the task at hand that we forget to stop to appreciate and recognize the extraordinary efforts that our people have made. During the change process, it is important to send positive messages that the change is paying off and that progress is happening. Upon reaching a waypoint, take the time to acknowledge and celebrate the achievement.

Dan Emerson, director for the northeast
region at Cassella Waste Systems, does this
particularly well. He holds regular awards
ceremonies that recognize the individual
contributions of his various divisions: safest,
most growth, innovative, etc. These really
boost the morale and energy of his team.

Sometimes leaders who are diligent about reporting progress upward to their stakeholders forget to share these successes downward with their own teams. Identify and communicate the small wins to internal as well as external stakeholders.

SUMMARY OF ORGANIZATIONAL CHANGE

1. Understand organizational change.
   - ■ Manage transitions.
   - ■ Manage fear.
   - ■ Manage reactions.
2. See and communicate the need for organizational change.
   - ■ Anticipate change.
   - ■ Communicate why change is necessary.
   - ■ Explain the return on change.
3. Create readiness for organizational change.
   - ■ Instill a sense of urgency.
   - ■ Build confidence.
   - ■ Foster a culture of continuous improvement.
4. Support organizational change.
   - ■ Make room for creativity.
   - ■ Remove roadblocks to change.
   - ■ Develop proactive leadership.
5. Implement the organizational change.
   - ■ Choose a strategy.
   - ■ Establish waypoints.
   - ■ Communicate how the change will occur.
6. Manage the organizational change.
   - ■ Support new behaviors.
   - ■ Use forcing agents.
7. Sustain the organizational change.
   - ■ Celebrate successes.
   - ■ Maintain flexibility.
8. Look ahead toward what's next.

Maintain Flexibility

As you work your way through the various phases of the change process, you will inevitably need to adjust your strategy, approach, and people in order to address the situational changes encountered due to growth, changes in the marketplace, and unanticipated challenges.

> *As Crossbeam Systems has grown, the company has had to continually make adjustments in its strategy and the people it needs in order to execute the strategy. This near-continual state of change has been embraced by employees, in large part due to the constant open, honest communication from the CEO and other leaders in the company. The leadership team regularly shares with those working with them in the company their current assessment of the business and what and who may be needed to make the business successful.*

LOOK AHEAD TOWARD WHAT'S NEXT

As you approach your goals, you should always be asking yourself these questions: "What's next? How can we continue to grow or improve the business? Where do we want to be in the next three years? What will we need to do to get there? Do we have the right people in place to get us there?"

> *At Crossbeam Systems, the senior management team was reconfigured as changes in the business required it to have a different set of skills and makeup. A skilled corporate financial officer was brought in with the experience needed to help position and manage the company for going public. Growing international sales required a change in the sales management leadership and strategy. As part of the company's organizational review, today all options are constantly being evaluated and adjusted as needed to achieve the strategic goals and vision.*

Most often, some type of change will be required, and it is much better to be driving the change than reacting to it. Good leadership in the workplace anticipates what the next challenge might be.

CASE STUDY 3
PLAYING A NEW TUNE AT MARTIN GUITAR

by Jim Garrett

What would it be like to become, at the age of thirty-one, chief executive officer of one of the world's premier makers of acoustic guitars? Further, how would you live up to the expectations inherent in bearing the family name of the five generations who had owned and run this famed company for more than 170 years? And what if you had a strong sense that the company was in turmoil and required some major changes if it was to preserve its fine reputation by continuing to produce what you considered "the best of its kind in the world"?

Christian Frederick Martin IV accepted those challenges in 1986 when he moved up from vice president for marketing and took over from his grandfather, C. F. Martin III, as chairman of the board and CEO of C. F. Martin & Company, Inc., of Nazareth, Pennsylvania. Grandfather Martin had led the company for forty-one years, from 1945 until his death that year at the age of ninety-two. Additionally, Chris's father, Frank Herbert Martin, had served as the company's president beginning in 1970 and throughout Chris's formative years as a Martin Guitar employee.

As you read through Chris Martin's story, below, imagine how you might have dealt with the issues that Chris faced and what resources you would have drawn upon to assist in making the difficult decisions that inevitably must be made for a company in transition. As you get a sense of Chris's leadership style, anticipate how that style might dovetail with the organizational culture of Martin Guitar. Look over the discussion questions interspersed throughout the text, and check out the in-depth follow-up questions in the appendix to deepen your learnings from the Martin Guitar story.

By the time Chris Martin IV took the helm of C. F. Martin & Company, known familiarly as Martin Guitar, he had already spent some fourteen years working at the plant doing everything from packing guitar strings for shipment to apprenticing in the shop, where he learned every operation in the construction of a Dreadnaught (full-sized) guitar, to attending trade shows. He experienced, from the bottom up, how his family's business worked.

But even though he knew how the company operated and had worked alongside many of its employees, he felt weighed down by the baggage of being the next C. F. Martin to run the family business. Not only did he feel himself not to be a born leader, now he had been elevated to a position of boss over hundreds of people, many of whom were his father's peers, some of them having worked at Martin Guitar for decades.

What's more, both his father and his grandfather had practiced a leadership style that resembled the practices of the old "Theory X" School: "I'll tell you what to do; don't give me any lip." He was concerned that he might have to learn how to be a kind of leader that didn't feel right for him.

In his business administration courses at Boston University, from which he graduated in 1978, Chris had been exposed to a very different concept of leadership, one that extolled the virtues of a more personal, friendly, participatory way of leading. Instead of a hierarchical, top-down, "do as I tell you" style, Chris had learned from the example of companies such as Toyota that, as he puts it, "you've got to engage the people who do the work; they're the ones who've got the expertise; you've got to put them in a position to let them grow." Chris knew from observing his father's management experience that some of the unrest at Martin Guitar stemmed from the fact that the dogmatic "Theory X" approach wasn't working, and he felt that the companies that were engaging their workers were the ones that would prosper.

QUESTIONS

1. Do you think Chris Martin IV's early experiences working in his family's company helped or hindered his role as CEO? What are some of the difficulties of trying to lead people you've worked with as a peer? As a subordinate? What are some of the difficulties of trying to lead people much older than you?

2. Why do you think Chris Martin IV felt he wasn't a born leader? Was his worry about having to adopt a leadership style that didn't suit him a realistic one?

3. Do you think that Chris's business education prepared him for taking on the role of company leader? How helpful do you think it was for him to be exposed to such different leadership styles? Might this shake his confidence as a leader, or would it give him tools as a leader?

Chris eagerly tried to introduce this new style of leadership at Martin Guitar. His employees, especially his father's peers, as he calls them, didn't see the merits of this way of doing business. The way they were used to doing things, Chris says, was "multigenerational: that's what my grandfather did, and my father inherited it, and my father didn't try to reinvent the wheel—to his detriment, unfortunately." The employees were used to and shaped by that old "we'll tell the workers what to do" approach, and when Chris tried out a new way of doing things, they resisted. In fact, the employees called a strike. "We had a lot of problems around that," Chris recalls.

What's more, the company had strayed from its core business—guitars and related acoustic stringed instruments—during his father's presidency, borrowing money to make a series of acquisitions, while also experiencing a significant decline in sales as the guitar lost popularity in the late '70s and '80s. So Chris wasn't able to build on any positive momentum at Martin Guitar; instead, he had the job of "rebuilding a multigenerational family business that had gone through some rough times."

And then Chris remembered what he had heard about Outward Bound. With the hope that from Outward Bound he could learn more about how to be an effective leader, especially in situations of stress, he went off to the mountains of Colorado for a five-day Outward Bound Professional renewal course for managers. He returned to Pennsylvania deeply impacted by the experience.

"It was a profound experience for me," Chris remembers. "Even though it was only five days, I felt that I had learned a lot—about people I didn't know coming together and accomplishing something. There was the physical element, but it was so much more mental—taking that time to sit and think and, in my case, coming to terms with the fact that maybe I could figure out that I could be the kind of leader that would work for me. It made me realize that I am who I am, [that I should] work with the strengths that I have [and not] try to be someone else. I just had to learn how to be more *me*."

QUESTIONS

4. What obstacles did Chris face in introducing a new leadership style to Martin Guitar? How might Chris have been more successful in introducing his new leadership methods to an older generation?

5. Do you think Chris might have avoided the strike? How?

6. What are some of the first steps Chris could have taken to resolve the company's business problems, such as debt, acquired businesses, and declining sales? Should he have tried to restore the company to its core business? How?

7. Based on what you know about the Outward Bound process as it is portrayed in this book, list as many as you can of the different Outward Bound elements that are likely to have been operant during the Colorado mountain expedition that Chris Martin IV describes here. Why do you think Chris felt empowered to learn how to be more himself?

Once back home, Chris wanted to take his whole senior management team off to Outward Bound immediately, to share with them what he had experienced. He wanted them to see "that if this group of people who didn't know each other in Colorado could accomplish this, what could a bunch of people who did know each other and did have enough of a common goal around them [accomplish]?" At that time, Chris was also working with some consultants, who firmly advised him that taking his managers right off to Outward Bound was not going to work, that his staff would rebel. He would have to do some preliminary work with them first: off-site meetings, discussions of how best to work with the new CEO, what he expected from the business, etc.

Once that had been done, Chris scheduled the first Martin Guitar group for a five-day canoeing expedition on the Upper Potomac River with Outward Bound Professional. During a campfire discussion on the trip on the Potomac River, and as related later by David Starnes of Outward Bound, one of the management team members spoke up, evaluating Chris's leadership role during the day's activities: "If this company's going to go anywhere, you've got to be a leader, and if you lead the way

you led today—which is trying to get everybody to be happy all the time, not wanting to step on anybody's toes—it will never succeed. So, Chris, the ball is in your court. We're here to support you; we love Martin Guitar; it is a marvelous company, with a great culture and wonderful products. But if you want to be the CEO, then you have to take the responsibility of being the CEO and not just get it because you're the family heir . . ."

Chris notes that he listened to and learned from criticisms such as this. About that first course, Chris has only one regret: "The president of the company at that time was the most obstinate. He had some health issues, but he just decided he wasn't going to go, and I wished that he had gone to a doctor and had the doctor say, 'I can certify that you are not able to go.' He didn't do that; he just said, 'I've decided I'm not going to do this.' He and I could have had a beneficial relationship, but it became not beneficial; if I said 'black,' he said 'white.' Sometimes that's good; I don't want to surround myself with yes-men. But that was my only regret—that he never went [on an Outward Bound course]."

All the rest of the senior managers went, however, and Chris says that they each got a great deal more from the experience than they had ever thought they would. "What I have found out for us about the weeklong expedition is that it's around about Wednesday when things start to change. The first day or two, you're still who you were, and the last day or two, you're different. It's that middle of the week . . . Some companies do a one-day retreat, but that's not the same. It takes a good three days to get to the point where you're starting to think about changing, and by the fourth or fifth day, you're beginning to change."

QUESTIONS

8. Do you think Chris's first impulse—to have his managers immediately take an Outward Bound course—was a wise one? Do you think his consultants' advice was important to the eventual success of the Outward Bound experience?

9. How do you think Chris should have responded to his manager's criticism that he was avoiding stepping on people's toes, that he should take responsibility for being the CEO and not just walk into it because he's the family heir? Is this sort of comment acceptable even in an off-site setting such as an Outward Bound course?

10. What do you think were the impacts of the company president's refusal to participate in the Outward Bound course? Of a senior manager's refusal to participate in a team-building experience?

11. Do you think Chris might have been able to salvage his adversarial relationship with the company president? How?

12. Do you agree with Chris that change occurs more effectively on a weeklong retreat than on a one-day retreat? Why or why not? Is the potential for such a gain in individual and corporate growth a justifiable company investment?

After several years of annual Outward Bound expeditions, once most of the upper- and mid-level managers had been on one, Chris opened up the opportunity to all employees, which now number more than 800. He says, "What has happened with these broader groups, particularly with the hourly workers, is, no matter what the particular experience is for them and me, the two things I can say is, I know them better than I ever would have if we had never done [Outward Bound], and they know me better than they ever would have if we had never done it. They know Chris Martin as a human being, rather than just as Chris Martin the Boss."

The kinds of change that Chris has seen in his employees—his colleagues or co-workers, as he calls them—are a combination of feeling freer to talk openly about things that they feel are road-blocks to their operations, gaining a greater sense of bonding and confidence in the team and its ability to solve problems creatively and collaboratively, and getting to know one another in much greater depth. "And," as Chris says about his first Outward Bound experience, "fortunately, it also worked for everybody else, maybe, because it made me more genuine."

Chris Martin remains enthusiastically committed to the Outward Bound experience: "I have tried to create an environment that is inclusive and participatory, and [Outward Bound] is an intensive course in that. You might be able to learn the same thing in a semester somewhere else, but with Outward Bound you can learn it in a week." The widespread impact of Outward Bound on the company's employees is evidenced by the number of offices, cubicles, and workrooms where

Martin's co-workers have prominently posted their Outward Bound course certificates on the walls for all to see.

The number of orders for new guitars has slacked off in recent years. "Now, with interest rates creeping up and gas [prices] creeping up, we're a little more challenged," Chris comments. "And that is also where some of [those lessons are] in our kit-bag. When times get tough, we can fall back on [the fact that] we've had these shared experiences; we can work as a group in good times and bad. It's great when times are good, but I think it's almost more valuable when times are bad, because that's the last time you want to begin to snipe or go into your silo I always say to my colleagues, 'The competition is out *there*, not in here. We should not be competing with each other unless it's beneficial.'"

QUESTIONS

13. What type of leadership style do you think Chris is using, based on this narrative? In what ways do you think the Outward Bound expeditions might have helped Chris to introduce his new leadership style?
14. Does Chris Martin IV's belief that the lessons derived from the Outward Bound experience—about communication, teamwork and collaboration, trust and inclusiveness, etc.—will enable the company to weather the stormy times more successfully make sense to you? Why or why not?

Just as there have been many changes at Martin Guitar since Chris Martin IV took the reins, there have been equally significant changes in the man himself. From a young man who was a reluctant CEO that, again according to David Starnes, "wasn't sure he was ready to be the real, live, drive-it-down-the-road kind of guy," Chris has learned what it means for him to lead, to make decisions, to step in and take command when necessary, while still giving his colleagues and his company the room and the encouragement to be the best they can be.

He says, "I give people a lot of freedom. If I let people look at the whole picture, they'll very often divvy up the work and get things done, which is nice. But the other thing I learned—and I don't know if I learned it in the field with Outward Bound—is that sometimes I'm too reliant on taking a step back. At some point, I realize I do have to step in. When I am out in the field, when I see people struggling, getting overwhelmed, I don't need to sit there and watch them spin. 'You're in deep doodoo; can I help?' And they say, 'Thank God; somebody knows what they're doing!' So that's one of the things I have learned: that, as much as I am the kind of boss that will stand back and watch people, when they can't figure it out, I have to help them. And sometimes it's just a matter of saying, 'We're good to go; let's move forward.' When they won't make the decision, if I don't make it, they just get more confused . . ."

And then Chris reflects a bit on the office politics that plague so many organizations and how the environment at Martin Guitar is different. He recalls the words of a former high-level employee from a couple of years ago: "This is the only company I've ever worked for where people don't go out of their way to make themselves look good by making me look bad. This is the only place I've worked where that isn't the natural order of things. Everywhere else, the way people looked good was to make me look bad. And here, I'm on my own; they don't make me look bad, and they might not make me look good, but they don't sabotage my career."

The culture of C. F. Martin & Company itself has been significantly changed for the better during Chris Martin's twenty-plus-year tenure as the company's leader. The lowered productivity of an antagonistic relationship between boss and workers that existed in the early '80s has been replaced by an upbeat, modernizing, and expanding company with a work force that really believes, as Chris says, "The one thing that we have is that we make the best guitar of its kind. When people walk in the door, they know they're coming to work for a company that doesn't make a copy or a commodity; we make the best of its kind."

In 1986 Martin Guitar made $16 million; in 2004 it made $80 million. In 1986, production was around 5,000 instruments; 2004's production was 70,000 instruments. The factory was expanded in 1999, almost doubling its size. The Martin Guitar Museum and Visitors Center was opened in 2006. And through all of this growth, high standards of quality have been maintained: in 2006, *Acoustic Guitar Magazine* awarded nine "Player's Choice" awards to C. F. Martin & Company.

The colleagues of the Martin Guitar Company have figured out how to excel beyond the constraints of their motto, *Non Multa Sed Multum* ("not many but much"); they have maintained their quality while vastly increasing their quantity. They are living proof to themselves and to the world that they had more in them than they knew.

QUESTIONS

15. Do you think that Chris Martin IV knows himself pretty well and knows what his strengths and weaknesses as a leader are? Do you think that much of this awareness has come from the feedback others have given him?

16. What sort of leadership style does Chris Martin exemplify? Does it seem as though he's able to adapt his leadership style when necessary?

17. What do you think it is about Martin Guitar that has made the issue of office politics so unimportant? Why do people have such a high regard for the company and their co-workers?

PART IV

TAKING LEADERSHIP INTO YOUR COMMUNITY

About the Writer: Joan Welsh

Joan Welsh has been a leader in Outward Bound since the early 1980s after taking an Outward Bound course on vacation while executive director of a human services agency in Boulder, Colorado. She volunteered for and then became an instructor with the Colorado Outward Bound School. Joan later became an associate director for the Pacific Crest Outward Bound School and then the Colorado Outward Bound School before serving as president and CEO of the Hurricane Island Outward Bound School. During more than twenty years' involvement with Outward Bound, she led and participated in countless courses, including courses in Baja, Nepal, and Kenya.

Joan was a founder and executive director of Boulder County Safehouse and was also the director of academic and student affairs at Rockport College, Maine. She has been a volunteer leader on many community and national nonprofit boards.

Joan attended Pomona College and the University of Colorado, earning a bachelor's degree. She has also taken graduate and executive courses at the University of Colorado, University of Phoenix, and Harvard University.

Joan currently serves as the deputy director for the Natural Resources Council of Maine and is a board member of three nonprofit organizations. She lives in Rockport, Maine.

Personal Introduction: Joan Welsh

When I was forty, I wanted an adventurous vacation, so I took an Outward Bound sailing course on Penobscot Bay in Maine. On that trip with nine other people—men and women from all walks of life, ages eighteen to fifty-four, from all over the country—I experienced Outward Bound's ethic of service: helping each other, working together to solve problems, gaining confidence in ourselves while learning a new skill.

After introducing ourselves on the first day, we provisioned a 30-foot, ketch-rigged open boat and rowed out into the harbor. Our instructor said, "OK, here's the mainsail, and this smaller sail is the mizzensail. See if you can get the sails up and get this boat to sail."

Now, none of us were sailors, but we began to puzzle it out and help each other. One person held the lines while another positioned the sail. One figured out the proper knots. Another discovered how to work the tiller. By combining our various skills and using our common sense and intuition, together we managed to get the sails up and began moving along the water.

We were elated. We were a community of strangers who, when brought together, served each other and served a greater purpose. Being together on a small boat was a metaphor for being together in a larger community. We could never have reached our goal—getting the boat to sail—without all of us helping.

At that time, I was the executive director of a shelter for battered women and children. One of the challenges was helping survivors of violence feel that they are stronger than they know. I felt that the lessons I had learned on that sailboat in Maine would benefit the women and children at Safehouse. I contacted the Colorado Outward Bound School about bringing its activities to Safehouse and other domestic violence programs in Colorado. We began to provide programs for the women and children and do team building with staff and the board. Everyone began to work better together and to feel excited about the potential of serving one another better. These programs grew throughout the state.

Through my personal ethic of service to my community and my discovery of Outward Bound's ethic of service, I spent twenty years working for Outward Bound. This service ethic can be applied to a wide variety of community leadership situations, as you'll see in Part IV, Taking Leadership into Your Community. Chapter 13, Serving Others as a Community Leader, introduces you to volunteer service. Chapter 14, Leading a Volunteer Organization, gives insight into successfully leading volunteers. Chapter 15, Leading Youth in Your Community, offers leadership strategies for volunteer work with young people. Chapter 16, Leading Your Community in the Political Arena, focuses on leading an issue campaign. Whether you're a leader in a volunteer organization, working with youth, or entering the arena of political issues, this section of the book will help you incorporate Outward Bound's effective leadership strategies and service into your own community leadership opportunities.

CHAPTER 13

SERVING OTHERS AS A COMMUNITY LEADER

The value of helping, of serving, one another is central to the fabric of our communities. America has a high propensity for not-for-profit organizations wherein individuals and groups volunteer to carry forward this value. The following old Hasidic parable epitomizes this value:

A rabbi wanted to see both Heaven and Hell. As he pleaded with God, he found himself before a door that bore no name. The door opened into a room where all was prepared for a feast. A great dish of steaming food sat on the huge table, around which sat scores of diners with great spoons in their hands but all shrieking with hunger and fainting with thirst. Each time they attempted to feed themselves, they found that they could not maneuver the spoons into their mouths, for the spoons were so long that no food ever touched their tongues. The rabbi could see and hear from the cries of these people that he stood on the threshold of Hell. He closed his eyes and begged God to remove him from that terrible place. When he opened them again, he found himself standing before another door that bore no name. As it opened, his heart sank: There was the same table, with the great dish of steaming food and around the table people sat just the same and in their hands the same spoons.

Yet there was no crying, and the curses had become blessings. With the same long spoons, each individual reached to one another, feeding the food to each other across the table. "Here," said the rabbi, "is Heaven," and he thanked God, who had shown him the nature of Heaven and Hell, as well as the chasm—a hair's breadth wide—that divides them.

—from the Talmud

Being a leader in your community is grounded in this principle of serving others. This chapter focuses on the characteristics of service work and how you, as a leader, can cultivate and nurture this work, both in yourself and in others.

SERVICE AND COMPASSION: CORE VALUES OF COMMUNITY LEADERS

Outward Bound believes that successful experience leads to self-respect, which leads to concern

---

THE IMPORTANCE OF SERVICE

Before founding Outward Bound, Kurt Hahn, an educator and headmaster of the Salem School in Germany, held these views:

- From successful experience in an elemental setting, one can learn better to respect self.
- From respect for self can flow compassion and concern for others.
- From compassion for others one draws commitment for service to humankind.
- In genuine service to the benefit of others, one best expresses on a day-to-day basis reverence for life itself.

— Outward Bound Instructor Manual

for others, which leads to compassion, service, and reverence for life. Outward Bound is based on the importance of learning through one's experience and furthering that learning into compassion and service to others.

We often forget that throughout our lives we are continually learning, beyond traditional education, in ways that can then be applied to situations that call us to become leaders in service to others. At Outward Bound, instructors guide participants through challenging experiences that call upon their inner strengths and help them become aware of those strengths—and, more importantly, become thoughtful about how to put those strengths to good use in service to others. As you read through this chapter, consider the challenges you have faced that give you inner strength and compassion for others, that have led you to become a leader in helping others. So much about leadership comes from within our own realm of experience.

Helping Others—A Foundation of Outward Bound Programs

Just as on my first Outward Bound course we needed to help and work with one another to begin to get the boat to sail, so every Outward Bound course teaches that it is through helping each other and working together that goals and destinations are reached. The curriculum of every Outward Bound course relies on this principle. Courses also usually include a service project of some sort, a project that gives something to others beyond the group.

For example, rescue and evacuation techniques are taught on Outward Bound courses as part of the skills training that Outward Bound provides. They are important techniques to know when you are in the wilderness. But they are also useful because sometimes a rescue is necessary when a teammate sprains an ankle or gets sick. Having these skills provides a safety net for the group. Further, others in distress often call upon Outward Bound groups to help with emergency evacuations. It is relatively common for hikers to

become lost or hurt in the wilderness areas where Outward Bound operates its programs.

In the White Mountains of western Maine—one of the locations of Outward Bound's land programs—searchers are often needed to find a lost or injured hiker. Local authorities know to call the Outward Bound base to ask for assistance from the students and staff in the field as well as all staff who are at the base or who live in town. These Outward Bound staff and students are quickly mobilized to help the search and to help carry an injured person down from the mountains.

Another example of rescue service in Outward Bound is the night watch that occurs on Maine's Hurricane Island. Every night that a group of sailing students is on the island, students volunteer to monitor the very-high-frequency (VHF) radio in the watch station in case there is a boat in trouble. If they hear a distress call, their duty is to then notify the U.S. Coast Guard, awaken their comrades and leaders, and mobilize any aid the students and staff on the island can provide.

Some years ago, Roland Barth was sailing with his family in Penobscot Bay, where Hurricane Island is located. It was a dark night, and the fog was rolling in. Barth was watching the chart closely and knew that he was very near some dangerous rocks, but due to the intense fog, he was uncertain exactly where he was. (This was before the days of global positioning systems.) The wind was increasing from the west, and it began to push his boat onto a rocky shore. Knowing he was in danger, he began blowing his foghorn again and again and calling for help on his VHF radio.

Outward Bound students in the watch station heard the call and mobilized the other students and staff on the island, who took an Outward Bound motor vessel to search for the vessel in distress. Directed by the sound of Roland's foghorn, they found his boat through the fog. They threw him several

lines and towed him to Hurricane Island.
This was Roland's first exposure to
Outward Bound and its ethic of service.
He was immensely grateful and became
a strong advocate of the program (later
becoming a trustee of the Hurricane Island
Outward Bound School), not only because
of this rescue but also because of the type
of educational experience Outward Bound
provides to young people and adults.

Outward Bound's staff on Hurricane Island are also useful to local lobster fishermen, who work in small boats for long hours from before dawn until well after dark in all kinds of weather. When the lobstermen haul up traps from the bottom of the ocean, it is not uncommon for the lines to become tangled in the propellers of the boats. Outward Bound staff, skilled not only in land rescue but in water rescue, are often called to don their scuba gear and go out to the disabled craft, dive down, and untangle the line from the lobster boat's propeller. Staff lobster feasts are common on the island, a grateful gift to the Outward Bound staff for helping these hard-working lobstermen.

Serving Through Emergency Training

Are you an outdoorsperson who would like to become more confident in your ability to help others while you are hiking, climbing, boating, or sailing? Much of leadership is seeing a need and responding to that need.

Courses in first aid, wilderness first response, and rescue techniques will give you the opportunity to learn and upgrade your skills, to expand your base of rescue experience and competence. Outward Bound teaches these skills, but there are also many other ways to gain and hone such abilities. Every community has courses in first aid, first responder training, and emergency medical care. The American Red Cross as well as local community centers and even outdoor stores offer such courses. Excellent first responder and wilderness first-aid books are also available, some published by Out-

ward Bound. Your local library and bookstore can help you locate these. See the resources for Chapter 13 in the Bibliography at the back of this book.

There are many opportunities for community leadership in emergency work. You may decide to volunteer for your local volunteer fire department or search-and-rescue group. Small rural and mountain communities, especially, rely on volunteers for these important services. Such groups often provide in-depth training as well. In the mountain communities in Colorado, the volunteer fire department is the hub of community equipment and fire trucks.

One of the most challenging areas of leadership and emergency training is becoming an emergency medical technician (EMT). This rigorous training enables you to be on call at any time to aid in the rescue efforts and emergency response to almost any kind of accident or calamity. Although EMTs are often paid (and EMT certification is required of most professional firefighters), many people acquire this certificate in order to be more proficient in their personal emergency response abilities.

Performing Service Projects

The type of service projects conducted on Outward Bound courses are as varied as the opportunities around the country and the interests of the hundreds of staff leaders who work for Outward Bound. Many Outward Bound instructors of wilderness courses work with the National Park Service and other public or private landowners to build trails or spend a day doing a project that would otherwise be difficult to accomplish.

For instance, Maine Outward Bound courses often work on the Appalachian Trail to repair damage done by erosion from winter storms. Students clear away fallen trees, move rocks, and build steps up steep embankments. Park rangers are very grateful to have this valuable help since their budgets are never sufficient for all the needed repair and maintenance work. In another example, Outward Bound sailing courses often stop over on islands to paint local churches or schools or help elderly people repair their homes. Other programs, such as Outward Bound's urban courses, take underprivileged children out for a day to a local park and teach games that further teamwork and cooperation.

Outward Bound courses in other countries also offer unique opportunities for service projects. An adult women's course traveled to Kenya and Tanzania to climb Mount Kilimanjaro, but first they wanted to do something to benefit the nearby village of Loitokitok. Working with the Kenya Outward Bound School, located a few miles outside of Loitokitok, the group learned that the local community center was badly in need of painting. They contacted village officials, who were greatly pleased to have the group's help.

On a clear, crisp morning we finished our breakfast at the Kenya Outward Bound School and began the hour's walk to Loitokitok. We carried the supplies we had purchased: pale yellow paint, many paintbrushes, and large black plastic garbage bags. As we walked along the dusty unpaved road, Mount Kilimanjaro stood grandly to the southwest. We paused to gaze at the massive snowcapped mountain shining in the early morning light, knowing we would be hiking up it within the next few days. Its beauty and majesty awed us, and each woman secretly wondered if she would be able to make it to its 19,340-foot summit. But this day, our minds were on a different challenge: working in a foreign village, with few supplies and among people we did not know but hoped to befriend.

We arrived at the community center, which was right in the middle of the village. It was a large two-room building made of concrete blocks and stucco. The paint was peeling off the interior walls and in places had worn completely away.

We each cut holes in the top and sides of our garbage bag for our head and arms.

This would be our painting uniform! We must have looked strange—white American women, from ages twenty-six to fifty-seven, draped in garbage bags. But we went to work with enthusiasm.

When we began painting, a few men stood around observing us. Slowly, word spread in the village that a group of white women were painting their community center. Gradually others started to gather and watch, many gaping at us. We eventually discovered that we were considered very strange because women in Kenya do not paint houses; the men do it.

As women of the village started coming closer, we invited them to come into the building and join us. We offered them paintbrushes and garbage bags, and soon we had several new friends laughing and painting alongside us. We learned stories of their lives, their children, and their families; we told them of our lives, children, and families. As the day wore on, we all made new friends. We also had the feeling that many of the Kenyan women might consider taking up paintbrushes of their own!

As the villagers learned of our work, the local leaders gathered people to offer to cook us a meal at the end of the day. When the center was freshly painted and we were cleaning up late in the day, pots of food began arriving. Men, women, and children came to see what we had done and to have a meal with us. They built a fire outside and brought benches out for everyone to sit on. As the evening darkened, we all sat around the fire. The Kenyans sang songs of their land and their village. Then we sang "America" and "Amazing Grace." There was a glow in all of us and a keen awareness that we American women, from our simple day of painting the community center, had gained just as much from the experience as had this little village and these beautiful people.

Projects such as these are examples of things you can do within your own community. You can join groups who are already organized to do projects, or you can easily gather your friends and neighbors together to do something that will enhance your community or help someone in need.

Being a leader means seeing an opportunity for a project and then finding a way to accomplish it. You and your group will also gain from the experience, as we American women in Kenya did.

Identifying Your Moral Values

Outward Bound believes that people, especially youth, gain strength and character through serving others. Josh Miner, founder of Outward Bound in the United States, wrote in *Outward Bound USA* that "through help to those 'in danger and in need' youth can strike the deepest chords of the human spirit. It would become a creed: 'He who drills and labors, accepts hardship, boredom, and dangers, all for the sake of helping his brother in peril and distress, discovers God's purpose in his inner life.'" Although Outward Bound has never identified itself as "religious," its fundamental philosophies are based on moral values that are often identified in the world's religions.

As you think about service to others and to your community, what are your moral values and philosophies? Your values, as are Outward Bound's, will be fundamental to your actions and choices. They are a part of your history and experience, and they are invaluable. They provide the bedrock for your ability to lead in your community.

Moral values generally are instilled by our families, our heritage, religious teachings, and events in the world that affect us. Reading and learning about the Holocaust of World War II, for example, teaches about compassion and standing up for others.

Moral values also come from our personal experiences. Outward Bound believes that moral values can be taught through service to others, that when you feel needed you become instilled

with a greater purpose. You discover something larger than yourself, something that gives meaning to your life besides your own private and individual needs.

As a community leader, reflect upon your own life, your own upbringing, your experiences, and what has helped you to want to lead and help others.

Sara is a woman in her fifties whose mother died of cancer several years ago. During her mother's long and, at times, painful illness, the hospice organization came to her home and provided help that Sara could not manage on her own. Sara's mother eventually was moved from her home to a hospice center, where she died peacefully and with dignity.

Sara was so moved and inspired by the hospice workers, by their values of dignity, respect, and immense care for every individual, that she decided she would like to become a hospice volunteer. She decided that the values of the hospice organization not only had helped her and her mother but were fundamental to her own values of individual dignity, no matter what the circumstances.

Sara became a volunteer leader in her local hospice organization. She and her co-workers continue to build the organization and to recruit others to serve, especially others who have benefited from hospice care for their loved ones.

WHAT INSPIRES YOU TO SERVE?

I arise in the morning torn between a desire to improve (or save) the world and a desire to enjoy (or savor) the world. This makes it hard to plan the day.
—E. B. White, *in* The New York Times

We read in newspapers and on the Web about human and environmental disasters and places where volunteer help is needed; we see the images on television. But how do we discern when and how to act? How do we choose between saving and savoring the world? How do any of us move out of our inertia, the habits of our daily lives that focus on our own personal daily needs, desires, and obligations?

Listening to Your Inner Callings

Leadership demands inner knowledge and awareness. This does not mean that you mustn't act until you feel wise and all-knowing. If this were the case, nothing would ever get done! In fact, much of what we learn and teach at Outward Bound is to step out and take risks, even when we're not too sure of what the outcome will be.

You can never respond to all the needs that exist in your family, your community, and the world at large. It would be a mistake to jump into every opportunity you see. Therefore, it is important to know yourself and learn about what within you responds to the needs you see around you. Finding ways to be a leader through service in your community and world comes from being aware of what inspires you and paying attention to your inner voice.

Finding Time for Reflection

For example, reflection—a time of quiet and being alone—is a part of every Outward Bound course as a Solo (see Chapter 9, Going Solo, in Part II, Taking Leadership into the Outdoors). Time to write and reflect, time to think and connect our daily experiences to our values and desires for a good life is vital in discerning what is important to us and what inspires us.

In her book *The Measure of Our Success*, Marian Wright Edelman writes: "Listen for the 'sound of the genuine' within yourself and others . . . There is,' Howard Thurman told Spelman College students in 1981, 'something in every one of you that waits and listens for the sound of the genuine in yourself.' It is 'the only true guide you'll ever have.' " Edelman advocates learning how to be quiet within yourself, to be by yourself, to meditate, pray, or just have times of silence to discern your true needs, desires, and inspirations.

This is hard to do in our society, filled as it is with music, news, and busy-ness. Yet it is important to pay attention to your inner callings and understand what personally leads you to feel good about yourself and your actions.

What do you do in your daily life that provides this opportunity? Do you walk or run each day by yourself? Do you find time to be alone? Finding quietness and attending to your inner voice takes commitment.

Journal Writing

Reflection at Outward Bound is also taught through daily journal writing. Taking time to record your thoughts and ideas is an excellent way to begin to notice what inspires you. You may not choose to write every day, but becoming disciplined about finding time to write your thoughts, feelings, and ideas is invaluable. Keeping a journal is a very good way to reflect and consider what is important to you.

We at Outward Bound have found that over the years keeping a journal helps provide a roadmap of your thoughts and experiences. Writing helps bring to your consciousness those things that are most important to you, and it helps you identify what inspires you.

Being a Good Samaritan

Sometimes inspiration comes from an immediate and demanding situation. The Good Samaritan happened upon a person on the road who needed help right then, and the Good Samaritan responded with openness and willingness. Our society today often emphasizes privacy and not interfering in others' affairs, as well as the fear of lawsuits. Yet we have "Good Samaritan" laws that protect those who respond to an immediate need, acknowledging the importance of such actions. Core to the early teachings of Outward Bound's founder was this notion of responding to needs when we see them.

A local newspaper article recently described two men who were driving home from work on a quite icy, dark winter night. While driving through their rural area, they passed a lake and saw that a car had just gone off the slick road into the lake. They quickly stopped, called 9-1-1 on their cell phone, conferred about what to do, and waded into the chilly waters to help the elderly couple trapped inside their car. The men's quick, instinctive actions saved the lives of this couple.

Having an ethic of service means that when you are needed, you help. This isn't something that one has to learn; it is something that comes from within. Much about leadership is about how we respond intuitively.

Acting on Your Intuition

Everyone has intuition. Yet having the confidence to *trust* your intuition and then the courage to act on its messages comes with practice and with increasing your awareness that you always can do *something*, even if it is to find someone else to participate. What is learned is the consciousness of having the responsibility to act.

Some things you just *know* you should do. You know you should return the proper change in the grocery store if the clerk gives you more than is due. You know you should help an elderly or disabled person by opening a door. In an emergency, do you feel able to act to help? Would you help organize the people who might gather at the place of an emergency? It helps to think about these questions so that if there is a time when you are faced with an emergency, you will at least have given your actions some forethought.

Responding to an Emergency

Outward Bound teaches the importance of staying calm and gathering your wits in the face of an emergency. Michael Lindsay, Colorado Outward Bound's program director in the 1980s, taught the staff to mentally brew a cup of tea when confronted with an emergency. Of course, he didn't mean this literally; what he meant was that we should take the time to think and not panic, to stay calm.

Often, leadership in emergency situations means being a good follower. In a medical emergency, if a doctor or other trained medical person is present, he or she may organize the immediate care necessary; your important actions are to follow his or her requests and to help others gathered there do the same.

This is situational leadership: The nature of the emergency itself and what resources and knowledge are at hand determine how you can be of service. You must assess the situation and determine what will make your service most successful. Mentally brew a cup of tea for a moment before you act.

Following Role Models

Often we are inspired by others, people we know or people we read or hear about.

A high school teacher inspired Nelson Chase by talking about the Peace Corps. Nelson felt something within himself respond to and resonate with what his teacher had done; when he listened to his teacher, it rang a bell inside him. He felt drawn to doing something similar himself; his intuition told him that it was something he, too, wanted to do. So Nelson became a Peace Corps volunteer and served in 1972 and 1973. He was inspired to serve in the Peace Corps because of his teacher.

Nelson later began working with Outward Bound and in the late '70s and early '80s was an early proponent and organizer of the community programs that are now so fundamental to Outward Bound's work.

After working for the Colorado Outward Bound School for many years, Nelson left Outward Bound in 1985 to follow his dream of bicycling around the world. For the next five years, he pedaled on every continent in the world, and his letters to friends throughout that time were filled with great stories of

> **EMERGENCY ACTION STEPS**
> 1. Stay calm.
> 2. Assess the situation and get yourself and anyone you're responsible for out of immediate danger.
> 3. If someone you are responsible for is injured or in danger, call 9-1-1. Speed is especially important if life-threatening situations occur, such as profuse bleeding, cardiac arrest, unconsciousness, or lack of breathing.
> 4. If you're working with an organization, call its contact person and pass on your information about the situation. Follow the organization's policy about calling relatives of the injured person and speaking to the press.

his adventures. He witnessed and participated in many opportunities for service during those years, and when he again decided to return to work, he applied to the Peace Corps to be a country director. Although this was a paid position, it still took commitment and willingness to undergo hardship.

During those later years when Nelson worked for the Peace Corps, several of his young Peace Corps volunteers who were finishing their Peace Corps service called Outward Bound to inquire about work with us. Nelson had inspired them to consider working for Outward Bound. He had been inspired by a role model, and he in turn became an inspiring role model for others.

Putting Yourself in Another's Shoes

Finally, a common way we feel inspired comes from putting ourselves in someone else's shoes. Can you imagine what it would be like if you lived alone and broke your leg and had no family nearby to help? The phrase "There but for the grace of God go I" can move us to be of service to others who might well have been us.

The natural disasters of 2005 are a good case in point. What if you had been in Sri Lanka when the tsunami hit? What if you had lost your home and belongings to Hurricane Katrina or the earthquake in Pakistan? Understanding the randomness of catastrophe and that it could happen to anyone often inspires us to action.

On an Outward Bound course high in the Sierra Nevadas in California, the terrain was difficult and steep and the backpacks were heavy, the group having just been resupplied with food and gear for the coming week. Among the group of sixteen- to twenty-year-olds, ten young men and women were laboring up the trail. Steve was serving as sweep that day, walking last in line to make sure everyone made it up the trail. The group was quite spread out as each person focused on the personal challenge of making it to the top of the pass with a very heavy pack.

As Steve rounded a curve in the trail, he saw Julie resting on a rock with tears in her eyes. She was a physically small woman of seventeen who was extremely tired and feeling unsure that she could make it to the top. Steve sat down next to her and offered encouragement. He then picked up her pack and added it to his own, thus carrying two heavy packs. He carried both packs slowly to the top of the pass, giving Julie the break she needed to rest her hips and shoulders and walk weight-free for awhile.

At the top, Julie felt revived and able to take her own pack back and continue. Steve's help had given her just the break and encouragement she needed to carry on. She never needed help again on the course. At the end of the course, she remarked how she would never forget what Steve had done for her and that she would always try to remember how meaningful that small act of service had been for her, that she would always try to remember to do that for others.

What inspired Steve's action? After all, his own pack was heavy as well. Simply put, he felt that he could easily have been in the same situation as Julie. Steve felt moved to help Julie, despite his own discomfort and tiredness, because he knew that, under trying circumstance, he might have experienced her exhaustion. He reached beyond his own needs when he saw someone else's.

In the account above, we also see that Julie felt inspired by Steve's example. Thus, our actions as leaders can inspire others to perform acts of service too. Helping others, being inspired to help others, is something that gets passed on. Frequently we feel that we must repay someone who helps us, yet repayment is usually impossible. But "passing it forward" is very possible and perhaps the best repayment. These acts, both small and large, of helping others inspire others to also be of service. You, yourself, are inspiration for someone else.

PUTTING YOUR STRENGTHS TO WORK FOR OTHERS

What are your strengths? What are your gifts? What is in you that can help others? These questions may seem very similar to those regarding what inspires us to serve. Yet being *inspired* to serve and seeing where you are best *suited* to serve are two different things.

Our deepest fear is not that we are inadequate. Our deepest fear is that we are powerful beyond measure. It is our light, not our darkness that most frightens us. We ask ourselves, 'Who am I to be brilliant, gorgeous, talented, and fabulous?' Actually, who are you not to be?

You are a child of God. Your playing small does not serve the world. There is nothing, nothing enlightened about shrink-

ing so that other people won't feel insecure around you. We were born to make manifest the glory of God that is within us.

It is not in just some of us; it is in everyone. And as we let our own light shine, we unconsciously give other people permission to do the same. As we are liberated from our fear, our presence automatically liberates others.
 — *Nelson Mandela, from his 1994 inaugural speech*

Determining Your Strengths

How, then, do you think about using your strengths for service in your community? Identifying your strengths will help you make better choices about where to put your time and energy.

Following Your Preferences

Several aptitude tests can give some answers to what your natural preferences and skills are. The Strong Campbell Interest Test, the Meyers Briggs Personality Inventory (a personality preference test based on Carl Jung's studies), and others give clues into what your natural aptitudes, preferences, and strengths are (see the Bibliography at the end of this book). These tests are often used to guide educational and career choices.

There is a correlation between what we like and what we do well. What do you enjoy? What do you like to do? What do you feel passion for? What in the world would you like to see changed? Asking these questions usually leads to understanding what your strengths are and where best to apply them.

Throughout our lives, most of us pursue different careers and different interests. Thus our interests, skills, and strengths change over time. It is helpful to realize that we are never tied to one course of action; we are always able to change course if we find we are not in the right place doing the thing that serves others and ourselves well.

Learning from Your Mistakes

Sometimes we learn from something that does not go well for us. Trying something and discovering that, in fact, it is not your strength is worth learning. No experience is worthless or a waste of time. Everything you do teaches you about what to do better next time: it helps you learn about yourself and where your talents lie.

Outward Bound believes in the value of making mistakes and learning from those mistakes. It is not uncommon for participants on an Outward Bound course to make bad decisions and discover that the path that was charted was not the right one. Writer Rita Mae Brown said something that's become a favorite Outward Bound saying: "Good judgment comes from experience, and often experience comes from bad judgment." Taking the longer, more difficult way can be worth more than any words can teach about learning what *not* to do next time.

Benefiting from Your Service Work

It is important to remember that service work is not a one-way street: It is not simply something that goes outward—it also affects *you*. Each of us needs to feel the benefits from our service work. You should enjoy using your skills; you should enjoy seeing positive outcomes from your efforts. Some people enjoy travel, if that is involved in their service work.

> *Don and Jean Morrison are retired. Every year they travel to a different part of the United States or to some foreign country and do service work. They have been volunteer hosts at national parks; they have built homes for Habitat for Humanity; they have helped Doctors Without Borders. They find work that provides them with a community and frequently also provides them with room and board. They get to see the world by going to places that need their help. Every year is a new adventure.*
>
> *Many learn new skills from volunteering that serve them in new and unforetold ways. For instance, you may well have a better chance of being accepted into graduate school or a new job because of your service experi-*

ences. And many appreciate the change that service work engenders in people, in communities, and in society as a whole.

INTEGRATING PUBLIC SERVICE INTO THE REST OF YOUR LIFE

I don't know what your destiny will be, but one thing I know; the only ones among you who will be really happy are those who will have sought and found how to serve.
—Dr. Albert Schweitzer, in Prophet in the Wilderness, *by Hermann Hagedorn*

How do you begin to even think about serving others in the midst of your already overly busy life? How do you find the time? How do you prioritize serving your community among the many demands of family, work, hobbies, recreation, and more? These are not easy questions, but being driven to action by guilt is not the answer.

Fitting Service into Your Existing Activities

One answer lies in paying attention to what you are currently doing and what might fit into the activities, interests, and patterns of those things in your daily and weekly path. Think about what opportunities are already there in your life.

Do you have children in school, and do you go to their school frequently? Volunteering and helping out in the classrooms of any of our schools is much needed and greatly appreciated. It is invaluable to spend time one-on-one with special-needs children, help drive on field trips, or teach a special session on something of interest to you for which you have unique talents. Taking schoolchildren into your workplace and giving them opportunities to understand varieties of careers they might consider is the focus of "Take Your Daughters and Sons to Work Day" and other similar projects.

Working with People You Enjoy

Maintaining friendships is an important part of our daily lives. If you integrate service work with people you enjoy and for issues and causes that are important to you, you will combine your values and your priorities. A good way to visit with a valued friend is to agree to do a community service project together. Serving in a soup kitchen while standing next to a friend you haven't seen for awhile is enriching to those you serve as well as to you and your friend.

Some important community service projects have been taken on by a group of friends who decide to come together to accomplish something—somewhat like the Kenya Outward Bound course that painted the community building in Loitokitok. Habitat for Humanity often relies on groups of people who know each other to work for a day to help build a house. Busy lives can fulfill more than one thing at a time, and doing service work while cultivating valued friendships is possible.

Taking on a Time-Limited Project

Sometimes you can take on a service project that is time limited. It may be easier for you to participate if you see that a specific length of time is required. This way, if serving means you need to let go of other things for awhile, you can see when your service work will end and you can resume your other desired activities.

Many organizations have benefit dinners with auctions that raise substantial amounts of money. These events usually have a committee that works to obtain the auction items and manage the fundraiser. These volunteer committees usually exist for a few months to plan and execute the event. This is a great way for some people to help the organization for a specified duration, and when the event is finished, they know they are done.

Maximizing Your Time by Being Organized

Take time to think about what you are doing and how you use your time. Evaluate how your days and weeks are spent. Making service work a priority usually means making adjustments to an already busy schedule. It means making service work a priority. Often those who are successful at integrating service work into their lives are also the people who are the busiest. There is a common saying that if you want to get something done, ask those who are the busiest.

Being organized, an important skill of every leader, is a key ingredient to finding time for service work while maintaining the other obligations in your life. What does "being organized" mean, then?

Different people have different styles of being organized. Taking time to reflect and plan in your head is one way; again, a journal helps here. Making lists and organizing your thoughts on paper is often very helpful. Everyone has their own methods of ordering their days and weeks, but thinking ahead about what needs to be done, making lists, and combining tasks in ways that best use your energy and time are fundamental. Time-management books, seminars, and trainings can be very useful; for some recommendations, see the resources for Chapter 13 in the Bibliography at the end of this book.

Outward Bound leaders tend to be excellent organizers. They must pack every minute of an Outward Bound course full of meaningful activities, follow the curriculum, and anticipate the unexpected. They spend a good deal of time thinking and planning before students ever arrive. They make lists and then review and edit their lists. They think about their itinerary, the food, where to spend each night, and how to accomplish the goals of the course.

Becoming disciplined about taking the time to plan can be invaluable, and it will help you carve out time to address your priority activities. In any case, taking the time to stop and think and to give *prioritizing* a priority is imperative.

Making Service a Habit

Public service and exercise have something in common: they both are most easily accomplished when they become a habit.

At Outward Bound, every morning of almost every course includes a run and dip. This "run and dip" can consist of a run, jog, or walk of varying lengths followed by a plunge into a river, stream, or ocean. There's no cancelling because the weather is too cold, we're too tired from the activities of the previous day, or we didn't sleep well the night before. Many Outward Bound leaders would prefer to stay warm in their sleeping bags than have to get up and get going. Yet the run and dip is integrated into the rhythm and activities of the day. It becomes automatic.

So it is with service. It becomes integral to how you think about living out your life. Here's an example of integrating service into your life:

Mary Amory and her husband were Outward Bound instructors years ago and now are professionals in their community who have raised three children. A year or so ago, Mary happened upon the book Mountains Beyond Mountains *by Tracy Kidder. It is the true story of Dr. Paul Farmer and his medical work to improve the conditions of people in Haiti, Peru, the then Soviet Union, and this country. Dr. Farmer, through his work in these countries and through his vision and perseverance under great odds, founded a nonprofit called Partners in Health.*

Mary was so inspired by the book and by what Dr. Farmer is doing that she wanted to help in some way. She contacted Partners in Health to ask them how she might help. After talking with them, she decided to organize several events that would tell the story of Dr. Farmer and the work his organization is doing. She also wanted to raise money to support the medical costs for the people in Haiti.

Mary talked to many of her friends, and together they organized a series of educational and social events that were great fun and that raised approximately $4,000. Later, when Christmas approached, Mary organized a sale of select donated second-hand items in early December, raising additional dollars, and a year later, organized another holiday sale, again raising several thousand

dollars. Now Mary asks her friends to think about saving useful items throughout the year, storing them in her barn, and then helping sort and tag them for an annual sale.

Mary has integrated this event into her life. Doing this project has become a habit for her. It has become organized in such a way that it is easily repeated and has become something the community looks forward to each year.

As you find ways to serve and as you begin to experience the benefits of community service, you will find that it becomes integrated into your life. Once you begin, it does become a habit, a meaningful habit. It becomes something that you learn you really can't do without and that it enhances your life . . . that you "do well by doing good." And, just as the type of daily exercise you engage in changes with the weather, the time of year, and your age, so the service work you do changes and adapts to the life changes you're experiencing and to the seasonal changes that occur regularly.

An example of service work changing as your life changes is this: When I had young children, I volunteered at their elementary school; I helped with field trips and supported the teacher when she or he had special needs. When my children were in junior high and high school, I began volunteering instead with the local women's center, which later became Safehouse. My children's needs changed and my interests changed as we grew older.

Joining a Service Group or Board of Directors

Service groups such as the Kiwanis Club, the local Rotary Club, and similar civic organizations meet regularly, enjoy programs and members' company, and also include community service as part of their regular activities. Sometimes joining a service group is a good way to bring service into your life more easily. This often can expose you to different community needs, which then may draw you to volunteer more fully in one particular organization.

Volunteering on boards of directors for community nonprofits is another excellent use of your talents and interests. Boards are always looking for people to serve, and it is an excellent way to provide leadership in your community. United Way and other organizations that support the nonprofit enterprises in your community can give you information about what boards are looking for members and where you might volunteer your skills.

OPPORTUNITIES FOR SERVICE IN THE WORLD

Let the beauty we love be what we do. There are hundreds of ways to kneel and touch the earth.
—*Jalal al-Din Rumi, in* Essential Rumi

The term "outward bound" refers to a ship leaving its harbor, its place of safety. The term means that when a ship is well stocked and ready, it sails away on its destination; it is outward bound. So it is said that the Outward Bound experience truly begins when people leave their Outward Bound courses and go back to their homes and their communities equipped with and aware of new skills and experiences that will help their life's voyage. They are compelled to take what they have learned to apply a greater understanding of service and compassion in their daily lives.

Service has many forms and avenues. There are so many ways to serve. You can serve within your family, with your friends, in your community, in your country, and internationally throughout the world. In the past few years we have witnessed natural disasters around the world: devastating tsunamis, floods, and earthquakes taking the lives of thousands. Volunteers from around the world leave their comfortable homes to go to the aid of the victims of these disasters.

At Home

My mother always said, "Charity begins at home." Certainly, this is where we all start from, and it is where we find the most opportunities—though often home can be the most difficult place to find ways to serve! Where do we find opportunities at home? Do we offer to help a family member without being asked? Do we care for an aging relative with compassion and selflessness?

Leadership begins at home as well. We talk a

SERVICE OPPORTUNITIES ALL AROUND YOU

Close to Home
- Appalachian Mountain Club (trail maintenance): *www.outdoor.org*
- Big Brothers/Big Sisters: *www.bbbs.org*
- a local hospice: *www.hospicefoundation.org/hospiceInfo/volunteer.asp*
- Kiwanis Club: *www.kiwanis.org*
- Rotary Club: *www.rotary.org*
- Domestic violence hotlines: *www.mincava.umn.edu*
- United Way: *www.unitedway.org*

In the Larger World
- Red Cross: *www.redcross.org*
- Doctors without Borders: *www.doctorswithoutborders.org/volunteer/field*
- Habitat for Humanity: *www.habitat.org/cd/local*
- National Park Service: *www.nps.gov/gettinginvolved*
- Partners in Health: *www.pih.org/youcando/volunteer.html*
- Peace Corps: *www.peacecorps.gov*

lot about how our actions on an Outward Bound course impact our team members and how our actions at home impact our family members. Although we sometimes forget, because our family life is so close to us, thinking about leadership at home forms the basis for the work we do beyond our homes . . . the ripples spreading outward in the water.

Mingma, our Sherpani on an adult Outward Bound course in Nepal, is a woman whose leadership both in the outdoors and in her home I will always remember. . . . She is the wife of the owner of the trekking company that Outward Bound hired for its programs in Nepal. Mingma and two male Sherpas were the guides for our sixteen-day trek in the Gannesh, an area in the middle of the country, a trek that went from 2,000 feet where we started in the city of Gorka to 15,000 feet as we crossed Patang Pass.

Mingma is a quiet, strong woman with a broad smile, flashing white teeth, and warm dark eyes. She was open and helpful to our group as we trekked through her beautiful and physically challenging country. She encouraged the participants and explained the history and culture of the different villages and locales we passed as we gained altitude.

When the course ended and the course participants had departed, Mingma invited the Outward Bound leaders into her home for lunch. It was a modest home, clean and spare. She had prepared spicy and delicious Nepali food. She and her husband were gracious hosts and kept offering us more to eat. Also in the house were several elderly people. We learned that they were an uncle, an aunt, and Mingma's mother. Mingma was as gracious to these elders as she was to us, her guests. She told me that they lived there with her, her husband, and their two children.

Mingma's and her husband's care of and service to their elders were, to them, nothing unusual. It was impressive, though, to us westerners to see such a strong and obvious ethic, which indeed is part of the Nepali culture. I learned something from being with her: not only about her country and how to navigate the challenging trail system of Nepal but, further, about being strong and gracious within one's own family. As my mother ages and faces increasing challenges, I often think of Mingma.

Here is another example of leadership at home:

Gregg was a fourteen-year-old middle schooler in Connecticut. He was a good student, and his parents were proud of him. He told his parents that he wanted to take an Outward Bound course and learn to sail.

Gregg took an Outward Bound sailing course in Chesapeake Bay and had a great time. He loved learning the points of sail, how to cook on the boat, how to reef sails, how to navigate. He also liked being in the company of other energetic and fun young people.

Upon his return home, after a few weeks his mother reported that, though he'd always been a great kid, something had changed in him. He seemed to see things that needed to be done, and she didn't have to ask or remind him about family chores. He did more than he was asked. He did more small things: bringing in the groceries from the car, carrying out the garbage cans on pickup day. He was more considerate of his family and siblings. He talked often of his course and of the importance of helping his boat mates and how they had helped him.

Gregg had learned that service is in the smallest acts as well as in large commitments such as giving years to work in the Peace Corps or to be a teacher for Teach for America.

In Your Community

There are opportunities for service everywhere in our communities. Where do you see opportunities for yourself? If you are a student, are there student groups that do projects in your community? If you are a member of a church, are there programs for helping others in your congregation? What about the local boys and girls club? Many young people need "Big Brothers" and "Big Sisters." Is there a local Habitat for Humanity in your area that needs help building a house for a low-income family? How about simply holding a door open for an elderly person?

In the World at Large

Where do you find out about opportunities for service elsewhere in the world? How about joining the Peace Corps? The World Wide Web has information on vast numbers of organizations looking for volunteers to do thousands of different types of service work, from local community opportunities to opportunities within this country or internationally.

Perhaps a commoner way to find out about opportunities is through your friends and word of mouth. Hearing of interesting service work and talking with the people who have done it are excellent sources of information. They can not only help you discern what types of work are available but also give you an excellent reality check on what this work really entails and whether it is something that appeals to you to do yourself. Here is an example of someone who found interesting opportunities for leadership and service in the world.

Lucy is a young woman who graduated several years ago from Vassar College. She is the daughter of two former Outward Bound instructors and has done an Outward Bound staff training herself. Having been raised with the ethics of Outward Bound and service to others, she decided that she wanted to pursue something that would give back to society and would be of use. She also wanted

a new kind of experience for herself. She applied for and was accepted into the Teach for America program.

Lucy is in the second year of this two-year program, teaching kindergarten in Marianna, Arkansas. It has not been easy. She had never taught school before and had not majored in education. Her classroom the first year had no windows. It was hot and humid. The children needed a lot of classroom discipline, which is not easy even for a trained first-year teacher under any circumstances. The school has a 50 percent turnover rate in its teachers.

So why is Lucy doing this? What are her reasons for staying and continuing? She wasn't at all sure she could do it, but she is learning that yes, in fact, she can do it—just as in an Outward Bound course! She is gaining confidence. She is giving to children she has grown to care about. She is living in a different culture and part of the United States that she didn't know about before. She is meeting new people, different from her family and friends at home and at school. She believes that this experience will enrich and enhance her personal and professional skills and life, that this experience will give her a good background for whatever future endeavors she pursues.

Serving in foreign countries or, like Lucy, working somewhere with a different culture, even though it is within your own country, puts you outside your comfort zone and requires commitment and a willingness to risk the unknown. Don't volunteer for service of this type if you are reluctant. It takes a strong desire for a new experience despite difficult circumstances to successfully complete this type of assignment.

Yet despite hardships, the rewards are remarkable—everything from feeling the satisfaction that you have made a difference in peoples' lives to learning about a new culture and gaining new skills that will serve you well for years to come, both in your profession and in a richer and fuller personal life. This type of service work reaps many benefits, most of all a sense of having done very worthwhile work.

A FINAL NOTE

The circles of service spread outward like ripples from a stone dropped in water. Giving of yourself, helping those in need, begins close to us and then spreads outward and even moves to encompass the world. There are as many opportunities for service as there are individuals and places in our communities and the world. Saying yes to those opportunities and willingly leading when needed gives a richness and completeness to our lives.

CHAPTER 14

LEADING A VOLUNTEER ORGANIZATION

There is no better work than being involved with a volunteer organization. Everyone there cares about a common purpose, a common mission. Everyone is there to share in the work of the world, ready to harness their energies together, focused and harmonized, to bring meaningful work to their community.

Volunteers are core to service work in the United States, which has more nonprofit service organizations than any other country in the world. Service- and mission-driven organizations usually do not have the resources to do all the work they want to accomplish through paid staff. Thus volunteers are of huge importance for addressing the variety of social, economic, and environmental needs in our communities.

When you choose to volunteer in your community, you usually seek out an organization that serves the need or population that interests you and the issues you have already become involved in. When you engage in activities and issues for which you have passion, you may find that you gradually gravitate toward a leadership role. You may see a need to fill, or it may be a time in your life when you are ready to do more, or perhaps the issue compels you to step out and take a stronger role.

In the late 1970s, I was volunteering at a women's resource center in Boulder, Colorado, doing peer counseling and advocacy work primarily for disadvantaged and low-income women. More and more women fleeing from domestic abuse began coming to the center asking for assistance. They would be waiting at the center's doorstep first thing in the morning, often in their bathrobes and with their children in tow. We had nowhere to send them, and few community resources were available.

The organization quickly realized that services for these women and children were badly needed, and a volunteer task force was organized. At the time, I was volunteering one day a week as a peer counselor. I had become very interested in the work of the resource center and participated in extra trainings when they were offered. I took advantage of every opportunity to be involved and to learn more about the issues the center was addressing. Because of my interest and other volunteer experience in the community, I was asked to become the volunteer leader of a task force to develop services for battered women and their children, including a residential "safe house."

We worked for more than a year, organizing community services to provide housing and services for these families in need. My volunteer work for that year took on the aspects of a full-time job: recruiting and coordinating other volunteers; coordinating community services; writing grants to fund our goal, which was to buy a home for a safe house; and developing a full program of counseling and advocacy for these women and children.

A year and a half later, I became the paid executive director of the program, which eventually became an agency, the Boulder County Safehouse, which not only provides programs and housing for women and children in need but also works to train community helpers and advocates for programs for the abusing husbands and partners. In the early 1980s during the first years of Safehouse, we had four paid staff and more than one hundred volunteers. The organization recently celebrated its twenty-fifth anniversary.

I worked at that agency for seven years before I went to work full-time for Outward Bound (I had been working part-time as an Outward Bound instructor during vacations and holidays). Much of what I know today came from that experience—an experience that began as a volunteer. I believe that my experience at that agency particularly suited me for a career at Outward Bound. Outward Bound is about experiential learning—learning by doing—and my skills in organizing and leading have largely come from learning by doing, especially at Safehouse.

Just as you can learn skills such as knot tying, how to read a chart or map, how to work a compass, and how to prepare for an expedition, so, too, you can learn basic skills in organizing, communicating, and working with others that help you become a successful leader. The preceding sections of this book cover leadership fundamentals, outdoor leadership, and professional leadership, and much of that also applies to leading in volunteer organizations. This chapter, however, focuses specifically on issues to think about that apply to volunteer, usually nonprofit, organizations.

WHAT SETS VOLUNTEER ORGANIZATIONS APART FROM OTHER LEADERSHIP SITUATIONS?

Volunteer organizations are most commonly nonprofit organizations that have tax-exempt 501(c)(3) status with the federal government. They differ from for-profit businesses in that they are formed for the purpose of serving the good of society. They are mission driven rather than profit driven. They exist to be of service to others, whether people, the community, the environment, or some other identified entity. The U.S. economy has an entire nonprofit sector including churches, hospitals, arts centers, human service agencies, and educational institutions. They exist to help society and the world be a better place. Some utilize volunteers; others do not. A for-profit business, even though

it may, indeed, help others, exists to make a profit, to support the owner, and to give money to the owner, a group of owners, or, if a publicly held company, the shareholders.

This does not mean that nonprofit organizations don't make a profit—they often do (though usually small); indeed, they *should* make a profit in order to be healthy, viable, and sustainable organizations. Having nonprofit status merely refers to the fact that any excess revenues beyond the expenses of the organization are kept by the organization and used to further the organization rather than going to owners or shareholders of the business or company.

There are certainly similarities between nonprofit and for-profit organizations. Many practices are the same. Working with people, motivating teams, managing finances, and accomplishing objectives are all done through very similar processes. More and more nonprofit organizations are using methods and business practices shown to be successful in the for-profit world. Yet there are some differences, too, which are worth noting.

Unique Motivations

A major difference between for-profit and nonprofit organizations is that volunteers and paid staff who work for a nonprofit don't really have to be there. Volunteers can choose to offer their time and talents anywhere. Paid staff could work elsewhere and probably earn better salaries doing so. Outward Bound is full of people who left higher-paying corporate jobs to join the ranks of this institution. Several of Outward Bound's talented leaders first learned their skills in the for-profit world. Many took significant pay cuts to do this work. Volunteers and paid staff work at a nonprofit organization primarily because they believe in the work of the organization and want to help.

Allen Grossman was the longtime owner and corporate executive officer of a New York company. He also volunteered time on nonprofit boards, as did his wife, Jane. Allen decided to sell his company, and when he looked around at what he wanted to do next, he looked at the nonprofit sector.

It was a serendipitous decision: Outward Bound USA was searching for a new president and CEO. Allen applied for the position and was hired in 1991. He successfully led Outward Bound for eight years, working more hours and earning less pay than he had as a business owner. Yet he loved the work, and it was a rewarding experience. Today, Allen teaches courses in management of nonprofits and public school districts at the Harvard Business School, courses that focus on the nonprofit sector.

Thus, people who work for a volunteer, non-profit organization, whether they're paid or not, care deeply about the success of the organization and about how it accomplishes its mission. People working in volunteer organizations tend to be there because they love the work and what that work accomplishes. They are highly motivated and invested in the organization.

Leaders who work with these motivated people find them eager to be engaged and to share their thoughts and ideas. This usually means that leaders of volunteer nonprofit organizations must work hard to involve volunteers and paid staff, to help them feel valued.

Workers in a nonprofit volunteer organization need to be motivated beyond the assurance of a salary. As is discussed in "Appreciation and Rewards" later in this chapter, motivating and focusing volunteers to accomplish the goals of the organization's mission require thoughtful inclusiveness and effective communication. Awareness of these needs is important when leading a group of volunteers or undertaking a project for a nonprofit.

Often Less Hierarchy

Another difference is that mission-driven non-profits are rarely completely hierarchical in their organization, but rely more on teams and groups for decision making. Consensus decision making is often a goal in nonprofits, especially in smaller-community grassroots nonprofits. Thus, decision making generally takes more time than decision making in a for-profit business where the owner, CEO, or senior staff are the primary decision-makers—though many for-profits now use more-inclusive decision-making models than were used years ago.

Generally, nonprofit workers, whether paid or volunteer, are not as motivated by their pay as are many of their for-profit counterparts. They are working because they believe in the mission of the organization. They want to be involved in decisions and to have their voices heard because of this investment. It may be only a slight differentiation between the two sectors, but it is significant.

Often Smaller Budgets

Nonprofit organizations are usually challenged to find adequate resources, both human and financial. Because mission-driven organizations usually want to accomplish far more than their human and financial resources will allow, they often struggle to meet the many needs and demands requested of them.

For-profit businesses sell something, whether it be services or products, and receive money for those services and products. Nonprofits usually are not able to provide their services at a price equal to the cost of running the organization. The people they serve may not be able to pay for the services, or the work of the organization may not lend itself to earning any income. Such organizations therefore depend on fund-raising from individuals, foundations, and corporations in order to sustain their operations. Many nonprofits depend entirely on fund-raising. Some receive federal, state, and/or local tax-supported grants.

In any case, resources rarely meet all the organization's financial demands, and it is a large part of a nonprofit's work to raise the dollars needed to fund operations and programs. This is often a difficult reality for new employees of a nonprofit who may have come from the corporate world, where there is usually working capital available for projects or at least a willingness to borrow money to invest in a project.

Decisions Based on Furthering the Organization's Mission

Finally, perhaps the most important quality of a volunteer organization is that decisions are made to support and further the mission of the organization. What must the organization do to help *more* people, to deliver its services *more* effectively, and to improve those services? Decisions in a for-profit organization focus on that which brings in the most profits or other gain to the company and that increase the financial "bottom line." The fundamental purpose of a volunteer organization is to do *more* good. This puts a different pressure on decision making in the non-profit world.

BECOMING A LEADER IN A VOLUNTEER ORGANIZATION

At Outward Bound, most participants on longer courses have the opportunity to lead for a day, because this leadership role is rotated to a different person each day. Each person, with the support of the group, learns from the experience. On professional courses in particular, feedback is given to the leader to help him or her better understand and evaluate the experience, what he or she did well and what could have been improved. This expectation at Outward Bound serves as a model for other organizations.

Work Your Way Up

As a volunteer, look for opportunities wherein you might take on a leadership role for something you see the organization needs. Keep your eye out for something that you could do, a project you could lead that would enhance and add capacity to the goals of the mission.

Then, when you have completed the task, ask for feedback, and be open to it. How did others see your performance? How were you to work with? Could you have done something differently that would have improved the outcome or improved the teamwork? Or, even better, ask for feedback in the midpoint of the project. That will give you an opportunity to make corrections if any are needed. And you will learn by doing.

Learning from others around you is another common way to learn to lead in volunteer organizations. The longer you volunteer, the more you learn about how the organization works and the key actions that bring successful outcomes. As is discussed in "Training and Orientation" and "Supervision" later in this chapter, training, formal guidance, and supervision are important. But also of importance is watching other leaders and identifying what you see is successful about their leadership. Modeling other leaders whom you admire and would like to emulate is a great way to learn. Asking for their feedback and guidance as you take on more responsibilities will help you hone your skills and become more successful within the organization.

Key to becoming a leader as you volunteer is responsibility. Make sure you do what you say you will do. Volunteering is just like any job, and how responsible you are about it and how seriously you take that responsibility indicate to others your readiness to take on more duties. Other volunteers and paid staff will notice your behavior, see you as competent, and begin to look to you to do more for the organization.

> *Susan volunteered helping teach migrant workers to speak and read English. These workers wanted to improve their communication and to become citizens of the United States. They needed to improve their English in order to take citizenship classes. Susan showed up on time, and when she saw needs in the small organization providing these services, she pitched in and helped. She began expanding her hours as more workers asked for more services. She was so effective and dependable that as the needs*

for service increased and more volunteers were recruited, Susan was asked to take on a leadership role as the trainer and supervisor for the new volunteers.

Watch for opportunities and become familiar with as many aspects of the organization as you can. Often there will be a planned project that is in the annual work plan. Current leadership may be in place to accomplish the plan, or, as in Susan's case, leadership capacity may need to be added. Ask to be considered. Don't be reluctant to give your ideas about how you would see a project being accomplished. As you build credibility through your ongoing volunteer work, you will find ample opportunities to give input and to be heard.

Have Confidence in Yourself

It is common at Outward Bound and elsewhere for potential leaders to feel that they need more training and more experience; they do not feel competent.

Marie was an outstanding Outward Bound instructor who had worked for the organization for several years. Everyone respected her abilities and skills. The program director felt that Marie was ready to become a course director, overseeing the instructors for a group of courses. At first Marie declined, saying she didn't feel she was ready to take on the larger responsibilities of course directing.

The program director and I both talked with her at length, helping her to see her own capabilities and persuading her to take on the position. We showed her how we would support her and give her extra training for the few areas in which she felt weak. Marie finally agreed; she went on to become one of the best course directors at that time.

Certainly there are times when a lack of confidence may be well grounded, but more often than not, you really do have the ability within you

to take on greater tasks and a larger role. It comes back to risk taking and being willing to step into something that feels a bit beyond you. This is a classic Outward Bound tenet. You are more than you know—you have more in you than you think, *plus est en vous.*

If you are asked by an organization to take on a greater leadership role, or if you see an opportunity and want to be considered, don't hesitate to try it just because you feel that you don't know everything needed to do the job. Be willing to step outside your comfort zone. Be willing to stretch your skills and knowledge. Take a risk.

Ask for Support

It is responsible, though, to think through what you feel competent doing and where you would need help and support. A good leader can never do it all, so who around you, either inside or outside the organization, can give you that support? You have to be willing to ask for help. You have to be willing to realize that you can't do it alone.

A favorite metaphor in Outward Bound is thinking about the belay system, wherein the person climbing up or rappelling down a cliff is made safe by being on belay: as you climb up or step off the top of the cliff, you are attached to a rope being held and supported by someone else, someone who will catch you if you fall. So who can be "on belay" for you as you take on a new leadership role? Who can you go to when you're unsure about something? Or with whom can you brainstorm to help you become clearer about the direction you want to take a project?

Consider the skills of your friends and whom among them you might ask for counsel and advice. Consider staff in the organization whom you trust and believe will help you. Is there a course or workshop you could take that would teach you what you need to know as you begin the work? Many resources outside yourself are available that will support you in a new role. Just as the student leader on an Outward Bound course relies on his or her group to help read the map, give ideas, and provide expertise, so your leadership can and should rely on others to help.

> *When I was asked to take on volunteer leadership of the task force to start Safehouse, I was very unsure of my ability to take on such a large project. I talked to friends for their thoughts and their ability to help me. I talked with the staff about how much help I could expect to get from them. When I said yes, the organization agreed to send me to a grant-writing workshop and to a course on "Managing Volunteers" at the local community college. I discovered that a great deal of help and support existed both within and without the organization, and I utilized all of it.*

Finally, think about teamwork. You can't be a leader all by yourself. You need to lead others. It would be hard to be effective by yourself. Chapters 4 and 10 discuss teamwork, and those thoughts are also useful in volunteer roles. You must motivate others, communicate constantly, and provide the day-to-day and long-term vision of what you're trying to accomplish. Remember what it has been like for you as a member of a team and what you liked best from your team leader. Practice that artful balance between guiding and directing your team and giving them plenty of opportunity for input and participation. Again, learn by doing, see what works for you and your team, and don't be afraid to make mistakes. The key is to learn from mistakes and be willing to make adjustments along the way.

LEADING VOLUNTEERS

An organization must deserve to have volunteers working for it and with its leaders. No one *has* to volunteer; people have a choice—not only whether they will volunteer but also where they will spend their valuable time and energy.

A good cause and mission are very significant, but equally important is having a quality organi-

zation that has a culture of good spirit and a reputation for being effective. An organization must be a good place to work, even if the "work" is done by volunteers. It needs to be organized and of high quality in order to attract good people.

Conversely, an organization is only as good as the people doing the work, so it's important to attract and retain high-caliber volunteers. And people need to have fun and celebrate accomplishments, both large and small.

Set the Tone

Whether you are leading a project, a work team, or a whole organization, your leadership is key to the spirit and culture of that group or organization. A professor in a nonprofit management class once said that the leader is like a queen bee. Every hive of bees has only one queen, and it is her job to lay all the eggs in the hive, which then become the worker bees. Whatever the temperament of the queen, so it is with the whole hive. Hives that are aggressive, collecting and producing lots of honey, have a queen who is energetic and productive. Some hives are mellower and more easygoing; they don't collect and produce as much honey. This also is the result of the type of queen in that particular hive. Beekeepers see big differences in their various hives, all due to the queens.

> *Mark Udall was a longtime Outward Bound instructor, course director, and program director. He is also a world-class mountaineer and adventurer who has summited the world's 3rd highest peak, Kanchenjunga, as well as peaks in Russia, and attempted other 8,000-meter peaks in the Himalaya, including Mount Everest. He became the executive director of the Colorado Outward Bound School in the 1980s.*
>
> *During those years, Colorado Outward Bound developed many foreign courses, adventuring in Nepal, Alaska, Kenya, and elsewhere. There was a spirit of exploration and adventure throughout the organization.*

Many Colorado Outward Bound instructors came back from their personal international adventures with ideas for courses in Peru, Kenya, and the Himalaya of northern India. We also did annual staff trips on Utah rivers in April, "practicing what we preached," often being caught in snowstorms.

Mark's adventuresome spirit permeated the organization, causing new course areas to be explored and acted upon. Today, Mark is a member of the U.S. House of Representatives for Colorado's 2nd Congressional District—yet another adventure!

Work groups and organizations often take on the attributes of their leader. Your commitment and hard work toward your vision and goal will set the tone for all those around you. You must exemplify the attributes you want others to maintain. A culture of communication and inclusiveness will come from you. A culture of risk taking and support for taking risks will come from you. The ability to laugh at yourself and be open to feedback will come from you. The ability to have fun and celebrate will come from you. Setting the tone is a very important responsibility, one about which you as a leader should be thoughtful and intentional.

Just as Outward Bound leaders show by example how to be leaders in the wilderness and to be accomplished in the different skills they are teaching students, so leaders in volunteer organizations must show by their examples. Setting the tone, creating the culture, and walking the talk of the mission of the organization is key to attracting, motivating, and retaining volunteers.

Draft a Plan

As you take on more and more leadership—whether it is leading a project, work group, or a department, or serving as a board member or high-level leader—spend time thinking through how you want to organize the work you are leading. Draft a plan, knowing that it well may change, but start leading by mapping a course of action for your group. Talk with others invested in the work to assure that your plan will be in keeping with the general direction and overall strategies of the organization.

As you form your group or begin the project, take time to talk with your group about your plan. Get feedback and be open to ideas that may well change your plan, hopefully for the better. The beauty of working with volunteers is the broad range of knowledge that they bring to the task. Many people together build an even better plan than one person alone can do, but it helps to have a draft to work with in the beginning.

Another approach, though, is to start with a blank slate with your group. If you are leading a project and have a team of people to work with to accomplish the project, it can be very empowering to the group to have a planning meeting wherein everyone brainstorms the various strategies that will lead to completion.

As the leader, it is your choice to decide which planning method to use. In any case, it is important to spend time with your group of volunteers so you arrive at a final plan together that everyone feels involved in and, hopefully, can agree to.

Use an Established Volunteer Program

Over the years, a lot of thought has gone into working with volunteers. Because the United States relies so much on mission work being performed by volunteers, organizations now commonly provide structure regarding how volunteers are recruited, trained, and managed.

Does your organization have such a volunteer program? If so, your task is to learn the parameters of that program and then implement it according to the organization's desires. This is also an opportunity to give feedback to your organization. How might the experience for volunteers be improved? How might the current program be enhanced? Make sure you spend enough time in the program. Spend at least one session, and as you build relationships and experience, begin to give feedback. Offer to help implement the recommendations for improvement you may have.

It is not unusual for a volunteer organization to have volunteer leaders—people responsible for a project or department, or someone who has the job of overseeing the organization's volunteer program. Having people volunteer to take on these roles can be of immense value to the organization. It saves the organization from having to pay a salary, or, if funds are just not available, it makes the difference between providing services or not.

For example, a small organization may have many volunteers but not enough full-time paid employees to manage the volunteers and assure their work is organized and meaningful. Having someone volunteer to organize fellow volunteers and to provide leadership and structure will help build the organization's success, both with its volunteers and in its work to provide its services.

Create a Volunteer Program

If your organization doesn't have such a volunteer program in place, you may want to consider the ideas in the next section on creating a more formal volunteer program. Having a more structured program is helpful, especially as you increase the number of volunteers and their duties.

WHAT ARE THE COMPONENTS OF A VOLUNTEER PROGRAM?

Volunteers need to be treated as professionals. Working with a system of volunteer policies and procedures will help you and will help the volunteers. Written policies and procedures help everyone understand how the organization works, what you expect of them, and what they can expect of you, the leader. A volunteer program provides a clear structure that prevents misunderstandings and sets up realistic expectations. A volunteer manual that is kept current and that outlines how everything in the organization works is immensely valuable. The following subsections outline the components of a good volunteer program.

Job Descriptions

What will the volunteers for your organization do? It is very, very important to clearly define their roles and responsibilities. Give job titles to each type of volunteer task that needs to be done. Volunteers can perform work within the organization that would otherwise require many, many paid staff.

At Safehouse for Battered Women and Children, volunteers work as, among other jobs, crisis counselors on the telephone, in-house peer counselors, child advocates, women advocates, victim assistance advocates helping people through the court system, and outreach advocates working with families outside the shelter. Each job has its own title and separate job description.

Job descriptions, especially in complex volunteer organizations where many different jobs exist, also help people decide what kind of volunteer work they want to do. In a smaller organization, there may be only a few job descriptions, but even with a few, it is helpful to be clear about what each job entails. A job description should include the following:

- job title
- who supervises the work
- hours of work per week or month
- description of duties
- length of commitment requested
- any meeting requirements
- how feedback will be given and received—performance review
- qualifications—what qualities and skills you are looking for
- any benefits given and how to access them

This last point is important: Will you provide any meals while the volunteer is working? Will the volunteer have access to any special benefits enjoyed by the organization? For instance, because of the high level of stress involved in working at Safehouse, the organization arranged with students at the Boulder Massage School to volunteer to give free massages to other volunteers and paid staff. Perks like this can help attract and retain good volunteers.

Recruitment and Screening

Once you have job descriptions in place for the different volunteer jobs, think about when volunteers are needed.

Consider Timing

Is your organization small, and does it have an ongoing need for volunteers? Do you have the means to train and orient volunteers one at a time? Do you desire an ongoing open recruitment process?

Or do you have significant training requirements due to the complexity of tasks that volunteers need to perform? Is it important to recruit volunteers for certain time periods? If you live in a university community with many student volunteers, recruiting each semester works well.

Put Out the Word

There are many ways to recruit volunteers. Word of mouth is probably the most effective. People who hear good things about your organization, about what you are doing, will want to volunteer.

Do members of your organization do public speaking about your organization? Speaking to civic and church groups, telling them about the organization's mission and goals, is an excellent way to attract volunteers. By providing a speech or program at their meeting, you let these groups know about your needs and spread the word.

Make flyers and post them strategically in the community. It can also be effective to place announcements that you are looking for volunteers in such locations as your local library, town hall, churches, and other public places.

Sometimes newspapers, radio stations, and even television stations will give public service announcements. These free advertisements for needs in the community are a common venue for volunteer recruiting. Any written or spoken recruitment tool will require a well-written and succinct description of what you are recruiting for and the requirements you desire in your volunteers. This is easy to provide if you have those job descriptions in place.

A relatively new place to announce your need for volunteers is the Internet. Organizations have successfully put out the word on websites such as *craigslist.com*.

Conduct Job Applications and Interviews

Have a volunteer application available for people to fill out. Consider the traits, skills, and qualities your organization needs in its volunteers. Ask enough open-ended questions in the application to understand the background and motivation of each applicant.

Interview and screen each applicant before accepting him or her into your program. Ask them why they are interested and what talents and skills they believe they will bring to the work of the organization. Ask for references. Remember that the organization is only as good as the people who are doing the work, whether they're paid staff or volunteers.

Training and Orientation

Volunteers' value to an organization is built on the training they receive. Quality organizations are careful to make sure they give thought and time to how they orient and train new people coming into the organization. Think through all the tasks that volunteers will do. Then think of everything they will need in order to do those tasks—where supplies are located, procedures for the activities, any legal or organizational requirements for record keeping, where to go for help. See the sidebar "Volunteer Handbook" for suggestions on a document you can provide to all new volunteers.

Establish Training Requirements

Are there special skills volunteers need that might require training? Do you want to make the training mandatory, a requirement for volunteering? Some volunteer work depends upon being well trained and attending all trainings. For example, for peer counselors, a session on active listening and feedback is essential.

Your organization may want to find others in the community to help with specialized training. It is common to find volunteer experts to train volunteers. This is usually a nice opportunity for a professional to do something helpful for your organization. Therapists, lawyers, nurses, doctors, youth specialists, and others who have expertise you may need for your training are usually very willing to help.

Set Up a Training Schedule

Establish a training schedule and make it available during recruitment so volunteers can plan for their training. How long each training session is and how frequently they are offered will depend on the content of the trainings and the availability of the trainers. Some types of volunteer work may require one or two nights a week of training for many weeks. Some may require only one evening. Schedule volunteer trainings at a time when most people can come; usually this will be in the evening.

Welcome Volunteers to the Organization

Whether you are a leader of the training or not, make sure that a welcoming tone is set at the train-

ing. It is important that the organization's leaders be available at the beginning to welcome the new volunteers and give them an opportunity to get to know them. Whoever is leading the volunteer program needs to make sure the volunteers feel appreciated and acknowledged by the organization and its representatives.

Rockland, Maine, has become quite famous for the Farnsworth Museum and its extensive collection of paintings by the Wyeth family—N. C., Andrew, and Jamie. The museum recruits and trains many volunteer docents to lead educational trips for Maine schoolchildren as well as events for adults.

Being a docent at this museum has become one of the favored volunteer opportunities in the area. Always, at the beginning of the extensive training, the executive director of the museum talks to the new volunteers not only about the unique qualities of this small museum but why he is excited to be a part of it. He sets the tone and inspires the new members of the museum family: the new volunteers.

During the trainings, make sure to build in time for people to get to know each other. You

---

VOLUNTEER HANDBOOK

Giving each volunteer a manual outlining the important things they should know is very helpful. This is their handbook, their guide to the work they will do. Be creative as you think of what you would like your volunteers to know. It may include the following:

- welcome letter from the organization leaders as well as the volunteer program's leaders
- mission and vision of the organization
- organizational chart
- names and titles of any paid staff
- list of current volunteers
- contact information for paid staff and volunteers
- volunteer job descriptions
- the organization's policies and procedures, including its process for conflict resolution
- annual calendar of important events and required meetings and trainings

want to build a culture of community for your volunteers. These people are giving their time to your organization, so it is important to think of ways to make their time rewarding, even during the training. It is always helpful to have refreshments, such as cookies, coffee, and tea.

Give people a tour of the facility where they will be working or an overview of where they will be going if they will be working in various places. Orient them to what their surroundings will be when they arrive to do their volunteer work. Make sure they meet the staff they'll work with.

Build realistic expectations about what their volunteer experience is likely to be. If you are also a volunteer, this is a great opportunity for you to talk about your experience with the organization.

Supervision

Volunteers need supervision, especially when they're getting started with an organization. Supervision assures them that they have the support they need to be successful in their volunteer work, and it helps the organization use their talents to the best advantage. Volunteer work takes time and effort, and it serves everyone well to make sure this time and effort is allocated appropriately.

Maintain personnel files for your volunteers, with emergency contact information and any waivers or signed policies. Each file should also include the dates when the person started, the job description, and any performance evaluations that occur. The file should provide a history of the work this volunteer has had with your organization. Files should always be open for the person to view but should otherwise be treated confidentially, as with all staff personnel files.

Make sure each volunteer has a way of checking in at the beginning of his or her work time. Find a way for volunteers to pick up on the work that preceded them, whether it is a written log or a person who briefs them verbally. Volunteers who feel lost or perplexed about what they should be doing don't often last long. You want volunteers to be successful, and adequate supervision is vital to their success.

If a volunteer is having problems or the organization is having problems with the volunteer, immediate intervention is needed. Offer honest feedback and provide clear requests and methods for making a correction. Handle such a situation immediately rather than delaying until a routine performance review is scheduled.

A volunteer at Safehouse had all the right intentions. She really wanted to help and showed up on time for her shifts. However, the other volunteers and staff began to complain to me that she was not always appropriate in her work with the residents of the shelter. She often shared too much of her own dilemmas in her personal life and sometimes gave them advice that was not correct or contained a different message than what the organization conveyed.

I talked with the volunteer coordinator, and we outlined the problems with specific examples of the things we wanted her to change. The next time she came in for her shift, the coordinator sat down with her privately and gave her the feedback. The coordinator described specifically how the problem incidents could have been handled differently.

The volunteer really appreciated the feedback and began to realize how and where she had erred. She improved and went on to finish her six-month commitment successfully.

Performance Reviews

In any meaningful work, feedback and means for improvement are always beneficial. This is also true with volunteer work. Quality volunteer organizations treat the volunteers as professionals by taking the time to sit down at predetermined intervals to tell the volunteer how he or she is doing and recommending any improvements that may be necessary or desired.

There are many, many forms for performance reviews. Usually the job description provides the basis for identifying the areas to be discussed. Whatever method you use, make sure that it is used uniformly with all volunteers. Consistency and fairness are very important in treating volunteers as professionals.

Also, remember to give adequate time for the volunteer to comment and give feedback to the organization as part of the performance review. Performance reviews are not just about the worker; they are also an opportunity to learn how the organization can be more effective through the eyes and thoughts of those closest to carrying out the organization's mission.

Document these volunteer performance assessments, and include them in each volunteer's personnel file. This can be very useful if a volunteer should want to use your organization as a reference for future employment or for application to graduate school, etc. Just as businesses maintain files on their paid employees, so too it is important to maintain files on volunteer workers.

Appreciation and Rewards

All volunteer programs have ways to recognize and appreciate the work that has been given to the organization. Of course, the most useful and important recognition is steady feedback and ongoing communication with the individual volunteers. However, celebrations and rewards also have their place, especially in mission-driven volunteer organizations.

Setting aside a particular time and place to celebrate volunteers is important. Your organization's resources will determine how you want to do it. Thank-you gatherings can range from a simple potluck dinner to a formal catered event. The important thing is to do something for your volunteers. Be creative. Make the celebration fun. Sometimes skits are a great way to highlight events and people.

At Outward Bound, we have Final Dinners. On the last night of an Outward Bound course, a special meal is prepared and course participants plan skits that highlight key events during the course. The skits offer a great way to reminisce about both the hard times and the peak times. It enables the group to laugh and to share pride in its accomplishments.

This type of celebration can also be the setting for giving special awards to people who have performed outstanding service for the organization. The problem with "outstanding" awards is that you might leave someone out. Really, every volunteer is outstanding, and you want to find ways to acknowledge each one of them. It's important to make sure to find a way to recognize every individual who is contributing.

If your organization has a newsletter, highlighting volunteers in each issue is a way to recognize their service. Occasional press releases to local newspapers are another method. But remember, often the most cherished rewards for volunteer work is a compliment of "good job" and of seeing the results in the community of the work that has been done. Make sure that letters of appreciation from the community are shared with volunteers. That is often the greatest reward.

Conflict Resolution

Any time you work with groups of people, conflicts are likely to arise once in a while. At Outward Bound, where course participants are often confined to tight and close quarters (especially on boats), conflicts are common. But conflict is a normal part of the formation of an effective working group or team, as described in Chapter 4, Building Trust, Building a Team, in Part I, Leadership Fundamentals.

As a leader, it is important that you stay involved in your organization and keep an eye out for conflict so that you are able to identify it as soon as possible. Conflict management is important in every organization because it helps deal with problems before they become significant. It is important to identify the conflict with the people involved and then facilitate resolving it, as with an Outward Bound group.

It is important that you, or whoever is facilitating the conflict, stay neutral and objective during these conversations. Any bias will compromise the results. Your organization's process for conflict resolution is an item to include in your volunteer handbook (see the sidebar above) as part of its policies and procedures.

First, facilitate calm listening. Bring the people who are having the conflict together privately at a time when they are able to be calm. Ask each person in turn to give his or her point of view, identifying his or her feelings, while the others listen until each is finished. After everyone has heard the differing points of view, see whether there is enough understanding to resolve the conflict.

Next, mediate reasonable requests. If there is not, ask each person to state what he or she needs to be able to move forward and continue to work with the other people involved. Then ask if each can accommodate the stated requests. Usually this resolves the problem.

As a last resort, consider termination. If it does not, or if the conflict continues despite these conversations, the next step is deciding whether one or all of the parties can continue to volunteer, knowing that it undermines the morale of others.

Termination

We always think of volunteer organizations in the most positive way. We are all working together to carry out a mission that we care about. We are "doing well by doing good." Yet occasionally problems arise, and it is critical for the health and well-being not only of the recipients of your organization's service or work but also of the culture and health of the organization itself to deal with such situations. Letting a problem with a volunteer escalate or continue can be a huge disincentive to other volunteers trying to carry out their duties successfully and happily.

Charles was a volunteer with a local youth organization. He and other volunteers staffed the after-school activities, provided snacks, organized games, and helped students with their homework. Charles signed up for a one-semester commitment and attended all the volunteer trainings provided by the organization.

Several months into the semester, Charles started coming in late or not showing up at all for his shift. He also didn't notify anyone that he was going to be absent or late. It was difficult for the students with whom he had bonded, who looked forward to seeing him, and it was difficult for the staff, because they depended on him to help run the program. It was also difficult for other volunteers who were called at the last minute to take his place.

The director of the program spoke to him about the problem, and Charles promised to show up on time. He did for a few weeks but then started falling into the same pattern of tardiness or being absent. It became apparent that he was not committed to the program, and other volunteers were becoming resentful of having to fill in for him. He was asked to leave the program.

Develop a policy stating when and how a volunteer may be asked to discontinue their work with the organization. Place this policy in your organization's volunteer handbook (see the sidebar above). All conversations with a problem volunteer should be confidential and documented in writing; place the documentation in that volunteer's personnel file. The termination policy should include the following points:

■ If a volunteer is doing anything illegal, he or she will be asked to leave immediately. Charges may be filed.

■ If a volunteer is not operating within the policies of the organization, he or she will be informed about the problem and will be asked to comply. If the volunteer fails to comply, he or she will be asked to leave.

■ If there are recurring complaints about a volunteer, either from people in the community or from within the organization, the volunteer will be informed of the complaints and will be given the opportunity to discuss the complaints with his or her supervisor. A plan of action will be designed to address and rectify the complaints. If complaints continue and are not resolved, the volunteer will be asked to leave.

■ If a volunteer is having performance problems, is not successfully completing the work, is continually tardy, or has poor-quality work, a verbal discussion will occur with a time set for improvement. If improvement does not occur, a written warning will be given. If the written warning still does not resolve the problem, the volunteer will be asked to leave.

Maintaining Momentum

Organizations and even working groups are like people: Each one has its own character and personality or culture. Each one is different and changes as leadership changes. It is a leader's role and responsibility to keep the spirit and the morale of the group and/or organization high and to keep the group performing. As a leader, you set the tone for the group, as mentioned above. Like the beehive's queen bee, your manner will affect those around you.

Stay Positive

This is not always an easy thing to do. The saying "It's lonely at the top" is quite true because your job is to present a positive attitude even though you may not be feeling positive. Showing good spirit, especially in a time of difficulty, is very, very important in any organization. This is especially true in a volunteer organization where people are not paid to be there, but choose to be there. For example, Outward Bound leaders of a group in the field must show courage and calmness when encountering challenging events, even though they may not be feeling courageous or calm.

I was once leading an Outward Bound group with another instructor in Joshua Tree National Monument in California. We had planned a rigorous itinerary because the group looked strong on their applications and medical forms.

The fifth day of the course was an especially long day with difficult routefinding through several different canyons. One of the participants turned her ankle, which slowed her down and, in turn, slowed the group down. As late afternoon approached, we realized that we still had far to go. The group's progress was slow. We were making our way through canyons with a lot of boulders and fallen trees to climb over and around. It would be very difficult to find our way in the dark, even though everyone was equipped with headlamps. Also, there was no place to camp except our destination, due to the difficult terrain.

As darkness began to fall, people were getting tired and grumpy. The other instructor and I were also pretty tired and worried about the group, but we kept up a banter of conversation and said (in truth) that this was what Outward Bound is all about: having a difficult time of it but knowing that we can do it! As we hiked through the difficult terrain, the other instructor and I moved from one person to the next, spending time with each one. This was very effective in keeping their energy up and helping them see the progress they were making.

We finally arrived at our designated campsite around 10:00 at night, having left at 7:00 that morning. Amazingly, once we had finished dinner, everyone wanted to sit in the circle for the debrief longer than usual to talk about the day and the accomplishment.

Acknowledge Teamwork

Another key to maintaining your organization's momentum is acknowledging the important contributions of your volunteers as part of the team. Give recognition to those who have enabled the organization to reach its goals. Peter Drucker, in his book *Managing the Nonprofit Organization*, writes:

The leaders who work most effectively, it seems to me, never say "I." And that's not because they have trained themselves not to say "I." They don't think "I." They think "we"; they think "team." They understand their job to be to make the team function. They accept the responsibility and don't sidestep it, but "we" gets the credit.

Respond to Changing Circumstances and Setbacks

Another element is to remember those who are your organization's constituencies and to keep in touch with them. Drucker mentions that an organization is serving community constituents, and he talks about keeping abreast of changes needed to serve them. These constituents whom the organization is serving will signal when any changes may be needed.

Be willing to be innovative. Be willing to change. Make sure you and the organization stay open and notice when changes and adjustments to activities and services are needed. Momentum and forward movement for a group or organization is rarely in a straight line. Being open to different ways of operating and willing to make adjustments, depending on the needs of your constituents, yet all the while staying within your mission, keeps the organization fresh and motivated.

Sometimes projects suffer setbacks and are beset by obstacles. Members of the group become discouraged, just as our group in Joshua Tree did. Help the group see their successes to date. Break down the project into smaller tasks so that your volunteers don't become overwhelmed with the big picture. Spend time with the most disaffected in your group, giving them encouragement and recognition. Spending time with them one-on-one, hearing their concerns, and working to address those concerns is very effective.

Give Your Team a Boost

Have fun! Plan something that gives your group members a boost. Perhaps spend some time to-gether besides just working on the goal and instead let people enjoy each other. Usually this involves food. Or bring in something silly to a meeting that makes people laugh. Is your group stumped by a problem? Offer a quick puzzle that they can work on and solve. It's a great metaphor for how your group really can succeed.

Be creative. Use your own ingenuity to come up with ideas that you believe will keep your team moving forward. This is inherent in leadership. Spend time thinking about what might help your group the most and take the risk of trying it. Don't worry if it flops; at least you're trying, and your group will appreciate that. Remember to play.

My teenage son had a skinny, weird-looking rubber chicken. He loved using it to tell chicken-crossing-the-road jokes. Once I took it to work with me in my briefcase because we were going to have an all-day meeting trying to solve some difficult budget problems. In the middle of some contentious discussions, I dropped the chicken onto the middle of the table. It surprised everyone and immediately broke the tension. We had a good laugh and renewed our discussion in an easier mood.

Most of all, don't feel that you have to control or be responsible for your group's feelings and attitudes. As a leader, you want to be responsive to morale, keeping it up and moving the group forward. But ultimately, it is every individual's responsibility to be present and to do his or her best as a participating team member.

MAKING MEETINGS WORK

How often have you attended meetings that lost direction, went past their allotted time, and failed to meet the goals of the meeting's original purpose? Many times I have heard leaders say, "I wasted so much time today. I was in meetings constantly and never got my work done."

But I believe that meetings *are* the work of

leaders. Leaders work through other people, and so meetings are necessary to develop understanding of the tasks and goals at hand, to receive input, to make decisions, and to build an inclusive organization. Meetings bring people together to discuss problems, to solve problems, and to agree on next steps. Meetings are where you share information. Meetings build teamwork. Meetings give others the opportunity to participate, to feel involved and valued.

Meetings are even more important with volunteers. This is where they see the big picture, where they are informed of what is happening, and where they are able to spend time with others who are also invested in the mission for which all are working.

Meetings take thoughtful planning, however, to be effective. In *The Tao of Leadership*, John Heider says, "The wise leader establishes a clear and wholesome climate in the group room. In the light of awareness, the group naturally acts in a wholesome manner." Making sure that meetings are effective is an important leadership skill, and it's especially important when working with volunteers, who prize their time and want their volunteering to be worthwhile.

First of all, consider whether a meeting is truly needed. Unnecessary meetings are sure to discourage people from attending future ones. Be willing to cancel a meeting if you do not have a clear and compelling agenda.

What Kind of Meeting?

Now consider what type of meeting you need to hold. Different kinds of meetings serve different purposes. It is important to be clear about what type of meeting you are calling so that the meeting participants have appropriate expectations for what their responsibilities will be and so that they can be prepared.

Regular Information-Sharing Meetings

Standing meetings occur on a regular basis—usually weekly or monthly. This is a large meeting, a monthly volunteer meeting, for instance, that is required for all volunteers. These meetings bring people together to update each other on the ongoing work of the organization, report back on accomplishments since the last meeting, and outline the key strategies of the next week or month. This is important in helping volunteers see where their individual work fits into the whole organization.

Be clear with volunteers that such a meeting is not a decision-making meeting but, rather, is for communicating new information, giving reminders of important information, and providing opportunity for feedback. Have a schedule of these meetings posted in the volunteer handbook (see the sidebar above) or in the orientation materials the volunteers receive when they first begin their volunteer time with your organization. Setting regular dates and times for this type of meeting is very helpful, such as the first Tuesday of every month, 7:00–8:30 PM.

Planning Meetings

In planning meetings, people with different perspectives are involved so they can give input to the creation of a new plan of action. These meetings may occur over a specific period of time to create a new initiative, program, or event. Their focus is much narrower than a regular information-sharing meeting.

Information-Gathering Meetings

Sometimes meetings are needed solely to seek input about a problem or challenge facing the organization. When a variety of perspectives are needed in order to make an informed decision, you hold an information-gathering meeting just to receive feedback, and you, as a leader, primarily listen. Public hearings are this sort of meeting: no decisions are being made; public officials are simply gathering input from their constituents. This type of meeting is often part of a strategic planning process as well, wherein a planning committee poses certain questions to members of the organization and listens to their comments and observations about those questions.

Decision-Making Meetings

When a group needs to summarize the information at hand and make a decision—whether it's a decision about an issue facing the organization, a new policy to take to the board, or a new initiative to implement—a decision-making meeting is appropriate. The number of people needed in a decision-making meeting is usually less than for an informational meeting. It is very hard to have a large group making decisions. Seven to fifteen people is an optimal number for problem solving and decision making.

Crisis-Management Meetings

When something difficult happens and all involved with the organization need to be briefed about what has happened and how the event is being handled, you need to convene a crisis-management meeting. This is very important for building trust in the organization's leadership and the organization's ability to meet difficulties competently. If you are on the board of an organization, assuring that good information is provided in a timely way will be one of your roles.

Occasionally Outward Bound has a significant field emergency involving a serious injury or even a fatality. Although these events are rare, one of the first things we do as leaders is clearly communicate to the members of the organization the three critical elements of who, what, and where. A meeting is held for all available staff and volunteers to brief them on the circumstances and what is being done to address the problem. We have found that quick and decisive information sharing (making sure that the information is accurate) builds trust that everything is under control. This greatly reduces rumors and keeps crisis events from becoming magnified in the rumor mill.

This also happens with the student group in the field. If there is a serious

event during the course, the course participants are gathered together and given the information, as it is known. They are most often given the choice, as a group, whether to continue the course. Almost without fail, students decide to continue on with the course, feeling assured that the event has been and is being handled well by Outward Bound and that they can and should continue on. In fact, it is usually helpful to stay together to continue to process the event.

Set an Effective Agenda

When you announce a meeting, identify the type of meeting it will be and include an agenda. Create and distribute the agenda, identifying the items to be discussed, well ahead of the meeting time. This allows everyone to think about the items to be discussed. It also allows people to identify additional items that you may not have considered.

Allocating time for each agenda item also helps give structure and organization to the meeting. On the draft agenda, be clear about what time will be set aside for announcements only and what agenda items will include discussion and feedback. Be sure to allocate appropriate times for both types of items as well as for questions and clarifications, if needed.

Be careful to keep the agenda reasonable for the amount of time you have scheduled for the meeting. It is frustrating to everyone if the agenda is too packed with items you're not able to either fully present or discuss or if a too-full agenda makes the meeting run later than scheduled.

It is also a good idea to assign specific agenda items to different people. This is a nice way to be inclusive and build team spirit.

When setting an agenda for a decision-making meeting, be clear before the meeting and on the agenda about what items need a decision. It is also important to identify agenda items that are for input only, rather than discussion or decisions.

Who Should Attend the Meeting?

This very important question deserves considerable thought. Who attends a meeting will have a significant effect on what happens at the meeting. The question of who should attend any given meeting also is affected by the type of organization you are involved in. Is your organization hierarchical, with the leader as an authority figure and a top-down management style? Or is your organization more horizontal, one that includes as many people and as many points of view as possible in decisions?

Most successful mission-driven volunteer organizations have a culture of inclusiveness. They work to provide a voice and a means for input on decisions, especially those decisions that affect the volunteers. Most paid and volunteer staff work at a particular organization because they believe in its goals and want very much to be involved and to help in every way they can. They are invested, and you want them to be.

It is a good idea to think about those who will be most affected by a decision. Some of the biggest organizational conflicts result from different expectations about who will make a decision. Including group members who represent those most affected is often a guideline for who should attend a decision-making meeting. This builds trust in and transparency for the organization.

The Outward Bound Sea Program in Maine was recently undergoing a lot of change. One of the most important was deciding on a new design for the boats to be used for future sailing courses. The existing wooden pulling boats were revered among the sea staff as stable, seaworthy, and excellent for teaching sailing. They had served the program well since the 1960s.

A weekend meeting was held on Hurricane Island, in Maine, by Outward Bound's wilderness board, the decision makers. The draft plans for the new boat were posted for all to see. The proposed new boats would be made of fiberglass and would contain fewer students.

This change was very controversial among the sea staff. Meetings were held during the weekend to explain the reasons for the proposed change and to get input from these staff. It was significant that these meetings were held on Hurricane Island, the historical home of the Sea Program.

Although it was clear that the staff were not decision makers, this was an opportunity for the board members to hear from the staff and consider their input when making a final decision. This also helped the staff feel that they had an opportunity to voice their concerns and that their opinions were valued.

Homogenous or Heterogeneous Groups?

Much has been discussed and studied about homogenous versus heterogeneous groups and the kinds of decisions they make. If a focused perspective—one in alignment with the proposal being put forth for a decision—is preferred, a homogenous group will arrive at the decision fairly quickly.

If a variety of points of view and different perspectives are desired, make sure that your group is mixed, with many differing opinions. Although a heterogeneous group can sometimes make for a contentious meeting, with good facilitation and good ground rules all these views will be valued and considered worthwhile for consideration.

Recently I was in a meeting wherein a major decision had to be made about a significant position our environmental organization was about to take on a very public issue. The position would have significant press coverage and might not be unanimously supported by the organization's 8,000 members and donors.

There were varying points of view among the group that had gathered to make the decision. The participants in the meeting represented the different constituencies and opinions within the organization: the policy and program people, the staff focused on membership, the development department representing the donors to the organization.

The proposal and the reasoning behind it were presented. Each group member was given ample time to ask questions and pose concerns. As each concern was discussed and the proposal modified to address each concern, the final decision encompassed far more than the original proposal had. This thoughtful discussion that included all points of view led to a much better decision than would have happened without the meeting. And, very importantly, everyone in the group could support the decision and work very hard to carry it out.

Although heterogeneous decision making takes more meeting time, it usually saves implementation time because the differing points of view within the organization have been worked out. This type of meeting also usually gets buy-in from those who might oppose the decision otherwise.

How to Facilitate an Information-Sharing Meeting

So you've determined what type of meeting you will be holding, you've created and distributed an agenda well ahead of time, and you've decided who will attend the meeting. The meeting is about to begin—now what do you do? What follows are some tips for being a good meeting facilitator of an information-sharing meeting, then a decision-making meeting. These are the most common types of meetings that volunteer organizations regularly convene. The other meeting types noted above are variations on the themes outlined in these two primary types of meetings. The key for you as facilitator is to achieve that balance between moving the meeting along, not letting it become hijacked by other individuals or agendas, and assuring there is full participation by all members.

Setting Up the Meeting Space

Think about the seating arrangement you want. Depending on the size of the group and the avail-

able meeting space, a circle or semicircle is always preferable to a lecture seating arrangement. Make sure the room is set up the way you want it before the meeting is scheduled to begin.

It is a good idea to post the agenda in some way, such as written on a blackboard or a flip chart, so all who are at the meeting can see it. Remember that agendas should always be considered drafts until the meeting begins and you have given participants the opportunity to add any additional items they would like discussed.

It is a good idea to provide refreshments. Having some simple snacks available is a small gesture of thanks to the volunteers. Make sure the food is set out before the meeting begins so people have a chance to get some refreshments and chat a bit before you start the meeting.

Getting Started

Begin the meeting on time, even if everyone is not there. This sets an important tone: It lets the participants know that it is important to be on time and that you will proceed as scheduled. Those who make the effort to be on time will greatly appreciate it. If you wait for latecomers to arrive before you start the meeting, you reward tardiness; by starting on time, you reward timeliness and show respect for your volunteers' time.

Open the meeting with something that sets a positive tone for the meeting: an inspirational story, reading, or account of something that has happened since your last meeting. As much as possible, tie your opening remarks to the work the volunteers are doing. Something I have found valuable is to read a letter from a constituent who benefited from the organization's services. Sharing this gratitude from a recipient of services inspires everyone and reminds them why they are there.

Make sure everyone is introduced and knows one another. Nametags help, especially if it is a new or large group. Volunteers who work different shifts don't always know each other if they work at the organization at different times. If necessary, allow time for brief introductions or an ice-breaking activity (for some ideas, see "Building Your Team" in Chapter 4, Building Trust, Building a Team, in Part I, Leadership Fundamentals).

Confirm the agenda and ask for additional items. Adjust the time allotments to reflect the added items, making sure you can end the meeting at the designated time. If an additional agenda item will take significant time, negotiate with the person who added it and with the group as a whole, deciding what on the agenda can be replaced and held for the next meeting; or ask the person if the added item could be addressed at the next meeting.

It's important that meetings stay within their allocated time. It is often helpful to ask for a volunteer timekeeper who will alert you and the group five or ten minutes before an agenda item's allocated time is up.

Designate a note taker to document your meeting and provide information to those not able to attend. The note taker can also make notes on the flip chart summarizing the agenda items as they are covered in the meeting. Post the meeting notes in a prominent place so everyone is able to see them after the meeting.

Set ground rules, especially at a group's first meeting. Ground rules include things such as asking people to stay present at the meeting until break time, to raise their hand if they have something to say, to allow each speaker to finish without interruption, etc. It is a good idea to ask the group what ground rules they want to include, but have some of your own in mind to get them started. It is also important for you to know the ground rules you feel are necessary in order to have a successful meeting.

Keeping the Meeting Focused

As the facilitator, you have two primary tasks: keeping the agenda moving and making sure everyone in the group stays engaged.

To keep the agenda moving, pay attention to the topic at hand; if someone starts straying off into other topics, bring the discussion back to the current agenda item. You may want to create a "tabled bin" or space on another flip chart to list items that come up that can't be discussed at that meeting, just so people know these items will not be forgotten and will come up at another meeting.

Rely on your timekeeper to help you and the group keep track of the agenda. If an agenda item begins to run over its alloted time, you may need to negotiate with the group to allot more time for that item and take time away from another item. Or you might have to adjust the agenda by moving items to the "tabled bin." But it is important to keep to the overall meeting schedule.

Most of all, be a leader in the meeting. Be a clear and strong facilitator. Don't hesitate to intervene if the meeting starts to go off course. Bring it back to the agenda. Meetings that amble and lose focus generally lose participants.

Keeping Everyone Engaged

To keep everyone in the group engaged in the meeting, there are a few pitfalls to watch out for.

First, share the podium! Arrange the agenda so that items that will be presented by others alternate with your presentations. Having one person do all the talking will quickly put people to sleep!

If the group is new, you will need to learn what the needs of the particular group are. Sometimes certain people talk a lot and dominate the discussion; sometimes the group is shy and no one asks questions.

Be careful not to let one person monopolize the meeting with questions or comments. Gently interrupt these "talkers" by thanking them for their input and perspective and then ask if someone else would like to comment. It also is appropriate to say something such as, "Your comments have been very helpful. Now I'd like to hear from others on this subject."

Getting a quiet group to participate more fully can be daunting. Reward any quiet person who speaks up by showing enthusiasm for their comments. Encourage questions by always beginning your response with something like, "I'm glad you asked that!" or "That's a really important point."

Ask for additional comments from others. Usually once a few people start commenting, others will follow, especially if you keep your speaking to a minimum, thus leaving lots of room for others. Make your comments positive and encouraging.

If necessary, you can use timed group go-arounds to ensure that everyone gets a chance to contribute and no one person dominates. For instance, you can ask everyone to give their opinion in one or two minutes as you go around the circle. As the group matures, the nature of its interactions will change and these kinds of interventions will become less necessary.

And finally, make sure you end the meeting on time. This is as important as beginning on time. Make sure participants know what's expected of them as a result of the meeting and that they know when the next meeting will occur.

Managing Conflicts

What if an argument occurs within the meeting? Conflicting and differing points of view occur normally, and they are actually very constructive for an organization. The key is to ensure that these heated discussions are respectful and that they follow the ground rules you've established.

What you want to avoid is a monopoly of the meeting by two people having such a discussion. Asking for other perspectives and calling on others wishing to speak by turns as hands are raised usually prevents such a monopoly. If it seems that no one else is as interested in the argument as the two people involved, suggest that they table their discussion for a smaller meeting focused on that topic; then make sure that meeting occurs, and facilitate it if necessary.

How to Facilitate a Decision-Making Meeting

A decision-making meeting shares many of the elements of an information-sharing and discussion meeting, but it also has its own unique differences. First, be clear in the beginning about who will be the final decision makers. The determination of who will make a certain decision may be yours alone to make, or it may be the result of the organization's structure, such as bylaws—or it may be decided by another decision-making meeting, such as a board of directors' meeting. Also, guard against changing a decision unless the decision-making process is revisited by this original group.

Agreeing on a Decision-Making Process

Next, clarify ahead of time what process you will use for making the decision. Will you make a decision by a simple majority, by a two-thirds majority, by consensus, or by some other means? If you use a majority basis to make a decision, you will facilitate discussion on the various points of information, then call for a vote.

Consensus decision making is the more common process used in volunteer organizations. However, it's important to be sure that everyone understands what consensus really is. There are many misunderstandings about consensus decision making.

Preparing for Consensus Decision Making

The goal of consensus is to reach agreement with everyone in the room so that when the meeting is over, everyone will work to support the actions resulting from the decision.

I was recently part of a large effort in the state of Maine to bring together many nonprofits with similar goals to form an entity that would be more persuasive and effective toward meeting our common goals. In forming the group and deciding how we would govern ourselves, an agreed-upon method for decision making became a key question.

We decided we wanted to reach agreements by consensus, but many in the group had not used this process before. We hired an experienced consultant to lead a half-day session of consensus decision-making training in which we actually used this method to make a significant decision.

332 LEADING A VOLUNTEER ORGANIZATION

Consensus decision making is not always easy to achieve, but it is the best way to engage the strategic participants in accomplishing the goal or goals of the decision.

First, give the participants time to think about a clear written proposal and to discuss it with others if necessary before coming to the meeting. Then make sure the proposal is also presented in writing in some way at the meeting; it could be written on a blackboard or it could be handed out on a printed agenda.

Next, make sure that everyone understands the proposal, has the same information, and is "on the same page" so that there are no misunderstandings during the discussion.

Make sure you give ample time for full discussion. Also, as with an information-sharing meeting, see that a few people do not dominate the discussion. I have found it is helpful to go around the room and specifically ask the participants for their thoughts. Some may choose to pass, but at least they have been given the opportunity to speak.

Building Consensus

As everyone gives their thoughts and opinions, begin to judge for yourself whether you are beginning to hear agreement or if there are a few items that are preventing agreement. Be a keen listener so that you can distill those certain items that may be sticking points.

Point out to the group the areas of agreement you are hearing. If they all agree, note these agreements somehow—on a flip chart or blackboard, for instance.

Then identify those items where there still is disagreement. Work to break down the progressing discussion into smaller segments. Build agreement on certain aspects, make a note of them, and move on to items that need further discussion.

Big, general discussions lead to frustration. Identifying where agreements have been found will give the group a feeling of accomplishment and encourage them to keep working.

Keep track of the time and remind the group when necessary. A timekeeper in this setting is also helpful. If you feel the group is getting close to full agreement and time is running out, ask the group whether they are willing to stay a bit longer. If some participants are unable to stay, try to move the issue to closure.

If time is running out, sometimes you will have good results by stopping the discussion and noting

---

STEPS TOWARD BUILDING CONSENSUS

Your role as the facilitator of a consensus decision-making meeting is to make sure that these steps are followed:

1. See that a clear and concise proposal is made to the group, preferably ahead of time and preferably in writing.
2. At the beginning of the discussion of the proposal, make sure that everyone understands it. Allow time for questions and clarifications.
3. Ensure that all perspectives are communicated at the meeting, that all participants have an opportunity to speak about their point of view.
4. List in writing the points of agreement.
5. Identify items where there still is disagreement, and break the discussion down into smaller segments.
6. Describe the emerging solution and ask each member to state whether they can support it. Everyone does not need to agree with the decision, but everyone needs to agree to *support* the decision and not work against it.

the time constraint. Identify and state what you believe is the prevalent solution for the decision, then go around the room and ask each member to state whether they can support the stated solution.

What you want to accomplish is building agreement. That does not mean that everyone has the same feelings about the solution; it means they will agree to support it. This is the greatest misunderstanding about consensus decision making—not everyone needs to be in full support of the decision, but everyone needs to agree to support the decision and not work against it once the meeting is finished.

If you cannot reach agreement, discuss the next steps with the group. Do they want to schedule another meeting? Are there some things that can be done in the meantime to address the key concerns? Identify the next steps clearly, note them on the flip chart or chalkboard, and put them in the meeting notes. Set a time for the next meeting, making sure that all participants can attend.

Getting Feedback

It is helpful in these types of meetings to save five or ten minutes at the end to get feedback on how the meeting went. Outward Bound uses the plus-delta model (see Figure 8 in Chapter 12, Managing Change in the Workplace, in Part III, Taking Leadership into Your Professional Life): Participants say what they liked and what went well in the meeting (the "plus") as well as what could be improved for the next meeting (the "delta"—a Greek letter used as a mathematical and scientific symbol for change). This helps identify any underlying complaints that may exist and also helps everyone see the positives. It is also good feedback for you as the meeting facilitator.

STARTING A NEW VOLUNTEER ORGANIZATION

If you have been growing in your work in the community and find yourself in more and more leadership roles, you may come upon a need in your community that you would like to address through the creation of a new program or orga-

nization. Maybe you have seen a need and have gotten an idea about how to address that need.

Mary O'Rear was a high-school English teacher who began to notice that quite a few girls in her classes were struggling with problems related to eating disorders. She began to read about this problem and decided that she wanted to do something to prevent this problem, which was becoming more and more prevalent at this high school.

Mary began to talk with other women in the community about what she was seeing to find out whether other adults in the community were also seeing this problem. They were. Mary decided to hold a conference for teenage girls, focusing on presentations and discussions on body image, society's messages about body image, the way food is presented to us as consumers, and education about healthy eating. She had a good idea, and others joined her. All were volunteers.

Mary organized this conference around ten years ago, with great success. Each year the conference grew, focusing on other issues facing teenage girls but always relating to self-esteem and body image. Well-known speakers who had done research on the issues were invited. Mary raised money to pay for these speakers and for other aspects of the conference. Adults began to attend, along with teenage girls, to learn more so they could do better work with young women.

Mary's efforts grew into the formation of a nonprofit called "Mainely Girls." It functions today all over the state of Maine as an organization that addresses issues specific to teenage girls. Mary left teaching to become its executive director. Now conferences and other programs for girls occur in many places in the state.

This all started from Mary's seeing a need, learning about the issues, gathering others around her, and creating a service to address the needs. Mary includes girls in the organizing and running of this organization, and it has become well known throughout the state and nationally.

Develop a Clear Vision for the Organization

Volunteer organizations, whether informal or organized into legal 501(c)(3) entities, start with a vision, an idea of something that you believe needs doing. Josh Miner, founder of Outward Bound in America, writes in *Outward Bound USA* about the importance of "having a good idea." All kinds of things can, and generally do, happen from that point. An important part of leadership is having that vision, that good idea, and charting a way to carry that idea forward. Josh had the idea of bringing Outward Bound to the United States from England, and he led the way to make it happen by talking to others about his good idea and gaining their support and involvement.

Volunteer organizations exist to make a difference in the world, in a nation's society, and in the lives of individuals. An important task is to carefully and thoughtfully define and clarify what it is you want your specific program or organization to do. As you begin to think about forming a volunteer organization, consider the following six steps:

1. **Think about your commitment to your idea:** Will it really make a difference? Are you excited about it? Does this idea give you energy and a desire to work on it? To work hard on it? Are you committed to the idea?

   Nothing is ever done well without a high sense of commitment. Leadership is not about *thinking* about leading. It is about being *committed* to your idea and wanting your idea to be a reality and to successfully accomplish the goal of enriching society and your community through your idea.

2. **Talk with others about your idea:** Begin to explore your idea with others and get their feedback. Organizations are all about teamwork, so for your idea to succeed, it's

important that you to begin to see whether others can feel the same excitement about it that you do. Communicating the vision of your idea to others is critical. Leadership is about communicating with others, persuading others of the worth of your idea, and getting others excited in a way that will motivate them to help you.

Motivating others about your idea is important. You can't make an idea a reality on your own. You will need help. A leader is not a leader without followers. You must convince others of the merits of your idea and begin the process of building a team of supporters and helpers. Plus, others' ideas may broaden, flesh out, and enrich your idea. Does their feedback expand your thinking?

3. **Find out what volunteer organizations already exist in your community:** Is another organization already implementing your idea or something similar to it? Duplicating what already exists is not something you should consider doing. Research what volunteer activities and services addressing your idea already exist in your community.

   The United Way or Volunteers for America are two places to start. Often communities have resource centers that can guide your search. Community foundations and other grant makers usually have good information about what volunteer organizations exist. The local library may also have community lists of nonprofits in your area. If you find an organization that is doing what your idea entails, go and visit this organization to see if you can become involved in its efforts.

4. **Find out if an organization that already exists in your community will work for your idea:** As a result of your search, is there an organization that might take on your idea? If you find an organization that is doing similar work but not exactly the work that you are inspired to do, go and talk with the organization's leaders

and find out if there is any interest in your idea. Leadership often means being a salesperson, convincing others that your idea has merit and deserves their help.

5. **Find out if there is a need in the community for your idea:** The search in step 3 can tell you what activities and services already exist in your community, but assessing the true need for your service is critical. Document your thoughts about the reasons why the need for your idea exists. As you talk with community people, get them to define the need as well, and document what they say. This will be important later as you work to gather resources to support your organization.

6. **Think through what activities you see your program or organization doing:** What will it look like when people are at work in your organization? Who will it serve? What will you do to serve those people? How will you serve them? The particulars of where and when can be decided later, after you have defined your organization's mission and developed a plan of action (see below).

Decide on Structure: Informal or Formal Nonprofit Status?

How do you know whether you want your idea to be carried out within the structure of a nonprofit organization or an informal volunteer organization? Usually it depends on what resources you need.

Do you need money to accomplish your idea? Will you want to ask others to give money to your idea? Do you want to be able to offer the incentive of a tax deduction to those who contribute? Do you want to ask charitable foundations or corporations for money? If the answer to any of these questions is yes, a federal nonprofit 501(c)(3) status is necessary.

However, if you can accomplish your idea solely through your own efforts or the volunteer efforts of others and do not require significant fund-raising, informal not-for-profit status might suffice. Can you support your idea through simply doing the work to make your idea happen? Are you willing to donate materials or funds yourself or to find others to give these without any kind of tax deduction?

Setting Up a Formal Nonprofit

If you are planning on starting a formal nonprofit organization, you will need to do several things after defining your organization's purpose and identity:

- You will need to find a lawyer—hopefully pro bono—who will help you with the legal requirements of articles of incorporation, bylaws, etc.
- You will need to recruit founding board members.
- You will need to submit a letter to the Internal Revenue Service requesting 501(c)(3) status and send in accompanying legal documents.

Decide on Staffing Structure

Another thing to think about is how complicated or simple you want your organization to be. In addition to having volunteers to implement different aspects of your idea, do you need to hire a few paid employees? How will you manage the volunteers? If you plan on paying staff, you must be sure to follow worker compensation laws and overall compensation laws. Will you need to pay employment taxes? Do you need any kind of liability insurance to protect yourself and others from any accident, injury, or some kind of emergency? Consulting a lawyer or accountant is important if you are doing this on your own.

Develop a Mission Statement

Once you have gone through the above six steps to develop a clear vision for your idea and have decided to move forward, begin to think about crafting your mission statement. Whether your organization will be a nonprofit or an informal volunteer organization, defining the purpose of your organization is best done through a mission statement.

TIPS FOR A MISSION STATEMENT

An organization's mission statement should meet these criteria:

- Be short and focused.
- Be easily understood.
- Tell what you are trying to do and why you exist.
- Be about the end result, not the means to get there.
- Be sufficiently broad so that it gives room to grow and be flexible.
- Direct the activities in the right direction and keep activities on track.
- Inspire dedication and commitment.

A mission statement is usually a statement of no more than a paragraph that provides the long-range view of what you want your idea to accomplish. The mission statement talks about the end result, not the means of getting there. It should tell others what the core of your idea is. The two examples below pack a lot of information into few words, yet they clearly state the primary focus of each organization:

> *Outward Bound's mission statement says, "Our mission is to inspire character development and self-discovery in people of all ages and walks of life through challenge and adventure, and to impel them to achieve more than they ever thought possible, to show compassion for others and to actively engage in creating a better world."*
>
> *The mission of the Natural Resources Council of Maine is "to protect, conserve, and restore Maine's environment, and to ensure the wise use of its resources for now and for future generations."*

Creating a mission statement that defines the purpose of your organization, or reviewing and updating an existing mission statement, can often be an arduous process. Yet it provides a critical role in helping to keep the organization focused on its primary intent. It is used for all people involved in the organization so they know what the focus is, and it helps outsiders understand what you

are trying to accomplish. The mission statement provides the basis for planning, budgeting, and fund-raising. It is used to recruit volunteers and paid staff, if you decide to use them. It provides inspiration and vision for the long-term accomplishments you hope to attain.

Do you have a group of people interested in your idea? If so, and if you want them to become a part of your volunteer organization, include them in the creation of the mission statement. Allow plenty of time to do this. Here are some basic steps for writing a mission statement:

1. **Identify the core people who care about your idea and set a meeting time.** Make sure the key people whose input you value and want engaged in your idea can attend. Try to include people who may be opinion leaders in your community or who might have access to opinion leaders.

   Choose a room that has good light with windows. Set aside at least half a day. Bring flip charts and multicolored markers. Bring food and drinks; it always helps to keep peoples' energy up!

2. **Create a draft agenda and write it on a flip chart that is clearly visible to all.** Include time allotments for each agenda item. The agenda might include:
   - goal of the meeting
   - welcome and introductions
   - housekeeping: where are the bathrooms, phones, etc.

- ground rules: Do you want the conversations to be confidential at this early stage? Encourage full participation by all; welcome all comments. The group can identify what is needed. Make sure these rules are clearly written for reference during the meeting.
- introduction to the idea and why you have asked people for their participation
- brainstorming
- consolidation of ideas
- identification of key ideas and phrases to be included in your mission statement
- draft of a mission statement by the group or an assigned subgroup
- feedback on the meeting: what went well, what could be improved
- identification of next steps
- adjournment

3. **Make your opening remarks to the group.** This is an important time for giving your sales pitch. You want to set the initial tone for this meeting by clearly outlining your goals and sharing your enthusiasm for the possibilities you see, then describe why you have invited their participation. Hopefully everyone attending will be familiar with your idea and enthusiastic about helping you with it.

   Answer questions, but avoid long discussions. At this point, try to limit questions to those for clarification about your idea. Then present the agenda and describe the process and desired outcomes of the meeting.

4. **Describe what a mission statement is.** (See sidebar "Tips for a Mission Statement," above.) You could post some examples (see above). Draw on the expertise in the group. Some in the group may have worked on mission statements before.

5. **Begin the brainstorming session.** Ask everyone to briefly state their thoughts about this vision and to freely give their comments

that will help articulate this vision. There should be no discussion during this session, only openness to all ideas.

Make sure you write down on a flip chart each and every statement that is said so that everyone can be assured their statement is recorded accurately. Another method of brainstorming is to use Post-it notes. Have everyone write each idea on a separate Post-it. Give the group several minutes, but ask them to keep ideas short and brief. Then have everyone put his or her Post-its up on the flip chart.

6. **Begin consolidating the similar phrases or words, those that are most alike, and distill them into groupings so you have a statement or two.** Circle similar comments with the same color of marker. Or, if using Post-its, group together the Post-its with the same or similar words, phrases, and meanings. Take each idea grouping at a time and consolidate this group of similar ideas or key phrases into one or two statements.

7. **Refer back to the contents of a mission statement.** (See the sidebar above.) How many statements do you now have? Although you may not yet have one coherent mission statement pulled together, do the ideas in the several statements fit the outline of what a mission statement should include? Are there any consolidated statements you could eliminate?

   This is a very challenging part of writing a mission statement. Paring down and consolidating many words into a few while maintaining the critical, core ideas is not easy, but it's very necessary.

8. **Write a draft mission statement.** Now there are two ways to proceed. If you are making good progress and have plenty of time, the group can begin to wordsmith the several consolidated statements together to form two or three sentences for a true mission statement.

Or, more likely, time may be coming to a close. In this case, ask for two or three volunteers who will work with you to write a draft mission statement from the several consolidated statements.

9. **Stop the process and think about the work you have done.** If you have drafted a statement as a group, give people time to go home and think about it. In the next few days, send notes of your meeting around to everyone so they can review the process and see if there are any other ideas that they think would be important to include. Or if you and a group of others are going to get together to pull a draft statement together, set a time to do that, with the promise to send your draft out to the full group for comments and suggestions.

10. **Call a second and final meeting to finalize the mission statement.** From the feedback you have received, via email or phone, create an edited version of the draft mission statement. Then reconvene the group to finalize and agree on the newly created mission statement. Bring treats to this meeting to show your appreciation and to celebrate the accomplishment.

A Shorter Option

The above process is certainly necessary if you are forming a new nonprofit organization or are wanting to review or change an existing nonprofit's mission statement. However, a less formal process could be used for starting a new program idea within an existing nonprofit or for starting an informal volunteer organization that does not need federal 501(c)(3) status.

If you are more interested in an informal organization, you could modify the above process by either doing it yourself or including only a handful of others. It is always preferable to have help from others, but if you do not want to hold a meeting, you could instead include others by sending drafts of your proposed statement to them electronically or in hard copy for their feedback.

NURTURING FUTURE LEADERS

Good work needs good people. In *Managing the Nonprofit Organization*, Peter Drucker says, "You develop people, not jobs." It is therefore important to think about nurturing others not only to lead within your organization but also to move out beyond your organization to bring their abilities and energies to other organizations that are working to do good in the community and the world. This is true whether you are leading an established organization or a new volunteer organization that you've started.

Your good idea is an opportunity for the future, far beyond your initial time and energy. Your good idea will hopefully grow far beyond what you initially envisioned and will provide a benefit to more people than you can imagine. Your good idea needs people to carry it forward, to add to it, to build upon it, and, yes, even to change it if that is what is best for the community. Your good idea needs to become something bigger than you; you want it to become self-sustaining so that it no longer depends on you for leadership but continues on with other inspired leaders. That is a true legacy.

Founding an organization and working to pass it on requires a selfless leader. It means leading in a role of grace and working to keep your ego in abeyance. This is not easy to do, especially if your organization becomes successful and well known. You will become—and should be—proud of what has been accomplished. Yet we have all heard of the "founder's syndrome," in which it is difficult for the founder to let go of control and to empower others to further his or her good idea. Founders become proprietary of the organization and get caught up in thinking "I" rather than "we." This can also happen to leaders of established organizations if they stay a long time in their leadership role and become entrenched in their position.

So to develop leadership within a volunteer organization, whether you started it or not, you must begin to nurture those people who share your love of and enthusiasm for the work. Skills can always be taught, but passion and commitment for the work and mission are the key ingredients for the successful leader.

Give Them Opportunities

Begin to think about the opportunities you can give to the people who have this passion and interest. Expand their duties while making sure you give them the tools to be successful. This may mean spending more time with them or agreeing to send them to training workshops. Start encouraging them to do more; push them a bit. Err on the side of being more demanding and setting high standards that will help them improve their performance. But also be patient. Allow them to make mistakes. Remember your own experiences as you learned to lead and what helped you.

Just as Outward Bound leaders allow their groups to make mistakes that cause them more difficulties but, in the end, greater learnings, so you too should support these future leaders to learn by doing. This is the ultimate learning tool, which again and again proves successful at Outward Bound and in all walks of life.

Don't waste time, though, on people who won't try. Future leaders need to meet you halfway at least. They must be willing to give it their best, to take risks, and to fail, with your support. Give people responsibility, but mentor them. Giving them responsibility without support dooms them to failure and stands to hurt the organization.

Encourage Mentoring

Nurturing a future leader can often depend on the chemistry between you. You have to like someone in order to mentor that person well. If someone with whom you may not connect well has potential, think about whether there are others in the organization who would like to work with that person. Don't limit yourself to be the only person mentoring others. Building it into the culture of your organization will enhance its reputation as a wonderful place to learn and grow. This is a great recruitment tool for bringing in good people.

Set a Good Example

Make sure you set a good example. People learn by doing, and they also learn by watching others. Think of the things you've learned over the years by watching others. Walk your talk. It is key to being credible and to encouraging and inspiring others to do good work.

A FINAL NOTE

Working and leading in volunteer organizations, shaping the work, furthering the mission, and nurturing future leaders provide a lifetime of benefit, for you as well as for those you are serving. It is hard work. It tends to be selfless work. Yet it usually gives back tenfold in the form of life satisfaction and the knowledge that you are "doing well by doing good."

TIPS FOR NURTURING FUTURE LEADERS

- Help them have a bigger view of what they can do—build their confidence.
- Give them constructive feedback.
- Give them positive reinforcement—point out what they have done well.
- Ask questions; don't give answers—stimulate their thinking. Any student who asks an Outward Bound leader a question will almost always get this response: "And what do you think?"
- Facilitate brainstorming.
- Give people time to explore and try new things.
- Include them in the team—teamwork is great for learning.

CHAPTER 15

LEADING YOUTH IN YOUR COMMUNITY

Driving home from work recently, I heard a radio report about a group of teenagers in a small fishing town in Maine who wanted to renovate a building for an arts center. They wrote a grant for the materials they would need, but did not succeed in raising the money. Rather than being deterred and giving up, they went to various stores and convinced people in the community to help them with their project. On their own, they raised the money locally and received enough donated materials to successfully renovate the building, which now serves the whole town. They did it themselves, with their own ingenuity and ambition. It was an inspiring account.

What great energy and initiative youth have. How important young people are to making our communities interesting and lively places to live. This chapter focuses on the importance of and ways to include youth in your service work and in your thoughts about being a community leader.

WHAT'S IT LIKE TO LEAD YOUNG PEOPLE?

Think about your community. Can you imagine it without young people? Young people are the foundation of our future, and they provide the stimulation, creativity, and enterprise that will help to make our communities, country, and world a better place. They are the seedlings of the healthy garden of tomorrow; the care we give them now will determine how successful they will be in the future. In her book *The Measure of Our Success*, Marian Wright Edelman, president of the Children's Defense Fund, writes:

> *Diverse opportunities for young people to serve their communities can play a major role in restoring hope and moral example to our nation. Young people need to believe*

they are needed, and adults need to be reminded that our children and youth all have something to contribute and are precious resources to be nurtured and cherished.

Recognize the Importance of Youth in Your Community

Young people stretch us. Teenagers of today know a great deal about current events, the Internet, and the latest in technology. They push us to think more broadly. They challenge us to learn new things and to keep current. They stimulate us to keep growing.

Look around your community. I am convinced that you will see evidence of young people working in your community and contributing their time and talent in remarkable and beneficial ways. For example, Baltimore, Maryland, has a program wherein youth volunteer to take care of public places. They do service work that encourages pride in their city and that serves everyone in the city. This program, the Parks & People Foundation, is featured in the case study at the end of Chapter 16, Leading Your Community in the Political Arena.

Young people are critically important to our communities and to our nation's future. As a person interested in your community, consider how youth can help meet some of your community's needs. Facilitating their involvement and including them can be an important part of your work.

Draw on Outward Bound's Expertise in Working with Youth

Outward Bound has successfully worked with youth for decades. It has developed expertise in working with many populations, primarily fourteen- to twenty-year-olds. Outward Bound today serves youth through its wilderness courses, public- and private-school programs, urban programs, and renowned youth-at-risk programs. This chapter offers ideas that you, as a community leader, can learn from Outward Bound in working with this age group.

Outward Bound's first courses in Colorado in the early 1960s were with teenage boys recruited from a variety of backgrounds and locations. Prep-school boys from Colorado were mixed with inner-city youth from the Bronx, and they learned from each other about overcoming physical adversities and getting along. Outward Bound found that mixing youth from different backgrounds led to building new understandings and friendships. This practice continues in Outward Bound today, and I encourage you to consider it as you think about forming and working with groups of young people.

Outward Bound began working with girls in the 1970s. At first it was felt that girls couldn't do the same physical activities that the boys' courses included—these activities were thought to be too strenuous. The first girls' courses were modified to be shorter and less arduous than the boys' courses. Initially just a few women instructors were hired to teach these courses, so most of the courses were taught by men.

Gradually, however, vocal women working at Outward Bound began challenging these assumptions and pushing for courses equal in challenge to the boys' courses. It didn't take long for the curricula for both boys and girls to become the same. It was also at about that time that Outward Bound started adult women's courses as well.

From the beginning, and continuing today, fundamental to Outward Bound's work with youth is founder Kurt Hahn's Seven Principles of Character Development:

- Give the opportunity for self-discovery.
- Make your followers meet with triumph and defeat.
- Give the opportunity for self-effacement in the common cause.
- Provide periods of silence.

- Train the imagination.
- Make competition important but not predominant.
- Free the children of the wealthy and powerful from the enervating sense of privilege.

—Martin Flavin, *Kurt Hahn's Schools and Legacy*

These fundamentals have served Outward Bound well for more than sixty-five years. As you think about working with youth in your community, these principles are worth remembering and applying to your work.

Be Aware of the Challenges Facing Youth

Youth are faced with huge challenges today, which range from pressure to achieve, to material enticements for all kinds of products, to the availability of illegal substances. Yet such challenges are not new. Fifty years ago, Outward Bound founder Kurt Hahn said this:

> There can be no doubt that the young of today have to be protected against certain poisonous effects inherent in present-day civilization. Five social diseases surround them, even in early childhood.
>
> There is the decline in fitness due to modern methods of locomotion; the decline in initiative due to the widespread disease of spectatoritis; the decline in care and skill due to the weakened tradition of craftsmanship; the decline in self-discipline due to the ever-present availability of tranquilizers and stimulants; and the decline in compassion, which William Temple called 'spiritual death.' "
>
> —*Kurt Hahn as quoted by His Royal Highness Prince Philip, Duke of Edinburgh, at Colorado Outward Bound's 25th anniversary in 1987*

Although Hahn first said these words more than half a century ago, they seem appropriate for our world today. So you can see that, as a community leader serving young people, you can still find guidance and perspective from the legacy of Outward Bound's early philosophies.

Understand the Characteristics and Needs of Teenagers

Adolescence is a time of significant growth and change. Physically, emotionally, socially, and cognitively, young people are developing from children into adults, and the rate at which these changes occur vary tremendously from individual to individual. "Normal" development has a long continuum. For instance, there can be as much as a six- to eight-year physical maturation difference between boys and girls, although girls tend to mature sooner emotionally. Still, you cannot expect a clear norm.

Further, just as differences in growth rates are large, so too differences in conceptual and abstract thinking are large. Although the way we think differs among individuals, even as adults, this is especially true for adolescents.

There are also big differences within a single young person. If an adolescent can think abstractly about one thing, it does not necessarily mean he or she can think abstractly about something else. As you work with young people, remember that it may not be realistic to expect them to be able to extrapolate learning experiences on a consistent basis.

For example, imagine that a youth group is building a community garden project, and there is quite a good discussion about the need for cooperation. There is agreement on outlining how the garden will look, what vegetables to plant, and even what low-income groups will be given the produce when it matures. The tasks are divided up, and the group gets to work marking the boundaries of the garden, digging it up, and lining out the rows for planting.

But in following-up at the end of the day, the group may have little understanding about the need for taking adequate care of all the tools required for the garden project. The

decisions about what tools should be cleaned and stored for ongoing maintenance might require more leadership from you than the earlier discussion did.

Characteristics of Moral Development

Although adolescents have internal conflicts, they do not necessarily experience the feelings of disenfranchisement and isolation from society that are sometimes portrayed in the popular media. In fact, teenagers are often keenly tuned in to the needs of their community and want to help. They often can be very aware of injustices and the suffering of others, as can young children. Teenagers have the capacity for empathy and thoughtfulness and are not always the consistently internally focused youth they are made out to be. See the sidebar on characteristics of adolescent moral development, below.

How does understanding these moral characteristics help you as a leader of youth volunteers? Well, teenagers really do want to make the world a better place, as do you. That's a great place from which to start working together. Appealing to this desire can be the motivator for helping them organize a project or activity. Adolescents also have compassion for those who are suffering, for animals, and for environmental problems. This can help you guide their choice of activities.

When conflicts arise (see "Challenges in Leading Youth" later in this chapter), remember that teenagers are able to consider the rights and feelings of others. Frame the solutions so they can see the conflict in these terms. For instance, if you are organizing a youth group to take a shift in a soup kitchen and you see conflict in the decision regarding who will be servers and who will clean up, focus their thoughts on the goal of the work—helping provide a meal to disadvantaged people—and engage them in sharing time for both tasks so that the distribution of work is equal and fair to all.

Your words and opinions matter to youth. Encourage them to think about what you say, and

CHARACTERISTICS OF ADOLESCENT MORAL DEVELOPMENT

The National Middle School Association describes, in its 1995 report *This We Believe*, the following characteristics of moral development in young adolescents:

- They are generally idealistic, desiring to make the world a better place and to become socially useful.
- They are in transition from moral reasoning that focuses on what's in it for them to that which considers the feelings and rights of others.
- They often show compassion for those who are downtrodden or suffering and have special concern for animals and the environmental problems that our world faces.
- They are moving from acceptance of adult moral judgments to development of their own personal values; nevertheless, they tend to embrace values consonant with those of their parents.
- They rely on parents and significant adults for advice when facing major decisions.
- They increasingly assess moral matters in shades of gray rather than the black-and-white terms characteristic of younger children.
- At times, they are quick to see flaws in others but slow to acknowledge their own faults.
- Owing to their lack of experience, they are often impatient with the pace of change, underestimating the difficulties in making desired social changes.
- They are capable of and value direct experience in participatory democracy.
- They greatly need and are influenced by adult role models who will listen to them and affirm their moral consciousness and actions by being trustworthy role models.
- They are increasingly aware of and concerned about inconsistencies between values exhibited by adults and the conditions they see in society.

encourage them to formulate their own opinions. Ask them what they think. Encourage group discussions of moral questions and values, guiding their opinions if necessary.

This is a great opportunity to talk about how our actions affect others on many different levels, whether what is affected is the environment (driving a car rather than walking might contribute to global warming, for instance), animal versus human rights and needs (such as protecting wolves that may be attacking the livestock of ranchers), or an election (which can be changed by just a few votes). Your goal is to encourage respect for different points of view and to show them that these issues are complex and not solved by simple solutions.

Behavioral Characteristics

Knowing some other characteristics of how adolescents generally behave can make it easier to work with them.

They have short attention spans. If you are working with a group of teenagers, remember that their attention spans are often short and they like doing rather than listening! The more you engage them in creating activities and in problem solving, the better their attention spans will be. Help them to plan the garden rather than offering them a ready-made plan.

They are very emotive. Teenagers' emotions are often very close to the surface, and it is not unusual for them to readily show their emotions. It is important to assure safe avenues for sharing these emotions, and it is important to assure that your own emotions are kept in check and that you are steady and consistent. For a discussion of establishing guidelines and safe boundaries for behavior, see "Challenges in Leading Youth" later in this chapter.

They are impulsive. Teenagers don't always think of the consequences before they act. Thus it is very important to give clear instructions. Teenagers think of themselves as immortal and often are willing to engage in overly risky behavior. Finding the balance between allowing some appropriate risk-taking with good safety backups and curtailing excessive risk-taking is a challenge for anyone working with youth.

This means that you must make sure you understand the possible risks involved in any activities you are planning. Create clear rules about the behaviors that you know you must prevent. See "Dealing with Safety Concerns" later in this chapter. Then try to allow as much freedom as possible for them to use their judgment up to that point.

> *For example, say you are working with a teenage group to do a neighborhood cleanup, and you want to include a swim at a nearby lake at the end of the day. In the morning, outline clear safety rules: stay in pairs; identify the perimeters of the neighborhood; know how to find you if they need help. Beyond these few safety rules, allow the group to plan how the day will go, who will go where, and other aspects of building a successful day.*
>
> *Then, before the swim, again review safety procedures: don't swim alone; don't swim beyond the identified swimming area. Find out who in the group may be a weak swimmer, and talk privately with these youth about how they will handle their swim.*

They are self-conscious. Be mindful that adolescents are focused on themselves a good deal. Although they have great capacity for compassion and quickly seeing injustice, their primary frame of reference is their own identity. As a youth leader, you must be careful not to single out an individual in front of his or her peers or embarrass anyone. This is hard on adults, too, but it's especially so for teenagers. They like to conform to their peers and not be seen as different, though they often choose ways of being different—but within the boundaries of their peer group. It may be helpful to have small groups work together on a problem, rather than assigning individual tasks.

> *I worked at a small arts college for a few years with students ages eighteen to twenty. They were bright and creative, and I truly enjoyed being around them. Their dress and hair styles were typically weird but fit right in with their arts-crowd peer group—blue hair or hair of all colors, partly shaved heads, old-style clothing from used-clothing stores in unusual combinations.*
>
> *Underneath this affect, they wanted to do the right things; they wanted to do well at the school; they wanted to create art that received positive feedback from their teachers. They liked to test the limits and the rules but, on the whole, were good about staying within these rules once they knew we were serious about them. They were delightful as well as colorful, and today I enjoy seeing them every now and then in the community and hearing of their successes.*

HOW CAN YOU INVOLVE YOUTH IN COMMUNITY WORK?

Everything that you do as a leader in your community affects youth in some way: Helping adults indirectly helps the children in their lives. Beautifying your city or town helps children have nice places to play in and simply be in. Working for the environment is an effort that benefits the health of children. Everything we do has an impact on children.

Yet youth themselves also want to be involved. They want to be needed and to be useful. Finding opportunities for them to help improve their community is a win-win for them and for your community.

Be Open to Their Ideas

Probably one of the first ways you can involve youth is to be open to them and to their ideas. It's not only adults who have good ideas. Adolescents often have marvelous ideas that help them and the community. The youth that renovated the arts building for their town in Maine, described earlier in this chapter, is just one example of what can happen when youths' ideas are listened to and supported. CBS News correspondent Steve Hartman reported another example on February 17, 2006:

> *A car that can go from zero to sixty in four seconds and gets more than 50 miles to the gallon would be enough to pique any driver's interest. So who do we have to thank for it—Ford? GM? Toyota? No—just Victor, David, Cheeseborough, Bruce, and Kosi, five kids from the auto-shop program at West Philadelphia High School.*
>
> *The five kids, along with a handful of schoolmates, built the soybean-fueled car as an after-school project. It took them more than a year—rummaging for parts, configuring wires, and learning as they went. As teacher Simon Hauger notes, these kids weren't exactly the cream of the academic crop.*
>
> *"We have a number of high-school dropouts," he says. "We have a number that have been removed for disciplinary reasons, and they end up with us."*
>
> *One of the Fab Five, Kosi Haron, was in a gang at his old school—and he was a terrible student. The car project has changed all that.*
>
> *"I was just getting by with the skin of my teeth, Cs and Ds," he says. "I came here, and now I'm a straight-A student."*
>
> *To Hauger, the soybean-powered car shows what kids—any kids—can do when they get the chance.*
>
> *"If you give kids that have been stereotyped as not being able to do anything an opportunity to do something great, they'll step up," he says.*

This story reflects the leadership of a teacher, yet anyone interested in auto mechanics could have been helpful to these enterprising young men who, through having their good idea and implementing it, became better students—they became more than they knew they could be. But they needed first to be given the opportunity.

Use Existing Programs

Often adolescents participate in their community by teaching summer programs to younger children. They work, either for pay or as volunteers, to teach and help day camps, such as those operated by the YMCA, local towns, and private camps. Many summer camps hire teenagers as staff members and staff assistants. Adolescents frequently work for city parks and recreation departments building trails and maintaining facilities and grounds, again either as paid or as volunteer staff. These kinds of activities not only teach teenagers skills and responsibility but are also useful to list on their future job and college applications.

Youth Service Programs

Youthlinks is a nonprofit organization whose mission, according to their website, is to "empower youth to commit to themselves and their community, broaden their horizons, and acquire healthy life skills through focused enrichment programs and meaningful volunteer work." The organization works with children ages eleven to seventeen to help them develop leadership skills and to encourage civic-mindedness.

The young people who participate in Youthlinks engage in all kinds of activities in their community. They teach senior citizens how to use email; they mentor elementary-school students; they work in community gardens. Recently, Youthlinks started a program wherein the participants research as much as they can about the assets and needs in their community, then they discuss their findings and choose a service project that will address their top-priority need. They create a work plan, develop a budget and fund-raising plan, assign roles and responsibilities, and implement the plan. They also reflect upon and evaluate the effectiveness of the project after it's completed. What a good way for youth to learn skills and help their community at the same time.

Youthlinks is just one example of what young people can do in their community to make a significant impact on a local need. What is important is that they have driven the process. They have been responsible for all aspects of the work they have done.

What Inspires You?

Just as Chapter 13 describes how to think about what kind of service work you might want to do in the world, thinking about what specific work to do with youth should follow the same process:

■ What appeals to you? Remember, follow your intuition!

■ What is in your life already that would lead to working with youth?

■ What are your interests and skills?

■ Do you have youth experience, or should you work and learn under someone who does?

I was a beekeeper for many years and loved the many hours I tended them: catching swarms, building more hives, extracting honey. One year the local junior high school had a Career Day for introducing the students to different kinds of activities and careers, and I volunteered to do a day on beekeeping.

I took an empty hive and all the equipment, plus samples of honey. I talked about how the students should think about whether or not to become a beekeeper: if you think "sting" when you think of bees, you probably shouldn't become a beekeeper, but if you think "honey," you have potential!

I discussed the "dance" bees do at the hive entrance to show the other bees where to find good pollen; how the queen behaves; and the life cycle of a bee. We talked about how centrifugal force works when we're extracting the honey.

It was fun for me because I talked about a hobby that I love, and it seemed to be fun for the students. It was a great opportunity for me to work with young people in a way that matched my interests.

Another example of finding inspiration in working with youth comes from Boulder, Colorado, where, in the mid-1990s, music programs were being eliminated in the schools due to budget cuts.

A group of concerned adults gathered to talk about the importance of music, how it helps children learn and develop many skills, such as math. Gradually an idea was formed to start an after-school music program made up of local music teachers, both volunteer and paid. These concerned adults worked with interested young people and raised money to provide scholarships for students who wanted to work with paid teachers but couldn't afford it.

As more and more children began to participate, the adults found they needed a building to house the program. Gradually the program evolved into an ongoing and important organization fulfilling an unmet need of youth in the community. It started and then grew through the interests and concerns of local volunteers.

Sports Programs

Do you like sports? Would you enjoy volunteering in youth sports programs? Soccer, baseball, T-ball, football, tennis, and swimming are some of the more popular sports programs for young people that are sponsored through the community. These are wonderful opportunities, when coached and led properly. You have an opportunity to help children learn and improve skills, develop their physical abilities, and learn about fairness, teamwork, and good sportsmanship.

Outward Bound founder Kurt Hahn cautioned,

however, against too much emphasis on games. As quoted in *Outward Bound USA* by Joshua Miner and Joe Boldt, Hahn once said this:

> *It is my mission in life to dethrone games. Competitive sports provide exercise, recreation, physical development, the social experience of team effort, and the personal and social values of acquired skills and competitive experience. Inevitably, however, the stress on competition denies to the athletically inferior youngster the chance to know authentic competitive pressure. When the contest is close, coaches are reluctant to use substitutes. Even a class E league has its bench sitters . . . the physically gifted youngster . . . could loaf. . . . He could satisfy himself with a mediocre effort. He could gloss over his shortcomings by basking in the stardom of his specialty.*

I believe this is an important thought. If you are interested in working with youth through athletics, think of ways to nurture the less physically gifted to feel good at accomplishing improvement as well as ways to challenge the gifted youth to work harder and stretch to reach new goals. This, to me, is one of Outward Bounds' most important ideas: to challenge all people, no matter what their ability; to help them achieve success on whatever level is appropriate for them.

Programs for At-Risk Youth

What about working with a youth-at-risk program? Were you troubled as an adolescent? Did you struggle in school? Some of the best youth workers are people who have "been there" and can truly relate to teenagers who are struggling with behavior problems, abuse, or addictions. There is no more important work than giving a hand to these youth and to programs designed for them. You may have experiences in your life that make you especially able to relate to struggling young people. Some of the most successful and accomplished staff at Outward Bound were at-risk youth themselves.

> *Peter Athens, an Outward Bound mountaineering instructor in Colorado, was revered by all who knew him for being an exceptional mountain climber, lead instructor, and course director. Today he is a world-renowned guide and mountaineer in the Himalaya and around the world. He participated in several famous rescues on Mount Everest, including the events chronicled by Jon Krakauer in his book* Into Thin Air.
>
> *While I was working for Outward Bound in Colorado, I was surprised to learn that Peter had struggled as a teenager and had taken an Outward Bound course because of those struggles. His Outward Bound course inspired him to become not only a world-class mountaineer but also an exceptional leader of teenagers and adults.*

The use of your experiences to do good in the world is far reaching. You can use what you know and what you have been through to help others, which gives you credibility and competence, especially with youth.

IS LEADING YOUTH RIGHT FOR YOU?

Critical to involving youth in your community is the attitude you have. Seeing young people as an important resource, valuing their abilities, and listening to their ideas opens doors for them to participate. As a leader in your community, you will have opportunities to include youth. Seeing young people as a significant constituency and community participants enriches all.

Do You Want to Work Directly with Youth?

Do you wonder about working with youth? Do you worry that you might not be capable of dealing with the many challenges they present? When considering working with youth, here are a few things to ask yourself:

- Do you like and respect young people? Although this seems a simple question, answering it honestly is key to your success in this line of work.
- What about young people do you like? Think about the qualities you notice in youth around you or that you can identify.
- Do you like learning from youth? Are you open to new ideas and eager to think differently?
- Do you gain energy from the energy of young people? Teenagers are active and inquisitive. Does this energize you or aggravate you?
- Do you remember your adolescence? What was it like for you? What was it like for your friends? Remembering your own experiences and those of your friends will help you relate to the experiences of the youth you work with.
- Are you patient? Teenagers require a lot of patience!

Would You Rather Support Youth and Their Work?

Many community leaders prefer to support youth work rather than work directly with youth. What are signs that you might not be the right person to work directly with youth?

- Do you need personal validation from young people? They are usually more focused on themselves than on you, and your role is to be there for them. If you want to be liked by youth, perhaps working directly with them isn't as fulfilling as helping those who do.
- Do you prefer to be directive and in control? Teenagers need to be taught and encouraged to take control themselves, and if letting go of control might be hard for you, it may be better not to work directly with adolescents.
- Do you find yourself easily drawn into power struggles with youth? Getting into "win-lose" situations is frustrating for everyone involved.
- Do you like situations to be highly organized? As young people learn to take responsibility, some chaos usually occurs; helpers need to have tolerance for disorganization.

- Do you need quite a bit of time to build trust with others? Youth need to know that you trust them until or unless they give you reasons not to trust them.
- Do you prefer adult conversation? Talking with youth often entails more listening than dialog, and often it is imperative that you hold your tongue.

Thinking about these questions will enhance your success as a leader working with young people, either directly or in support of them. There are many varieties of ways you can use your best skills and talents, and an honest assessment of yourself, your likes, and your needs will help you decide where you are best suited to serve youth.

What Youth Workers Say about Leading Youth

Youth: *1. state or quality of being young; 2. the period of adolescence; 3. an early stage of development; 4. young people.*
—Webster's New World Dictionary and Thesaurus

Outward Bound youth workers are some of the most dedicated staff people I know. When I asked staff from the Philadelphia Outward Bound Center why they do the work they do, their answer was this: "Knowing you have a profound impact on the growth and development of these young people and being able to share experiences that are so new and exciting to them make it truly fulfilling."

Beth Dimond works in my office at the Natural Resources Council of Maine. She's cheerful and fun loving and brings a lot to the spirit of the organization. I noticed that every once in a while, she took long weekends off, saying she had "youth camp" that weekend. I also noticed that she often spoke of spending time with a troubled young person from her youth group. While writing this chapter, I asked Beth to tell me more about what she does.

I learned that Beth is the youth director for her church's youth camp. These camps, which occur several times a year, are retreats where about sixty teenagers gather for long weekends. Beth works with a council of nine student leaders to organize and lead these retreats. I learned that she has been director for ten years and was a chaperone before that for five years. I asked her why she does it and what motivates her.

Beth was a participant of her church's youth camp during her high school years and gained a lot from the experience. She had struggled as a young person, and church camp had really helped her gain confidence and accomplish much in her life. She decided to become involved as a young adult because of her own experiences as a youth.

But there's more: She says she gets so much from the work. She feels that she's making a real difference. She feels very close to the group, which has grown tremendously during her tenure as leader. This group obviously loves Beth and thinks she's cool, which we at the Natural Resources Council of Maine think too! Working with youth has become a big, rewarding part of her life.

Then I talked to another person in our midcoast Maine community who is well known for his work with youth. Emanuel Pariser founded the Community School, a small alternative residential high school, thirty-three years ago. I asked Emanuel why he is so dedicated to teenagers and why he continues to do the work that he does.

Emanuel says it is important work because there is so much potential. Young people's lives are not yet fully formed, and there are so many directions they can go. Most teenagers are not at all sure about their future and what they want to do. A caring adult can steady them and help them find a place to start a process of discovery. To have a positive influence when a person is starting to form basic goals and direction in his or her life is immensely rewarding.

Emanuel also says that he loves the honesty and straightforwardness of young people. They tell the truth as they see it, and it's not covered up by what they might think you want to hear. You learn about yourself from young people. They don't have the social screens that adults have. They may well pinpoint an issue in their relationship with you that challenges you and makes you look more closely at your own thoughts and actions. For instance, if you have an issue with authority and tend to resist setting clear boundaries, youth will call you on it and force you to think more about it and probably change.

Emanuel feels that it's important to remember that one shoe doesn't fit all sizes. You can't approach working with youth using a cookie-cutter philosophy. You have to learn who they are from each adolescent, and you end up learning more about who you are as well. Emanuel finds it very stimulating and interesting.

Last, Emanuel talks about the wonderful energy of young people. It's exciting to be around them, and their energy often touches parts of yourself that you may have kept hidden or, if you're older, have lost touch with. Although Emanuel doesn't say it quite this way, he seems to be saying, "Young people keep you young!"

As Beth and Emanuel describe, fundamental to working with youth are the respect and faith that you have for them and in them. They, like adults, have more in them than they know—*plus est en vous*. Working with them to facilitate their discovery and knowledge of their capabilities and strengths is extremely rewarding work. And it is *fun*. Just as leading volunteers requires being a good role model, in working with youth, your words and actions will have more impact than *you* know!

LEADERSHIP STRATEGIES FOR WORKING WITH YOUNG PEOPLE

One reason for Outward Bound's success with troubled youth is the amount of one-on-one attention given to each student. So many young people yearn for an adult to listen to them, to pay attention to them, to take them seriously. Being interested—truly interested—in a young person is one of the most important things you can do as a leader of youth. Just stop what you're doing to listen and take the time to hear what he or she is thinking. It can be a tremendous gift to anyone, but especially to a young person. Engage in a real conversation and be open about your thoughts and values. It will be a truly positive experience for that young person and will help build his or her character in a way you may never realize.

May Sarton writes in *Journal of Solitude* and *Plant Dreaming Deep* of the importance of relationships and how each one influences our growth and attitudes. These relationships may be for only a few hours, a few days, or many decades, but they may well have an impact far beyond our knowing. I remember such an experience once:

I was at a ski area and happened to be riding up a chairlift with a nineteen-year-old young woman. I asked her about herself, what she was doing there in Colorado. She began sharing with me her dilemma about whether to go to college or to strike out on some adventures she was dreaming about. She wanted to go to Alaska. She wanted to go to Nepal. I listened, intrigued with her ideas and thoughts. I asked more questions and pointed out some things she might want to think about.

We were strangers, but in that short chairlift ride, we became friends. She had already done some amazing things on her own that impressed me. She clearly could do anything she set her mind to. Even though this happened many, many years ago, I still remember her. She made an impression on me and taught me to be even more willing to take on adventures and challenges. Perhaps I helped her consider more as well. I will never know, but I believe we both had an influence on each other.

A relationship that you as an adult have with a teenager, whether it is in a brief conversation or occurs over time, can have a real impact. Think of things you have learned through talking with

---

TIPS FOR DEVELOPING TRUST

- Tell the truth. Youth are usually very quick to detect wishful thinking or exaggerations.
- Be honest about yourself. Although you shouldn't disclose personal details about your private life, at least in the beginning, you can share your honest feelings and concerns. Don't feel that you need to know everything to have these young folks trust you. It's better to say, "I don't know" or, "I worry about that, too" than to bluff.
- As stated many times above, *listen*. Be open to every person and be quiet so that you can truly hear their words and understand their thoughts.
- Show that you believe their ideas and thoughts are important. Ask questions about what they think. Show that you are honestly considering what they have offered.
- Show that you care. Offer compassion. Laugh with them. Sympathize with their concerns.
- Use your intuition to sense their needs and the timing for when to respond to those needs.
- Trust yourself. You are a good human being wanting to do something productive, useful, and fun with these young people. Trust that the right words and reactions will be there for you.

someone you admired or perhaps even knew only briefly. Some conversations or ideas just stick in your mind and change your frame of reference. Being open and caring, being willing to listen and also sharing your beliefs and ideas with a teenager allows her or him to be more open with you.

Build Trust

Inherent in a good relationship is trust. Youth are often suspicious of adults and people they don't know. It takes time to build trust, and it is something earned. Don't be put off or feel a sense of failure if initially you feel that some individuals don't trust you.

Staff from Outward Bound say that the most important thing an instructor can do to create trust and respect on a course is to follow through on your actions. If you say you are going to do something, then do it.

Develop Credibility by Maintaining an Appropriate Role

As much as students say they hate authority, they love structure and guidance. Setting clear expectations, leading by example, sticking to your guns, and being the adult will command respect from your students.
—Vanessa Mendillo, community liaison and curriculum coordinator, Philadelphia Outward Bound Center

It is always important to remember that you are the adult and, by necessity, the one who ultimately is responsible for the group or young individual. This does not mean that you can't have fun with your group, but always keep in mind that you are not their peer.

One thing to consider is that wanting young people's approval can get you in trouble. Remember the lists in "Is Leading Youth Right for You?" earlier in this chapter, of things to think about when you're deciding whether to work directly with youth? It includes asking whether you need personal validation. Keep in mind that working

with youth is not an appropriate setting for expecting or needing validation or approval.

Sometimes you will need to set limits on the young people's inappropriate behaviors or to guide the group away from an activity or decision that could be harmful to themselves or others (see "Challenges in Leading Youth" later in this chapter). You will not be effective in doing this if you have not established credibility in your role as being the adult leader.

I always caution our Outward Bound instructors about disclosing their personal lives. Talking with youth about your personal life or personal problems is not appropriate. Remember, you are there to work *with* them and *for* them. Talking about yourself draws them into a different relationship with you, one of being more a peer of yours or even becoming a helper to you. It's fine to be friendly, share feelings, and give your point of view on issues, but be careful to keep appropriate boundaries between your personal life and problems and your role as a helping, caring adult working with young people. See "Healthy Boundaries" later in this chapter.

Set the Tone for a Positive Group Culture

Generally, I believe all kids want to have fun, be productive, have friends, and generally do well. Providing students with a supportive, structured (yet relaxed), and open environment that allows them to drop their "cool" shell and be themselves allows the students first to respect themselves and in turn gives them the perspective to see other people for who they are and love and respect those people as well.
—Vanessa Mendillo, community liaison and curriculum coordinator, Philadelphia Outward Bound Center

When you first begin working with a new group of young people, or a group that is new to you, be very mindful of the tone you set at the very beginning. Outward Bound is very thoughtful about initial impressions and setting the tone for a new group, which establishes their relationships with

TIPS FOR SETTING A POSITIVE TONE

- Learn everyone's name as quickly as you can.
- Spend some time getting to know each individual.
- Identify why you are there and the broad goals that you see for the group.
- Ask the group to identify other goals they may have. Confirm their agreement with your goals. Be willing to change or revise your goals.
- Discuss and identify a group code of conduct. As much as possible, this should come from the youth themselves. Write it down for everyone to see. It could include such items as these:
- Everyone will have a chance to speak.
- Everyone will speak with respect for one another.
- No one will use foul language.
- It is OK to ask for help; the group will reach out to one another.
- Everyone will try.
- At the end of each group meeting, spend ten minutes doing a debrief. Ask the group how the day or event went, what was good about it, what could have been done better. This will help the group assess itself and build a culture of wanting to improve their experiences.

each other and with you. See the sidebar "Tips for Setting a Positive Tone."

Another tool in building group culture is to keep a record of what the group is doing. Chapter 13, Serving Others as a Community Leader, discusses journal writing as a valuable tool figuring out what motivates you. Keeping a group journal is another useful way to create a positive culture. Give each member of the group an opportunity to add something to the group journal: write a narrative or a poem, or perhaps draw something that represents the activities or actions that occurred during that meeting or day. Most groups enjoy doing this type of journal and reviewing it at the end of the project. It's also a great record of the progress the group has made.

And don't forget to exemplify and model the behaviors and actions you are trying to instill. Are you using the equipment properly? Are you speaking respectfully? Are you dressed appropriately for the project at hand?

Work to Provide a Culture of Inclusion

These days, much is being discussed and studied about the problems of bullying and exclusiveness among young people. These phenomena are seen as the cause of disastrous events such as the Columbine High School shootings in Colorado in 1999.

Outward Bound instructors create situations that require all group members to be involved in order for the group to succeed. This approach prompts students to work with each others' strengths for ideal results. This is the best scenario, but there will be many times when teenagers must work through a failure before they realize the potential they have as a team.

Outward Bound tries to set its students up for success by making the nonnegotiable rules very clear from the beginning. These rules begin with (1) there will be no exclusive relationships, and (2) everyone will respect one another. Outward Bound begins with these two rules so that everyone in the group very clearly knows what is expected of him or her. Jon Mark Howard, Mark Wheeler, and Hepsi Barnett et al. have this to say in *Outward Bound Instructor's Guide to Managing Adolescents in the Field*:

> *Fitting in and being perceived as somewhat competent, capable, and cool is a need for*

all participants, no matter how much they protest [otherwise]. A task, a place to be, and someone to be with are basic social needs. Any kind of social isolation or social ostracism needs to be dealt with immediately to ensure the success of the . . . experience. It can't be said too strongly: Social needs of the adolescent are at the core of their existence. If these needs are not met, it is more serious than not having enough to eat!

The next important step in discouraging exclusive relationships or bullying is to be sure that the adolescents know and practice effective communication styles. The Outward Bound course curriculum includes instructions regarding how to give and receive feedback, how to make assertive and direct statements and requests, how to read body language, and methods for conflict resolution. When youth are given these tools and instructions for enhancing positive communication, they almost always respond positively.

As you work to create a healthy culture in your youth group, be aware of any exclusiveness or scapegoating behavior. The *Outward Bound Instructor's Guide to Managing Adolescents in the Field* makes the following suggestions:

- At the beginning, give assigned places for everyone: a space to sit at meetings, meals, etc. However, keep switching who sits next to whom and who spends time with whom for the first few days. This cuts down on the feelings of "finding your place" or feeling left out. A fine bit of balancing is required to keep the group together long enough to create a team effect and yet change the subgrouping of its members to promote interaction with everyone and diminish any cliquishness. One example is to keep the day-hiking groups the same but change cleanup crews.
- Social isolates—people who are excluded— almost always cause negativity for both the individual and the group. Most budding social isolates act in ways that influence the condi-

tion. It is very important to have a private conversation that addresses this directly during check-in time. If you see social isolation beginning to develop, change your tactics and begin to assign working duos, for example, to ameliorate the problem. Social isolation rarely clears up on its own.

- The amount of Outward Bound instructor time each participant needs each day will vary hugely. It is almost always in direct inverse proportion to the amount of attention that a participant gets daily from his or her peers. Your compensatory attention to such individuals during check-in time should be as inconspicuous as possible so they are not perceived as needing special help.

Develop Their Independence

Helping adolescents become independent is an important role you play as a youth leader. It's a time of life when they are trying to become independent, sometimes in unproductive ways. Yet young people also need and want to depend on adults. Sometimes this push and pull of dependence and independence is confusing both to the adolescent and to you—and especially to parents! Yet key to building successful citizens is nurturing responsible adolescents as they try out their independence and giving them opportunities to practice this independence.

This is how Outward Bound nurtures and develops independence in the young people who take its courses: The last section of an Outward Bound course is called Final Expedition. At this stage, all the teaching of skills has been completed and the group has had ample time to practice those skills. For the students' Final Expedition, the staff assesses their readiness and, depending on the level of ability, the group is given control of planning and executing their last challenging trip—such as hiking a new route or canoeing, sailing, or kayaking primarily on their own. They are given full responsibility for using what they have learned and for being in charge.

If a group has not mastered the skills to the desired level, the staff will modify the parameters of their Final Expedition but still give them control in the planning and execution within this modification. For instance, the staff will give them different route options from which to choose. The groups whose skills are excellent will be given more difficult route choices than a group whose skills are not quite at the highest level. Staff judgement is important in assessing each group's abilities.

Although staff are available in case of an emergency and have built-in checkpoints to assure that all is well, Final Expedition is an important time for the students to test their skills and to see that they really can do it on their own. It is heartening and exciting to see them succeed. That is not to say they don't have difficulties and make mistakes—they do. But they almost always turn their mistakes around to the benefit of their expedition and their time together. What is important is that they are given the opportunity to exercise their independence and to show to themselves and to others the competency they have acquired.

An Outward Bound group was on a five-day Final Expedition at the end of a twenty-three-day course in the San Juan Mountains of Colorado. They had learned their mountaineering skills well and were now proficient at using their maps and compasses as well as other techniques needed in the terrain they were covering. The group achieved their daily checkpoints and seemed to be making good progress toward their destination, where they would rejoin the staff, have a final celebration, and board the buses to go home.

On the fourth day, a surprise snowstorm hit. It was late August, and even in the Colorado Rockies, this was unusual for that time of year. The storm dumped a good foot of wet, heavy snow. The instructors had met the students at their checkpoint the previous day,

but there was no sign of the students at their fourth day's checkpoint, and the instructors were worried about the students. The staff waited and waited. Six hours passed; there was still no sign of the group. Darkness fell. The instructors relayed a message to the base camp that the group was missing.

The next morning, all available staff at the base came out to search. The snow made it difficult. Day Five was the day the students were supposed to come out of the field, have their dinner, and board the buses to return home, but there was still no sign of them. A helicopter was called in to search for them. Day Six came, bright and clear, one of those glistening days that follows a snowstorm. Everyone was becoming more worried. Parents had been called.

The helicopter began searching again and spotted the group. They were hiking through deep drifts, making their way toward the appointed rendezvous. The instructors hiked in, meeting the students not far from the final destination. All the students were jubilant and in good health.

The students reported that when the storm hit, they had kept together, moved down off the mountain ridge into a secluded and protected spot, pitched their tents, and stayed together, keeping warm and dry. They had plenty of food and were not afraid. In fact, they reported having a great time telling stories and sleeping.

The students had done exactly what they should have. They were safe. They had stayed together, and they had made excellent decisions. And they had become a tight group of friends who stayed in touch with each other for many years afterward.

As this account illustrates, an important aspect of Outward Bound's work to encourage responsible independence is the training that its students receive prior to their Final Expedition. It is a gradual progression of learning skills. The students are given more and more responsibility as they learn the skills and as the course progresses, culminating in the Final Expedition.

Turning Over Control

Gradually turn over control to your young people. Allow them to be successful but also to make mistakes. As you plan activities, think about the sequence of events. Think about how to assure that they have ample training and information. Then plan how to gradually turn the activity or project over to them. Find a way to be present, to be "on belay" for them, supporting them, as you gradually relinquish control and they take on more.

> *For instance, when your group builds that community garden, after you have engaged them in planning it and have made sure all the elements for success are included, then step back and watch them implement it, giving encouragement when needed and answering questions if asked. But by all means, don't step in if you see them making a mistake. Let them spot it and make the correction. Or if they don't spot their mistake, let them live with the consequences.*

Seeing a youth group make mistakes and letting them live with the consequences is one of the hardest things to do, for me personally. We all want so much for our young people to be successful and to learn from what we know—which we learned largely from making our *own* mistakes. But young people will always remember a mistake and will likely not repeat it. If, however, you feel that a mistake or consequence has the potential for a safety problem, be sure to intervene (see "Dealing with Safety Concerns" later in this chapter).

Letting Go

Being in control is a central issue for many teenagers and the adults they are with. Beware of power struggles; they usually lead to no good. Therefore,

being aware of your own needs regarding control is also important as you work with adolescents.

How capable are you of gradually letting go, of giving over more responsibility? There are two sides to adolescents gaining responsibility and independence: yours, and theirs.

> *When I was working for Outward Bound in California, I helped teach parent seminars at the beginning and end of twenty-eight-day youth-at-risk courses in the Sierra Nevadas. We had learned over the years that, as important as it was for the young people to gain new skills and self-confidence and to be able to make better decisions for themselves, it was also important for the parents to allow them to change and to use this newly learned independence and responsibility.*
>
> *It was very hard for some parents to allow their children to practice their new skills and to trust their abilities to make responsible choices. The parents were so used to their old behaviors, it was hard for them to believe the new ones were possible. It was helpful for the parents to think ahead about specific ways to give their children more responsibility and to redevelop the trust that had been lost in the past.*

Letting go, though, also means carefully assessing adolescents' ability to successfully take on the responsibility. You must always use your judgment as a leader to make sure the youth have the tools and training that will enable them to be successful. You may want to review the methods for weighing risk in Chapter 5, Taking Risks and Making Decisions, as you think about turning over control.

CHALLENGES IN LEADING YOUTH

The preceding section on leadership strategies for working with young people—building trust, developing credibility by maintaining an appropriate role, setting the tone for a positive group culture, and working to provide a culture of inclusion—will help you to help prevent discipline problems. However, it's probably unavoidable to have some challenges to face when leading youth.

Dealing with Inappropriate Behavior

We have found that holding students accountable for their own behavior while with Outward Bound is the most powerful learning that takes place. In some cases, students have been removed from their course for violation of verbal behavioral contracts. These students almost always return to try again to complete their course—and the difference in their behavior is profound.
—Vanessa Mendillo, community liaison and curriculum coordinator, Philadelphia Outward Bound Center

Human behavior being what it is, it would be naïve to think you won't ever have to deal with behaviors that are negative for the group and for the experience you are working to create for the teenagers you're working with.

Mike was a twenty-eight-year-old man who loved being active, loved being outdoors, and wanted to share his enthusiasm with young people. He volunteered to lead a group of adolescents from a local teenage club in a trail improvement activity in a park just outside town; the park was an asset to the town and drew people from near and far to hike. The group consisted of about ten boisterous boys who admired Mike and wanted to do this outdoor project with him.

On the appointed morning, they all met at the trailhead with brown-bag lunches. Mike had brought all the needed tools as well as snacks and drinks, figuring it would be a rather hot and dusty day. He outlined the duties they were to perform, then counted off the group into two teams of three and one of four. He went over the safety rules, including fire safety cautions

because the fire alerts were high. He assigned the three teams the areas of the trail they were to work on.

All went well for the first few hours. Mike walked around, checking in with each team. Late in the morning, he checked in with team number two. He could tell something was going on from their furtive looks and lack of progress. He also thought he could smell cigarettes. He asked them if they had been smoking. They denied it. He emphasized the dry conditions and the danger of fire. He also told them they'd stop for lunch in half an hour, so they should keep going until noon. Then he told them where to gather for lunch.

At noon, team number two didn't arrive at the designated place. Mike got the others started on lunch and went to find the missing boys. They weren't at the trail site where they had been working. Worried, Mike began to search for them off the trail. After about fifteen minutes, he thought he smelled cigarette smoke again. He found them seated below a big rock, trying to stay out of sight.

Mike confronted their behavior, saying that they not only had broken one of the primary rules of the day but they were also posing serious danger: to the forested park where they were as well as to the nearby town, should a forest fire start. The boys seemed nonchalant and unrepentant.

Mike wanted to give them a warning and a second chance. He knew that they would be proud of having completed this project with the others. But because they did not seem to care or want to cooperate, Mike decided that the risks were too great and that they would need to leave the project. He walked them down to the lunch meeting area and called one of their parents to come and get the three boys. The parent was briefed on the problem and promised to communicate with the other parents.

The rest of the group discussed the situation and agreed that the rules were important and had been broken. Mike was clear with them that, although he hated to see the other three youths leave, their behavior created danger for the forest and the town. The remaining boys continued with their day, and a local photographer came out to take their pictures for the local paper. It was a positive experience for them, and they talked about it for some time afterward. They even became regular stewards of the park and formed an ongoing working group that Mike worked with every summer to do volunteer trail maintenance and repair.

As you can see from this anecdote, Mike had to be clear both to himself and to the boys about what the rules were. He had to decide what actions to take when the rules were broken. It would have been helpful if he had outlined the consequences of breaking the rules when he was orienting the boys to the project. Note, too, that he wanted to give a warning first, but their attitude made him feel that a warning would not have been effective. He used his intuition and his judgment in confronting inappropriate behavior.

Dealing with Conflict

What about dealing with conflict, especially conflict between two youths? What if two or more of Mike's boys had had a serious disagreement or even a physical fight?

Conflict is a common fact of life. Disagreements happen. When working with youth, don't be afraid of conflict, but look for ways to resolve it. High-school students today learn a lot about conflict resolution. In fact, some schools train high-school students as peer counselors who work with their peers, their problems, and their disagreements.

When dealing with conflicts between two teenagers, bring them together with you acting as the unbiased mediator. The goal is not to determine right and wrong, but to get each person to

listen to the other and to understand that there are different points of view. The intent is to facilitate the two in finding a mutually satisfactory solution, one that will satisfy the desires of both of them. Make sure that each person has an equal opportunity to present his or her point of view.

Then see if you can present areas of agreement or, better, ask each of them if they hear any areas where they can agree. Hopefully they will. If no areas of agreement can be reached, ask them to respectfully agree to disagree. You may need to check in with each one afterward to coach them and help them see the benefits of this method. Praising them verbally for resolving their conflict will not only help them move forward but will also help the rest of the group see that conflicts can be resolved and that you will help them to resolve their differences.

Sometimes it helps to remove the people having a conflict from the group and from each other for a short period of time—a cooling-off period. This may be a helpful tactic to use before bringing them together for resolution. It gives them time to think things through rather than acting out of emotion.

Recognizing Gender Differences

Yes, there are gender differences, and much has been written about the different needs that adolescents have based on gender. As you work with youth, it is helpful to understand what some of these differences are and to be aware of any preconceived notions or unconscious attitudes you may have that might influence how you perceive and respond to young men and women. Try to the best of your ability to treat young men and women equally and fairly. It is very, very important.

In order to treat them fairly, though, you may need to incorporate several strategies to meet the needs of both genders. Although gender differences are based in actual physical and cognitive predispositions such as hormonal and neurological maturation, youth workers should think in terms of styles and preferences by which young men and women

DIFFERENCES IN COGNITIVE DEVELOPMENT

Gender: Predispositions / Strengths	Behavioral Description
Female: Detailed thinking	When given directions, girls remember the details better. Girls are better at following a sequence of tasks. Example: Girls will have everything they need in their backpacks the first time.
Male: General or global thinking	When given directions, boys get the gist or the idea. Boys are better at getting to the goal. Example: Boys may have their backpacks in the van faster.
Female: Hearing and listening	Girls remember more of what they hear and can listen for longer uninterrupted times than most boys can. Example: If you recite a list of things to put in a backpack, most girls will remember it.
Male: Seeing and watching	Boys do better remembering what they see or looking at something while they are listening. Example: If you recite a list of things to put in a backpack, boys will remember the first and last things, but not much in the middle of the list. If they *see* the things they need to pack, they will remember it better.
Female: Language and talking	Girls are more verbally facile and detailed. They like to express their thoughts and feelings and often do so in much more detail than boys do. Likewise, they readily absorb information through language. Example: Girls don't mind reading manuals to put things together or watching the instructor passively for a while.
Male: Doing and showing	Boys would rather *do* than talk. They'd rather see an instructor show how to tie a knot while they have the rope in their hands than hear about it first or, worse, read about it. Example: Boys prefer to just begin to assemble and learn by doing.

absorb information and learn. The preceding chart, taken from the Outward Bound guide *Outward Bound Instructor's Guide to Managing Adolescents in the Field* describes some of these differences. Note, however, that approximately 20 percent of girls and boys cross over into the other category. In other words, approximately 20 percent of girls have the style that is the male stereotype, and 20 percent of boys have the style that is the female stereotype. Still, it is helpful to have a general understanding of some differences and how to approach them.

Dealing with Safety Concerns

An important role for you as a youth leader is assuring the safety, both physically and emotionally, for your teenagers. Almost everything discussed so far in this chapter will help you assure safety: building trust, maintaining appropriate roles, creating a culture of respect and inclusion, and building independence and empowering your group. Yet just as with discipline problems, prevention is the best remedy. This means thinking through the rules and codes of conduct you expect and want to establish in your first meetings. Here are some additional thoughts about safety.

Physical Safety

Safety is of the highest priority at Outward Bound, and it should be your highest priority as well. When planning your group's activities, think through the worst that could happen. Then think through (1) what would be necessary to prevent that worst thing from happening and (2) what you would do if that worst thing happened.

For example, in the anecdote described above when Mike was orienting his crew of boys to do trail work, he carefully outlined the appropriate use of tools and the cautions about preventing forest fires, but another consideration would have been to make sure the boys had appropriate clothing and footgear. Safety glasses and even helmets are useful for trail crews, especially if there is danger of falling rock or other objects.

After I have thought through both aspects of the worst that can happen—how to prevent it and what to do if it occurs—I plan how to address each of these questions; then I feel prepared to undertake the activity. See the next section for details.

As for prevention and what to do: utilize others' expertise if needed. Bring along an expert to help, such as a forest ranger to talk about the do's and don'ts of trail work or a rock-climbing specialist to illustrate the rules of climbing. Make sure you have an adequate number of adults to help supervise the group's activity. If you feel there is not enough supervision, ask for parents or others to volunteer to help.

If you still feel the level of supervision is inadequate, don't hesitate to delay or cancel the activity. One of the most important safety lessons is that if conditions are not safe, *delay or call off the activity*.

Most outdoor accidents happen when people are so focused on the goal, they neglect to really scrutinize problems such as changes in the weather that tell them they should wait or cancel. In 1986, a school group was caught in a snowstorm while trying to climb Mount Hood in Oregon and nine

people died. It was a classic case of trying to get to the summit when they should have stopped or even not gone at all. The result was a tragic incident, with several students losing their lives. Make sure canceling is an option in your mind if you have the slightest inkling that the activity or conditions might not be safe.

Safety Planning

Volunteer activities and outings with youth groups can present a wide range of safety issues. An activity such as volunteering in a soup kitchen, where the environment is relatively controlled, may involve limited safety concerns. Outings such as studying a pond or conducting a census of a city neighborhood, which take place in environments that are less easily controlled, require significant preparation and forethought on the part of both the leaders and the participants.

The information in this section is adapted from *Safety Habits of Mind*, by Katrina Abbott and Scott Hartl. It also draws heavily from the *Ropes Course Safety Manual* from Project Adventure and the *Manual of Accreditation Standards for Adventure Programs* from the Association for Experiential Education. In planning for each activity, the leader should consider the following questions:

What potential safety risks might you encounter during this outing? What are the neighborhoods like that you will be working in? Will you be walking on busy streets? Will you be near open water or rock faces? What about the weather?

Have you thought through the what-ifs, the worst-case scenarios? Proactive thinking about potential safety issues such as those listed below will reduce the chances of their ever occurring and increase the chances of your responding effectively if they do; for example:

- What if someone gets split from the group?
- What if someone gets hurt?
- What if you come across hostile people or animals?
- What if a young person needs to be sent back to the organization or home?

Do you have a dependable communication link to help? This might be a cell phone or two-way radio if you will be away from an area where phones are usually available.

Does a trustworthy contact person have copies of your plans for the outing? Designating one contact person that you know can be reached while you are out is an important link in the safety system. The contact person should have a copy of your activity information and a list of the youth who will be with you. Leave a written itinerary of your plans with a designated person at your organization. The itinerary should outline what you are doing, where you are going, when you are going and when you are returning, and the potential hazards of your outing or activity.

Are you taking the smallest group possible? Keeping the group size small is one of the most effective ways to keep a trip safe and productive. Conversely, a large group or, worse, a busload on an outing is very difficult for anyone to keep under control and on task. Figure out a way to create smaller groups. If the outings site is local you may be able to cycle all the students through the experience by breaking them into smaller groups taken out during the day or over a series of days. If you can't help being out with a larger group, small subteams can be created by recruiting parents and other adults to help.

Is the youth-to-adult ratio appropriate for the activity and the group and as low as possible? If you have more than five or six teenagers, then you may need to arrange for extra adult help. The appropriate ratio of adults to youth will vary depending primarily on the nature of the outing, the location, and the age and behavioral maturity of your students. Outward Bound schools and centers maintain a student-to-instructor ratio of six to one for all field experiences, and lower student-to-instructor ratios are standard for adolescent programs.

Have you compiled a safety kit for the outing? Some basic items can be gathered into safety kits to be carried by each adult during any outing. Safety kits can be assembled once and then made available for all future outings. The safety kit could include items such as these:

- several quarters or a phone card for pay-phone calls
- basic first-aid supplies—bandages, antiseptic, compress, latex or other synthetic gloves, etc.
- list of emergency phone numbers
- The following trip-specific items can be arranged for each outing:
- map of the area where you will be
- copy of your trip itinerary
- emergency money for cabs, etc.

Do you know your participants' medical histories? Do they have any potentially serious medical conditions (for example, allergic reactions to bee stings or medications, heart problems, asthma, etc.)? Do they have severe phobias? Are they nonswimmers? Do they have food allergies? When participants fill out a medical form for the trip, it should be carried along by the group leader.

Are you familiar with the outing site? When you venture beyond common resources such as an after-school program or a city park and into less controlled environments, then your knowledge of the current conditions of the area in which you will be traveling and working is one of the most important dimensions of keeping an outing safe. Scout the area before you take your young people there. Know the route that you will take; choose a safe meeting place in case the group gets separated or any incident occurs. Take cell phones but also familiarize yourself with where pay telephones are that could be used in case of an emergency. Locate the nearest medical facilities with emergency care capacity. See the next sections for additional concerns.

Are the adults and youth briefed on the safety issues of the trip? What do the adults need to know to manage their groups safely? What do the youth need to know to manage themselves safely? When do the adults and young people need to know this information so that they can be prepared?

Discuss safety issues with participants and assisting adults before each outing. In your pretrip discussion with them, discuss the what-ifs; go over the Outing Information Sheet (see the sidebar in this section); talk about your expectations for

OUTING CHECKLIST

Before the trip:
1. Fill out appropriate paperwork and give it to a designated staff member at your organization or to an adult helper.
2. Ask an appropriate number of adults to assist with the trip. Adult helpers must be sufficiently fit and physically capable of completing the activities intended, socially skillful enough to work with youth and other adults, and it must be clear to all adults as well as youth just who is in charge. It might also be appropriate to get medical histories for the adults, as well as youth, depending on the activities planned, their rigor, and remoteness.
3. If adults will drive private vehicles, determine whether they have credentials as stated by your organization's policy and whether paperwork is on file if necessary.
4. Prior to the trip, provide all adults and drivers with the following:
   - information on location
   - driving directions to location
   - time to meet
   - appropriate clothing
   - a schedule of the day
   - what their role will be
5. Have first-aid kits for each independent group on the outing.
6. Have adults arrive with enough time so they can get a briefing on the flow of the day and any last-minute information.
7. Listen to a weather forecast if your activity will depend on weather.
8. Brief students on the trip or activity beforehand, including:
   - the schedule for the day
   - proper clothing and footwear (keep the weather forecast in mind)
   - food or meals they should bring

Day of the trip:
1. Brief adults on any last-minute changes and updates.
2. Hand out and explain the first-aid kits; ascertain if any of the adults have medical or first-aid training.
3. Brief participants on the activity site once you are there; indicate boundaries of the activity area and any potential hazards.
4. Be aware of youth and adult needs and changing weather conditions.
5. If there is an emergency, refer to the information you have gathered regarding the location of the nearest hospital and where to call for help. If the program is within a 9-1-1 response area, the leader should first call 9-1-1 and let medical professionals respond.
6. Before leaving the site, account for all the students and adults.
7. If any incidents occurred during the trip, fill out an Outing Incident Report (see sidebar) and give it to your organization.

street travel or behavior on public transportation (see "Travel Safety," below). Go over what to do if anyone is lost or separated from the group.

Do you know what the weather forecast is? Are you prepared for unprepared participants? Extremes of weather can quickly complicate an outdoor activity if you are not prepared for it. It is always advisable to bring extra clothes and food for unprepared participants (see "Travel Safety," below).

Are the tasks engaging and well organized? One of the most effective strategies for managing outings safely is to have well-planned and engaging activities that will keep the youth focused and on task.

Travel Safety

Below are some common practices for traveling and working with a youth group. This list is not exhaustive, but it begins to capture the combined experiences and best practices of a growing group of Outward Bound instructors and students.

Group travel: When working and traveling as a group, stay together within sight and sound of each other. In certain situations with older youth, their maturity level (which is not always correlated to age level) may allow for traveling and/or working with less supervision. Parents should always be aware of the amount of supervision that their children will be getting.

- Establish a safe place to meet if the group is separated and ensure that this is understood by all youth and adults in the group.
- Assign a number to each adolescent and count off at selected points of the trip to ensure that everyone is present.
- Identify a person who will be in front of the group, a "lead," and a person who will stay at the end, a "sweep." The lead and the sweep should be either adults or trusted youth, as appropriate.
- Ask students to dress appropriately for the

environment in which they will be traveling. Some types of clothing or flashy jewelry may send messages of aggression or be an invitation for conflict.

Street travel: Brief participants on street crossings before arriving at their first crossing. Many youth are used to treating street crossings casually and will need to be reminded to cross streets only at a designated cross walk or corner, wait for the entire group, and cross with the "walk" signal.

Walking on roads without sidewalks should be avoided if possible. If it is necessary to travel on a street without sidewalks, then walk single file on the shoulder facing traffic.

Avoid stopping to talk in congested areas; find a well-lit, out-of-the-way place to talk as a group. Avoid dark and deserted streets and shortcuts through parks, tunnels, etc.

Public transportation: When traveling in a subway or trolley, have everyone in your group travel in the same car. When traveling on buses or subways, avoid crowded cars where a large group will be intrusive. Try to use two doors for boarding to cut down on crowding. Adults should count participants once they are all in the bus or subway car and again when they get off.

While waiting for a bus or subway, have participants stand well away from the side of the road or the edge of the platform. Stay out of dark, unlit, isolated places and within sight of the station attendant where possible.

Private vehicles: Be clear on the policies that your organization has on minors traveling in private vehicles, and make sure these policies are enforced. As a leader, you should follow the same requirements as those for other drivers. Create a safe policy for older adolescents driving younger participants to activity sites.

Advise parents of how their children will be transported.

If you feel that a driver or a car is unsafe, find an alternative or cancel the trip.

OUTING INFORMATION SHEET

This should be filled out and discussed with each person prior to leaving for the outing.

Date of outing: _____

Leader(s): _____

Cell phone numbers for trip leader(s): _____

Cell phone number for primary support contact outside the trip: _____

Duration of outing, including travel: _____

Site location /address: _____

Telephone or location of closest telephone: _____

How you are getting to the site (transportation): _____

Contact person at the site: _____

Activities: _____

Possible safety issues: _____

Precautions to address safety issues: _____

Emergency plan: nearest hospital / clinic
(with emergency care capabilities): _____

Address: _____ Telephone: _____

OUTING INCIDENT REPORT

Date: _____

Name of injured / ill party: _____

Location where accident / incident occurred: _____

Narrative on incident: Describe the incident completely. Include how the incident happened and the final outcome. Attach physician's or other care provider's report if the participant was examined by one. _____

_____

_____

Analysis: Include any observations or suggestions regarding how the incident could have been prevented. _____

_____

_____

Additional comments: _____

_____

_____

Report prepared by: _____

Position / relationship: _____

Signature: _____

Other adults involved: _____

Emotional Safety: Harassment

Harassment of any kind, including sexual harassment, should never be permitted—in your organization or anywhere else you observe it. This issue can be addressed by working to ensure that the culture of your group is inclusive. Laughing or joking about another person or telling jokes that are offensive to another, whether they are about gender or culture or anything else, should not be tolerated.

Harassment is any unwanted, persistent, or excessive behavior that is verbally or physically malicious, humiliating, offensive, or intimidating. Harassment can be of a general nature, sexual, racial, ethnic, or related to sexual orientation.

If someone in your group makes offensive remarks unintentionally, quietly point out to the offender that the remark could well be hurtful to another member of the group, and remind the offender of the agreement the group reached in the beginning about being respectful of one another. If harassment continues, the perpetrator should be asked to leave the activity or program, and you should report the behavior to the offender's parents or guardians.

General Harassment. According to the *Outward Bound Instructor's Guide to Managing Adolescents in the Field,* general harassment may include but is not limited to the following:

■ unwelcome remarks, jokes, or behaviors that are intimidating or humiliating

■ jokes, innuendoes, or taunting because a person refuses to conform to community norms or fails to do something he or she has said he or she will do

■ statements that make an individual feel "put down"

■ refusing to accept a particular person's ideas

■ refusing to accept a person's decision not to participate in or complete a particular activity if that person feels threatened by it

Sexual Harassment. Sexual harassment may include but is not limited to the following:

■ unwelcome remarks, jokes, taunting of a sexual nature, leering, and posture or attire that causes awkwardness or embarrassment to the recipient

■ refusing to work, participate, or associate with a person because of his or her gender

■ unwelcome physical contact such as touching, patting, or pinching

■ requesting sexual favors; this may start out as innocent gestures, comments, or jokes and progress to unwanted advances

■ inappropriate display of sexual organs

Racial and Other Types of Harassment. Racial, ethnic, or sexual-orientation harassment may include but is not limited to the following:

■ unwelcome remarks, jokes, innuendoes, or taunting about a person's racial or ethnic background, color, place of birth, citizenship, ancestry, or sexual orientation

■ writings or drawing that are racist or derogatory in nature

■ refusing to work, participate, or associate with a person because of his or her racial or ethnic background or sexual orientation

THINKING ABOUT LEGAL RESPONSIBILITIES

It is difficult here to outline specific legal responsibilities in leading youth because each state has different laws and mandates. However, if you are working with a youth agency or organization, it will have information about any legal obligations you have as a youth leader.

The guiding philosophy that this section can give you is to remember that safety comes first. If you learn about behaviors or actions that have the potential to harm an individual youth or someone else, you should notify the legal authorities. This always takes precedence over the relationship you have with the young person, but it is very important that you make this clear up front to the youth you are working with. When you begin your work with them, this is one of the ground rules they will need to know about. If someone is likely to get hurt, the choice of reporting it to the authorities is out of your hands.

Dealing with Illegal Activity

If you learn that a youth is involved in an illegal activity, you need to decide how you wish to respond to it and whether your organization requires you to report that to authorities. Say, for instance, that you find some boys and girls smoking pot. You need to decide what action you will take. Should you give them a warning? Should you ask them to leave the program? Should you report the activity to local law enforcement? Whatever method you choose, make sure you have told your group ahead of time how you plan to handle this type of situation, should it arise.

Sometimes your decision is based on your personal standard, your own bottom line. What level of tolerance do you have? If an action by a youth, or knowledge of an action by a youth, is completely offensive or intolerable to you, then be honest with yourself and the young person and tell him or her that you cannot tolerate that behavior and that the youth must stop this behavior or leave the program. You may even feel compelled to inform authorities, but make sure you tell the person of your intention.

At Outward Bound, we sometimes have problems with minors smoking cigarettes, an illegal activity in Maine and a clear violation of Outward Bound rules. Generally, we go by the standard of "three strikes and you're out." The first time, they get a warning; then the second time they get a second warning; and by the third time they're found engaging in the activity, they're removed from the course, which also means informing their parents. However, their attitude and the situation itself will often dictate the appropriate response from their leader.

What if someone discloses to you that he or she has participated in an illegal activity, say, stealing something? These are very difficult situations because you have a relationship with this teenager, and trust may well be the reason he or she has disclosed this information to you. Yet you need to be honest with the person and let him or her know that you cannot ignore or hide illegal behavior. The best thing you can do is to convince the person to go to authorities him- or herself. Offer to go with the teenager. Offer to find help for him or her to ameliorate the situation. But be honest with him or her.

Reporting Abuse

The same principles hold true if you suspect or learn of any kind of child abuse that may be oc-

curring. In most states, schools and organizations have a legal responsibility to report such abuse to that state's social services agency. As an individual youth leader, you may not have the strict legal responsibility to the same degree that a teacher has, but you have a moral responsibility. Again, let the teenager know that you are obliged to notify authorities.

I know of a situation wherein a girl began to disclose to a youth leader that her father was abusing her. Before the girl could go on with her disclosure, the adult explained to her, in a caring and supportive way, that if she continued to tell her story, the adult would need to speak to someone at the county social services department. The adult told the girl that she would get help through that department, that a social worker would talk with her, and that the father would most likely be confronted. The adult told the girl that the social worker would help her and make sure that she would be kept safe. The adult also acknowledged how difficult this situation was and how difficult it would be to confront it, but that by getting help, the girl's life would improve.

The girl thought about it. She then decided to go ahead and talk about it, knowing that it would lead to help for her. The benefit of this early disclosure by the youth worker was that it gave the girl the opportunity to decide and to have control of her situation. However, if the girl had not decided to divulge her complete story, the youth worker still would have had to call the social services department with these concerns.

These are terribly difficult situations. You should be prepared for animosity and anger from the teenager, who may feel betrayed by you. In this case, you must hold to your knowledge that in the end, intervention will help this young person, even though he or she may not see it now. Yet these events can also lead to the greatest benefits for the teen with whom you are working. Your presence, your caring, your honesty with the youth may lead to a rewarding and safer outcome.

Confidentiality is of utmost importance in these cases. Yet you need to get support for yourself. Talk to a professional in your youth organization, or find a teacher or someone who has experience with youth to confirm the hard choices and actions you are taking. A social services worker may also be helpful to you.

Setting Healthy Boundaries

Like most people interested in working with teens, you probably have only the best of intentions, for them and for their community. Unfortunately, sometimes adults have been attracted to youth work because it gave them access to young people who were vulnerable to emotional, physical, or sexual abuse. Whether teens come to your organization for homework help, guidance in a crisis, community service, or just to have fun with friends, they need assurance that it is a safe place where the adults can be trusted.

An opposite problem has also occurred when teens and/or their parents have made false accusations of abuse against youth workers they know. Whether caused by malice, mental instability, or misunderstandings, such accusations can be devastating, both to the individual and to the whole organization.

As a youth worker, you need to set good boundaries so that you avoid unhealthy relationships with youth and are protected against possible claims of misconduct. If you work with a well-established organization, good policies—often called "child and youth protection policies" or "policies for abuse prevention"—are probably already in place. If so, learn these policies and take them seriously. Here are some questions that youth workers should ask:

■ How does the organization check volunteers for past history of abuse before allowing them to interact with the youth? Are all volunteers

carefully interviewed? Are their references checked? Does the organization run a criminal background check?

■ What types of physical contact are appropriate between an adult volunteer and a teen? Can volunteers hug freely or only return a hug offered by a youth? What about contact sports or rough-housing?

■ What if a teen asks a volunteer if they can speak together privately? How can this situation be handled so that it's clear to everyone that nothing abusive or inappropriate is happening behind closed doors, while still respecting the young person's need for confidentiality?

■ How is the organization prepared to respond if a charge of abuse is made against a volunteer?

If your organization doesn't have answers to these questions, that's an area in which you can show some real leadership. By helping develop abuse prevention policies, you might unknowingly protect a teenager from a predator—or protect your organization from a damaging lawsuit.

Good resources about setting boundaries, abuse prevention, and risk management are available (see the resources for Chapter 15 in the Bibliography at the end of this book). Some of this material has been written with church youth work in mind, but much of the practical and legal advice is also valid for secular youth work.

NURTURING YOUNG LEADERS

Mentoring a young person may well be one of your most rewarding opportunities as a youth leader. Seeing potential in a young person and deciding to spend significant and intentional time helping this person mature and grow in his or her leadership skills may build into a relationship that lasts a lifetime.

Finding Them Leadership Opportunities

Are you on the board of a youth organization? Are you an adult who is working in some way with youth? Can you spot a teenager who you think has good potential for leadership that you would be interested in helping? As a community worker and leader, keeping your eye out for potential youth leaders is very useful—for the young person, for the community, and for your sense of making a difference.

One-on-One Mentoring

If a young person comes to you for help or for your opinion about something, this is a great way to build a friendship that may have potential to be a mentoring or a coaching relationship. Thus, one of the best ways to build youth leaders is making use of the chance for one-on-one interaction. It is important to watch for these kinds of opportunities and to be open to them.

If you take on a mentoring or coaching role with a youth leader, remember some of the characteristics of adolescents in "Be Aware of the Challenges Facing Youth" earlier in this chapter. A mentoring role requires even more patience and remembering to allow this youth to make mistakes. One of the most valuable things a youth mentor can do is to celebrate accomplishments but also ask probing yet supportive questions after a negative experience. You can help the young person see this as a learning experience rather than a defeat. Encouragement and support are important aspects of the mentoring role.

One-on-one support may not be convenient or present itself, but there are many additional ways to further leadership among talented young people. As mentioned above, including youth representatives on boards of directors is increasingly popular. This gives youth a great opportunity to sit at the table and observe how an organization is governed. It is important, though, to be sure to give this young representative a voice at the board table. It is important for a board to listen to what young people have to say. They have much to offer, and it would be a big mistake and a lost opportunity if the board doesn't listen well.

Leadership Programs

Certainly, leadership programs for youth are another option, with Outward Bound programs leading the way. The Boy Scouts and the Girl Scouts have very challenging badge systems that emphasize leadership skills. Many Outward Bound instructors are proud of reaching the highest level in these systems, which take years and determination to finish.

School programs also nurture future leaders. Boys State and Girls State programs have been available for a long time; student leaders are chosen to attend a statewide program that teaches about our government, develops citizenship, and promotes citizen action.

Encouraging young people to lead school student groups is a good learning experience. Student council positions and offices in honor societies and school organizations are great opportunities. Although teachers may be the primary supporters to youth in these school activities, you may have a chance through other youth work you are doing to encourage your young friends to participate in these leadership roles.

Youth-Developed Programs

Probably one of the best ways to nurture youth leadership is to work with young people who are developing their own programs and organizations. Just as Youthlinks had a project wherein young people create their own projects, some communities have entirely youth-led organizations. These youth truly learn by doing.

Station Maine is an organization dedicated to offering boating opportunities to youth of all ages. It was organized and is led by local teens. They recruit students from five area schools to participate in local and international sailing and rowing contests. Youth work with the participants, and graduates of the program serve on the board. The adults who work with the program are careful to assure that students lead much of the organization's work. Coaching these young people in organizational leadership skills is a terrific leadership learning experience for these adolescents.

Giving Positive Reinforcement

Nurturing young leaders mostly comes from keeping your ears and eyes open to serendipitous moments. As we know, young people are very aware of what adults say and do. A word of encouragement here and there may have more effect than you know.

A young person who is taking on a challenging opportunity or is offering a kind, quiet gesture of help to someone deserves your acknowledgment. Notice what young people are doing. Tell them when you see them do something good. Give them positive reinforcement and feedback. Even the smallest action that shows usefulness deserves praise, which will help that young person do it again—and do even more next time.

Leadership is built on step-by-step actions. You can encourage someone to keep taking those steps. Who knows? Perhaps your encouragement will play a small—or even a large—part toward this young person becoming president of the United States!

And isn't this the great pleasure of working with youth? They have so much potential. All of us have become, and are becoming, who we are because of many, many people in our lives. What more worthwhile work can there be than being a part of someone becoming "more than they know"!

Making Them Feel Needed

There are three ways of trying to win the young. There is persuasion; there is compulsion; and there is attraction. You can preach at them; that is a hook without a worm. You can say, "You must volunteer"; that is of the devil. Or you can tell them, "You are needed!" That appeal hardly ever fails.
—Kurt Hahn, *in* Readings from the Hurricane Island Outward Bound School, *edited by Allison Kuller*

The notion that we are needed is so powerful for all of us. Teenagers need to feel that they have something to contribute and are valued. Real responsibilities in organizations and roles in the community give them pride and a real sense of purpose.

Many youth organizations have a place on the board of directors for a youth representative. Churches often have a slot on their board for a young person. There are many ways to include adolescents in the important tasks of the community, and empowering them to take these responsibilities is the best learning tool we can give them.

Advocating for Youth in Your Community

Once you begin leading young people, being with them, learning from them, and engaging in their development as important community citizens, you will find that you are compelled to be their advocate. Adults who work with youth cannot help but see many opportunities to make sure young peoples' needs and voices are heard within the many facets of a community.

Because youth are affected by so many decisions at the local, state, and federal levels, they need caring adults to carry their voices to the decision makers of our society. That is not to say that youth cannot voice their own needs. They can and should. But their voices are not always heard, and you can play an important role in helping them perfect their message and then finding an entrée into the various decision-making systems.

The organization for which I currently work helped draft and gained sponsors for a state legislative bill to stop industry polluters from contaminating a river that local students like to swim in and boat upon. The legislative hearing for the bill included many testimonies from local merchants, environmentalists, and industry representatives. Students decided that they wanted their voices to be included too. A board member from my organization worked with this group of students to help them draft their testimony and then coached them on what the hearing would be like and what to expect when they gave their testimony.

Hearing from these young people was important to the proceedings. The adults whose testimonies followed the students' referred back to their words as important reasons for having a clean river—because it is important for the well-being and interests of these young people. They made a difference by their presence and their words.

Being an advocate for youth can happen in any setting. It can take place in your neighborhood: making sure that it is safe for children and adolescents. It can take place within your local government: making sure that there are facilities for youth in your town. Do you have safe, drug-free events in your town or city for youth to go to in the evenings? Where do youth congregate in your city or town? Are there good activities for them that are age appropriate? Is there support in your community for learning about what young people want? Is there a way to have them lead a project to develop what they want?

Do you know community merchants who might want to help young people accomplish an endeavor of their choosing? Could you open some doors for these youth? Remember the young people who recruited all those materials for their town's arts center in Maine? There must have been some adult advocates who opened some merchant doors for them.

Do you buy Girl Scout cookies? Do you encourage others to buy their cookies? That's youth advocacy at work.

There are small and large ways to be advocates and as many situations as there are individual youths and adults—and communities. The key is to be open and alert for opportunities—*and* to not be silent. If you see an opportunity to open a door for a youth project or to include a young person in a community discussion, take that opportunity. The potential is huge, both for the young people and for the community.

A FINAL NOTE

As a leader in your community, you must consider many different constituencies. This includes the elder population, disadvantaged populations, and young families. Yet remembering the importance of young people, even though you may not be working directly with them, is an important aspect of cultivating a healthy and thriving place, in which all can live and grow. The children and grandchildren of all the people in your community are its future.

CHAPTER 16

LEADING YOUR COMMUNITY IN THE POLITICAL ARENA

Never doubt that a small group of thoughtful, committed citizens can change the world.
Indeed, it's the only thing that ever has.
—Margaret Mead, The World Ahead

Pulitzer Prize-winning author David Mc-Cullough, in his book *1776*, chronicles the events of the Revolutionary War during that critical year in this country's history. It tells the incredible story of the participation of many, many regular people involved in winning the war and creating a government. Most of the leaders of this momentous time in our history were not trained to do what they eventually managed to do. They learned as they went and relied on their intellects and ingenuity. They gave of themselves for a cause they believed in. They were thoughtful, committed citizens. They changed the world.

So, too, can we all. Outward Bound teaches over and over the importance of being responsible citizens, of going back from an Outward Bound course to one's community and being of use. All during an Outward Bound course, participants are impelled to act responsibly for the good of their patrol or watch, their group. This behavior, then, becomes a metaphor for behavior at home and within their community. Being engaged in furthering the well-being of your community leads to political activity in one way or another. In *The Measure of Our Success*, Marian Wright Edelman writes:

> *America's fate and direction depend on citizen leaders in every nook and cranny of our great nation. Change will come … not from the top down, but from millions of people like you and me raising our voices from the bottom up, telling our religious and political and professional spokespeople what is important to*

us and holding them accountable. Remember that leaders come in both genders; all sizes, colors, and ages; and from all geographic areas and neighborhoods. And they don't all have obvious or special talents.

WHY SERVE YOUR COMMUNITY THROUGH POLITICAL LEADERSHIP?

Politics today is often thought of with disparagement. Regrettably, some—but not all—in powerful political positions have abused their power and betrayed the trust of the people they govern.

Yet politics is so necessary for democracy. According to David McNally in *Another World Is Possible*, politics is merely the process by which "communities of people organize their common life, allocate their resources, and tackle their shared problems. Politics is about the rules we make, the values we honor, the processes we follow so that large groups of people can live together with some measure of fairness, order, and peace." Politics are central to the fabric of our society and certainly of our communities.

Too many people feel that they cannot make a difference. They feel that the systems of local, state, and national government are too big and monolithic to be influenced by the "little people." Yet democracy is founded on the notion that one person with one vote can, in fact, make a difference. And when people gather together others who share their concerns, one voice becomes several and may become many. This leadership can and does make a difference.

Making a difference, though, usually begins

with small steps and actions. Entering into politics doesn't just happen through one single decision. It begins with becoming involved in your community. By volunteering in your community, you help make possible the improvements you, as a community leader, envision.

Chellie Pingree took an Outward Bound course as a teenager. After finishing college, she and her soon-to-be husband moved to a small island off the coast of Maine to farm and raise a family. Using what she had learned on her Outward Bound course and from her upbringing, she became integrally involved in island life: She volunteered at the school. She helped neighbors when they were ill. Although islanders are often standoffish, she and her husband gradually became accepted into the tight island community, largely because of her volunteer actions. Chellie raised livestock and vegetables, and her husband built boats.

As their family grew, Chellie became more and more involved in the school and local activities. She ran for the school board and was elected. She became its chairperson. She also started a small business selling yarn, a product made from the sheep on her farm. The venture grew into a thriving mail-order business.

In the early 1990s, Chellie and her oldest daughter, Hannah, went to hear then Congresswoman from Colorado Pat Schroeder, who spoke at an event in Portland, Maine. Schroeder talked of the need for people, and especially women, to run for public office. She spoke about how good people, everyday citizens, are needed to participate and to bring their common sense and good intentions into public life. She pointed out that all politicians come from the broad range of American life, from the humblest to the most highly educated. It just takes a willingness to say yes.

Toward the end of the talk, Hannah nudged her mother and said, "Mom, you should run, you should do it." There was then a seat open for the state senate in the district where Chellie lived. Chellie decided to do it. She would be a young woman from a very small island running for election to the Maine State Senate.

Chellie won. She served her full allowable number of terms for eight years, becoming Senate Majority Leader along the way. She found that she loved politics. She emerged as a political leader in the state and ran for the U.S. Senate in 2002. Although she was defeated in that race, she went on to become the current president and corporate executive officer of Common Cause and still hopes to serve again in public office someday. There is more to this story:

After graduating from Brown University, Hannah Pingree designed a political section for the women's website iVillage during the national election in 2002. Hannah then went to work on her mother's U.S. Senate campaign. Hannah decided that she, too, loved politics and wanted to run for office. Today, Hannah serves in the Maine House of Representatives representing the island communities on the coast of Maine and has been elected House Majority Leader. She is one of Maine's youngest legislators.

WAYS TO SERVE THROUGH POLITICAL LEADERSHIP

You can be a leader in the political arena in many ways; running for office is just one. There are many varieties of offices for which you can run for election or to which you may apply or be appointed.

You can also help direct issue campaigns. These campaigns work on an idea rather than for a candidate—for example, motivating people to write letters and vote for a local initiative, such as a bond measure that would help your school, or getting people to write to their federal elected representatives, for example, to urge them to pro-hibit oil drilling in the Alaska National Wildlife Refuge.

You can serve on citizen boards—every com-munity needs participants. Some examples are planning boards that review development and zoning or citizen boards that oversee local recre-ation and human service efforts.

As you become more involved in leadership in your community, consider where you might give energy to help form and influence policies that affect the issues about which you care most deeply. Do you value literacy and use the public library? How about serving on the library board? Are you involved in your children's school? How about running for a seat on the school board? Your local newspaper and town or city office can give you information about openings on such boards.

This is a great way to learn about local activ-ism. Learn by doing. Entering the political arena can start at the very local level, the way that Chellie Pingree started. All it takes is the willingness to serve. You are needed.

This chapter focuses primarily on leading an issue campaign. What you may find, though, is that after you've worked on an issue, especially if you are successful, you will want to consider doing more. You may be interested in becoming a candidate for public office. Working in the politi-cal arena can be infectious, yet another way to feel that you are doing well by doing good!

IDENTIFYING PROBLEMS TO SOLVE AND ISSUES TO ORGANIZE AROUND

If you have an interest in serving your commu-nity, you probably care deeply about something that you want to see improved or dealt with in a more systematic way. To begin to be a leader in the political process, follow your natural interests. Usually issues choose you.

When I was working in domestic violence services, dealing with families in need gradu-ally led to my wanting to gain more help from the structures and systems within the community. The police, the district attorney, the victim witness system all are systems that interact with such families. We found that state and federal laws and resources were sorely lacking in giving these community helpers the appropriate tools to deal with domestic violence problems. This led us to work for change within the federal, state, and local governmental systems, usually through state legislatures and Congress.

In the beginning of our volunteer work, we didn't think that this would be necessary. But as we did the work, we found time and again that the laws and practices that guided and instructed the police and the legal system were not adequate to really help these families. Today, because of the political work done to make these improvements and additions to our laws, there are many state and federal statutes that guide and mandate certain actions when service agencies are working with abuse victims, perpetrators, and their children.

Research the Issues

As you gather information, develop four to five themes around which to organize the facts that will help communicate your issue campaign. Clearly identify the problems that your issue ad-dresses. It is very important to have facts to back up your reasons for addressing an issue, facts to support your position. If you want to ask local or state government or an agency to take a specific action regarding an issue, they will need data to convince them of the need for this action.

If you are working in a volunteer organization and your issue has emerged from that work, collect information from the organization. Information can be found in the needs assessments from fund-raising grant applications; information can be found in data collected about clients, the recipi-ents of service; information can be obtained from interviewing and documenting those interviews

LEADING AN ISSUE CAMPAIGN

If you find an issue you care about and want to take on a campaign to address that issue, consider the following:

- Research the issue—start with a solid foundation of information about your issue.
- Focus on solutions—prioritize your goals and keep them at the forefront.
- Develop a strategy—map out the activities and the steps you will take. Create a plan.
- Make a budget—utilize your resources carefully toward your goals.
- Form an effective team—use your knowledge about working with volunteers.
- Organize the work—the skills you have from your personal and professional life are the same skills you will need to organize an issue campaign.
- Work effectively with the media—find ways to voice support for the issue publicly and to use influence with others.
- Think about connections—what larger group of people can be reached and organized?
- Stay current—keep aware of new developments and open to new ideas and ways to be better organized. Stay tuned to current events, new technology, and trends.
- Learn by doing—you have the passion and commitment.
- Be patient—your knowledge and skills will grow the longer you are involved.
- Keep your spirits up—fight complacency and flagging morale.
- Never give up—losses and setbacks are temporary.
- Work for the long haul—continue to increase your support base.

with volunteers, paid staff, and the recipients of service.

Depending on your issue, you may also be able to research public documents to support your cause. Most municipal and state agencies and departments keep information that is usually readily available to the public. The federal Freedom of Information Act guarantees that a U.S. citizen can obtain public documents from federal, state, and local government.

Talk with other organizations and people who are working in your area of concern. It's amazing how the network of people will grow as you begin to do your research. Solicit help from other concerned citizens in doing the research. Spread the word that you are interested in developing a campaign around the issue. You will begin to find others to help you.

Make sure that as you gather data, you keep track of the sources of the information. Quoting information without a good reference source can lead not only to a lack of credibility but possibly to legal problems later on in your issue campaign.

Choose Your Issue

As you are thinking about and researching your issue, you may come upon other aspects of the same issue that could prove to be more productive toward solving the problems that your issue addresses. Or, as you talk with people, other ideas may emerge regarding the problems and possible goals for solving them. As you make a final selection of an issue to work on, consider the list in the sidebar below.

Over the years, Outward Bound has been involved in several environmental issue campaigns. Because the wilderness is the organization's classroom, preserving wilderness areas and preventing development or incompatible uses in wilderness areas comes up more frequently than Outward Bound would like.

In the 1980s, Canyonlands National Park in Utah was identified as a site for storing nuclear waste. This was of great concern to Outward Bound not only because of the beautiful nature of the park but because

*Outward Bound uses this area for its
canyoneering and multi-element courses.
Outward Bound mounted a letter-writing
campaign among our staff and the many
students who participated in courses in the
area. Happily, Canyonlands was not chosen
as a nuclear dump site, and it was felt that
the many letters that were written on the
park's behalf had helped. It was also a great
educational tool that helped Outward Bound
students understand the importance of
citizen action and participation.*

We hope the Outward Bound alumni now often write letters expressing their thoughts to their political leaders. Perhaps some of them have gone into politics!

*The Holy Cross Wilderness Area in Colorado
was also a target for change within the U.S.
Forest Service's management plan for the
area. Outward Bound staff went to many
Forest Service meetings and joined with
other outdoor leaders in working to keep the
threatened changes from occurring.*

*In Maine, Outward Bound was a
key member in working to preserve the
Allagash River as a federally designated
"wild and scenic river," which means that
no motorized boats or vehicles have access
to the river. Outward Bound worked
hard with others to reach an agreement
called the River Driver's Agreement,
which protected the river's wild quality.
Other people wanted to provide access for
motorized boats with roads and launching
ramps. This issue reemerged in the 2006
state legislative session, and activists
around the state are still working to
protect this valued river.*

All these actions took time to organize, plan, and carry through. Sometimes Outward Bound leads certain efforts; other times, it is a member of a coalition working on issues such as in the River Driver's Agreement. Outward Bound staff and participants have worked to make a difference in the future of wilderness in the United States.

ENVISIONING A SOLUTION

Once you have chosen your issue, you then need to decide exactly what solution you want for the problem that exists. Sometimes this may be defeating a proposed change in something you hold dear, such as a development project in a wild and pristine area. Sometimes you will want to create a solution to an existing problem in your community, such as a shelter for homeless people or a safe house for abused women and children.

In any case, it is important to be clear about what it is you want and define it carefully so it is understandable to many. The list in the sidebar above for choosing an issue also can be used when thinking about your solution to the issue you choose.

You may want to bring a group of people together to help you envision the solution. Including other people is a good way to begin to build support and help for your issue campaign. It is good to include people who know the issue well, including what solutions are possible and what is likely to succeed. If you are working within an organization, it is important to bring the leaders and the board of directors into alignment around your solution. They may have important input and insight into what would be best.

Stay open to many ideas. Then work to build consensus around agreement on one solution and goal. This will direct your issue campaign.

DEVELOPING A STRATEGY

Once you decide on your solution, begin to think about your strategy, which will be the groundwork for building a campaign plan. In developing your strategy, consider the five sections below. Take a look at each of these key questions from the United Church of Christ's *Public Policy Briefing Book*, look at the resources you have to

TIPS FOR CHOOSING AN ISSUE

According to Kim Bobo, Jackie Kendall, and Steve Max in *Organizing for Social Change*, your issue should do the following:

- The issue's solution should result in a real improvement in people's lives. If you can see and feel the improvement, then you can be sure that the problem has actually been solved.
- The issue should be worthwhile. People working on the issue campaign should feel that they are working for something about which they feel good and that merits the effort.
- The issue should be winnable. The problem should not be so large or the solution so remote that you and others are overwhelmed by them. You should see that you have a good chance of winning, or at least that there is a good strategy for winning. Ask who else has won on an issue and how, and then call on people with experience and ask for advice.
- The issue should be widely felt. Many people must feel that this issue addresses a real problem, and they must agree with the solution. It is not enough that a few people feel strongly about it.
- The issue should be deeply felt. People must not only agree that the issue is significant but feel strongly enough about it to do something about it. It is not enough that many people agree about the issue but don't feel strongly about it.
- The issue should be easy to understand. It is preferable that you don't have to convince people that the problem exists, that your solution is good, and that they want to help solve the problem.
- The issue should have a clear target. That target is the person or groups—for example, a town council, a legislative committee, a mayor—who can give you what you need to win your issue.
- The issue should have a clear time frame that works for you. An issue campaign has a beginning, a middle, and an end. You should have an approximate idea of what those times are and that they work for you.
- The issue should be nondivisive. Avoid issues that divide your present constituency. Don't pit neighbor against neighbor, old against young, or black against white.
- The issue should build leadership. The campaign should have many roles that people can play. Issue campaigns that meet most of the other criteria also build leadership.
- The issue should raise money. Have some idea of how you will obtain funding sources for your campaign. Figure out how much money your campaign will cost both you and any opponents.
- The issue should be consistent with your values and vision. The issue you choose to work on must reflect your values and your vision for an improved society.

work with—people power, information, money endorsements, etc.—and develop a strategy that makes the most sense for you.

Objective: What Do You Want?

A campaign must begin with a clear sense of what you want to achieve. It should be easily explained and understood. An initial objective (such as a change in a law) should be big enough to attract peoples' interest, yet small enough to win some concrete results within a reasonable time—six months to a year.

Audience: Who Can Give Your Objective to You?

The first question to ask is, who has the "authority" to give you what you want? Is it Congress, your state legislature, your city council, your local school board, the local health department? Identify the decision makers that you will need to influence. Whoever it is, this is your primary audience.

Second, who will most directly influence your audience's decision making? This could be the media, local business leaders, or other community groups. They also need to be a target of your efforts.

Message: What Does Your Audience Need to Hear?

A campaign must have a message that is clear, true, persuasive, and consistent for the audiences that the campaign has targeted. Advocates often make the mistake of believing that the most effective message is the one most persuasive to themselves. What do your *audiences* think, and what will genuinely move them to your side? That message must be repeated, over and over again, with clarity.

Messengers: Who Does Your Audience Need to Hear Your Message From?

The same message will have a very different effect depending on who communicates it. In general, an issue campaign should have some messengers who have credibility as experts, some who can speak from personal experience, and others who have special credibility or connection to the person or group you have targeted.

Identify individuals and groups that you will need as allies to help you carry your message. What people do you know who have good relationships with the decision makers and can be your messengers?

Delivery: How Can You Get Your Audience to Hear Your Message?

Campaigns can deliver their message in many different ways, from lobbying or media work to protest and direct action. Campaigns need to evaluate their options for action and weave the right methods together in a winning mix.

FORMING A TEAM

When you have thought through your strategy, it is time to build a team of people who believe in your issue and will help you lead the campaign. They should be people who share your passion and will bring resources of knowledge, community connections, and the ability to help strategize and troubleshoot as the campaign evolves.

The size of your team should be between six and fifteen people. You want it to be big enough

and inclusive enough to include the attributes described in the sidebar below and also to ensure there is enough capacity and energy at each meeting. Make it large enough so that if one or two people cannot make it to a meeting, work can still get done without them. Too large a group, however, makes it harder to stay focused and stay on task.

If you are working within an organization, most of the necessary people may already be available within the organization. Or you may want to include others outside the organization as well. In any case, the organization's leadership should be integrally involved in the selection of this team and the ongoing work of the team.

The duties of this team are to guide the campaign by strategizing and organizing the work. This is the group of people who will agree on a finalized work plan and make decisions during the course of the campaign. They, with you, will help lead the various aspects of the campaign and work to ensure its success. Other volunteers will be needed to implement the various strategies within the campaign, but this is the group who will work together consistently to ensure the campaign is going smoothly. Regularly scheduled meetings will be important to assure this happens.

ORGANIZING THE WORK

Once you have formed your team, you need to draft a plan for the campaign that the group agrees to and from which they can work. A definite written plan, a work plan with time lines, will guide your campaign and be a road map for everyone working on the campaign. This very important step will help keep the campaign focused. It also helps volunteers working on a campaign see that there is structure and good organization to the campaign. As mentioned in Chapter 14, Leading a Volunteer Organization, it is important for volunteers to have clarity about what their work will be and, for a campaign, to have a clear goal in mind that everyone rallies around.

Think of every activity and event you want to have. Identify time lines for each of them. Some

TIPS FOR BUILDING YOUR TEAM
- Find someone who knows the issue and can help develop the message.
- Find someone who is a good strategic thinker.
- Find someone who knows the community well and can help identify key messengers.
- Find someone who can help with fund-raising.
- Find someone who can act as treasurer to assure careful management of the money.
- Find people who are willing to meet regularly and have the time to commit.
- Find someone who is willing to manage volunteers.
- Find people who do not polarize your issue, whose presence won't automatically alienate important messengers or decision makers.

actions, such as large events and getting out the vote, will need to have a subplan of their own.

Think about the different stages of the campaign: the beginning, the middle, and the end. What are the different needs during these stages?

Beginning. Sometimes issue campaigns have a media kickoff event, similar to a candidate announcing a run for an office. This event could be a press conference, with press releases distributed well ahead of the event. Choose your best public messengers who have the most credibility in your community. It also helps to have people who are or will be affected by your issue give testimonials and tell stories illuminating the importance of the issue in their lives, their children's lives, etc. Speakers should clearly identify and describe the issue using simple language and your four to five message points. Speakers should urge support from the community and tell people how to get in touch with you to help. Large photos or pictures showing your issue visually are also helpful at a kickoff event. People remember pictures and stories the best.

Middle. This is probably the hardest stage. Once you announce your campaign with a beginning splash, then you need to begin an intense letter-writing campaign to the decision makers and to the general community via letters to the editor of local media. It is also important to organize people to speak individually with the targeted decision makers to persuade them of the merit of your campaign. If there will be public

hearings or debates about your issue, you need to organize people to go to these hearings and to voice their opinions. If there is a debate, make sure people attend and show their support for those participating in the debate who support the issue. Working effectively with the media is very important during this phase as well.

It is also important in the middle of a campaign to step back to assess your progress and effectiveness. Ask for feedback from people not engaged in the campaign. Listen to their thoughts. Perhaps a poll would be helpful to see if your message is getting out. Polling is expensive, so it needs to be included in your planning budget, yet it is an effective way to test your message and see if people are paying attention to your issue. Be willing to change your tactics or to innovate strategies if you find you are not being effective so far. See "Some Midpoint Measures" later in this chapter.

End. This is when you want to get out the vote or, if the issue is not on a ballot, have many, many phone calls and letters going to the decision makers. A barrage of good information supporting your cause is needed in the final stage. You may want to use public service announcements or advertising in some way. You may want to do mailings to everyone who is affected by the decision. Citizen activism, such as supporters carrying signs about your issue, may be appropriate. Lawn signs and public displays are also used at the end of a campaign.

Now let's take a detailed look at how to implement these various activities on an issue campaign.

Planning Information Outreach

Will you do door-to-door canvassing, wherein you hand out written literature describing your issue? When would be the most opportune time to do that canvassing? What printed material will you need to hand out door to door, and by when do you need it? When do materials need to be drafted, reviewed, and taken to the printer?

What events are happening in your community that offer an opportunity to talk to people and pass out materials? Are there fairs and community celebrations where it would be good to have a booth and visibility? Carefully think through all potential activities in which you could participate that would help you reach your goal. What information and materials would you want to be able to give people at these events?

Most issue campaigns these days have a website where supporters can turn for information, quick updates, and suggestions for getting involved and supporting your issue. Have some-one on your team put up a website, or hire someone to do this for you. You'll also need someone to manage the website and keep it updated and useful.

Creating a Detailed Time Line

As you identify all activities and dates for when these activities need to occur, identify what people will be responsible for each activity and include these dates and people in the plan. Charts such as the one below are often helpful.

Plans can, of course, change and be adapted to meet the variety of needs that arise during a campaign, but having an outline and guide helps you make decisions about the proposed variations to the plan and their effectiveness compared to the plan you have already devised.

Building a Budget

Once you have identified all your activities, build a budget based on each activity.

Expenses. Identify all your expense items and research the costs involved for each. Think of every type of expense you may need to be success-ful. Research prices so the costs you identify are

ACTION	WHO	WHEN
Develop the message		
Develop 4–5 themes		
Research facts		
Develop outreach material		
■ brochure		
■ fact sheet		
■ mailings		
■ website		
Plan events		
■ receptions		
■ coffee meetings		
■ information fairs		
■ conferences		
Plan a door-to-door campaign		
Work with the media		
■ press releases		
■ letters to the editor		
■ editorials		

based in reality. For instance, how many printed items will you need? What does it cost to print a certain number? Do you gain a cost advantage by printing a certain quantity or by printing at certain times? Be realistic and don't budget too low.

Revenues. Once you identify how much money you need based on your expense budget, identify where you will get that money. Again, be realistic and, if anything, budget conservatively. How will you raise the money to pay for materials and events?

The most common way to raise funds is to ask supporters to give to your campaign. Is it possible to talk with a few people of means to help you in a sizable way? Will any coalition partners provide funds? (See "Building a Coalition" later in this chapter.)

Fund-raising will be an important discussion to have with your team. You may want to hold a fund-raising event to talk about your issue, with donated music, food, and beverages, where people will bring their checkbooks. Sometimes other organizations will help with the campaign either with cash or by providing some of the services and goods needed for the campaign.

Balancing the budget. Once you carefully assess the revenues you believe it is possible to raise, compare your expenses against these revenues. Generally, expenses start out being more than revenues. This is the time, then, to scale back the activities you want to do and the events you want to hold. It is always easier to add to a budget midway through a campaign than to have to cut back once you're underway. This is always the hardest part: balancing, realistically, what you want to do with how much money you will be able to raise.

Carefully think through what the absolutely key and necessary expenses are, the ones you cannot do without. Then make a list of optional expenses; if you get more money, you can do these, but without more money, you will be forced to omit them.

Consider building a three-tiered budget, one based on minimum resources, one based on moderate resources, and one based on doing everything you desire.

You don't want to end a campaign owing money. That is not only very difficult personally for the team of individuals most responsible for the campaign but also does not reflect positively on the campaign and your abilities to manage and lead a successful campaign. Even if you lose on your issue, you will most likely want to come back again to work on the issue later, and your credibility will be important for the future.

Working with the Media

Once you and your team have worked on and agreed to a plan and a budget, it is time to really begin reaching out to the community and start the real work of the campaign. The media is extremely important in any campaign, whether it's an issue or an individual running for office. It helps get the word out to a far broader audience than you or your team, organization, or coalition can do on your own.

A section of your campaign work plan should

TIPS FOR FUND-RAISING
- Ask for donations at every opportunity.
- Hold a raffle at an event sponsored by another organization.
- Hold a food-tasting event in conjunction with neighborhood restaurants.
- Ask a sympathetic restaurant to donate 10 percent of its revenue on a certain day to your issue.
- Organize a phone-a-thon. Though these take a lot of organizing, they can be effective.
- Organize benefit concerts and performances.
- Organize benefit dinners.
- Hold a rummage sale.

be exclusively about media work. If you can find someone to volunteer to oversee this part of your campaign, so much the better. Media work is most effective when it has focus and continuity so that the message you are trying to convey builds over time and is consistent.

Whatever media techniques you use, remember to make copies or tapes of the results. These can be used in future events, mailings, and fund-raising efforts. The shelf life of media coverage can be quite lengthy and can help build your campaign's credibility.

Contact Lists

There are many different methods for working with the media. However, no matter what the varieties of methods you choose to use, it is very helpful to have a list of media contact people to whom you will send press releases and also try to gain as allies in getting your message out.

Identify the key media people in your area,

including message makers in broadcase media (radio and television), print media (local newspapers, magazines, and community publications), and online media (websites, blogs, and listserves). Then meet with them and work to build relationships with them. Remember that all good political work is about building relationships with people who will then become interested in your issue and want to help.

Make a contact list of all these media people and their email addresses, phone numbers, and mailing addresses. Also note on the list the deadlines the different media sources have, such as hours before airing time or days before publication of a newspaper or magazine. This will also help you decide on the timing of any events you want covered by specific media.

Press Releases

The standard way to inform the public about a newsworthy event during your issue campaign is

---

PRESS RELEASE GUIDELINES

These guidelines are from *Getting the Word Out in the Fight to Save the Earth* by Richard Beamish:

- Be sure of your facts.
- Stick to essential details. Don't try to be all-inclusive.
- Leave no important question unanswered. Assume that your reader has never heard of your cause and has little or no familiarity with your subject.
- Keep it simple, clear, and direct.
- Convey a sense of urgency without being histrionic, perhaps through a quote from a leader.
- Go easy on how many quotes you use, however, and make sure they sound like something a real person would say.
- Never use a long word when a short word will do.
- Avoid jargon of any kind, especially legalese and computer jargon.
- Favor short sentences over long ones. When you do use a long sentence, try to follow it with a short, declarative one.
- Be sparing in the use of acronyms. When you do use one for the first time, be sure it appears parenthetically after the full name of whatever it represents; for example, "The United States Forest Service (USFS)."
- Include visual aids when you can. A photocopied map, photograph, or other image illustrates your message and can add interest to your release.
- Have a friend, preferably one not involved in your campaign, read the press release to be sure it is interesting, understandable, and free of typographical errors and misspellings.

to issue a press release. Press releases can be issued to any type of media. The key to an effective press release is to clearly include the *when, what, where, who,* and *why* of the event.

Be sure to include your campaign's contact names and phone numbers at the top of the page for further information. Use a headline to highlight your message and attract attention, then try to engage your reader with a catchy lead paragraph. Get to the point and then elaborate on it, with increasingly less important (but still essential details) in the paragraphs that follow. Limit your release to one or two pages, preferably double-spaced for easy reading and editing. Be neatly professional: produce a clean, clearly printed, easy-to-read press release.

The press release needs to be straightforward, clear, and succinct without unnecessary words and details. See the "Tips for Press Releases" sidebar for more details.

Media will not always choose to broadcast or publish your press release, but it may help to make follow-up calls to your key media contacts asking if they received the press release and calling their attention to it. This is where having a volunteer in charge of the media work can really make a difference, if that person takes the time to develop relationships with key media contacts.

Besides the kickoff event, any noteworthy happening can warrant a press release. For instance, if you are holding a benefit concert, dance, or dinner that is raising money for your campaign, a press release is useful to notify the public without having to advertise for it. Also, any new information about your issue that occurs during the course of the campaign deserves a press release, calling attention to the ongoing issue you are trying to address. Is there a prominent leader who is lending his or her name to your issue? This would deserve a press release. Use your imagination and look for opportunities. Any coverage you can gain through the media will help you.

Be cautious, however, about being too aggressive with press releases. You should know when *not* to issue a release. Issuing too many releases or releases that are not very interesting to the public may lead to your media contacts losing interest in what you are doing. Here are some questions adapted from *Getting the Word Out* to help you determine whether a press release will be effective:

- What do you hope to accomplish by issuing this press release?
- Who, outside your organization, really cares?
- Is what the press release announces truly newsworthy?
- Will the resulting press coverage help?
- Can you accomplish your purpose better in another way?

Print Media

Decision makers pay a great deal of attention to all the media, but especially local newspapers, magazines, and community publications. Try as many of these strategies as possible to reach many levels of print media—locally, regionally, statewide, even nationally.

Letters to the editor. It is very useful to have different voices throughout the community writing their support to local publications; this shows that there is a broad base of concern regarding your issue. Decision makers carefully read letters to the editor, especially in their districts and community. Ask people who volunteer with you to write letters to the editor. Think about allies in the community whose letters might be influential; ask them to write as well.

Also, think about the timing of letters to the editor. It's good to have them written throughout the life of the campaign, but they are especially important in the few weeks before a final decision is scheduled.

Editorials. Visit with editorial boards at your local newspapers and try to get their support. A newspaper editorial in support of your issue can have a very significant influence in your community. Always remember to write a note of thanks to these boards for meeting with you. The same is true for any news reporter who covers an event you have sponsored.

Columns and interviews. Visit newspaper and magazine columnists as well, and ask them to write about the work your campaign is doing and the solution to the issue you are working toward. A favorable newspaper or magazine column can be very helpful to an issue campaign. Columnists are likely to be especially interested if there are personal stories to be told. They might choose to interview you as well; if you will be photographed for print media, think about how to present yourself (see interview tips under "Broadcast Media," below).

Opinion editorials. Get opinion leaders to write "op-ed" pieces, as they are called. A prominent person in your community who supports your issue and is willing to write of his or her support can be very influential as well. Sometimes it will help him or her if you draft the talking points or at least give the person a good fact sheet with data that will help make the correct points. You want to make sure that the desired message is conveyed. Usually, a person writing an op-ed piece will let you review it before it is sent to a newspaper or magazine for publication.

Broadcast Media

Local radio and television stations are a very effective way to get your message out to a lot of people at once. Today's reality is that fewer people use print media, so don't forget about broadcast media.

Editorials. Also visit with editorial boards at your local radio and television stations; talk with them about your issue and ask for their support. A radio or TV editorial in support of your issue can have a very significant influence over voters, decision makers, and the public at large. Always write a thank-you note to these boards for meeting with you.

Interviews. If you persuade any of the media in your community to interview you about your campaign, prepare carefully and think through your message. Think of the same principles that are used in a press release (see sidebar above), keeping your message clear and concise.

Be prepared to tell stories that illuminate your issue, but don't have more than three or four messages, and make sure they all support your issue. Make sure you know all the facts. If you are asked a question to which you don't know the answer, don't be afraid to say you don't know, but promise to find the answer. That is better than trying to bluff.

If you will be interviewed on TV, think about how to present yourself. It is a good tactic to wear a little makeup. An interview is a time when some color on your cheeks and lips helps present a professional image, even for women who don't normally wear makeup. A little cheek color is useful for men, too. But make sure your makeup is not too heavy.

Wear bright-colored clothing; solids are best. Women should not wear heavy jewelry. Suits of gray or navy work well, with light- or cream-colored shirts. Busy, printed clothes, ties, or scarves do not look attractive on TV (or in print photographs).

Know who you are talking to when you are going to be interviewed. Try to learn that person's point of view and try to think of what questions will be asked. Stay calm and don't get angry. If the interviewer begins to go off on a tangent, bring him or her back to your message point. It doesn't hurt to repeat your essential points. If the interviewer misinterprets your answer, speak up and make a correction.

Electronic Media

The online world offers many new opportunities for getting your message out. Make sure someone on your team is Web savvy so you can make the most of these emerging media. And don't forget that many traditional print and broadcast media also have electronic venues as well.

Listserves. These days, you don't have to simply snail-mail your printed materials; you can send them electronically either in the body of an email message or as an attached file. You'll want to develop email address lists for your supporters just as you do your print mailing addresses. It's often effective to build listserves for supporters with varying levels of interest in the campaign so you can target your messages most effectively.

Blogs. An extremely effective emerging electronic medium is the web log, or blog. Information is exchanged nearly instantaneously, and bloggers are increasingly shaping our political dialogs. For example, relative newcomer Senator Barack Obama has astounded political pundits by his web fund-raising bringing in more money than well-established Democratic Senator Hillary Clinton's more traditional campaign.

BUILDING A COALITION

Identify the key people you want to involve, and identify the key organizations with which you want to work closely. The more voices and support you have for your issue, the greater your chance for success. It is very important to build as broad a base of support as possible, including any interested groups but also as many individuals as possible. This is grassroots organizing at work, and it has always been historically important in the politics of the United States.

Brainstorm Who to Include

Early in your planning, have your team identify all the groups you can think of that are compatible with your issue. Include organizations, businesses, and any interested groups. Consider nonprofits, government agencies, interest groups, churches, and neighborhood associations. Churches are wonderful allies that have contacts with many varieties of people to whom you might not otherwise have access.

Is your campaign about a health issue? How about talking with local hospitals and any doctors' associations, nurses' associations, and patient support groups? Are you organizing around an environmental issue? How about talking with local hiking clubs, local chapters of national organizations such as the Sierra Club and the Audubon Society, and local conservation groups?

Make as comprehensive a list as you can. Think broadly. There may be groups interested in your issue that do not immediately come to mind, such as employer groups wanting to work on health issues to prevent absenteeism.

Approach Potential Organizations

Once you've identified as many possibilities as you can, have members of your team go and talk personally to key leaders of these groups. Carefully explain your issue, the reasons you are mounting a campaign on the issue, and what the goal of your campaign is. Ask these groups to join your effort. The intent is to have all the targeted groups join your campaign simultaneously, if possible. That way, everyone in the coalition has the same information and you're able to mount a unified and further reaching effort. Launching your effort with a large number of supporting organizations strengthens your campaign.

Plan a Coalition-Building Meeting

Set up an information-sharing meeting at which you will devise a plan on how all these groups can work together, how they can become a coalition to coordinate efforts for working on and winning the campaign. Invite a representative or two from every group you have talked with to come and hear more about your issue. Plan this meeting carefully, using some of the same methods for organizing meetings discussed in Chapter 14, Leading a Volunteer Organization. It is important that all invited organizations participate fully, so good facilitation is a priority.

At this meeting, the goal is to have the participating organizations' representatives give commitments from their organizations to support and work on your campaign. Ideally, these representatives will go back to their organizations, share the information you have given them, and broaden the base of support and campaign activity throughout their organizations. Your goal is to widen the web of support for your campaign and to gain even more people who will join your efforts, discuss your issue, and bring more influence to the decision makers you want to persuade.

Will the Coalition Be Temporary or Permanent?

When forming a coalition, consider whether it will be permanent or temporary. Sometimes coalitions are formed to further ongoing issues; such coalitions have more than a single campaign in mind. They are formed to bring their collective voices together to improve and coordinate their efforts toward longer-term goals.

> *When working at Safehouse, we found that many of our concerns were shared with other domestic-abuse shelters in Colorado and even around the country. We began to talk with one another and decided to form a coalition of domestic-violence programs around the state that became the Colorado Coalition Against Domestic Violence.*
>
> *This group of more than twenty-five different organizations pooled money together to lobby the state legislature for laws to protect and help survivors of domestic violence and their families. The coalition shared information and best practices. It worked to further educate the state and its leaders about the importance of addressing issues of abuse in the workplace, in schools, and in communities. Together, the unified voice of many provided a stronger message and better results.*

If your issue has long-term implications and your campaign is just one among many ongoing solutions, you may find that you are building a permanent coalition. It may be that when you've formed a coalition for your campaign, the coalition discovers that the needs go beyond your campaign and the coalition wants to continue its work. This decision will be an item to consider as the groups meet together and organize themselves into a coalition and as the work the coalition does evolves.

WORKING WITH OTHER ALLIES

Some allies won't be part of your coalition but you will want to cultivate their support nonetheless. These may be individuals or organizations, businesses, or other entities that may not wish to participate in a coalition but whose support you need. Ask them for their advice. Keep them informed of your progress in the campaign, and when the time comes, ask them to advocate for your issue in a specific way, such as voting for your campaign.

You may find that you have allies within the body you are trying to influence, such as a state legislature, town council, or planning board. These insiders are extremely helpful. They help you with strategy. They help you understand the opposition. If you are trying to get a bill through a state legislature or other legislative body, you will need legislators to sponsor your bill. Bill sponsors help you draft the legislation's language and guide you through the necessary steps.

Most of all, you want these allies to advocate for your issue. When talking with these potential allies, be specific. See the sidebar "Remember Your ABCs," below.

DEALING WITH OPPOSITION

Opposition is inevitable, but it usually is a good sign that you are being effective. Taking on an issue invariably indicates that something needs to change; otherwise you wouldn't be doing it. In any campaign, there are people who object to change or who have vested interests in maintaining the status quo. In your initial strategy sessions, try to identify who might oppose your campaign and plan for what you may need to do to address their opposition.

TIP: REMEMBER YOUR ABCS

The United Church of Christ's *Public Policy Briefing Book* has this advice:

- **A**sk for something specific.
- **B**e persistent.
- **C**ourteousness—remember to be appreciative.

WHAT YOU SAY ABOUT YOUR ISSUE	WHAT YOUR OPPONENT SAYS ABOUT THEIR APPROACH OR ISSUE
WHAT YOUR OPPONENT SAYS ABOUT YOUR ISSUE	**WHAT YOU SAY ABOUT YOUR OPPONENT'S APPROACH OR ISSUE**

Identify and Approach Your Opponents

Identify who your opponents are likely to be. How strong are they? What will attaining your goal mean to them? What will they do to oppose you? What will they say?

Once you have identified your opponents, consider going to meet with them. I am a firm believer in talking with people about their concerns. You may be able to dispel any unrealistic fears they may have about the effects that your proposed solution might have on them. You may even convince them to remove their opposition and, even if they are not willing to support your issue, not overtly oppose the campaign.

If you don't feel able to meet with your opponents, think about what person or people in the community might be a bridge between your efforts and your opponents' concerns. Consider taking a person like that with you when you meet with an opponent, or ask that person or persons to try to work something out with the opposing side.

In fact, before you even announce your campaign, it might be worth going to talk with anyone you feel may oppose you to see if you could manage this opposition preemptively. It could save you a great deal of work if you could manage the opposition before it becomes entrenched.

Face Your Opposition

If, however, your conciliatory efforts are not possible or do not work, devise a plan to address what you believe your opponents' criticisms about your issue will be. One method is to devise a chart like the one above. This will help you clearly understand the differences between your approach and your opponents'.

Avoid Negative Tactics

Be careful to avoid personal attacks. Although some political strategists say that negative campaigns actually gain voters and, thus, work, I believe they should be avoided, especially regarding issue campaigns.

The Natural Resources Council of Maine (NRCM) is currently involved in a campaign to prevent real estate development on 400,000 acres of Maine's North Woods. It is the largest real estate development ever proposed in the state of Maine. NRCM's campaign is a major effort involving local outreach, obtaining 5,000 citizen signatures on petitions and media coverage; developing, printing, and distributing an alternative vision for the area; fund-raising; and motivating people within the state to attend hearings before the Land Use Regulation Commission (the decision makers) to oppose the proposed development. The campaign will go on for more than a year before the commissioners make a decision.

The proponent of the development is the largest land-development company in the United States. It has vast resources compared to the small advocacy nonprofit NRCM. Yet through the campaign's organizing, getting out the message, and building support, the people of Maine seem to have major concerns about the development.

NRCM is careful, however, to focus its campaign on the company's plan and to never personally criticize the employees of the development corporation. NRCM works hard to differentiate this large development plan from NRCM's vision for the North Woods. It takes a lot of work and care to carefully craft the messages that delineate these differences.

During the campaign, on Halloween 2006, unknown individuals vandalized several homes and offices of some of the development company's officials. Quite a bit of damage was done, and it was deeply upsetting to everyone. NRCM and other environmental organizations publicly denounced these actions and called for civil and restrained interactions between the proponents and the opponents of the development. This negative activity has not happened again.

This example shows that tensions can run very high around issue campaigns. It is important that those involved in the issue maintain civility and respectfulness for differences of opinion. This is important for us not only as a democratic country but, further, for the credibility of your campaign.

EVALUATING THE EFFECTIVENESS OF YOUR ISSUE CAMPAIGN

The best sign of the effectiveness of your issue campaign, of course, is winning and achieving your goal. But even if you lose the campaign, you may have been very effective in changing public knowledge and opinions about your issue.

Whether you win or lose, though, it is important to take time to reflect on the campaign and look at the lessons learned. What went well? What didn't work? Where could you have done better? If you had it to do over again, what would you have done differently? What lessons can you apply the next time you want to undertake an issue campaign, or what can you tell others who may want to undertake an issue campaign?

But if you are only partway through your campaign, as NRCM is, how can you tell if you are on the right track? How do you evaluate whether your efforts are effective toward achieving your end goal?

It is important to evaluate your campaign in its midpoint in case it is necessary to change directions and alter your plan. Events can often change the course of your original plan. New circumstances may emerge that alter the validity of your earlier solution. Other pressures may come to bear on the decision makers whom you are trying to influence. Political work is never static, so evaluating how you are doing along the way should be ongoing, but especially during the midpoint in the campaign.

Some Midpoint Measures

Many measures can tell you whether or not your campaign is being effective. Begin with the basics of your plan and how successful you have been in reaching the key organizations and opinion leaders. How is your coalition operating? Is it being effective? Are there any changes that should occur in its leadership or its members? Spend considerable time asking questions during your team and coalition meetings to get peoples' assessment on the progress to date.

Are your planned activities on track and actions being completed on time? Have you met your deadlines? Are there any problem people who say they will do things but don't follow through? Should you replace any of the people who originally signed on to help? Should you recruit more people?

Invariably you will need to make adjustments. Issue campaigns are made up of a whole mix of people, so no campaign will run completely smoothly or without any glitches.

> *An Outward Bound expedition runs into unexpected weather, personality conflicts, sickness, or other obstacles. At the beginning of an Outward Bound course, plans are made and supplies are acquired. But during the several weeks of the course, plans change. The group may not be as fit as was initially thought. Rain may have soaked the food. Someone may have sprained an ankle. Course leaders need to adjust their plans for the route and for their resupplies, and they need to work to keep the morale of the course participants high.*

Similarly, an issue campaign encounters obstacles. So, too, in a campaign, you must assess the needs of the group or groups, be willing to make adjustments, and keep everyone focused on the goal. You, a key leader, need to be willing to adjust your thinking and tackle the hard choices.

MAINTAINING PROGRESS

Key to an issue campaign, as with other types of community organizing, is keeping the goal in mind but breaking the components of the campaign down into achievable segments. All those action steps that you created early in the planning phase of the campaign will aid in maintaining progress.

Celebrate Achievements

Work to accomplish the short-term goals and celebrate their achievements. Consider a midpoint event to celebrate the successes to date. Find ways to celebrate every step forward, whether it be obtaining a great op-ed piece, bringing in more dollars, or gaining an opinion leader to support your issue.

Conversely, don't be afraid to name the disappointments and talk about how to overcome them. They are inevitable, so don't ignore or gloss over them. Acknowledging disappointments helps people "get things off their chest." They may also discover that they're not alone in their feelings. This helps build teamwork as well as an understanding of what can be done better next time.

Show Appreciation

Say "thank you" often. Help people feel appreciated for their efforts, and give yourself a pat on the back too. Campaigns are not easy, and they take commitment. Acknowledge this to yourself and others.

Avoid Burnout

Take a look at elements of burnout, both for yourself and for other workers on the campaign. Think about the time you and others are putting into the campaign. This is never nine-to-five work, and there may be times when you and others are putting in exorbitant hours.

Pace yourself. You need to find ways to have a steady, predictable pace and to see the more intense times as unusual and limited. Key to maintaining progress is helping everyone, including yourself, stay rested and optimistic about attaining your goal.

Take a break. Make sure you and others still have private time, to spend with family or to engage in leisure activities that are not driven by the campaign. Campaigns can be all-consuming, so find ways for you and others to take a break.

Build stamina. Everyone has their own capacity for dedicated work, no matter what that work entails. Pay attention to your own needs for regeneration, and respect others' needs. Try to build stamina—for the duration of the campaign and, hopefully, beyond.

A FINAL NOTE: WORKING FOR THE LONG HAUL

Really, what entering the political arena is about is becoming a lifetime advocate for things you believe in. It is about becoming committed to working in your community for the improvements and betterment of society. This is the long haul. Your issue campaign is really just one effort in a very long run.

You may never choose to participate in another issue or political campaign. However, most people find that it's energizing and invigorating. In any case, because of your work in the political arena, you become a better citizen leader and a stronger person, in every way. You participate in the privilege that we have as citizens of a democracy. You participate in a system that, no matter what our individual political leanings or goals, is held sacred in our culture and is envied by other cultures.

Finding ways to stay committed to this ongoing work is a goal in itself. And by so doing, you are doing well by doing good.

CASE STUDY 4
LEADING PARKS AND PEOPLE

by Jim Garrett

Some real-life situations consist of leadership vacuums, opportunities for natural leaders to step in and help guide a positive outcome. Consider, for example, the following description of a city government that had an unmet need and the enterprising citizen who had the vision and leadership skills to create a solution for the city's problem. Community volunteer Sally Michel co-founded the Parks & People Foundation in the city of Baltimore, Maryland, to help the city's children.

As you read the narrative, try to put yourself in Sally's shoes and envision how you would approach the obstacles she faced as if you were actually experiencing what she faced. Pay particular attention to the methods she used, to her interactions with city officials, and to her leadership style as her organization grew. Also think about the discussion questions and how you might have responded to these situations if you had been there yourself. In the appendix, you will find follow-up questions that revisit these discussion questions, providing more food for thought and encouraging you to think more deeply about this scenario.

In 1971, Sally Michel was a young wife raising a family in Baltimore, Maryland, and—as she felt was expected of most women of her generation—she volunteered in her community. She and a friend were doing research for a Junior League project to address the problems of drug abuse in the city. Although many different programs existed, none of them knew about nor were collaborating with the others, so Sally felt that there needed to be a citywide coordinator of drug abuse-prevention programs. Sally Michel wanted to tell her idea to Baltimore's mayor—but how?

QUESTIONS

1. Do you think Sally Michel, in her day, was an exception or the norm in her desire, as a stay-at-home mother, to volunteer in her community? What is the norm today?
2. Why would a young mother like Sally be motivated to do something about the issue of drug-abuse prevention? What level of volunteer service did Sally's idea exhibit?
3. Why do you think Sally wanted to express her idea to her mayor? Do you think that would be effective?

Sally Michel attended a local school's fundraising auction, and one of the items up for bid was lunch with Baltimore's new mayor, William Donald Schaefer. Sally made the winning bid for that auction item.

At Sally's lunch with the mayor, whom she expected to be just another boring bureaucrat, she discovered that he in fact "got teary when he started talking about the potential for the city." The mayor invited her to attend his press conference the next day at City Hall, during which he announced the appointment of a drug coordinator for the city. Sally relates: "So everybody thought I had reached my goal in twenty-four hours. My phone was ringing off the hook: 'How can I help? How can I help?' " The Junior League created a task force to assist the city's drug coordinator. That was the beginning of Sally Michel's long involvement in public-private partnerships with the City of Baltimore and the state of Maryland.

Then Sally got a call from the mayor asking for a payback lunch. Mayor Schaefer said, "I want to have lunch with you because you're so upbeat, and I just had the worst experience: I took all the leading businesspeople out to dinner two nights ago—paid for it myself, no press, no announcement about it—because I have a lot of good people who work for me, but no one goes beyond the boundaries of their job description, and I want to know how to get creative ideas." Sally asked the mayor why the experience hadn't worked as he'd expected, and eventually she discovered that the business leaders the mayor had met with were all men. She said, "Well, you really should try meeting with women, because they have a whole different agenda: they care about schools, and they care about kids." The mayor said, "Set it up!"

QUESTIONS

4. What leadership qualities did Sally exhibit in her bid for lunch with her mayor? Why do you think her lunch with the mayor was so effective?

5. What type of leader did Mayor Schaefer turn out to be? Why do you think Sally connected with him and wanted to work with him?

6. What could have contributed to the mayor's dinner with businessmen failing to meet his goals? Do you agree with Sally's assessment about the different agendas that men and women have? Why or why not?

So Sally Michel rented a hall, hired a caterer, and invited twelve women—a mixed group of people—and the mayor. She told him he was not allowed to speak until the end of the dinner; then he would get to speak and nobody else could. Rules for brainstorming were posted on every table, and many new ideas came forth.

At the end of the evening, the mayor said, "I want to do this every week!" Sally said, "No, I can only do them once a month. And the next one's at my house." All told, she organized seventy-six monthly dinners, and some great things happened because of ideas suggested at those dinners.

The mayor hadn't known anything about education—he had no children; he had never married—but when he heard an idea with potential benefits to his city, he moved. "He was so empowering," Sally says, "that if you had some idea about a solution to a city problem and you wanted to help, you were on. He just let you go; if you had the energy and could figure out the finances, you were on."

QUESTIONS

7. What type of leadership did Sally show when the mayor told her to "set it up"? Why do you think Mayor Schaefer felt comfortable asking Sally to do something he didn't have experience with?

8. Why was it that Sally limited the dinner to twelve people? All women? What reasons do you think she might have had for the ground rules she set for the dinner? Why do you think her dinner was so effective?

9. Was Sally's decision to hold her innovative dinner meetings monthly due to her time constraints a good one? Would it have been advisable to delegate other people to host those meetings as well so they could be held weekly as the mayor asked?

10. Do you think Mayor Schaefer needed to have been married and to have had children in order to be an effective leader on education issues? Why or why not?

After that, Sally Michel became a regular member of an informal, nongovernmental group of advisors to the long-serving mayor. On being reelected for the fourth time, Mayor Schaefer sought to set up a plan to accomplish the things he had promised to do during the campaign, one of which was to establish more public-private partnerships that could work with various city agencies.

At that time, some twenty-five years ago, the city of Baltimore was faced with aging and deteriorating parks and public recreation facilities. Mayor Schaefer had a vision for creating public-private partnerships that would rejuvenate the urban park system as well as improve the academic skills of the city's school-age population. The mayor asked Sally to set up two partnerships—one to focus on public education and one to work with the Recreation and Parks Department—and then he asked her to recruit the leadership for the partnerships.

First Sally Michel created the Fund for Educational Excellence, which she turned over to a friend who was a prominent business leader. Shortly thereafter, she says, "I got on to the Rec and Parks thing. I didn't really know anything about Rec and Parks, but it seemed like a good idea . . . I was very naive about it." When Sally told the mayor that she didn't know anything about recreation and parks, he told her that he didn't either, and he wanted her to chair it so that she could educate him about recreation and parks. Soon after, Mayor Schaefer hired a young, energetic, and creative man named Chris Delaporte to head the Department of Recreation and Parks. Together, Michel and Delaporte started their public-private partnership, the Parks & People Foundation, in March 1984.

QUESTIONS

11. What do you think led Mayor Schaefer to invite a community volunteer such as Sally Michel to participate in an informal, nongovernmental group of advisors? What leadership qualities did Sally exhibit that led to her progression from concerned citizen to mayoral advisor?

12. Why might Sally have accepted the mayor's challenge to work on an issue she was unfamiliar with? Do you think her steps in setting up two new organizations were typical? Effective?

Initially, Parks & People Foundation had no money and no staff—"That's what public-private partnerships working with government means: no money and no staff," remarks Sally. So to raise money for the recreation centers, they sold raffle tickets for a donated automobile. Other than that, she says, "We didn't have anything to do; I mean, we didn't know *what* to do."

But then two months later, out of the blue, Sally got a phone call from someone whose sister lived in Baltimore. Jonathan Nolan, who worked at the Hurricane Island Outward Bound School (HIOBS) in Maine, was trying to find a city that would raise $25,000 to match a scholarship endowment for sending inner-city kids to Outward Bound courses in Maine during the coming summer.

"This was like a sign from above about what this new foundation should do," Sally remembers. "As I look back on it, it was insane—taking that dare from Jonathan Nolan [in 1984]. 'Of course, yes,' we said; 'you've got $25,000? Sure, we'll match it.' And we'd had only one meeting as a foundation before that!" she remembers. "I saw Outward Bound as an opportunity to solve problems such as black-white [racial] issues with young people."

Sally Michel worked night and day for weeks to recruit, equip, and provide medical screening for the kids, as well as sponsors to donate the tuition money. That summer, ninety-five Baltimore kids—a mixture of black and white kids, from public and private schools—journeyed to Maine aboard yellow school buses. The only things they had in common when they headed north was that they all knew where York Road, a major city thoroughfare, was and they had each been equipped by Sally Michel with two plastic baggies: one contained pencils and stationery so that the students could write a thank-you letter to their sponsors; the other contained a batch of Michel's freshly baked chocolate chip cookies.

Four weeks later, after the buses brought the first group of kids back to Baltimore, they were invited to City Hall to tell about their experience. One of the students, still tanned, scratched-up, and tousle-haired from the expedition, said that when they left for Maine, most of them didn't know one another at all, but "now we're family; what do you want us to do?"

Everyone in attendance, especially the mayor, was convinced of the program's significance. The kids had been caught up by the spirit of Outward Bound and were ready to work together to make a difference in their hometown.

QUESTIONS

13. In financing her fledgling community organization, what else, besides raffling off a car as a fund-raiser, might she have done?
14. What qualities of leadership did Sally exhibit in her response to the call from Maine? What might have happened had she considered the Outward Bound scholarship an irrelevant opportunity or impossible goal?

During the summer of 1985, another hundred or so high-schoolers from Baltimore traveled to the Outward Bound base in Maine, but then Mayor Schaefer came up with another novel idea. Why, he wondered, did they have to send their kids to Maine on an uncomfortable fourteen-hour school-bus ride, when there are mountains, rivers, bays, forests, and wooded city parks right there in Maryland? The seed for the first urban Outward Bound base in the United States was sown.

Beginning in 1986, under the sponsorship of Parks & People Foundation, Hurricane Island Outward Bound School came to Baltimore and established its urban base of operations in Leakin Park. Part of one of the largest municipal park tracts in the United States, at 1,200 acres, Leakin Park is located in the southwest quadrant of the city. When asked whether a city park, even one composed largely of woods and natural areas rather than open fields and playgrounds, was an appropriate place for a wilderness program like Outward Bound, Sally Michel remarked: "Do you know what it's like for city kids to be in a park at night and hear an owl? It's terrifying!"

Parks & People's executive director of that time, joined by Michel and other members of the Parks & People board, worked hand-in-hand with Phil Costello and Arthur Pearson from HIOBS to establish the Baltimore–Chesapeake Bay Outward Bound Program. They researched more distant areas of Maryland for expedition sites, gathered all the necessary group gear, planned the course curriculum, and oversaw the construction of the first of four Outward Bound pulling boats to be built for the sailing courses in Chesapeake Bay.

Over the ensuing twenty years, backpacking, canoeing, rock climbing, a ropes course (a jungle gym high in the air, where participants are protected with climbing gear as they swing on ropes, balance on cables, etc.), initiative activities, and orienteering have been added to sailing as course activities, and more than 50,000 students and teachers have experienced Outward Bound through the Baltimore Center, thanks to the inspiration—and hard work—of Sally Michel, Mayor Schaefer, their teams, and their supporters.

Sally and the Parks & People Foundation did not stop with Outward Bound, however. Once the Baltimore–Chesapeake Bay Outward Bound Program was launched, Parks & People worked with the city to help restore the nineteenth-century grandeur of Druid Hill Park, the crown jewel of Baltimore's Olmstead Brothers–designed park system, at the time of the parks' 150th anniversary. After that, Parks & People created, staffed, or sponsored seven "Motivating Youth" sports and environmental education programs, which have a strong academic component as well as a recreational one, plus six "Green Parks, Clean Streams & Green Communities" programs, which use a community organizing model to build the capacity of communities to improve the quality of life in Baltimore. All told, these Parks & People programs have added another 50,000 adults and children to the 50,000 served by Outward Bound in Baltimore over the years.

QUESTIONS

15. What type of leadership did Mayor Schaefer demonstrate in his idea to move the outdoor experience for youth to a park in his city rather than the Maine wilderness? Why do you think this idea worked?

16. What qualities of leadership did Sally Michel demonstrate in building a coalition with Outward Bound?

17. Why do you think a single opportunity to send city kids to summer camp in Maine resulted in so many different outcomes in Baltimore? A new coalition was established; a significant park was restored; many new parks programs evolved—how did one woman's leadership accomplish this?

For years, Parks & People Foundation had tried to address more effectively the problem of chronic reading deficiencies in the city's elementary schoolchildren by combining a reading and studying component to its after-school sports programs. Despite the foundation's determined efforts to improve this situation, the results were less than satisfactory. "We found," Sally Michel recalls in an interview in *Style* magazine, that "it was very, very difficult for fourth graders to read—and for some, impossible. That was phenomenal to me. Two things occurred to me: summers should be used for kids that are behind in school, and we as a community should not find it acceptable that our kids can't read. It hurts all of us when kids can't read."

So in 1997, under Michel's energized and directly involved leadership, Parks & People Foundation gave birth to SuperKids Camp, a seven-week academic and cultural enrichment camp that combined exciting, literacy-based educational opportunities during the mornings with cultural enrichment and experiential activities all over the city each afternoon. In whirlwind trips to Ivy League college campuses, Michel personally recruited college students to participate in the program as teachers. "We called it SuperKids Camp," says Michel, because "we wanted it to feel not as though they were in summer school but, rather, that they were on an adventure. And we wanted to show kids why reading is important and how it links to other things."

In its inaugural year, 460 kids were served by 132 teachers. Since then, SuperKids Camp has grown to enroll an average of 1300 children each year. According to *The Daily Record*, "This simple idea has made a significant difference in the lives of participants and their families. Campers not only receive intensive reading instruction, they have fun—lots of fun."

So, once again, Sally Michel and her supporters saw a pressing need in the city and devised an innovative—and effective—solution; they brought together people from both private and public institutions in the city and combined volunteer and paid-staff energies to make attainable the vision of Baltimore as "the City that Reads"—all for the benefit of the least advantaged members of the metropolitan area and their neighborhoods.

When she was asked a few years ago what advice she would give to anyone thinking about volunteering to work on a cause, Sally said, "You have to be a risk-taker, you have to be creative, you have to raise money, and you have to have help. There's no great science to it. You find your issue that you feel passionate about, and you find people to help you. If you know your facts, people will listen to you. They may not always give you money, but they'll listen."

Recently, Sally Michel quipped, "For someone who didn't finish college, I sure am throwing myself around like an expert!" And why does she do it? Because "what we keep, we lose, and only what we give remains our own."

"So," she concludes, "think of how rich I am, in that way!"

QUESTIONS

18. What types of vision and leadership skills did Sally Michel exhibit in starting a literacy program with a parks foundation? Which of her strategies were effective?

19. Do you agree with Michel's assessment of what it takes to lead an issue campaign? What other qualities or qualifications come to mind?

POSTSCRIPT: LEADERSHIP LESSONS FROM MOUNT KILIMANJARO

BY MARK GERZON

As fighting rages in the Middle East between Arabs and Jews, violence persists between Muslims and Hindus in India and Kashmir, and tensions intensify globally between Al Qaeda's *jihad* and the United States's "war on terror," my experience climbing to the summit of Mount Kilimanjaro in the summer of 2006 with emerging leaders from twelve nations is a fitting way to close a book by Outward Bound about becoming more effective leaders. In the company of four Americans and four Muslim fellow trekkers and more than a half dozen others from nations ranging from Canada to Liberia, New Zealand to Slovenia, I learned more about the world—and myself—than I would ever have imagined.

Hundreds of thousands of men, women, young people, and children who experience Outward Bound in one of the thirty-three countries where the organization is active could make the same enthusiastic statement about their expeditions. But our journey was unique for two reasons: We were a microcosm of the world, and our focus was how to lead in a world filled with differences. In partnership with a four-person team from Outward Bound International, my Kenyan colleague Kimani Njogu and I co-led the first Outward Bound expedition designed specifically for global leaders—Global Leaders Program (GLP)—with emerging leaders from a dozen nations to the summit of Africa's highest peak.

During our five-day ascent and two-day descent, we faced many of the same challenges and breakthroughs that other Outward Bound expeditions have experienced over the generations. We experienced, as the Outward Bound process is described in this book's chapters, the stresses and anxieties that led to mastery and competence, resulting in an expanding capacity to lead—and to live. But because of the unique composition and purpose of our group, we experienced something more profound as well: we experienced renewed hope for the world.

To understand why so many of us were inspired by the trek to be more committed global citizens, consider the words of our group. At the end of the third day of trekking, we held a council in our blue mess tent at the high camp called Barafu (altitude 15,000 feet). Kimani and I asked each person to share what made this expedition as a *global* team different from a single-nation or single-culture trek. Whether or not you ever climb a mountain as part of a global team, I think you will find our team's reactions to the expedition compelling because they capture the unique challenge of leadership in a shrinking world. Here are a few excerpts of their dialog (not attributed in order to protect confidentiality):

- "What makes this different from the United Nations is that here we can't write anybody off; we know that we *need* each other."
- "My awareness has been heightened; I can't operate on automatic with the usual assumptions."
- "I can explore what people from Afghanistan think of Americans. How two countries feel about each other is brought down to the level of two people on a mountain. Here I can listen to a Thai colonel talk about war and peace, which gives me a whole new perspective. I am more deliberate and intentional because I am not surrounded by my nation's citizens."

■ "I never knew a Muslim before today. I have much more understanding of their world now and what I have to do to understand it."

■ "Each of us is many layers. When we face challenging situations, we get to know the real person. We get to see how each person reacts at a deeper level."

■ "None of us has a single identity; each of us has a multiplicity of them. Becoming aware of that gives us more ways to connect with each other."

■ "My life started on an island, then it embraced a whole archipelago, then international work. When I look at my climbing partners, I don't think of the countries they come from; I think of them as people who were there when I needed them the most. We are three days away from any health center, and my life depended on you."

■ "I am noticing that no one is saying that this is about reaching the summit of Kilimanjaro. Everyone here is focused on other people. The way I would put it is, 'You will remember the mountain, but you will remember each other more.' "

Or, as another one of the participants said, "Maybe we can bring the whole world into our small blue tent."

During our twelve days in Tanzania, both on the mountain and in community, we learned some practical lessons that are relevant to anyone who wants to learn—or teach—about leadership.

1. **Leadership begins with our missions and our challenges, and all content should connect to that fundamental human starting point.** My colleague Kimani and I, and the Outward Bound team, could not begin this expedition by *telling* the participants what they had to learn from us. We began by *asking* them what they needed to learn in order to achieve their mission in life—and what obstacles they were facing. Everything we taught was based on their mission and obstacles, not on our preconceived notions.

2. **Leadership means working with both the global and local, both the universal and the personal, and includes an active engagement with the inner life of each individual as well.** The natural tendency on a *global* leadership program is to focus on what everyone shares. Conversations were filled with references to global movies (*Pirates of the Caribbean*), global music (Madonna), global events (the World Cup), global conflicts (such as the war in Iraq and Afghanistan and the war raging around Israel and Palestine), and other media-magnified phenomena. But we also stressed that the local is as important as the global. We also discussed our differences, not just our similarities, and asked each participant to share what was unique about their own lineage and culture. For global leadership to be vibrant and alive, it must—absolutely *must*—be grounded in the richness of the local and in the very individual challenges that each person faces.

3. **Leadership is not about concepts but about experience. Concepts must be linked to real life: of nature, of others, of one's inner self.** As several comments in the blue tent underscored, leadership is not a spectator sport. We learn about the world by being in it, interacting with it, and being affected by it.

■ "This is a totally different experience from having a *conference* on global leadership. It is as different as day is from night. Seven days with our lives on the line is a feeling that no hotel conference can possibly create."

■ "On a mountain, you find out who you really are. You are together twenty-four hours a day for seven days. When things get difficult, you can't go back to your hotel room and close the door."

I have taught leadership workshops around

the world in hotel conference rooms, and it is true that this was not the same. The participants may learn some concepts; they may experience some powerfully transformative dialog. But they cannot put that dialog into action without getting out of their chairs and going into the world. The experiential dimension of this program, which my Outward Bound colleagues handled with such skill and sensitivity, is therefore a critical part of this leadership experience.

4. **Learning about leadership is enhanced by ensuring that those who are present, by their very composition, evoke the diversity of the "whole."** Whether one is working with a company, a community, or even the world, the most powerful leadership learning happens when a microcosm of the "whole" is involved. If one wants to change the way a group or organization behaves, then it is best to include all the "parts" in the leadership experience.

The world's full complexity and diversity is too vast to be *contained* by any small team. Nevertheless, with a conscientious selection process, the whole can be *evoked*. Our program did not include a single Latin American, a representative of an indigenous tribe, or a single person who (like more than a billion people) lives on US $2 a day or less. It was certainly not an accurate statistical sample of humanity. But it was so powerfully and beautifully diverse that it awakened our global consciences and our global consciousness. A team does not have to be a perfect microcosm of the whole to teach us what we need to learn as leaders. It simply needs to stretch our identities and widen our sense of self.

There is no other wilderness-based program in the world that has reached so many people for so many years in so many countries around the world. This single fact, I believe, is a clue to what Outward Bound's global calling is. This organization is well positioned to become a training ground for the leaders of tomorrow, for the men and women who will one day run the companies, countries, armies, and nonprofit organizations of the world. If these men and women have had their minds stretched and their hearts opened, through experiences like ours on Kilimanjaro, the possibility of a just, sustainable, and peaceful world will be greatly enhanced.

But—in the spirit of Outward Bound, which always involves challenging ourselves to extend ourselves beyond the comfortable—let me close by challenging the organization and each of us.

When I first encountered the leadership of Outward Bound on Thompson Island a few years ago, I was struck by the way in which the organization was a mirror of the challenges that most leaders face. At the time there were thirty-three countries with Outward Bound programs, each dealing with its own triumphs and struggles. But there was no truly collaborative global initiative in which all the countries worked together. To varying degrees, many of them were part of Outward Bound *International.* But it was clear that, when push came to shove, the primary loyalty of each national program was, quite understandably, to itself. It seeks first its *own* survival, its *own* growth, its *own* unfolding. As one executive director of an endangered country program put it: "First, we have to look after our own program; only *then* can we collaborate."

In today's interdependent world, most of us are "global leaders" because, in our workplaces and our communities alike, we are challenged to lead across many kinds of borders: national, cultural, religious, ideological, ethnic—and more. Whether you are a leader in a school or a community organization, a city council member or a corporate executive, you face the same dilemma. You have to make sure that those you are leading feel that their needs are being addressed. Only then will they be more willing to open their minds and hearts to the needs of others.

Leadership the Outward Bound Way symbolizes, I believe, exactly the kind of leadership that the world urgently needs. The collaborative, value-based leadership that is described so eloquently in the chapters of this book is an approach that has proved effective on frigid mountains and on stormy seas, on arduous treks and dangerous climbs. Just as we used it while taking a global team up Mount Kilimanjaro, you can use it to face the unpredictable and demanding challenges in your life.

APPENDIX: CASE STUDY FOLLOW-UP QUESTIONS

These follow-up, or follow-*through*, questions for the case studies' questions are designed to encourage you to go beyond the simple and superficial answers you might be tempted to supply while reading through the case study narratives and to investigate the issues more thoroughly.

CASE STUDY 1: THE PALESTINIAN-ISRAELI UNITY PROJECT
Question 1:

A. Think back over occasions when you have been in charge of an argumentative or even oppositional group. What did you try to do to get them to work together or at least tolerate one another? Were you successful? If not, what do you wish you had done to facilitate the group?

B. Ian Randall, in his master's thesis titled "Education, Human Agency, and Compassion: Outward Bound as a Case Study in Empowering Young People as Agents of Social Change" (University of Newcastle-upon-Tyne, UK, 2004), interviewed Outward Bound instructor Dave Genova about his critical motivating experience with the encounter between the two crews. What do you think compassion has to do with the issues this encounter raised?

Question 2:

A. What other kinds of discrimination can there be in addition to the usually listed types—for example, racial, ethnic, economic, age? Have you witnessed or been directly involved with discrimination based on weight? Height? Clothing? Table manners? Dialect or accent?

Question 3:

A. While the group of characteristics in question 2A, above, may seem less significant, consider your own reactions to the differences you see in others and whether those perceptions change the way you react to other people, especially with regard to your first impressions of them. What can you do to minimize negative (first) impressions so that they do not have a negative effect on your ability to lead people effectively?

B. If you were faced with the task of leading a group of teenagers who are of two (maybe three) different ethnic or racial backgrounds, would you feel at all challenged? Defensive? Trying to decide what sort of self-image you will project? Thinking about what you need to anticipate in terms of the group's interaction, with the hope of preventing any heavy friction among them? Or would you be more laid-back, deciding to just wait and see, hoping for the best and going with the flow?

Question 4:

A. Which of your organization's values are you especially committed to modeling? What steps might you take if you saw a disconnect between what was written in mission and policy statements and what was actually happening?

Question 5:

A. Really! How much actual "social change" can be accomplished anyway, especially through so-called compassion?

B. What do you think of all this talk about "compassion," "meaningful dialog," "ideal community," "social justice," and "trust"? Does it sound like 1960s "encounter-group" jargon—baring your soul to strangers, liberal philosophizing, etc.?

C. Or maybe you have actually experienced a business or social context (other than family) that was characterized by trust, respect, and openness. If so, how did you react? Were you a productive and/or enthusiastic participant? Or was your attitude negative and your productivity reduced?

D. In thinking about your own leadership approach or style in general, what place does compassion have as one of your characteristics? After going through the preceding questions, will you consider increasing your level of compassionate interaction with the people you lead? Why or why not?

Question 6:

A. Breaking the Ice was founded by a group of European businessmen led by Heskel Nathaniel (an Israeli born in Haifa in 1962 who lives in Germany, where he is the managing director of a real estate investment and development company) and Doron Erel (an Israeli-born professional mountain climber; see *www.breaking-the-ice.de*). Is Heskel Nathaniel a traitor to his country, as some claim? What could transform a veteran Israeli military man into a "peacenik"?

Question 7:

A. How can knowledge of the demographics and social dynamics of the home communities of your group help you to lead them more effectively?

Question 8:

A. In spite of these students' expressed commitment when they signed on to the course to communicate with honesty and openness and to strive to work cooperatively throughout the course with students from the "other side," what might it feel like to them once the wilderness component of their experience actually begins and they all come face to face with the challenges of traveling, working, and living together under backcountry conditions?

Question 9:

A. Do you have personality traits you want to modify because they have proved to be ineffective, even counterproductive, in facilitating emotional safety in the group you're leading?

Question 10:

A. How well do you want those whom you are leading to know you? Do you feel that your authority, your power, is enhanced if you are a bit mysterious? Or do you think that your students or clients are more willing to follow your lead if they have a fuller sense of your personal history and values?

Question 11:

A. Have you developed strategies for changing gears, for re-engaging the group you are leading during those parts of the day when attention spans shorten and commitment flags?

Question 12:

A. Is your style of leadership more autocratic or democratic? Do you adjust your leadership style to fit specific situations or objectives?

Question 13:

A. How could you explain to students or clients the importance of making a last-minute change in plans, especially one that moved from a hands-on experience such as climbing on the cliffs to sitting around and doing more talking about difficult subjects?

Question 14:

A. Have you found successful strategies for initiating meaningful discussions and then pulling back and letting the group keep things going?

Question 15:

A. Have you had any experiences that have confirmed or deepened your prejudices? Have you been well served by thinking, acting, or living in compliance with your prejudices?

B. Which of the stereotypes and prejudices that you grew up with have you succeeded in eliminating from your thinking or at least seriously questioning? Which ones are you still working on?

Question 16:

A. In general, whose personal stories tend to have the greatest impact on you: Those of your peers? Elders? Younger colleagues or acquaintances? Why?

Question 17:

A. An old Chinese maxim says, "What I hear, I forget. What I see, I remember. What I do, I understand." And a Native American saying requests you to "walk a mile in my moccasins." To what extent can you truly understand or empathize with others without experiencing what they have experienced? Can leaders really be effective without themselves having done what they are asking their followers to do?

B. How much is your credibility as a leader enhanced when those whom you are leading know that you won't ask them to do anything you have not done or are not willing to do?

Question 18:

A. Imagine that you have accompanied the Unity Project students back to Haifa. Envision the scene at the Haifa airport when they come out through customs and are met by their families and friends. How will they be greeted? Do you think the students will divide again into their two ethnic groups?

B. Will Levi, who encountered the hornets' nest on the rock face, bring his parents over to meet Shafik's family? Will Mona and Jon, who have each lost family members or close friends to interethnic violence, still be able to talk freely with each other, now that they are surrounded by the folks back home?

C. What kinds of projects could you suggest that the Unity Project students might undertake

in Haifa that would keep them working together throughout the rest of their high school years and beyond?

Question 19:

A. Consider the people you lead and the experiences they have shared under your leadership. How can you ensure that those experiences will have a long-lasting and positive impact on them, an impact that will affect how they live out their lives in the future?

CASE STUDY 2: SEA KAYAKERS STRANDED IN DARKNESS AND FOG
Question 1:

A. How much control or influence, directly or subtly, should trip leaders exert during a group's planning for and organizing of its "final expedition" or on their sticking to a schedule en route? Would you be more likely to turn over the group's leadership to the students if the course were a longer one? For example, what if the trip were two weeks or longer, rather than eight days?

B. Does the age or the gender of the participants matter when considering the preceding question? What about the socioeconomic or education level of the group?

Question 2:

A. Who tends to follow the agreed-upon course "contract" guidelines better, teens or adults? Is a different set of strategies needed for corralling adults than for teenage students?

B. What consequences would be appropriate for an adult who won't comply with basic expedition rules and behavioral expectations?

Question 3:

A. Who should assume responsibility for ensuring that all the gear issued for an expedition is accounted for and in the best possible condition? How can this be ensured? What policies and procedures should be followed? Should the organization insist that all trip leaders follow iron-clad procedures, or should decisions about gear and equipment be left largely in the hands of the instructors?

B. If and when a serious incident occurs that might, at least in part, be attributable to equipment failure or inadequacy, who should take the blame? Why?

Question 4:

A. How should the senior leader constructively respond when confronted by an assistant leader's opposing views? Have you experienced this dynamic as a leader? As an assistant leader?

Question 5:

A. What kind of leadership style would be most appropriate in this case—in these conditions, with this student population—especially as the afternoon wore on and there were still miles to go? Why would this style be best?

B. What factors do you take into consideration when deciding what leadership style to use in a changing outdoor situation?

Question 6:

A. How do you feel about changing your plans when situations change?

B. What methods do you use to assess both current and predictable conditions, including students' (and leaders') physical and emotional states, which can affect energy levels and also judgment? What is your personal "what-if?" questioning process?

Question 7:

A. Is there a difference between male and female students in terms of their compliance with rules and guidelines? Does age make a difference within each gender group?

B. Do you find yourself responding differently to participants depending on their gender? What steps could you take to become more self-aware on this issue?

C. How about with a co-leader? Do you work differently with a co-leader of the same gender as you do with one of the opposite gender?

Question 8:

A. What sorts of advanced learning does your organization expect its leaders to know? Can outdoor leaders be trained to handle every possible scenario in the wilderness?

Question 9:

A. Would it be a good idea to have either a formal or a mental checklist for steps to take when conditions begin to worsen? How would you balance the need for timely decision making under stressful conditions with the need to make changes in equipment or preparation to meet any anticipated dangers?

Question 10:

A. There's an old saying that "an army marches on its stomach." What do you do to ensure that your participants will be able to maintain a more-than-adequate energy level and remain properly hydrated, especially during long, stress-filled travel days?

Question 11:

A. Were the actions of the distressed crew members a result of their earlier training on the expedition? Did their initiative contribute to the crew's safety?

B. Do you encourage your participants to be self-reliant when conditions worsen? Do you make sure they're learning skills during an expedition to help them become more self-reliant?

Question 12:

A. What, if any, differences in behavior and in trip leader actions would you expect if Zach and Shannon's crew had been made up of students in the fifteen- to nineteen-year-old age range instead of having an average age of thirty-six years? Would you prefer to work with adults or teens in times of danger and distress? Why?

Question 13:

A. What strategies can leaders use to assess participants' individual needs, psychologies, etc., and then use that information to good advantage as they conduct the course? Because Zach had denied Kelly's earlier request for a buddy tandem kayak team, should he have taken that into consideration when she was stranded on the ledge with Ruth?

Question 14:

A. What pieces of equipment do you want to always have on hand and easily accessible in the event of an especially challenging situation? How do you strike the best balance between having everything you could possibly need right at your fingertips and being so encumbered by gear that your freedom of movement is adversely hindered?

Question 15:

A. What is the proper role and appropriate course of action for an assistant leader when he or she has knowledge, opinions, or intuitions that are in conflict with those of the senior leader?

Question 16:

A. Are you familiar with the concept of cascading decision-making mistakes? How does this case study illustrate the accumulation of many small errors in judgment leading to a potentially large mishap?

CASE STUDY 3: PLAYING A NEW TUNE AT MARTIN GUITAR

Question 1:

A. What kinds of baggage do you bring to your leadership situations? Are there obstacles that stand in the way between you and those whom you are intending to lead? Do you have allies who can help you carry this baggage? Friends, co-workers, mentors who are standing by, ready and willing to lend a hand? Are you the sort of person who looks for ways to help others with their baggage?

B. If you were the new leader of a team with a wide age range, how would you address the issue of ageism (a form of prejudice and discrimination that can interfere with the functioning of a team) right from the start and minimize the likelihood that members might judge one another because of age?

Question 2:

A. When you first found yourself in the role of leader, did you feel prepared for the job? What sort of advance training did you have?

B. Can anyone really be trained ahead of time to be a leader, or must leadership be learned by doing on-the-job training?

C. Looking back, what do you wish you had known ahead of time that would have made your task simpler or easier?

Question 3:

A. How useful were any business management courses you have taken when you were actually faced with leading a group or a company? How would you reconstruct your business education to make it of even greater practical usefulness?

B. What other managerial or leadership styles have you investigated?

C. Do you consider yourself reasonably adept at choosing among the different leadership styles—collaborative, autocratic, democratic, consensus-building—for different situations?

Question 4:

A. Working with people from several different generations or age groups is often very challenging; the perspectives of the different generations on how to get things done can be quite different. What strategies do you know about or have you used that provide effective bridges across a generation gap?

Question 5:

A. Have you been a leader in a company that experienced a strike? What leadership skills did you bring to that experience?

Question 6:

A. Have you been a leadership position in a company that was facing problems such as declining sales, debt, or mergers and acquisitions? What leadership skills did those challenges require?

Question 7:

A. Have you had an experience of five (or fewer) days in length that has profoundly affected you, changing the ways you see yourself and the people you lead? What was it like? What did you learn from the experience?

Question 8:

A. What has been your experience in working with consultants? Was it time (and money) well spent? Why or why not?

B. How hard is it to find a consultant who can really make a positive difference to you and your organization? What can a consultant do to help you ensure that the benefits of the consultant's work with your group will be lasting ones?

Question 9:

A. How open are you to feedback? Do you solicit it? Or do you hope that you won't be subjected to it?

B. Have you experienced criticism from someone you manage? How did you handle it? Do you think your team members feel comfortable enough to freely give you their honest opinion?

Question 10:

A. Have you had to deal with a subordinate manager's refusal to participate in a team-building experience? To participate in a major business initiative or project?

B. What ways can you think of to reduce or eliminate the unfavorable effects of a top manager's refusal to participate? Alternatively, how could you go about getting him or her to join in the activity, even if at a reduced level?

C. Have you ever been the one to say "no" to a boss's request that you take part in a new kind of activity? What sort of dynamic did that set up in your relationship?

D. How would you feel if you had agreed to engage in an activity or participate in an initiative even though you really were against it, but you felt compelled to go along with the boss's request? Or if you felt compelled to go along with the group because you didn't want to be left out or be called a wimp, etc.?

Question 11:

A. Have you experienced an adversarial relationship with another leader in your workplace? How did you deal with the relationship?

B. Have you had a difficult working relationship with a supervisor or other type of boss? With a subordinate? What are the differences in dealing with these two types of adversarial relationships?

Question 12:

A. Have you experienced a team-building or other management-type program or retreat in your work? What was it like for you as an employee? Personally?

B. Have you found longer or shorter retreats to be more effective? Why?

Question 13:

A. What kind of organizational structure are you most comfortable in? Do you prefer a formal, hierarchical structure or a more horizontal, open, friendly one? In your experience, which is the most efficient, productive structure for you to work in?

B. What tools have you used to figure out what kind of working atmosphere is preferred by you and your colleagues? Have you used a Myers-Briggs or equivalent test and then discussed the results as a group? Do you think that working together effectively is enhanced when each person knows the nature of everyone's else's style and preferences?

Question 14:

A. Have you had any experiences with downturns at your workplace? What characteristics of the organization's culture either helped or hindered the conditions?

B. The old saying goes, "When the going gets tough, the tough get going." What motivates your colleagues to dig in and make it through difficult times? In your opinion, to what extent does a close bond of collegial friendship, formed within a nurturing organizational culture, make the prospects brighter for an ultimately successful outcome?

Question 15:

A. What style of leadership is most appealing to you, the step-back type or a more hands-on, assertive type?

B. When you are in the role of a follower or a subordinate, do you prefer the security of being told exactly what to do and how to do it, or do you like to have the freedom to innovate, set your own pace, etc.?

C. Are you good at giving constructive feedback to others? Is there a culture of constant improvement in your organization, with provision made for regular feedback exchanges? If not, would you want to institute it? Why or why not?

Question 16:

A. Are you able to change and adapt your leadership style when the situation warrants it? How comfortable with this are you?

Question 17:

A. Is the atmosphere of your workplace tainted by negative interpersonal interaction? Can you envision ways to make your workplace more like Martin Guitar's?

B. Have you ever been the target of negative office politics? Have you figured out any ways to counteract the negative impact of sniping, gossiping, back-biting, etc., in your place of business?

C. How is a team's effectiveness affected by office politics? Could negative office politics have a calculable affect on a company's bottom line?

CASE STUDY 4: LEADING PARKS AND PEOPLE
Question 1:

A. Have you ever volunteered in your community? Are you currently volunteering your services in your community? What type of volunteering do you do or have you done?

B. How do you juggle family obligations along with your volunteer service? Work obligations? Other types of responsibilities?

Question 2:

A. Are you bothered by problems that plague your community? Whether or not such problems impact your own daily life directly, do you recognize their long-term effects on your quality of life and the lives of your family and friends?

B. When you think about a problem in your community that you'd like to volunteer to help with, do you look for an existing program or organization to work with? Or do you look at the larger picture for what might be missing? How empowered do you feel to envision a new solution to urban problems?

C. What types of urban or social needs do you see in your community to which you feel you could contribute your talents? What inspires you to think creatively about solving your community's difficulties?

Question 3:

A. Is talking to your mayor an approach you might consider if you had an idea for solving a problem in your community? Why or why not?

B. Who else would you approach besides your mayor? Your city council or equivalent? Why or why not?

Question 4:

A. Have you shown the type of initiative that Sally showed as a community volunteer in gaining access to the people in power? What strategies have you used? How effective were they?

B. In what other ways could you get the attention of city leaders you want to work with?

Question 5:

A. Which elected officials in your community have you worked with? Why did you choose to work with them?

B. What leadership styles in others are you interested in working with? Why? How does this fit with your leadership style?

Question 6:

A. In your community, do you see a difference between the agendas that businessmen have and those that business- or other women have? Are the dynamics different in your era and community from what Sally Michel experienced forty years ago? If so, how? Why do you think that is?

B. What other kinds of community groups can you think of that would expand your elected officials' pool of problem-solving allies?

Question 7:

A. Have you ever been asked to bring together a new group for brainstorming? If so, who asked you to do this? Why?

B. Can you think of other ways to involve city leaders with citizens who have great ideas?

Question 8:

A. Who would you invite to a brainstorming session such as Sally's dinner with the mayor? Would you limit your session to one gender? Why or why not?

B. What type of ground rules would you establish for a brainstorming session? Why?

Question 9:

A. As a community volunteer, have you ever had an effective idea that someone in power appreciated and wanted you to implement? What type of idea was it? Was it implemented?

B. Did you feel comfortable shaping that idea in your own vision rather than bowing to pressure from an elected official? Would you have said "no" to your mayor if he wanted your dinner meetings to be held weekly instead of monthly?

Question 10:

A. Do you think people in power have to directly experience an aspect of an issue in order to be an effective leader on that issue? Why or why not?

B. Is it effective for elected officials to fill in the gaps in their personal experience and knowledge with that of community volunteers? Why or why not?

Question 11:

A. Have you ever served on an advisory board in your community? What kinds of issues might you as a volunteer leader bring to such a community group?

B. What other types of community organizations can you think of in addition to advisory groups that could inform your elected officials?

Question 12:

A. Have you ever been asked by an elected official in your community to create an organization for addressing an issue you know little about? If so, what was the issue? What organization did you initiate? If not, what sort of organization could you envision creating around what issue?

B. Have you volunteered with a fledgling organization? What sorts of allies did you enlist? What type of coalitions did you build? What other steps did you or could you envision taking?

Question 13:

A. Have you experienced the difficulties of financing a fledgling community organization? What ways have you found for fund-raising?

Question 14:

A. What enables a community leader to see a windfall as an opportunity rather than irrelevant? How would you go about raising the matching money for an opportunity like the one that Outward Bound offered to Sally Michel?

Question 15:

A. Have you had an innovative idea that reinvented an existing program? What helped you to create your new idea?

Question 16:

A. What types of coalitions have you worked with in your community? How effective have they been? Why or why not?

Question 17:

A. Have you been involved in coalitions and partnerships that created significant new opportunities in your community? What were they? How would you envision a program that could be built upon and expanded successfully?

Question 18:

A. Have you ever broadened the mission of an organization you volunteer with? What types of innovative programs have you envisioned?

Question 19:

A. Looking at Sally Michel's assessment of what it takes to be a volunteer leader in your community, would you say you have those qualities? Have you used some of them in service to your community? All of them? What else?

BIBLIOGRAPHY

INTRODUCTION
References
Hahn, Kurt. *Harrogate Address on Outward Bound.* Address at the Conference at Harrogate. Harrogate, England. May 9, 1965.

CHAPTER 1, WHY LEARN LEADERSHIP FROM OUTWARD BOUND?
References
Hahn, Kurt. "The Seven Laws of Salem (1930)," Appendix I in *Ten Years of Gordonstoun: An Account and an Appeal.* Welshpool, Wales: Country Times Printers, 1944.

———. "Training for and through the Sea." Notes for an address given to the Honourable Mariners' Company, Glasgow, Scotland, 1947. Source of the quotation "Training for all through the sea or the mountains—that is my plea."

———. Address at the Forty-Eighth Annual Dinner of Old Centralians. In *The Central: The Journal of Old Centralians.* No. 119. London, 1959. Source of the quotation "the highest dynamics of the human soul."

———. "Outward Bound." Address, annual meeting of the Outward Bound Trust, London, July 1960.

———. Address, Founding Day Ceremony of the Athenian School, Danville, California, November 21, 1965.

Miner, Joshua L., and Joe Boldt. *Outward Bound USA: Crew Not Passengers.* 2nd ed. Seattle: The Mountaineers Books, 2002.

Walsh, Victor, and Gerald Golins. "The Exploration of the Outward Bound Process." Paper, Colorado Outward Bound School, Denver, 1976.

Ylvisaker, Paul. "The Missing Dimension." Keynote address, International Outward Bound Conference, Cooperstown, NY, 1987.

Resources
Flavin, Martin. *Kurt Hahn's Schools and Legacy.* Wilmington, DE: Middle Atlantic Press, 1996.

Godfrey, Robert. *Outward Bound: Schools of the Possible.* New York: Anchor Books, 1980.

Hahn, Kurt, *www.kurthahn.org.* This nonprofit website is a good source for the writings and speeches of Kurt Hahn.

James, Thomas. *Education at the Edge.* Denver: Colorado Outward Bound School, 1980.

———. "Kurt Hahn and the Aims of Education." *Journal of Experiential Education* (Thunder Bay, Ontario) 13, no. 1 (May 1990).

Outward Bound, *www.outwardbound.org.* Information about the current programs offered by Outward Bound USA.

Zelinski, Mark. *Outward Bound: The Inward Odyssey.* Hillsboro, OR: Beyond Words Publishing, 1991.

CHAPTER 2, BECOMING A LEADER
References
Alexander, Caroline. *The Endurance: Shackleton's Legendary Antarctic Expedition.* New York: Knopf, 1998.

Blair-Smith, Caroline, Landon Fake, Bill Frederick, Ashley Lodato, and Gretchen Ostherr. *Outward Bound Instructor Manual.* Rockland, ME: Hurricane Island Outward Bound School, various years.

Calloway, Wayne. "Arrogance greatest threat to business." (PepsiCo Inc.'s Wayne Calloway addresses National-American Wholesale Grocers Association 1992 Midyear Executive Conference). Ryan Mathews. *Grocery Marketing* vol. 58 no. 10 (Nov. 1992): p. 39(1).

George, Bill. *Authentic Leadership: Rediscovering the Secrets to Creating Lasting Value.* San Francisco: Jossey-Bass, 2003.

Godin, Seth. *Wisdom, Inc.: 26 Business Virtues that Turn Ordinary People into Extraordinary Leaders*. London: HarperBusiness, 1995.

Hammarskjöld, Dag. *Markings*. 1964. Reprint. New York: Ballantine Books, Epiphany Edition, 1983.

Kouzes, Jim, and Barry Posner. *The Leadership Challenge*. 3rd ed. San Francisco: Jossey-Bass, 2002.

Morrell, Margot, and Stephanie Capparell. *Shackleton's Way*. New York: Viking, 2001.

Priest, Simon, and Michael Gass. *Effective Leadership in Adventure Programming*. Champaign, IL: Human Kinetics, 1997.

Willing, Steve. *NOLS Leadership Education Toolbox*. Lander, WY: National Outdoor Leadership School, 1991.

Resources

Graham, John. *Outdoor Leadership: Technique, Common Sense, and Self-Confidence*. Seattle: The Mountaineers Books, 1997.

Harvey, Mark. *The National Outdoor Leadership School's Wilderness Guide*. New York: Fireside, 1999.

CHAPTER 3, COMMUNICATING EFFECTIVELY
References

Blair-Smith, Caroline, Landon Fake, Bill Frederick, Ashley Lodato, and Gretchen Ostherr. *Outward Bound Instructor Manual*. Rockland, ME: Hurricane Island Outward Bound School, various years.

Graham, John. *Outdoor Leadership: Technique, Common Sense, and Self-Confidence*. Seattle: The Mountaineers Books, 1997.

Interaction Associates. "Facilitative Leadership" workshop. See *www.interactionassociates.com*.

Maslow, Abraham. *Toward a Psychology of Being*. Princeton, NJ: Van Nostrand, 1968.

Resources
Conflict Resolution

Association for Conflict Resolution, *www.acrnet.org*.

Conflict Resolution Network, *www.crnhq.org*.

Learning Styles

Armstrong, Thomas. *Multiple Intelligences in the Classroom*. New York: Basic Books, 1993.

Gardner, Howard. *Frames of Mind*. New York: Basic Books, 1993.

———. *To Open Minds*. New York: Basic Books, 1991.

CHAPTER 4, BUILDING TRUST, BUILDING A TEAM
References

Blair-Smith, Caroline, Landon Fake, Bill Frederick, Ashley Lodato, and Gretchen Ostherr. *Outward Bound Instructor Manual*. Rockland, ME: Hurricane Island Outward Bound School, various years.

James, William. "The Moral Equivalent of War." In *The Writings of William James*, ed. by John J. McDermott. New York: Random House, 1967.

Miner, Joshua L., and Joe Boldt. *Outward Bound USA: Crew Not Passengers*. 2nd ed. Seattle: The Mountaineers Books, 2002.

Priest, Simon, and Michael Gass. *Effective Leadership in Adventure Programming*. Champaign, IL: Human Kinetics, 1997.

Tuckman, B. W., and M. A. Jensen. "Stages of Small Group Development Revisited." *Group and Organization Studies* 2, no. 4:419–27.

Resources

Collard, Mark. *No Props: Great Games with No Equipment*. Beverly, MA: Project Adventure, 2005.

Priest, Simon, and Karl E. Rohnke. *101 of the Best Corporate Team-Building Activities We Know*. Tulsa, OK: Learning Unlimited Corp., 1999.

Rohnke, Karl E. *Cowtails and Cobras II: A Guide to Games, Initiatives, Ropes Courses & Adventure Curiculum*. Dubuque, IA: Kendall/Hunt Publishing Co., 2003.

Rohnke, Karl E. *Silver Bullets: A Guide to Initiative Problems, Adventure Games and Trust Activities*. Dubuque, IA: Kendall/Hunt Publishing Co., 1989.

Rohnke, Karl E., and Steve Butler. *Quicksilver: Adventure Games, Initiative Problems, Trust Activities and a Guide to Effective Leadership.* Dubuque, IA: Kendall/Hunt Publishing Co., 1996.

Rohnke, Karl E., and Jim Grout. *Back Pocket Adventure.* Beverly, MA: Project Adventure, 1998.

Snow, Harrison. *Indoor/Outdoor Team Building Games For Trainers: Powerful Activities From the World of Adventure-Based Team Building and Ropes Courses.* Columbus, OH: McGraw-Hill, 1997.

CHAPTER 5, TAKING RISKS AND MAKING DECISIONS
References

Blair-Smith, Caroline. *Teaching Leadership and Decision Making.* Rockland, ME: Hurricane Island Outward Bound School, 2004.

Blair-Smith, Caroline, Landon Fake, Bill Frederick, Ashley Lodato, and Gretchen Ostherr. *Outward Bound Instructor Manual.* Rockland, ME: Hurricane Island Outward Bound School, various years.

Graham, John. *Outdoor Leadership: Techniques, Common Sense, and Self-Confidence.* Seattle: The Mountaineers Books, 1997.

Hahn, Kurt. *Outward Bound.* Address at the annual meeting of the Outward Bound Trust, London, July 1960.

Leamer, Laurence. *Ascent: The Spiritual and Physical Quest of Legendary Mountaineer Willi Unsoeld.* New York: Harper Perennial, 1999.

Miner, Joshua L., and Joe Boldt. *Outward Bound USA: Crew Not Passengers.* 2nd ed. Seattle: The Mountaineers Books, 2002.

Priest, Simon, and Michael Gass. *Effective Leadership in Adventure Programming.* Champaign, IL: Human Kinetics, 1997.

Shedd, John A. *Salt from My Attic.* Portland, ME: The Mosher Press, 1928.

Resources

Wade, Ian R. "Safety Management." In *Adventure Education*, by John C. Miles and Simon Priest. State College, PA: Venture Publishing Inc., 1990.

Walbridge, Charlie. *American Canoeing Association River Safety Anthology.* Birmingham, AL: Menasha Ridge Press, 1996.

———. *American Canoeing Association River Safety Reports.* Birmingham, AL: Menasha Ridge Press, 2000.

Williamson, John E. (Jed), ed. *Accidents in North American Mountaineering.* Golden, CO: The American Alpine Club, published annually.

CHAPTER 6, FINDING COURAGE, OVERCOMING FEAR
References

Bacon, Stephen. *The Conscious Use of Metaphor in Outward Bound.* Denver: Colorado Outward Bound School, 1983.

Logue, Christopher. *New Numbers.* London: Jonathan Cape, 1969.

Hipp, Earl. *Fighting Invisible Tigers: A Stress Management Guide for Teens.* Minneapolis, MN: Free Spirit Publishing, 1995.

Outward Bound Readings Book. Outward Bound International, multiple editions, no date.

Zunin, Leonard, as quoted in *Tempered Radicals: How Everyday Leaders Inspire Change at Work,* by Debra E. Meyerson. Watertown, MA: Harvard Business School Press, 2003.

Resources

Graham, John. *Outdoor Leadership: Technique, Common Sense, and Self-Confidence.* Seattle: The Mountaineers Books, 1997.

CASE STUDY 1, THE PALESTINIAN-ISRAELI UNITY PROJECT
References

Breaking the Ice, *www.breaking-the-ice.de.*

North Carolina Outward Bound School, *www.ncobs.org.*

Pitt, Jesse. *The Unity Project—Community Instructor Manual.* Rev. ed. Asheville, NC: North Carolina Outward Bound, 2005.

———. *The Unity Project—Community Instructor Workbook.* Rev. ed. Asheville, NC: North Carolina Outward Bound, 2005.

Randall, Ian. "Education, Human Agency and Compassion: Outward Bound as a Case Study in Empowering Young People as Agents of Social Change." Master's thesis, University of Newcastle-upon-Tyne, UK, 2004.

Randall, Ian, and Dave Genova. *The Unity Project—Community Instructor Manual.* Asheville, NC: North Carolina Outward Bound, 2002.

CHAPTER 7, PREPARING TO LEAD AN EXPEDITION
References
Petzoldt, Paul. *The New Wilderness Handbook.* New York: W. W. Norton and Co., 1984.

Simpson, Stephen. "The Intrinsic Value of Minimum Impact." *Journal of Experiential Education* 6, no. 2 (1993).

Resources
Backpacking
Cox, Steven M., and Kris Fulsaas. *Mountaineering: The Freedom of the Hills.* 7th ed. Seattle: The Mountaineers Books, 2003.

Curtiss, Rick. *The Backpacker's Field Manual.* New York: Three Rivers Press, 1998.

Jardine, Ray. *Beyond Backpacking: Ray Jardine's Guide to Lightweight Hiking.* Arizona City, AZ: AdventureLore Press, 2000.

O'Bannon, Allen. *Allen & Mike's Really Cool Backpackin' Book.* Evergreen, CO: Chockstone Press, 2001.

Randall, Glenn. *The Outward Bound Backpacker's Handbook.* Guilford, CT: Lyons Press, 1999.

Townsend, Chris. *The Backpacker's Handbook.* Camden, ME: Ragged Mountain Press, 2005.

———. *The Backpacker's Pocket Guide.* Camden, ME: Ragged Mountain Press, 2002.

Environmental Ethics
Hampton, Bruce, and David Cole. *NOLS Soft Paths: How to Enjoy the Wilderness without Harming It.* Mechanicsburg, PA: Stackpole Books, 2003.

Leave No Trace®: *www.lnt.org.* Leave No Trace also publishes educational booklets for different regions of the country (for example, Northeast Mountains, Temperate Coastal Zones, etc.), with specific considerations for each region.

McGivney, Annette. *Leave No Trace: A Practical Guide to the New Wilderness Etiquette.* Seattle: The Mountaineers Books and *Backpacker Magazine,* 1998.

Waterman, Laura, and Guy Waterman. *Wilderness Ethics: Preserving the Spirit of Wildness.* Woodstock, VT: The Countryman Press, 1993.

First Aid: Books
Isaac, Jeff, and Peter Goth. *The Outward Bound Wilderness First-Aid Handbook.* Rev. ed. New York: Lyons and Burford, 1998.

Wilkerson, James A., ed. *Medicine for Mountaineering and Other Wilderness Activities.* Seattle: The Mountaineers Books, 2001.

First Aid: Classes and Certifications
American Heart Association, 1-800-AHA-USA-1 (1-800-478-7653), *www.americanheart.org.*

American Red Cross, 1-202-303-4498, *www.redcross.org.*

Stonehearth Open Learning Opportunities (SOLO), 1-603-447-6711, *www.soloschools.com.*

Wilderness Medical Associates, 1-888-WILD-MED (1-888-945-3633), *www.wildmed.com.*

Wilderness Medical Institute, 1-866-831-9001, *www.nols.edu/wmi.*

Food and Cooking
Mendenhall, Ruth Dyer. *Backpack Cookery.* Glendale, CA: La Siesta Press, 1974.

Miller, Dorcas. *Good Food for Camp and Trail: All-Natural Recipes for Delicious Meals Outdoors.* Boulder, CO: Pruett Publishing, 1993.

———. *More Backcountry Cooking: Movable Feasts from the Experts.* Seattle: The Mountaineers Books, 2003.

National Outdoor Leadership School. *NOLS Cookery.* 5th ed. Harrisburg, PA: Stackpole Books and NOLS, 2002.

Prater, Yvonne, and Ruth Dyer Mendenhall. *Beyond GORP: Favorite Foods from Outdoor Experts.* Seattle: The Mountaineers Books, 2005.

———. *Gorp, Glop and Glue Stew: Favorite Foods from 165 Outdoor Experts.* Seattle: The Mountaineers Books, 1982.

Maps

Local outdoor supply stores generally carry maps and/or guidebooks for popular backcountry trips in their area.

National Park Service publishes maps for all of the national parks; 1-202-208-6843, *www.nps .gov.*

United States Forest Service publishes maps of all the national forests; 1-202-205-8333, *www.fs.fed.us.*

United States Geological Survey publishes detailed topographic maps of almost all regions of the United States in a variety of scales; an index to the maps for each state is available online; 1-888-ASK-USGS (1-888-275-8747), *www.usgs.gov.*

Navigation

Burns, Bob, and Mike Burns. *Wilderness Navigation.* Seattle: The Mountaineers Books, 1999.

Grubbs, Bruce. *Basic Essentials: Using GPS.* 2nd ed. Guilford, CT: Falcon Publishing, 2005.

Kals, W. S. *Land Navigation Handbook: The Sierra Club Guide to Map, Compass, and GPS.* 2nd ed. Berkeley, CA: Sierra Club Books, 2005.

Kjellström, Björn. *Be an Expert with Map and Compass.* New York: Hungry Minds, Inc., 1994.

Letham, Lawrence. *GPS Made Easy: Using Global Positioning Systems in the Outdoors.* 4th ed. Seattle: The Mountaineers Books, 2003.

Randall, Glenn. *Outward Bound Map and Compass Handbook.* Guilford, CT: The Lyons Press, 1989.

Other Modes of Travel
Canoeing

American Canoeing Association. *Introduction to Paddling: Canoeing Basics for Lakes and Rivers.* Birmingham, AL: Menasha Ridge Press, 1996.

Foster, Nigel. *Open Canoe Technique.* Guilford, CT: A Falcon Guide, 2004.

Gullion, Laurie. *The Canoeing and Kayaking Instruction Manual.* Birmingham, AL: Menasha Ridge Press and American Canoeing Association, 1987.

Landry, Paul, and Matty McNair. *The Outward Bound Canoeing Handbook.* Guilford, CT: The Lyons Press, 1992.

Ray, Slim. *The Canoe Handbook: Techniques for Mastering the Sport of Canoeing.* Harrisburg, PA: Stackpole Books, 1992.

Canyoneering

Allen, Steve. *Canyoneering 3.* Salt Lake City: University of Utah Press, 1997.

Van Tilburg, Christopher. *Canyoneering: Beginning to Advanced Techniques.* Seattle: The Mountaineers Books, 2000.

Sea Kayaking

Hanson, Jonathan. *Essential Sea Kayaking.* Guilford, CT: The Lyons Press, 2000.

Johnson, Shelley. *The Complete Sea Kayaker's Handbook.* Guilford, CT: Ragged Mountain Press, 2002.

Seidman, David. *The Essential Sea Kayaker.* 2nd ed. Camden, ME: Ragged Mountain Press, 2001.

Whitewater Safety

Walbridge, Charlie. *American Canoeing Association River Safety Anthology.* Birmingham, AL: Menasha Ridge Press, 1996.

———. *ACA River Safety Reports.* Birmingham, AL: Menasha Ridge Press, 2000.

Winter Travel

Hindman, Steve. *Cross Country Skiing: Building Skills for Fun and Fitness.* Seattle: The Mountaineers Books, 2005.

Lanza, Michael. *Winter Hiking and Camping.* Seattle: The Mountaineers Books, 2003.

O'Bannon, Allen. *Allen & Mike's Really Cool Backcountry Ski Book.* Evergreen, CO: Chockstone Press, 1996.

Osborne, Samuel P. *The Cross-Country Skier's Handbook*. Woodbridge, CT: Charles Scribner's Sons, 1995.

Parker, Paul. *Free-Heel Skiing: Telemark and Parallel Technique for All Conditions*. Seattle: The Mountaineers Books, 2001.

Prater, Gene. *Snowshoeing*. Seattle: The Mountaineers Books, 2002.

Weiss, Hal. *Secrets of Warmth*. Seattle: The Mountaineers Books, 1988.

CHAPTER 8, TAKING RESPONSIBILITY FOR YOURSELF AND OTHERS OUTDOORS
References

Blair-Smith, Caroline, Landon Fake, Bill Frederick, Ashley Lodato, and Gretchen Ostherr. *Outward Bound Instructor Manual*. Rockland, ME: Hurricane Island Outward Bound School, various years.

Glasser, William. *Control Theory in the Classroom*. New York: HarperCollins, 1986.

Graham, John. *Outdoor Leadership: Technique, Common Sense, and Self-Confidence*. Seattle: The Mountaineers Books, 1997.

Kalisch, Kenneth R. *The Role of the Instructor in the Outward Bound Educational Process*. Three Lakes, WI: Honey Rock Camp, 1979.

Priest, Simon, and Michael Gass. *Effective Leadership in Adventure Programming*. Champaign, IL: Human Kinetics, 1997.

Resources

Bacon, Stephen. *The Conscious Use of Metaphor in Outward Bound*. Denver, CO: Colorado Outward Bound School, 1983.

Dewey, John. *Experience and Education*. New York: Touchstone, 1997.

Glasser, William, MD. *Reality Therapy in Action*. New York: HarperCollins, 2000.

Hershey, Paul, and Kenneth H. Blanchard. *Management of Organizational Behavior: Utilizing Human Resources*. 4th ed. Englewood Cliffs, NJ. Prentice-Hall, 1982.

Knapp, Clifford E. *Lasting Lessons: A Teacher's Guide to Reflecting on Experience*. Charleston, WV: Clearinghouse on Rural Education and Small Schools, 1992.

Miles, John, and Simon Priest. *Adventure Education*. State College, PA: Venture Publishing, 1990.

Outward Bound West. *Outward Bound Instructor Manual*. Golden, CO: Outward Bound, 2004.

Tuckman, B. W., and M. A. Jensen. "Stages of Small Group Development Revisited." *Group and Organization Studies* 2, no. 4:419–27.

Willing, Steve. *NOLS Leadership Education Toolbox*. Lander, WY: National Outdoor Leadership School, 1991.

Safety and Risk Management: Books

Abbott, Katrina, and Scott Hartl. *Safety Habits of the Mind*. Garrison, NY: Expeditionary Learning Outward Bound, 1995.

Ajango, Deb. *Lessons Learned II: Using Case Studies and History to Improve Safety Education*. Eagle River, AK: SafetyEd, 2005.

Barton, Bob. *Safety, Risk and Adventure in Outdoor Activities*. London: Paul Chapman Publishing, 2006.

Broze, Matt, and George Gronseth. *Sea Kayaker's Deep Trouble: True Stories and Their Lessons from Sea Kayaker Magazine*. Camden, ME: Ragged Mountain Press, 1997.

Cox, Steven M., and Kris Fulsaas. *Mountaineering: The Freedom of the Hills*. 7th ed. Seattle: The Mountaineers Books, 2003.

Haddock, Cathy. *Managing Risks in Outdoor Activities*. Wellington, New Zealand: New Zealand Mountain Safety Council Inc., 1993.

Leemon, Drew. *Risk Management for Outdoor Leaders*. Lander, WY: National Outdoor Leadership School, 2005.

National Outdoor Leadership School. Annual proceedings of the Wilderness Risk Management Conference, Lander, WY, 1995–2006.

Petzoldt, Paul. *The New Wilderness Handbook*. New York: W. W. Norton and Co., 1984.

Tilton, Buck. *Outdoor Safety Handbook*. Mechanicsburg, PA: Stackpole Books, 2006.

Walbridge, Charlie. *American Canoeing Association River Safety Reports.* Birmingham, AL: Menasha Ridge Press, 2000.

Williamson, Jed, ed. "59th Annual Report of the Safety Committees of the American Alpine Club and the Alpine Club of Canada," *Accidents in North American Mountaineering* (Golden, CO) no. 59 (2006). Also available for prior years.

Safety and Risk Management: Conferences

The annual Wilderness Risk Management Conference (*www.outwardbound.org /event-wrmc07.vp.html*) is sponsored by Outward Bound, the National Outdoor Leadership School, The Student Conservation Association, and the Wilderness Risk Managers Committee (WRMC), engaging some of the top wilderness leaders in North America. The WRMC serves as a platform for the collaboration of various wilderness practitioners, program administrators, recreation degree students, lawyers, and insurance representatives to discuss, share, and learn risk management, practical safety skills, and field and administrative techniques. The goal of the WRMC is to raise overall standards in the wilderness adventure and education industry. Attending this unique conference is the best way to familiarize yourself with wilderness risk management and safety issues.

CHAPTER 9, GOING SOLO
References

Hahn, Kurt. Address at the Forty-Eighth Annual Dinner of Old Centralians. In *The Central: The Journal of Old Centralians* (London), no. 119 (February 1959): 3–8. Address delivered at Grocer's Hall, London, November 17, 1958.

Blair-Smith, Caroline, Landon Fake, Bill Frederick, Ashley Lodato, and Gretchen Ostherr. *Outward Bound Instructor Manual.* Rockland, ME: Hurricane Island Outward Bound School, various years.

Lindbergh, Anne Morrow. *Gift from the Sea.* 50th anniversary ed. New York: Random House, 1975.

Ralston, Aron. *Between a Rock and a Hard Place.* New York: Atria Books, 2004.

Rilke, Rainer Maria. *Letters to a Young Poet.* Reissued ed. Translated by M. D. Herter Norton. New York: W. W. Norton and Co., 2004.

Thoreau, Henry David. *Walden Pond.* New York: Houghton Mifflin, 1949.

Unsoeld, Willi. "The Spiritual Values of the Wilderness." Keynote address, third conference of the Association for Experiential Education, Estes Park, CO, 1978.

CHAPTER 10, TEAM BUILDING IN THE WORKPLACE
References

Brimm, Michael, Ram Charan, Dale Lake, Hiro Takeuchi, and Noel M. Tichy. *A Model for Improving Team Effectiveness.* Ann Arbor, MI: University of Michigan Global Leadership Program, 1988.

Covey, Stephen R. *The Seven Habits of Highly Effective People.* New York: Free Press, 2004.

Drucker, Peter F. *The Daily Drucker: 366 Days of Insight and Motivation for Getting the Right Things Done.* London: Collins, 2004.

French, Gordon. Testimonial. North Carolina Outward Bound School website (*www.ncobs .org*), 2005.

Interaction Associates. *Facilitative Leadership® Workshop Manual.* San Francisco, CA: 2007. See *www.interactionassociates.com.*

Kaplan, Robert S., and David P. Norton. "Using the Balanced Scorecard as a Strategic Management System." *Harvard Business Review* (January-February 1996): 76.

King, Angus. Confirmed via email to Robert Gordon, July 18, 2007.

Tuckman, B. W., and M. A. Jensen. "Stages of Small Group Development Revisited." *Group and Organization Studies* 2, no. 4:419–27.

Resources

Kaplan, Robert S., and David P. Norton. *The Balanced Scorecard: Translating Strategy into Action*. Watertown, Mass.: Harvard Business School Press, 1996.

Kilmann, Ralph H., and Kenneth W. Thomas. Thomas-Kilmann Conflict MODE Instrument. Mountain View, CA: Xicom and CPP, Inc., 1974.

Kouzes, James M., and Barry Z. Posner. Leadership Practices Inventory in *The Leadership Challenge*. 4th ed. San Francisco: Jossey-Bass, 2007.

Outward Bound Professional. *www.outwardbound-pro.org*.

CHAPTER 11, WORKPLACE COMMUNICATION SKILLS
References

Argyris, Chris. *Overcoming Organizational Defenses*. New York: Prentice Hall Press, 1990. Pages 88-89.

Argyris, Chris, Robert Putnam, and Diana McLain Smith. *Action Science: Concepts, Methods, and Skills for Research and Intervention*. San Francisco: Jossey-Bass, 1985. pp. 57-58.

Kotter, John. *Leading Change*. Watertown, MA: Harvard Business School Press, 1996.

Senge, Peter M. *The Fifth Discipline: The Art and Practice of the Learning Organization*. New York: Currency Business Books, 2006.

Wilson Learning Library. *The Social Styles Handbook*. Herentals, Belgium: Nova Vista Publishing, 2004.

Resources

Pyzdek, Thomas. *The Six Sigma Handbook: The Complete Guide for Greenbelts, Blackbelts, and Managers at All Levels*, Revised and Expanded Edition. New York: McGraw-Hill, 2003.

CHAPTER 12, MANAGING CHANGE IN THE WORKPLACE
References

Bridges, William. *Managing Transitions: Making the Most of Change*, 2nd ed. New York: Perseus Books Group, 2003.

Interaction Associates. *Facilitative Leadership® Workshop Manual*. San Francisco, CA: 2007. See *www.interactionassociates.com*.

Kotter, John P. *Leading Change*. Watertown, MA: Harvard Business School Press, 1996.

Resources

Johnson, Spencer. *Who Moved My Cheese?* New York: Penguin Putnam, 1998.

CASE STUDY 3, PLAYING A NEW TUNE AT MARTIN GUITAR
References

Landers, Rick. "Interview with Christian F. Martin IV." *Modern Guitars Magazine*, December 30, 2005. *www.modernguitars.com/archives/001426.html*.

C. F. Martin & Company, Inc. "The Martin Story: A Brief History of the Martin Guitar Company." Nazareth, Penn.: C. F. Martin & Company, Inc., 2006. Adapted from a story that originally appeared in *The Music Trades*, March 1993. Updated and used with permission, May 2006.

———. "Our Story." April 2007, *www.mguitar.com/history/ourstory.php*.

Martin, Christian F. IV, chairman of the board and CEO of C. F. Martin & Company, Inc. Interview with Jim Garrett, April 9, 2007.

Martin Guitar Museum and Visitors Center, Nazareth, PA. Visit by Jim Garrett, April 9, 2007.

Starnes, David, executive director of Baltimore Chesapeake Bay Outward Bound Center. Interview with Jim Garrett, April 3, 2007.

CHAPTER 13, SERVING OTHERS AS A COMMUNITY LEADER
References

Blair-Smith, Caroline, Landon Fake, Bill Frederick, Ashley Lodato, and Gretchen Ostherr. *Outward Bound Instructor Manual*. Rockland, ME: Hurricane Island Outward Bound School, various years.

Brown, Rita Mae. *Starting from Scratch: A Different Kind of Writers' Manual.* New York: Bantam, 1989. Page 204.

Edelman, Marian Wright. *The Measure of Our Success, A Letter to My Children and Yours.* New York: HarperCollins, 1993.

Hagedorn, Hermann. *Prophet in the Wilderness.* New York: Macmillan & Company, 1949.

Kidder, Tracy. *Mountains Beyond Mountains.* New York: Random House, 2003.

Mandela, Nelson. Inaugural speech, South Africa, 1994.

Miner, Joshua L., and Joe Boldt. *Outward Bound USA: Crew Not Passengers.* 2nd ed. Seattle: The Mountaineers Books, 2002.

Rumi, Jalal al-Din. *Essential Rumi.* Translated by Coleman Barks et al. New York: Harper Collins, 1995.

White, E. B. In Israel Shenker, "E. B. White: Notes and Comment by Author," *New York Times,* July 11, 1969.

Resources

Center for Applications of Psychological Type. *www.capt.org*

Hessler, Peter. *River Town: Two Years on the Yangtze.* New York: HarperCollins, 2001. This is an account of a Peace Corps volunteer in China.

Kiersey, David, and Marilyn Bates. *Please Understand Me: Character and Temperament Types,* 3rd ed. Del Mar, CA: Prometheus Nemesis Book Company, 1984. Discusses the Myers Briggs Personality Inventory.

McKenzie, R. Alec. *Time Management.* 2nd ed. New York: AMACOM, American Management Association, 1997.

Morgenstern, Julie. *Time Management from the Inside Out: The Foolproof System for Taking Control of Your Schedule and Your Life.* 2nd ed. New York: Henry Holt & CO., 2004.

Personalitydesk. *www.personalitydesk.com.* A good source for Myers-Briggs Type Indicator® personality inventory and Strong Campbell Interest Test materials.

CHAPTER 14, LEADING A VOLUNTEER ORGANIZATION
References

Drucker, Peter. *Managing the Nonprofit Organization.* New York: HarperCollins, 1990.

Heider, John. *The Tao of Leadership.* Atlanta: Humanics Limited, 1985.

Miner, Joshua L., and Joe Boldt. *Outward Bound USA: Crew Not Passengers.* 2nd ed. Seattle: The Mountaineers Books, 2002.

Resources

Chrislip, David D., and Carl E. Larson. *Collaborative Leadership: How Citizens and Civic Leaders Can Make a Difference.* San Francisco: Jossey-Bass Inc., 1994.

Collins, Jim. *Good to Great and the Social Sectors: A Monograph to Accompany Good to Great.* Boulder, CO: Jim Collins, 2005.

Crenshaw, Larry, ed. *The Outward Bound Earth Book.* 3rd ed. Birmingham, AL: Menasha Ridge Press, 1995.

Dees, Gregory, Jed Emerson, and Peter Economy. *Enterprising Nonprofits, A Toolkit for Social Entrepreneurs.* New York: John Wiley and Sons, 2001.

Doyle, Michael, and David Straus. *How to Make Meetings Work.* New York: The Berkley Publishing Group, 1982.

Kass, Amy A. *The Perfect Gift: The Philanthropic Imagination in Poetry and Prose.* Bloomington: Indiana University Press, 2002.

McAdams, Terry W. *Careers in the Nonprofit Sector.* Washington, DC: The Taft Group, 1986.

CHAPTER 15, LEADING YOUTH IN YOUR COMMUNITY
References

Abbott, Katrina, and Scott Hartl. *Safety Habits of Mind.* Outward Bound Expeditionary Learning.

Edelman, Marian Wright. *The Measure of Our Success, A Letter to My Children and Yours.* New York: HarperCollins, 1993.

Flavin, Martin. *Kurt Hahn's Schools and Legacy*. Wilmington, DE: The Middle Atlantic Press, 1996.

Hartman, Steve. "Kids Build Soybean-Fueled Car." CBS Evening News, February 17, 2006. *www.cbsnews.com/stories/2006/02/17 /eveningnews/main1329941.shtml*.

Howard, Jon Mark, Mark Wheeler, Hepsi Barnett, JoAnn Deak, and Cate Huisman. *Outward Bound Instructor's Guide to Managing Adolescents in the Field*. 3rd ed. Garrison, NY: Outward Bound Inc., 2003.

Krakauer, Jon. *Into Thin Air*. New York: Random House, 1997.

Kuller, Allison, ed. *Readings from the Hurricane Island Outward Bound School*. Rockland, ME: Hurricane Island Outward Bound, 1986.

Leemon, Drew, Steve Pace, Deb Ajango, and Henry Wood. *Manual of Accreditation Standards for Adventure Programs*. 4th ed. Boulder, CO: Association for Experiential Education, 2005.

Miner, Joshua L., and Joe Boldt. *Outward Bound USA*. 2nd ed. Seattle: The Mountaineers Books, 2002.

National Middle School Association. *This We Believe: Developmentally Responsive Middle Level Schools*. Report. 1995. *www.etsd.org /ems/endorsement/characteristics.htm*. Accessed August 2006.

Philip, Duke of Edinburgh. Kurt Hahn Award address at 25th anniversary, Colorado Outward Bound, October 24, 1987. Denver, Colorado.

Sarton, May. *Journal of Solitude*. New York: W. W. Norton & Company, 1973.

———. *Plant Dreaming Deep*. New York: W. W. Norton & Company, 1968.

Webster's New World Dictionary and Thesaurus. New York: Simon & Schuster, 1996.

Webster, Steven E. *Project Adventure Ropes Course Safety Manual: An Instructor's Guide to Initiatives, and Low and High Elements*. Dubuque, IA: Kendall/Hunt Publishing Company, 1994.

Youthlinks. *www.youthlinksonline.org*. Accessed August 2006.

Resources

Crenshaw, Larry. *The Outward Bound Earth Book: Activities and Readings for Environmental Education, Appreciation, and Celebration*. Morganton, NC: North Carolina Outward Bound School, 1994.

Csikszentmihalyi, Mihaly, and Reed E. Larson. *Being Adolescent: Conflict and Growth in the Teenage Years*. New York: Basic Books, 1984.

James, Thomas. *Education at the Edge: The Colorado Outward Bound School*. Denver: The Colorado Outward Bound School, 1980.

McGillicuddy-De Lisi, Ann, and Richard De Lisi (editors). *Biology, Sex, and Behavior: The Development of Sex Differences in Cognition*. Greenwich, CT: Ablex Publishing, 2001.

Nabhan, Gary Paul, and Stephen Trimble. *Why Children Need Wild Places*. Boston: Beacon Press, 1994.

Safety and Legal Responsibilities

Boy Scouts of America. "Guide to Safe Scouting." In Chapter 1, "Youth Protection and Adult Leadership." *www.scouting.org/pubs/gss/*. Accessed in March 2007.

Church Pension Group of the Episcopal Church USA. "Model Policies for the Protection of Children and Youth from Abuse." *www.cpg .org/productsservices/modelpolicies.cfm*. Accessed in March 2007.

Crabtree, Jack. *Better Safe Than Sued: Keeping Out of Trouble in Youth Ministry*. Loveland, CO: Group Publishing, 1998.

Melton, Joy Thornburg. *Safe Sanctuaries for Youth: Reducing the Risk of Abuse in Youth Ministries*. Nashville, TN: Discipleship Resources, 2003.

National Alliance for Youth Sports. "Background Checks in Youth Sports: Guidelines for Your Organization." *www.nays.org/timeout /screening2-06.pdf*. Accessed in March 2007.

Patterson, John C., and Barbara B. Oliver. *The Season of Hope: A Risk Management Guide for Youth-Serving Nonprofits*. Washington, DC: The Nonprofit Risk Management Center, 2004.

Peterson, Marilyn R. *At Personal Risk: Boundary Violations in Professional-Client Relationships.* New York: W. W. Norton & Company, 1992.

Twedt, Steve. "The Fearful Flip Side of Child Protection." *Youth Today,* December 2004–January 2005. *www.youthtoday.org /youthtoday/Dec04/story2_12_04.html.* Accessed in March 2007.

White, Leslie T., John C. Patterson, and Melanie L. Herman. *More than a Matter of Trust: Managing the Risks of Mentoring.* Washington, DC: The Nonprofit Risk Management Center, 1998.

CHAPTER 16, LEADING YOUR COMMUNITY IN THE POLITICAL ARENA
References

Beamish, Richard. *Getting the Word Out in the Fight to Save the Earth.* Baltimore: The Johns Hopkins University Press, 1995.

Bobo, Kim, Jackie Kendall, and Steve Max. *Organizing for Social Change.* Santa Ana, CA: Seven Locks Press, 1996.

Edelman, Marian Wright. *The Measure of Our Success, A Letter to My Children and Yours.* New York: HarperCollins, 1993.

McCullough, David. *1776.* New York: Simon & Schuster, 2005.

McNally, David. *Another World Is Possible: Globalization and Anti-Capitalism.* Winnipeg: Arbeiter Ring, 2002.

Mead, Margaret. *The World Ahead: An Anthropologist Anticipates the Future.* Edited by Robert Textor. New York: Berghahn Books, 2005.

United Church of Christ. *Public Policy Briefing Book 2005–2006.* Cleveland, OH: Justice and Witness Ministries, United Church of Christ, 2005.

Resources

MacCrae, Melissa. *It Takes a Woman: Women Shaping Public Policy.* Brewer, ME: Goddess Publications, 1999.

Minck, Holly, Kim Haddow, and Laura Iaponara. *Loud and Clear in an Election Year.* San Francisco: Spin Project and the Independent Media Institute, 2004.

Salzman, Jason. *Making the News: A Guide for Nonprofits and Activists.* Boulder: Westview Press, 1998.

Wallack, Lawrence, Katie Woodruff, Lori Dorfman, and Iris Diaz. *News for a Change: An Advocate's Guide to Working with the Media.* Thousand Oaks, CA: Sage Publications, 1999.

CASE STUDY 4, LEADING PARKS AND PEOPLE
References

Achenback, Sarah. "At Home with Sally Michel: A 'Model Citizen' talks about Brainstorming, Risk-taking and Making the Impossible Possible for Baltimore's Kids?" *Style* magazine, May–June 2002.

The Daily Record. "Parks & People: The Foundation for Baltimore Recreation and Parks." *The Daily Record,* July 2004. *www.mddailyrecord.com.*

Michel, Sally (chair of the board, Parks & People Foundation). Interview with Jim Garrett, March 29, 2007.

Resources

Carrera, Jackie (executive director, Parks & People Foundation). Interview with Jim Garrett, March 15, 2007.

Parks & People Foundation. *Annual Report.* Baltimore, Md.: Parks & People Foundation, 1997.

Parks & People Foundation. *Draft Strategic Plan 2011.* Baltimore, Md.: Parks & People Foundation, January 2007.

ABOUT THE CONTRIBUTORS

Caroline Blair-Smith (Part III contributor) is an Outward Bound course director and a writer and editor of Outward Bound USA publications. She is a Registered Maine Guide and runs a dog sledding guide service in Albany Township, Maine.

Jimmy Carter (Foreword) was the thirty-ninth president of the United States. He founded the nonpartisan and nonprofit Carter Center in 1982 to address national and international issues of public policy, including conflict resolution, promotion of democracy, protection of human rights, and prevention of disease and other afflictions. President Carter won the Nobel Peace Prize in 2002 and is the author of twenty-one books.

Rob Chatfield (Introduction, co-editor) is the Communications Director for Outward Bound International and was the Chief Safety Officer for the former Hurricane Island Outward Bound School. He has worked as an Outward Bound instructor and program administrator in Canada and the United States for over twenty-five years.

Greg Farrell (Expeditionary Learning sidebar author, Chapter 1) is President of Expeditionary Learning Schools/Outward Bound, as well as being one of its original creators and developers. Previously, he led quality-of-life and antipoverty programs in the New York-New Jersey area, and worked as a newspaper reporter, assistant dean of admissions, U.S. Army private, English teacher, and coach.

Jim Garrett (Case Studies author) is currently the director of Outward Bound's National Service Initiative. He adapted the case study method developed by Harvard Business School into a system called Instructor Judgment Training for Outward Bound USA. For thirty years, he taught middle and high school students in the fields of English, world religions, and human values. He also established outdoor adventure programs for International College, Beirut, Lebanon, and The Gilman School in Baltimore.

Mark Gerzon (Postscript) is founder and co-director of the Global Leadership Network, which collaborates with Outward Bound International on programs for the promotion of global leadership. He has worked as a facilitator and leadership trainer for the United Nations, the U.S. House of Representatives, and a wide range of corporate and civic organizations around the world for more than a decade. Among his several published books is *Leading Through Conflict: How Successful Leaders Transform Differences into Opportunities* (Harvard Business School Press: 2006).

Bob Gordon (Part III author) has been a leader with Outward Bound USA since 1981 and is now president of Outward Bound Professional, *which* creates results-focused programs for business clients in the areas of team building, leadership development, cultural change, communication, and trust building. An accomplished sailor and climber, Gordon was a member of the 1991 American Karakoram Expedition to Gasherbrum II.

Ashley Lodato (Part I contributor and Part II author) is an Outward Bound instructor with over twenty years' experience. Formerly a spokesperson and freelance writer for New England land conservation efforts, she is currently a full-time mom and part-time Outward Bound employee.

John Raynolds (Part I author) is a former Navy frogman, a business executive in the fields of investment banking, manufacturing, and distribution, and the former CEO and president of Outward Bound USA. Through his writing, speaking, advising, and personal example he has championed the cause of volunteer service and commitment. He has been on the board of the International Executive Service Corps and A Better Chance; authored *The Halo Effect: How Volunteering to Help Others Can Lead to a Better Career and a More Fulfilling Life* (Golden Books Adult Publishing, 1998); and served as spokesperson for a group advising former President George H.W. Bush on implementing a national volunteer program.

Joan Welsh (Part IV author) is a longtime Outward Bound instructor and was the president and CEO of the Hurricane Island Outward Bound School from 1991 to 2001. Since 2004, Joan has been the deputy director of the Natural Resources Council of Maine. She has a long and distinguished record of volunteer service and currently serves on the boards of three nonprofit organizations.

INDEX

THE MOUNTAINEERS, founded in 1906, is a nonprofit outdoor activity and conservation club, whose mission is "to explore, study, preserve, and enjoy the natural beauty of the outdoors. . . . " The club sponsors many classes and year-round outdoor activities in the Pacific Northwest, and supports environmental causes through educational activities, sponsoring legislation and presenting educational programs. The Mountaineers Books supports the club's mission by publishing travel and natural history guides, instructional texts, and works on conservation and history.

Send or call for our catalog of more than 500 outdoor titles:

The Mountaineers Books
1001 SW Klickitat Way, Suite 201
Seattle, WA 98134
800-553-4453
mbooks@mountaineersbooks.org
www.mountaineersbooks.org

OUTWARD BOUND pioneered the field of wilderness experiential learning in the U.S. beginning in 1961 and has continued to deliver unparalleled expertise and experiences in the outdoors ever since. Today, Outward Bound delivers adventure and challenge in the wilderness, urban settings, workrooms and classrooms as a catalyst to help students push past perceived limitations and achieve their potential, and to inspire them to serve others and care for the world around them.

OUTWARD BOUND

To learn more about Outward Bound:
Outward Bound
100 Mystery Point Road
Garrison, NY 10524
866-846-7745
www.outwardbound.org

OTHER TITLES YOU MIGHT ENJOY FROM
THE MOUNTAINEERS BOOKS

Outdoor Leadership: Technique, Common Sense, & Self-Confidence
By John Graham
This essential handbook explores outdoor leadership skills and attributes, including advice and personal anecdotes.

Strange and Dangerous Dreams:
The Fine Line Between Adventure and Madness
By Geoff Powter
Adventurers are among the world's most celebrated heroes, but when they overreach, potential glory can become madness and death.

The Art of Rough Travel: From the Peculiar to the Practical, Advice from a 19th-Century Explorer
By Francis Galton, Edited by Katharine Harmon
Deliciously bizarre and surprisingly relevant travel advice from the 19th century.

Walking The Gobi:
A 1600-Mile Trek Across a Desert of Hope and Despair
By Helen Thayer
Baby-boomer and adventurer Helen Thayer tells the remarkable story of her 1600-mile trek across the Gobi desert. Fierce temperatures, drug smugglers, inhospitable terrain, and natural history mark her journey.

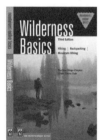

Wilderness Basics: Hiking, Backpacking, Paddling, Mountain Biking, 3rd Edition
Edited by Kristi Anderson and Arleen Tavernier
This classic handbook for the outdoor novice covers it all—from planning an adventure to selecting the right gear to navigating in the wild.

Wake Up and Smell the Planet: The Non-Pompous, Non-Preachy Grist Guide to Greening Your Day
By Grist magazine, Edited by Brangien Davis
From Grist.org, the hottest online magazine covering sustainability and popular culture, comes this quirky, humorous, entertaining, and sometimes irreverent guide to greening your day.